Scammell and Densha...
Law of Agricultural Holdings

Scammell and Densham's Law of Agricultural Holdings

Ninth edition

Supplement

Peter R Williams BA, FCIArb, HonRICS
Solicitor of the Supreme Court
Partner, Wilsons Solicitors LLP

Michael N Cardwell MA(Oxon)
Professor of Agricultural Law,
School of Law, University of Leeds

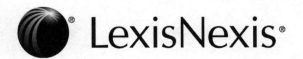

Members of the LexisNexis Group worldwide

United Kingdom	LexisNexis, a Division of Reed Elsevier (UK) Ltd, Halsbury House, 35 Chancery Lane, London, WC2A 1EL, and London House, 20–22 East London Street, Edinburgh EH7 4BQ
Australia	LexisNexis Butterworths, Chatswood, New South Wales
Austria	LexisNexis Verlag ARD Orac GmbH & Co KG, Vienna
Benelux	LexisNexis Benelux, Amsterdam
Canada	LexisNexis Canada, Markham, Ontario
China	LexisNexis China, Beijing and Shanghai
France	LexisNexis SA, Paris
Germany	LexisNexis GmbH, Dusseldorf
Hong Kong	LexisNexis Hong Kong, Hong Kong
India	LexisNexis India, New Delhi
Italy	Giuffrè Editore, Milan
Japan	LexisNexis Japan, Tokyo
Malaysia	Malayan Law Journal Sdn Bhd, Kuala Lumpur
New Zealand	LexisNexis NZ Ltd, Wellington
Poland	Wydawnictwo Prawnicze LexisNexis Sp, Warsaw
Singapore	LexisNexis Singapore, Singapore
South Africa	LexisNexis Butterworths, Durban
USA	LexisNexis, Dayton, Ohio

© Reed Elsevier (UK) Ltd 2011

Published by LexisNexis

A CIP Catalogue record for this book is available from the British Library.

ISBN 978-1-4057-4493-5

9 781405 744935

Typeset by Letterpart Ltd, Reigate, Surrey

Printed and bound in Great Britain by CPI Antony Rowe, Chippenham and Eastbourne

Visit LexisNexis at www.lexisnexis.co.uk

Preface

As in the case of the writing of the 9th Edition, the preparation of the Supplement to it has proved to be a much larger task than I had envisaged. I am indebted to a number of people for their help. My former articled clerk, now Professor of Law at Leeds University, Michael Cardwell, has not only largely re-written the chapter dealing with the Mid-Term Review of the Common Agricultural Policy, now renamed Payments to Farmers under the Common Agricultural Policy, but he has also updated the chapter on Milk Quota. Ben Sharples has revised the chapter on the Agricultural Land Tribunal, following the wholesale change in the rules relating to conduct of proceedings in that forum. Gary Soloman has re-written the section dealing with compulsory purchase. I have also had invaluable input from the researches undertaken for me by Josie Edwards and Louise Brown.

As with the 9th Edition, the Supplement has been typed by Paula Marlton, which has allowed my long-term secretaries, Jenny Howell (who this year celebrates 30 years of working with me) and Toni Mead, to focus on client work. I am grateful to all three for the work that they have undertaken over many years.

In November 2010 I left Burges Salmon after more than 30 years with the firm to establish Ebery Williams LLP. That was always to be an interim arrangement. In April 2011 I became a Partner in Wilsons. Preparing the Supplement at the same time as I was moving firms created an extraordinary workload. I would not have survived had it not been for the support of Miles Farren, Dinah Close and Emma Nigogosian.

Lastly, my wife, Anne and my three sons, Thomas, Harry and Edward, have again put up with home life being entirely disrupted. I am grateful to them all.

I have endeavoured to state the law as at 1 January 2011.

P R Williams
Wilsons Solicitors LLP

April 2011

Contents

Contents

Section 5 Milk Quota and the Mid-term Review of the Common Agricultural Policy

Appendix I Legislation

Supplementary Table of Statutes

References in the right-hand column are to paragraph number. Paragraph references printed in **bold** type indicate where the provision is set out in part or in full.

Supplementary Table of Statutes

Supplementary Table of Statutory Instruments

References in the right-hand column are to paragraph number. Paragraph references printed in **bold** type indicate where the provision is set out in part or in full.

Supplementary Table of European Legislation

References in the right-hand column are to paragraph number. Paragraph references printed in **bold** type indicate where the provision is set out in part or in full.

Supplementary Table of Cases

A

B

PARA

C

Supplementary Table of Cases

PARA

G

H

PARA

Supplementary Table of Cases

xl

PARA

PARA

DECISIONS OF THE EUROPEAN COURT OF JUSTICE ARE LISTED BELOW
NUMERICALLY. THESE DECISIONS ARE ALSO INCLUDED IN THE PRECEDING
ALPHABETICAL LIST.

PARA

Chapter 1

PROTECTION OF AGRICULTURAL HOLDINGS TENANTS – HISTORICAL INTRODUCTION

AGRICULTURE ACT 1986: MILK QUOTA

1.15 In April 1984[1] milk quota was introduced into the United Kingdom arising from quantitative controls imposed on the production of milk and other dairy products under the Common Agricultural Policy of the European Economic Community, now the European Community (EC). Initially, the quota system, introduced on 2 April 1984, operated for five years. It has subsequently been amended and extended, particularly in 1992[2]. The milk quota system continues, notwithstanding the Mid-term Review of the Common Agricultural Policy[3].

The notable thing about milk quota is that it was the first time that EC legislation directly affected the landlord and tenant relationship applying in respect of agricultural holdings. Between 1984 and the mid-1990s, milk quota increased in value very substantially. As a consequence, a significant value attributed to an agricultural holding was regarded as having passed to the separate asset of milk quota. The question as to whether milk quota 'attached' to land and how it was to be dealt with between the landlord and the tenant exercised practitioners after 1984.

It was as a consequence that in 1986 the Agriculture Act 1986 was enacted to ensure that on the termination of a tenancy, the tenant should share in such part of the value of the quota as was attributable to the quota attached to the agricultural holding being vacated[4].

Because in recent times the value of milk quota has fallen, it is now much less of an issue both between landlords and tenants and, indeed, mortgagors and mortgagees. Nevertheless, it represents the first significant incursion of EC law into the law of agricultural holdings. That has since been followed as a consequence of the Mid-term Review of the Common Agricultural Policy and the introduction of Entitlements[5]. Again, both Entitlements and the right to the Single Payment income represent significant issues for landlords and tenants in respect of agricultural holdings, including lettings under the Agricultural Tenancies Act 1995 (ATA 1995).

[1] See para 49.1.
[2] See para 49.1.
[3] See para 49.1.
[4] See para 49.28.
[5] See para 52.1.

1

THE MID-TERM REVIEW AND THE FUTURE

1.22 Although freedom of contract has continued to be the touchstone for agricultural tenancies in the United Kingdom, it has to be considered within the broader constraints that operate both at EC and world trade levels.

It may be argued that the Mid-term Review of the Common Agricultural Policy[1] has unshackled farmers from the detailed rules of earlier, more specific subsidy regimes, in that the Single Payment embraces most of those regimes and is not dependant upon any particular form of production or production at all[2]. Conversely, the reforms have been characterised as 'decoupling with strings attached'[3].

Although for the purposes of Council Regulation (EC) 1782/2003, governing the introduction of the Mid-term Review of the Common Agricultural Policy, 'agricultural activity' is defined as 'the production, rearing or growing of agricultural products including harvesting, milking, breeding animals for farming purposes, or maintaining the land in good agricultural and environmental condition'[4], what is clear is that, for the purpose of the cross-compliance obligations imposed by Council Regulation (EC) 1782/2003, the farmers obligations are to comprise first, statutory management requirements and, second, a requirement to maintain all agricultural land in good agricultural and environmental condition[5]. This represents a considerable departure from the role of agriculture as described by Lord Salmon in *Johnson v Moreton*[6]. Indeed, as Mrs Margaret Beckett, the then Minister at DEFRA, put it at the Labour Party Conference in September 2005, farmers must redirect their activities from food production to land management[7].

[1]   See Ch 52.
[2]   See 2003 Horizontal Regulation [2003] OJ L270/1, Annex VI, as amended.
[3]   For instance, see: Centre for World Food Studies, Amsterdam, and Netherlands Bureau for Economic Policy Analysis, the Hague, The CAP-reform Proposal of the Mid-Term Review: Decoupling with Strings Attached (Brussels, European Commission, 2002).
[4]   See para 52.4.
[5]   In respect of this obligation, a European Community framework is set out in Annex VI to the 2003 Horizontal Regulation [2003] OJ L270/1.
[6]   [1980] AC 37, [1978] 3 All ER 37, HL.
[7]   The editor is grateful to HAC Densham and MN Cardwell for permission to use material from their essays in Susan Bright (ed), *Landlord and Tenant Law: Past, Present and Future* (2006) Falcon Chambers, Hart Publishing.

Chapter 3

FORMATION OF A FARM BUSINESS TENANCY

WHAT IS A FARM BUSINESS TENANCY?

The section 4 exceptions

Tenancies granted and variations made on or after 19 October 2006

3.12 TRIG2[1] acknowledged that the operation of s 4(1)(f) of the ATA 1995 and the doctrine of implied surrender and re-grant had caused confusion to landlords and tenants alike, and their professional advisers. As a consequence, TRIG2 made the following recommendations:

(a) An additional provision to be included within s 4(1)(f) enabling existing parties to an AHA 1986 tenancy, by mutual consent, to include additional land and buildings within their holding resulting in the 'new' holding being governed by the AHA 1986 and on the same terms (mutatis mutandis) as the original tenancy.

(b) It should no longer be necessary for the 'original' holding to form a substantial part of the 'new' holding either by area or value (whichever is the more significant).

DEFRA accepted the recommendations of TRIG2 and put forward proposals for reform contained in the RRO 2006[2]. As set out in DEFRA's Explanatory Note[3]:

(i) The proposal would amend s 4(1)(f) of the ATA 1995 with the effect that the AHA 1986 will apply to the tenancy in the cases where:
   • the parties come to an agreement (eg to add land to the holding) but which, without their knowledge or intention that it should do so, has effect as a surrender and re-grant; and
   • the parties come to such an agreement and *are* aware that it will have effect as a surrender and re-grant.

(ii) In both the above cases the original holding must be the whole or a substantial part of the new holding.

(iii) The proposal would add a new s 4(1)(g) which would provide that the AHA 1986 will apply where there is a written contract of tenancy which states that the AHA 1986 is to apply, and the tenant previously held an AHA 1986 tenancy of all or a substantial part of the holding.

(iv) The proposal would introduce an anti-avoidance provision (new s 4(2B)), to stop parties from using the amended s 4(1)(f) or new s 4(1)(g) to add land incrementally to a holding and so get around the 'whole or substantial part' requirement. The proposal would also define

3

'substantial' in s 4(1)(g) as meaning either substantial in area or substantial in value, widening the cases in which the new s 4(1)(g) could apply to a proposed restructuring of a holding.

The proposals have been enacted in the RRO 2006[4] with effect from 19 October 2006.

(A)   For the words:

'("the previous tenancy") and is so granted merely because a purported variation of the previous tenancy (not being an agreement expressed to take effect as a new tenancy between the parties) has effect as an implied surrender followed by the grant of the tenancy',
there has been substituted:

', and is so granted because an agreement between the parties (not being an agreement expressed to take effect as a new tenancy between the parties) has effect as an implied surrender followed by the grant of the tenancy, or'[5].

(B)   A new s 4(1)(g) has been inserted[6]:

'(g) is granted to a person who, immediately before the grant of the tenancy, was the tenant of the holding, or of any agricultural holding which comprised the whole or a substantial part of the land compromised in the holding, under a tenancy in relation to which the AHA 1986 applied, and is so granted by a written contract of tenancy indicating (in whatever terms) that the AHA 1986 is to apply in relation to the tenancy'.

As a consequence of the amendments, the parties to an existing 1986 Act tenancy are able to apply the AHA 1986 to a new tenancy by express provision in the contract of tenancy, provided that the tenant previously held an AHA 1986 tenancy of all or a substantial part of the holding[7].

The significant amendments to s 4(1)(f); a new s 4(1)(g) and an anti-avoidance provision contained in s 4(2) of the ATA 1995, have made it easier for landlords and tenants of AHA 1986 tenancies to add land and make other changes without the risk of losing AHA 1986 security, while ensuring that this section cannot be manipulated beyond what was intended by repeated surrenders and re-grants leading to incremental changes in the land let.

1   See para 1.19.
2   SI 2006/2805.
3   Explanatory Document: The Regulatory Reform (Agricultural Tenancies) (England and Wales) Order 2006: Statement by the Department for the Environment, Food and Rural Affairs, March 2006.
4   SI 2006/2805.
5   SI 2006/2805, art 12(4).
6   SI 2006/2805, art 12(5).
7   As to a substantial part of the holding, see the AHA 1986, ss 69(1A) and 73(1A).

4

The definition of a farm business tenancy

The business conditions

FARMED

3.23 The requirement is that all or part of the land comprised in the tenancy must be farmed for the purpose of a trade or business. Minimal commercial farming will, therefore, suffice, although, as will be seen, the character of the tenancy has to be primarily or wholly agricultural at the outset, whether the parties choose to serve notices or not[1]. Diversification within the farm business tenancy regime is only possible for those businesses which were primarily agricultural at the beginning of the tenancy. However, for the business conditions, there is no requirement that the part farmed should be substantial, that it should be a self-sufficient business or that the business it supports should itself be agricultural. Further, there is no requirement that the part of the holding which is farmed should be the same throughout the tenancy.

The condition is that part of the land should be *farmed*, not that it should be used for agriculture. This can be compared with the notice conditions and the agriculture condition which both refer to 'agriculture' and not 'farming'. No definition of farming is given, although s 38(2) of the ATA 1995 provides that references to farming the land include the carrying on in relation to land of any agricultural activity. It can be assumed, therefore, that farming may go beyond agricultural activity and include activities which do not fall within the definition of agriculture.

'Agriculture' is defined in s 38(1) of the ATA 1995. It is the same definition as appears in the AHA 1986[2]. The definition includes livestock breeding and keeping, but the definition of livestock, also in s 38, is not the same as the AHA 1986. The AHA 1986 definition, but not the ATA 1995 definition, includes any creature kept for the purpose of carrying on in relation to land of any agricultural activity but it is arguable that such words were in any event superfluous.

When will an activity be 'farming' which will not be 'agricultural'? In part, the choice of the word 'farmed' is to cater for future changes in the industry which cannot yet be foreseen. However, certain activities which have been held not to be agricultural can be seen as farming. For example, the growing of crops for the testing of pesticides[3] or the breeding of livestock for research purposes. Whilst such activities may satisfy the business conditions they will not satisfy the agriculture condition which requires primary agricultural use at the time of challenge, nor the notice conditions which requires the tenancy to be primarily agricultural at the outset. The non-agricultural-farming activities are, therefore, regarded as diversification activities. If the intention at the outset is for the entire or a substantial part of the holding to be used for such purposes, the tenancy will not be a farm business tenancy.

Whilst the tenant must act in accordance with his obligations under the tenancy, it is not a requirement of the business conditions that the tenant personally farm the holding.

In determining whether the tenancy is being farmed for the purposes of the ATA 1995, it is necessary to disregard commercial use being carried out in breach of the user covenant or a cessation of activities defined in the user covenant[4].

[1]   See the notice conditions (ATA 1995, s 1(4)) and the agriculture condition (ATA 1995, s 1(3)).

[2]   See Ch 19.

[3]   *Dow Agrochemicals v Lane (EA) (North Lynn)* (1965) 192 Estates Gazette 737, 115 L Jo 76, CCA.

[4]   ATA 1995, s 1(8), discussed in relation to the business conditions.

FORMALITIES

Formalities

A contract

3.34 All lettings of land involve a contract between the parties. As such, the agreement between the parties on the basic terms must be sufficiently certain. In the context of letting land this means that the agreement must be clear on the following basic matters:

(a)   parties;
(b)   the extent of the land demised;
(c)   the payment or consideration for the occupation;
(d)   the term[1].

In addition there are particular formal requirements which relate only to contracts for the sale or other disposition of an interest in land which the parties and their advisers need to be aware of. All contracts for the sale or other disposition of an interest in land (and hence including a tenancy or lease) concluded on or after 27 September 1989 must, in accordance with the Law of Property (Miscellaneous Provisions) Act 1989 (LP(MP)A 1989), be in writing and incorporate all the terms which the parties have expressly agreed in one document or, where contracts are exchanged, in each[2]. That document must be signed by, or on behalf of, each party to the contract. If there is an exchange of contracts, each party must sign the document, but not necessarily the same one[3]. Any contract which does not comply with the requirements of the LP(MP)A 1989 is void and ineffective unless it falls within one of the very limited exceptions in the Act. An oral agreement for the grant of a tenancy for a term of five years is void by virtue of s 2 of the Law of Property (Miscellaneous Provisions) Act 1989. The tenant cannot be estopped from relying on that Act. However, where the tenant had entered into possession under a void agreement and had paid an annual rent, this had created an enforceable periodic tenancy. The tenant had failed to terminate it by effective notice when the tenant served notice which did not expire on the relevant quarter day[3A]. Two exceptions of relevance may be mentioned:

(a) short leases such as fall within s 54(2) of the Law of Property Act 1925 (LPA 1925) (see below);
(b) contracts made in the course of a public auction.

Whilst the Act requires the terms to be contained in one document, s 2(2) allows that one document to incorporate terms by reference to some other document rather than to set them out verbatim[4].

It has not been common in the past for the contract for the tenancy and the grant of the tenancy itself to form separate transactions. If there is no preliminary contract, the actual tenancy will be the contract and must (subject to the exceptions for short leases) comply with both the LP(MP)A 1989 and the formal requirements of the LPA 1925. With the increase in fixed-term tenancies, the additional searches and enquiries which a tenant may wish to conduct, and in many cases the need for a deed, a separate contract leading to completion (as with sales of freeholds) may become more common. In which case, the contract must comply with the LP(MP)A 1989 and the disposition itself with the LPA 1925.

[1]   In the absence of a specified date for the commencement of a lease, it may be construed by the court: *Liverpool City Council v Walton Group plc* [2002] 1 EGLR 149.

[2]   LP(MP)A 1989, s 2(1). An arrangement which fails to comply with s 2(1) may be saved by s 2(5) which expressly preserves the creation and operation of constructive trusts: see para 19.30A. Such a trust which arises in relation to an agreement, arrangement or understanding is closely akin to, if not indistinguishable from, proprietary estoppel. See *Yaxley v Gott* [2000] Ch 162, [1999] 2 EGLR 181, CA. Cf *James v Evans* [2000] 3 EGLR 1, [2000] 42 EG 173, CA, where proprietary estoppel can operate through a constructive trust, s 2(5) may help to save oral agreements or incomplete contracts. Also see, para 22.1 fn 10. See *McCauseland v Duncan Lawrie Ltd* [1996] 4 All ER 995, [1997] 1 WLR 38, CA: agreements to vary the contract must likewise comply with s 2.

[3]   LP(MP)A 1989, s 2(3).

[3A] *Hutchison v B&DF Ltd* [2008] EWHC 2286 (Ch), [2009] L&TR 12. Also see, *Looe Fuels Ltd v Looe Harbour Comrs* [2008] EWCA Civ 414, [2008] All ER (D) 305 (Apr). Also see, paras 19.30A and 20.1A.

[4]   *Record v Bell* [1991] 4 All ER 471, [1991] 1 WLR 853; *Tootal Clothing Ltd v Guinea Properties Management Ltd* (1992) 64 P & CR 452, [1992] 2 EGLR 80, CA; *Commission for New Towns v Cooper (Great Britain) Ltd* [1995] Ch 259, [1995] 2 EGLR 113, CA; *Firstpost Homes Ltd v Johnson* [1995] 4 All ER 355, [1996] 1 EGLR 175, CA.

Failure to comply with formalities

3.40 While specific performance is a discretionary remedy[1], it is usually granted where the contract is for the disposition of an interest in land. If the parties are entitled to a decree of specific performance, the equitable maxim 'equity treats as done that which ought to be done' and the principle in the case of *Walsh v Lonsdale*[2] means that, in equity, the tenant is the rightful occupant of the land, but only under an equitable lease, albeit on the same terms and conditions as the intended lease. He can also call for the grant of the lease by deed.

If, in the above circumstances, the tenant has gone into possession and paid rent, he may have acquired a legal periodic tenancy, the period being referable to the frequency of the rental payments[3], This may improve the tenant's position vis-à-vis third parties whilst, against the landlord, he is still entitled to rely upon the equitable rights in the contract including, therefore, any agreement to a fixed term of years and is not, vis-à-vis the landlord forced to rely on the legal periodic tenancy[4].

Legal interests bind the whole world. More needs to be done to protect an equitable interest against third parties. An equitable lease may not bind a later purchaser (including a later tenant) of the legal estate even if he is aware of the letting[5] unless:

(a)   if the land is unregistered, the contract for the lease has been registered as an estate contract[6];

(b)   if the land is registered, it is protected by a notice on the register of the superior title[7];

(c)   if the land is registered and the tenant is in occupation, that occupation will protect his equitable rights provided that the purchaser does not make inquiries of the tenant who fails then to disclose his interest[8].

The position in relation to registered land and the failure to register a lease of more than seven years or a lease to take effect in possession after the end of the period of three months from the grant[9], is dealt with in para 3.38 above. It should be noted that there is a discretion to extend the time limit[10].

Lastly, it should be noted that on 6 April 2010 the Perpetuities and Accumulations Act 2009 came into force for property transactions entered into on or after that day. The Act sweeps away centuries of complex law and simplifies what remains. It relegates the rule against perpetuities to trust law. It substitutes a fixed period of 125 years for all transactions that remain subject to the rule regardless of the period specified in the governing document.

1   See para 45.23.
2   (1882) 21 Ch D 9.
3   *Martin v Smith* (1874) LR 9 Exch 50; *Inntrepreneuer Estates Ltd v Mason* [1993] 2 CMLR 293, [1993] 2 EGLR 189; *Long v Tower Hamlets London Borough Council* [1998] Ch 197, [1997] 1 EGLR 78.
4   *Walsh v Lonsdale* (1882) 21 Ch D 9. As to the application of this principle to agricultural tenancies, see *Padgham v Rochelle* [2002] PLSCS 197.
5   *Midland Bank Trust Co Ltd v Green* [1981] AC 513, [1981] 1 All ER 153, HL; *Lloyds Bank plc v Carrick* [1996] 4 All ER 630, 73 P & CR 314, CA.
6   Land Charges Act 1972, ss 2 and 4.
7   LRA 2002, ss 32–39.
8   LRA 2002, ss 11, 12 and Sch 1 para 2.
9   LRA 2002, s 27(2)(b).
10   LRA 2002, s 6(5).

Chapter 7

USER COVENANTS

ABSOLUTE V QUALIFIED

7.4 When interpreting a user covenant, it is important to consider the distinction between a covenant expressed in the active voice, such as 'not to use' and a covenant expressed in the passive voice, such as 'shall not be used'. The distinction is well established[1]. Where the covenant is in the active voice, a covenant will not be broken if the prohibited act is not undertaken by the covenantor but by a third party, such as a sub-tenant[2].

[1] *Berton v Alliance Economic Investment Co* [1922] 1 KB 742 at 759.
[2] *Roadside Group v Zara Commercial Ltd* [2010] EWHC 1950 (Ch), [2010] 33 EG 70 (CS), [2011] 1 P & CR D11. Also see, *Mackusick v Carmichael* [1917] 2 KB 581.

Chapter 8

ASSIGNMENT AND SUB-LETTING

GENERALLY

8.3 It has been held, in relation to commercial premises, that there is no precise test of the meaning of 'sharing occupation'. The starting point is to consider the nature of the permitted use. The fact that the tenant remained 'exclusively responsible for everything concerned with the property' indicated that the premises had not been shared[1].

In *Akici v LR Butlin Ltd*[2], Neuberger LJ (as he then was) acknowledged that the difference between possession and occupation can be elusive, but it is a difference which is recognised and should be adhered to. Where the owner had unrestricted access to the property, on the facts in *Akici*[3], it was found that there had been no parting with possession.

What was also noteworthy about the *Akici*[4] decision is that the judge limited the impact of the *Scala House and District Property Co Ltd v Forbes*[5] decision to cases where a legal interest had either been created or transferred. Where, as in the *Akici* case, the tenant had allowed a company in which the tenant had no formal interest to operate a business from the premises, if such an act was in breach of covenant it was remediable.

The developments in relation to this area of law were given a further twist by the Court of Appeal in *Clarence House Ltd v National Westminster Bank plc*[6]. In relation to commercial premises, it reversed the decision at first instance holding that a 'virtual assignment' – an arrangement under which only the economic benefits of a lease are transferred – made without the landlord's knowledge did not amount to a parting with possession.

The Court of Appeal's decision in the *Clarence House* case is not quite as it might appear from a cursory reading of the headnote. A 'virtual assignment' is not in fact an assignment per se but a form of management agreement. It can include assigning the right to receive rent from a sub-tenant: a chose in action. However, the issue as to whether this was a breach of the alienation provision is illusory because there was no change in occupation and/or possession. Throughout the property was occupied by the sub-tenant.

It should also be noted that in the High Court in the *Clarence House* case the landlord succeeded in the argument that 'possession' turned on the right to receive rent in accordance with the provisions of s 205 of the Law of Property Act 1925.

¹ *Mean Fiddler Holdings Ltd v Islington London Borough Council* [2003] EWCA Civ 160, [2003] 2 P & CR 102, [2003] 2 EGLR 7 at 10H.
² [2005] EWCA Civ 1296, [2006] 2 All ER 872, [2006] 1 EGLR 34, overruling *Tulapam Properties Ltd v De Almeida* (1981) 260 Estates Gazette 919.
³ [2005] EWCA Civ 1296, [2006] 2 All ER 872, [2006] 1 EGLR 34.
⁴ [2005] EWCA Civ 1296, [2006] 2 All ER 872, [2006] 1 EGLR 34.
⁵ [1974] QB 575, [1973] 3 All ER 308, CA.
⁶ [2009] EWCA Civ 1311, [2010] 2 All ER 201, [2010] 2 All ER (Comm) 1065. Note that the Supreme Court declined to give permission to appeal.

FULLY QUALIFIED COVENANTS

8.4 If the prohibition against alienation is fully qualified, the landlord is under statutory duties in connection with the exercise of his discretion. These duties are contained in the Landlord and Tenant Act 1988 (LTA 1988) and breach may result in a damages claim against him[1].

The LTA 1988 provides that where the landlord receives a written request from the tenant for consent to a disposition, he must, within a reasonable time, give consent, unless it is not reasonable for him to do so, and serve written notice of his decision on the tenant specifying any conditions attached to the consent or, if he is refusing consent, specifying the reasons for the refusal.

While the LTA 1988 shifts the burden of showing reasonableness onto the landlord[2], it does not interfere with the common law as to what will, and what will not, amount to an unreasonable refusal of consent. In the context of non-agricultural commercial lettings, it is usual to have a qualified prohibition. There is extensive case law as to whether or not a landlord has acted reasonably. The extent to which these cases easily translate into the agricultural setting remains to be established, but the following indications from the case law may be useful.

(a)   The landlord is required to act reasonably. It does not matter that there may be other landlords who would not have reached the same conclusion. It is a question of whether a reasonable landlord could have refused consent in these circumstances[2A].

(b)   It is not a question of whether the landlord's concerns can be justified, but simply whether he acted reasonably[3].

(c)   The reason for refusal may be to do with the assignor, rather than the assignee. For example, if the assignor is in breach of covenant and the landlord reasonably suspects that he will not put it right or that the assignee will not put it right, he may be justified in refusing consent if the breach is serious[4].

(d)   It may be reasonable to refuse consent for reasons to do with the personal and financial attributes of the assignee, particularly if the concern is whether or not the assignee will be able to pay the rent and perform the covenants. Unsatisfactory references procured by the landlord may be sufficient reason to refuse consent[5]. Further, in the context of farm business tenancies, it may be legitimate for the landlord to consider the training and practical experience of farming of the proposed assignee and require references as to his husbandry skills.

Potential damage to the landlord's reversion by poor farming techniques may be a reason for refusing consent. Personal considerations of race, sex, age, sexual orientation or disability as reasons for refusing consent will not be reasonable in view of the fact that discrimination on such grounds is unlawful in most cases under the Race Relations Act 1976, the Sex Discrimination Act 1975, the Employment Equality (Age) Regulations 2006[6], the Civil Partnerships Act 2004 and the Disability Discrimination Acts 1995 and 2005.

(e) Can the landlord refuse consent for considerations of sound estate management? It was held in *International Drilling Fluids Ltd v Louisville Investments (Uxbridge) Ltd*[7] that the refusal of the landlord must have something to do with the particular landlord and tenant relationship. Conversely, it has been held in *Town Investments Ltd Underlease, Re, McLaughlin v Town Investments Ltd*[8] that the landlord is entitled to take into account the effect of the assignment on his entire estate. The landlord is not allowed to refuse consent to force the tenant to surrender so as to achieve the collateral advantage of getting the holding back in hand[9]. The answer must depend on the particular facts of the case, but to refuse consent to an assignment where the assignee intends to use the holding for a use which is within the user covenant (and which, therefore, the original tenant himself could have carried out) because it does not fit with the farming pattern on the estate as a whole may not be reasonable[10].

(f) Refusing consent where the intended use would be in breach of the user covenant (and hence where consent would amount to a waiver by the landlord in relation to the breach) is likely to be reasonable[11].

[1] Landlord and Tenant Act 1988, s 4.
[2] At common law, the burden is on the tenant to show that the landlord was acting unreasonably: *Shanly v Ward* (1913) 29 TLR 714.
[2A] Generally see *Homebase Ltd v Allied Dunbar Assurance plc* [2002] EWCA Civ 666, [2003] 1 P & CR 75, [2002] 24 LS Gaz R 38; *Mount Eden Land Ltd v Folia Ltd* [2003] EWHC 1815 (Ch), [2003] NPC 95; *NCR Ltd v Riverland Portfolio No 1 Ltd* [2005] EWCA Civ 312, [2005] 2 EGLR 42, [2005] 22 EG 134; *Crestford Ltd v Tesco Stores Ltd* [2005] EWHC 805 (Ch), [2005] 3 EGLR 25, [2005] 37 EG 148; *Lombard North Central plc v Remax Herbarne Ltd* [2008] EWHC 3161 (Ch), [2009] L&TR 14.
[3] *Air India v Balabel* [1993] 2 EGLR 66, [1993] 30 EG 90, CA; *Beale v Worth* [1993] EGCS 135, CA.
[4] *Goldstein v Sanders* [1915] 1 Ch 549; *Orlando Investments Ltd v Grosvenor Estate Belgravia* (1989) 59 P & CR 21, [1989] 2 EGLR 74, CA.
[5] *Shanly v Ward* (1913) 29 TLR 714.
[6] SI 2006/1031.
[7] [1986] Ch 513, [1986] 1 EGLR 39, CA.
[8] [1954] Ch 301, [1954] 1 All ER 585.
[9] *Bromley Park Garden Estates Ltd v Moss* [1982] 2 All ER 890, [1982] 1 WLR 1019, CA.
[10] Although see *Bates v Donaldson* [1896] 2 QB 241, CA.
[11] *Killick v Second Covent Garden Property Co Ltd* [1973] 2 All ER 337, [1973] 1 WLR 658, CA and cf *Bates v Donaldson* (ante). See also *Ashworth Frazer Ltd v Gloucester City Council* (1999) 80 P & CR 11, [2000] 1 EGLR 44, CA.

LANDLORD AND TENANT (COVENANTS) ACT 1995

8.5 This Act came into force on 1 January 1996. Some of its provisions apply to all existing leases[1] and some only to leases entered into after 31 December

1995 ('new leases')[2]. It abolishes privity of contract between landlord and tenant[3] to new leases so that, on assignment, the tenant is released from his obligations, including that of paying rent[4]. The landlord is also released from his covenants[5]. For leases entered into before 1 January 1996, privity of contract still applies and the original tenant remains liable under the tenancy throughout the term even after he has assigned, leaving the tenant vulnerable to actions on the covenants where the assignee defaults.

While the tenant under a new lease is better off, the landlord is clearly worse off[6] and the Landlord and Tenant (Covenants) Act 1995 makes some provision to compensate by the provision in s 16 that a landlord may, as a condition of consent to assignment where there is a qualified prohibition, require the original tenant to enter into an authorised guarantee agreement (AGA) whereby he guarantees the performance of the tenant covenants by his immediate assignee, although there are strict controls over what can be contained in such an agreement[7].

[1]   The Agricultural Tenancies Act 1995 (ATA 1995), ss 17–20. As to the relevance of the Landlord and Tenant (Covenants) Act 1995 to remedies, see Ch 45.
[2]   As defined in the ATA 1995, s 1(3). It should be noted that delivery of the lease in escrow is not the relevant date: *Dyment v Boyden* [2004] EWCA Civ 1586, [2005] 1 WLR 792, [2005] 1 EGLR 19.
[3]   ATA 1995, s 5.
[4]   Provided that the assignment is not in breach of covenant or results from, for example, the tenant's bankruptcy. In these cases, the tenant continues to be bound until the next assignment.
[5]   ATA 1995, s 2.
[6]   *Scottish & Newcastle plc v Raguz* [2008] UKHL 65, [2009] 1 All ER 763, [2009] 2 All ER (Comm) 447.
[7]   For the creation of a valid AGA, see the requirements set out in the ATA 1995, s 16.

Chapter 9
RENT AND RENT REVIEW

INTRODUCTION

9.3 TRIG2[1] agreed that the provisions of the ATA 1995, as originally enacted, were unnecessary in principle and led to needless complication in some cases. The parties should be given greater flexibility to agree their own arrangements.

There was a political expedient leading to the dismantling of the previous compromise. TRIG2 noted that a relaxation in the rules governing rent review provisions would remove a major reason why some AHA 1986 tenants would not consider surrendering their 'protected' tenancies in exchange for better holdings let on farm business tenancies. Under the original rent review provisions under the ATA 1995, TRIG2 observed that a 1995 Act rent could not easily be reviewed adopting the 1986 Act formula.

TRIG2 also considered it appropriate that the arbitrator (including any other person appointed to determine the rent) should be entitled to fix the rent by reference to all provisions within the tenancy agreement including those by reference to which the rent is to be determined. The ATA 1995 prohibited the arbitrator from considering rent review criteria previously agreed between the parties[2].

TRIG2 recommended that:

(a)   section 9 of the ATA 1995 should be modified to apply Pt II in every case, except where the parties agree otherwise in writing, provided that no such agreement be permitted which would result in an upwards-only rent review provision;

(b)   the parties to an ATA 1995 tenancy should be precluded from proceeding to arbitration under the statutory rules in cases where the tenancy agreement itself provides another mechanism for settling disputes as to the amount of the rent;

(c)   it should be open to an arbitrator to fix the rent by reference to all provisions of a tenancy agreement, including those by reference to which the rent is to be determined.

These recommendations have been adopted and implemented by the Regulatory Reform (Agricultural Tenancies) (England and Wales) Order 2006 (RRO 2006)[3] coming into force on 19 October 2006[4].

14

Accordingly, the RRO 2006 now enables the parties to reach a *binding* agreement to review the rent on any basis they choose (including reference to the AHA 1986 rent review formula) provided that certain conditions are satisfied[5].

Article 14 of the RRO 2006, which introduced these amendments, provides that the amendments will only apply 'where the provision in the instrument creating the tenancy referred to in the new section 9(c)' is made on or after 19 October 2006. In the ninth edition of this book it was suggested that this does not confine the amendment to tenancies granted on or after that date. The parties can agree to vary the rent review mechanism in any existing tenancy[5A]. However, it should be recognised that this is arguable as Article 14 is capable of being read to mean that it only applies to agreements concluded after the RRO 2006 came into force[5B].

The original options under s 9 are still available after 19 October 2006 and, if the parties choose to adopt them, will continue to attract the same issues which existed before the amendments introduced by the RRO 2006. It is unlikely that, save in very limited circumstances, any post-RRO 2006 tenancy considering a rent review other than on the statutory open market basis would do anything other than rely upon s 9(c)[6].

This represents a move away from the rent review compromise originally contained in the ATA 1995 to almost total freedom of contract for the parties. It is in part in recognition of the problems of managing AHA 1986 tenancies. The vast majority of issues which have arisen since the ATA 1995 came into force in relation to rent review have not been with farm business tenancies, but the resultant lack of flexibility for landlords and tenants in connection with AHA 1986 protected tenancies. The changes introduced by the RRO 2006, whether in relation to surrender and re-grant (where the risk to a tenant of losing AHA 1986 security has been reduced) or in relation to rent review (where the amendments have removed one of the major hurdles to moving AHA 1986 tenants onto farm business tenancies) have greatly eased the management of AHA 1986 tenancies.

[1]   Tenancy Reform Industry Group (2002), see para 1.19.
[2]   ATA 1995, s 13(2), as originally enacted. See para 9.16ff.
[3]   SI 2006/2805.
[4]   SI 2006/2805, art 1(1).
[5]   See para 9.13.
[5A] A view shared by guidance issued by the Central Association of Valuers.
[5B] See C P Rodgers, *Agricultural Law* (3rd edn, 2008) Tottel, para 3.100.
[6]   See para 9.14.

THE STATUTORY RENT REVIEW FORMULA

The rent properly payable in respect of the holding

Introduction

9.17 This wording is familiar from Sch 2 to the AHA 1986. Like the AHA 1986, s 13 of the ATA 1995 sets out what the rent properly payable is; what the arbitrator must have regard to; and to determine the ambit of his inquiry by imposing disregards[A1].

Section 13(2) provides that the rent properly payable in respect of the holding is:

> '... the rent at which the holding might reasonably be expected to be let on the open market by a willing landlord to a willing tenant taking into account (subject to subsections (3) and (4) below) all relevant factors, including (in every case) the terms of the tenancy (including those which are relevant for the purposes of section 10(4) to (6) of this Act, but not those which (apart from this section) preclude a reduction in the rent during the tenancy)'[1].

From this definition, it can be seen that, save in so far as it impacts upon the determination of the open market rent, the arbitrator does not have to have regard to the productive capacity or related earning capacity of the holding. It is clear that in many cases the earning capacity of the holding will have an impact on demand and therefore on the rent which the market is willing to pay. Neither, in contrast to the AHA 1986, is the arbitrator *directed* to consider the rent of comparable holdings[2] or the character and situation of the holding and, while he has to assume that the parties are willing, he does not have to assume that they are prudent[3].

The review of rents on an open-market basis does reflect the move away from security of tenure to freedom of contract. Supply and demand governs the level of rents payable. On review, it is supply and demand for the particular letting and, therefore, the terms of the tenancy must be taken into account by the arbitrator. Some terms will have more impact that others. User covenants which restrict the tenant's ability to develop and diversify, while assisting the protection of the tenancy's status as a farm business tenancy, may depress the rent. Conversely, user covenants which allow for significant diversification may increase the rent, even though that tenant is not actually diversifying, the potential non-agricultural income from diversification is a matter which will be taken into account.

Full repairing leases may at first seem attractive to a landlord of a dilapidated estate, but will undoubtedly have an impact on review. The length of the term will be important as will be the tenant's ability to escape his obligations by utilising break provisions or by assigning the remainder of the term. The frequency of reviews and whether rent is payable in advance of arrears will also have an impact. The arbitrator is specifically directed to consider these factors.

Prior to the RRO 2006, when an arbitrator was determining the open market rent under s 13(2) of the ATA 1995, he was not permitted to take into account any terms in the tenancy agreement relating to the criteria by reference to which any new rent was to be determined. As seen above, this restriction no longer applies. The only term which the arbitrator is now to ignore is any provision which would preclude a reduction in the rent. This amendment applies to all tenancies or rent review provisions under the ATA 1995, whenever entered into, and it is not limited to tenancies granted on or after 19 October 2006 when the RRO 2006 came into force[4].

[A1] See *Morrison-Low v Paterson* (2010) SLC/233/08. Also see, para 29.18A.
[1] ATA 1995, s 13(2), as amended by the RRO 2006, SI 2006/2805, arts 11 and 15.

2   And note the restriction on his considering other arbitrator's awards: *Land Securities plc v Westminster City Council* [1993] 4 All ER 124, [1992] 2 EGLR 15.
3   Cf Sch 2 to the AHA 1986.
4   ATA 1995, s 13(2), as amended by the RRO 2006, SI 2006/2805, arts 11 and 15.

The basis of valuation

9.19 A rent review clause contemplates the assessment of the rent which would be achieved on a hypothetical letting. This exercise, involving a hypothetical transaction, contains four stages in the arbitrator's analysis:

(a)   the hypothetical landlord and tenant;
(b)   the property to be valued;
(c)   the duration of the hypothetical letting; and
(d)   the terms of the hypothetical letting.

The hypothetical willing landlord and willing tenant have been the subject of judicial scrutiny in the context of contractual provisions in commercial leases. From the case of *Evans (FR) (Leeds) Ltd v English Electric Co Ltd*[1], it is worth noting the explanation of the willing landlord and the willing tenant given by Donaldson J where he clarifies the extent of the hypothesis. He makes it clear that the willing party is an abstraction and a hypothetical person so that circumstances personal to the particular party should not be taken into account. The landlord is not affected by personal ills such as a cash flow crisis but neither is he to be taken to be willing to wait to let. The assumption is that he is willing, though not desperate, to let at the review date. Similarly, the willing tenant is to be taken to be actively seeking premises but unaffected by liquidity problems. However, the parties are not to be taken to be totally isolated from the real world. In the words of Donaldson J, they are not to be taken to be negotiating in a vacuum. Those real factors that would have an impact on every landlord or tenant negotiating the hypothetical letting, such as the availability of other land, the rent on comparable holdings, etc, should be taken into account.

The property to be valued is the demised property let by the farm business tenancy[1A]. It is necessary for the arbitrator to consider the physical subject matter of the property to be valued as it stands at the date of valuation[2]. The exercise in valuing the property to be valued is not as straightforward as it first appears. First, it is subject to the statutory disregards which are contained in ss 13(3) and 4(b)[3]. Second, there are other factors which have a bearing on the assumed physical subject matter. In the context of commercial leases, this has given rise to a number of issues such as the valuation of property in an assumed state[4]. The issue of an assumed state is not one which may have exercised values of agricultural property in the past, but with increasing diversification, issues about assumed state may have greater prominence. For example, an assumption that the property is fully fitted out and equipped for occupation does not require the rentalisation of equipment which is not fixed to the property[5].

As to the duration of the hypothetical letting, this is a difficult point in the case of farm business tenancies, which are typically quite short and often

17

periodic. In commercial rent review cases, there is a strong assumption that the duration of the hypothetical letting is equal to the unexpired term of the actual lease. In the case of AHA 1986 tenancies, it has never been a live issue because the tenant had security of tenure and the rent review would be triennial.

There is no guidance in s 13 of the ATA 1995 as to the notional term of the hypothetical new letting. In commercial leases, with express rent review provisions, the notional term is often expressly stated. The parties to farm business tenancies do not have the freedom to add to the s 13 formula[6]. The question is whether the arbitrator is to assume a new letting for the unexpired term of the old or is to assume a new letting for the same original term as the subject tenancy or for some other term.

In the absence of guidance in s 13 of the ATA 1995 as to the length of the new hypothetical letting, the common law position must be relied upon. The position is that the arbitrator should value the unexpired residue of the term as at the review date. This accords with the case law on commercial lettings[7]. A 12-year term with three years left to run will, therefore, be looked at as a three-year term for the purposes of review, but as a letting on the terms of the original tenancy which may, of course, be wholly inappropriate or unduly onerous against the assumption of a letting for three years.

Lastly, the arbitrator is required by s 13(1)(a) of the ATA 1995 to take into account the terms of the hypothetical letting, including those relating to the review of rent. These will include restrictions on user and repairing[8] and similar obligations[9].

[1] (1977) 36 P & CR 185, [1978] 1 EGLR 93.
[1A] The wording of the rent review provision needs careful consideration. For example, in *Coors Holdings Ltd v Dow Properties Ltd* [2007] EWCA Civ 255, [2007] 2 P & CR 461, the Court of Appeal considered the rent review provisions in a 90 year lease of a public house. The issue was whether the words 'the site comprised in the demised premises' had the effect that the rental value was to be assessed by reference only to the land on which the public house was built or to the land and building as erected on it. In other words, did the phrase 'the site comprised in' mean that the building was to be disregarded for rent review purposes? The Court of Appeal held that it did. Also see, *Elmbirch Properties v Schaefer Tsoropatzadis* [2008] 2 P & CR 8, [2007] 2 EGLR 167.
[2] *Ponsford v HMS Aerosols Ltd* [1979] AC 63, [1978] 2 All ER 837, HL.
[3] See para 9.20.
[4] See *Woodfall: Landlord and Tenant* (Looseleaf edn, 1994) Sweet & Maxwell, para 8.032.
[5] *Ocean Accident & Guarantee Corpn v Next plc* [1996] 2 EGLR 84, [1996] 33 EG 91.
[6] Other than adopting it as an express review.
[7] *R & A Millett (Shops) Ltd v Legal and General Assurance Society Ltd* [1985] 1 EGLR 103, 274 Estates Gazette 1252; *Norwich Union Life Insurance Society v Trustee Savings Banks Central Board* [1986] 1 EGLR 136, 278 Estates Gazette 162 and *Ritz Hotel (London) Ltd v Ritz Casino Ltd* [1989] 2 EGLR 135, [1989] 46 EG 95.
[8] See para 9.17.
[9] As to the treatment of entitlements and Single Farm Payments, see paras 25.29 and 52.31.

SEVERED REVERSIONS

9.23 The problems of the service of rent review trigger notices following the severance of the landlord's reversionary interest arise also in connection with

AHA 1986 tenancies[1]. Following the severance of the reversion, where the original tenancy remains, the severance does not itself create separate tenancies[2]. If that is all that has happened, the severance has no impact on rent review at all, save to make it more difficult for one landlord to review the rent without the concurrence of the other[3]. However, separate tenancies of each severed part will arise if either:

(1) there is an express agreement with the tenant to enter into new tenancies; or
(2) the tenant is a party to the deed of severance and agrees to apportion the rent between the severed parts.

It may be in the interest of the landlords to seek agreement in relation to new tenancies to get around the problem of the service of notices. Where they do so, then provided that the rent payable under each new tenancy is merely the apportioned part of that payable under the old tenancy, the rent review cycle will continue through to the new tenancy[4]. If, for example, the rent had been reviewed under the old tenancy two years previously, and assuming three-yearly reviews, the first review under the new tenancy will be one year after the severance.

[1]   See paras 25.6ff and 29.10.
[2]   Cf *Jelley v Buckman* [1974] QB 488, [1973] 3 All ER 853, CA.
[3]   *Stiles v Farrow* (1977) 241 Estates Gazette 623.
[4]   ATA 1995, s 11.

PROCEDURE AND THE ARBITRATION

Triggering the rent review procedure

9.24 The trigger mechanism necessary to commence the review procedure depends upon whether the rent review formula is one which falls within s 9 of the ATA 1995 or not. If the parties are seeking to review the rent by reference to a section 9 option, it may be that no trigger is necessary. If the choices are mechanical (ie one of the original section 9(a) or (b) options), the parties may have chosen to make the review automatic rather than provide for it to be instigated by one of the parties[1]. If the parties do require there to be a trigger, they will have to provide for it specifically. A trigger is likely for a section 9(c) option. If there is a trigger, such provision should make clear:

(a) who is entitled to trigger the review[2];
(b) when the trigger notice can be served;
(c) the form of the notice and whether writing is required[2A];
(d) service requirements – as the trigger will not be a notice or document required or authorised to be served under the ATA 1995, the provisions of s 36 will not apply;
(e) whether the notice needs to set out the amount of rent required by the landlord; and
(f) whether time is to be of the essence[3].

One issue which can arise is the relevant date for the rent review. In *Bisichi Mining Ltd v Bass Holdings Ltd*[4], the High Court held that where the lease entitled the landlord to give notice seeking a review during the first six weeks of certain specified years of 'the said term', this meant the term commencing on the execution of the lease and the first rent payment and not, as the arbitrator had decided, the term date specified in the lease.

[1] Although in the commercial sector see the case of *Stylo Shoes Ltd v Wetherall Bond Street W1 Ltd* (1974) 237 Estates Gazette 343 where it was held that if the lease did not expressly require the service of a trigger notice, one would be implied. The implication could only be necessary in relation to the section 9 option which is the application of a mechanical formula and will depend upon the wording of the review formula. See, on the other hand, *Woodhouse (Edwin) Trustee Co Ltd v Sheffield Brick Co plc* [1984] 1 EGLR 130, 270 Estates Gazette 548.

[2] *First Property Growth Partnership LP v Royal & Sun Alliance Property Services Ltd* [2002] EWHC 305 (Ch), [2002] 12 LS Gaz R 36, [2002] 2 EGLR 11, affd [2002] EWCA Civ 1687, [2003] 1 All ER 533, [2003] 1 EGLR 39.

[2A] Note that a letter marked 'subject to contract and without prejudice' will not be sufficient to trigger a rent review: *Maurice Investments Ltd v Lincoln Insurance Services Ltd* [2006] EWHC 376, [2007] 1 P & CR 235.

[3] It will not be unless the clause expressly so provides or it is implied by other terms of the lease (*United Scientific Holdings Ltd v Burnley Borough Council* [1978] AC 904, [1977] 2 All ER 62, HL). A deeming provision – which provides that a tenant will be deemed to have agreed to a rent level proposed by the landlord in the absence of the service of a counter notice with a set time – will not of itself make time of the essence *Starmark Enterprises Ltd v CPL Distribution Ltd* [2001] EWCA Civ 1252, [2002] Ch 306, [2002] 4 All ER 264, following *Mecca Leisure Ltd v Renown Investments (Holdings) Ltd* (1984) 49 P & CR 12, [1984] 2 EGLR 137, CA. Also see, *McDonald's Property Co Ltd v HSBC Bank plc* [2002] 1 P & CR 333, [2001] 3 EGLR 19.

[4] [2002] EWHC 375 (Ch), [2002] 2 EGLR 4, (2002) 18 EG 159. Also see *Riverside Housing Association Ltd v White* [2005] EWCA Civ 1385, [2006] 1 EGLR 45, [2005] 50 EG 91 (CS).

Chapter 10

REPAIRS

PARTICULAR COVENANTS AND THE STANDARD OF REPAIRS

To keep in repair

10.6 An obligation to keep in repair includes an obligation to put premises into repair[1] where they are dilapidated at the beginning of the term. The general state of the premises, even in the light of such an obligation, is still of relevance in providing guidance as to the standard of repair contemplated by the parties, even though there may be specific items requiring repair immediately upon commencement of the tenancy. To keep in repair generally means to keep in repair at all times. Hence there will be a breach of the repairing obligation as soon as a defect occurs[2]. Where the obligation is on the landlord to repair, his obligation only arises when he has knowledge of the defect or of facts which would put a reasonable landlord on inquiry. Such a limitation is implied into the contract of tenancy[3]. A tenant is unlikely to succeed in the argument that a landlord may be responsible for repairs or defects, beyond the landlord's contractual repairing obligations, arising from the law of nuisance[4].

[1] *Proudfoot v Hart* (1890) 25 QBD 42, CA. Note that the *Proudfoot* test may not apply in longer leases: *Anstruther-Gough-Calthorpe v McOscar* [1924] 1 KB 716, CA (a lease of 95 years).
[2] *British Telecommunications plc v Sun Life Assurance Society plc* [1996] Ch 69, [1995] 2 EGLR 44, CA.
[3] *Makin v Watkinson* (1870) LR 6 Exch 25.
[4] *Jackson v JH Watson Property Investment Ltd* [2008] EWHC 14 (Ch), [2008] 1 P & CR D45, [2008] 1 EGLR 33.

To leave in repair/to yield up in repair

10.9 If the only covenant given by a tenant is to leave or yield up the holding in repair, the landlord has no dilapidations claim until the tenancy has terminated. However, such a clause is usually combined with an obligation to keep the demise in repair. Where the covenant was to deliver up the premises in 'good and substantial condition', the extent of the repairs that a tenant may be required to undertake to comply with such a covenant can give rise to significant dispute[1]. Further, a covenant to leave in good repair and condition has been held to require a tenant to remove any equipment which is redundant[2]. This may be particularly relevant to a tenancy of a dairy farm.

[1] *Carmel Southend Ltd v Strachan & Henshaw Ltd* [2007] EWHC 1289 (TCC), [2007] 35 EG 136.
[2] *Shortlands Investments Ltd v Cargill plc* [1995] 1 EGLR 51, [1995] 08 EG 163.

Roof repairs

10.11A Although it is beyond the scope of this book to consider repairing obligations in relation to individual items in detail, some comments in relation to roofs and windows are necessary because this is a regular area of dispute in respect of farmhouses and farm buildings.

A reference to a roof will include both the external covering of the roof and the supporting structure, such as rafters and beams. It would not include things which are not, strictly speaking, part of the roof properly so called, such as chimney stacks, parapet walls and guttering. However, the context may show that the parties intended some or all of these to be within the obligation. In *Taylor v Webb*[1] (not appealed on this point), the landlord covenanted to repair 'outside walls and roofs'. At some stage there had been an addition to the original building, in that a passage had been built over the roof of the rear ground floor premises which led to an upper storey behind. The passage was lit from above by means of glass skylights, which appear to have formed a very substantial part of the passage. The Judge held that these were within the landlord's obligation. He said: 'I have no doubt that the skylights are part of the building, and I also think that they are part of the roofs, and that was the intention of the parties. If they were not, it would mean that over that part of the building there would be no roofs'. However, as Lord Evershed MR pointed out in *Holiday Fellowship Ltd v Viscount Hereford*[2], it does not follow from this that skylights are always part of the roofs in which they are set. The question in every case depends upon the proper construction of the lease.

The expression 'window' refers to all parts of a window, including its frame and glazing. One problem arising in practice is whether the expression extends to skylights or other horizontal glazing. Such authority as there is appears to suggest that it does. Thus, in *Easton v Isted*[3] Joyce J said: 'A window is not less a window because it is not capable of being opened, nor is it less a window because it is not fixed in a vertical plane. I think the glazed top of a conservatory was just as much a window as the fixed portions of the vertical side'. The question whether skylights were 'windows' arose in *Ayling v Wade*[4] in which the tenant had covenanted to repair 'the interior of the premises including all ... windows'. Danckwerts LJ recorded counsel's concession that the tenant's obligation did not extend to the glass in a skylight on the flat roof of part of the premises in the following terms: 'Apparently, it is accepted that a window does not include a skylight in the present case, a matter on which I think I should have felt some difficulty'.

[1]   [1937] 2 KB 283, [1937] 1 All ER 590, CA.
[2]   [1959] 1 All ER 433, [1959] 1 WLR 211, CA.
[3]   [1903] 1 Ch 405.
[4]   [1961] 2 QB 228, [1961] 2 All ER 399, CA.

Competing or no obligations to repair

10.11B Unlike the AHA 1986, the ATA 1995 does not have the fallback of the 'model clauses'[1]. Accordingly, if the repairing obligations in the tenancy agreement fail to make the landlord or the tenant responsible for a particular item of repair, a genuine lacuna may exist.

Conversely there may be competing landlord and tenant repair covenants in a tenancy agreement. In such cases it is necessary for the Court to consider where the primary obligation lies[2].

¹   See para 23.5.
²   *Janet Reger International Ltd v Tiree Ltd* [2006] EWHC 1753 (Ch), [2007] 1 P & CR 24.

REMEDIES

The landlord's remedies

10.12 The landlord may have four options:

(a)   to sue for damages[A1];
(b)   to enter, carry out the repairs and sue for debt;
(c)   to forfeit the lease[1];
(d)   apply for specific performance.

Until recently it was thought that a landlord could not obtain a decree of specific performance against the tenant[2]. However, it would seem that, on the authority of *Rainbow Estates Ltd v Tokenhold Ltd*[3], a decree may be available in appropriate circumstances. In the *Rainbow* case, there was no power for the landlord to enter to carry out repairs, nor was there a valid forfeiture clause. These factors were considerations in the court's decision to grant specific performance.

The Leasehold Property (Repairs) Act 1938, which requires a landlord to obtain the leave of the court before suing for damages for forfeiting for breach of a repairing covenant during the term of certain leases, does not apply to farm business tenancies[4].

The amount of damages recoverable, whether during the term or at the end, is circumscribed by s 18(1) of the Landlord and Tenant Act 1927 (LTA 1927). The LTA 1927 provides that the landlord's damages are in no case to exceed the amount by which the value of the reversion is diminished by reason of the breach[5]. From this it can be seen that, the earlier during a term a landlord brings an action, the less will be the damage to the reversion in most cases and the lower the ceiling on the damages. Towards the end of the term, particularly where, as with farm business tenancies, there is no security of tenure, the more likely it is that the breach of covenant will lead to a substantial diminution in the value of the landlord's interest. It is important to note that s 18(1) does not affect the measure of damages at all, but simply places a cap on recovery[5A].

It has long been established that generally, where the landlord intends to carry out the repairs or he has carried them out, the measure of damages will be the cost of the repairs[6].

10.12   *Repairs*

A landlord should beware of over-stating the claim for damages as to do so may result in the landlord being penalised in costs[7]. Also, the landlord's costs in negotiations in relation to repair works are not costs incurred in connection with any steps taken in or in contemplation of proceedings under the Law of Property Act 1925[8].

[A1]   In *Hawkins v Woodhall* [2008] EWCA Civ 932, [2008] All ER (D) 375 (Jun), the court was prepared to order that the landlord should be responsible for the tenant's loss of profits as a consequence of the landlord's breach of his repairing obligations.

[1]   See Ch 13.

[2]   *Hill v Barclay* (1810) 16 Ves 402; *Jeune v Queens Cross Properties Ltd* [1974] Ch 97, [1973] 3 All ER 97.

[3]   [1999] Ch 64, [1998] 2 EGLR 34.

[4]   ATA 1995, Sch para 8.

[5]   LTA 1927, s 18(1). Also see, *Van Dal Footwear Ltd v Ryman Ltd* [2009] EWCA Civ 1478, [2010] 1 All ER 883, [2010] 1 WLR 2015.

[5A]   It has been suggested by Mr Guy Fetherstonhaugh QC that breaches should be analysed 'dynamically, rather than through the termination dilapidations telescope, which tends to focus on a snapshot analysis of the breaches at the contractual term date': see Estates Gazette, 17 July 2010 p 82. Cf *Brew Bros Ltd v Snax (Ross) Ltd* [1970] 1 QB 612, [1970] 1 All ER 587, CA. Also see, the Blundell Lecture of Mr Kirk Reynolds QC, Estates Gazette, 14 August 2010 p 53.

[6]   *Jones v Herxheimer* [1950] 2 KB 106, [1950] 1 All ER 323, CA. Also see *Mason v Totalfinaelf UK Ltd* [2003] EWHC 1604 (Ch), [2003] 3 EGLR 91, where *Crewe Services & Investment Corpn v Silk* (1997) 79 P & CR 500, [1998] 2 EGLR 1, [1998] 35 EG 81, CA was not cited; *Latimer v Carney* [2006] EWCA Civ 1417, [2007] 1 P & CR 213.

[7]   *Business Environment Bow Lane Ltd v Deanwater Estates Ltd* [2008] EWHC 2003 (TCC), [2008] 3 EGLR 105.

[8]   *Agricullo Ltd v Yorkshire Housing Ltd* [2010] EWCA Civ 229, [2010] 2 P & CR 173, [2010] L&TR 9.

10.13   In *Crewe Services & Investment Corpn v Silk*[1], the letting was of an AHA 1986 tenancy. The landlord sued for damages for disrepair during the term of the tenancy. At first instance, referring to *Jones v Herxheimer*[2], the judge assessed damages at £15,940. The Court of Appeal allowed the appeal. The court confirmed that the test at common law for assessing damages for breach of a repairing covenant during a continuing tenancy is the diminution in the value of the freehold reversion. The judge was found to have relied too much on the general principle stated in *Jones v Herxheimer*[3] that the cost of repairs may represent the damage to the value of the reversion. The permissible heads of damage and the measure of damages must in principle be arrived at by an objective test. At the end of a tenancy, the cost of repairs, or that cost only slightly discounted, may be the best evidence of the diminution of the value of the freehold reversion if the tenant fails to establish, by leading evidence, that the diminution is less. However, it was wrong to treat the undiscounted costs of repairs as a safe guide to the damage to the value of the reversion where the landlord owned the farm subject to a continuing, protected tenancy of an unpredictable duration, and where there was no evidence that the landlord intended to undertake the repairs. The judge would have been assisted by evidence of the effect of the disrepair caused by the tenant's breaches of covenant on the value of the freehold reversion if it had been put on the market, subject to and with the benefit of the tenancy, at the date of the hearing. In the absence of such evidence, the judge was not bound to award nominal damages. The cost of repairs was discounted by almost three-quarters to take account of the uncertainties.

Once the amount of damages has been assessed, it must be compared with the diminution in the value of the landlord's reversion. This is done by looking at the value of the reversion with the premises in their actual state and the value it would be had there been no breach of covenant.

If an action is brought for damages at the end of the term (the landlord's dilapidations claim) the same limitation applies. Further, LTA 1927, s 18(1) provides that no damages will be payable if it can be shown that the premises, in whatever state of repair, are going to be demolished. This may be the case where, for example, the land is to be acquired under a CPO or where the landlord is intending to redevelop.

It should be noted that where a landlord pursues an exaggerated claim, even when he succeeds in being awarded damages, he may be penalised in costs where the tenant has protected himself by an offer of settlement under Part 36 of the Civil Procedure Rules or otherwise[3A].

A well drawn tenancy agreement will reserve to the landlord the right to enter the holding and to carry out repairs which the tenant has failed to execute[4]. It will usually go on to provide that the repairs executed by the landlord will be at the tenant's expense. The sums expended by the landlord are recoverable as a debt from the tenant and not as damages[5]. The balance of authority seems to suggest that, in such circumstances, the ceiling on damages in s 18(1) of the LTA 1927 would not apply[6].

Forfeiture is the only remedy available to a landlord with a tenant in breach of repairing covenant which gets the holding back in hand, subject to the tenant's right to apply for relief. Forfeiture is dealt with in detail in Chapter 13.

[1]   (1997) 79 P & CR 500, [1998] 2 EGLR 1, [1998] 35 EG 81, CA. Also see, *Latimer v Carney* [2006] EWCA Civ 1417, [2007] 1 P & CR 213.
[2]   [1950] 2 KB 106, [1950] 1 All ER 323, CA.
[3]   [1950] 2 KB 106, [1950] 1 All ER 323, CA.
[3A] *Business Environment Bow Lane Ltd v Deanwater Estates Ltd* [2009] EWHC 2014 (Ch), (2009) PLSCS 234.
[4]   The landlord has no implied right of entry to carry out the tenant's repairing obligations, although he does to carry out his own.
[5]   This is important for commercial lettings as a way of avoiding the strictures of the Leasehold Property (Repairs) Act 1938 which applies to damages claims only – see, inter alia, *Colchester Estates (Cardiff) v Carlton Industries plc* [1986] Ch 80, [1984] 2 All ER 601; *Elite Investments Ltd v TI Bainbridge Silencers Ltd* [1986] 2 EGLR 43, 280 Estates Gazette 1001.
[6]   See the cases at fn 1 above.

Dilapidations protocol

10.16 In 1998, the Civil Procedure Rules introduced the concept of pre-action protocols. The aim was to reduce litigation. Since June 2000, the Property Litigation Association has sought to promote a dilapidations protocol for commercial landlords and tenants[1]. So far it has not been implemented[2] and currently it has no relevance to the agricultural sector.

10.16   *Repairs*

[1]   See an article in the Estates Gazette, 11 November 2006, 'Further debate needed by all parties', P Stell.
[2]   Note that it is annexed to the RICS Dilapidations Guidance Notes, the fifth edition of which came into effect in 2008. That too has been the source of some 'heated' discussions: see an article in the Estates Gazette, 10 April 2010, 'Sought-after clarification', B Woolhouse.

Chapter 11
OTHER TERMS

EARLY RESUMPTION OR BREAK CLAUSES

11.5 There is nothing in the ATA 1995 to prevent the parties agreeing an early resumption clause or option to break a fixed-term tenancy before its term date[1]. For fixed-term leases of over two years there is a requirement that any notice necessary to exercise the option must be of at least 12 months' duration[2]. Such a requirement will override any shorter notice provision in the lease.

For longer fixed-term tenancies, break clauses will be important to the tenant, who might otherwise be locked in for the entire fixed term with a rent he can no longer afford and if he is unable to assign[3]. It may be important for the landlord where changes in fiscal policy, personal circumstances or redevelopment opportunities may lead to a change in priorities for the land.

An option to break can be exercisable by the landlord or the tenant or by both. It can be limited to the happening of specific events or to specific times (perhaps to coincide with rent review) or can be unrestricted. Where there are no conditions which need to be met (either events or time), the motive of the person exercising the option is irrelevant[4]. While the courts are astute to ensure that break clauses based on the default of the tenant are properly interpreted as forfeiture clauses (thus allowing the tenant to apply for relief)[5], it is not possible to look at the motive of a landlord exercising an open option to break.

Options to break will be strictly construed both in relation to any conditions which must be met before exercise[6] and, subject to s 7 of the ATA 1995, any time limits which are laid down. Time is of the essence[7].

The impact of a break clause on, for example, the rent; the ability of the tenant to raise finance and the willingness of the tenant to invest in the holding, will depend upon the circumstances in which the option can be exercised and how frequently it can be exercised. If the parties are concerned, and particularly if the purpose of the break is to enable a landlord to take advantage of possible development opportunities, it may be possible to grant a separate, periodic, or short fixed-term tenancy of part of the holding. Such a split may have an impact at rent review. Furthermore, depending upon the intended use of the holding, it could mean that part of the letting is not then 'primarily or wholly agricultural' so as to comply with the notice conditions[8] or the agriculture condition[9]. In the alternative, for a fixed-term tenancy, the parties may agree that the tenancy of the part, which is not primarily or wholly agricultural, to be excluded from the security of tenure provisions of Pt II of the Landlord and Tenant Act 1954, if protection under that Act would otherwise arise[10].

1   See Ch 12.
2   ATA 1995, s 7.
3   Cf the Agricultural Holdings Act 1986 where the tenant can always serve a 12-month notice to quit. See para 28.10.
4   *Batty v Vincent and City of London Real Property Co* (1921) 90 LJ Ch 302, 65 Sol Jo 311; *Re Knight and Hubbard's Underlease* [1923] 1 Ch 130.
5   See Ch 13.
6   *George Francis (Provinces) Ltd v Ruxdra Investments Ltd* (1960) 176 Estates Gazette 871, CA. Also see, *Fitzroy House Epworth Street (No 1) Ltd v Financial Times Ltd* [2006] EWCA Civ 329, [2006] 2 All ER 776, [2006] 1 WLR 2207; *Hotgroup plc v Royal Bank of Scotland plc* [2010] EWHC 1241 (Ch), [2010] 2 P & CR D59, [2010] 23 EG 107 (CS).
7   *United Scientific Holdings Ltd v Burnley Borough Council* [1978] AC 904, [1977] 2 All ER 62, HL.
8   ATA 1995, s 1(4).
9   ATA 1995, s 1(3).
10 Such an agreement is possible, see the Landlord and Tenant Act 1954, s 38(A). See para 3.1.

AGRI-ENVIRONMENT SCHEMES/CONSERVATION

11.11 The ATA 1995 makes no provision relating to agri-environment schemes or conservation. Although technically the tenant's adoption of conservation, objectives could put him in breach of the rules of good husbandry[1], this does not carry with it the potentially draconian consequences which apply under the AHA 1986[2]. The parties may nevertheless wish to deal with conservation expressly in the farm business tenancy agreement[2A].

There is a wide range of agri-environment schemes[2B]. Schemes vary as to their requirements in relation to the landlord's participation of express consent. A landlord may wish to include a covenant that he is to be consulted and that his consent is required before the tenant can enter into any such scheme. This issue is more important as a consequence of the minimal farming requirements imposed by the Mid-term Review of the Common Agricultural Policy[3].

1   See para 23.4.
2   See para 30.7.
2A   As to the types of issues that can arise in relation to environmental impact, see *R (on the application of Wye Valley Action Association Ltd) v Herefordshire Council* [2009] EWHC 3428 (Admin), [2010] 2 All ER 863, [2010] PTSR 1561.
2B   As to Sites of Special Scientific Interest (SSSIs), note the case of *R (on the application of Boggis) v Natural England* [2009] EWCA Civ 1061, [2010] 1 All ER 159, [2010] PTSR 725 where the Court of Appeal reversed the High Court decision. The High Court had upheld a challenge by an individual to a SSSI designation by Natural England.
3   See para 52.26.

LANDLORD'S ACCESS

11.12 One area which gives rise to disputes is the landlord's reservation of the right to access. In the Scottish case of *Possfund Custodial Trustee Ltd v*

Kwik-Fit Properties Ltd[1], the court held on appeal, reversing the court at first instance, that a landlord was not entitled to access to dig boreholes to test for environmental contamination in reliance upon a clause which provided that the tenant was to 'permit the landlord and its agents at all reasonable times with or without workmen ... to enter upon the premises generally to inspect and examine the same, to view the state of repair and condition thereof and to take a schedule of the landlord's fixtures and of any wants of compliance by the tenant with its obligations hereunder'.

[1]   [2009] 1 EGLR 39, [2008] CSIH 65.

Chapter 12

STATUTORY SECURITY OF TENURE UNDER THE AGRICULTURAL TENANCIES ACT 1995

FIXED-TERM TENANCIES

Lettings of more than two years

12.3 Section 5 of the ATA 1995 interferes with the common law position for farm business tenancies for a fixed term of more than two years by providing the following:

(a)   a farm business tenancy which is for a fixed term of more than two years will not automatically terminate by effluxion of time on its term date[1];

(b)   if a landlord or a tenant wants to end the tenancy on the term date, he must take positive action to do so by serving a written notice on the other party of his intention to terminate the tenancy on that date[2];

(c)   the notice must be served[3] at least 12 months[4] before the term date. There is no prescribed form for the notice[5], but prescribed methods of service are set out in ATA 1995, s 36.

---

[1]   ATA 1995, s 5(1). 'Term date' is defined in s 5(2) as meaning the date fixed for the expiry of the term. If there is any doubt as to the need to serve a notice (arising, for example, in connection with the validity of the tenancy or the length of the grant, a notice may be served 'without prejudice' to any contention by the landlord as to the existence or length of term: *Grammer v Lane* [2000] 2 All ER 245, [2000] 1 EGLR 1, CA.

[2]   ATA 1995, s 5(1).

[3]   Or 'given' in the words of the ATA 1995. For service methods, see ATA 1995, s 36 and see also Ch 17.

[4]   Until 19 October 2006, the notice also had to be of less than 24 months' duration. That upper limit was removed by the Regulatory Reform (Agricultural Tenancies) (England and Wales) Order 2006, SI 2006/2805 (RRO 2006), art 13.

[5]   For a precedent, see Form C1.

Leases for life

12.6A Where there is a severance of the freehold reversion, arising from a sale of part of the freehold by the original landlord, each of the landlords of the severed parts has the right to serve a notice to quit that part[1]. Section 140 of the Law of Property Act 1925 entitles a tenant who receives a notice to quit from the landlord of a severed portion of the reversion to opt to quit the whole holding by serving notice to quit on the other reversioners within one month. The ATA 1995 provides its own additional overlay. Section 5(3) of the ATA 1995 provides that a notice of termination given by one freehold reversioner to prevent the continuance of a fixed term will be taken as a notice to quit for these purposes. This will entitle the tenant to serve notice to terminate the tenancy on the other reversioners, provided that he does so within one month of receiving the notice of termination. This enables the tenant to prevent the continuation of the tenancy after the term date in relation to the entirety of the holding where he has only been given notice of termination in relation to part of the holding by one reversioner.

1   See para 29.6.

Chapter 13
FORFEITURE

WAIVER OF THE RIGHT TO FORFEIT

Acts amounting to waiver

13.7 Most problems in relation to waiver arise from the demand for, or acceptance of, rent following a breach of covenant or condition. Either will be a waiver of the landlord's right to forfeit for an existing breach as amounting to an act recognising the continued existence of the lease. Increasingly, landlords or their agents make use of systems for the collection of rent which rely upon automatic demands being sent out to tenants or rely on clerks to deal with the rent demands who may have no direct knowledge of circumstances on the holding. As the intention of the landlord is irrelevant to the question of whether or not the breach has been waived, the fact that a rent demand may have been sent out in error is equally irrelevant. The landlord will have been taken to have waived the breach[1]. It is important that the landlord or his agent managing an estate has a system in place for stopping demands being made for rent once a breach is known or until such time as the landlord has decided what to do.

The following points arise in relation to demands for and acceptance of rent:

(a)   The demand for rent accruing after the breach or acceptance of rent 'under protest' or 'without prejudice' will still result in a waiver[2].

(b)   Waiver will not arise where the rent which is demanded or accepted accrued due before the facts giving rise to the right to forfeit[3].

(c)   A demand for rent is not treated as having been made if it is not received by the tenant[4].

(d)   Where the tenant pays rent, as a matter of course, into the landlord's bank account, it may amount to a waiver even if the bank has been instructed by the landlord not to accept it[5]. In *Lewis (John) Properties plc v Viscount Chelsea*[6], it was stated that had there been a breach of covenant in that case, the receipt of rent by the landlord's bank would not have amounted to a waiver because the landlord had made it clear, in writing, that it was not accepting or demanding rent following the alleged breach and, when rent was received, it was returned to the tenant.

(e)   Where the rent is payable in advance, the demand or acceptance of rent will waive the right to forfeit in respect of breaches before the demand or acceptance and those which continue beyond the demand but which the landlord knew about at the time and knew would continue through the period covered by the rent[7]. Demand or acceptance will not waive for future breaches which may arise during the period covered by the rent but about which the landlord had no knowledge at the date of demand or acceptance.

(f)   As a matter of law, the right to forfeit might therefore be waived by acceptance of rent by the landlord and with knowledge of the breach even though the landlord had no intention to waive. The test is objective, namely whether the landlord has acted so as to recognise the continued existence of the lease and the continuing relationship of landlord and tenant. In *Seahive Investments Ltd v Osibanjo*[7A], it was held by the Court of Appeal that, on the facts of that case, an objective observer would have no ground for supposing that an amount re-paid by the tenant had been accepted by the landlord as rent. The processing of a cheque was not in itself conclusive of the question whether the payment was accepted as rent.

(g)   A landlord who distrains for rent, whether accruing before or after the breach, will waive the right to forfeit[8].

[1]   *Matthews v Smallwood* [1910] 1 Ch 777; *Central Estates (Belgravia) Ltd v Woolgar (No 2)* [1972] 3 All ER 610, [1972] 1 WLR 1048, CA; *Lewis (John) Properties plc v Viscount Chelsea* (1993) 67 P & CR 120, [1993] 2 EGLR 77; *Thomas v Ken Thomas Ltd* [2006] EWCA Civ 1504, [2007] Bus LR 429, 150 Sol Jo LB 1396.
[2]   *Davenport v R* (1877) 3 App Cas 115, PC; *Segal Securities Ltd v Thoseby* [1963] 1 QB 887, [1963] 1 All ER 500; *Windmill Investments (London) Ltd v Milano Restaurant Ltd* [1962] 2 QB 373, [1962] 2 All ER 680.
[3]   *Price v Worwood* (1859) 4 H & N 512; *Re a Debtor (No 13 A 10 of 1995)* [1995] EGCS 58. As to appropriation of rent in the case of a voluntary arrangement by the tenant, see *Thomas v Ken Thomas Ltd* [2006] EWCA Civ 1504, [2007] Bus LR 429, 150 Sol Jo LB 1396.
[4]   *Smith's (Henry) Charity Trustees v Willson* [1983] QB 316, [1983] 1 All ER 73, CA.
[5]   *Pierson v Harvey* (1885) 1 TLR 430.
[6]   (1993) 67 P & CR 120, [1993] 2 EGLR 77.
[7]   *Segal Securities Ltd v Thoseby* [1963] 1 QB 887, [1963] 1 All ER 500.
[7A]   [2008] EWCA Civ 1282, [2009] 1 P & CR D18, [2009] 2 P & CR 9.
[8]   *Green's Case* (1582) Cro Eliz 3, 78 ER 269.

HOW TO FORFEIT

Re-entry

13.10 Forfeiture occurs upon the exercise by the landlord of his right of re-entry. That re-entry may be physical[1] or by the service of court proceedings[2]. The vast majority of forfeiture occurs by the service of court proceedings for the following reasons:

(a)   Physical re-entry onto premises is not permitted where there is somebody lawfully residing on the premises or any part of them where the premises are let as a dwelling[3].

(b)   Even after physical re-entry, the tenant is entitled to apply for relief from forfeiture and there is no guarantee that prolonged court proceedings will be avoided. There is no more certainty for the landlord following re-entry[4].

(c)   The re-entry must be peaceable. If there is any violence or threat of violence to person or property, the landlord leaves himself open to criminal prosecution under s 6 of the Criminal Law Act 1977 where there is, to the knowledge of the landlord, someone on the premises who is opposed to the re-entry.

(d)   The landlord will have the problem of dealing with the tenant's goods. This may include livestock and in respect of which the landlord will have bailor's obligations[5]. There is no guarantee that a tenant whose lease is forfeited by court proceedings would not have, eventually, to be evicted when the problem with his goods would be the same unless there is also a judgment for unpaid rent or otherwise.

(e)   The problem of re-entry itself and of securing the land[6]. Most well-drafted forfeiture clauses will allow the landlord to re-enter part of the land in the name of the whole. If this is the case, re-entering part of the holding may be sufficient.

In appropriate cases, where there is little chance of an application for relief; where the holding consists of bare land only; and where re-entry can be effected without the presence of the tenant, peaceable re-entry may be a cheaper and quicker option. The re-entry should be unequivocal, clear and for the purpose of forfeiting the lease. It is usual to change the locks on commercial premises. For farmland, this may not be appropriate although locks on gates can be changed; gates can be chained and clear notices placed around the land stating that the landlord has re-entered.

To exercise his election to treat the lease as forfeited by court proceedings, the landlord must commence proceedings. Under the Civil Procedure Rules, proceedings commence upon the issue by the court of the claim form (whether the action is commenced in High Court or county court).

[1]   Or, more accurately, actual, as re-entry can occur, for example, by the landlord reletting premises to a sub-tenant who is already in occupation: *London and County (A & D) Ltd v Wilfred Sportsman Ltd* [1971] Ch 764, [1970] 2 All ER 600, CA; *Ashton v Sobelman* [1987] 1 All ER 755, [1987] 1 EGLR 33. As to peaceable re-entry prior to the purchaser of the reversion becoming the registered proprietor of the land, see *Rother District Investments Ltd v Corke* [2004] EWHC 14 (Ch), [2004] 2 P & CR 311, [2004] 1 EGLR 47.

[2]   In the Law Commission Report Number 142 'Report on Forfeiture of Tenancies', these two methods were called 'actual re-entry' and 'constructive re-entry'. Note that the proceedings should be brought in the name of the correct landlord: *Mountcook Land Ltd v The Media Centre (Properties) Ltd* [2006] PLSCS 189.

[3]   Protection from Eviction Act 1977, s 2. As to whether premises are let as a dwelling, see *Wolfe v Hogan* [1949] 2 KB 194, [1949] 1 All ER 570, CA; *Ponder v Hillman* [1969] 3 All ER 694, [1969] 1 WLR 1261; *Patel v Pirabakaran* [2006] EWCA Civ 685, [2006] 4 All ER 506, [2006] 1 WLR 3112. Note also the restrictions upon forfeiting a long lease introduced by the Commonhold and Leasehold Reform Act 2002.

[4]   *Billson v Residential Apartments Ltd* [1992] 1 AC 494, [1991] 1 EGLR 70, CA.

[5]   Torts (Interference with Goods) Act 1977.

[6]   As to re-entry generally, particularly in the context of mortgagees and mortgagors, also see *Ropaigealach v Barclays Bank plc* [2000] QB 263, [1999] 4 All ER 235, CA; *Royal Bank of Scotland v Miller* [2001] EWCA Civ 344, [2002] QB 255, [2001] 3 WLR 523; *Aurora Leasing Ltd v S Morgan & Sons Ltd* [2009] EWHC 3066 (Ch).

Preliminaries

Other breaches

13.14 The landlord can proceed to forfeit after the expiry of a reasonable time from the date of the service of the notice. What is a reasonable time will depend on the facts of each case and, where the breach is remediable, on what is a reasonable time to remedy all of the breaches complained of[1]. What is reasonable, particularly in the context of repairing obligations, will very much depend upon the facts of the case, but landlords should err on the side of generosity[2].

If the breach is irremediable, sufficient time should be given to allow the tenant to consider his position; whether or not he should admit the breach; whether he should offer any compensation and whether or not he ought to apply for relief from forfeiture[3]. Even in cases of irremediable breach, what is a reasonable time will depend upon the facts. In *Horsey Estate Ltd v Steiger*[4], two days was insufficient, but in *Civil Service Co-operative Society v McGrigor's Trustee*[5], 14 days was held to be sufficient.

The notice must contain sufficient details of the breach to enable the tenant to know what is required of him[6]. In the case of breaches of a repairing covenant it will be insufficient to state that the tenant has not repaired. The particular item in disrepair should be mentioned. The landlord does not need to inform the tenant what he needs to do to remedy the breach[7].

The notice must require the tenant to remedy the breach if it is capable of remedy. Accordingly, the distinction between remediable and irremediable breaches is of importance.

Examples of remediable breaches are:

(a)   non-payment of rent;
(b)   failure to repair;
(c)   failure to carry out works on time[8];
(d)   unauthorised alterations;
(e)   unauthorised use[9].

Examples of irremediable breaches are:

(i)   unauthorised assignment, sub-letting on parting with possession[10];
(ii)   bankruptcy or liquidation[11];
(iii)   illegal or immoral user[12].

Section 146(9) of the Law of Property Act 1925 provides that a s 146 notice is not required where the forfeiture is for the tenant's bankruptcy[13] if the forfeiture clause is contained in certain types of lease. One type of lease is a lease of agricultural or pastoral land. What this means is that for cases falling within s 146(9), the tenant has no right to relief against forfeiture[14]. If a particular case does not fall within s 146(9), a s 146 notice will be required and relief will be available when forfeiting for bankruptcy or liquidation if the tenant's interest is sold within one year of the bankruptcy or liquidation on the taking of that interest in execution, but otherwise will apply only for the first year[15].

1   *Kent v Conniff* [1953] 1 QB 361, [1953] 1 All ER 155, CA.

2   Some cases suggest that, in normal circumstances, three months will generally be sufficient, but it would be dangerous to rely on this rather than seek to estimate a genuine reasonable time: *Gulliver Investments Ltd v Abbott* [1966] EGD 299; *Bhojwani v Kingsley Investment Trust Ltd* [1992] 2 EGLR 70, [1992] 39 EG 138.
3   See Lord Russell LJ in *Horsey Estate Ltd v Steiger* [1899] 2 QB 79 at 91, CA.
4   [1899] 2 QB 79, CA.
5   [1923] 2 Ch 347.
6   *Fox v Jolly* [1916] 1 AC 1, HL; *Cardigan Properties Ltd v Consolidated Property Investments Ltd* [1991] 1 EGLR 64, [1991] 07 EG 132; *Adagio Properties Ltd v Ansari* [1998] 2 EGLR 69, [1998] 05 LS Gaz R 30, CA.
7   *Fox v Jolly* [1916] 1 AC 1, HL; *Lewis (John) Properties plc v Viscount Chelsea* (1993) 67 P & CR 120, [1993] 2 EGLR 77.
8   *Expert Clothing Service and Sales Ltd v Hillgate House Ltd* [1986] Ch 340, [1985] 2 EGLR 85, CA.
9   See eg *Cooper v Henderson* (1982) 5 HLR 1, 263 Estates Gazette 592, CA; although not where the user has a stigma attached to it where the taint will linger even after the user has ceased – see para 7.1ff.
10 *Scala House and District Property Co Ltd v Forbes* [1974] QB 575, [1973] 3 All ER 308, CA. Cf *Akici v LR Butlin Ltd* [2005] EWCA Civ 1296, [2006] 2 All ER 872, [2006] 1 EGLR 34. See para 8.3.
11 *Civil Service Co-operative Society Ltd v McGrigor's Trustee* [1923] 2 Ch 347.
12 Where the taint will remain even after the user has ceased: *Rugby School v Tannahill* [1935] 1 KB 87, CA.
13 This includes liquidation: *Horsey Estate Ltd v Steiger* [1899] 2 QB 79, CA.
14 Either under the statutory provisions or otherwise: *Official Custodian for Charities v Parway Estates Developments Ltd* [1985] Ch 151, [1984] 1 EGLR 63, CA.
15 Law of Property Act 1925, s 146(1).

RELIEF FROM FORFEITURE

Jurisdiction and time limits

Non-payment of rent

Issue of proceedings in the High Court

13.18   The court has an equitable jurisdiction to grant relief from forfeiture. However, if a tenant being at least six months' rent in arrears[1] pays all of the arrears of rent and costs before judgment, he is entitled to have the proceedings stayed by virtue of s 212 of the Common Law Procedure Act 1852. If payment is not made before judgment, s 210 of the 1852 Act limits the discretion of the High Court to a period of six months following the execution of the order for possession where the tenant owes six months' rent. If during that time the arrears and costs are paid, it is almost certain that the tenant would obtain relief. If the tenant does not apply during that six-month period[2] and his rent is at least six months in arrears, he is banned from all remedy.

It would appear that where the tenant owes less than six months' rent, he may apply, under the inherent equitable jurisdiction at any time, although delay in applying will be a relevant factor in deciding whether or not to grant relief[3].

1   *Standard Pattern Co Ltd v Ivey* [1962] Ch 432, [1962] 1 All ER 452.
2   Senior Courts Act 1981, s 38.

3   *Thatcher v CH Pearce & Sons (Contractors) Ltd* [1968] 1 WLR 748, 19 P & CR 682. Also see, *Ayala v Newnham Borough Council* [2010] EWHC 309 (Ch).

Chapter 14

OTHER METHODS
OF TERMINATION

SURRENDER

14.1 The Agricultural Tenancies Act 1995 (ATA 1995) does not prevent the termination of the tenancy by surrender[1]. Sections 5 to 7 of the ATA 1995 govern one method of termination and, while contracting out of these sections is not permitted, it does not prevent the parties from choosing to terminate in some other way.

If a tenancy is to be surrendered, it must be by all of the tenants. One cannot act unilaterally[2]. An express surrender must, to be effective at law, be by deed[3] and must be accompanied by the tenant giving up possession. There must also be conduct by the landlord accepting that the tenancy is at an end[4]. An agreement to give up possession at some date in the future is not a surrender. An agreement to surrender may also be void if it is in reality an attempt to contract out of the notice requirements of ss 5 to 7 of the ATA 1995.

Surrender may be implied by operation of law. It may, but need not, result from the tenant actually delivering up possession of the holding in an unequivocal way such as returning all keys to the landlord and vacating the holding[5], although ultimately it is a matter of the intention of the parties to be established from their conduct[6]. Other circumstances in which a surrender will be implied have been discussed in relation to ss 3 and 4 of the ATA 1995[7] and include, for example, the extension of a term date[8] or the addition of land[9] or the grant of a new lease of the same land[10]. Note that a surrender does not prejudice the rights of sub-tenants or mortgagees[11].

---

[1]   As to surrender under the Agricultural Holdings Act 1986, see Ch 33 and para 33.5, in particular in relation to the effect of an agreement to surrender under the Housing Act 1988.

[2]   *Greenwich London Borough Council v McGrady* (1982) 81 LGR 288, 46 P & CR 223, CA; *Hammersmith and Fulham London Borough Council v Monk* [1992] 1 AC 478, [1992] 1 EGLR 65, HL.

[3]   Law of Property Act 1925, s 52(1).

[4]   *Bellcourt Estates Ltd v Adisina* [2005] EWCA Civ 208, [2005] 2 EGLR 33, [2005] 18 EG 150.

[5]   *John Laing Construction Ltd v Amber Pass Ltd* [2004] 2 EGLR 128, [2004] 17 EG 128 (CS).

[6]   For examples, see *Proudreed Ltd v Microgen Holdings plc* (1995) 72 P & CR 388, [1996] 1 EGLR 89, CA; *Filering v Taylor Commercials Ltd* [1996] EGCS 95, CA; *Borakat v Ealing London Borough Council* [1996] EGCS 67.

[7]   See para 3.10ff.

[8]   *Savile Settled Estates, Re, Savile v Savile* [1931] 2 Ch 210; *Friends' Provident Life Office v British Railways Board* (1995) 73 P & CR 9, [1995] EGCS 140, CA.

[9]   *Jenkin R Lewis & Son Ltd v Kerman* [1971] Ch 477, [1970] 1 All ER 833; *Friends' Provident Life Office v British Railways Board* (1995) 73 P & CR 9, [1995] EGCS 140, CA; *Well Barn Farming Ltd v Backhouse* [2005] EWHC 1520 (Ch), [2005] 3 EGLR 109.

[10] *Jenkin R Lewis & Son Ltd v Kerman* [1971] Ch 477, [1970] 1 All ER 833.

[11] *Mellor v Watkins* (1874) LR 9 QB 400.

REPUDIATORY BREACH

14.1A There are circumstances in which a lease may be terminated for a repudiatory breach of contract. These cases have not related to the agricultural sectors[1].

[1]   *Antaios Cia Naviera SA v Salen Rederierna AB, The Antaios* [1985] AC 191, [1984] 3 All ER 229, HL; *Rice (t/a Garden Guardian) v Great Yarmouth Borough Council* [2003] TCLR 1; *Dominion Corporate Trustees Ltd v Debenhams Properties Ltd* [2010] EWHC 1193 (Ch), (2010) 23 EG 106 (CS).

Chapter 16

COMPENSATION FOR IMPROVEMENTS

AMOUNT OF COMPENSATION – IMPROVEMENTS OTHER THAN PLANNING PERMISSION

The statutory formula

16.24 While one is to assume that the land is to continue to be let, the assumption is not that a tenant could be found who would want or need the improvement. That is part of the investigation into whether the improvement would result in an increased rent being attainable. If the improvement is particularly esoteric or of a particularly specialised nature so that any tenant is unlikely to use it, it may actually result in a decrease in the rent to compensate the tenant for maintenance obligations. In these circumstances, no compensation would be payable.

There is no guidance on the terms of the assumed letting. If, for example, a tenant has accepted a conditional consent from the landlord on condition that he agrees to particularly onerous repairing obligations in respect of the improvement, is one to assume that those obligations are in the hypothetical letting?

Whether or not the improvement will increase the letting value of the land is determined at the termination of the tenancy upon the tenant quitting the holding. All of the risk is on the tenant. Changes in technology, fashion or regulatory controls may all mean that an improvement with an otherwise long anticipated remaining life does not add any value to the holding as land comprised in a tenancy at the end of the term. Indeed, the investigation into the anticipated remaining life of the improvement, which will determine the years' purchase to be applied to capitalise the rental increase, will take into account the likelihood of such changes after the termination of the tenancy. For example, the uncertainty surrounding the future of milk quota may well mean that a relatively low year's purchase could be justified. Combine that with the application of the section 20(1) formula and a tenant may find that the statutory compensation for milk quota (assuming that it is an intangible advantage and falls to be compensated under the ATA 1995) is less than its capital value were it to be sold on the open market.

Single payment scheme (SPS)[A1] entitlements give rise to their own issues. When the tenancy agreement is silent in relation to the handling of SPS entitlements at the end of the tenancy, the tenant is not obliged to transfer those entitlements to the landlord[B1]. Where the tenant does transfer the entitlements to the landlord, the issue arises as to whether these rights form part of the tenant's statutory right to compensation. The point remains to be litigated to a reported decision[C1].

The same valuation formula is applicable to all improvements[1] whether that improvement is a building or an act of husbandry such as fertilising or growing crops. Industry attempts to persuade DEFRA to provide a different basis of valuation for routine improvements, possibly based on the value to an incoming tenant, failed. Accordingly, the compensation for growing crops, fertilising, liming, cultivations, unexhausted and residual manurial values, etc is the capitalised increased rent which a tenant would be prepared to pay as a result of these improvements. The calculation could be difficult, and more difficult than the sums would often justify given the relatively minor nature of some of the works and the fact that many such improvements will be relatively short-lived. In response to concerns expressed along these lines, the only comfort offered was a statement by Michael Jack (the then Minister of State at the Ministry of Agriculture Fisheries and Food) in the House of Commons as follows:

> 'Some concern has been expressed that [the valuation formula] could result in routine improvements, which may have a small value relative to the overall value of the holding, being overlooked. However, the same principles of valuation will apply for small and routine improvements as for large ones. If they add value, they should be compensated accordingly'[2].

The need is for an agreed professional practice will establish itself amongst land agents and valuers, either informally or through the guidance of the professional bodies[3].

A1   See Ch 52.
B1   Case C-470/08 *Van Dikj v Gemeente Kampen* [2010] All ER (D) 141 (Feb).
C1   As to rights arising in relation to a share farming agreement, see *National Trust for Places of Historic Interest v Birden* [2009] EWHC 2023 (Ch), [2009] All ER (D) 154 (Sep).
1   Save for planning permissions, as to which, see paras 16.20 and 16.29ff.
2   *Hansard* 19 April 1995, Col 245.
3   See CAAV Publication No 166, 'Commentary on the Valuation of Improvements under the Agricultural Tenancies Act 1995' December 1995.

16.25   The assumption in the valuation formula in s 20(1) of the ATA 1995 is that each improvement should be identified and its impact on the value of the holding assessed separately. Where each improvement is looked at, it should be remembered that the comparison is with the holding without that improvement but with all of the other improvements in place. The base rent should be identified accordingly. The circularity and double counting that this could lead to is unfortunate. This could result, in appropriate cases, in an agreement between valuers to take a more global view of the overall impact of the improvements in question[1].

Planning permissions may attract compensation in their own right. Such compensation is only payable where the specified physical improvement has not been completed or the change of use effected[2]. Section 20(4) of the ATA 1995 makes it clear that this restriction on separate compensation does not mean that no account is to be taken of implemented planning permissions.

16.25 *Compensation for improvements*

Where a physical improvement or intangible advantage (resulting from a change of use) adds more value to the holding because it was authorised by planning permission, this is something which can be taken into account when determining the amount of compensation payable in respect of the physical improvement or intangible advantage.

Once the amount of compensation payable in respect of the improvement has been determined in accordance with the section 20(1) formula, the next stage is to establish whether there are any deductions to be made from that base sum. Subsections (2) and (3) of s 20 contain provisions for reducing the amount payable in respect of benefits provided by the landlord and grants obtained by the tenant.

[1] The advice of the CAAV to its members (see their 'Commentary on the Valuation of Improvements under the Agricultural Tenancies Act 1995') is that valuers should consider each improvement separately but should recognise that a claim which would unjustly enrich the tenant may not be upheld.

[2] ATA 1995, s 18(1)(c).

The contractual formula

16.28 Until the RRO 2006[1], it was not possible to contract out of the statutory provisions relating to compensation under the ATA 1995. Those provisions created a problem in practice. Landlords who agreed to permit tenants to make improvements had no way of determining in advance what the compensation payable at the termination of the tenancy would be.

TRIG2[2] recommended amending the ATA 1995 to allow the level of compensation for tenant's improvements to be capped at the amount of the tenant's investment in making that improvement. As a consequence, s 20 of the ATA 1995 has been amended to introduce a new subsection 29(4A)[3]. The effect of the new provision is to allow the landlord and the tenant the option of agreeing an upper limit to the amount of compensation payable. Where they agree that there should be a limit, but are unable to agree on the amount of the limit, the amount is the cost to the tenant of making the improvements.

It should be noted that the amendment to the statutory formula is only so as to allow the parties to fix an upper limit on the compensation payable. Perhaps surprisingly, in the context of the underlying freedom of contract ethos of the ATA 1995, the parties cannot fix a minimum level of compensation.

[1] The Regulatory Reform (Agricultural Tenancies) (England and Wales) Order 2006, SI 2006/2805, effective from 19 October 2006.

[2] Tenancy Reform Industry Group (2002), see para 1.19.

[3] RRO 2006, SI 2006/2805, art 16.

Chapter 17

MISCELLANEOUS PROVISIONS

SERVICE OF NOTICES OR DOCUMENTS

Posting

17.3 While it is not absolutely clear from the wording of s 36(2), it is not thought that personal service is required by the words 'delivered to him' or 'left' at his proper address. Postal service should be sufficient[1]. As to the issues concerning registered post and recorded delivery, see Ch 42.

---

[1] The Agricultural Holdings Act 1986 (AHA 1986), s 93 provides that notices are given if delivered; left at the recipient's proper address; or sent by post in a registered letter or by recorded delivery service. It is clear that ordinary post has been considered sufficient under that section. As to the rules on service by post, see Ch 42.

Change of landlord

17.12 The tenant is entitled to serve notices on a particular landlord unless or until he receives notice that that landlord has ceased to be entitled to receive the rents and profits from the holding and has been given the name and address of his successor[1]. There is no requirement that the notice of the successor should be in writing but it is obviously preferable, from an evidential point of view, that it should be[2]. As with s 93 of the AHA 1986, there is no corresponding provision the other way. If a tenant can, and does, assign without notifying the landlord, it would seem that service on the previous tenant would not be good service[3].

---

[1] ATA 1995, s 36(7).
[2] See Ch 42 and para 42.25.
[3] Note that ss 47 and 48 of the Landlord and Tenant Act 1987 apply to agricultural holdings: see para 31.29.

Chapter 18

EXTENT OF THE AGRICULTURAL HOLDINGS ACT 1986 CODE

WHAT IS AN AGRICULTURAL HOLDING?

No security of tenure

Gladstone v Bower tenancies

18.5 These were tenancies granted before 1 September 1995 for a fixed term for more than one but less than two years[1]. In *Gladstone v Bower*[2], the Court of Appeal determined that such tenancies did not confer security of tenure under the AHA 1986.

It has been suggested that such tenancies, while attracting no security of tenure, also fell wholly outside the definition of an agricultural holding. It is submitted that this view is mistaken[3].

[1]   These tenancies are of mostly historic significance as it has not been possible to grant one since 1 September 1995: see para 3.3.
[2]   [1960] 2 QB 384, [1960] 3 All ER 353, CA. See 20.13.
[3]   *EWP Ltd v Moore* [1992] QB 460, [1991] 2 EGLR 4, CA.

Chapter 19

WHAT IS AN AGRICULTURAL HOLDING?

AGRICULTURAL HOLDING: DEFINITIONS

Agricultural land

Used for agriculture

19.5A The definition of 'agriculture', contained in s 96(1) of the AHA 1986, provides as follows:

> ' "agriculture" includes horticulture, fruit growing, seed growing, dairy farming and livestock breeding and keeping, the use of land as grazing land, meadow land, osier land, market gardens and nursery grounds, and the use of land for woodlands where that use is ancillary to the farming of land for other agricultural purposes'.

It has already been noted that the same wording is retained by the ATA 1995, applicable as a general rule to lettings on or after 1 September 1995[1]. Despite the fact that, for example, the common definition contained in the AHA 1986 and the ATA 1995 does not include the most prevalent form of agriculture, namely the growing of corn, the opportunity to update the definition was not taken upon the enactment of the ATA 1995 nor its review undertaken by the RRO 2006[2].

Although some other legislation adopts a similar definition of agriculture, for example, in relation to town and country planning[3], other statutes do not. The Inheritance Tax Act 1984 provides that:

> ' "agricultural property" means agricultural land or pasture and includes woodland and any building used in connection with the intensive rearing of livestock or fish if the woodland or building is occupied with agricultural land or pasture and the occupation is ancillary to that of the agricultural land or pasture; and also includes such cottages, farm buildings and farm houses, together with the land occupied with them, as are of a character appropriate to the property'[4].

Similarly, as regards non-domestic rating, the Local Government Finance Act 1988 contains a definition of 'agricultural land' which expressly excludes:

'(a)   land occupied together with a house as a park,
 (b)   gardens (other than market gardens),
 (c)   pleasure grounds,
 (d)   land used mainly or exclusively for purposes of sport or recreation, or
 (e)   land used as a race course'[5].

19.5A *What is an agricultural holding?*

By contrast, the Income Tax (Trading and Other Income) Act 2005 defines 'farming' as meaning 'the occupation of land wholly or mainly for the purposes of husbandry, but does not include market gardening'[6].

1   ATA 1995, s 38(1).
2   In parliament, during the passage of the Agricultural Tenancies Bill, it was contended that the definition should suggest the future direction of the industry, including, for example, crops for industrial and fuel uses and land entered into set aside; Hansard HC Vol. 254, col. 82 (Mr Clifton-Brown).
3   Town and Country Planning Act 1990, s 336(1).
4   Inheritance Tax Act 1984, s 115(2).
5   Local Government Finance Act 1988, Sch 5, para 2.
6   Income Tax (Trading and Other Income) Act 2005, s 876(1).

19.6A Cases relating to agriculture in respect of other legislation provide some guidance as to the principles that the courts apply[1]. For example:

(a)   In relation to activities such as farm shops, in respect of Town and Country Planning legislation, in *Williams v Minister of Housing and Local Government*[2], it was emphasised that there is 'a significant difference in character between a use which involves selling the produce of the land itself, and a use which involves importing goods from elsewhere for sale'. The sale of imported goods would amount to a change of use unless it was de minimis. In that case a material change of user occurred where the owner of a nursery garden imported fruits to the extent that they accounted for approximately 10% of the total sales.

(b)   In *Allen v Secretary of State for the Environment and Reigate and Banstead Borough Council*[3], it was accepted that even significant sales of home grown products would be ancillary to agricultural use. Sales of imported products are different and would, in principle, amount to a material change of use.

(c)   In *Fletcher v Bartle*[4], it was held that a room used for retail sales did not constitute an agricultural building, exempt from non-domestic rates, notwithstanding that the only produce sold was that produced by the appellant.

(d)   The extension of agriculture into processing has been considered by the Courts in relation to Town and Country Planning legislation. In *Millington v Secretary of State for the Environment, Transport and the Regions*[5], the Court was asked to consider whether or not wine making from grapes grown on the farm was an agricultural use. It was argued by the Secretary of State that, when the grapes were crushed so as to produce juice, a new product was created. It was submitted that the creation of a new product could not be described as using the land for the purposes of agriculture. The Court rejected the submission on the basis that the making of wine or, indeed, cider or apple juice, was a normal farming activity.

(e)   In relation to rating, in *Cartwright v Cherry Valley Farms Ltd*[6], the Court considered a plant where duck feathers were washed, dried and baled. The Court decided that the plant was exempt from non-domestic rates on the basis that it was a building used in connection with operations carried on in buildings used for the keeping or breeding of livestock. The use of the feather plant was ancillary to or consequential on the operations carried on in the duck rearing buildings.

(f)   *R (on the application of Hall Hunter Partnership) v First Secretary of State*[7] concerned planning issues surrounding the erection of poly tunnels for the growing of soft fruit. One of the points considered was the possible resultant change in use of the land from agricultural. It was held that the fact that Parliament had exempted the use of land for agricultural purposes from planning permission could not be of any assistance in deciding whether a particular activity carried on by a farmer amounted to a use of his land for agricultural purposes or operational development for agricultural purposes within s 55(1) of the Town and Country Planning Act 1990. If it were the latter, the erection of poly tunnels would not in any event be covered by the GPDO. If Parliament were persuaded that changes in agricultural practice meant that certain types of agricultural buildings were required, the remedy was to amend the GPDO to permit the erection of such buildings. The existence of blocks of poly tunnels for up to nine months of the year within the single planning unit of the farm could not be reasonably regarded as 'required temporarily' for the purposes of the GPDO.

[1]   Generally see, Cardwell and Bodiguel, 'Evolving Definitions of "Agriculture" for an Evolving Agriculture?', The Conveyancer and Complete Property Lawyer (Issue 5, 2005).
[2]   (1967) 65 LGR 495, per Widgery J at 500, 18 P & CR 514.
[3]   [1990] 1 PLR 25, [1990] JPL 340.
[4]   [1988] RA 284.
[5]   [1999] 3 PLR 118, [2000] JPL 297, CA.
[6]   (2003) Land Tribunal, unreported.
[7]   [2006] EWHC 3482 (Admin), [2007] 2 P & CR 73. Also see, *Tapecrown Ltd v First Secretary of State* [2006] EWCA Civ 1744, [2007] 2 P & CR 113, a case where a planning inspector held that a building erected on agricultural land was non-agricultural.

Trade or business

Horses

19.10 The requirement for commerciality can best be illustrated by land used for horses. The trade or business does not itself need to be agricultural so long as the user is[1]. Land let for grazing (an agricultural use) by animals which are not agricultural (because it is outside the definition of 'livestock') in connection with a non-agricultural business (for example, a riding school) will fall within the definition of an agricultural holding if the other requirements of the definition of an agricultural holding are met as well.

The use of land for horses frequently has given rise to problems in practice. The result of a series of cases upon the effect of the letting of land for use by horses is as follows:

(a)   Horses are not 'livestock' unless used in the farming of land or for the carrying on in relation to land of any agricultural activity (for example cart horses). This is because they are not kept 'for the production of food, wool, skins or fur' (except in the rare instance of horses destined for dog food or the continental meat trade). Therefore, land used for

keeping horses rather than grazing by horses is not land used for
agriculture within the meaning of s 96(1)[2].

(b)   If the land is let for grazing, then even though the animals which graze
the land are not 'livestock', the land is agricultural land within the
meaning of AHA 1986, ss 1(4) and 96(1). The definition of 'agriculture'
includes the use of land as grazing land without restriction on the
animals that graze.

(c)   If the land is used not merely for grazing by horses but also for a trade
or business (for example for the grazing of horses forming part of a
commercial riding school), then the holding will be an agricultural
holding if the requirements of that definition are met. This is because
the trade or business need not necessarily be an agricultural trade or
business. If the land is let for grazing by horses for non-commercial
purposes, for example, a pony paddock let for the tenant's personal
hunters, hacks or show jumpers or those of his children, then the land
will not constitute an agricultural holding[3].

1   *Rutherford v Maurer* [1962] 1 QB 16, [1961] 2 All ER 775, CA.
2   *Belmont Farm Ltd v Minister of Housing and Local Government* (1962) 60 LGR 319,
13 P & CR 417. Also see, *Minister of Agriculture, Fisheries and Food v Appleton* [1970]
1 QB 221, [1969] 3 All ER 1051 and *South Oxfordshire District Council v Secretary of
State for the Environment* [1981] 1 All ER 954, [1981] 1 WLR 1092. Note that for the
purposes of the Town and Country Planning Acts there is a similar but not identical
definition of agriculture. Accordingly, the keeping and breeding of horses on agricultural
land constitutes a change of use and requires planning consent which, if obtained, might
entitle a landlord to serve notice to quit under s 26 and Sch 3, Case B, on the basis that the
land was required for a use other than agriculture for which planning consent had been
obtained, as to which see para 31.20. Also see, *Gainsborough-Field v Hyde* [2005] EWHC
2229 (QB); *Sykes v Secretary of State for the Environment* (1980) 42 P & CR 19, [1981]
1 EGLR 137, DC.
3   See *McClinton v McFall* (1974) 232 Estates Gazette 707, CA. In relation to rating the
House of Lords indicated that a concession that land used for grazing horses was
agricultural land for rating purposes had been correctly made: see *Hemens (Valuation
Officer) v Whitsbury Farm and Stud Ltd* [1987] QB 390, [1987] 1 EGLR 172, CA. Also in
relation to planning, see *Sykes v Secretary of State for the Environment* (1980) 42 P & CR
19, [1981] 1 EGLR 137, DC. Note that a stricter approach has been adopted for the
purposes of Inheritance Tax. In *Wheatley v IRC* [1998] STC (SCD) 60, grazing solely by
horses which were believed to be used for leisure pursuits did not result in a meadow being
'occupied for the purposes of agriculture' within s 117 of the Inheritance Tax Act 1984. It
was stated that some connection with agriculture was required, for example grazing by
draught horses.

MIXED USER: AGGREGATE OF AGRICULTURAL LAND

19.15   Since the enactment of the AHA 1984, and its subsequent consolidation in the AHA 1986, the issue of mixed user has been considered by the
courts.

In *Short v Greeves*[1], the issue was not what statutory protection applied at the
outset of the tenancy, but what was the effect of a change in the user during
the course of the letting. Initially the tenancy was protected as an agricultural
holding where a garden centre was let with some six acres of agricultural land

which provided all of the produce for the garden centre. Subsequent develop-ments led to some 60% of the garden centre's produce being bought in. Nevertheless, the court held that this was insufficient to deprive the tenancy of its 1986 Act protection[2].

In *Gold v Jacques Amand Ltd*[3], the primary issue was whether a licence to occupy agricultural land gave rise to protection under the AHA 1986. In finding that it did, the court also determined that such protection was unaffected by the fact that no retail sales in relation to a business of buying and selling bulbs was to be carried out from the land and the holding only provided some 15–20% of the production for the business. Further, it was relevant that there was a wholesale bulb business.

It is submitted that the principles set out in para 19.14 have been affected by the amendment to the statutory definition by the AHA 1984, now consoli-dated in the AHA 1986. Whereas under the AHA 1948, the terms of the tenancy (if any) was the dominant factor in determining whether protection arose under that Act, s 1(2) of the AHA 1986 provides that this is just one of three matters to have regard to[4]. It is likely that the court would have regard to implied as well as express terms. This would be consistent with the way in which the court has construed the word 'contemplation' when dealing with cases under s 2 of the AHA 1986 (and its statutory predecessor)[5]. It is nevertheless submitted that the court is still governed by express terms in the tenancy agreement unless sham is alleged[6]. If the tenancy agreement is silent, then the court is entitled to look at other matters relevant to the contempla-tion of the parties[7].

Accordingly, it appears that the combined effect of the pre-AHA 1984 case law, the AHA 1986 statutory definition and the post-AHA 1984 decisions establish that:

(a) If, as a matter of substance, the land comprised in the tenancy agreement, taken as a whole, was an agricultural holding at its commencement, then the whole of the holding is entitled to the protection of the AHA 1986. If it was not, then none of the holding is so entitled.

(b) In determining what the substantial purpose was, the terms of the tenancy granted must be considered, if those terms provided for or contemplated the use of the premises for a particular purpose. Then, subject to any subsequent agreement, that purpose is the essential factor in deciding whether or not the holding was let as an agricultural holding so as to be entitled to the protection of the AHA 1986[8].

In carrying out its assessment, in the absence of clear contractual agreement as to the use of the premises, the court may consider a number of factors, including:

(i) the contribution made to the income or profits of the tenant[9];
(ii) whether the use is continuous or intermittent[10];
(iii) the proportion of the land used for various purposes[11];
(iv) evidence as to the paramount purpose of the letting[12].

49

19.15   *What is an agricultural holding?*

1   [1988] 1 EGLR 1, [1988] 08 EG 108, CA. Also see *Lester v Ridd* [1990] 2 QB 430, [1989] 1 EGLR 114, CA.
2   Note *Monson (Lord) v Bound* [1954] 3 All ER 228, [1954] 1 WLR 1321, where only 10% of agricultural production was generated on the holding and protection under the AHA 1948 was not found to apply.
3   (1991) 63 P & CR 1, [1992] 2 EGLR 1.
4   See para 19.14.
5   See *Scene Estates Ltd v Amos* [1957] 2 QB 205 at 211, [1957] 2 All ER 325, CA.
6   See para 19.54.
7   See *Scene Estates Ltd v Amos* [1957] 2 QB 205 at 213, [1957] 2 All ER 325, CA.
8   See *Tan v Sitkowski* [2007] EWCA Civ 30, [2007] 1 WLR 1628, [2007] 06 EG 165 (CS); *Jewell v McGowan* [2002] EWCA Civ 145, [2002] 3 EGLR 87, where the court appeared to place much weight on the fact that the tenancy agreement obliged the tenant to use the lead for agricultural purposes only. Also see para 32.12.
9   *Monson (Lord) v Bound* [1954] 3 All ER 228, [1954] 1 WLR 1321; *Deith v Brown* (1956) 167 Estates Gazette 513.
10   *McClinton v McFall* (1974) 232 Estates Gazette 707, CA.
11   *McClinton v McFall* (1974) 232 Estates Gazette 707, CA.
12   *Howkins v Jardine* [1951] 1 KB 614, [1951] 1 All ER 320, CA.

CHANGE OF STATUS

Reduction of agricultural use and increase of non-agricultural use

19.20   A more difficult problem is where a holding was undoubtedly an agricultural holding at its inception but due to the adoption, for example, of a diversification scheme then a non-agricultural use has been introduced or intensified so as to affect the character of the holding and the tenancy. In such circumstances, will the holding cease to be an agricultural holding only possibly to return to being one again when the balance changes and reverts to the original position?

The present law following the passing of the AHA 1984 and AHA 1986 was extensively considered and applied in *Short v Greeves*[1]. The test applied in *Wetherall v Smith*[2] was held to apply:

'The cases show that the tenancy is not to be regarded as alternating between being within and outside the Agricultural Holdings Act 1948 [now the AHA 1986] as minor changes of use take place, and that, when the tenancy is clearly an agricultural one to start with strong evidence is needed to show that the agricultural use has been abandoned'.

This can mean that a holding whose current use is predominantly non-agricultural may still be an agricultural holding if it was one at the outset and the agricultural use has not been abandoned but merely reduced[3].

1   [1988] 1 EGLR 1 [1988] 08 EG 109, CA. The wording from *Wetherall v Smith* was quoted in *Short v Greeves*.
2   [1980] 2 All ER 530, [1980] 1 WLR 1290.
3   Also see, *R (on the application of Dean Fewings) v Secretary of State for Communities and Local Government* [2008] EWHC 2401 (Admin); *R (on the application of Williams) v Secretary of State for Communities and Local Government* [2009] EWHC 475 (Admin), [2009] All ER (D) 112 (Jul).

THE RELATIONSHIP BETWEEN THE AHA 1986 AND OTHER PROTECTIVE CODES

The Landlord and Tenant Act 1954 and agricultural land

Licences/tenancies at will

19.23 Neither a licence nor a tenancy at will of business premises is protected by the LTA 1954[1]. Conversely, a licence conferring exclusive possession of an agricultural holding entered into before 1 September 1995 is statutorily protected under the AHA 1986 by way of the statutory conversion contained in s 2 of the AHA 1986[2]. Likewise, a tenancy at will of agricultural land is a letting 'for an interest less than a tenancy from year to year' and therefore if granted before 1 September 1995, it too is protected by s 2 of the AHA 1986.

[1] As to tenancies at will, see *Cardiothoracic Institute v Shrewdcrest Ltd* [1986] 3 All ER 633, [1986] 2 EGLR 57; *Uzun v Ramadan* [1986] 2 EGLR 255. As to licences, see the LTA 1954, s 23. Also see, *Catalyst Communities Housing Ltd v Katana* [2010] EWCA Civ 370, [2010] 26 EG 92.

[2] See para 20.5. It should be noted that neither a licence nor a tenancy at will entered into on or after 1 September 1995 will be protected as a farm business tenancy under the ATA 1995: ATA 1995, s 38.

JOINT VENTURES AND PARTNERSHIPS

Introduction

19.30A As noted in Chapter 3[1], s 2 of the Law of Property (Miscellaneous Provisions) Act 1989 requires that all contracts for the sale or other disposition of an interest in land must be in writing and incorporate all of the terms that the parties have expressly agreed in one document. There are limited exceptions. Section 2(5) provides that nothing in this section 'affects the creation or operation of resulting, implied or constructive trusts'. In *Yaxley v Gotts*[2], the Court of Appeal held that a representation in relation to a joint venture gave rise to proprietary estoppel which in turn resulted in a constructive trust. The fact that it was not in writing did not matter.

In the context of residential premises, the House of Lords held in *Stack v Dowden*[3] that where property was conveyed into joint names by cohabitants, in the absence of a declaration of trust, they held the property jointly and equally. Exceptions to that rule would be rare. In relation to commercial property, the principles arising in relation to resulting trusts were applied by the Court of Appeal in *Laskar v Laskar*[4]. The presumption of equality was not applied.

[1] See para 3.34.
[2] [2000] Ch 162, [1999] 2 EGLR 181, CA.
[3] [2007] UKHL 17, [2007] 2 AC 432, [2007] 2 All ER 929.
[4] [2008] EWCA Civ 347, [2008] 1 WLR 2695, [2008] P & CR 245. Also see, *Pallant v Morgan* [1953] Ch 43, [1952] 2 All ER 951; *Adekunle and Ben v Ritchie* [2007] BPIR 1177 (CC); *Yeoman's Row Management Ltd v Cobbe* [2008] UKHL 55, [2008] 4 All ER 713, [2008] 3 EGLR 31.

19.31 *What is an agricultural holding?*

General partnership

19.31 Partnership is defined as 'the relation which subsists between persons carrying on a business in common with a view to profit'[1]. Partners may occupy land either pursuant to:

(a)   a tenancy held outside the partnership; or
(b)   a tenancy held as an asset of the partnership; or
(c)   a licence (express or implied).

In the case of a tenancy granted by the landowner to himself and another or others, there has been a longstanding issue as to whether, as a matter of property law, this is possible[2].

Licences under the AHA 1986 are converted by the 'statutory magic' of s 2 of the AHA 1986 into fully protected tenancies[3]. In the case of partnerships, it was found by the Court of Appeal in *Harrison-Broadley v Smith*[4] that a licence was capable of being a 'non-exclusive' licence, ie one not conferring exclusive possession, and as such the 'statutory magic' would not apply. The 'non-exclusive' licence would not obtain protection under the AHA 1986[5].

The Court of Appeal's decision in *Harrison-Broadley v Smith*[6] was followed by the House of Lords in *Bahamas International Trust Co Ltd v Threadgold*[7]. As a consequence of those decisions, partnerships have been widely used by landowners as a means of avoiding security of tenure under the AHA 1986[8].

If the licence to occupy is to be found to be a non-exclusive licence, and not subject to statutory conversion, not only must the form of the agreement itself show that the parties intended to enter into a non-exclusive licence, but also it must be shown that, in fact, the licence granted was non-exclusive[9]. This might be shown by the licensor being a member of the partnership and retaining rights to carry on, in common with his partners, the agricultural activities on the holding and retaining the right whether or not it has been exercised to continue to occupy the holding. If the right to continue to occupy the holding is not exercised, there may be a degree of sham[10].

1   Partnership Act 1890, s 1(1). Also see, *Stekel v Ellice* [1973] 1 All ER 465, [1973] 1 WLR 191.
2   See para 19.36ff.
3   See para 20.5.
4   [1964] 1 All ER 867, [1964] 1 WLR 456, CA. A different perspective as to the position of a non-landowning partner should be noted from the unreported High Court decision of Forbes J in *Brooks v Brown* (1986) unreported: see para 21.18.
5   Or its statutory predecessor, the AHA 1948.
6   [1964] 1 All ER 867, [1964] 1 WLR 456, CA. Also see, *Orgee v Orgee* [1997] EGCS 152.
7   [1974] 3 All ER 881, [1974] 1 WLR 1514, HL.
8   As to licences and the AHA 1986 generally, see para 21.15ff.
9   See para 21.16.
10   See para 19.54.

Share farming agreement

19.34 The expression 'share farming'[1] is not a term of art but has been frequently used to define an arrangement between a landowner and a farmer for the farming of the land. The objectives of share farming agreements are to avoid the arrangement being characterised either as a partnership or a letting. A share farming arrangement is generally distinguished from a partnership on the basis that it is an agreement to share gross receipts and for net profits. The cautious landowner prefers sharing only grass profits. Although the term is wholly undefined and is used in different contexts by different people to mean different things, normally a share farming agreement involves an arrangement entered into between two or more persons to make available from their separate businesses assets or services for the carrying out of specified farming operations, the gross receipts from which are to be divided between and paid to the separate businesses in agreed proportions. Rights to occupy land for the purposes of this sort of venture will not have involved either the grant of a tenancy or an exclusive licence if, upon its true construction, the arrangement made did not give the non-landowning party rights of exclusive possession[2].

A great many share farming agreements may be found on their true construction to be general partnerships or lettings. Where such an agreement is found to be a joint venture[3] which is not a general partnership, any licence granted by one party to the other to occupy agricultural land must have been carefully constructed and carefully scrutinised to ensure that the rights granted to the non-landowning party did not amount to an exclusive licence with the licensor receiving a fluctuating return[4].

1   See Cardwell, 'Arable Farming in the Short Term' (1993), The Conveyancer, 138.
2   See *McCarthy v Bence* [1990] 1 EGLR 1, [1990] 17 EG 78, CA, for a case in which a 'share milking' agreement was considered by the Court of Appeal. Also see, *Lam Kee Ying Sdn Bhd v Lam Shes Tong (t/a Lian Joe Co)* [1975] AC 247, [1974] 3 All ER 137, PC; *Tulapam Properties Ltd v De Almeida* (1981) 260 Estates Gazette 919; *Akici v LR Butlin Ltd* [2005] EWCA Civ 1296, [2006] 2 All ER 872, [2006] 1 EGLR 34. Also see, *Gibbons (a firm) v Pickard* [2002] EWCA Civ 1780, [2002] All ER (D) 476 (Nov).
3   Also see, *Rowan v Dann* [1991] EGCS 19, CA; affd (1991) 64 P & CR 202, [1991] EGCS 138, CA; *National Trust for Places of Historic Interest v Birden* [2009] EWHC 2023 (Ch), [2009] All ER (D) 154 (Sep). See para 19.52.
4   Turnover leases for public houses in the licensed victuallers trade are well known. The fact that the rent is a fluctuating sum does not detract from the fact that there is a grant of a tenancy. For a case of an agricultural holding with a fluctuating rent, see *Bolesworth Estate Co Ltd v Cook* (1966) 116 NLJ 1318.

Dissolution of a partnership

19.42   On dissolution of a partnership it is therefore necessary to consider the general rules which apply in relation to:

(a)   a tenancy (one or more of the partners being tenants) which is partnership property or held on trust for the partnership; and

(b)   a tenancy which is not partnership property and which is not held on trust for the partnership.

In the case of (a) above, one or more of the outgoing partners (or in the case of death, their executors) can insist on realisation of the value of the tenancy by sale either by virtue of s 39 of the Partnership Act 1890 or by insisting on the execution of any trust for sale involved. The latter, however, needs to be considered in the context of the Trusts of Land and Appointment of Trustees Act 1996 (TLATA 1996)[1].

It is beyond the scope of this book to consider the application of TLATA 1996 in detail[2], nevertheless it should be noted that in relation to a property which is the subject of either a trust of land[3] or a trust of sale of proceeds of land[4], the court has a discretion to make such order as it thinks fit in relation to:

(i)   the exercise by trustees of their functions[5]; and

(ii)   the nature or extent of a person's interest in property which is subject to the trust[6].

In exercising its discretion, the matters to which the court is required to have regard include:

(A)   the intentions of the person or persons (if any) who created the trust;

(B)   the purpose for which the property subject to the trust is held;

(C)   the interests of any minor who occupies or might reasonably be expected to occupy the land which is subject to the trust as his home; and

(D)   the interests of any secured creditor of the beneficiary[7].

All beneficiaries have the right to apply to the court under TLATA 1996 for an order to resolve disputes in relation to trust property[8]. In exercising its discretion, the court may order sale; the payment of an occupation rent[8A]; exclusion from occupation of one or more of the beneficiaries; or partition[9].

Dissolution needs to be contrasted with retirement. It is beyond the scope of this book to consider and compare the two concepts in detail[10]. It should be noted that retirement only arises where there is provision for this in the partnership agreement or it arises with the consent of all of the partners[11]. The Partnership Act 1890 contains no rules governing the retirement of a partner. The court will enforce any retirement arrangement agreed between the partners.

---

1   As to authorities prior to the Trusts of Land and Appointments of Trustees Act 1996, see *Re Mayo* [1943] Ch 302, [1943] 2 All ER 440, and *Thompson's Trustee in Bankruptcy v Heaton* [1974] 1 All ER 1239, [1974] 1 WLR 605, as to the extent of the fiduciary duties.

2   See Charles Harpum, *Megarry and Wade: The Law of Real Property* (6th edn, 2000) Sweet & Maxwell, Chs 8 and 9.

3   TLATA 1996, s 14(1).

4   TLATA 1996, s 17(2).

5   TLATA 1996, s 14(2)(a).

6   TLATA 1996, s 14(2)(b).

7   TLATA 1996, s 15(1).

8   TLATA 1996, s 14(1). As to the extent to which equitable principles have been replaced by the statutory regime under TLATA 1996, and the extent to which set-off can be applied in the event of sole occupation of the property, see *Murphy v Gooch* [2007] EWCA Civ 603, [2007] 3 FCR 96, [2007] 2 FLR 934. Also see, *Bassford v Patel* [2007] BPIR 1049.

8A   TLATA 1996 does not preclude a beneficiary with no right to occupy claiming an occupation rent. Accordingly, a trustee in bankruptcy can make such a claim: *Barcham, Re, French v Barcham* [2008] EWHC 1505 (Ch), [2009] 1 All ER 145, [2009] 1 WLR 1124.

9   TLATA 1996, ss 12–14. It should be noted that in cases of valuing a minority interest, it has been customary to discount the vacant possession value by 10 per cent: see *Cust v IRC* (1917) 91 Estates Gazette 11, EGD 236. Also see, *Wight v Commissioners of Inland Revenue* [1982] 2 EGLR 236.

10 Reference should be made to Blackett-Ord, *Partnership* (2nd edn, 2002) Butterworths and *Lindley and Banks on Partnership* (18th edn, 2002) Sweet & Maxwell.

11 It can be unclear as to whether an agreement is one of retirement or dissolution: see *Sobell v Boston* [1975] 2 All ER 282, [1975] 1 WLR 1587. Also see generally, *Mullins v Laughton* [2002] EWHC 2761 (Ch), [2003] Ch 250, [2003] 4 All ER 94.

19.45 It is clear from *Popat v Shonchhatra*[1] that a distinction must be drawn between the capital and profit sharing entitlements of the partners and the assets of the partnership. Nourse LJ states this, referring to the 1983 decision of *Reed (Inspector of Taxes) v Young*[2], where he himself had said:

> 'The capital of a partnership is the aggregate of the contributions made by the parties, either in cash or in kind, for the purpose of commencing or carrying on the partnership business and intended to be risked by them therein. Each contribution must be of a fixed amount. If it is in cash it speaks for itself. If it is in kind, it must be valued at a stated amount. It is important to distinguish between the capital of a partnership, a fixed sum, on the one hand and its assets which may vary from day to day and include everything belonging to the firm …'.

In *Popat v Shonchhatra*[3], Nourse LJ made it clear that:

> '… while each partner has a proprietary interest in each and every asset, he has no entitlement to any specific asset and, in consequence, no right without the consent of the other partners or partner, to require the whole or even a share of any particular asset to be vested in him'[4].

Nourse LJ also considered the size of a partner's share in the assets of the partnership during the currency of the partnership (as opposed to his share in the capital or in the profits). He concludes that 'subject to any agreement, all the partners are entitled to share equally in the partnership property'[5].

In reaching his conclusion, Nourse LJ found no answer in s 24 of the Partnership Act 1890, which deals only with 'the capital and profits of the business'. Agreements between the parties relating to capital and profit sharing ratios are, therefore, irrelevant. *Popat v Shonchhatra*[6] makes it clear that:

(a)   the fact that one partner introduced the assets (and hence any capital value it has resides in his capital account) is irrelevant; and

(b)   the agreements relating to capital and profits are irrelevant.

Where no agreement has been reached in a partnership as to how the parties would share the assets of the partnership, in accordance with the well established rule referred to by Nourse LJ, they must share equally. During the currency of the partnership no one partner has any greater rights than the others in relation to the assets.

A further issue which arises in practice is the basis for valuation of farm land where a partnership agreement provides for an option for continuing partners to buy out the interest of a retiring partner[7].

19.45 *What is an agricultural holding?*

1   [1997] 3 All ER 800, [1997] 1 WLR 1367, CA.
2   [1986] 1 WLR 649, 59 TC 196 at 215, HL.
3   [1997] 3 All ER 800, [1997] 1 WLR 1367, CA.
4   At 1372.
5   At 1372G.
6   [1997] 3 All ER 800, [1997] 1 WLR 1367, CA.
7   See *Hunter v Dowling* [1893] 3 Ch 212; *Cruickshank v Sutherland* (1923) 92 LJ Ch 136;
    Re White, White v Minnis [2001] Ch 393, [2000] 3 All ER 618, CA; *Gadd v Gadd* (2002)
    PLSCS 30; *Drake v Harvey* [2010] EWHC 1446 (Ch), [2010] 2 BCLC 688. Also see, para
    19.46 fn 4. Also see the Scottish cases: *Noble v Noble* 1965 SLT 415; *Shaw v Shaw* 1968
    SLT (N) 94; *Clark v Watson* 1982 SLT 450; *Russell's Executor v Russell's Executors* 1983
    SLT 385.

Non-assignable tenancies

19.46 Upon the dissolution of the partnership, the non-landowning tenant, as partner, is entitled to his due proportion of the realisable equity in the value of the tenancy which, being protected by the AHA 1986 and assignable in the absence of an express covenant against assignment, may have considerable value[1]. The tenancy, as an asset of the partnership, may be sold in the winding up of the partnership. The non-landowning tenant will not be allowed to bid for the tenancy, unless authorised by the terms of the partnership or with the agreement of his partners. Further, if the partnership assets are administered by the court, the court may be asked to direct an assignment to the non-landowning tenant beneficially at a price to be fixed by the court on the basis of independent valuation advice.

A problem arises where the tenancy is non-assignable. This may arise from an express provision in the partnership agreement or an ancillary tenancy agreement. Alternatively, the landlord, or his personal representatives, may serve a notice under s 6 of the AHA 1986[2], thereby introducing a prohibition upon assignment[3].

Where there is an express covenant against assignment it is submitted, in the absence of any authority on the point, that the correct approach is to value the tenancy as a partnership asset on the basis that it is non-assignable[4]. That value would be credited to the partnership account for distribution upon dissolution[5].

It is beyond the scope of this book to consider the position of a farming partnership dissolution in respect of jointly owned land which is the subject of a tenancy in favour of the partnership. It is submitted that the principles set out above are of equal application where they arise. Regard must also be had to the fiduciary duties of a joint trustee[6] and the rights of a beneficial co-owner who is excluded from occupation to receive an occupation rent[7]; and the provisions of the Trusts of Land and Appointment of Trustees Act 1996[8].

1   Unless the partnership agreement provides otherwise.
2   AHA 1986, s 6(5) provides for the immediate imposition of a conditional prohibition upon
    assignment, sub-letting or parting with possession of the holding. See para 23.3.

3   It has to be considered whether the service of s 6 notice at the time of the dissolution of a
     partnership may constitute a breach of trust by the landlord: see *Harris v Black* (1983)
     46 P & CR 366, 127 Sol Jo 224, CA, especially per Slade LJ at 374.
4   A task often undertaken for Revenue purposes. As to valuation, see: *Layzell v Smith
     Morton & Long* [1992] 1 EGLR 169, [1992] 13 EG 118; *Baird's Executors v IRC* [1991]
     1 EGLR 201, 1991 SLT (Lanwds Tr) 9; *IRC v Gray (Executor of Lady Fox)* [1994] STC
     360, [1994] RVR 129, CA; *Walton v IRC* [1996] STC 68, [1996] 1 EGLR 159, CA;
     Greenbank v Pickles (2000) 81 P & CR D28, [2001] 1 EGLR 1, CA; *Wight v
     Commissioners of Inland Revenue* [1982] 2 EGLR 236. Also see, para 19.42 fn 9.
5   *Sobell v Boston* [1975] 2 All ER 282, [1975] 1 WLR 1587.
6   *Regal (Hastings) Ltd v Gulliver (1942)* [1967] 2 AC 134n, [1967] 1 All ER 378, HL.
7   *Pavlou (a bankrupt), Re* [1993] 3 All ER 955, [1993] WLR 1046.
8   See para 19.42.

Distribution on dissolution

19.47 When the rights in relation to partnership property are resolved, s 44
of the Partnership Act 1890 provides that, in settling accounts between the
partners after a dissolution of a partnership, the following rules shall (subject
to any contrary agreement) be observed.

(a)   Losses (including losses and deficiencies of capital) shall be paid first
       out of profits, next out of capital and lastly (if necessary) by the
       partners individually in the proportion which they are entitled to share
       in profits.
(b)   The assets of the partnership, including the sums (if any) contributed by
       the partners to make up losses of deficiencies of capital, shall be applied
       in the following manner and order:
    (i)   in paying the debts and liabilities of the partnership to persons
           who are not partners in it;
    (ii)   in paying to each partner rateably what is due from the partner-
           ship to him for advances, as distinguished from capital;
    (iii) in paying to each partner rateably what is due from the partner-
           ship to him in respect of capital; and
    (iv)   the ultimate residue (if any) shall be divided among the partners
           in the proportion in which the profits are divisible[1].

1   Note that where a partner has failed to draw his share of partnership profits, this does not
     imply that he has formally released his entitlement to it or that it otherwise affects his
     interest in the partnership: *Hodson v Rowlands* [2009] EWCA Civ 1042, [2009] All ER
     (D) 168 (Oct).

Tax

19.48 It is likewise beyond the scope of this book to consider the tax
implications of a farming partnership dissolution or tax generally. The
following points may assist practitioners before they consult specialist tax
publications:

(a)   an AHA 1986 tenancy is an asset for the purposes of capital gains tax
       (CGT)[1];
(b)   the extinction of an asset is a disposal for CGT purposes[2];

(c)   the receipt of a capital sum by way of compensation for the loss, destruction or dissipation of an asset is a disposal for CGT purposes[3];

(d)   in addition to standard reliefs, the incidence of CGT on a partnership dissolution may be ameliorated by the application of the extra statutory concession D26.

If a farm is partnership property and sold upon the dissolution of a farming partnership, it will be a chargeable transfer for the purposes of stamp duty and land tax (SDLT). If the farm is transferred to one of the partners in its entirety, then SDLT may often be avoided, particularly if the parties are 'connected'[4].

For a farming partnership, agricultural property relief (APR) will have considerable significance in relation to inheritance tax (IHT). Section 116 of the Inheritance Tax Act 1984 (ITA 1984) contains the relief from the charge to IHT. Relief is provided for 'the value transferred where that value is attributable to the agricultural value of agricultural property'.

The amount of the relief is either 100% or 50%. The former applies where the transferor can recover possession within 24 months or where he satisfies the pre-1981 full-time working farmer relief provisions[5]. In all other cases, it is 50%. APR takes precedence over business property relief. It should be noted that, by contrast, if the tenancy commenced on or after 1 September 1995, then 100% APR is available to the landownder[6].

Agricultural property means:

'... agricultural land or pasture including woodland and any buildings used in connection with the intensive rearing of livestock or fish if the woodland or building is occupied with agricultural land or pasture and the occupation is ancillary to that of the agricultural land or pasture; and also includes such cottages, farm buildings and farmhouses, together with the land occupied with them, as are of a character appropriate to the property'[7].

Section 116 of the ITA 1984 does not apply to any agricultural property unless:

(a)   it was occupied by the transferor for the purposes of agriculture throughout the period of two years ending with the date of the transfer; or

(b)   it was owned by him throughout the period of seven years ending with that date and was throughout that period occupied (by him or another) for the purposes of agriculture[8].

The issue which has emerged from these definitions is whether the house lived in by the farmer is a farmhouse attracting APR or whether it stands separately as a residential unit attracting IHT[9]. To be a farmhouse it must be 'a dwelling for the farmer from which the farm is managed' and is occupied by 'the farmer of the land [who] is the person who farms it on a day-to-day basis'[10].

Consideration also needs to be given to the possible availability of business property relief[11], in particular where the farm or estate includes a mixture of in hand land and buildings and investment properties.

1   The Taxation of Chargeable Gains Act 1992 (TCGA 1992), s 21 which provides that 'all forms of property shall be assets for the purposes of this Act'.
2   TCGA 1992, s 24.
3   TCGA 1992, s 22.
4   See Finance Act 2003, Sch 15 para 18, as amended by the Finance Acts 2006, 2008.
5   See ITA 1984, s 116(2)(b).
6   ITA 1984, s 116(2)(c).
7   ITA 1984, s 115. See *Starke v IRC* [1994] 1 WLR 888, [1994] STC 295; on appeal [1996] 1 All ER 622, [1996] 1 EGLR 157, CA.
8   ITA 1984, s 117.
9   See *Lloyds TSB Private Banking plc (Personal Representative of Antrobus, Deceased) v IRC* [2002] STC (SCD) 468; *Lloyds TSB Private Banking plc v Twiddy (Inland Revenue Capital Taxes)* [2006] 1 EGLR 157, [2006] RVR 138; *Arnander (executors of McKenna, decd) v Revenue and Customs Comrs* [2006] STC (SCD) 800, [2007] RVR 208.
10 *Arnander (executors of McKenna, decd) v Revenue and Customs Comrs* [2006] STC (SCD) 800, [2007] RVR 208.
11 ITA 1984, s 104. Also see, *Brander (Representative of James (dec'd), Fourth Earl of Balfour) v Revenue and Customs Comrs* [2010] UKUT 300 (TCC), [2010] STC 2666.

Chapter 20

INTERESTS PROTECTED BY THE AGRICULTURAL HOLDINGS ACT 1986

CONTRACT OF TENANCY

20.1A Regard should also be had to the common law requirements of the formation of a tenancy. In *Street v Mountford*[1], Lord Templeman stated that 'the only intention which is relevant is the intention demonstrated by the agreement to grant exclusive possession for a term at a rent'[2]. More recently, in *Islington London Borough Council v Green*[3], Blackburne J said: 'A lease or tenancy is a contractually binding agreement, not referable to any other relationship between the parties, by which one person gives another the right to exclusive occupation of land for a fixed or renewable period or periods of time, usually in return for a periodic payment of money'.

A lease or tenancy will only come into existence if it is intended to be binding and is supported by consideration[4]. It does not need to be for a fixed or renewable period. A tenancy at will is a legally binding contract under which the tenancy is on terms that either party may determine it at any time[5].

In addition to the common law requirements, ss 52 to 54 of the Law of Property Act 1925 provide that a tenancy must be created by a deed unless it falls within s 54(2) as a lease 'taking effect in possession for a term not exceeding three years (whether or not the lessee is given power to extend the term) at the best rent which can be reasonably obtained without taking a fine'[6]. A contract to create a tenancy entered into after 27 September 1989 must comply with s 2 of the Law of Property (Miscellaneous Provisions) Act 1989. If it does not, it will be void. Section 2 requires a written contract signed by both parties[7]. It does not apply to a lease governed by s 54(2) of the Law of Property Act 1925[8].

It should be noted that in a case where documents were not effective to create a valid and binding lease they were sufficient to constitute an effective acknowledgement of title[9].

[1] [1985] AC 809, [1985] 1 EGLR 128, HL. Also see, para 21.16.
[2] [1985] 1 AC 809 at 826, [1985] 1 EGLR 128, HL. Also see, para 21.15.
[3] [2005] EWCA Civ 56, [2005] HLR 591, [2005] L&TR 494.
[4] Also see, para 21.15.
[5] Also see, para 21.20.
[6] Also see, para 43.10.
[7] Also see, para 3.34 and para 19.30A.
[8] An oral agreement for the grant of a tenancy for a term of five years is void by virtue of s 2 of the Law of Property (Miscellaneous Provisions) Act 1989. The tenant cannot be estopped from relying on that Act. However, where the tenant had entered into possession under a void agreement and had paid an annual rent, this had created an enforceable

periodic tenancy. The tenant had failed to terminate it by effective notice when the tenant served notice which did not expire on the relevant quarter day: *Hutchinson v B&DF Ltd* [2009] L&TR 12. Also see, *Looe Fuels Ltd v Looe Harbour Comrs* [2008] EWCA Civ 414, [2008] All ER (D) 305 (Apr).

9   *Rehman v Benfield* [2006] EWCA Civ 1392, [2007] 2 P & CR 317.

20.2 It should be noted that the definition in s 1(5) of the AHA 1986 created a problem in the case of tenancy for a term certain of more than one but less than two years[1]. Such a letting fell outside the statutory conversion provisions contained in ss 2 and 3 and never, therefore, became a tenancy from year to year, but was it nevertheless an agricultural holding? If so, the other provisions of the AHA 1986 would have applied to it. After a period of some doubt the matter was finally resolved by the Court of Appeal in *EWP Ltd v Moore*[2]. A *Gladstone v Bower* tenancy was a tenancy of an agricultural holding albeit excluded from the security of tenure and succession provisions. Therefore, for example, the compensation on quitting, freedom of cropping provisions etc, applied.

It should also be noted that there must be a single contract of tenancy for the formation of a single agricultural holding. If there are two or more contracts of tenancy, even between the same landlord and the same tenant, these will create separate agricultural holdings and the contracts of tenancy will not be aggregated, nor will separate concurrent agreements between the same parties be read together as a single agreement for the purposes of conferring security of tenure[3]. If, therefore, a grazing agreement was entered into in respect of the grassland and a *Gladstone v Bower* (18-month) tenancy agreement was entered into in respect of the arable land comprised within the same farm, the two will not be read together to be converted into a tenancy of a single agricultural holding.

Where land is 'added' to an existing holding and a single rent is agreed upon without apportionment, then the doctrine of termination and regrant will apply so that all the land will then be comprised in one single contract of tenancy[4]. However, where there are two separate lettings of two blocks of land to the same tenant and later a single unapportioned rent is agreed upon on review for all the land together, the doctrine of surrender and regrant will not be invoked and the two holdings will remain two separate agricultural holdings[5].

1   This is popularly known as a *Gladstone v Bower* tenancy by reason of the decision of the Court of Appeal in that name: [1960] 2 QB 384, [1960] 3 All ER 353. For a commentary on such lettings generally, see para 20.13.
2   [1992] QB 460, [1991] 2 EGLR 4, CA.
3   *Darby v Williams* (1974) 232 Estates Gazette 579, CA.
4   See *Jenkins R Lewis & Son Ltd v Kerman* [1971] Ch 477, [1970] 1 All ER 833.
5   *Childers (JW) Trustees v Anker* (1995) 73 P & CR 458, [1996] 1 EGLR 1, CA. As to surrender and re-grant generally, see para 33.5ff.

Tenancies of one year and tenancies at will

20.4A As regards an agreement for a lease, currently, following the decision of the Court of Appeal in *Mexfield Housing Co-operative Ltd v Berrisford*[1], where a contract that purports to grant a lease fails to do so because the term of the lease is uncertain, such a contract cannot survive independently of the failed lease so as to be enforceable as between the original parties. In the absence of a trust or estoppel, equity will not enforce such a contract[2]. However, the *Mexfield* case is under appeal to the Supreme Court. In the Court of Appeal, Mummery LJ observed:

> 'I must add that I do not reach this conclusion with enthusiasm. It is clear what the parties intended to contract and it is equally clear that because of the old rule about "uncertainty of term" in a lease the parties' contractual intentions cannot be fulfilled in this case. As Mr David Neuberger QC (as he then was) argued in *Prudential*: "It is undesirable that parties should not be bound by bargains they had freely entered into. In the general law of contract there is no reason why an agreement cannot be of an indefinite duration or perpetual": see p 388G of the report. The law has held for centuries that this cannot be done with tenancy agreements. It is time that this rule was re-examined by parliament'.

1   [2010] EWCA Civ 811, [2010] HLR 711, [2010] 2 EGLR 137.
2   *Prudential Assurance Co Ltd v London Residuary Body* [1992] 2 AC 386, [1992] 2 EGLR 56, HL.

A letting for two years or more

20.7   Section 3 of the AHA 1986 converts into annual tenancies at the end of the fixed term any lease or tenancy for a period of two years or more[1]. This still applies to fixed-term leases which began before 1 September 1995 which expire after that date. This is achieved by providing that such a tenancy shall, instead of terminating 'on the expiration of the term for which it was granted', continue 'as from the expiration of the tenancy' from year to year[2].

1   For the position regarding a tenancy of more than one but less than two years, see para 20.13.
2   Section 3 of the Agricultural Holdings Act 1948 (AHA 1948) (which s 3 of the AHA 1986 very closely follows) contained an express prohibition upon contracting out (see AHA 1948, s 3(4)). Section 3 of the AHA 1986 contains no such express prohibition. This is because agreements entered into after 12 September 1984 are subject to the special provisions excluding succession: see para 35.8. Also see, *Calcott v JS Bloor (Measham) Ltd* [1998] 1 WLR 1490, [1998] 3 EGLR 1, CA.

AGRICULTURAL HOLDINGS WITH NO SECURITY OF TENURE

Gladstone v Bower agreements

20.14   Following the enactment of the ATA 1995, *Gladstone v Bower* agreements are likely to be of limited or no relevance. Nevertheless, the following points should be noted:

(a)   A *Gladstone v Bower*[1] agreement could not be 'back-dated'[2]. The tenancy took effect from the date of execution and completion of the tenancy agreement for the purpose of assessing the duration of the term. If a tenancy, expressed to run from, say, 25 March, for a term of, say, 18 months, was not executed and completed until a date during the last year of the term created, ie after 25 September, the tenancy would have been converted into a tenancy from year to year by operation of s 2 of the AHA 1986.

(b) It is submitted that if the true agreement between the parties was that there should be a series of *Gladstone v Bower* agreements, each one restricted to a period of more than one but less than two years, that the true agreement between the parties would be found to have been for the aggregate of such term which, if it exceeded two years, would have been converted into a tenancy from year to year by s 3 of the AHA 1986[3]. Thus, people holding over after the expiration of the last of a line of *Gladstone v Bower* agreements may still be able to maintain that they have AHA 1986 security beginning before 1 September 1995.

(c) It has been held by the Court of Appeal in *EWP Ltd v Moore*[4] that although a tenancy for more than one but less than two years was not converted into an annual tenancy by either s 2 or s 3 of the 1948 Act (as it then was), nevertheless the tenancy fell within the definition of a 'contract of tenancy' and within the definition of an 'agricultural holding'. It did not attract security of tenure under the Landlord and Tenant Act 1954, Pt II[5], but did attract compensation on quitting and all the other incidents (apart from security of tenure, and now succession) of an agricultural holding.

(d) In *Calcott v JS Bloor (Measham) Ltd*[6], it was decided by the Court of Appeal that where there was a grant of a tenancy for 13 months from 1 November 1992, but the tenancy agreement was not signed until 11 June 1993, it did not take effect as a *Gladstone v Bower* agreement. Further, the Court decided that the anniversary date of the annual tenancy was not the date on which the original term was to expire but 11 June.

1   [1960] 2 QB 384, [1960] 3 All ER 353, CA.
2   *Keen v Holland* [1984] 1 All ER 75, [1984] 1 WLR 251, CA following *Bradshaw v Pawley* [1979] 3 All ER 273, [1980] 1 WLR 10 and *Hoveringham Group Ltd v Scholey* (1982) unreported – a case of a letting for a year and a day accepted just after the start of the term. Also see, *Calcott v JS Bloor (Measham) Ltd* [1998] 1 WLR 1490, [1998] 3 EGLR 1, CA.
3   There is no authority directly upon this proposition but the comparable decisions in the context of agreements for a succession of grazing licences or tenancies would appear to apply equally to a succession of *Gladstone v Bower* agreements. See *Short Bros (Plant) Ltd v Edwards* (1978) 249 Estates Gazette 539, CA; *Scene Estate Ltd v Amos* [1957] 2 QB 205, [1957] 2 All ER 325, CA; *Rutherford v Maurer* [1962] 1 QB 16, [1961] 2 All ER 775, CA.
4   [1992] QB 460, [1991] 2 EGLR 4, CA.
5   Section 43(1)(a) of the Landlord and Tenant Act 1954, Pt II, was amended by s 8 of the Agriculture Act 1958, and Sch 1 para 29, to exclude from the 1954 Act grazing agreements and agreements subject to prior Ministry consent, but not (understandably since *Gladstone v Bower* was decided in 1960) tenancies for more than one but less than two years.
6   [1998] 1 WLR 1490, [1998] 3 EGLR 1, CA.

Chapter 21

INTERESTS NOT PROTECTED BY THE AGRICULTURAL HOLDINGS ACT 1986

EXPRESS STATUTORY EXCEPTIONS

Grazing and/or mowing agreements

General points

21.8 The possibility of a grazing agreement falling outside the definition of an agricultural holding, but being caught by the Landlord and Tenant Act 1954, Pt II, in the case of a tenancy for grazing or mowing only was expressly excluded by para 29 of Sch 1 to the Agriculture Act 1958.

Although a full tenancy enjoying security of tenure can be surrendered by operation of law in consideration of the grant of a grazing agreement[1], clear evidence that the transaction is genuine is required[2]: once a sham always a sham[3].

Grazing agreements are quite separate from rights of common grazing and pasturage[4].

1 *Foster v Robinson* [1951] 1 KB 149, [1950] 2 All ER 342, CA (a Rent Act case).
2 *Somerset County Council v Pearse* [1977] CLY 53; *Short Bros (Plant) Ltd v Edwards* (1978) 249 Estates Gazette 539, CA.
3 *Short Bros (Plant) Ltd v Edwards* (1978) 249 Estates Gazette 539; cf *Foster v Robinson* [1951] 1 KB 149, [1950] 2 All ER 342, CA.
4 As to whether registration of rights of common grazing are capable of transforming non-severable rights of pasturage into severable rights, see *Bettison v Langton* [2001] UKHL 24, [2002] 1 AC 27, [2001] 3 All ER 417.

IMPLIED EXCLUSIONS

Gratuitous and non-contractual licences

21.15 Before there can be any contract of tenancy, there must first be a contract. That means that there must be an agreement supported by valuable consideration or under seal. A purely gratuitous licence, as an act of kindness between neighbours has been held not to constitute a contractual licence and not to be converted into a tenancy from year to year[1].

The fact that no periodic payment is demanded, or payable, does not mean that the arrangement is purely gratuitous. Consideration can take other forms, for example, an obligation on the part of the farmer to bring the land into good heart[2]. The occupier's agreement to reseed the land farmed after he had harvested his crop was sufficient consideration to support the agreement as a legal contract[3]. An agreement whereby the farmer was allowed to occupy rent free during a probationary period, before a decision as to him having a full tenancy, was held not to be a gratuitous licence[4]. A non-contractual licence, even though it may confer exclusive possession upon the licensee, will not be converted if there was no intention to create legal relations because, for example, the arrangements were made between closely related members of the same family[5]. Conversely, a letting by a mother to her son, at a very concessionary rent was held to have involved an intention to create legal relations giving rise to protection[6].

The intention to create legal relations has not always been treated entirely consistently by the courts. For example, in the context of trespasser cases, in *Burrows v Brent London Borough Council*[7], Lord Browne-Wilkinson said: 'It cannot be right to impute to the parties an intention to create a legal relationship such as a secure tenancy or licence unless the legal structures within which they made their agreement force that conclusion'. In *Lambeth London Borough Council v O'Kane*[8], Arden LJ observed that *Street v Mountford*[9] 'established that, provided the parties intended to enter into legal relations, the question whether their relationship was one of landlord and tenant depended on whether the indicia of that relationship were present. The *Burrows* case, on the other hand, decides that the question whether the parties entered into a new tenancy turns on what the parties' intentions were when the former tenant remained in occupation'.

1   *Verrall v Farnes* [1966] 2 All ER 808, [1966] 1 WLR 1254.
2   *Mitton v Farrow* [1980] 2 EGLR 1, 255 Estates Gazette 449, CA. Also see, *Secretary of State for Social Services v Beavington* (1981) 262 Estates Gazette 551; *Ashburn Anstalt v Arnold* [1989] Ch 1, [1987] 2 EGLR 71, CA; *Davies v Davies* [2002] EWCA Civ 1791, [2003] 01 EGCS 65, 146 Sol Jo LB 281; *Well Barn Farming Ltd v Backhouse* [2005] EWHC 1520 (Ch), [2005] 3 EGLR 109.
3   *Davies v Davies* [2002] EWCA Civ 1791, [2003] 01 EGCS 65, 146 Sol Jo LB 281.
4   *Verrall v Farnes* [1966] 2 All ER 808, [1966] 1 WLR 1254; *Isaac v Hotel de Paris Ltd* [1960] 1 All ER 348, [1960] 1 WLR 239, PC.
5   *Booker v Palmer* [1942] 2 All ER 674, 87 Sol Jo 30, CA; *Holder v Holder* [1968] Ch 353, [1966] 2 All ER 116, CA; *Nunn v Dalrymple* (1989) 59 P & CR 231, [1990] Fam Law 65, CA; *Padgham v Rochelle* [2002] PLSCS 197.
6   *Collier v Hollinshead* [1984] 2 EGLR 14, 272 Estates Gazette 941.
7   [1996] 4 All ER 577, [1996] 1 WLR 1448 at 1454, HL.
8   [2005] EWCA Civ 1010, [2006] HLR 21, [2005] 32 EG 67 (CS).
9   [1985] AC 809, [1985] 2 All ER 289, HL.

Non-exclusive licences

21.16 A very important category of licence which was not converted into a tenancy from year to year, and did not therefore attract security of tenure, is a non-exclusive licence. Indeed, the great majority of arrangements made before 1 September 1995 between landowners who do not farm for active farmers to occupy and farm their land without creating tenancies and security of tenure, relied upon the general rule of law as specified in *Harrison-Broadley v Smith*[1] and *Bahamas International Trust Co Ltd v Threadgold*[2], that for the statutory conversion of s 2 to have operated, the licence must, upon its true construction, have conferred upon the licensee rights of exclusive possession.

An essential ingredient of a lease is that the tenant should enjoy exclusive possession of the property. Possession is not the same as occupation, although the distinction between the two is, as Lord Neuberger MR said in *Akici v LR Butlin Ltd*[2A], 'technical and elusive'. Exclusive possession does not necessarily mean that the tenant is in occupation of the property[2B].

It is now clear from the decision of the House of Lords in *Street v Mountford*[3] that a licence granted for valuable consideration, conferring exclusive possession[4] upon the licensee necessarily involves the creation of a tenancy at common law without regard to the provisions of s 2 of the AHA 1986, so that no statutory conversion is involved.

In the last edition of this book, it was submitted that, in these circumstances, it was difficult to see how the statutory conversion of a licence, as provided by s 2 of the AHA 1986, can have operated at all. If a non-exclusive licence is not converted[5] and an exclusive licence for consideration is not a licence at all but a tenancy under another name[6], and a gratuitous or non-contractual licence is not converted either[7], it is unclear as to what form of licence Parliament can have intended to be capable of creation and then conversion by the statutory operation of s 2.

[1]   [1964] 1 All ER 867, [1964] 1 WLR 456, CA.
[2]   [1974] 3 All ER 881, [1974] 1 WLR 1514, HL. Also see, *McCarthy v Bence* [1990] 1 EGLR 1, [1990] 17 EG 78, CA.
[2A]   [2005] EWCA Civ 1296, [2006] 2 All ER 872, [2006] 1 EGLR 34.
[2B]   *Clear Channel UK Ltd v Manchester City Council* [2005] EWCA Civ 1304, [2006] 1 P & CR D49, [2006] 1 EGLR 27.
[3]   [1985] AC 809, [1985] 2 All ER 289. For an excellent analysis of the impact of *Street v Mountford*, see 'Street v Mountford Revisited', an essay by Professor Susan Bright in *Land and Tenant Law: Past, Present and Future* (2006) Hart Publishing/Falcon Chambers.
[4]   As to the issue of sharing occupation of possession, see *Akici v LR Butlin Ltd* [2005] EWCA Civ 1296, [2006] 2 All ER 872, [2006] 1 EGLR 34.
[5]   Which it clearly is not: see *Harrison-Broadley v Smith* [1964] 1 All ER 867, [1964] 1 WLR 456, CA and *Bahamas International Trust Co Ltd v Threadgold* [1974] 3 All ER 881, [1974] 1 WLR 1514, HL.
[6]   *Street v Mountford* [1985] AC 809, [1985] 2 All ER 289, HL.
[7]   *Goldsack v Shore* [1950] 1 KB 708, [1950] 1 All ER 276, CA.

HOLDOVER/EARLY ENTRY

21.19   Issues as to the rights arising from the payment and acceptance of rent are commonplace in relation to the law of agricultural holdings and in landlord and tenant generally. There are three common situations where issues arise:

(a)   when a new occupier is allowed into occupation of premises pending the conclusion of negotiations or the formal grant of an interest in the land, whether a tenancy or indeed the acquisition of the freehold. This is commonly known as 'early entry';

(b)   where an existing licence or tenancy has come to an end and the tenant or licensee remains in occupation. This is commonly known as 'holdover';

(c)   the third area where it arises is where a tenant has committed a breach or breaches of the terms of his tenancy and the landlord is in a position to forfeit. The impact of the payment and acceptance of rent after the landlord has knowledge of a breach is critical in relation to whether the landlord is then found to have waived the breach[1].

A further issue which arises is the legal effect of 'subject to contract' or 'subject to licence'. The former is commonly used. In *Yeoman's Row Management Ltd v Cobbe*[2], Mummery LJ said that: 'where that well-known expression is used, an intention has been expressed to reserve the right for either party to withdraw from the negotiations at any time prior to the exchange of formal contracts. It is made clear that there are no legally enforceable rights before that happens'. However, as the Judge himself acknowledged, where 'subject to contract' is used, it does not necessarily prevent a proprietary estoppel[3] from arising in the event of a subsequent representation that leads a party to believe that 'subject to contract' would not be relied upon[4]. Even when 'subject to contract' is used, and there is no basis for proprietary estoppel, in testing whether the phrase prevents an otherwise concluded agreement being binding, the court will ask whether the parties intended to create legal relations[5].

[1]   This issue is dealt with Ch 13.
[2]   [2006] EWCA Civ 1139, [2006] 1 WLR 2964, [2006] 3 EGLR 107;revsd [2008] UKHL 55, [2008] 4 All ER 713, [2008] 3 EGLR 31.
[3]   See para 21.24.
[4]   Also see, *Chartbrook Ltd v Persimmon Homes Ltd* [2009] UKHL 38, [2009] AC 1101, [2009] 4 All ER 677, where the House of Lords reversed the decisions of the High Court and Court of Appeal determining that, after considering pre-contract negotiations, the agreement did not mean what it literally appeared to mean.
[5]   *Proforce Recruit Ltd v Rugby Group Ltd* [2005] EWHC 70 (QB), [2005] All ER (D) 22 (Feb); *Business Environment Bow Lane Ltd v Deanwater Estates Ltd* [2007] EWCA Civ 622, [2007] 32 EG 90; *Birmingham College of Food, Tourism & Creative Studies v University of Central England in Birmingham* [2007] EWHC 1442 (Ch); *Jirehouse Capital v Beller* [2009] EWHC 2538 (Ch), [2009] All ER (D) 204 (Oct). As to 'subject to licence', see *Prudential Assurance Co Ltd v Mount Eden Land Ltd* (1996) 74 P & CR 377, [1997] 1 EGLR 37, CA. Also see, para 9.24(c).

Holdover

21.22 In deciding whether the parties have reached an agreement for a new tenancy, the ordinary principles relating to the formation of contracts apply. There must be a consensus as to the terms of the proposed tenancy. There must be an offer, express or implied, by the landlord to grant a tenancy on those terms. There must be acceptance by the tenant, express or implied, to take the tenancy on the terms offered. There is certainly no presumption that a new tenancy will be created by the payment and acceptance of a sum in the nature of rent[1]. In all of those cases no new tenancy was found to have come into existence. For a case where a tenancy was found to exist, see the Scottish case of *Morrison-Low v Paterson*[2].

21.22 *Interests not protected by the Agricultural Holdings Act 1986*

The type of problems which have arisen in practice are illustrated by the following cases:

(a) In *Walters v Roberts*[3], a purchaser entered into a contract to buy a sheep farm with vacant possession for £100,000. There was a discrepancy in relation to the area described in the contract as 3,156 acres. On admeasurement it was found to be 1,515 acres. A further contract was entered into and the purchaser was allowed into possession. Problems arose and the sale was never completed. It was held by the High Court that the occupier's rights:

> 'resulted from the second contract and the Agricultural Holdings Act 1948 did not extend to the rights of a person who had contracted to purchase the land and was let into occupation pursuant only to that contract and whose occupation was never intended to survive its extinction and that accordingly the Plaintiffs were entitled to a decree of specific performance'.

Nourse J continued:

> 'If a licence for a purchaser to occupy pending completion of the purchase were to be transformed into a tenancy from year to year ... it would be the transformation of a licence of a special and subordinate character liable to be determined without notice and with no existence independent of the purchaser's equitable interest in the land into an agreement for a tenancy ... with an independent existence of its own. In my judgement that must be a most remarkable state of affairs if the 1948 Act did catch an arrangement of this kind and afforded a protection which was clearly never intended'.

(b) In *Dockerill v Fitzpatrick*[4], a tenant of an agricultural holding had an option to purchase at a price to be agreed or determined by arbitration. The tenant exercised the option to purchase as to part only of the holding and ceased paying rent. He maintained that he was in occupation as a prospective purchaser of part and as tenant of the balance and that he had no need to pay rent until the rent had been apportioned. The landlord served a notice to pay, which was not complied with, followed by a notice to quit. The notice to pay related to the rent of the entirety of the holding, including the land over which the option had been exercised. The Court of Appeal held that a tenant who remains in occupation of land pending the conveyance of land to him in performance of an agreement to buy it is entitled to occupy only as tenant and not as a potential purchaser. Accordingly, he remains obliged to pay rent until such time as the contract for the purchase is completed. The notice to quit was upheld.

(c) In *Gold v Jacques Amand Ltd*[5], the owner of 6 acres of land negotiated for the sale of the property to a prospective purchaser. The purchaser undertook to erect an agricultural building on the land at its own expense and to pay £40 per week for use and occupation. Negotiations broke down, resulting in the owner seeking an order for possession. The High Court held that the negotiations which had led to an agreement in principle did not give rise to an enforceable contract because there was uncertainty as to a number of elements. However, the prospective purchaser was allowed into possession in anticipation that the negotiations would be successful and on terms that the agricultural building would be erected. After the company had entered onto the land and had started to build, it was under an obligation to complete the building. The court inferred the existence of an implied contractual licence granted for value. The licence was to occupy the land for agricultural purposes. Accordingly, the licence was converted into a tenancy from year to year by s 2 of the AHA 1986.

(d)   In *Javad v Aqil*[6], a prospective tenant was allowed to enter into possession and thereafter he paid periodic payments of rent while negotiations proceeded as to the terms of a tenancy to be granted to him. It was inferred, in the absence of any other material factors, that the parties intended to create a tenancy at will rather than a periodic tenancy pending the outcome of the negotiations. As the land in question was not agricultural land, the tenancy at will did not give the occupier any protection. The owner was entitled to possession upon terminating the tenancy at will.

(e)   In *VG Fraulo & Co Ltd v Papa*[7], without the owner's authority, the owner's surveyor gave the occupier a key to the property and the occupier moved in. The owner's solicitor wrote two letters to the occupier. In the first, an open letter, the solicitor stated that the occupation was unlawful and that possession was required. The second, marked without prejudice, offered a tenancy which would be back-dated. In a telephone conversation the occupier confirmed that she would enter into the agreement. The occupier did not sign any tenancy agreement did not pay rent. In proceedings for possession, the County Court Judge decided that the without prejudice letter and telephone conversation were admissible and dismissed the claim for possession. The Court of Appeal allowed an appeal. The court held that the without prejudice letter constituted an offer upon conditions which were never satisfied. The reference within to any tenancy relating back did not make the defendant's occupation lawful. It was not possible to impute a licence resulting from acquiescence in the defendant's occupation. There was never a concluded agreement between the parties and therefore it was not possible to look at the without prejudice letter.

Where a tenant for a term of years holds over and continues to pay rent at a yearly rate, there will be a presumption that a tenancy from year to year has been created implied by law[8]. Where a tenant holds over and pays rent at a weekly rate, only a weekly tenancy will result[9]. Where a tenant holds over and pays rent on a six month basis, a six monthly tenancy arises. Such tenancies may at common law be determined by a notice equal to at least one complete period of the tenancy[10]. It should be noted that the notice to quit must expire at the end of the current period or on the first day of any subsequent period. To determine a monthly tenancy, a month's notice expiring at the end of a month of the tenancy is required[11].

[1]   See *Clarke v Grant* [1950] 1 KB 104, [1949] 1 All ER 768, CA; *Sector Properties v Meah* (1973) 229 Estates Gazette 1097, CA; *Longrigg Burrough Trounson v Smith* [1979] 2 EGLR 42, (1979) 251 Estates Gazette 847, CA; *Cardiothoracic Institute v Shrewdcrest* [1986] 3 All ER 633, [1986] 2 EGLR 57; *Land v Sykes* [1991] 1 EGLR 18, [1991] 06 EG 125; affd [1992] 1 EGLR 1, [1992] 03 EG 115, CA; *Bennett Properties v H & S Engineering* [1998] CLY 3683; *Stirling v Leadenhall Residential 2 Ltd* [2001] EWCA Civ 1011, [2001] 3 All ER 645, [2002] 1 WLR 499.

2   1985 SLT 255, HL.
3   (1980) 41 P & CR 210, 258 Estates Gazette 965.
4   [1989] 1 EGLR 1, [1989] 02 EG 75, CA.
5   (1991) 63 P & CR 1, [1992] 2 EGLR 1.
6   [1991] 1 All ER 243, [1990] 2 EGLR 82, CA.
7   [1993] 2 EGLR 99, [1993] 39 EG 127, CA.
8   *Hyatt v Griffiths* (1851) 17 QB 505.
9   *Adler v Blackman* [1953] 1 QB 146, [1952] 2 All ER 945, CA.
10 *Doe d'Peacock v Raffan* (1806) 6 Esp 4.
11 *Queen's Club Gardens Estates Ltd v Bignell* [1924] 1 KB 117, DC.

ADVERSE POSSESSION

21.23 The rights of a mortgagee to bring an action for possession subsist for 12 years from the date on which the mortgagor made the last payment to the mortgagee[A1]. In the case of fraud, time runs from when the claimant has knowledge of the deceit[B1].

It is beyond the scope of this book to consider the issue of adverse possession. Reference should be made to the leading textbook: Jourdan and Radley-Gardner, *Adverse Possession*[1].

A1   *Ashe v National Westminster Bank plc* [2008] EWCA Civ 55, [2008] 1 WLR 710, [2008] 2 P & CR 183.
B1   *Barnstaple Boat Co Ltd v Jones* [2007] EWCA Civ 727, [2008] 1 All ER 1124, 151 Sol Jo LB 987.
1   Second Edition (2011) Bloomsbury Professional. Also see cases relating to agricultural land: *J A Pye (Oxford) Ltd v Graham* [2000] Ch 676, [2000] 2 EGLR 137, affirmed by the House of Lords [2002] UKHL 30, [2003] 1 AC 419, [2002] 3 All ER 865; *Lambeth London Borough Council v Blackburn* [2001] EWCA Civ 912, 82 P & CR 494, 33 HLR 847; *King (t/a Oakland Services UK) v Job* [2002] EWCA Civ 181, [2002] 2 P & CR DG7; *Purbrick v Hackney London Borough Council* [2003] EWHC 1871 (Ch), [2004] 1 P & CR 553, [2003] 27 LS Gaz R 39; *J A Pye (Oxford) Ltd v United Kingdom (Application 44302/02)* (2005) 43 EHRR 43, [2005] 3 EGLR 1, ECtHR; *Beaulane Properties Ltd v Palmer* [2005] EWHC 1071 (Ch), [2006] Ch 79, [2005] 3 EGLR 85; *Tower Hamlets London Borough Council v Barrett* [2005] EWCA Civ 923, [2006] 1 P & CR 132; *Tennant v Adamczyk* [2005] EWCA Civ 1239, [2006] 1 P & CR 485; *Batt v Adams* (2001) 82 P & CR 406, [2001] 2 EGLR 92; *Williams v Jones* [2002] EWCA Civ 1097, [2002] 3 EGLR 69, [2002] 40 EG 169; *Clarke v Swaby* [2007] UKPC 1, [2007] 2 P & CR 12; *J Alston & Sons Ltd v BOCM Pauls Ltd* [2008] EWHC 3310 (Ch), [2009] 1 EGLR 93.

TRESPASS

21.23A Landowners sometimes encounter unlawful occupation of their land by gypsies and travellers or others. It is beyond the scope of this book to consider this issue. However, it should be noted that landowners have not only the power to obtain a court order for possession[1], but also the ability to seek an injunction to restrain trespass[2]. The courts have not to date allowed a trespasser to succeed in opposing an order for possession in reliance upon Article 8 of the European Convention on Human Rights[3].

1   Civil Procedure Rules Pt 55.
2   *Secretary of State for the Environment, Food and Rural Affairs v Meier* [2009] UKSC 11, [2010] 1 All ER 855, [2009] 1 WLR 2780.

3   *Central Bedfordshire Council v Taylor (Secretary of State for Communities and Local Government intervening)* [2009] EWCA Civ 613, [2010] 1 All ER 516, [2010] 1 WLR 446. Also see, *Lambeth London Borough Council v Kay* [2006] UKHL 10, [2006] 2 AC 465, [2006] 4 All ER 128.

PROPRIETARY ESTOPPEL

21.24 It is also beyond the scope of this book to consider the doctrine of proprietary estoppel. Nevertheless, it should be noted that, in a rare case, it is possible for a tenant, with full protection under the AHA 1986, to lose that protection by reason of his conduct giving rise to a claim for possession by his landlord based upon the doctrine of proprietary estoppel[1]. It may also be relevant to the landlord's ability to enforce the terms of the tenancy agreement[2].

In short, pursuant to the doctrine of proprietary estoppel, an equity arises where:

(a)   the owner of land (O) induces, encourages or allows the claimant (C) to believe that he has or will enjoy some right or benefit over O's property;
(b)   in reliance upon this belief, C acts to his detriment to the knowledge of O; and
(c)   O then seeks to take unconscionable advantage of C by denying him the right or benefit which he expected to receive[3].

The classic formulation of the doctrine is contained in the speech of Lord Kingsdown in *Ramsden v Dyson and Thornton*[4]:

'These factors ordinarily are considered to be an expectation created or encouraged by the owner of the land that a person will have a certain interest in it, that person then taking no occupation, and upon the faith of the expectation, with the knowledge of the owner of the land and without objection, lays out money upon the land'[5].

The House of Lords has considered the application of the doctrine of proprietary estoppel in two leading property cases since the publication of the ninth edition of this book[6]. It is submitted that the decisions do not change the law but it is clear that the context in which a claim arises is critical to the outcome.

The Court of Appeal has also found that, despite persistent delays in the payment of rent and the landlords' submission that the tenant occupied pursuant to a tenancy at will, the tenant was able to establish his claim to a tenancy of 21 years under the doctrine of proprietary estoppel[7].

1   *JS Bloor (Measham) Ltd v Calcott* [2002] 04 LS Gaz R 31, [2002] 1 EGLR 1.
2   *Hazel v Hassan Akhtar* [2001] EWCA Civ 1883, [2002] 2 P & CR 17, [2002] 07 EG 124.
3   See Charles Harpum, *Megarry & Wade: The Law of Real Property* (6th edn, 2000) Sweet & Maxwell, para 13–001ff.
4   (1866) LR 1 HL 129. Also see, *Gillett v Holt* [2001] Ch 210, [2000] 2 All ER 289, CA; *Clarke v Swaby* [2007] UKPC 1, (2007) 2 P & CR 2; *Brightlingsea Haven Ltd v Morris* [2008] EWHC 1928 (QB), [2009] 2 P & CR 169, [2009] 1 EGLR 117. For a case where the claim of proprietary estoppel failed, in the alternative to a claim for protection under the AHA 1986, see *Orgee v Orgee* [1997] EGCS 152, CA.

⁵ Also see, *Sutcliffe v Lloyd* [2007] EWCA Civ 153, [2007] 22 EG 162.
⁶ *Yeoman's Row Management Ltd v Cobbe* [2008] UKHL 55, [2008] 4 All ER 713, [2008] 3 EGLR 31; *Thorner v Majors* [2009] UKHL 18, [2009] 3 All ER 945, [2009] 1 WLR 776. Also see, *Fisher v Brooker* [2009] UKHL 41, [2009] 4 All ER 789, [2009] 1 WLR 1764; *Henry v Henry* [2010] UKPC 3, [2010] 1 All ER 988, [2010] 2 P & CR D17.
⁷ *Nazam (t/a New Dadyal Cash and Carry) v Manton Securities Ltd* [2008] EWCA Civ 805, [2008] 2 P & CR D46, [2008] NPC 85.

21.25 The practice of the landlord to renew tenancies does not found proprietary estoppel[1]. But it may be relevant where there has been a failure to conclude a tenancy[2].

Cause of action or issue estoppel may also be relevant to a party's ability to enforce contractual rights[3].

As to the need to comply with the requirements of s 2(1) of the Law of Property (Miscellaneous Provisions) Act 1989, see paras 20.1A and 22.1 fn 10.

¹ *Keelwalk Properties Ltd v Walker* [2002] EWCA Civ 1076, [2002] 3 EGLR 79, [2002] 48 EG 142.
² *James v Evans* [2000] 3 EGLR 1, [2000] 42 EG 173, CA; *Charlton v Hawking* [2003] EWHC 570 of 2002 (Ch) Leeds, unreported.
³ *Thoday v Thoday* [1964] P 181, [1964] 1 All ER 341, CA; *Arnold v National Westminster Bank plc* [1991] 2 AC 93, [1991] 3 All ER 41, HL; *Meretz Investments NV v ACP Ltd* [2007] EWCA Civ 1303, [2008] Ch 244, [2008] 2 WLR 904.

CONSTRUCTIVE TRUST

21.26 It is likewise beyond the scope of this book to consider the law of constructive and resulting trusts, although these concepts may be relevant to a claim for a tenancy.

There is no accepted definition of a constructive trust. It is 'a judicial remedy giving rise to an enforceable equitable obligation'[1]. A constructive trustee may be personally liable to account for any improper gain which he has made or for any loss which his acts or omissions have caused, or in appropriate circumstances, he may hold specific property in his hands on trust[2].

Where the court found that negotiations for a joint venture failed, it decided that the tenant held the tenancy on a resulting trust for the landlord. The court ordered that the tenant had to give up possession to the landlord[3].

In *Charlton v Hawking*[4], where the court rejected claims to a tenancy protected under the AHA 1986 and found that there was no implied agreement giving rise to a constructive trust, it decided that the application of the doctrine of proprietary estoppel should provide the occupier with a licence for so long as the occupier wished to carry on her business.

Particular difficulties can arise in cases of unmarried couples. The issue which arises, and which has wider application, is whether the presumption that a conveyance into joint names indicated both legal and beneficial joint tenancy.

The Court of Appeal has held that conduct can infer a severance of the joint tenancy so that the parties hold as tenants in common[5].

1   *Westdeutsche Landesbank Girozentrale v Islington London Borough Council* [1996] AC 669 at 714, [1996] 2 All ER 961, HL, per Lord Browne-Wilkinson.
2   *Megarry and Wade: 'The Law of Real Property* (6th edn, 1999), Sweet & Maxwell, para 10–017ff.
3   *Rowan v Dann* [1991] EGCS 19, CA; affd (1991) 64 P & CR 202, [1991] EGCS 138, CA. Also see, *Kilcarne Holdings Ltd v Targetfellow (Birmingham) Ltd* [2005] EWCA Civ 1355, [2006] 1 P & CR D55; *Lalani v Crump Holdings Ltd* [2007] EWHC 47 (Ch), [2007] 08 EG 136 (CS).
4   [2003] EWHC 370 of 2002 Leeds, unreported. Also see, *Stack v Dowden* [2007] UKHL 17, [2007] 2 AC 432, [2007] 2 All ER 929.
5   *Jones v Kernott* [2010] EWCA Civ 578, [2010] 3 All ER 423, [2010] 1 WLR 2401. Also see, *Stack v Dowden* [2007] UKHL 17, [2007] 2 AC 432, [2007] 2 All ER 929.

Chapter 22

INTRODUCTION: THE TENANCY AGREEMENT

INTRODUCTION

22.1 As with all other provisions in this section of the book, the following provisions only apply to agricultural holdings falling within the provisions of the Agricultural Holdings Act 1986 (AHA 1986).

Unlike the freedom of contract applying under the Agricultural Tenancies Act 1995 (ATA 1995), the mutual rights and obligations of landlords and tenants of agricultural holdings during the currency of the tenancy derive from four sources:

(a)   the contract of tenancy;
(b)   supplemental provisions derived from common law and custom[1];
(c)   'model clauses' as to repair and maintenance of fixed equipment implied by the AHA 1986[2]; and
(d)   standards of good husbandry and sound estate management applying under statute[3].

The statutory provisions have the effect of supplementing, varying or overriding the terms of the agreement reached between the landlord and tenant whether oral or written.

The obligations arising in relation to the AHA 1986 tenancies have their origin in the political agenda following the Second World War, namely to increase productivity and to ensure that agricultural land was farmed[4]. The freedom of contract contained in the ATA 1995 reflected the change in priorities. The Mid-term Review of the Common Agricultural Policy moved the process on again by releasing the obligations imposed upon farmers in relation to farming[5].

Under the AHA 1986, the tenancy agreement need not be in writing, but three points should be noted:

(i)   either the landlord or the tenant may require the other to agree that certain statutorily prescribed terms are reduced into writing[6];
(ii)   a tenancy for a fixed term of three years or more must be made by deed if it is to create a legal lease[7];
(iii) the lease must comply with the requirements of the Land Registration Act 2002[8].

It should also be noted that:

(A) no formality is required for the creation of a lease which takes effect in possession for a term not exceeding three years, at the best rent obtainable without taking a fine[9];

(B) a contract to grant a lease taking effect in possession for a term not exceeding three years is exempt from the requirements of the Law of Property (Miscellaneous Provisions) Act 1989 as to the formalities necessary for the creation of land contracts[10]. Such contracts can therefore be made orally.

[1] The common law provisions for supplementing tenancy agreements which did not contain minimal provisions, eg an implied obligation to farm in a good and tenantlike manner, the doctrine of emblements and an implied obligation to maintain premises in a good and tenantlike manner, have now, since the passing of the agricultural holdings legislation, been largely superseded by the statutory provisions.

[2] AHA 1986, ss 6–24.

[3] Agriculture Act 1947, ss 10 and 11.

[4] See the speech of Viscount Simon in *Johnson v Moreton* [1980] AC 37, [1978] 3 All ER 37, HL.

[5] See Ch 52.

[6] AHA 1986, s 6: see para 22.2 below.

[7] Law of Property Act 1925, s 52(1) and (2).

[8] See para 3.38 et seq.

[9] Law of Property Act 1925, s 54(1).

[10] Law of Property (Miscellaneous Provisions) Act 1989, s 2(1) and (5)(a). As to the position in the case of a claim for proprietary estoppel, see the remarks (obiter) of Lord Scott in *Yeoman's Row Management Ltd v Cobbe* [2008] UKHL 55, [2008] 4 All ER 713, [2008] 3 EGLR 31; and those of Lord Neuberger MR in *Thorner v Majors* [2009] UKHL 18, [2009] 3 All ER 945, [2009] 1 WLR 776.

Chapter 23

WRITTEN TENANCY AGREEMENT AND FIXED EQUIPMENT

WRITTEN TENANCY AGREEMENT

Section 6 notice

23.1 Section 6 of the Agricultural Holdings Act 1986 (AHA 1986)[1] contains provisions for either landlord or tenant to refer to arbitration the provision of a written 'agreement' containing the rights and obligations of the parties. The right to do so arises either when the tenancy agreement is purely oral or when it is in writing[1A], but provision is not made in the written agreement for all the terms agreed between the parties or for one or more of the matters specified in Sch 1 to the AHA 1986[2].

In order to activate the provisions of s 6, there must first be a request by either landlord or tenant to the other to enter into a written agreement containing these provisions. The request does not need to be in writing, but it must demand the inclusion of all of the terms contained in Sch 1 of the AHA 1986 and not just some of them. Where the request is made by the landlord, the tenant may not, without the landlord's written consent, assign, sub-let or part with possession of the holding or any part of it between the date on which the landlord's request was served on the tenant and either an agreement is concluded between landlord and tenant or the award of an arbitrator appointed under s 6 takes effect[3]. Any such transaction is statutorily rendered void[4]. Therefore, if a tenant after such a request assigns his tenancy, a landlord cannot give a valid notice to quit under Case E[5].

It should be noted that it is only if the demand under s 6 is made by the landlord that the tenant's right to assign is postponed until after the arbitration. A tenant's demand does not have that consequence.

There is no time limit prescribed by the AHA 1986 for the parties to enter into an agreement after the service of a request under s 6. In the event of no agreement being concluded between the landlord and the tenant following the request, the matter will be determined by arbitration. Only the party who has made the request under s 6 can refer the terms of the tenancy to arbitration[6]. In the absence of agreement as to the appointment of the arbitrator, the party that made the s 6 request may apply to the President of the Royal Institution of Chartered Surveyors (RICS) for an appointment.

---

[1] Formerly the Agricultural Holdings Act 1948 (AHA 1948), s 5(1).
[1A] As to what may constitute a tenancy agreement in writing, see *Grieve & Sons v Barr* 1954 SLT 261.

2   AHA 1986, s 6(1). The request to enter into an agreement need not necessarily be made in writing, although for evidential purposes this is advisable. The request may be made at any time during the subsistence of the tenancy and is a condition precedent to arbitration.

3   Unless restricted by the terms of the lease, the tenant may freely assign or sub-let without the landlord's permission: *Church v Brown* (1808) 15 Ves 258.

4   AHA 1986, s 6(5) and (6). These provisions were first introduced by Sch 3, para 3(3) to the Agricultural Holdings Act 1984, with the object of preventing a pre-emptive assignment or other disposition of the tenancy by the tenant between the request to enter into the agreement in writing and the arbitrator's award. The use of the word 'void' eliminates any argument to the effect that although the disposition was unlawful it nevertheless was effective to vest the tenancy in the assignee: see *Old Grovebury Manor Farm Ltd v Seymour Plant Sales and Hire Ltd (No 2)* [1979] 3 All ER 504, [1977] 1 WLR 1397, CA.

5   This conclusion was reached in *Wilson v Hereford and Worcester County Council* (1991) County Court, unreported. Also see para 23.3.

6   AHA 1986, s 6(1).

Arbitration under section 6

23.3 The arbitrator's jurisdiction is expressly limited by s 6(2) of the AHA 1986 so that his award can only deal with three matters:

(a)   It must specify the existing terms of the tenancy, subject to variations agreed between the landlord and the tenant.

(b)   In so far as the existing terms (as varied or otherwise) neither makes provision for the matters specified in Sch 1 nor makes provision inconsistent with the matters contained in Sch 1, the award must make provision for all those matters having such effect as may be agreed between the parties or, in default of agreement, as appears to the arbitrator to be 'reasonable and just between them'.

(c)   The award can also include any further provisions relating to the tenancy which may be agreed between the landlord and the tenant.

It should be noted that Sch 1 matters will only be included in the tenancy agreement pursuant to the arbitrator's award if either the tenancy is silent or it makes no inconsistent provision. If the arbitrator determines that the tenancy agreement makes contrary provision to the Sch 1 matters, then the agreement prevails. The arbitrator cannot impose Sch 1 provisions for those previously agreed between the parties. If the tenancy agreement expressly permitted sub-letting, then the arbitrator's award will permit sub-letting. The arbitrator can only incorporate Sch 1 matters where he determines that it is 'reasonable and just' to do so. That will be an issue of fact between the parties.

The arbitrator is given no general power to rewrite the tenancy agreement so as to bring it up to date. His task is to determine the existing terms of the tenancy and then only add to or vary those terms in accordance with the express provisions of the legislation.

If it appears to the arbitrator that, by reason of any provision which he is required to include in his award, it is equitable that the rent of the holding should be varied, he may vary the rent accordingly[1].

The incorporation of a prohibition against alienation is of major importance to landlords, particularly following the change in the wording of notices to quit given by reason of death[2]. It should be noted that assignment in the face of a prohibition constitutes an irremediable breach of the term of the tenancy giving rise to the possibility of a notice to quit under Case E[3]. But an assignment following a section 6 notice before such a prohibition is agreed upon or imposed does not[4].

Section 19 of the Landlord and Tenant Act 1927, requiring a landlord's consent to an assignment not to be unreasonably withheld, does not apply to agricultural holdings[5]. The landlord's consent to assignment can therefore be withheld for any reason. It is not subject to the requirements of reasonableness. Where the statutory covenant in Sch 1 is included, the tenancy becomes non-assignable as the statutory covenant does not include any provision relating to reasonableness[6].

The procedure under s 6 is as follows:

(a)   The landlord or tenant who wishes to have a written agreement established must first request the other to enter into such an agreement.

(b)   If the request is not accepted, the party making the request may then demand arbitration and, in default of agreement, apply to the President[7] for an arbitrator to be appointed.

(c)   The arbitrator appointed, following the arbitration hearing, must make an award specifying the existing terms of the tenancy, subject to agreed variations or additions and such of the Sch 1 items, whether agreed or not, which the arbitrator considers are reasonable and just to be included, unless they would be inconsistent with the terms otherwise agreed[8]. There is no need to convert the award into a formal tenancy agreement since the award is effective as an agreement. If such a conversion is made there is a potential liability to stamp duty which otherwise would be avoided. Moreover, the unco-operative party may well refuse to execute such an 'agreement' which is in reality not an agreement at all. The terms and provision in the arbitrator's award take effect by way of variation of the tenancy agreement previously in force, either from the date of the award or such later date specified in the award. The making of an award does not affect an existing notice to quit served by the landlord or any notice served by the tenant.

A problem, in relation to which there is as yet no authority, is whether a notice given under s 6 which is not further activated for many years will eventually lapse or otherwise be rendered ineffective[9].

---

1   AHA 1986, s 6(3). Any such variation is to be disregarded for the purpose of applying the three-year rent cycle: AHA 1986, Sch 2, para 4(2)(a). Note also that this does not permit a general rent review by reference to changed economic circumstances. It is only a revision of rent to take account of the revised terms which is provided for.

2   See the AHA 1948, s 24(2)(g) as amended by s 16 of the 1976 Act – now repealed and re-enacted in Sch 3 of the AHA 1986 as Case G. For a commentary on assignments and their interrelationship with succession, see para 35.18ff.

3   As to which, see para 31.76ff.

4   *Wilson v Hereford and Worcester County Council* (1991) unreported. Also see para 31.88ff.

5   Landlord and Tenant Act 1927, s 19(4).

6   This could give rise to a case where, exceptionally, the arbitrator applies the 'reasonable and just' requirement so as to introduce the concept of reasonableness and the criteria approved in *International Drilling Fluids Ltd v Louisville Investments (Uxbridge) Ltd* [1986] Ch 513, [1986] 1 EGLR 39, CA.

7   As with all references in this book to 'the President' this means the President of the Royal Institution of Chartered Surveyors.

8   AHA 1986, s 6(4) provides that the arbitrator's award shall take effect 'by way of variation of the agreement previously in force in respect of the tenancy'. These words were originally added by Sch 3, para 4 of the Agricultural Holdings Act 1984 in order to make clear that an arbitrator's award does not create a fresh tenancy. The decision in *Hollings v Swindle* (1950) 155 Estates Gazette 269 is thereby inapplicable since 1984.

9   See the Limitation Act 1980, ss 5, 34 and especially 34(6). Note the distinction between statutory and contractual arbitrations in the context of delay: *Bremer Vulkan Schiffbau und Maschinenfabrik v South India Shipping Corpn Ltd* [1981] AC 909 at 962, [1981] 1 All ER 289, HL.

MAINTENANCE, REPAIR AND INSURANCE OBLIGATIONS

Incorporation of model clauses

23.7 Section 7(3) of the AHA 1986 provides that the model clauses are to be incorporated into every contract of tenancy of an agricultural holding 'except insofar as they would impose on one of the parties to an agreement in writing a liability which under the agreement is imposed on the other'. Accordingly, the model clauses will apply where the tenancy agreement is oral. The proviso to section 7(3) of the AHA 1986 reserves the principle of freedom of contract by excluding the model clauses where the tenancy agreement makes contrary provision[A1].

The AHA 1986 nevertheless seeks to promote standardisation of repairing obligations by providing in s 8 that where the terms of a tenancy agreement substantially modify the operation of the model clauses, either party can request a variation so as to bring the tenancy into conformity with the latter. If the parties are unable to reach agreement, the terms are referred to arbitration under the AHA 1986[1]. Section 8(3) of the AHA 1986 imposes upon the arbitrator a duty to consider whether the terms concerned are justified, having regard to the circumstances of the holding and the circumstances of both the landlord and the tenant (but not the rent). If the arbitrator is satisfied that the terms concerned are not justifiable, he can vary them 'in such a manner as appears to him to be reasonable and just as between the landlord and tenant'[2]. This might involve varying the tenancy agreement to bring it into conformity with the model clauses, or varying its terms in a way which reflects the special circumstances of the holding or the parties. In doing so, the arbitrator can vary the rent, if appropriate[3]. Where an award has been made, no further reference under s 8 can be made for three years from the date of the award[4].

Where an arbitration (or agreement) pursuant to s 6 or s 8 of the AHA 1986 transfers the liability for repair or maintenance from one party to the other, s 9 of the Act enables any dispute as to prior failure to carry out repairing obligations to be decided at the date of the variation of the tenancy (and not later on termination) by arbitration[5]. Where a variation is effected by the issue of new regulations, s 9(4) of the AHA 1986 empowers an arbitrator, for a prescribed period, to disregard the variation when settling the terms of the tenancy on a reference under s 6 of the AHA 1986[6].

The Court of Appeal considered the proviso to s 7(3) of the AHA 1986 in *Burden v Hannaford*[7]. The court considered the exclusion of the model clauses where 'they would impose on one of the parties to an agreement in writing a liability which under the agreement is imposed on the other'. The tenancy agreement expressly relieved the tenant of the liability to repair hedges and fences, an obligation which would have been imposed upon the tenant under the model clauses. The court decided that where there was any inconsistency between the tenancy agreement and the model clauses, this had to be resolved by giving effect to the contractual terms and not the model clauses. The model clauses were incorporated, as there was no positive obligation in the tenancy agreement to fence which was at variance with the regulations, but in construing the contract of tenancy and the model clauses together, the former prevailed. The consequence was that neither party was liable to repair the hedges and fences.

The effect of the court's decision in *Burden v Hannaford* is that there may be cases in which no liability to repair items of fixed equipment exists, as a consequence of the tenancy agreement relieving one party of an obligation, without imposing it on the other. Conversely, it is possible to impose on one party an obligation which is placed on the other by model clauses. This occurred in *Roper v Prudential Assurance Co Ltd*[8], where the tenant's express repairing obligations extended to electrical wiring in the context of a general obligation to repair and maintain the farmhouse, cottages and buildings on the holding. Repair in this case was held to include replacing the existing electrical wiring and installations in the farmhouse, an obligation which the model clauses placed on the landlord where the wiring was in need to replacement due to age (and not the neglect of the tenant). Liability therefore was imposed on the tenant, reversing the model clause liability for replacement which would have fallen on the landlord.

[A1] See para 23.7A.
[1] This important right for tenants to request an arbitration is frequently overlooked and rarely invoked. If shortly after the grant of the tenancy the tenant demands arbitration so as to have the 'model clauses' substituted for full repairing obligations, the liability for dilapidations is not likely to be great because of the rule in *Evans v Jones* [1955] 2 QB 58, [1955] 2 All ER 118, CA, as to which see para 39.7.
[2] AHA 1986, s 8(3).
[3] AHA 1986, s 8(4).
[4] AHA 1986, s 8(6).
[5] AHA 1986, ss 9(2) and 71.
[6] By virtue of the Agriculture (Time Limit) Regulations 1988, SI 1988/2821, the prescribed period during which an arbitrator could ignore the amendments made to the model clauses by SI 1988/281 was the three months following their commencement on 24 March 1988. Clearly, s 9(4) of the AHA 1986 is of sporadic importance, remaining dormant in the intervals between the issue of fresh regulations, which itself is an infrequent occurrence.
[7] [1956] 1 QB 142, [1955] 3 All ER 401, CA.
[8] [1992] 1 EGLR 5, [1992] 09 EG 141.

23.7A An issue which remains to be resolved is whether the exception in s 7(3) of the AHA 1986 applies only to a written tenancy agreement so that the model clauses cannot be overridden where the tenancy is oral[1]. In the 12th edition of Muir Watt on Agricultural Holdings[2], the author comments on the decision in *Burden v Hannaford*[3] as follows:

'The absence of a written contractual term positively imposing liability on the other party is thus a condition precedent to the incorporation of the relevant part of the statutory clause but once it is incorporated it has still to be read with the contract and in case of inconsistency the contract prevails'.

The comments recognise that the three separate judgments given by Lord Denning, Hodson LJ and Morris LJ reached the same conclusion but for different reasons. In an earlier article[4], Mr Muir Watt had more fully analysed the Court of Appeal's decision in *Burden v Hannaford*, concluding by expressing regret that the Court had not probed more deeply into the meaning of 'incorporated' or the effect of s 7 of the AHA 1986[5].

1   Although the point was not decided in *Stodday Land Limited v Mashiter* [2009] EWHC (Ch), unreported, Judge Behrens QC acknowledged 'force' in the arguments that the model clauses could not be overridden when the tenancy is oral.
2   (1967) Sweet and Maxwell.
3   [1956] 1 QB 142, [1955] 3 All ER 401, CA.
4   [1956] JPL 15. Where Mr Muir Watt expressed the opinion that the reasoning of the Court of Appeal applied to oral tenancies.
5   Then s 6 of the AHA 1948.

MODEL CLAUSES

Part III: General provisions: obsolete and redundant buildings

23.19 Part III, para 13 of the 1973 Regulations contains the obligations of the parties in relation to items of fixed equipment redundant to the farming of the holding. Either a landlord or a tenant who is of the opinion that any item of fixed equipment is redundant (or was so before it was damaged or destroyed by fire) is entitled to give two months' notice in writing to the other requiring the question of redundancy to be determined in default of agreement by arbitration. The arbitrator must then determine whether or not the item of fixed equipment is (or was before damage or destruction by fire) 'redundant to the farming of the holding'[1].

When deciding the issue of redundancy, the arbitrator must consider whether repair or replacement of the item is reasonable having regard to:

(a)   the landlord's responsibility to manage the holding in accordance with the rules of good estate management; and

(b)   the period for which the holding may reasonably be expected to remain a separate holding; and

(c)   the character and situation of the holding and the average requirements of a tenant reasonably skilled in husbandry[2].

It is noted that these provisions are phrased in the negative, ie the arbitrator is not to determine the item as redundant in his award unless he is satisfied that the repair or replacement of the item is not reasonably required, having regard to these criteria. In practice, the general provisions are of little assistance to an arbitrator in determining whether or not an item is redundant. It is submitted that the word 'redundant' has its normal dictionary meaning and is not synonymous with obsolete. Accordingly, the arbitration procedure referred to above is available only in the case of redundant fixed equipment that is surplus to the needs of the holding. Correspondingly, arbitration is not available where the fixed equipment is merely 'obsolete' or obsolescent, ie where old buildings which are expensive to maintain and repair exist on the holding and would be better replaced with modern buildings, but until then are still needed for the purpose of farming the holding efficiently. Accordingly, the parties are only relieved from their obligations in respect of obsolete fixed equipment if they have agreed in writing that the item of fixed equipment is obsolete.

The effect of agreement as to redundancy or obsolescence or an arbitrator's award that an item is redundant is that both parties are then relieved of any further liability to maintain or repair the item in question[3]. Furthermore, the landlord is entitled to remove the redundant item[4]. However, the right given to a landlord to enter onto a holding to demolish a redundant building is expressed in para 13 of the 1973 Regulations to arise following a determination by an arbitrator. The power is not expressly granted when the parties have agreed that a building is redundant.

In deciding whether to agree that an item of fixed equipment is redundant the parties should bear in mind that the consequence will often be more than merely a relieving of contractual repairing obligations. The planning consequences and the possibility of a Case B notice to quit and the possible loss by removal of the building should also be taken into account before agreement is reached as to redundancy. Consideration should also be given to consequent insuring liability, especially for personal injury to third parties from falling masonry.

As stated above, in addition to redundant and obsolete buildings, there is a third category of items of repair, maintenance, etc from which the parties are or can be relieved. This is any item of work which is 'rendered impossible (except at prohibitive or unreasonable expense) by reason of subsidence of any land or the blocking of outfalls which are not under the control of either the landlord or the tenant'[5].

Unreasonable or prohibitive expense does not relieve liability if it is occasioned by any other failure, for example, cracked or blocked field drains, although it might well assist a tenant if the field drains had become out of alignment over the course of time consequent upon the occurrence of subsidence.

[1]   SI 1973/1473, Sch para 13(1).
[2]   SI 1973/1473, Sch para 13(2).
[3]   SI 1973/1473, Sch paras 13(1) and 14.
[4]   SI 1973/1473, Sch para 13(1).
[5]   SI 1973/1473, Sch para 14(2).

TENANT'S APPLICATION TO THE AGRICULTURAL LAND TRIBUNAL

Procedure

23.29 If the landlord refuses to carry out the work on being requested in writing to do so by the tenant, or refuses to do so within a reasonable time of being so requested[1], the next stage is for the tenant to make an application to the ALT.

The landlord, if he wishes to oppose the application, must serve a reply within one month.

The tenant's application must specify the 'agricultural activity' which the tenant proposes to carry on.

The procedure before the ALT is discussed later in this book[2].

1   AHA 1986, s 11(3)(b).
2   See Ch 46.

Sub-tenants

23.32 Where work has been done by a head tenant under a direction made by the ALT on the application of a sub-tenant, the head tenant may claim compensation for the improvement from his landlord at the end of the head tenancy[1]. If the head tenant has failed to comply with the ALT's direction, and the sub-tenant carries out the work, the head tenant can claim against the head landlord for compensation at the end of the tenancy since the sub-tenant has a right to recover the reasonable cost of the work from the head tenant[2]. In such circumstances any grant out of public money paid to the sub-tenant is treated for the purpose of calculating compensation as if it had been made to the head tenant[3]. Where the whole or any part of an agricultural holding has been sub-let, every landlord, tenant and sub-tenant is deemed to be a party to the proceedings before an ALT with respect to the holding and is entitled to be heard by the ALT[4].

1   AHA 1986, s 68(2).
2   AHA 1986, s 68(2)(b).
3   This provision was not included in the Agriculture Act 1958 and derives from para 2 of the Appendix to the Report of the Law Commission on the Agricultural Holdings Bill (Cmnd 9665).
4   Agricultural Land Tribunals (Rules) Order 2007, SI 2007/3105, r 4(1)(b).

Chapter 24

FARMING: GOOD HUSBANDRY AND STANDARD LEASEHOLD COVENANTS

STATUTORY RIGHTS

Compensation for damage by game

24.11 Section 20(1) of the AHA 1986 sets out provisions which entitle a tenant to recover damages where his crops have sustained damage from any wild animals or birds, where the sporting rights are vested in the landlord or anyone (other than the tenant himself) to whom the landlord has granted the sporting rights[1]. This right does not apply to damage by animals or birds where the tenant himself has permission in writing from the landlord to kill the animals or game in question[2].

There is as yet no authority on two problems of construction. First, does the adjective 'wild' qualify both animals and birds? It is submitted that it does, in the same way as 'farm labourers' was held to qualify both 'cottages and other houses' in *Paddock Investments Ltd v Lory*[3]. Second, if so, are hand-reared pheasants which after release exhibit tendencies of tameness really 'wild birds'? It is submitted that once released into the wild, they are then 'wild birds' despite their origins and propensities.

The right gives a remedy to recover damages from the landlord[4], even though the landlord may have let the shooting rights elsewhere.

An occupier of land has the right, as an incident of his occupation, to kill hares and rabbits, and any agreement which purports to divert or alienate this right is void[4A]. Where a landlord interfered with this right, the tenant was entitled to damages which was found to be an adequate remedy, rather than an injunction[4B]. Permission in writing to the tenant to kill any game excludes compensation for damage caused by that game[4C].

The right to recover compensation[5] is excluded unless the following applies:

(a) The tenant gives notice in writing to the landlord of the occurrence of the damage within one month after he first became, or ought reasonably to have become, aware of it[6].

(b) The tenant gives the landlord a reasonable opportunity to inspect the damage before the crop in question is harvested, if the damage is to a growing crop, or before the crop is removed from the land, if the damage in question is to a crop already harvested[7]. Seed once sown is treated as a growing crop whether or not it has germinated[8].

(c)   Written notice of the claim, together with particulars of it, must be given to the landlord within one month after the expiry of the year in which the claim is made[9]. It is to be noted that 'year' in this context means any period of 12 months ending, in any year, with 29 September or such other date as may by agreement between the landlord and the tenant be substituted for that date[10].

[1]   The revised wording contained in the AHA 1986 protects the tenant's position and enables him to make a claim if the landlord enjoys the sporting rights following a sub-letting by the tenant to him, rather than by means of a reservation.

[2]   By the former s 14 of the AHA 1948, the right to compensation was restricted to game which by s 14(4) was defined as meaning 'deer, pheasants, partridges, grouse and black game'. These restrictions on the right to compensation were removed by the AHA 1984, Sch 3 para 7.

[3]   [1975] 2 EGLR 5, 236 Estates Gazette 803, CA.

[4]   AHA 1986, s 20(1).

[4A]   Ground Game Act 1880, ss 1, 3, 8.

[4B]   *Ross v Watson* 1943 SC 406, 1944 SLT 228.

[4C]   *Mason and Shepton Mallet Transport Co v Clarke* (1953) 161 EG 519.

[5]   Contracting out is prohibited: AHA 1986, s 78(1).

[6]   AHA 1986, s 20(2)(a).

[7]   AHA 1986, s 20(2)(b). The notice under s 20(2)(a) and (c) and the giving to the landlord of a reasonable opportunity to inspect the damage under s 20(2)(b) are essential prerequisites to the recovery of compensation. The question of whether or not reasonable opportunity has been given to the landlord will depend on all the circumstances.

[8]   AHA 1986, s 20(3)(a). This provision removes a doubt previously existing as to whether ungerminated seed amounted to a growing crop. The provision was first introduced by the AHA 1984, Sch 3 para 7(2)(c). It is very important because pheasant damage to seed corn is more detrimental normally than any damage caused by the birds just before harvest.

[9]   AHA 1986, s 20(2)(c).

[10]   AHA 1986, s 20(3)(b). The provision as enacted in s 14(1)(b) of the AHA 1948 provided for notice of the claim to be given to the landlord within one month after the expiration of the calendar year, or such other period of 12 months as may have been substituted by agreement between landlord and tenant.

STANDARD LEASEHOLD COVENANTS

Conservation

24.23 A covenant which is not regularly seen in tenancy agreements of agricultural holdings protected by the AHA 1986 is one relating to conservation. However, clearly the pursuit of conservation objectives could operate contrary to a tenant's obligations to farm in accordance with the rules of good husbandry[1]. The AHA 1986 provides protection to a tenant by reason of Sch 3 para 9(2). This provides that a tenant will be protected in proceedings brought by the landlord before the Agricultural Land Tribunal for a certificate of bad husbandry if the practice complained of is adopted pursuant to a provision in the tenancy, or any other agreement with the landlord, which indicates (in whatever form) that its object is the furtherance of one or more stated conservation objectives, namely the conservation of flora or fauna, the protection of buildings of archaeological/historical interest, and the conservation or enhancement of the natural beauty of the countryside. The ALT must disregard the practice alleged only if it is permitted by a provision in the tenancy or some other written agreement with the landlord (for example, a management agreement to which the landlord is a party). Often such provisions are contained in separate management agreements, for example, if the holding has been notified a Site of Special Scientific Interest under the Wildlife and Countryside Act 1981[2] or it is in an Environmentally Sensitive Area designated under the Agriculture Act 1986. It is submitted that if the rules of good husbandry have been incorporated as a term of the tenancy agreement, then the inclusion of a conservation covenant should remove the possibility of a landlord seeking to pursue a complaint against the tenant under, for example, Case D.

1   See para 24.4.
2   As to Sites of Special Scientific Interest (SSSIs), note the case of *R (on the application of Boggis) v Natural England* [2009] EWCA Civ 1061, [2010] 1 All ER 159, [2010] PTSR 725 where the Court of Appeal reversed the High Court decision. The High Court had upheld a challenge by an individual to a SSSI designation by Natural England.

LANDLORD'S ACCESS

24.27 One area which gives rise to disputes is the landlord's reservation of the right to access. In the Scottish case of *Possfund Custodian Trustee Ltd v Kwik-Fit Properties Ltd*[1], the court held on appeal, reversing the court at first instance, that a landlord was not entitled to access to dig boreholes to test for environmental contamination in reliance upon a clause which provided that the tenant was to 'permit the landlord and its agents at all reasonable times with or without workmen ... to enter upon the premises generally to inspect and examine the same, to view the state of repair and condition thereof and to take a schedule of the landlord's fixtures and of any wants of compliance by the tenant with its obligations hereunder'.

1   [2009] 1 EGLR 39.

Chapter 25
RENT REVIEW

GENERAL RENT REVIEW

Introduction

Outline of the current law

25.4 Section 12 and Sch 2 to the AHA 1986 set up a procedural code which is generally informal, but contains a number of technicalities which need careful consideration.

In outline, the rent review procedure commences when either the landlord or the tenant may demand arbitration as to the rent properly payable. The new rent then takes effect from the earliest date on which the tenancy could next have been terminated by notice to quit, ie the first annual term date of the tenancy not earlier than 12 months following the date of the demand. Subject to specified exceptions, such reviews can take place not more than once every three years.

Where the AHA 1986 applies to a new tenancy by virtue of the operation of s 4(1)(g) of the Agricultural Tenancies Act 1995 (ATA 1995), and the rent is unchanged from the rent payable under the previous tenancy, disregarding any changes resulting from adjustments to the boundary of the holding, the three-year rent review cycle is uninterrupted[1].

The arbitrator must determine the rent properly payable in accordance with the statutory rental formula. The rent properly payable in respect of a holding is the rent at which the holding might reasonably be expected to be let by a prudent and willing landlord to a prudent and willing tenant[2], taking into account all relevant factors, including (in every case):

(a)   the terms of the tenancy (including those relating to rent)[3];
(b)   the character and situation of the holding (including the locality in which it is situated)[4];
(c)   the productive capacity of the holding[5] and its related earning capacity[6]; and
(d)   the current levels of rents for comparable lettings[7].

He is required to disregard factors such as tenant's improvements, tenant's fixtures, the grant-aided element of landlord's improvements, 'high farming', the fact that the tenant is in occupation, any tenant's dilapidations and the like[8].

25.4 *Rent review*

The arbitrator is expressly directed to disregard certain matters.

The arbitrator must determine whether the rent should be increased, reduced or remain the same and must award the appropriate rent in consequence.

Both The Royal Institution of Chartered Surveyors and The Central Association of Agricultural Valuers publish excellent Guidance Notes for valuers acting in relation to valuations under the AHA 1986[9].

The tenancy continues with the arbitrator's awarded rent substituted for the rent previously payable. The parties can, of course (and usually will) agree the rent rather than go through the entire statutory arbitration procedure.

1   AHA 1986, Sch 2 para 7, inserted by the Regulatory Reform (Agricultural Tenancies) (England and Wales) Order 2006 (RRO 2006), SI 2006/2805, art 8.
2   AHA 1986, Sch 2 para 1(1).
3   AHA 1986, Sch 2 para 1(1). The arbitrator must take account of the existing rent: *Enfield London Borough Council v Pott* [1990] 2 EGLR 7, [1990] 34 EG 60.
4   AHA 1986, Sch 2 para 1(1). See para 25.20.
5   AHA 1986, Sch 2 paras 1(1) and (2)(a). See para 25.21.
6   AHA 1986, Sch 2 paras 1(1) and (2)(b). See para 25.21.
7   AHA 1986, Sch 2 para 1(1). See para 25.30ff.
8   AHA 1986, Sch 2 paras 1(3) and 2(1), (2). See para 25.36ff.
9   Available respectively from Surveyor Court, Westwood Business Park, Coventry CV4 8JE and Market Chambers, 35 Market Place, Coleford, Gloucestershire GL16 8AA.

The valuation formula: the amount of the rent properly payable

25.18 In the leading case of *Childers (JW) Trustees v Anker*[1], the Court of Appeal had to consider the statutory formula for the level of rent and the statutory disregards. The court provided the following assistance:

(a)   The rent envisaged by the statutory formula is not 'the open market rent' – 'Section 12(2) and Schedule 2 ... provide a complete statutory code to fix a rent and that code should be applied without addition or subtraction;'[2]. Schedule 2 does envisage the rent being set at a market rent level, but the assumptions made (eg as to what the market would know or not know about the holding in an open market rental valuation) would not apply when the statutory formula was being given effect to[3].

(b)   All relevant information that the arbitrator required (even if confidential to the tenant) was admissible and must be supplied to enable the arbitrator to determine the rent properly payable. This would normally include quota details, Single Farm Payment information, information relating to grants, etc.

(c)   Where a holding was subject to any management agreement that had been or could be expected to be obtained, any payments under such an agreement fell to be taken into account not as part of the productive capacity of the holding, but as another 'relevant factor'.

(d)   Marriage value (ie the special value to an established farmer in the district in being able to take on the subject holding and farm in conjunction with his other land as one single enlarged agricultural unit) did not fall to be disregarded, but to be included in the rent properly payable.

As to scarcity value, although the correct treatment of scarcity value was not in issue in *Childers (JW) Trustees v Anker*[4], there were strong indications in the judgment of Morritt LJ that if that matter had been put in issue, the court would have determined that scarcity value does not fall to be disregarded.

The existing rent can be one relevant factor to be taken into account[5], but the existence of a preferential rent will not prejudice the application of the Sch 2 rent formula.

There is no obligation on either party to activate a rent review every three years. Failure to do so is irrelevant in determining the new rent at arbitration.

Non-farming income generally is a relevant factor in fixing the rent under Sch 2, particularly given the increased extent of diversification: for example, farm shops and caravan sites. It nevertheless remains unclear as to what extent income generating potential from non-agricultural sources can be taken into account. Productive capacity expressly includes the situation in which the tenant has permission to diversify into non-agricultural land uses. The user covenant is clearly relevant in relation to this issue[6].

One area which gives rise to difficulties is the treatment of dwellinghouses, for example, the treatment of bed and breakfast income derived from such use of the farmhouse and rental income from cottages[6A]. Each case falls to be considered on its individual facts. It should nevertheless not be assumed that rental income derived from a lawful sub-letting of a cottage should be passed in full to the landlord of the agricultural holding. For example, the repairing obligations between the head landlord and the head tenant are unlikely to reflect the obligations between the tenant and the sub-tenant. Also, the valuer of the AHA 1986 tenant may seek to factor into the assessment of the rent management charges[7].

[1] (1995) 73 P & CR 458, [1996] 1 EGLR 1, CA. See also, *Enfield London Borough Council v Potts* [1990] 2 EGLR 7, [1990] 34 EG 60.

[2] *Childers (JW) Trustees v Anker* [1996] 1 EGLR 1, per His Honour Judge Bromley, approved in the Court of Appeal.

[3] *Childers (JW) Trustees v Anker* [1996] 1 EGLR 1, per Morritt LJ in the Court of Appeal.

[4] *Childers (JW) Trustees v Anker* (1995) 73 P & CR 458, [1996] 1 EGLR 1, CA.

[5] *Enfield London Borough Council v Pott* [1990] 2 EGLR 7, [1990] 34 EG 60.

[6A] See *Morrison-Low v Paterson* (2010) SLC/233/08. See para 25.18A.

[6] See the county court case of *Tummon v Barclays Bank Trust Co Ltd* (1979) 39 P & CR 300, 250 Estates Gazette 980, in which it was decided that the holding fell to be valued *rebus sic stantibus*, ie as it stands. If the holding had potential for enhanced value use which was not realised by the tenant, then that latent value did not fall to be assessed and added to the rent. It may be that now the arbitrator is directed to take into account 'the productive capacity' of the holding which suggests the potential rather than realised capacity that the county court case is no longer applicable in that respect. Furthermore, potential non-agricultural income available to the tenant who is permitted by his tenancy agreement to 'diversify' would be relevant as an 'other relevant matter'. Note further that the *Tummon* case was decided before the substantial changes in the provisions of the rent

formula were introduced by the AHA 1984. Also see, *Jewell v McGowan* [2002] EWCA
Civ 145, [2002] 3 EGLR 87: see para 24.21.
7   For further discussion of these issues, see the Guidance Notes issued by the RICS and the
CAAV: see fn 2 of para 25.3.

25.18A *Morrison-Low v Paterson*[1] is arguably the most important rent
review case since *Childers (JW) Trustees v Anker*[2]. Although a decision of the
Scottish Land Court[3], it addresses issues common to rent review in England
and Wales. The court's opinion cites English cases alongside Scottish authorities. The case deals with a contested rent review governed by s 13 of the
Agricultural Holdings (Scotland) Act 1991, so amended by the Agricultural
Holdings (Scotland) Act 2003. The 79 page opinion of the court contains a
detailed review of issues which impact widely upon rent reviews including an
analysis of the approach to comparables; the treatment of comparable
evidence not under the 1991 Act; scarcity; the treatment of Single Payment
Scheme Payments (Single Payments)[4]; marriage value; and the use of dwellings.

In summary, the decision of the court was as follows:

(a)   In considering comparables, the court adopted a narrow approach,
      determining that adjustments should be made for distinctions, for
      example, where in determining the rent of a comparable holding the
      income potential of cottage lettings has been ignored.
(b)   The court decided that the Scottish equivalent of farm business tenan-
      cies[5], Limited Duration Tenancies, could be used as comparable evi-
      dence.
(c)   In the court's opinion neither Single Payment Scheme entitlements nor
      Single Payments are attributes of the holding. Nevertheless, a modest
      rental element was ascribed to the existence of these rights, recognising
      the operation of the market and the fact that eligibility of the landlord's
      land assisted in meeting the rent.
(d)   Having reached the conclusion that the ability to claim the Single
      Payment lies solely with farmers and does not derive from the land and
      so does not directly give rise to rent, the court recognises that the
      holders of sufficient suitable entitlements are the most likely successful
      bidders for tenancies. While the occupation of the existing tenant is to
      be ignored, he (or the business with which the entitlements are
      registered) was found to be best placed as the hypothetical bidder. The
      disregard of his occupation means that he has a greater area of
      entitlements than the remaining eligible land area he otherwise has (if
      any).
(e)   Following *Childers (JW) Trustees v Anker*, the court found that, while
      marriage value is taken out of comparables, in order to make them
      comparable, the marriage value of the subject holding in the market
      place is to be considered.
(f)   As to the impact of an attractive farmhouse upon rent, the court
      accepted that it was inappropriate to assess the farmhouse as a separate
      unit. Instead the court preferred to consider the farmhouse by analysing
      comparables with and without attractive farmhouses.

(g)   The court gave limited guidance as to the impact of letting cottages, in part because it was agreed between the parties that one half of the net rent (after an allowance for voids and management) would be added to the rent of the holding. The dispute centred on a third, larger cottage which was occupied by the tenant's son who worked on the holding. While it could be let, in the absence of a prohibition, the tenant had agreed to endeavour to use it for a full-time farm worker. Nevertheless, the court concluded that if it was more efficient to let the cottage, then that should be done. As a consequence, the court adopted the same approach to the rental impact which had been agreed between the parties in relation to the first two cottages.

The court recognised the need to have regard to the prevailing economic circumstances over the period of the next three years. The case also provides useful commentary for practitioners in relation to the use of farm budgets[6].

1   (2010) SLC/233/08.
2   (1995) 73 P & CR 458, [1996] 1 EGLR 1, CA.
3   At the time of writing this Supplement, it is understood that the decision is under appeal.
4   See Ch 52.
5   See Ch 3.
6   Generally, reference should be made to the excellent CAAV Discussion Paper – J Moody *Rent Review under the Agricultural Holdings (Scotland) Acts: Morrison-Low v Paterson – Scottish Land Court: CAAV Discussion Paper 12 June 2010.*

The valuation formula: factors to be taken into account

Productive capacity and related earning capacity: entitlements

25.29 As seen in Chapter 52, entitlements allocated to farmers under Mid-term Review of the Common Agricultural Policy only give rise to income to the farmer in the form of Single Payment[1] when matched against land in the region. Nevertheless, entitlements are not attached to the land. They are assets belonging to the farmer.

In the ninth edition of this book it was submitted that the entitlements registered in the name of the farmer fall to be disregarded, unless the parties make express provision for them to be taken into account in the tenancy agreement. Following the decision of the Scottish Land Court in *Morrison-Low v Paterson*[1A], it would seem to be established that the income stream from the Single Payment should not be included when assessing 'productive earning capacity', and that it 'cannot properly be viewed as part of the earnings of the farm'[1B].

As seen above, one of the factors that an arbitrator must take into account is the terms of the tenancy agreement. A quota provision which restricts or regulates the use and disposal of entitlements, affecting the income that can be generated by the tenant, will be a relevant consideration. Likewise, if the user covenant imposes upon the tenant an obligation to farm the holding in a manner which precludes him from just keeping the land in good agricultural and environmental condition, in accordance with the restrictions imposed by the European Regulations, then that will also be a relevant consideration.

The Single Farm Payment is expressly decoupled from production. Logically it cannot form part of the productive capacity or related earnings capacity of the holding. However, it will be a 'relevant factor'[1C], in a similar manner to income derived from management agreements[2].

It is submitted that entitlements do not fall to be disregarded on the basis of them falling within the definition of tenant's improvements or fixed equipment[3].

In *Childers (JW) Trustees v Anker*[4], the Court of Appeal also endorsed the approach taken by the Judge in that case that non-farming income was a relevant factor, an endorsement which arguably has the capacity to impact on the treatment of Single Payments on rent review[5]. That said, the analogy between sums received in respect of a Site of Special Scientific Interest and the Single Payment is not precise. In particular, a factor determining the amount received in respect of the former is income foregone, whereas the latter is kept characterised as income support. On the other hand, in both cases production is not necessarily a pre-requisite and land management obligations are imposed (albeit at a low level in the case of cross compliance under the Single Payment Scheme).

[1]   Known as the Single Farm Payment.
[1A]   *Morrison-Low v Paterson* (2010) SLC/233/08.
[1B]   *Morrison-Low v Paterson* (2010) SLC/233/08 para 138.
[1C]   *Morrison-Low v Paterson* (2010) SLC/233/08. See para 25.18A.
[2]   *Childers (JW) Trustees v Anker* (1995) 73 P & CR 458, [1996] 1 EGLR 1, CA.
[3]   See para 52.31. For further commentary on the impact of entitlements and Single Payments in relation to rent review, see 'Mid-Term Review, A Valuer's Interim Guide' (2004) Central Association of Agricultural Valuers and Moody J and Neville W, *Mid-Term Review, A Practical Guide* (2004) Burges Salmon LLP.
[4]   *Childers (JW) Trustees v Anker* (1995) 73 P & CR 458, [1996] 1 EGLR 1, CA.
[5]   A matter of some importance is that the Scottish legislation considered in *Morrison-Low v Paterson* differs materially from the legislation applicable in England and Wales. In particular, reference is instead made to 'information about rents of other agricultural holdings (including when fixed) and any factors affecting those rents (or any of them) except any distortion due to a scarcity of lets': Agricultural Holdings (Scotland) Act 1991, s 13(3)(a) (as amended by the Agricultural Holdings (Scotland) Act 2003, s 63).

Comparables

25.30 Schedule 2 para 1(3) of the AHA 1986 directs the arbitrator to have regard to any available evidence of rents which are, or (in view of rents currently being tendered) are likely to become, payable in respect of tenancies of comparable agricultural holdings on terms (other than terms fixing the rent payable) similar to the tenancy being the subject of the rent review. The arbitrator can consider rents arrived at either by agreement or as a consequence of arbitration, as well as current tenders for rent payable in respect of comparable holdings[1].

When assessing comparable holdings[2], Sch 2 para 1(3) of the AHA 1986 goes on to direct the arbitrator to disregard three factors in his assessment as to a true comparison with the subject holding. The three factors are:

(a)   'any element of the rents in question which is due to an appreciable scarcity of comparable holdings available for letting on such terms, compared with the number of persons seeking to become tenants of such holdings on such terms' (referred to henceforth as 'scarcity value');

(b)   'any element of those rents which is due to the fact that the tenant of or a person tendering for any comparable holding is in occupation of other land in the vicinity of that holding that may conveniently be occupied together with that holding' (referred to henceforth as 'marriage value'); and

(c)   'any effect on those rents which is due to any allowances or reductions made in consideration of the charging of premiums' (referred to henceforth as 'premium value').

---

[1]   These include those 'whether fixed by agreement or by arbitration' and even includes those which '(in view of rents currently being tendered) are likely to become payable'. Therefore the decision in the case of a commercial arbitration of *Land Securities plc v Westminster City Council* [1993] 4 All ER 124, [1992] 2 EGLR 15 has no application to AHA 1986 rent arbitrations.

[2]   See *Morrison-Low v Paterson* (2010) SLC/233/08. See para 25.18A.

Scarcity value

25.31 Since the widely recognised factors which in the past had given rise to the high level of open market rents were the high level of demand for agricultural holdings and the low level of supply, it soon became clear that if scarcity value had to be valued out of the comparable holdings this would involve a substantial adjustment in most cases. The first and most fundamental question that the AHA 1986 formula asks is whether, if the arbitrator has to value out scarcity from comparables, he is also obliged to eliminate scarcity value from the rent properly payable in respect of the subject holding[A1].

Perhaps surprisingly, although Sch 2 para 1(3)(a) requires scarcity value to be valued out of the rent of comparable holdings, the provision is silent as to whether it is to be disregarded in relation to the subject holding itself. It might be argued that if the intention of the legislature was that the scarcity value of the subject holding itself had to be disregarded, then it was surprising that this most important factor was not expressly mentioned in Sch 2. It is submitted that scarcity value should be disregarded in the subject holding, despite the fact that this is not expressly required by the AHA 1986. That conclusion is consistent with an analysis of the NFU/CLA package which resulted in the amendment of the rent review formula in the Agricultural Holdings Act 1984[1]. However, that view was challenged in *Childers (JW) Trustees v Anker*[2]. In that case the tenant placed reliance upon the decision in *99 Bishopsgate Ltd v Prudential Assurance Co Ltd*[3].

In *99 Bishopsgate Ltd v Prudential Assurance Co Ltd*, a building in the City of London had to be valued by reference to the rental values of comparable property 'let with vacant possession'. Lloyd J described as 'irresistible' an argument that 'there could be no conceivable point' in directing the arbitrator to have regard to comparable lettings with vacant possession if the subject premises were to be valued subject to existing occupational leases. The decision of Lloyd J was upheld by the Court of Appeal[4].

The same argument might be thought to apply to Sch 2 para 1(3)(a) of the AHA 1986. In *Childers (JW) Trustees v Anker[5]*, the tenant argued that both scarcity value and marriage value must be valued out of the rental of comparable holdings, on the basis that the objective was to arrive at an undistorted rental value for the subject holding. The Court of Appeal rejected this argument in relation to marriage value, deciding that marriage value in the subject holding is relevant and to be taken into account. The fact that it was to be disregarded in valuing comparables did not mean that it should be disregarded in respect of the subject holding. However, the Court of Appeal expressly left open to question whether the same analysis should be applied in relation to scarcity value. The court stated:

> 'This case is not concerned with whether scarcity (whether of demand or supply) is to be considered or excluded in the assessment of the rent for the subject holding, that question must await determination in a case in which it is raised'[6].

The Court of Appeal declined to determine the issue of scarcity value notwithstanding the fact that it was invited to do so. It was argued that, following the principle in *Pepper (Inspector of Taxes) v Hart[7]*, the court could have regard to Hansard, where in Parliament clear indications were given that scarcity value was to be excluded from the subject holding. Indeed, such a conclusion was critical to the whole basis of the NFU/CLA package[8] upon which the rent review formula in the AHA 1986 was founded. If scarcity value were allowed in respect of the subject holding it would undermine the central aim of the Sch 2 rental formula to link rent to productive capacity and related earning capacity, breaking the link with inflated tenders on the first lettings. The point remains to be resolved before the courts.

[A1]   See *Morrison-Low v Paterson* (2010) SLC/233/08. See para 25.18A.
[1]   See para 25.2.
[2]   (1995) 73 P & CR 458, [1996] 1 EGLR 1, CA.
[3]   [1985] 1 EGLR 72, 273 Estates Gazette 984.
[4]   (1984) 270 EG 950, [1985] 1 EGLR 72. As to a Scottish case in relation to the equivalent wording of the Scottish Act, see *Aberdeen Endowments Trust v Wills* 1985 SLT (Land Ct) 23.
[5]   (1995) 73 P & CR 458, [1996] 1 EGLR 1, CA.
[6]   *Childers (JW) Trustees v Anker* (1995) 73 P & CR 458, [1996] 1 EGLR 1, per Morritt LJ, CA.
[7]   [1993] AC 593, [1993] 1 All ER 42, HL.
[8]   See para 25.2.

Marriage value

25.32 After a period of doubt and controversy it has now been held authoritatively by the Court of Appeal in *Childers (JW) Trustees v Anker[1]* that although marriage value falls to be disregarded in the case of comparables, it does not for the subject holding. Therefore when assessing the rent of an agricultural holding (though not the comparable), any value the holding may have for farmers in the district with established and often equipped holdings to take on the subject holding to be farmed with the prospective tenant's existing established land holdings as part of an enlarged single agricultural unit, must be taken into account.

This does not mean that in every case, particularly where the actual tenant happens to farm other land as well, that some premium or additional rent is payable over and above the rent that would otherwise be payable. It does mean by contrast that the tenant cannot argue that the subject holding must be assessed as if it was farmed in isolation without other available land held by other prospective tenants in the district.

¹ (1995) 73 P & CR 458, [1996] 1 EGLR 1, CA. Also see, *Morrison-Low v Paterson* (2010) SLC/233/08. See para 25.18A.

Types of comparable

25.34 The statutory definition of the comparables which have to be taken into account in every case is contained in Sch 2 para 1(3) of the AHA 1986. As indicated above, such comparables are not confined to open market lettings, by tender or otherwise, but include rents fixed by agreement between parties, rents fixed by arbitration under existing tenancies, and rents which are 'likely to become payable in respect of tenancies of comparable agricultural holdings'[A1].

Under the general law, evidence of an arbitrator's award in another arbitration that determined the rent of a property on review is inadmissible as a comparable on a subsequent rent review[1]. However, under the AHA 1986, the arbitrator is expressly required to have regard to the current level of rents for comparable holdings and rent awards made by arbitrators in relation to such holdings[2].

The issue which follows from the statutory definition in the AHA 1986 as to what the arbitrator is to take into account in assessing the rent of an agricultural holding under the AHA 1986 is whether he can have regard to rents paid for farm business tenancies under the Agricultural Tenancies Act 1995. In practice, such rents under the Agricultural Tenancies Act 1995 (ATA 1995) have been significantly higher than those for comparable lettings of agricultural holdings under the AHA 1986.

Two cases concerning the basis of valuing a 'fair' rent for residential dwellings under the Rent Act 1977 provide support for the argument that the arbitrator under the AHA 1986 should be allowed to take into account rents payable in respect of lettings under the ATA 1995[3]. In *Curtis v London Rent Assessment Committee*[4], the court held that the starting point when valuing a 'fair' rent was the market rent. For the purposes of the Rent Act 1977, that market rent was then to be discounted to eliminate any element of scarcity value. It should be noted that it was accepted in *Spath Holme Ltd v Greater Manchester and*

Lancashire Rent Assessment Committee (Chairman)[5] (and confirmed in *Curtis v London Rent Assessment Committee*[6]) that if there is in fact no scarcity, then in theory the fair rent should equate to the market rent. The Court of Appeal held in *Curtis v London Rent Assessment Committee*[7] that the best evidence of market values was evidence of comparable rents for assured tenancies let under the Housing Act 1988. The court directed that these should be used instead of the diminishing number of registered fair rent comparables available under the Rent Act 1977.

It is submitted that the position relating to the interrelationship of rents payable under the AHA 1986 and those payable under the ATA 1995 is different to the relationship applying between the Rent Act 1977 and the Housing Act 1988. Schedule 2 para 1(3) of the AHA 1986 specifically directs the arbitrator consider the current level of rents payable or currently being tendered in respect of tenancies of *comparable agricultural holdings* [emphasis added]. This limits the comparison to agricultural holdings within the definition contained in the AHA 1986[8]. Further, the formula to be adopted under the AHA 1986 is quite different to that which applies under the Rent Act 1977 where there is no requirement on the part of the rent assessment committee in determining the fair rent to consider factors such as the productive capacity and the related earning capacity.

If lettings under a different code are preferred as comparables, eg farm business tenancies created under the ATA 1995, it would appear on parity of reasoning with the *Spath Holme* case that they cannot be rejected as inadmissible on that account alone. However, the difficulty arises as to whether a new letting of a farm business tenancy falls within the definition of an 'agricultural holding' within the meaning of para 1(3) of Sch 2 to the AHA 1986 since it refers to '... tenancies of comparable *agricultural holdings* on terms ...'. It is submitted that the effect on rent of the different levels of security and the difference in the terms of the letting must be evaluated and taken into account when undertaking the valuation exercise.

[A1] See *Morrison-Low v Paterson* (2010) SLC/233/08. See para 25.18A.
[1] *Land Securities plc v Westminster City Council (No 2)* [1995] 1 EGLR 245, [1994] 7 LS Gaz R 31.
[2] AHA 1986, Sch 2 para 1(1) and (3).
[3] *Spath Holme Ltd v Greater Manchester and Lancashire Rent Assessment Committee (Chairman)* (1995) 28 HLR 107, [1995] 2 EGLR 80, CA; *Curtis v London Rent Assessment Committee* [1999] QB 92, [1997] 4 All ER 842. Also, see *BTE Ltd v Merseyside and Cheshire Rent Assessment Committee* (1991) 24 HLR 514, [1992] 1 EGLR 116.
[4] [1999] QB 92, [1997] 4 All ER 842.
[5] (1995) 28 HLR 107, [1995] 2 EGLR 80, CA.
[6] [1999] QB 92, [1997] 4 All ER 842.
[7] [1999] QB 92, [1997] 4 All ER 842.
[8] AHA 1986, ss 1(1) and 96(1).

The valuation formula: factors to be disregarded

Tenant's improvements

25.39 As regards the definition of tenant's improvements, the following points should be noted:

(a)   Any grant obtained by the tenant for the carrying out of the improvement is for the benefit of the tenant in that the tenant obtains credit, not merely for that element of the improvement for which he paid out of his own resources, but also that element paid for out of parliamentary or local government funds.

(b)   An 'equivalent allowance' by the landlord will negative the disregard provision. For example, if the landlord agreed upon the improvement in consideration of the tenant being allowed to assign the tenancy to himself and his son, this might, on the facts of an individual case, be found to be an equivalent allowance. The allowance must be 'equivalent' to the value of the improvement. The provision that the landlord will pay compensation (which he is statutorily obliged to do anyway if his consent in writing is obtained) will be an allowance that would, as a matter of valuation, probably not be found to be nearly sufficient to constitute an equivalent allowance. Similarly, some minor benefit passing from the landlord to the tenant which was not equivalent in value to the improvement would be insufficient to negative the requirement that such an improvement should be disregarded.

(c)   The improvements must be carried out at the expense of the tenant. An improvement carried out by a third party (even if closely connected to the tenant) would appear not to fall to be disregarded. A problem arises in the case of improvements carried out by sub-tenants as to whether they too fall to be disregarded. It is submitted that the extended definition of tenant contained in s 96 of the AHA 1986 (including persons deriving title from the tenant) is sufficiently wide and all-embracing to include a sub-tenant[1].

(d)   In the case of a tenant who has held a tenancy of the agricultural holding under a series of tenancies, improvements carried out under a previous tenancy fall to be disregarded[2]. It should be noted that it is only a series of tenancies in favour of the same tenant which carry with them the rollover provision. If, for example, the tenant acquired his tenancy by succession, improvements carried out during the currency of, for example, his father's tenancy do not fall to be disregarded, unless special provision was made for this at the time of the grant of the succession tenancy. This is because the tenant in question had not held under a previous tenancy of the holding. The previous tenancy had been held by his deceased or retired close relation[3].

(e)   Where there is an agreement that, upon succession to a tenancy, the end of tenancy claims will be 'subsumed', it is submitted that the same position as set out in paragraph (d) applies.

(f)   The disregard provision does not apply if the tenant had received compensation on termination of the previous tenancy.

(g)   Improvements carried out in anticipation of the grant of a tenancy fall to be disregarded[4].

(h)   A problem can arise where the tenant carries out improvements for the benefit of the holding on adjoining land and not, therefore, physically on the holding itself. This would occur where the tenant builds a road to provide access to the holding for milk lorries. Such improvements are not 'executed on the holding' if a restricted or narrow construction of para 2(2)(a) of Sch 2 to the AHA 1986 is applied. It is submitted that nevertheless they fall to be valued out and the benefit of them falls to be credited to the tenant in arriving at the rent properly payable. A wider construction is likely to be favoured – 'on' meaning in connection with rather than merely physically within[5]. By contrast, tenant's buildings on an adjoining holding which are used to service both the tenant's own land and the subject holding do not fall to be disregarded for the purpose of rent reviews on the subject holding.

[1] Note the *ejusdem generis* rule and the genus of persons within the statutory definition, namely, 'executors, administrators, assigns or trustee in bankruptcy of tenant'; a list of persons all of whom derive title laterally from the tenant rather than subordinately.

[2] AHA 1986, Sch 2 para 2(3)(a). This provision was introduced to correct an injustice highlighted under the previous law by the decision in *East Coast Amusement Co Ltd v British Transport Board* [1965] AC 58, [1963] 2 WLR 1426, HL, and *Ponsford v HMS Aerosols Ltd* [1979] AC 63, [1978] 2 All ER 837, HL. See also *GREA Real Property Investments Ltd v Williams* [1979] 1 EGLR 121, 250 Estates Gazette 651, and, in the context of fixtures, *New Zealand Government Property Corpn v HM & S Ltd* [1981] 1 All ER 759, [1981] 1 WLR 870.

[3] AHA 1986, Sch 2 para 2(3).

[4] *Hambros Bank Executor and Trustee Co Ltd v Superdrug Stores Ltd* [1985] 1 EGLR 99, 274 Estates Gazette 590; *Scottish and Newcastle Breweries plc v Sir Richard Sutton's Settled Estates* [1985] 2 EGLR 130, 276 Estates Gazette 77.

[5] A similar construction is normally applied to agricultural work 'on the holding' which includes going to market to buy or sell produce when determining an applicant for succession's principal source of livelihood.

Tenant's occupation of the holding

25.44 A further factor to be disregarded is 'any effect on the rent of the fact that the tenant who is a party to the arbitration is in occupation of the holding'[1]. This direction eliminates any extra rent that the actual tenant might be shown to be prepared to pay because of the importance to him of retaining his occupation of the holding. In such circumstances a landlord might otherwise be able to show that the actual tenant in occupation would be prepared to pay more rent to avoid the upheaval of removal or because the holding is of some special or particular value to him. These factors have to be disregarded. The rent is assessed objectively by reference to the attributes of the holding and not subjectively by reference to the requirements or circumstances of the particular parties[2].

In *Childers (JW) Trustees v Anker*[3], it was held that this 'disregard' did not entitle the arbitrator to treat the sitting tenant as not being available as one of the potential tenants envisaged as 'prudent and willing'[3A].

It is submitted that it follows, by reference to this disregard, that any enhancement of rental value arising from the good husbandry (falling short of high farming) should be disregarded.

[1] AHA 1986, Sch 2 para 3(a).

[2] For a commentary on the similar words applied in the case of business premises under s 34 of the Landlord and Tenant Act 1954, see *Harewood Hotels Ltd v Harris* [1958] 1 All ER 104, [1958] 1 WLR 108, CA and in particular the judgment of Lord Evershed MR.

[3] (1995) 73 P & CR 458, [1996] 1 EGLR 1, CA.

[3A] See *Morrison-Low v Paterson* (2010) SLC/233/08. See para 25.18A.

Contracting-out and contracting-in

25.46 The statutory formula for revising the rent is extensive and makes no mention of whether the statutory procedures, or the rental formula, or any other matter prescribed by s 12 or Sch 2 to the AHA 1986 can be revised or varied by agreement or can be abandoned altogether. This could occur on the basis that the parties agreed there should be no rent review at all during the currency of the tenancy or that rent reviews should be carried out in accordance with the parties' own contractual formula. In *Johnson v Moreton*[1], Lord Russell remarked upon the absence of any statutory provision either authorising or prohibiting contracting-out, but as the matter was not directly in issue, came to no conclusion as to whether public policy demanded that the statutory procedures should override any agreement reached between the parties in the same way as the parties are precluded from contracting-out of the provisions protecting tenants in relation to notices to quit[2].

In the eighth edition of this book, the Editor advanced the proposition that there was no public policy reason for the parties not to be able to contract out of the statutory rent formula. Reliance was placed upon comments in *Goldsworthy v Brickell*[3] and *Childers (JW) Trustees v Anker*[4]. The ninth edition of this book recited the arguments contained in the eighth edition but added that support for the proposition could be found in the Court of Appeal decision in *Plumb Bros v Dolmac (Agriculture) Ltd*[5], a case not referred to in the eighth edition.

Since the ninth edition, the issue has been determined by Lewison J in *Mason v Boscawen*[6]. The Judge considered the passages in the eighth and ninth editions of this book. He observed that *Goldsworthy* was entirely neutral on the issue and *Childers* provided very slender support for the proposition. However, in deciding that a landlord and a tenant can contract out, the Judge found support for his view in the *Plumb Bros* case.

[1]   [1980] AC 37, [1978] 3 All ER 37.
[2]   Now the AHA 1986, s 26(1).
[3]   [1987] Ch 378, [1987] 1 All ER 853, CA.
[4]   [1996] 1 EGLR 1, [1996] 01 EG 102, CA.
[5]   (1984) 271 Estates Gazette 373.
[6]   [2008] EWHC 3100 (Ch), [2009] 1 All ER 1006, [2009] 1 P & CR 499.

25.47 In *Mason v Boscawen*[1], Lewison J recognised that one inconvenient consequence of his decision was that an exercise of the option to tax or a change in the rate of VAT impacted upon the triennial cycle of rent review causing it to start again. This unintended consequence of the decision was quickly remedied by the introduction of sub-paragraph 2(d) to paragraph 4 of Schedule 2 of the AHA 1986, inserted by s 79(1) of the Finance Act 2009[2]. The triennial rent review cycle is unaffected by an increase or reduction of rent arising from changes in relation to the impact of VAT on rent.

[1]   [2008] EWHC 3100 (Ch), [2009] 1 All ER 1006, [2009] 1 P & CR 499. Judgment was delivered on 18 December 2008.
[2]   The provision came into force on 21 July 2009 but had retrospective effect: Finance Act 2009, s 79(2).

Chapter 26

DISTRESS FOR NON-PAYMENT OF RENT

GENERAL

26.1 The Shorter Oxford English Dictionary defines 'distress' as, amongst other things, anguish. It certainly can be anguish for the tenant. Distress is an ancient[1] common law form of self-help available to a landlord where rent or a money payment reserved as rent[2] is due and unpaid[3]. It does not need to be specifically referred to in the tenancy agreement and, while it originally was limited to a power to seize and detain chattels, a power of sale was conferred by the Distress for Rent Act 1689.

It is beyond the scope of this book to consider distress in detail[4]. It is a highly technical remedy. Briefly, it enables a landlord to instruct a certificated bailiff to enter onto the holding and seize goods and chattels of the tenant. The bailiff may subsequently sell the goods and chattels to satisfy the unpaid rent. There are a number of provisions contained in ss 16 to 19 of the AHA 1986[5] modifying the application of the remedy of distress in relation to agricultural holdings protected under the Agricultural Holdings Act 1986 (AHA 1986).

On 19 July 2007, the Tribunals, Courts and Enforcement Act 2007 received Royal Assent. The Act includes provisions abolishing the common law right to distrain for non-payment of rent and introducing a new procedure for commercial rent arrears recovery (CRAR). The procedure will only be available in relation to commercial premises and to arrears of rent properly so-called. Much of the detail is to be set out in regulations which have yet to be made. The new procedure will be covered in a future release as and when it has become law. The remaining part of this Chapter is concerned with the existing law.

In anticipation of the Tribunals, Courts and Enforcement Act 2007 coming into force, the provisions of ss 16 to 19 of the AHA 1986 have been amended. These new provisions will come into force on a date to be appointed[6].

The new sections provide:

16   No distress for rent due more than a year previously

(1)   Subject to subsection (2) below, the landlord of an agricultural holding shall not be entitled to distrain for rent which became due in respect of that holding more than one year before the making of the distress.

(2)   Where it appears that, according to the ordinary course of dealing between the landlord and the tenant of the holding, the payment of rent has been deferred until the expiry of a quarter or half-year after the date at which the rent legally became due, the

100

rent shall, for the purposes of subsection (1) above, be deemed to have become due at the expiry of that quarter or half-year and not at the date at which it became legally due.

17 Compensation to be set off against rent for purposes of distress

Where the amount of any compensation due to the tenant of an agricultural holding, whether under this Act or under any custom or agreement, has been ascertained before the landlord distrains for rent, that amount may be set off against the rent and the landlord shall not be entitled to distrain for more than the balance.

18 Restrictions on distraining on property of third party

(1) Property belonging to a person other than the tenant of an agricultural holding shall not be distrained for rent if:

(a) the property is agricultural or other machinery and is on the holding under an agreement with the tenant for its hire or use in the conduct of his business, or

(b) the property is livestock and is on the holding solely for breeding purposes.

(2) Agisted livestock shall not be distrained by the landlord of an agricultural holding for rent where there is other sufficient distress to be found; and if such livestock is distrained by him by reason of other sufficient distress not being found, there shall not be recovered by that distress a sum exceeding the amount of the price agreed to be paid for the feeding, or any part of the price which remains unpaid.

(3) The owner of the agisted livestock may, at any time before it is sold, redeem it by paying to the distrainer a sum equal to the amount mentioned in subsection (2) above, and payment of that sum to the distrainer shall be in full discharge as against the tenant of any sum of that amount which would otherwise be due from the owner of the livestock to the tenant in respect of the price of feeding.

(4) Any portion of the agisted livestock shall, so long as it remains on the holding, continue liable to be distrained for the amount for which the whole of the livestock is distrainable.

(5) In this section 'livestock' includes any animal capable of being distrained; and 'agisted livestock' means livestock belonging to another person which has been taken in by the tenant of an agricultural holding to be fed at a fair price.

19 Settlement of disputes as to distress

(1) Where a dispute arises:

(a) in respect of any distress having been levied on an agricultural holding contrary to the provisions of this Act,

(b) as to the ownership of any livestock distrained or as to the price to be paid for the feeding of that stock, or

(c) as to any other matter or thing relating to a distress on an agricultural holding,

the dispute may be determined by the county court or on complaint by a magistrates' court and the court may make an order for restoration of any livestock or things unlawfully distrained, may declare the price agreed to be paid for feeding or may make any other order that justice requires.

(2) Any person aggrieved by a decision of a magistrates' court under this section may appeal to the Crown Court.

(3) In this section 'livestock' includes any animal capable of being distrained.

[1] It is founded upon the origins of the landlord and tenant system. Rent was considered as more than mere money and the obligation to pay it was, therefore, considered to be very much greater than the obligation to discharge a debt (even a secured debt). In consequence

the draconian and anachronistic remedy of seizing the tenant's property was given to landlords. It is unlikely that this remedy will endure much longer. The Law Commission has actively considered its total abolition – see the Law Commission Working Paper No 97 'The Law Commission provisionally recommends abolition' and see also para 26.13.

2 Or a money payment reserved as rent.

3 This is in addition to the other remedies available to a landlord, eg notice to pay, forfeiture, recovery by action through the court or the service of a statutory demand as a preliminary to bankrupt an individual tenant or put a corporate tenant into compulsory liquidation.

4 See *Woodfall: Landlord and Tenant* (Looseleaf edn, 1994) Sweet & Maxwell and Tanney and Travers, *Distress for Rent* (1st edn, 2000) Jordans.

5 Formerly, the Agricultural Holdings Act 1948, ss 18–22.

6 Tribunals, Courts and Enforcement Act 2007, s 148(5).

The future

26.13 As mentioned at the beginning of this Chapter, on 25 July 2006 the draft of the Tribunals, Courts and Enforcement Bill was published. It proposes to abolish the right for a landlord of commercial premises to distrain against the tenant's goods for rent arrears. Distress will be replaced by a procedure described as commercial rent arrears recovery. The Tribunals, Courts and Enforcement Act 2007 received Royal Assent on 19 July 2007. Part 3 of that Act contained the provisions to abolish distress. In 2009, the Justice Minister announced that Part 4 of the Act, containing changes to enforcement rules, would not be implemented. As to Part 3, a consultation paper was to be produced with a view to a permanent solution by 2012. Whether this proposal will be introduced, and whether the existing law relating to distress in respect of agricultural premises will be affected, remains to be established.

Chapter 27

INTRODUCTION: THE STATUTORY SCHEME AND SECURITY OF TENURE

OTHER METHODS OF TERMINATION

Surrender

27.13 Surrender can be effected at common law either expressly by a deed or following a surrender agreement or impliedly or by operation of law. The common law rules relating to surrender remain largely unaffected by the agricultural holdings legislation[1].

[1] See paras 14.1 and 33.4ff.

Repudiatory breach

27.13A There are circumstances in which a lease may be terminated for a repudiatory breach of contract. The cases have not related to the agricultural sector[1].

[1] *Antaios Cia Naviera SA v Salen Rederierna AB, The Antaios* [1985] AC 191, [1984] 3 All ER 229, HL; *Rice (t/a Garden Guardian) v Great Yarmouth Borough Council* [2003] TCLR 1; *Dominion Corporate Trustees Ltd v Debenhams Properties Ltd* [2010] EWHC 1193 (Ch), (2010) 23 EG 106 (CS).

TERMINATING A LICENCE

27.15A A licence can only be terminated by giving the contractual notice or, in the absence of a contractual provision, reasonable notice[1]. What is reasonable depends upon the circumstances of the case[2]. Where a licence includes a dwellinghouse, notice to terminate it should be in writing; contain the information prescribed by the Protection from Eviction Act 1977; and be given not less than four weeks before it takes effect[3].

The test as to whether an implied licence had been revoked is objective[4]. In *Fullard v DPP*[5], the appellants (F and R) appealed against their convictions for assaulting police constables in the execution of their duty. Two constables (G and J) had gone to F's house to investigate a traffic accident. While they were on the driveway F twice told them to 'fuck off'. G followed F to the house, where F told him to 'get out of my house' and immediately punched him. Then R punched J twice and F and R contended that the implied permission for the officers to remain on the property had been withdrawn and thus none of the officers had been acting in the execution of their duties. The appeals were dismissed. The two remarks were held not to amount to requests to leave. The words could simply have indicated a refusal to co-operate. Further, where implied permission was revoked, the licensee had to be given a reasonable period to withdraw.

1   *Minister of Health v Bellotti* [1944] KB 298, [1944] 1 All ER 238, CA.
2   *Greater London Council v Jenkins* [1975] 1 All ER 354, [1975] 1 WLR 155, CA.
3   Protection from Eviction Act 1977, s 5(1B), as inserted by the Housing Act 1988, s 32(2).
4   *Lambert v Roberts* [1981] 2 All ER 15, [1981] RTR 113, DC.
5   [2005] EWHC 2922 (Admin), [2005] All ER (D) 210 (Nov).

Chapter 28

NOTICES TO QUIT: GENERAL RULES

COMMON LAW REQUIREMENTS

Accuracy

28.4 An illustration of the court's approach can be found in *Peaceform Ltd v Cussens*[1]. In that case, the lease conferred on the tenant an option to purchase the freehold exercisable at any time before 6 February 2004 by giving not less than[2] three months' notice. A letter from the tenant's solicitor dated 27 August 2003 purported to give notice to exercise the option stating that 'you are entitled to not less than 3 months' notice and accordingly I confirm that this notice may be deemed to expire on 7 November 2003'. The landlords argued that, by giving a date for expiry that was less than three months from the date of service, the tenant had failed to serve a valid notice of the exercise of the option. Before *Mannai*[3] a notice containing this type of error would have been invalid. In this case, the court held in favour of the landlords, but not because of the wrong date. The deputy judge accepted that the wrong date did not invalidate the notice. The real issue was whether the letter would leave a reasonable recipient, with knowledge of the terms of the option, in any doubt as to how and when it was being exercised. Here (unusually) the notice period was not less than three months expiring no later than 6 February 2004. The expiry date in the letter purporting to give notice was neither clearly defined nor obvious from the context. Even assuming that a reasonable recipient would have realised that the tenant had intended to give a valid notice and that there had been a mere slip, the recipient would still not have known what the expiry date was intended to be.

The development of the application of the rules of construction to notices to quit and other notices to like effect given under the Landlord and Tenant Act 1954, Pt II, is that there has been a growing tendency of the courts to apply liberal rules of construction and to overlook even such matters as specifying an impossible term date[4], but there are limits to the courts' benevolence[5].

A court will treat a notice as invalid if it concludes that a reasonable recipient would not have understood its intention[6]. Also, a failure to provide core information required by legislation has also rendered a notice ineffective[7]. Likewise, a failure to reflect accurately the precise terms of a break clause may render a notice invalid[8], or not specifying the date correctly in relation to a rent review[9].

28.4 Notices to quit: general rules

Notwithstanding the above, the issue of ambiguity in relation to notices continues to be litigated. In *Baker Tilly Management Ltd v Computer Associates UK Ltd*[10], the tenant brought proceedings to determine the validity of a notice to quit it had served on the landlord relating to an underlease. When the underlease was granted, the tenant went by the name of Baker Tilly Services Limited. Subsequently, the tenant changed its name to Baker Tilly Management Limited but served the notice to quit using its old name. The landlord argued that the notice was ineffective as the tenant should have served it under the new name. The High Court determined that the important question was what the words would mean to a human taken to know the facts that formed the context of the transaction. It meant looking at the words used in the notice to quit from the perspective of a reasonable landlord. The landlord had been taken as knowing that despite the disparity in the name used by the tenant, the notice to quit was valid.

Prudential Assurance Co Ltd v Exel UK Ltd[11] is a case illustrating that notices must comply absolutely with the terms of the break clause and be given on behalf of the correct tenant. A lease was granted to two tenants. A trading company and a dormant company. Both were named as tenant because the lease contained an absolute prohibition on assignment to group companies. The tenant's solicitors served a break notice but did not refer to themselves as acting for the dormant tenant company and the notice was held to be ineffective. It was not obvious to the landlord receiving the notice what was intended. The landlord would not have known if there had been an unlawful assignment to the trading company alone or whether the solicitors were acting for both companies.

1   [2006] EWHC 2657 (Ch), [2007] 2 P & CR D2, [2006] 47 EG 182.
2   See para 42.27.
3   *Mannai Investments Co Ltd v Eagle Star Assurance Co Ltd* [1997] AC 749, [1997] 1 EGLR 57.
4   *Carradine Properties Ltd v Aslam* [1976] 1 All ER 573, [1976] 1 WLR 442.
5   *Morrow v Nadeem* [1987] 1 All ER 237, [1986] 2 EGLR 73, CA, wrongly identified landlord – notice bad. Cf *Parsons v Parsons* [1983] 1 WLR 1390, 47 P & CR 494 and *Frankland v Capstick* [1959] 1 All ER 209, [1959] 1 WLR 205. Also see *Pearson v Alyo* (1989) 60 P & CR 56, [1990] 1 EGLR 114, CA, following *Morrow v Nadeem*, a notice under the Landlord and Tenant Act 1954 naming the husband alone as landlord when the husband and his wife were joint landlords, was held to be invalid even though the husband was the sole equitable owner. Cf *Divall v Harrison* [1991] 1 EGLR 17, [1991] 14 EG 108: where a notice to quit an agricultural holding given by solicitors on behalf of equitable owners (beneficiaries under a will) and not on behalf of legal owners was held to be valid – tenants not likely to be misled. *Combey v Gumbrill* [1990] 2 EGLR 7, [1990] 27 EG 85: where a counter-notice demanding arbitration given by one of two joint tenants was held to be valid because authority to serve on behalf of both given by the courts to the wife-tenant in certain matrimonial orders. Also see *Hammersmith and Fulham London Borough Council v Monk* [1992] 1 AC 478, [1992] 1 EGLR 65, HL in which a joint tenancy was validly determined by one of two joint tenants without the knowledge or consent of the other.
6   *Barclays Bank plc v Bee* [2001] EWCA Civ 1126, [2002] 1 WLR 332, [2001] 37 EG 153.
7   *Speedwell Estates Ltd v Dalziel* [2001] EWCA Civ 1277, [2002] 1 P & CR D17, [2002] 1 EGLR 55.
8   *Peer Freeholds Ltd v Clean Wash International Ltd* [2005] EWHC 179 (Ch), [2005] 1 EGLR 47, [2005] 17 EG 124.
9   *Riverside Housing Association Ltd v White* [2007] UKHL 20, [2007] 4 All ER 97, [2008] 1 P & CR 237.

10   [2009] EWHC (Ch), unreported, 11 December 2009.
11   [2009] EWHC 1350 (Ch), [2010] 1 P & CR 90.

CONTRACTUAL REQUIREMENTS

28.9 The terms of the tenancy may impose further restrictions on the ability of a party to give a notice to quit[1]. Alternatively, the terms may seek to relax the common law requirements. The validity of any relaxation will depend on whether they conflict with an overriding statutory requirement. In the case of agricultural holdings, it is common to find a provision in the tenancy agreement that the landlord may give short notice to quit where the landlord intends to use the land for certain non-agricultural purposes[2]. Such provisions will be invalid if they provide for the landlord to give such period of notice that would prevent the tenant from making an effective claim to all relevant compensation under the AHA 1986[3].

1   *Datnow v Jones* [1985] 2 EGLR 1, 275 Estates Gazette 145, CA; *Prudential Assurance Co Ltd v London Residuary Body* [1992] 2 AC 386, [1992] 2 EGLR 56, HL.
2   *Coates v Diment* [1951] 1 All ER 890, 157 Estates Gazette 337; *Paddock Investments Ltd v Lory* [1975] 2 EGLR 5, 236 Estates Gazette 803, CA; *Rugby Joint Water Board v Foottit* [1973] AC 202, [1972] 1 All ER 1057, HL; *Floyer-Acland v Osmond* (2000) 80 P & CR 229, [2000] 2 EGLR 1, CA.
3   *Disraeli Agreement, Re, Cleasby v Park Estate (Hughenden) Ltd* [1939] Ch 382, [1938] 4 All ER 658; *Coates v Diment* [1951] 1 All ER 890, 157 Estates Gazette 337; *Parry v Million Pigs Ltd* (1980) 260 Estates Gazette 281. See also para 24.26.

STATUTORY REQUIREMENTS

28.10 In the case of a tenancy of an agricultural holding protected by the AHA 1986, the common law requirements as to the length of notice and the ability to serve a counter-notice or demand for arbitration are modified by the provisions of the AHA 1986.

The AHA 1986 does not expressly provide that a notice to quit must be signed. It should nevertheless be noted that, in the case of companies, it has been decided that where a notice has not been signed in accordance with the provisions of s 36 of the Companies Act 1985, it is defective[A1].

Where the property let includes a dwellinghouse as part of an agricultural holding protected under the AHA 1986, the premises are not 'let as a dwelling'. Accordingly, a notice to quit such premises does not need to comply with the provisions of s 5 of the Protection from Eviction Act 1977[1].

A1   *City & Country Properties Ltd v Plowden Investments Ltd* [2007] L&TR 15; *Hilmi & Associates Ltd v 20 Pembridge Villas Freehold Ltd* [2010] EWCA Civ 314, [2010] 3 All ER 391, [2010] 1 WLR 2750.
1   *National Trust for Places of Historic Interest or Natural Beauty v Knipe* [1997] 4 All ER 627, [1997] 2 EGLR 9, CA.

Chapter 29

NOTICES TO QUIT PART, JOINT INTERESTS AND SUB-TENANCIES

NOTICE TO QUIT PART

Severance of the landlord's reversion

29.6 Until 1925, if a landlord conveyed part of the freehold[1] (ie thereby severing the reversion), the various landlords of the various severed parts could not give notice to quit in respect of the individual part which each owned without joining in concert and giving notice to quit the whole holding[2]. Section 140 of the Law of Property Act 1925 (LPA 1925), as amended by the Law of Property (Amendment) Act 1926, remedied this difficulty[3].

Severance of the landlord's interest only applies where the reversion is divided up between two or more landlords. A disposal of the freehold to two landlords, for example, a husband and wife, who purchase the whole holding jointly, does not operate as a severance of the reversion. Conversely, if each were to take separate conveyances of separate defined parts, that would constitute a severance. Severance can be effected otherwise than by sale, for example, by gift.

Severance of the freehold reversion does not operate to create two or more new tenancies, whether or not accompanied by a legal apportionment of the rent[4]. If the landlord of the newly created severed part is a mere nominee or bare trustee of the landlord of the remaining part and, although not a sham, was a device to enable the service of a notice to quit part of the holding, it has been held that the severance is ineffective. The nominee landlord of the severed part will not be able to implement the provisions of s 140 of the LPA 1925[5].

---

1   Severance of the reversion can also apply where the landlord's reversionary interest is not that of a freeholder, eg because he is the head tenant.
2   *Bebington's Tenancy, Re, Bebington v Wildman* [1921] 1 Ch 559; *Smith v Kinsey* [1936] 3 All ER 73, 80 Sol Jo 853, CA.
3   The combined effect of the LPA 1925, the Law of Property (Amendment) Act 1926 and s 12 of the Agricultural Holdings Act 1923 were described in early editions as 'a nightmare to construe'.
4   *Jelley v Buckman* [1974] QB 488, [1973] 3 All ER 853; *Stiles v Farrow* (1977) 241 Estates Gazette 623. Cf *Paul v Caldwell* (1960) 176 Estates Gazette 743, 110 L Jo 704. Also see, *EDF Energy Networks (EPN) plc v BOH Ltd* [2009] EWHC 3193 (Ch), [2010] 2 P & CR 31, [2009] 49 EG 71 (CS).
5   *Persey v Bazley* (1983) 47 P & CR 37, 267 Estates Gazette 519, CA. This decision has been criticised. It is consistent with other decisions under s 140: *Clayton's Deed Poll, Re, Williams Deacon's Bank Ltd v Kennedy* [1980] Ch 99, [1979] 2 All ER 1133; *Nevill Long & Co (Boards) Ltd v Firmenich & Co* (1983) 47 P & CR 59, 127 Sol Jo 477, CA.

JOINT TENANCIES

Notice to quit by landlord

29.10 Where the freehold reversion is held by joint tenants on a trust of land, a notice to quit served by one such joint tenant is effective to terminate the tenancy[1]. The principle was stated by Brightman J (as he then was) in *Brenner v Rose*[2] as follows:

> 'In my judgment the right of a landlord in such circumstances either to have possession or to recover the rent is not to be whittled away by the mere fact that he is one of the partners and is a purchaser of the reversion expectant on the underlease. I do not see that the defendant's fiduciary capacity as a member of a partnership which includes the benefit and burden of the underlease raises any sort of equity which should be allowed to prevent him from exercising his rights as landlord that he would have had if he were a stranger to the partnership'.

If service of a notice to quit by one of several joint trustees causes expense which is greater than the benefit accruing, the trustee responsible may be liable for breach of trust[3].

At common law, it is equally clear that a notice to quit given to one of several joint tenants is sufficient for all unless the tenancy agreement on its true construction requires all to be served[4].

It has also been held that service by the landlord on one of the joint tenants of the property is not effective[5] unless it is addressed to all of the tenants[5A].

There are arguments that all of the joint tenants of an agricultural holding must be served with a notice to quit for that notice to be valid.

First, in *Jones v Lewis*[6], Denning MR stated:

> 'If work has to be done by two joint tenants to avoid forfeiture or to avoid losing their farm it is important that both should have notice of it'.

It might be argued that all tenants must be given the opportunity to challenge a notice to quit by being served with a copy of it. Support for this view may be derived from the fact that a valid counter-notice under s 26(1) of the AHA 1986 may only be served by all joint tenants acting together[7].

Second, in relation to a notice claiming compensation under the provisions of the Agricultural Holdings Act 1923, it was held that a notice claiming compensation by one only of joint tenants, being the one who actually suffered loss, was a sufficient notice for the purposes of the compensation provisions[8]. If only one of a number of joint tenants can make a valid claim for compensation, then arguably each of the joint tenants must be given the opportunity to make such a claim.

Where the reversion has been severed *Jelley v Buckman*[9] makes it clear that this has no effect upon the subsisting tenant: 'a severance of the lessor's reversion by conveyance does not bring two separate tenancies into being ... Severance, in our judgment, severs only the reversion, dividing the incidents attached to the reversion between the two reversions'. It follows that the landlords of the severed reversion should act in concert in relation to the service of notices. There is no case authority governing the position where one landlord declines, for example, to join with his fellow landlord in serving a s 12 notice in respect of a rent review. Based upon the authorities summarised in *Brenner v Rose* above[10], it would appear that a notice served by one landlord should be sufficient, but regard will be had to the trust obligations which exist[11].

1   *Brenner v Rose* [1973] 2 All ER 535, [1973] 1 WLR 443; *Parsons v Parsons* [1983] 1 WLR 1390, 47 P & CR 494; *Bevan v Webb* [1905] 1 Ch 620.
2   *Brenner v Rose* [1973] 2 All ER 535, at 539, [1973] 1 WLR 443.
3   See para 29.16.
4   *Doe d Bradford v Watkins* (1806) 7 East 551; *Quartermains v Selby* (1889) 5 TLR 223, CA.
5   *Jones v Lewis* (1973) 25 P & CR 375, 117 Sol Jo 373, CA.
5A   *Doe d Macartney (Lord) v Crick* (1805) 5 Esp 196.
6   *Jones v Lewis* (1973) 25 P & CR 375, 117 Sol Jo 373, CA. Also see, *Blewett v Blewett* [1936] 2 All ER 188 in the context of forfeiture.
7   *Newman v Keedwell* (1977) 35 P & CR 393, 244 Estates Gazette 469; *Featherstone v Staples* [1986] 2 All ER 461, [1986] 1 EGLR 6, CA. See para 29.13ff.
8   *Howson v Buxton* [1928] 97 LJKB 749. This decision has been doubted: see para 29.14.
9   [1974] QB 488, [1973] 3 All ER 853, CA.
10   [1973] 2 All ER 535, [1973] 1 WLR 443.
11   See para 29.16.

Notice to quit by tenant

29.11 A notice to quit which is signed by one of several joint tenants on behalf of the others is sufficient to terminate a tenancy from year to year[1]. The courts have also held that it is not necessary for the validity of a notice to quit that it is served by all joint tenants or with the concurrence of all joint tenants unless the terms of the tenancy provide otherwise[2]. It follows that the concurrence of all joint tenants is required to exercise a break clause in relation to a fixed term tenancy[3]. Provided that the tenant can establish that he was not limited in his ability to serve a notice to quit by the terms of the tenancy agreement, he will not be acting in breach of trust[4]. The position needs to be compared with that of a joint tenant failing to serve a counter-notice following a notice to quit from the landlord[5].

The operation of this old common law rule effectively sidesteps the need for a landlord to establish specific statutory grounds for possession. As such, the rule has been criticised. Nevertheless, the House of Lords upheld it in three cases[6], albeit all three were split decisions of the court, also holding that the remaining tenant has no separate proportionality defence under Article 8 of the European Convention on Human Rights. However, this conclusion is under attack by the European Court of Human Rights[7]. The Supreme Court has accepted that in making an order for possession of a person's home the court had to have the power to assess the proportionality of making the order and, in making that assessment, to resolve any relevant dispute of fact[8].

1 *Doe d Aslin v Summersett* (1830) 1 B & Ad 135; *Doe d Kindersley v Hughes* (1840) 7 M & W 139; *Greenwich London Borough Council v McGrady* (1982) 81 LGR 288, 46 P & CR 223, CA; *Hammersmith and Fulham London Borough Council v Monk* [1992] 1 AC 478, [1992] 1 All ER 1, HL; *Crawley Borough Council v Ure* [1996] QB 13, [1996] 1 All ER 734, CA; *Notting Hill Housing Trust v Brackley* [2001] EWCA Civ 601, 82 P & CR D48, [2001] 3 EGLR 11. Also see, *Smith v Grayton Estates Ltd* 1960 SC 349, 1961 SLT 38.

2 *Greenwich London Borough Council v McGrady* (1982) 81 LGR 288, 46 P & CR 223, CA; *Parsons v Parsons* [1983] 1 WLR 1390, 47 P & CR 494; *Hammersmith and Fulham London Borough Council v Monk* [1992] 1 AC 478, [1992] 1 All ER 1, HL; *Crawley Borough Council v Ure* [1996] QB 13, [1995] 3 WLR 92, [1996] 1 All ER 734; *Notting Hill Housing Trust v Brackley* [2001] EWCA Civ 601, 82 P & CR D48, [2001] 3 EGLR 11.

3 *Hammersmith and Fulham London Borough Council v Monk* [1992] 1 AC 478, [1992] 1 All ER 1, HL.

4 *Crawley Borough Council v Ure* [1996] QB 13, [1995] 3 WLR 92, [1996] 1 All ER 734.

5 See para 29.10.

6 *Harrow London Borough Council v Qazi* [2003] UKHL 43, [2004] 1 AC 983, [2003] 3 EGLR 109; *Lambeth London Borough Council v Kay* [2006] UKHL 10, [2006] 2 AC 465, [2006] 4 All ER 128; *Doherty v Birmingham City Council (Secretary of State for Communities and Local Government intervening)* [2008] UKHL 57, [2009] AC 367, [2009] 1 All ER 653. Also see, Cf *Lloyd v Sadler* [1978] QB 774, [1978] 1 EGLR 76, CA.

7 *McCann v United Kingdom (Application 19009/04)* (2008) 47 EHRR 913, [2008] 28 EG 114, ECtHR. Also see, *Connors v United Kingdom (Application 66746/01)* (2004) 40 EHRR 189, [2004] HLR 991, ECtHR; *Manchester City Council v Pinnock (Secretary of State for Communities and Local Government, intervening)* [2009] EWCA Civ 852, [2010] 3 All ER 201, [2010] 1 WLR 713; *Central Bedfordshire Council v Taylor (Secretary of State for Communities and Local Government intervening)* [2009] EWCA Civ 613, [2010] 1 All ER 516, [2010] 1 WLR 446; *Salford City Council v Mullen (Secretary of State for Communities and Local Government, intervening)* [2010] EWCA Civ 336, [2011] 1 All ER 119, [2010] LGR 559; *Solihull Metropolitan Borough Council v Hickin* [2010] EWCA Civ 868, [2010] 1 WLR 2254, [2010] 31 EG 62 (CS). Also see, Case Comment in relation to *McCann v United Kingdom (Application 19009/04)* in European Human Rights Law Review 2008 and 'The Rule in Hammersmith and Fulham LBC v Monk reconsidered', D Cowan and T Gallivan, Journal of Housing Law 2010. Also see, *Paulic v Croatia*, 3572/06 [2009] ECHR 1614.

8 *Manchester City Council v Pinnock* [2010] UKSC 45, [2010] 3 WLR 1441.

Tenant's counter-notice

29.14 There have been two cases in which the courts have construed the phrase 'the tenant' as meaning 'the joint tenants or any of them'. The first was *Howson v Buxton*[1]. That case concerned the notice provisions for the payment of compensation under s 12 of the Agricultural Holdings Act 1923. The case has since been distinguished in *Jacobs v Chaudhuri*[2] and *Newman v Keedwell*[3]. The relevance of *Howson v Buxton* in the context of the termination of a tenancy protected under the AHA 1986 was also commented on by the Court of Appeal in *Featherstone v Staples*[4].

The second case was *Lloyd v Sadler*[5]. That case related to a claim for protection under the Rent Act 1968 and was relied upon in the judgment of Nourse J at first instance in *Featherstone v Staples*[6]. In the Court of Appeal in *Featherstone v Staples*[7], Slade LJ, while accepting that 'there is no immutable doctrine that the phrase 'the tenant', when appearing in a statute, must always be construed as referring to all the joint tenants in any case where a joint tenancy is involved', preferred to place reliance upon what Megaw LJ described in *Lloyd v Sadler*[8] as 'the ordinary law as to joint tenancy, as it affects rights of property'. The Court of Appeal upheld the decision of Fox J in *Newman v Keedwell*[9] as to the meaning of the phrase 'the tenant' in relation to the provisions to terminate a tenancy protected by the AHA 1986[10].

[1]   (1928) 97 LJKB 749, [1928] All ER Rep 434, CA.
[2]   [1968] 2 QB 470 at 476, [1968] 2 All ER 124, CA.
[3]   (1977) 35 P & CR 393, 244 Estates Gazette 469 at 472.
[4]   [1986] 2 All ER 461, [1986] 1 WLR 861 at 871, CA.
[5]   [1978] QB 774, [1978] 2 All ER 529.
[6]   (1984) 49 P & CR 273, [1985] 1 EGLR 1.
[7]   (1985) 278 Estates Gazette 867 at 871.
[8]   *Lloyd v Sadler* [1978] QB 744, [1978] 2 All ER 529 at 783.
[9]   (1977) 35 P & CR 393, 244 Estates Gazette 469.
[10] See para 29.11.

SUB-TENANTS

Agricultural Land Tribunal

29.19 In proceedings before the Agricultural Land Tribunal (ALT) between the head landlord and head tenant, the sub-tenant is entitled to be heard. However, this will not assist him if the head tenant has not given counter-notice to a notice to quit given by the landlord as there will be no proceedings before the ALT in that case[1].

[1]   Agricultural Land Tribunals (Rules) Order 2007, SI 2007/3105, r 4(1)(b).

Chapter 30

THE STATUTORY RESTRICTIONS ON NOTICES TO QUIT: COUNTER-NOTICE

GENERAL

30.1 Under the AHA 1986, a notice to quit (if valid at common law) is, prima facie, effective to terminate the tenancy[1]. That general rule is subject to the ability of the tenant to serve on the landlord a counter-notice in writing requiring that s 26(1) of the AHA 1986 shall apply to the notice to quit. Such counter-notice must be served within one month of service of the notice to quit. This restriction on the operation of a notice to quit an agricultural holding applies equally to a notice to quit part given by a landlord to a tenant[2].

The notice to quit may be unqualified, i e state no reason for its being given[3], or contain one or more of the reasons contained in s 27(3) of the AHA 1986 or contain one or more of the reasons contained in Sch 3 to the AHA 1986 (the 'Special Cases')[4]. If it relies on one of the Special Cases, then there is *no* power to give a counter-notice[5].

Practitioners need to be aware that a notice may be given relying on one or more of the Special Cases and then state that it is given in the alternative as an unqualified notice[6]. In such a case, the tenant must serve counter-notice.

If a counter-notice is given and is appropriate, the notice to quit is thereby rendered ineffective unless and until the Agricultural Land Tribunal (ALT) for the area[7] in which the holding is situate consents to the operation of the notice to quit on one of the limited grounds specified in s 27(3) of the AHA 1986. Statutory rules have been made for the obtaining of the consent of the ALT[8].

---

[1] Subject to the extended period of notice required, as to which see para 28.10ff.
[2] AHA 1986, s 26(1)(a).
[3] It is rarely advisable to give such a notice to quit. If a ground as specified in s 27(3) is available, and that fact is not stated in the notice to quit, increased compensation on quitting for disturbance will be payable.
[4] In previous editions of this book these were known as the 'seven deadly sins'. They are also often, inappropriately, described as 'incontestable' notices to quit. They are not strictly 'incontestable' but different rules apply.
[5] See para 31.1 in relation to so-called incontestable notices and note that a demand for arbitration may be necessary instead.
[6] Such a notice must be very carefully worded and make the position perfectly clear to the tenant: *Cowan v Wrayford* [1953] 2 All ER 1138, [1953] 1 WLR 1340, CA.
[7] For details showing the areas covered by each tribunal, see para 46.3.
[8] The current rules are the Agricultural Land Tribunals (Rules) Order 2007, SI 2007/3105.

30.2 Such consent of the ALT must be sought by the landlord on an application made within one month of service of the counter-notice[1]. The application does not need to be in a prescribed form but in the style issued by the ALT.

Contracting out of the right to give a counter-notice, though not prohibited expressly by the AHA 1986, has been held by the House of Lords to be contrary to public policy and ineffective[2].

The general rule that a counter-notice is required does not apply in the case of a notice which sets out one of the Special Cases of Sch 3 to the AHA 1986[3].

There is no prescribed form for the counter-notice. All that is required is that the notice (which can be very informal, eg in the form of a letter) should be in writing and should specify in terms that it requires s 26(1) of the AHA 1986 to apply[4].

Care needs to be taken to ensure that the counter-notice is served on the correct landlord, particularly following a severance of the freehold reversion[5].

As to the calculation of the period of one month, the 'corresponding day' rule applies. One month from 1 February expires on 1 March regardless of whether February happens to fall in a leap year or not[6].

Until the passing of the AHA 1986, the equivalent provisions were contained in s 24(1) of the Agricultural Holdings Act 1948 (AHA 1948) and then in s 2(1) of the Agricultural Holdings (Notice to Quit) Act 1977. By virtue of s 99 of the AHA 1986, a counter-notice invoking s 24(1) of the AHA 1948 or 2(1) of the 1977 Act (though these are now repealed) will probably be valid and effective[7].

The one-month requirement is rigid and inflexible. There is no power to extend the period. But where the notice to quit is a dual one, relying on one of the Special Cases and stating that, in the alternative, it is to be treated as an unqualified notice, then in that case if the tenant goes to arbitration as to the reason stated in the notice to quit and fails, he may serve his counter-notice within one month from the termination of the arbitration[8]. Indeed, he *must* do so otherwise the notice to quit will take effect.

1   The Agricultural Land Tribunals (Rules) Order 2007, SI 2007/3105, r 39.
2   *Johnson v Moreton* [1980] AC 37, [1978] 3 All ER 37, HL.
3   See para 31.1.
4   In *Mountford v Hodkinson* [1956] 2 All ER 17, [1956] 1 WLR 422, CA, a tenant wrote an angry letter to the landlord saying, 'I don't intend to go. I shall appeal against it and take the matter up with' the County Agricultural Executive Committee (at that time the appropriate body), the Agricultural Land Tribunal at that time being an appellate body. This was before the passing of the Agriculture Act 1958. It was held that the language of the letter was insufficient to constitute an intention to invoke the provisions of s 24(1) of the AHA 1948 (now s 26(1) of the AHA 1986) and the letter did not operate as a counter-notice. For a more modern case in which the requirements of a valid counter-notice were judicially considered, see *Edlingham Ltd v MFI Furniture Centres Ltd* [1981] 2 EGLR 97, 259 Estates Gazette 421; and *Price v Mann* [1942] 1 All ER 453, 86 Sol Jo 252, CA and *Glofield Property Ltd v Morley* [1988] 1 EGLR 113, [1988] 02 EG 62. For a

case in which the decision in *Mountford v Hodgkinson* (above) was reconsidered and applied to an agricultural holding, see *Rous v Mitchell* [1991] 1 All ER 676, [1991] 1 EGLR 1, CA.

5   See para 32.6.
6   *Dodds v Walker* [1981] 2 All ER 609, [1981] 1 WLR 1027, HL. See also *Schnabel v Allard* [1967] 1 QB 627, [1966] 3 All ER 816, CA. See para 40.27ff.
7   For a similar situation, after the repeal of the equivalent provisions in the 1947 Act and their re-enactment in the AHA 1948, see *Ward v Scott* [1950] WN 76, 94 Sol Jo 97.
8   The Agricultural Holdings (Arbitration on Notices) Order 1987, SI 1987/710, art 10 and *Cowan v Wrayford* [1953] 2 All ER 1138, [1953] 1 WLR 1340, CA.

30.3 A landlord who has received a counter-notice must, within one month of receipt, apply to the appropriate ALT for consent to the operation of his notice to quit[1]. If he does not, his notice to quit is rendered ineffective by the counter-notice. However, unlike the one month available to the tenant, which is a statutory and inflexible time limit, the one month available to the landlord is provided not by the statute itself but by the Agricultural Land Tribunal (Rules) Order 1978. It is non-statutory and can be extended with the leave of the chairman of the ALT[2].

The power to give or withhold consent exercised by the ALT was, until 26 January 1959, exercised by the Minister through the County Agricultural Executive Committee, with the right of appeal to the ALT. From 26 January 1959, by virtue of para 8 of Sch 1 to the Agriculture Act 1958, the ALT became the tribunal at first instance, and the right of appeal was lost. The equivalent of an appeal from the ALT is by way of case stated to the High Court[3].

In the case of a tenant who is performing a period of service with the Armed Forces of the Crown, and who may be disabled or prejudiced in serving the counter-notice, there are powers to authorise some suitable person to do it and other necessary acts or conduct any proceedings on his behalf[4].

1   The form of application to the ALT, see Form 1 in the Appendix to the Agricultural Land Tribunals (Rules) Order 1987, SI 1978/259.
2   Agricultural Land Tribunals (Rules) Order 2007, SI 2007/3105, rr 4(2) and 51 and see *Kellett v Alexander* (1980) 257 Estates Gazette 494.
3   See para 46.24.
4   See the Reserve and Auxiliary Forces (Agriculture Tenants) Regulations 1959, SI 1959/84, and see also para A1.505.

APPLICATION FOR THE ALT'S CONSENT TO NOTICE TO QUIT

30.5 The application does not need to be in a prescribed form but in the style issued by the ALT. Non-compliance with the time limit renders the application invalid unless the chairman consents to an extension of time for making the application. This contrasts with the statutory inflexible time limit for giving a counter-notice. The time limit for applying to the ALT is non-statutory and contained in the regulations[1].

If the ALT consents to the operation of a notice to quit it may, either of its own motion or on the tenant's application[2], postpone the termination of the tenancy by the notice to quit for any period not exceeding 12 months if the notice would otherwise have come into operation on or within six months after the giving of the ALT's consent[3].

1   The Agricultural Land Tribunals (Rules) Order 2007, SI 2007/3105, r 39.
2   This must be made not later than 14 days after the giving of the consent. See the Agricultural Holdings (Arbitration on Notices) Order 1987, SI 1987/710, art 13.
3   Similar provisions apply where an arbitrator awards under Cases A, B, D or E that the reason stated in one of those notices to quit has been made out.

GROUNDS FOR CONSENT

30.6   Where an application has been made to the ALT for consent to the operation of a notice to quit, the ALT must first decide whether the landlord has made out any one or more of the six grounds available to him. Then, before consenting to the operation of the notice to quit, the ALT must, as a separate exercise, consider the fair and reasonable landlord requirement[1]. If satisfied that such a landlord would not insist on possession, then they must withhold their consent[2]. It should be noted that s 27(1) of the AHA 1986 requires that the ground upon which consent is sought must be 'specified by the landlord in his application for their consent'. That is a statutory requirement and not merely a requirement of the Agricultural Land Tribunals (Rules) Order 2007.

The grounds are as follows:
(a)   good husbandry;
(b)   sound management of the estate;
(c)   agricultural research, education, experiment or demonstration, or for the purpose of enactments relating to smallholdings;
(d)   a purpose desirable for enactments relating to allotments;
(e)   greater hardship would be cause by withholding than by giving consent;
(f)   the landlord proposes to terminate the tenancy for the purpose of the land being used other than for agriculture, not falling with Case B[3].

1   *R v Agricultural Land Tribunal for Eastern Province of England, ex p Grant* [1956] 3 All ER 321, [1956] 1 WLR 1240, CA; *Evans v Roper* [1960] 2 All ER 507, [1960] 1 WLR 814.
2   This is an obligation upon them; they do not merely have a discretion on the matter.
3   AHA 1986, s 27(3). As to Case B, see para 32.10.

Ground (b): Sound estate management

30.8   Ground (b) is:

'... the carrying out thereof is desirable in the interests of sound management[1] of the estate of which the land to which the notice relates forms part or which the land constitutes'[2].

This ground, like the good husbandry ground, involves a comparison between the existing system of farming carried on by the tenant and the proposed new system, but subject this time to the proviso that the ALT must consider not merely the land the subject of the notice to quit but also the remainder of the landlord's estate.

There is no definition of 'estate'. Technically the land which is the subject of the notice to quit may be the only land under consideration. Usually that will not be the case. It is not necessary for the landlord to show that the holding is being badly farmed. It is sufficient for the landlord to show that to combine the holding with other land will improve estate management of all of the land.

The classic example of sound estate management in the past has been the case where the landlord is able to show that by recovering possession of the land let, and by amalgamating it with other land, he is able to convert two uneconomic units into a single economic and efficient farm or unit. In the current agricultural economic climate the considerations specified in para 30.7 in relation to good husbandry apply equally to this ground.

The definition in s 10 of the Agriculture Act 1947 is of 'good' estate management and not 'sound' management of the estate, which is the expression which appears in s 27(3)(b) of the AHA 1986. It may be that there is more than a semantic difference between the two words in their respective contexts. The definition of 'good' estate management seems to be directed to the farming of the land in question. 'Sound' estate management seems to embrace a wider conception: the possible use of the land for other purposes altogether. Sound estate management envisages looking at the whole estate in the physical sense and considering what effect it would have on the management of the estate. The mere personal financial interest of the landlord in isolation is not sufficient, for example, where he merely wishes to alter financial terms of the tenancy[3].

As stated above, there is no statutory definition of an 'estate' in this context. The mere fact that the landlord may happen to own a number of scattered parcels in different parts of the country will not necessarily constitute those parcels an estate. The notion that an estate comprises all the assets of a landlord, as would apply when considering the distribution of the assets on death and the administration of his estate in that sense would not appear to be apposite in the context of sound estate management. That suggests a substantial block of land with some cohesive identity. In classic form, this would comprise a mansion house, some parkland, a home farm and some let farms. It is doubtful that the term 'estate' is as narrowly confined as that. There is no authority on the point.

A well thought-out scheme in detail is required, but this could be established by a proposal to sell off parts of the holding, including worn-out buildings, and applying the proceeds to improving the fixed equipment on the remainder of the holding[4]. A landlord who has persistently been in breach of his repairing obligations will normally have considerable difficulty in persuading an ALT to give consent to the dispossession of a tenant so that the landlord can sell at the enhanced vacant possession price and use the proceeds of sale to remedy the landlord's own breaches of covenant.

117

This ground does not enable a landlord to improve on the terms of the tenancy agreement by terminating the old tenancy subject to an undertaking to relet on terms more favourable to him[5]. It is possible that a landlord who has obtained planning permission to develop part only of the holding may be able to establish, if he is not empowered to serve a notice to quit part[6], that it would be sound estate management to give notice to quit the whole holding. If he is 'fair and reasonable', this may involve his offering to relet the balance of the holding to the existing tenant[7].

The ALT may not consider such matters as hardship to the tenant when considering whether the ground has been made out, but must take these factors into consideration when applying the fair and reasonable landlord requirement[8].

[1]   For the text of the rules of 'good' estate management, see para 24.5. Also see, para 30.11.
[2]   AHA 1986, s 27(3)(b).
[3]   *National Coal Board v Naylor* [1972] 1 All ER 1153, [1972] 1 WLR 908.
[4]   *Lewis v Moss* (1961) 181 Estates Gazette 685. For examples of what does not constitute sound estate management, see *Burnett v Smith* (1951) 159 Estates Gazette 3. Cf *Trustees of A Merchant v Sterry* (1954) 163 Estates Gazette 655; *Copeland v Ingram* (1956) Scottish Journal of the RICS, April, p 105; *Greeves v Mitchell* (1971) 222 Estates Gazette 1395. Also see, *Fowler v Cockerill* (2007) ALT/1/S/55.
[5]   *National Coal Board v Naylor* [1972] 1 All ER 1153, [1972] 1 WLR 908.
[6]   See Ch 29, as to notices to quit part generally.
[7]   But see the dicta of the Lord Chief Justice in *National Coal Board v Naylor* [1972] 1 All ER 1153, [1972] 1 WLR 908. In the circumstances quoted the landlord would probably be better advised to sever the freehold reversion so that the new owner of the severed part with development potential can then give a notice to quit in respect of the whole of that part of the holding vested in him – see para 29.6.
[8]   *Evans v Roper* [1960] 2 All ER 507, [1960] 1 WLR 814.

Ground (d): Allotments

30.11 Ground (d) is:

> '... the carrying out of the purpose is desirable for the purposes of the enactments relating to allotments'[1].

Allotments take two possible forms: allotments properly so called and allotment gardens. The special provisions relating to allotments are contained in the Allotments Acts 1908 to 1950. They are small agricultural holdings statutorily established for special purposes, for example, to rehabilitate retiring Great War Veterans and to provide to every man an acre, a cow, etc – 'a land fit for heroes to live in'. An allotment garden is a small parcel of land used for producing vegetables or fruit for the allotment holder or his family[2]; they can never be agricultural holdings because they are required to be used for the production of vegetables for consumption by the allotment holder and his family and not for the purpose of a trade or business.

Since many county councils are disposing of their allotments and allotments are thought by many to be anachronistic, it is unlikely that s 27(3)(d) will be evoked often in practice.

An interesting argument came before the Agricultural Land Tribunal in *Clophill Parish Council v Jones*[3]. The landlord served a notice to quit arguing reliance upon sound estate management and that it was desirable for the purposes of the enactments relating to allotments. The landlord's case was based upon its contention that the grant of the tenancy had put it in breach of its obligations under the Small Holdings and Allotments Act 1908. That Act provides in s 23 that a parish council must provide and let land for residents as allotments if it is satisfied that there is demand. By s 27(5), if an allotment is not able to be let under that Act, it may be let to any person at the best rent obtainable and on terms permitting the council to recover possession within 12 months if required for allotment use.

The Tribunal did not accept that the letting in this case was in breach of s 27(5) of the 1908 Act. Although there is no comprehensive definition of 'allotment' in that Act or in subsequent legislation, there is a species of allotment defined by the Allotments Act 1922 as an 'allotment garden' – ie an allotment less than 40 poles (10 acres/about 4ha) in size cultivated by the occupier primarily for crops consumed by himself or his family. The holding here was 14 acres, thus plainly not an allotment garden.

The Tribunal relied on *Halsbury's Laws*, 5th edn, vol 1, para 517 and para 19.12 of this book to conclude that the letting was of both an allotment and an agricultural holding. Although there are circumstances where s 27(5) might nevertheless apply, the Tribunal found nothing in the evidence before it to suggest that it did so here.

There was, on the contrary, evidence that the Council was in the habit of letting its allotment land as agricultural holdings under the powers granted by s 32 of the 1908 Act. The conclusion therefore was that there was a surplus of allotment land in the parish. Even if the Council had been in breach of s 27(5) in respect of the terms of this letting, it was permissible by s 32 and thus the Council's contention that it was not complying with the legislation was unfounded. If that were not sufficient to defeat the notice to quit, the Tribunal noted also Lord Widgery CJ's comments in *National Coal Board v Naylor*[4] that 'no purpose can be described as being desirable in the interests of sound estate management unless that purpose is connected with the way in which the land is managed'. Compliance with the statutory scheme is not a matter concerned with the way in which the estate is managed.

[1]   AHA 1986, s 27(3)(d).
[2]   The Allotments Act 1922, s 22 and the Agriculture Act 1947, s 109(3).
[3]   (2009) ALT, E26/621.
[4]   [1972] 1 All ER 1153, [1972] 1 WLR 908.

Chapter 31

THE STATUTORY RESTRICTIONS ON NOTICES TO QUIT: CASES A TO H

GENERAL PRINCIPLES

The statutory scheme

31.2 It is vital for a tenant who has received a notice under Cases A, B, D or E, if he wishes to dispute the reason stated for the giving of the notice, to do so by demanding arbitration within one month of receipt by him of the notice to quit[1]. If he fails to do so he is statute barred from raising any issue as to the reasons stated later, for example, when proceedings are taken for possession even where the reason stated for the giving of the notice to quit cannot be validly made out[2]. Further, the tenant must, within three months of giving a valid demand for arbitration, apply to the RICS for the appointment of an arbitrator or obtain the appointment of an arbitrator, otherwise the demand for arbitration will be rendered ineffective[3].

Special Case notices to quit do not have to be in a statutorily prescribed form or to draw the recipient's attention to the need to give a demand for arbitration.

The time limits and procedures are mandatory and inflexible. There is no power for any arbitrator or court to relax or extend them[4].

Given the inflexibility in relation to the time limits and procedures, this is balanced by more stringent rules applied to the landlord's adherence with the requirements of s 26(2) and Sch 3 to the AHA 1986[5]. The principles as to certainty and avoiding ambiguity which apply to notices to quit generally[6] have had a more stringent code applied by the courts to Special Case notices to quit[7]. It is submitted that, notwithstanding the commonsense approach adopted by the House of Lords in *Mannai Investments Co Ltd v Eagle Star Life Assurance Co Ltd*[8], the more rigorous approach applied by the courts in relation to Special Case notices to quit will continue.

---

1   See Chs 44 and 47.
2   *Magdalen College, Oxford v Heritage* [1974] 1 All ER 1065, [1974] 1 WLR 441, CA; *Harding v Marshall* (1983) 267 Estates Gazette 161, CA. Note that the notice to quit may be successfully challenged in these circumstances if fraud is established: *Rous v Mitchell* [1991] 1 All ER 676, [1991] 1 EGLR 1, CA.
3   The Agricultural Holdings (Arbitration on Notices) Order 1987, SI 1987/710, art 10. See para 31.11.

4 Cf time limits specified in regulations such as the Agricultural Land Tribunals (Rules) Order 2007, SI 2007/3105, which unlike the Agricultural Holdings (Arbitration on Notices) Order 1987, SI 1987/710, contains powers entitling the Chairman or Tribunal to extend time. See *Kellett v Alexander* (1980) 257 Estates Gazette 494; *Harding v Marshall* (1983) 267 Estates Gazette 161, CA.
5 *Pickard v Bishop* (1975) 31 P & CR 108, 119 Sol Jo 407, CA.
6 See para 28.11.
7 This is not surprising given that Cases A to H represent what Professor Rodgers has described as 'a species of statutory forfeiture': Agricultural Law, C P Rodgers (2nd edn, 1998), Butterworths, at para 7.38.
8 [1997] AC 749, [1997] 1 EGLR 57, HL. See para 24.3ff.

Certainty as to the type of notice

31.3 If the landlord is relying upon one of the Special Cases, then although no prescribed form of words is specifically required, he must make it clear as to which Special Case he is relying. If he employs ambiguous language[1], then his notice to quit will be invalid[2]. In *Budge v Hicks*[3], it was unclear as to whether the landlord was relying upon breaches which were remediable or irremediable. As a consequence, the notice was held to be ineffective.

This problem is often encountered when a landlord gives notice to quit in reliance upon a short notice clause in the tenancy agreement authorising the resumption of possession of the whole or part of the holding for non-agricultural purposes. Care must be taken when giving notice to quit in such circumstances to ensure that there is no ambiguity as to whether the landlord is relying upon Case B or s 27(3)(f) or neither.

1 Described as a 'calculated obscurity' in *Macnabb v Anderson* 1957 SC 213, 1958 SLT 8. Also see *Hammon v Fairbrother* [1956] 2 All ER 108, [1956] 1 WLR 490.
2 *Budge v Hicks* [1951] 2 KB 335, [1951] 2 All ER 245, CA.
3 *Budge v Hicks* [1951] 2 KB 335, [1951] 2 All ER 245, CA.

CASE A – SMALLHOLDINGS

31.18 Case A provides:

'The holding is let as a smallholding by a smallholdings authority or the Minister in pursuance of Part II of the Agriculture Act 1970 and was so let on or after 12 September 1984, and:
(a)   the tenant has attained the age of 65; and
(b)   if the result of the notice to quit taking effect would be to deprive the tenant of living accommodation occupied by him under the tenancy, suitable alternative accommodation is available for him, or will be available for him when the notice takes effect; and
(c)   the instrument under which the tenancy was granted contains an acknowledgment signed by the tenant that the tenancy is subject to the provisions of this Case (or to those of Case I in section 2(3) of the Agricultural Holdings (Notices to Quit) Act 1977),
and it is stated in the notice to quit that it is given by reason of the said matter'.

This new case was introduced by the Agricultural Holdings Act 1984 (AHA 1984). It was initially inserted as Case I in s 2(3) of the Agricultural Holdings

121

(Notices to Quit) Act 1977. Upon the consolidation of the legislation in the AHA 1986, it was moved to Case A. The former Case A applied where a notice to quit was given and the ALT had already consented to its operation on one of more of the grounds set out in s 3(3) of the 1977 Act. By 1984 this was recognised to be a 'dead letter'[1]. It was consequentially repealed by the AHA 1984[2].

Until the Court of Appeal decision in *Saul v Norfolk County Council*[3], there was doubt as to whether tenancies of statutory smallholdings[4] granted before the enactment of the Agriculture Act 1970 were subject to the statutory succession regime. The court decided that they were. The decision was in effect reversed by the AHA 1984, which amended s 18(4)(f) of the Agricultural Holdings (Notices to Quit) Act 1977 Act[5]. The AHA 1984 ensured that succession did not apply to smallholdings[5A].

The enactment of the new Case A in the AHA 1984 arose following considerable debate in the House of Lords. It was recognised that smallholdings were not effective as providing 'starter units' and that few farmers moved up the ladder to larger farms. The present provision[6] was intended to address this issue.

It should be noted that there is no equivalent power for any other landlord to dispossess his tenant who has attained the age of 65 on the provision of suitable alternative living accommodation. On the contrary, such tenants will normally be able to invoke the succession provisions[7].

There are four requirements of Case A:

(a)   the tenancy must have commenced after the AHA 1984 came into force[8];
(b)   the tenant must be 65 or older at the date of the giving of the notice to quit;
(c)   the tenancy agreement must contain a provision that the landlord may rely upon Case A;
(d)   where the tenant lives in the farmhouse, then the landlord must provide suitable alternative accommodation at the date of the expiry of the notice to quit.

There are extensive provisions set out in Pt II, paras 1 to 7 of Sch 3 to the AHA 1986 for determining whether suitable alternative accommodation is, or will be, available for the tenant[9]. These have to be complied with if the landlord is to give an effective notice to quit denying the tenant his right to give counter-notice.

1   J Muir Watt, Estate Gazettes Law Reports, 12 November 1983.
2   AHA 1984 Act, s 6(2) and Sch 4.
3   [1984] QB 559, [1984] 2 All ER 489, [1984] 3 WLR 84, CA.
4   See para 20.19.
5   AHA 1984 Act, Sch 1 para 2(b).
5A The AHA 1984 received Royal Assent on 12 July 1984 and came into effect on 12 September 1984.
6   Introduced in the Third Reading debate in the House of Lords by Lord Northfield.
7   See Chs 34–36.

8   12 September 1984: AHA 1984, s 11.
9   These are modelled on the provisions of the Rent Act 1977, Sch 15.

CASE C – CERTIFICATE OF BAD HUSBANDRY

A certificate from the Agricultural Land Tribunal

31.25 When granting a certificate, the ALT may specify (in the certificate itself) a minimum period of notice for termination of the tenancy. This is to prevent the holding deteriorating still further because of what could otherwise be between 12 and 24 months of notice. The period specified must be not less than two months and it does not need to expire on a term date of the tenancy[1].

There has in the past been considerable reluctance on the part of ALTs to grant certificates of bad husbandry. In previous editions of this book, it was observed that such certificates obtained some notoriety, particularly during the wartime era, when they were widely believed to have been abused by certain wartime Agricultural Executive Committees whose members then acquired the right to farm the land in question. Thereafter, landlords most frequently relied upon the notice to remedy procedures specified now in Case D[2]. However, since considerable restrictions were imposed, particularly by the Agriculture (Miscellaneous Provisions) Act 1976 upon the landlord's right to recover possession for breach of a term or condition of the tenancy involving the doing of work of maintenance, repair or replacement, notices to remedy have been more sparingly used since then and an application for a certificate of bad husbandry in the case of a neglected holding can now prove to be a more effective, expeditious and less expensive remedy for a landlord anxious to protect his holding from further deterioration and to recover possession.

In the Scottish Land Court it was held:

(a)   the Scottish Land Court (in England, the equivalent forum is the Agricultural Land Tribunal) had no discretion on equitable grounds to withhold their consent and had, therefore, to grant a certificate of bad husbandry when the grounds were proved;

(d)   temporary breaches of the rules of good husbandry, for example where a tenant was suffering from a physical or mental disability, would not be likely to establish a breach; but

(c)   the phrase 'other relevant circumstances' in s 11(1) of the Agriculture Act 1947 is restricted to circumstances relating to the unit itself and its production and not to mitigating factors relating to the tenant's personal circumstances[3].

Phillipps v Davies[3A] concerned 37.87 acres of bare land in Pembrokeshire. The landlord complained that two fields extending to some 10 acres had been abandoned and parts of the two fields had been used for dumping and burying scrap metal, asbestos and other non-agricultural waste brought in from off the holding. One field of some 2.5 acres was infested with docks but, save for general lack of attention to hedge trimming, no complaint was made about some 24 acres of grassland. The ALT found that the 10 acres had been abandoned and that the 2.5 acre field had a long-term dock problem and the tenant had not maintained a reasonable standard of efficient production in that field. The ALT found that the abandoned fields had in part been used for the dumping and burial activities complained of and that constituted *extremely bad husbandry* and that hedges had not been maintained for some years.

The tenant appealed to the High Court on the basis that the ALT failed to look at the holding as a whole but rather limited their assessment to the parts of the holding about which complaint was made and that, in not expressly resolving any of the arguments put forward by the tenant, they failed to give adequate reasons for the decision.

The court dismissed the tenant's application for the ALT to state a case[3B]. Sullivan J stated that:

> 'When one considers whether or not the reasoning of the Tribunal is adequate, it is important to bear in mind that the Tribunal is not addressing legal issues in a vacuum. It is responding to the arguments, which have been advanced before it. In the present case, if one looks at the manner in which the parties were putting their submissions, it is plain that there was no issue between the parties that the Tribunal had to look at the unit as a whole. This was not a case where the advocate on behalf of the tenant was submitting that the unit as a whole should be considered and the advocate on behalf of the landlord was submitting that it was sufficient if one looked at one part of the holding and found that on that part of the holding there was poor husbandry'.

In connection with the complaint about the adequacy of the ALT's reasons, Sullivan J observed:

> 'Considering the adequacy of the Tribunal's reasons generally, Mr Rodger submitted that the applicant was entitled to know why a certificate had been granted. I entirely agree, but I am satisfied that the applicant knows perfectly well why a certificate was granted. In summary, and using my terminology, it was because the Tribunal concluded that he had allowed about a third of the holding to go to pot and although reasonable standards of efficient production were being maintained on the remainder of the holding, the standards there were no more than that. Overall, there was no proper maintenance. In other words, this was not a case where a tenant might be able to make up for very obvious deficiencies in the husbandry of one part of the holding by a good standard of efficient production on the remainder of the holding'.

The tenant's application was made against and opposed by both the ALT and the landlord but the court ordered the tenant to pay only the costs of the ALT and not those of the landlord.

In *Tarmac UK Limited v Hughes*[3C], the holding extended to less than 2 acres consisting of farmhouse, a small range of buildings and just over an acre of pasture. The Applicant complained of the land being badly poached with stone from crumbling walls incorporated and redundant sheep fencing puddled into the ground; long-term serious neglect of fencing; gates not properly hung; hedging not attended to; weeds including ragwort and docks; redundant machinery littering the farm and metal sheets in hedges and ditches. Photographs spanning a two-year period supported the allegations. The state and condition had not improved, if anything it had got worse, in that time and the tenant had taken no steps to make any improvements in the nine months since he had been aware of the application. The ALT concluded that the management of the tenancy had been woefully inadequate because no steps had been taken to enforce the tenant's husbandry obligations for over 15 years. But this did not have any adverse impact on the tenant's ability to discharge his obligations of good husbandry. The ALT followed the approach of Sullivan J in *Phillipps v Davies*:

> 'In determining the Application the Tribunal adopts the principle stated by Sullivan J (as he then was) in *Davies v Phillipps & Phillipps* [2007] EWHC 1395 (Admin) that the Tribunal when considering whether the Respondent has been farming in accordance with the rules of good husbandry must have regard to the whole of the unit. A certificate will not necessarily be justified merely because there has been poor husbandry on part only of the holding. Equally, it is not necessary for the Applicant to demonstrate the rules of good husbandry having been breached over every part of the holding. The test is a pragmatic one. To satisfy Section 11(1) the breaches must "significantly affect the holding so that it can broadly be said that a reasonable standard of efficient production has not been maintained nor the unit kept in such a condition to maintain such a standard in the future". The cases to which Sullivan J referred in support of this proposition were *Ross v Donaldson* [1983] SLT 26 at p 27 (a Decision of the Scottish Land Court) and *Maggs v Worsley* (SW Agricultural Land Tribunal 11 May 1982). The Tribunal also applied the principle set out in *Goldsmid v Hick* (SE Agricultural Land Tribunal dated 15 February 2002), to the effect that the state of husbandry in a particular case is a "state of affairs" existing at the time of the Hearing and view, and not merely a matter of instant physical condition at that time; and the decision in *Cambusmore Estate Trustees v Little* 1991 STLT (Land Ct) 33 to the effect that the Tenant's personal circumstances, unrelated to any lapses by the Landlord from good estate management, are not to be taken into account'.

In *Goodwin v Clarke*[4], where a landlord had applied for a certificate of bad husbandry and before the hearing, on inspection, he had discovered that the breaches committed previously by the tenant had been remedied, it was held that since the landlord did not withdraw his application for a certificate, by continuing with the litigation he was then guilty of 'vexatious, frivolous or oppressive' behaviour and as such was liable for the costs of the tenant from that time onwards[5].

Applications for a certificate of bad husbandry usually give rise to intense activity on the part of the tenant to remedy the matters complained of. Particularly in the context of the decision in *Goodwin v Clarke*[6], this gives rise to the question as to when the state of husbandry is to be assessed by the ALT. In *Hale v Stone*[7], the ALT found that: 'notwithstanding the very recent ploughing and clearances, the holding gave the appearance of serious, previous neglect'. It was contended for the tenant that the state of husbandry should be assessed at the date of the hearing. The ALT decided that 'the state of husbandry is a state of affairs existing at the time, not merely a matter of instant physical condition at the time of the hearing'[8]. It is submitted that the starting point should be for the ALT to consider the evidence as to the state of the holding at the date on which the application for the certificate of bad husbandry is made.

1   AHA 1986, s 25(4).
2   See para 31.44.
3   *Cambusmore Estate Trustees v Little* 1991 SLT (Land Ct) 33. Followed in *Executors of Ewbank v Hodgson* (1998) ALT, 2/1508–09.
3A (2007) ALT, W/6209.
3B [2007] EWHC 1395 (Admin).
3C (2009) ALT, W/6229.
4   Decision of the Eastern Area ALT [1992] EA 605. For a similar decision of an ALT (Yorkshire and Humberside) in the case of a succession case, see *Clappison v Marr Trustees*.
5   As to the power to award costs, see para 46.21.
6   [1992] EA 605.
7   (1998) ALT, SW/27/71.
8   This direction was followed in *Goldsmid v Hicks* (2002) ALT, SE/1547.

CASE D – NON-PAYMENT OF RENT AFTER NOTICE TO PAY

Extra-statutory requirements

31.29 Part VI of the Landlord and Tenant Act 1987 (LTA 1987) applies to agricultural holdings which include a dwelling[1]. Section 47 provides that the landlord must serve written notice on his part specifying:

(a)   the name and address of the landlord; and
(b)   if that address is not in England and Wales, an address in England and Wales at which notices (including notices in proceedings) may be served on the landlord by the tenant.

This information must be contained in any written demand the landlord makes for rent or other sums payable to the landlord under the terms of the tenancy[2].

The penalty for non-compliance with s 47 is that the part of the amount demanded which consists of a 'service charge' is deemed not to be due[3]. 'Service charge' is widely defined to include any variable payments made directly 'or indirectly for services, repairs, maintenance or insurance'[4]. This will rarely apply to agricultural holdings. Normally where the 'model clauses' apply, the rent is not variable 'according to the relevant costs'[5].

More importantly in relation to agricultural holdings, s 48 of the LTA 1987 must also be complied with. Section 48 provides that the rent otherwise due from the tenant is not payable until notice of an address in England and Wales at which notices (including notices in proceedings) may be served on the landlord is given to the tenant. Section 48 is of wider application than s 47. It applies even where there is no 'service charge' payable. When s 48 applies, and not s 47, the notice only needs to be given once and not in every demand 'for rent or other sums payable to the landlord under the terms of the tenancy'[6].

Rent is not due until after the landlord has served notice under the LTA 1987, so that a notice to pay served before a s 48 notice had been given was invalid. After the s 48 notice is given, the accrued unpaid rent is treated as being immediately due. If a subsequent notice to pay refers to rent having become due on the earlier quarter days, it will still be valid and effective despite the fact that the rent was not due on those dates by reason of the non-service of the s 48 notice[7].

A 'correspondence address' for the landlord will not of itself be sufficient. Also, if an agent represents the landlord, the tenant must be given notice that all future documentation relating to the tenancy, including notices to the landlord, should be sent to the agent[8].

1   The Act is not primarily directed towards agricultural holdings. Part VI applies 'to premises which consist of or include a dwelling and are not held under a tenancy to which Part II of the Landlord and Tenant Act 1954 applies': LTA 1987, s 46(1).
2   LTA 1987, s 47(2).
3   LTA 1987, s 47(2) and (3). See also *Mannai Investments Co Ltd v Eagle Star Life Assurance Co Ltd* [1997] AC 749, [1997] 1 EGLR 57, HL. See para 28.3.
4   LTA 1987, s 46(2) and the Landlord and Tenant Act 1985 (LTA 1985), s 18(1).
5   LTA 1985, s 18(1).
6   *Dallhold Estates (UK) Property Ltd v Lindsey Trading Properties Inc* (1993) 70 P & CR 332, [1994] 1 EGLR 93, CA.
7   *Dallhold Estates (UK) Property Ltd v Lindsey Trading Properties Inc* (1993) 70 P & CR 332, [1994] 1 EGLR 93, CA. Cf *Rogan v Woodfield Building Services Ltd* (1994) 27 HLR 78, [1995] 1 EGLR 72, CA. The notice can take the form of the landlord's name and address being set out in the tenancy agreement itself.
8   *Glen International Ltd v Triplerose Ltd* [2007] EWCA Civ 388, (2007) 36 EG 164.

Rent due

31.30 In order for a landlord to utilise the notice to pay procedure he must first establish the 'rent due[1]. This involves two stages: first, identifying what is rent; and second, that it is due.

The terms of the tenancy will usually govern the amount of the rent and when and (in some cases) how it is to be paid. The rent may be varied in accordance with the statutory provisions contained in the AHA 1986[2]. The amount of rent due may also be affected by the general law applying to set-off[3].

A notice to pay rent should not include a claim for any other money due from the tenant. If interest on unpaid rent is contractually due to the landlord, it cannot be included in the notice to pay, unless it is expressly reserved as rent in the tenancy agreement. As the landlord must strictly comply with the statutory requirements applying to a notice to pay, he should err on the side of caution when inserting the amount of rent due in a notice to pay. A notice to pay must not include, for example, interest on improvements or an insurance premium.

Rent includes any element of VAT charged to the tenant on the underlying rent. Accordingly, a notice to pay which included the VAT charged on the rent had not overstated the amount of rent due and was valid[4].

1   In an unreported county court case, *Busk v Hallett* (1969) unreported, it was held that, not only must the amount claimed be due, but it must be as 'rent'.
2   See Ch 25. Under the Housing Act 1988 it has been held that if the tenant counterclaims for damages, extinguishing the liability for rent by set-off, rent is not lawfully due. In such a case the court has no jurisdiction to make an order for possession where the ground for possession is rent arrears: *Baygreen Properties Ltd v Gil* [2002] EWCA Civ 1340, [2003] HLR 119, [2002] 3 EGLR 42.
3   See para 31.32ff.
4   *Mason v Boscowen* [2008] EWHC 3100 (Ch), [2009] 1 All ER 1006, [2009] 1 EGLR 145.

Set-off

31.32   If the tenant has a valid claim to set-off, the rent otherwise payable will be reduced or extinguished. The existence of an arguable claim first creates a problem from the landlord who is required to state the precise amount of the arrears of rent in the notice to pay[1].

Whether an equitable set-off can be claimed against rent demanded in a notice to pay is open to doubt[2]. What is clear is that an equitable set-off cannot arise from a contingent liability on the part of the landlord[3]. In *Sloan Stanley Estate Trustees v Barribal*[4], the tenant sought to set-off against rent demanded in the notice to pay the landlord's part of the drainage rate. The rate was payable by the tenant, as occupier of the land, but recoverable against the landlord under the Land Drainage Act 1991. The Court of Appeal held that no set-off arose because the tenant had not paid the drainage rate to the authority before the service of the notice to pay. As a consequence, the notice to pay and subsequent notice to quit were found to be valid.

1   See para 31.35.
2   *Hanak v Green* [1958] 2 QB 9, [1958] 2 All ER 141, CA.
3   *Sloan Stanley Estate Trustees v Barribal* [1994] 2 EGLR 8, [1994] 44 EG 237.
4   [1994] 2 EGLR 8, [1994] 44 EG 237.

31.33   It frequently happens that the landlord is in breach of his obligations under the terms of the tenancy, for example, because he has failed to carry out repairs after due notice from the tenant[1]. At one time it was thought that the tenant had no right of set-off against the rent by reason of the landlord's breach. However, the modern law is that the tenant is entitled to counter-claim and to set-off against rent monies due by way of damages, whether liquidated or unliquidated, for breach by the landlord of his repairing obligations[2]. In the last edition of this book, it was submitted that it was probable, although there was no authority on this point, that in these circumstances a tenant who has defaulted on receipt of a notice to pay, and who can show that the landlord is himself in breach of his repairing or any other obligations, after having had due notice from the tenant, can thereby establish that the whole of the monies claimed to be due and owing as rent are not due and owing because of his entitlement to set-off against that rental payment the unliquidated damages due to him for breach by the landlord of his repairing obligations. This approach has been followed since in Scotland in relation to the like provisions of the Agricultural Holdings (Scotland) Act 1991[3].

In *Sloan Stanley Estate Trustees v Barribal*[4], the Court of Appeal left open the question as to whether the equitable set-off might be available against rent demanded affecting the validity of a notice to pay. Nevertheless, given the draconian consequences for a tenant failing to pay rent due in response to a valid notice to pay, the advice to a tenant must be 'pay under protest' and pursue the tenant's claims for equitable set-off separately.

The decision in *Muscat v Smith*[5] should also be noted. The case involved a statutory tenancy of a dwellinghouse. Following service of a repairs notice under the Housing Act 1985, the then landlord, W, carried out remedial work, which caused major disruption and inconvenience. The tenant withheld rent. The freehold was assigned with the right to recover the arrears of rent. At first instance, the court held that the tenant's claim against W could not be set off against the arrears of rent. The Court of Appeal overturned that decision. It accepted that the general principle of set-off did not assist the tenant because, inter alia, the breaches of contract were those of W. However, on the application of principles that differed from those of general equitable set-off, the tenant had been entitled to set-off against the successor landlord's claim for arrears of rent any damages due to him for W's breach of his repairing obligations. That was because the debt was a chose in action, vested in the successor landlord as assignee subject to all equities which were available to the tenant against W.

Conversely, if the landlord assigns the reversion to A, and A claims rent for a subsequent period, then the tenant cannot set-off his claim for damages against the original landlord for breach of a repairing obligation in defending against A's claim[6].

1   See para 23.17ff.
2   *British Anzani (Felixstowe) Ltd v International Marine Management (UK) Ltd* [1980] QB 137, [1979] 2 All ER 1063; *Melville v Grapelodge Developments Ltd* (1978) 39 P & CR 179, [1980] 1 EGLR 42; *Calabar Properties Ltd v Stitcher* [1983] 3 All ER 759, [1984] 1 WLR 287, CA. *Fuller v Happy Shopper Markets Ltd* [2001] 1 WLR 1681, [2001] 2 EGLR 32; *Baygreen Properties Ltd v Gil* [2002] EWCA Civ 1340, [2003] HLR 119, [2002] 3 EGLR 42; *Taylor v Blaquiere* [2002] EWCA Civ 1633, [2003] 1 WLR 379, [2003] 1 EGLR 52.
3   *Alexander v Royal Hotel (Caithness) Ltd* [2001] 1 EGLR 6, [2001] 16 EG 148.
4   *Sloan Stanley Estate Trustees v Barribal* [1994] 2 EGLR 8, [1994] 44 EG 237.
5   [2003] EWCA Civ 962, [2003] 1 WLR 2853, [2003] 3 EGLR 11.
6   *Edlington Properties Ltd v JH Fenner & Co Ltd* [2005] EWHC 2158 (QB), [2006] 1 All ER 98, [2006] 1 EGLR 29.

Form of notice to pay rent

31.35 If the notice to pay demands a sum in excess of the rent due and owing at the date of the notice to pay, then the notice to pay is invalid, whether or not the tenant was misled[1]. An inconsequential error in the form of the notice (but not the amount of rent) will not invalidate it[2].

The notice to pay must correctly state the amount of the rent due. Where a notice to pay stated that the arrears of rent amounted to £650, but were in fact £625, it was found to be invalid[3].

If the notice is despatched before the date on which the rent is due, but received, and therefore served, after it has become due, the notice is valid[4]. It should be noted that s 93 of the AHA 1986 provides that a notice may be sent by pre-paid registered post, which includes recorded delivery post. It is then deemed to be served when it would ordinarily be delivered in the normal course of post[5].

Service of a notice by leaving a notice at the farmhouse, where it slipped under the linoleum and remained undetected, was held to be sufficient[6].

In *Dockerill v Fitzpatrick*[7], a tenant who had exercised an option to purchase, but where the option had not been completed, was found still to be in occupation as tenant and required to comply with a notice to pay.

[1]   *Dickinson v Boucher* [1984] 1 EGLR 12, 269 Estates Gazette 1159, CA; *Busk v Hallett* (1969) unreported; *Pickard v Bishop* (1975) 31 P & CR 108, 119 Sol Jo 407, CA.
[2]   *Waller v Legh* (1955) 161 Estates Gazette 201, [1956] JPL 41; *Official Solicitor v Thomas* [1986] 2 EGLR 1, 279 Estates Gazette 407, CA. Cf *Pickard v Bishop* (1975) 31 P & CR 108, 119 Sol Jo 407, CA.
[3]   *Dickinson v Boucher* [1984] 1 EGLR 12, 269 Estates Gazette 1159, CA. This was not an application of the legal maxim: de minimis non curat lex – the law does not care for small things. Also see, *Dallhold Estates (UK) Property Ltd v Lindsey Trading Properties Inc* (1993) 70 P & CR 332, [1994] 1 EGLR 93, CA; *Official Solicitor v Thomas* (1986) 279 Estates Gazette 407; *Mason v Boscowen* [2008] EWHC 3100 (Ch), [2009] 1 All ER 1006, [2009] 1 EGLR 145 and para 31.30.
[4]   *French v Elliott* [1959] 3 All ER 866, [1960] 1 WLR 40. Cf *Beavers v Mason* (1979) 37 P & CR 42, CA.
[5]   The Interpretation Act 1978, s 7. For the position as to service of notices generally, see para 42.13ff.
[6]   *Newborough (Lord) v Jones* [1975] Ch 90, [1974] 3 All ER 17, CA.
[7]   [1989] 1 EGLR 1, [1989] 02 EG 75, CA.

Compliance

31.36   The general common law rule is that rent must be paid in cash before the end of the two-month period. Where the landlord and tenant have, by course of dealing between them, shown that the landlord has been willing to accept payment by cheque posted on or before the due date, then even though the cheque is received later, payment in that manner will suffice. Subject to due honouring of the cheque on presentation, the rent is deemed to have been paid from the moment of posting[1].

The law in this area was reviewed by the Court of Appeal in *Day v Coltrane*[1A]. This was a possession claim based on arrears of rent under the Housing Act 1988 in which five days before the hearing the tenant sent the landlord a cheque for the full amount of the arrears. The Court of Appeal allowed the tenant's appeal against the possession order: an uncleared cheque accepted by the landlord prior to the hearing was to be treated as payment at the date of delivery provided the cheque cleared at first presentation. The District Judge had therefore been right to adjourn to see whether the cheque would be paid and the Judge had been wrong to allow the landlord's appeal from that decision.

The law is set out in the judgment of Tuckey LJ at 1382, paragraphs 8–10 as follows:

> '8. It is common ground that in principle a landlord is entitled to have his rent in cash on the due date, unless the parties have expressly or impliedly agreed upon some other method of payment, such as by cheque. If they have agreed to pay by cheque per Lord Woolf at para 35 in *Homes v Smith* (2000) Lloyds Law Rep (Banking) 139:
>
> > "The general position in law ... is clear. Where a cheque is offered in payment it amounts to a conditional payment of the amount of the cheque which, if accepted, operates as a conditional payment from the time when the cheque was delivered."
>
> For this summary of the principle, Lord Woolf relied on earlier cases and in particular what Farwell LJ said in *Marreco v Richardson* (1908) 2 KB 584; 593:
>
> > "The giving of a cheque for a debt is payment conditional on the cheque being met, that is, subject to a condition subsequent, and if the cheque is met it is an actual payment ab initio and not a conditional one."
>
> *Marreco* was concerned with the effect of the Limitation Act, but Lord Woolf added that Farwell LJ's approach was of general application. This is demonstrated by three cases decided under the Agricultural Holdings Act 1948 to which we were referred.
>
> 9. Under the 1948 Act, effect must be given to a notice to quit served after failure to comply with a notice requiring the tenant to pay any rent due within two months of the notice. In *Beavers v Mason* (1978) 37 P&CR 452 the evidence showed that the landlord had previously accepted payment of the rent by cheque posted on the date it was due. The court held that a cheque posted in this way on the last day of the two month notice period was payment of the rent on that date if the cheque was honoured. The cheque was not received by the landlord until after the notice had expired. Nevertheless, as a result of the previous course of dealing, the court held that the tenant was entitled to pay by cheque and treated the post office as the landlord's agent for the purpose of deciding when the cheque was delivered. This court accepted that approach in *Official Solicitor v Thomas* (1986) 2 EGLR 1 although it did not apply to the facts of that case. It would also have applied in *Luttenberger v North Thoresby Farms Ltd* (1993) 1 EGLR 3 but for the fact that the tenant's cheque lacked a necessary signature.
>
> 10. There really cannot be any doubt about the principles of law to which I have referred in the last two paragraphs'.

In *Beavers v Mason*[2], the cheque was posted shortly before the end of the two-month period in circumstances where it would not in the ordinary course of post (and, in fact, did not) arrive within the two-month period. Nevertheless, it was held that the notice to pay had been validly complied with and the notice to quit was invalid.

---

[1] *Norman v Ricketts* (1886) 3 TLR 182, CA; *Beavers v Mason* (1979) 37 P & CR 42, CA.
[1A] [2003] EWCA Civ 342, [2003] 1 WLR 1379, [2003] 2 EGLR 21.
[2] (1979) 37 P & CR 42, CA.

Method of payment

31.38 In *Luttenberger v North Thoresby Farms Ltd*[1], the usual rule that payment is deemed to be made when the cheque is posted did not apply where the paying bank is not bound to honour the cheque. That happened in this case where the cheque only had one signature on it where two were required. The cheque was backdated to when the second signature was added which was outside the two-month period.

In *Hannacombe v Smallacombe*[2], the usual rule again did not apply where the cheque was returned marked 'refer to drawer, please re-present'.

Payment of rent by leaving a cheque for the landlord in the dairy was held to be insufficient compliance with the notice to pay[3].

Although a cheque sent by post is usually despatched at the tenant's risk, such risk passes to the landlord if he has impliedly accepted this method of payment. Accordingly, payment will be deemed to have been made even if the cheque is lost in the post[4].

1 [1993] 1 EGLR 3, [1993] 17 EG 102.
2 (1993) 69 P & CR 399, [1994] 1 EGLR 9, CA. also see, *Oakley v Young* (1970), an unreported decision of Judge Bulger in the Cheltenham County Court referred to in J Muir Watt, *Agricultural Holdings* (13th edn), Sweet & Maxwell. It is not referred to in the 14th edn of the work.
3 *Flint v Fox* (1956) 106 L Jo 828.
4 *Luttges v Sherwood* (1895) 11 TLR 233; *Pennington v Crossley & Son* (1897) 13 TLR 513.

CASE D – FAILURE TO REMEDY A BREACH OTHER THAN THE NON-PAYMENT OF RENT

Notice to do work: Form 2

Waiver

31.57 If, subsequent to the notice to remedy, the landlord takes some action which indicates his intention to waive the notice to remedy, for example, by signing a new tenancy agreement, or demanding arbitration as to the terms of the tenancy, then his right subsequently to rely upon a notice to remedy may thereby be waived[1]. It should be noted that waiver does not apply after the service of a notice to quit[2].

As an alternative to waiver, the tenant may argue that the actions of the landlord give rise to estoppel, discharging the tenant of his obligation to comply with a notice to remedy[3].

1 *Shepton Mallet Transport Ltd v Clark* (1953) 161 Estates Gazette 518, [1953] CPL 343, CA.
2 *Bolsom (Sidney) Investment Trust Ltd v E Karmios & Co (London) Ltd* [1956] 1 QB 529, [1956] 1 All ER 536, CA.

Challenging the validity of a notice to do work

31.60   The ability of the tenant to challenge the notice to remedy served upon him varies, depending upon whether a Form 2 notice (to do work) or a Form 3 notice (non-work) has been given[1].

In the case of a notice to remedy in Form 2 (notice to do work), the tenant has a number of opportunities to challenge the landlord.

The first opportunity which the tenant has to challenge a notice in Form 2 is by serving written notice requiring the matter specified in it to be referred to arbitration under the AHA 1986. If the tenant wishes to:

(a)   contest his liability to do the work, or any part of the work, required by the notice to do work; and/or

(b)   request the deletion from the notice of any item of work on the ground that it is unnecessary or unjustified; and/or

(c)   request the substitution, in the case of any item of work, of a different method or material for the method or material required to be used by the notice,

then he must, within one month after service of the notice to do work, serve written notice on the landlord requiring the questions identified by him to be referred to arbitration[2].

This is the only opportunity which the tenant has to challenge these three matters. If the tenant fails to do so, he is precluded from raising them again at the notice to quit stage.

The tenant's demand for arbitration does not need to be in a prescribed form[3]. It must set out clearly those items in respect of which the tenant denies liabilities; those items which he claims are unnecessary or unjustified; and also any method or material in respect of which he desires a substitution to be made[4]. If any of these matters are referred to arbitration, the tenant is not obliged to carry out the work which is the subject of the reference to arbitration until the arbitrator decides that he is liable to do it. He must carry out any other work which is undisputed[5].

¹   See para 31.56.
²   The Agricultural Holdings (Arbitration on Notices) Order, SI 1987/710, art 3(1) and (2).
³   For a precedent, see para A2.74.
⁴   SI 1987/710, art 3(3).
⁵   *Ladds Radio and Television Service Ltd v Docker* (1973) 226 Estates Gazette 1565. See para 31.58.

CASE E – IRREMEDIABLE BREACH

Anti-alienation provisions

31.84   The question as to whether there has been a parting with or sharing of possession sometimes arises in practice. In *Akici v LR Butlin Ltd*[1], Neuberger LJ (as he then was) acknowledged that the difference between possession and occupation can be elusive, but it is a difference which is recognised and should be adhered to[2]. Where the owner had unrestricted access to the property, on the facts in *Akici*[3], it was found that there had been no parting with possession.

What is also noteworthy about the *Akici*[4] decision is that the judge limited the impact of the *Scala House and District Property Co Ltd v Forbes*[5] decision to cases where a legal interest had either been created or transferred. Where, as in this case, the tenant had allowed a company in which the tenant had no formal interest to operate a business from the premises, if such an act was in breach of covenant it was remediable[6].

[1]   [2005] EWCA Civ 1296, [2006] 2 All ER 872, [2006] 1 EGLR 34.
[2]   Overruling *Tulapam Properties Ltd v De Almeida* (1981) 260 Estates Gazette 919.
[3]   *Akici v LR Butlin Ltd* [2005] EWCA Civ 1296, [2006] 2 All ER 872, [2006] 1 EGLR 34.
[4]   *Akici v LR Butlin Ltd* [2005] EWCA Civ 1296, [2006] 2 All ER 872, [2006] 1 EGLR 34.
[5]   [1974] QB 575, [1973] 3 All ER 308, CA.
[6]   Also see para 8.3 and the commentary relating to *Clarence House Ltd v National Westminster Bank plc* [2009] EWCA Civ 1311, [2010] 2 All ER 201, [2010] 2 All ER (Comm) 1065.

Chapter 32

RECOVERY OF POSSESSION FOR NON-AGRICULTURAL USE

NOTICE TO QUIT

Notice to quit part

32.3 At common, law a notice to quit part only of the property let by a tenancy is invalid[1]. The notice can only apply to the entirety of the premises[2]. However, in the case of agricultural holdings protected under the AHA 1986, there are three cases where a notice to quit part may be given:

(a)   those covered by s 31 of the AHA 1986[3];
(b)   those where express provision is made in the tenancy agreement for the notice to quit part to be given[4];
(c)   those covered by s 140 of the Law of Property Act 1925 (LPA 1925) (severance of the reversion)[5].

The impact of ss 32 and 33 of the AHA 1986 should also be noted:

 (i)   Section 32 gives the tenant the right to treat a notice to quit part validated by either s 31 of the AHA 1986 or by s 140 of the LPA 1925 as a notice to quit the entire holding. This is sometimes referred to as the right of 'enlargement'.

(ii)   Section 33 provides that where the landlord resumes possession of part of the holding, either by reason of s 31 of the AHA 1986 or by reason of a provision in the tenancy agreement, then the tenant will be entitled to a proportionately reduced rent which should also reflect any depreciation in the value of his retained land caused by the severance which the landlord has achieved or by the use intended for the severed land.

[1]   See para 29.1.
[2]   *Re: Bebington's Tenancy* [1921] 1 Ch 559.
[3]   See para 32.4.
[4]   See para 32.5.
[5]   See para 32.6.

Severance of the freehold reversion

32.6 Section 140 of the Law of Property Act 1925 provides that where the freehold reversion is severed, the landlord of any severed part may give an independent notice to quit in relation to that part. Thus if the original landlord of the entire holding sells or gives up his interest in a defined part of the land to a third party, that person will be entitled to serve on the tenant notice to quit in respect of the severed part which he now owns[A1].

135

Any severance which is relied on as validating a notice to quit part must be a genuine transfer of a part of the reversion and not merely a device designed to enable such a notice to be given. The courts have been prepared to look at the substance of the transaction rather than its mere form. For example, where a transfer of part of the reversionary estate to bare trustees was seen in substance to be merely a transfer to agents for the purposes of serving a notice to quit part, the court intervened finding that it was not a true severance and the notice to quit was invalid[1].

Severance of the freehold reversion does not of itself create two tenancies. The tenant continues to hold under one single lease, whether or not there has been any apportionment of the rent[2].

Section 140(2) of the LPA 1925 gives the tenant who is served with a notice to quit part of the premises the right to serve a counter-notice on the owner of the remainder of the reversionary estate which terminates the tenancy of the entire holding. Such counter-notice must be served within one month of the notice to quit and must expire at the same time as that notice. The counter-notice operates as a notice to quit by the tenant and s 140(2) effectively gives the tenant the right to enlarge the notice to quit part into a notice to quit the whole. In the case of agricultural holdings under the AHA 1986, a tenant wishing to exercise his right will do so under s 32 of the AHA 1986 rather than s 140(2) because the latter would disentitle the tenant to the payment of compensation for disturbance, which is available if the enlargement takes place under s 32 of the AHA 1986.

[A1]   As to severance generally, see *EDF Energy Networks (EPN) plc v BOH Ltd* [2009] EWHC 3193 (Ch), [2010] 2 P & CR 31, [2009] 49 EG 71 (CS).
[1]   *Persey v Bazley* (1983) 47 P & CR 37, 267 Estates Gazette 519, CA.
[2]   *Jelley v Buckman* [1974] QB 488, [1973] 3 All ER 853, CA.

CASE B

Key issues

32.13   There are nine key issues to be addressed in relation to the operation of Case B.

(1)   What does 'required' mean?
(2)   Is the planning permission for non-agricultural use?
(3)   Whether all of the land must be 'required'?
(4)   Does the requirement have to be for use by the landlord himself?
(5)   What sort of planning permission is required?
(6)   Does the notice to quit state the fact that the land is required pursuant to Case B?
(7)   Is there a bona fide intention to implement the change of use?
(8)   Are there reasonable prospects of the change of use being implemented?
(9)   What is the effect of a failure to implement the scheme?

The need for the notice to quit to state the fact that the land is required pursuant to Case B is self-evident.

Required for non-agricultural use

32.14 For Case B to be applicable, the land must be 'required' for non-agricultural use. The landlord must establish that there is a *present* intention to develop the land. A future intention, for example where the landlord intends to sell to a non-identified prospective developer, will not suffice[1]. The language of Case B suggests that the land must be required at the date of the giving of the notice to quit. It has been suggested that the requirement must be for use on the expiry of the notice to quit or a relatively short time thereafter[2]. This point has not been determined by the courts.

As the notice to quit cannot take effect immediately, the requirement must of necessity be to do something in the future. However, the verb is in the present tense: 'is required'. When planning permission is necessary, it must have already been obtained. The eighth edition of this book suggested that the provision seems to point to the need for a present requirement at the date of the notice to quit and not some possible future requirement which may never crystallise.

The cases decided in relation to s 30(1)(f) of the Landlord and Tenant Act 1954, Part II are of some assistance but do not provide a true analogy. Under the 1954 Act it is necessary for the landlord's intention to redevelop to be established at the date of the hearing[3]. The landlord's notice to terminate must state what on the termination of the tenancy the landlord intends[4]. These have been held to be words of futurity[5].

It is submitted that the proper approach to this issue under Case B is a two-stage process. First, the landlord must have a settled intention at the date that the notice to quit is given requiring the land which is the subject of the notice to quit (and, in most cases, subject to the planning permission obtained) for the stated purpose. The second stage is that the landlord must establish that such requirement is to be implemented at the date that the notice to quit expires or a reasonable period thereafter. It is submitted that it would not be reasonable for the period to be more than 12 months after the notice to quit expires.

---

[1] *Jones v Gates* [1954] 1 All ER 158, [1954] 1 WLR 222, CA; *Paddock Investments Ltd v Lory* [1975] 2 EGLR 5, 236 Estates Gazette 803, CA.
[2] Muir Watt and Moss, *Agricultural Holdings*, (14th edn, 1998), Sweet & Maxwell at para 12.50.1.
[3] *Betty's Cafes Ltd v Phillips Furnishing Stores Ltd* [1959] AC 20, [1958] 1 All ER 607.
[4] *Inclusive Technology v Williamson* [2009] EWCA Civ 718, [2010] 1 P & CR 7, [2009] 39 EG 110; *Somerfield Stores Ltd v Spring (Sutton Coldfield) Ltd (in administration)* [2010] EWHC 2084 (Ch), [2010] 47 EG 142, [2010] 33 EG 71 (CS).
[5] *Betty's Cafes Ltd v Phillips Furnishing Stores Ltd* [1959] AC 20, [1958] 1 All ER 607.

Planning permission for non-agricultural use

32.14A Allied to the first question as to whether the land is required is the issue as to whether the planning permission is for non-agricultural use. The question of law is whether on a true interpretation of Case B a landlord who seeks to serve a notice to quit on a tenant may do so:

(a)   if, but only if, the land is required for a use or uses (for which planning permission has been obtained) which are wholly and exclusively non-agricultural; or

(b)   if the land is required for two or more permitted uses which may be both non-agricultural and agricultural; or

(c)   if the land is required for two or more permitted uses which are predominantly non-agricultural but include the use of land for agriculture as a subsidiary or ancillary use.

It is submitted that, based upon the Court of Appeal decision in *Floyer-Acland v Osmond*[1], (a) is wrong in law. The correct answer is either (b) or (c). In *Floyer-Acland v Osmond*, Morritt LJ said:

'For my part, I would accept the argument for the tenant if it were shown that the landlords had two or more concurrent purposes, one of which involved the use of the land for agriculture. The liberty conferred on the landlord by clause 43 is "to resume possession … for any purpose or purposes not being the use of the land for agriculture". But the use of the land for agriculture by the Landlord would be a derogation from his grant to the tenant of the agricultural holding. If there were but one purpose, and that involved the use of land for agriculture, then, plainly, the landlord would not be entitled to determine the tenancy. I can see no reason to impute to the parties an intention that if the landlord has more than one purpose, then the second non-agricultural purpose should extinguish the adverse effect of a single agricultural use'.

Since the proposed uses were sequential and not concurrent, the court found for the landlord in relation to his contractual right to resume possession contained in the tenancy agreement (clause 43).

Morritt LJ's conclusions on the Case B point are set out in a separate passage at page 4H-L:

'The third and last point on Case B is very similar to the third point on clause 43. Does the condition that "the land is required for a use, other than for agriculture" operate so as to preclude the application of Case B on the ground that the uses for which the land is required include its use for agriculture? It is submitted, and I agree, that the singular "use" includes the plural "uses". No doubt it is possible to have two concurrent uses, one of which is agricultural, and the other not.

Case B does not involve any derogation from grant such as I referred to in connection with clause 43. Nor, in my view, is it appropriate to consider any particular predominant use if, as I think, the provision envisages the possibility of more than one use. But, in my view, it is clear that the possession of the land is not required [sc. in the instant case] for any agricultural use. Neither the winning and working of the sand and gravel, nor the subsequent activities of restoration and after care, are agricultural uses …'.

It is submitted that it is clear from this judgment that, in contrast with the position prevailing under clause 43, which was contained in the contract of tenancy and was therefore affected by considerations of derogation from grant, the Court of Appeal accepted that Case B could be invoked when the land was required for two or more concurrent uses one of which might be the use of the land for agriculture.

The decision of the Court of Appeal is, it is submitted, supported by sound policy considerations. The grant of planning permission in rural areas does not, on many occasions, involve a simple black and white choice between agricultural and non-agricultural uses. To hold that Case B could only be invoked when the planning permission on which reliance was placed did not permit, or rule out, any agricultural use would severely limit the ambit of Case B and prevent much development from being carried out in the countryside even though it had the support of the local planning authority. Landowners would have to argue strongly against the imposition of any ameliorating conditions requiring the continuation of some agricultural use on development land, and it would be difficult in appropriate cases to strike a proper balance between uses which, concurrently, would be beneficial to development.

[1]   (2000) 80 P & CR 229, [2000] 2 EGLR 1, CA.

The extent of planning permission

32.15 The better view is that all of the land which is the subject of the notice to quit must be required for the purpose specified in Case B. It is not sufficient if merely a substantial part of the land has the benefit of planning[1].

The whole or substantially the whole of the land should have the benefit of the planning permission. *Telford Development Corporation v Heath*[2] was a decision of HHJ Stuart-White in the Wellington County Court upon a special case stated for the opinion of the court. Only some 38% of the land which was referred to in the Case B notice to quit was subject to planning permission. The landlord submitted that this was immaterial, so long as a serious, significant and important part of the land was required. The tenant submitted that Case B was not satisfied unless the whole or (possibly) substantially the whole of the land to which the notice to quit relates was required. The court decided that there was 'a precise meaning available for the expression "the land" namely "the land to which the Notice to Quit relates", whether or not the Notice to Quit relates to the whole of the Agricultural Holding'. The court accordingly found in favour of the tenant.

A different question can arise where, although the whole of the land contained in the Case B notice to quit has the benefit of planning permission, for some reason an arbitrator decides that not all of the land is required by the landlord. It is submitted that the *Telford Development Corporation v Heath*[3] decision does not assist in dealing with this separate issue. The answer will lie in determining why the arbitrator has decided that not all of the land is required by the landlord[4].

[1]   *Public Trustee v Randag* [1966] Ch 649, [1965] 3 All ER 88. Cf *Fernandez v Walding* [1968] 2 QB 606, [1968] 1 All ER 994, CA. Also see, *Heath v Telford Corpn* (1988) unreported (CC); *Cawley v Pratt* [1988] 2 EGLR 6, [1988] 33 EG 54, CA; *Omnivale v Bolden Ltd* [1994] EGCS 63, CA.
[2]   (1987) unreported (CC).
[3]   (1987) unreported (CC).
[4]   See para 32.16.

Required for use by the landlord

32.16 The land does not have to be 'required' for the use of the landlord himself. The requirement of any person obtaining planning permission is included, whether that person is the landlord, a prospective purchaser of the landlord's reversion or a body intending to compulsorily purchase the landlord's interest[1]. If the landlord is intending to sell to a third-party developer, the latter must be identified and establish a bona fide intention to develop the land with a reasonable prospect of doing so[2].

The question as to the bona fide intention to implement the change of use and whether the landlord has a reasonable prospect of achieving the change of use being implemented may be considered together.

Goff LJ laid down the test in *Paddock v Lory*[3]: 'In my judgment, the test is, has the landlord a bona fide intention, and has he a reasonable prospect of carrying it out? (See *Jones v Gates* [1954] 1 WLR 222.)'. In *Jones v Gates*[4] the landlord said that he intended to sell the field as a sports ground. He had had some inquiries but had not had any offer and was not at the time in negotiations with anybody. The Judge said, at page 224, that 'in the absence of a definite person or persons willing to negotiate there could not be said to be such a reasonable prospect'. The Court of Appeal agreed. In *Paddock v Lory*[5] the landlord proposed to extract gravel from the farm. He was at the time in negotiations with Richard Biffa Ltd, gravel merchants, and he foresaw no difficulties in agreeing terms as to royalties with that firm so that it could commence extraction. But if terms could not be agreed then he would sell the land for gravel-working. The Court of Appeal held that, although meagre, that evidence was, in the absence of any challenge in cross-examination and taken at face value, just enough.

Cases under the Landlord and Tenant Act 1954, Part II provide some assistance. In *Yoga for Health Foundation v Guest*[6], Hart J said:

> 'The law to be applied is well settled. It is put by the learned editors of Woodfall (March 2002 release paragraph 22.106) in the following terms: "It is not sufficient for the landlord merely to assert that he 'intends' since he may change his mind once he gets possession. An intention connotes that the landlord does more than merely contemplate; it connotes a state of affairs which he decides, so far as in him lies, to bring about, and which, in point of possibility he has a reasonable prospect of being able to bring about, by his own act of volition; the landlord does not 'intend' if he has too many hurdles to overcome or too little control of events. The intention must be genuine and not colourable; it must be firm and settled, not likely to be changed. It must have moved out of the zone of contemplation, the sphere of the tentative, the provisional and the exploratory and have moved into the valley of decision. Thus the landlord's intention is composed of two main ingredients; a fixed and settled desire to do that which he says he intends to do and a reasonable prospect of being able to bring about the desired result.".'

The authority behind the test of intention referred to is *Cunliffe v Goodman*[7] which was recently applied in *Patel v Keles*[8] in which the Court of Appeal was concerned with a landlord's opposition to an application for new tenancy under s 39(1)(g) of the Landlord and Tenant Act 1954 which permits a landlord to oppose an application on the grounds that: '... on the termination of the current tenancy the landlord intends to occupy the holding for the purposes, or partly for the purposes, of a business to be carried on by him therein ...'. In dismissing the landlord's appeal from a decision that he lacked the requisite intention because he was likely to sell the premises after two years, Arden LJ, with whom Waller and Thomas LJJ agreed, described the test of intention as follows in paragraphs 14–15:

'14 If the landlord succeeds in showing that the requirements of s 39(1)(g) are satisfied, the tenant will have no right to renew his tenancy and will have to vacate the premises. Any goodwill attaching to his business at those premises will then either be lost or be acquired by the landlord when he starts to trade from the premises. In those circumstances, the courts have set a higher hurdle for establishing the necessary subjective intention. As was common ground before the judge, the landlord's intention has to satisfy the test of intention laid down in *Cunliffe v Goodman* [1950] 2 KB 237 with respect of a statutory predecessor of s 30(1)(f) of the 1954 Act, which provides the landlord may oppose the grant of a new tenancy if he intends to demolish or reconstruct the premises. In that case, Asquith LJ explored the requirement for an intention to be shown and, relevantly for the purpose of this appeal, held:

"An 'intention' to my mind connotes a state of affairs which the party 'intending' – I will call him X – does more than merely contemplate: it connotes a state of affairs which, on the contrary, he decides, so far as in him lies, to bring about, and which, in point of possibility, he has a reasonable prospect of being able to bring about, by his own act of volition ... Not merely is the term 'intention' unsatisfied if the person professing it has too many hurdles to overcome, or too little control of events: it is equally inappropriate if at the material date that person is in effect not deciding to proceed but feeling his way and reserving his decision until he shall be in possession of financial data sufficient to enable him to determine whether the project will be commercially worthwhile."

15 Asquith LJ went on to hold that there must be a "settled intention to proceed". A landlord would not have a settled intention if the project did not move "out of the zone of contemplation – out of the sphere of the tentative, the provisional and the exploratory – into the valley of decision" (page 254). The other members of this court made observations to similar effect (per Cohen LJ at 249 and 252, and per Singleton LJ 255 to 256)'.

Cunliffe v Goodman[9] was referred to in the argument in *Jones v Gates*[10] which was an agricultural holdings case. Lord Evershed MR said this at p 224:

'... the first question which the county court judge had to decide was whether the land was required for a need other than for agriculture for which permission had been granted on an application under the enactments relating to town and country planning. Nobody has suggested that a mere statement of the fact that the notice to quit is given on that ground is sufficient to satisfy subsection (2) and that the terms of the subsection are satisfied by the mere ipse dixit of the landlord. The conclusion of the county court judge was this:

"As to its being so required the plaintiff says that he intends to sell the field as a sports ground and would have no difficulty in doing so. He has, he says, had inquiries from a business firm and a football club but has so far had no offer and is not, I gather, now in negotiation with anybody. He does not propose either to let it for that purpose or so to use it himself. On that evidence Mr Phillips says that a reasonable prospect of use is shown and that that satisfied the word 'required'. I do not think that in the absence of a definite person or persons willing to negotiate there could be said to be such a reasonable prospect and I am not, therefore, satisfied that the holding is 'required' for purpose."

I agree entirely with that language of the county court judge: he said, there is no-one in negotiation with the landlord nor, as it seems to be on the evidence, was there anybody at any relevant time.

The matter may, I think, therefore, be put quite briefly thus: If the question be – Is this land required for a use referred to in section 24(2), then who now requires it? – it is clear that the landlord does not so require it, for he does not propose to use it or to let it; and there is no other user except what Mr Phillips calls "the prospective purchaser," who is an unidentified and possibly non-existent person. It follows, therefore, that, in my judgment, the county court judge rightly decided adversely to the landlord'.

In *Crossco No 4 Unlimited v Jolan Ltd*[11], Morgan J held that, in relation to s 30(1)(f) of the Landlord and Tenant Act 1954, there was no real dispute as to what is meant by the word 'intends'. The Judge stated that the law is conveniently summarised in Woodfall's Landlord and Tenant Looseleaf Edition, Volume 2 at paragraphs 22.106–22.109.2 as follows:

'It is not sufficient for the landlord merely to assert that he "intends" since he may change his mind once he gets possession. An intention connotes that the landlord does more than merely contemplate; it connotes a state of affairs that he decides, so far [a]s in him lies, to bring about, and which, in point of possibility he has a reasonable prospect of being able to bring about, by his own act of volition; the landlord does not "intend" if he has too many hurdles to overcome or too little control of events. The intention must be genuine and not colourable; it must be firm and settled, not likely to be changed. It must have moved out of the zone of contemplation – the sphere of the tentative, the provisional and the exploratory – and have moved into the valley of decision. Thus, the landlord's intention is composed of two main ingredients: a fixed and settled desire to do that which he says he intends to do and a reasonable prospect of being able to bring about the desired result.' [paragraph 22.106]

'The word "intends" is not to be equated with the words "is ready and able" so as to impose on the landlord the onus of proving that he has not only finally determined the course proposed but has also taken all necessary steps of the satisfaction of any requisite conditions to which the course proposed is subject. It is sufficient that there is a reasonable prospect that he will be able to bring about that which he says he intends. A "reasonable prospect" of obtaining planning permission is not the same as having to show that it is more likely than not that planning permission will be granted. In this context, a "reasonable prospect" means no more than "a real chance". A "reasonable prospect" is one which is strong enough to be acted on by a reasonable landlord rather than one which should be treated as merely fanciful or which should sensibly be ignored. There must not be so many obstructions yet to be surmounted that he cannot truly be said to "intend" it. That is the true relevance of ability in relation to intention. Whether the nature and extent of the obstructions prevent the landlord from having the requisite intention is a question of fact and degree. So where the landlord's scheme depended on finding a developer to develop other land owned by the landlord, and no developer had been found, the landlord did not have the necessary intention for the purposes of this ground. It is often convenient to consider the question of practical possibility under the two headings of legal ability to carry out the work, and practical ability to carry out the work. However the two headings are both part of a single aspect of intention: namely whether the landlord has a reasonable prospect of being able to implement his desire.' [paragraph 22.109]

'If it is proved that it is impossible to carry out the intention (e.g. because he cannot obtain the necessary finance) then it would seem that he must fail. However, the landlord may be able to satisfy the court that he has a reasonable prospect of raising any necessary finance even in the absence of a detailed financial plan.' [paragraph 22.109.2]

It follows that whether there is a bona fide intention on the part of the landlord to implement the change of use will be a question of fact in each case. Likewise, whether the landlord has a reasonable prospect of achieving the change of use will be determined on the facts of each case. For example, whether the landlord is able to comply with conditions applying to the planning permission[12].

1 *Rugby Joint Water Board v Foottit* [1973] AC 202, [1972] 1 All ER 1057, HL.
2 *Paddock Investments Ltd v Lory* [1975] 2 EGLR 5, 236 Estates Gazette 803, CA.
3 [1978] EGD 37 at 46.
4 [1954] 1 All ER 158, [1954] 1 WLR 222, CA.
5 [1978] EGD 37.
6 [2002] EWHC 2658 (Ch), [2003] 1 P & CR D27.
7 [1950] 2 KB 237, [1950] 1 All ER 720, CA.
8 [2009] EWCA Civ 1187, [2010] Ch 332, [2010] 2 WLR 1159.
9 [1950] 2 KB 237, [1950] 1 All ER 720, CA.
10 [1954] 1 All ER 158, [1954] 1 WLR 222, CA.
11 [2011] EWHC 803 (Ch), [2011] All ER (D) 13 (Apr).
12 The Editor wishes to acknowledge the contribution of Mr William Batstone to this section of this Chapter.

Planning permission

32.20 The courts have introduced an important check on the landlord's ability to rely upon Case B where they consider it to be inequitable for the landlord to do so by reason of estoppel[1]. Where the tenant supported an application for planning consent to convert farm buildings, as part of a renovation scheme under which his dairy parlour was to be re-located to new premises, the landlord was subsequently estopped from relying upon the planning consent to give notice to quit under Case B because the scheme had not been fully carried out as agreed between the landlord and the tenant.

It should also be noted that a Case B notice to quit will fail if the planning permission upon which it relies is subsequently quashed. This occurred in *R v Vale of Glamorgan District Council, ex p Adams*[2]. The freehold owners obtained planning permission to convert three barns into residential use. They served a notice to quit in relation to that part of the farm. The barns were essential to the continued use of the farm for its existing dairy business. The local authority applied the Planning Policy Guidance (PPG) and received the tenant's representations. The planning sub-committee granted permission following the planning officer's advice. The court held that the sub-committee had mis-directed itself in relation to the PPG as a consequence of the advice received. The permission was quashed and, as a result, the notice to quit failed.

1   *John v George* (1995) 71 P & CR 375, [1996] 1 EGLR 7, CA. Also see, *Inclusive Technology v Williamson* [2009] EWCA Civ 718, [2010] 1 P & CR 7, [2009] 39 EG 110; *Somerfield Stores Ltd v Spring (Sutton Coldfield) Ltd (in administration)* [2010] EWHC 2084 (Ch), [2010] 47 EG 142, [2010] 33 EG 71 (CS).
2   [2001] JPL 93, HC.

Chapter 33

OTHER METHODS
OF TERMINATION

SURRENDER

Agreement to surrender

33.5 An agreement between a landlord and a tenant of an agricultural holding protected by the AHA 1986 for the tenant to surrender his tenancy to the landlord is enforceable at common law. The AHA 1986 does not expressly impose any restrictions upon the freedom of the parties to contract to surrender and to effect a surrender by deed or operation of law. Following the decision of the House of Lords in *Johnson v Moreton*[1], doubts have been expressed as to whether an agreement to surrender in the future (as opposed to an immediate surrender) would be enforceable or whether it would be held to be unenforceable as being contrary to public policy[2].

In *Elsden v Pick*[3], the Court of Appeal decided that defect in a notice to quit could be waived by the recipient. It was commented, strictly obiter, by Buckley LJ, that an agreement to surrender within one year would be enforceable. It is open to question as to whether an executory agreement to surrender would be enforced if the tenant sought to resile from it before completion[4]. It is submitted that an agreement to surrender, entered into at the time of the grant of the tenancy governed by the AHA 1986, would almost certainly be found to be contrary to public policy[5].

In *Truro Diocesan Board of Finance Ltd v Foley*[6], the Court of Appeal considered the impact of an agreement to surrender in the context of the Housing Act 1988. An agreement was made between a landlord and a tenant, who claimed to have protection under the Rent Act 1977, that the tenant would surrender his existing tenancy and a new assured shorthold tenancy governed by the Housing Act 1988 would be granted to him 24 hours later. The court held that, for the purposes of s 34(1)(b) of the Housing Act 1988, since the tenant had surrendered his former tenancy the previous day, he could not have been a protected tenant immediately before the new tenancy was granted. Further, there was no need for the Housing Act 1988 to be construed differently as a result of the European Convention on Human Rights.

[1]   [1980] AC 37, [1978] 3 All ER 37, HL.
[2]   See para 19.50.
[3]   [1980] 3 All ER 235, [1980] 1 WLR 898, CA.
[4]   Also see, *Short Bros (Plant) Ltd v Edwards* (1978) 249 Estates Gazette 539, where the Court of Appeal expressed doubts as to the enforceability of an agreement to surrender under the Agricultural Holdings Act 1948.

33.5 Other methods of termination

  Applying the principles specified in *Johnson v Moreton* [1980] AC 37, [1978] 3 All ER 37, HL.
6   [2008] EWCA Civ 1162, [2009] 1 All ER 814, [2009] 1 WLR 2218.

Surrender by operation of law

33.6 An express surrender must, to be effective at law, be by deed[1] and accompanied by the tenant giving up possession. The basis of surrender by operation of law is estoppel. It arises where the tenant deliberately does some act which is inconsistent with the continuation of the tenancy and the landlord concurs or acquiesces. In those circumstances, it would be inequitable for the parties to rely upon the argument that there had been no surrender by deed in order to assert that the term of the tenancy was still continuing.

Surrender by operation of law will take place irrespective of the actual intentions of the parties[2] and despite the absence of any form of documentation. There is no requirement for the tenant actually to deliver up vacant possession of the holding. It is established that the following acts will give rise to a surrender by operation of law:

(a)   The tenant vacating the premises and handing back the keys to the landlord who accepts them unconditionally and not by mistake[3]. In *Artworld Financial Corporation v Safaryan*[3A], the Court of Appeal decided that by accepting the keys to the property 15 months before the end of the term, and allowing a member of the family to live in it, the landlord's actions completed a surrender by operation of law. The landlord had claimed that the family member was simply occupying as a caretaker of the property but the Court was not persuaded since the landlord had also redecorated the property, re-hung curtains and replaced furniture which the tenant had asked to be removed upon taking occupation under the lease.

(b)   The grant by the landlord, and the acceptance by the tenant, of a new tenancy of the premises, provided that it is a valid tenancy; it commences during the term of the old tenancy and it is not granted subject to the old tenancy.

(c)   The variation of the tenancy by an increase of the premises demised[4] or the increase of the length of the contractual term[5].

(d)   The variation of the tenancy by the insertion of a tenant's option to extend the original contractual term[6].

1   Law of Property Act 1925, s 52(1).
2   'This does not depend on the intention of parties but upon the impossibility of the two demises co-existing', per Buckley J in *Jenkin R Lewis & Son Ltd v Kerman* [1971] Ch 477, [1970] 1 All ER 833.
3   *John Laing Construction Ltd v Amber Pass Ltd* [2004] 2 EGLR 128, [2004] 17 EG 128 (CS); *Bellcourt Estates Ltd v Adesina* [2005] EWCA Civ 208, [2005] 2 EGLR 33, [2005] 18 EG 150.
3A   [2009] EWCA Civ 303.
4   *Jenkin R Lewis & Son Ltd v Kerman* [1971] Ch 477, [1970] 1 All ER 833; *Well Barn Farming Ltd v Backhouse* [2005] EWHC 1520 (Ch), [2005] 3 EGLR 109.
5   *Savile Settled Estates, Re, Savile v Savile* [1931] 2 Ch 210.
6   *Savile Settled Estates, Re, Savile v Savile* [1931] 2 Ch 210, *Baker v Merckel* [1960] 1 QB 657, [1960] 1 All ER 668, CA; *Friends' Provident Life Office v British Railways Board* (1995) 73 P & CR 9, [1995] EGCS 140, CA.

146

Chapter 34

INTRODUCTION TO SUCCESSION

THE AGRICULTURE (MISCELLANEOUS PROVISIONS) ACT 1976

34.2 The Agriculture (Miscellaneous Provisions) Act 1976 (A(MP)A 1976)[A1] introduced succession on death (but not on retirement) and provided the scheme for succession which, subject to amendment, particularly to the commercial unit occupation test of eligibility provided by the Agricultural Holdings Act 1984 (AHA 1984), is otherwise very largely the scheme as re-enacted in the consolidating AHA 1986.

The A(MP)A 1976 changed the wording of section 24(2)(g) of the AHA 1948. Section 16 of the A(MP)A 1976 provided that the right to give notice to quit on death accrued *not* on the death of the tenant (or the sole surviving tenant where there had been joint tenants) 'with whom the contract of tenancy was made' and provided for the right to arise on the death of the tenant for the time being, ie 'the tenant under the contract of tenancy'. Additionally, the definition of 'tenant' in the case of a notice to quit on death was changed so as to exclude executors and other persons deriving title by operation of law. Therefore, the decision in *Costagliola v Bunting*[2] would still apply, albeit for different reasons under the revised law, in the event of failure to give notice to quit on death and in consequence the tenancy devolving on the personal representatives of the deceased tenant.

Although following the A(MP)A 1976 the landlord still had his incontestable right to terminate the deceased tenant's tenancy, provisions were introduced for any one or more of a limited class of close relations of the deceased tenant, who satisfied the eligibility tests laid down in the 1976 Act, to make application to the Agricultural Land Tribunal (ALT) for the area in which the holding was situated for a new tenancy to take effect on termination of the old tenancy[3].

The eligibility tests to be satisfied by the successful applicant can be summarised as:

(a)   close relationship to the deceased tenant; and
(b)   derivation of principal source of livelihood from the holding for at least five of the seven years preceding death; and
(c)   the commercial unit occupation test, intended to ensure that the applicant does not occupy sufficient other agricultural land to enable him to make a living without the subject holding.

Apart from considering whether the applicant had satisfied the eligibility tests, the ALT had also to decide if the applicant was suitable. If so, the ALT was obliged to direct that the applicant should be granted a new tenancy unless it granted consent to the landlord for the operation of the notice to quit served following death.

The A(MP)A 1976 made provision for the possibility of there being several applicants and the basis on which the ALT should treat such applications. It also made provision for the landlord, where notice to quit had been given by him, to apply for consent to the operation of his notice to quit, as if the notice to quit was one of the class which did not specify an incontestable ground[4].

The A(MP)A 1976 also introduced provisions for arbitration as to the rent and the terms of the new tenancy and for destroying the old tenancy in the event of there being no (or no effective) notice to quit given by the landlord.

Regulations were passed pursuant to the A(MP)A 1976 setting out procedures which had to be adopted by applicants and by the landlord to implement the provisions of the A(MP)A 1976.

A1 The A(MP)A 1976 came into effect on 14 November 1976.
1   Cf the definition in AHA 1986, s 96 of 'tenant' for all other purposes.
2   [1958] 1 All ER 846, [1958] 1 WLR 580.
3   These were contained in Pt II of the A(MP)A 1976.
4   For a commentary on such notices to quit, see Chs 30 and 31.

Chapter 35
SUCCESSION ON DEATH

APPLICATION OF SUCCESSION RIGHTS

35.1 The general rule is that all tenancies of agricultural holdings carry with them succession rights and that, on the death or retirement of the tenant, an eligible person may apply for succession. The exceptions to that general rule are contained in ss 34, 36(2), 37 and 38 of the Agricultural Holdings Act 1986 (AHA 1986)[1].

[1]   Introduced by the A(MP)A 1976 on 14 November 1976: see para 34.2.

Two previous successions

35.16 The policy of the AHA 1986 is to exclude any further statutory succession after two successions have already occurred. The relevant rules are set out in s 37 of the AHA 1986, which on their face apply only to cases of retirement on death; but the combined effect of ss 37(6), 50(1) and 53(7) is that a succession under the retirement provisions also counts as one of the two permissible statutory successions.

Under s 37 the following events count as one statutory succession under the express terms of s 37 supplemented by other express provisions of Pt IV:

(a)   the grant of a tenancy to a single applicant obtained under a direction of the ALT;

(b)   the grant of a tenancy to two, three or four applicants jointly obtained under a direction of the ALT if the landlord agrees;

(c)   the grant of a tenancy by the landlord to a close relative who had become the sole or sole remaining application for a direction;

(d)   the grant of a tenancy prior to the date of the tenant's death, as a result of an agreement between the landlord and the tenant, to a person who would have been a close relative of the tenant if he had died immediately before the grant;

(e)   in relation to any time on or after 12 September 1984 the assignment of a tenancy, with the agreement of the landlord and tenant for the time being, to a person who, if the tenant had died immediately before the assignment, would have been his close relative. Except in the case of tenancies which were granted before 12 September 1984, or were obtained by virtue of a direction made by the Tribunal following an application made before 12 September 1984, or were granted (following such a direction) in circumstances falling within s 23(6) of the A(MP)A 1976, three further cases arise;

(f)   the grant or obtaining of a tenancy of part only of the land held by the previous tenant;

(g)   the grant of a joint tenancy by the landlord to persons only one of whom is or would have been a close relative;

(h)   an assignment to joint tenants only one of whom is or would have been a close relative.

Some aspects of these provisions were considered by Jowitt J in his decision in *Trustees of Saunders v Ralph*[1].

In *Saunders v Ralph*, the respondent's grandfather, Gilbert Ralph, had been granted a tenancy of the relevant holding on 9 June 1943. In 1957 the original landlord's trustees entered into a memorandum of agreement with Gilbert Ralph and his son Victor which provided that, with effect from 10 October 1957, Victor 'shall become joint tenant of the said holding and the said Gilbert James Ralph and Victor James Ralph shall jointly and severally become responsible for the due performance of all the agreements on the part of the Tenant' contained in the tenancy agreement. In 1988 Victor retired and his son, the respondent, applied to and obtained from the ALT a direction that he was entitled to a tenancy of the holding as Victor's nominated successor. The question between the parties was whether that was a first or second succession. The answer to that question depended upon whether the 1957 transaction was a first succession.

The judge held that it was not. The landlord's argument was that it took effect as a letting of the holding made, as a result of an agreement between the landlord and the tenant for the time being, under a new tenancy granted by the landlord to a person who, if the tenant had died immediately before the grant, would have been his close relative[2]. The judge dismissed that argument on the basis that the 1957 transaction was not a grant of a tenancy at all. It was merely a variation of the existing tenancy, adding an additional tenant to the previous sole tenant. An alternative analysis would have been that it took effect as an assignment of the tenancy by the father to the father and son jointly. Either way, it would not have been a 'grant' and, since it occurred before 12 September 1984, could not have fallen within s 37(2). This part of the judge's decision is correct.

The judge then considered a further argument advanced by the tenant. He held that, even if the 1957 transaction had taken effect as a surrender of the old tenancy and the grant of a new tenancy, it still would not have fallen within the terms of s 37(2). His starting point was the predecessor of s 37(2), ie s 18(5) of the A(MP)A 1976. Under that section he held that 'the statutory reference to a new tenancy granted to a person who would have been a close relative of the outgoing tenant is not apt to include a tenancy granted to that person and another who is not a close relative'. He then noted that the scope of s 18(5) had been enlarged by provisions in the AHA 1984 which are now s 37(4)(b) of the AHA 1986; but that this enlargement did not apply to tenancies falling within what is now subsection (8). The editor agrees with this conclusion, although it may have been reached by starting with s 37 of the AHA 1986 itself.

The judge further held that he would have reached the same conclusion if the transaction had taken effect as an assignment. In reaching this conclusion he was influenced by the provisions of s 37(5) which expressly capture assignments to joint tenants of whom only one is a close relative, and subsection (8) which excludes from subsection (5) any tenancy granted before 12 September 1984. Finally, the judge dealt with an argument advanced by the respondent's counsel in these terms.

'Retrospectivity

For the sake of completeness I deal with the issue of retrospectivity raised by Mr Denbin for the respondent. He submits that in any event a succession falling within subsection (2) of section 37 cannot be one which occurred before the passing of the 1976 Act. The submission, in my judgment, is misconceived. Before the passing of that Act there were no rights of succession. The Act created such rights and subsection (2), just as subsection (1) of what is now section 37, merely placed time limits upon the availability of those rights'.

This conclusion is not easily analysed or understood. Counsel appeared to be arguing that no transaction entered into before the succession provisions came onto the statute-book under the A(MP)A 1976 on 14 November 1976 could count as a succession because, on a proper interpretation of the A(MP)A 1976, it was not the intention of Parliament to treat as first (and possibly second) successions agreements between landlords, outgoing tenants and close relatives of outgoing tenants which had taken place many years and many times before 1976. The argument as formulated by the judge appears to be misconceived but the point is not straightforward and is discussed further below[3].

[1]   (1993) 66 P & CR 335 [1993] 2 EGLR 1.
[2]   AHA 1986, s 37(2), as amended by s 37(7).
[3]   See para 35.19.

Retrospectivity

35.19 The preceding paragraphs made the assumption, when considering Cases 6 to 10 inclusive, that the transactions under consideration had all occurred since 14 November 1976 when the A(MP)A 1976 came into force. The effect of s 37(7) of the AHA 1986 is that an assignment of a tenancy by the original tenant to a close relative with or without others cannot count as a succession if it took place at any time before 12 September 1984. However, that leaves open the question as to how far back in time it is permissible to enquire into a grant of a new tenancy falling within s 37(2).

Ignoring subsections (7) and (8), which have special provisions concerning dates, s 37 taken at its face value would appear to apply only to successions occurring after the AHA 1986 came into force. However, it is clear that successions occurring under the A(MP)A 1976, as amended by the AHA 1984, also count by virtue of the transitional provisions contained in para 1(1) of Sch 13 to the Act:

'Any reference, whether express or implied, in any enactment, instrument or document (including this Act and any enactment amended by Schedule 14 to this Act) to, or to things done or falling to be done under or for the purposes of, any provision of this Act shall, if in so far as the nature of the reference permits, be construed as including, in relation to the times, circumstances or purposes in relation to which the corresponding provision repealed by this Act has or has had effect, a reference to, or as the case may be, to things done or falling to be done under or for the purposes of, that corresponding provision'.

The unsurprising result of this is that, for example, a tenancy obtained by a direction of the ALT under the A(MP)A 1976 counts as a succession just as much as if it were obtained after the 1976 Act had been replaced by the AHA 1986. It is submitted that the same would apply to a voluntary surrender and new grant falling within s 37(2) made at an earlier time when the corresponding provisions of s 18(5) of the A(MP)A 1976 were in force.

The next question is: what about similar voluntary transactions which were entered into before the A(MP)A 1976 came into force? This is the question which appears to have been raised by counsel for the respondent in *Saunders v Ralph*[1] and which the judge did not properly answer.

The transaction under scrutiny in that case had occurred in 1957, some 19 years before statutory succession was introduced. As a matter of impression it would be very surprising if Parliament intended that landlords could exhume the past in this way. The purpose of s 18(5) of the A(MP)A 1976 and its replacement is to allow the parties to come to a voluntary arrangement over succession without having to wait for the original tenant to die. But that is all within the framework of the statutory scheme.

If any voluntary arrangement of the description, whenever made, counts as a first succession, the possible extent of retrospectivity is limitless. It would be possible for the owner of a traditionally managed estate to point to a succession of handovers from one family member to another stretching back over decades. In *Saunders v Ralph*[2], it is submitted that had Gilbert Ralph taken over the tenancy from his father, who had retired on the grounds of old age or disability in 1943, no statutory succession occurred either then or subsequently in 1957, as both events took place before the introduction of statutory succession.

To solve this problem it is submitted that it is legitimate to go back to s 18(5) of the A(MP)A 1976[3]. The voluntary surrender by the outgoing tenant of his tenancy followed by the letting of the holding under a new tenancy fell under subsection (5) if the new tenant was:

'a person who, if the outgoing tenant had died immediately before the grant, would have fallen within paragraphs (a) to (d) of subsection (1) above ...'.

Section 18(1) of the A(MP)A 1976 provided:

'Where after the passing of this Act the sole (or sole surviving) tenant of an agricultural holding dies and is survived by any of the following persons (a) ... (d) ... the following sections of this Part of this Act ... shall apply ...'.

It would also seem that the succession provisions contained in Pt II of the A(MP)A 1976 are wholly governed by those opening words 'Where after the passing of this Act ...'. The editor does not consider that a person who had taken a new tenancy of a holding, with the agreement of the outgoing tenant, before the Act was passed could have been a person who, if the outgoing tenant had died immediately before the grant, would have 'fallen' within paragraphs (a) to (d), since the Act was not in force. To put it another way, if the date of the grant of the new tenancy, and therefore the date on which the outgoing tenant hypothetically died, occurred before the passing of the Act the new tenant could not at that date have fallen within paragraphs (a) to (d) of the Act, because sub-s (1) did not, and could not, at that time, have applied to him.

Applying this analysis, it is not possible to agree with the judgment of Jowitt J in *Saunders v Ralph*[4] on this point. The judge's remarks on this point are plainly obiter. He deals with the argument 'for the sake of completeness', having already decided the case in favour of the respondent on the two major points previously discussed. It is submitted that this part of his judgment would not be followed in a case in which the point had to be fully argued and decided.

Since the ninth edition of this book, this point has been determined by the High Court in *Kemp v Fisher*[5]. HHJ Raynor considered the court's remarks in *Saunders v Ralph* and concluded that they were incorrect. The court found that the AHA 1986 deems these consensual transactions to be successions by direction of the ALT. Were this to operate retrospectively to arrangements made before the A(MP)A 1976 came into force, it would mean assuming a direction of a body which did not exist at that time. As the Judge observed:

> 'If the Act was retrospective in the way suggested by Jowitt J, as the editors of Scammell and Densham say, the possible extent of retrospectivity would be limitless and it would be possible for an owner of a traditionally managed estate to point back to a succession of handovers from one family member to another stretching back over decades. It would need very clear language to induce me to construe the Act in a way that would have that effect and I do not find that the Act was intended to be so construed'.

[1] (1993) 66 P & CR 335 [1993] 2 EGLR 1.
[2] (1993) 66 P & CR 335 [1993] 2 EGLR 1.
[3] AHA 1986, Sch 13 para 1(1).
[4] (1993) 66 P & CR 335 [1993] 2 EGLR 1.
[5] [2009] EWHC 3657 (Ch), [2010] 10 EG 118.

ELIGIBLE PERSONS

Treated as a child of the family

35.32 This category has given rise to difficulties[A1]. The ALT has accepted a distant cousin[1] and a stepson[2] who have lived with the deceased tenant and his wife as member of their family. However, where the nephew of a deceased tenant lived with him, but the deceased tenant was single, the ALT determined that the nephew was ineligible[3]. The ALT's approach may be affected by the introduction of civil partners as eligible successors.

A1   AHA 1986, s 35(2)(d).
1   *Williams v Lady Douglas* (1980) ALT, Wales Area.
2   *Ashby v Holiday* (1983) ALT, Yorks and Lancs Area.
3   *Berridge v Fitzroy* (1980) ALT, West Midlands Area. Also see, *Varley v Marquess of Northampton* (1984) ALT, East Midlands Area.

The principal source of livelihood test

Applicant fully eligible

AGRICULTURAL WORK

35.38 Agricultural work which is closely connected with, but not actually upon the holding causes problems, for example contract work on nearby holdings[1], cattle haulage with farm wagons and cattle dealing. Such work is typically connected with the holding because farm machinery and other equipment is kept on the subject holding and used for the contracting.

The distinction between farming on the holding or the larger unit and dealing in livestock unconnected with the holding is extremely difficult to determine in practice. At the one extreme, an applicant who purchases livestock at markets for the benefit of customers and sells them on without their visiting the holding at all, would probably, to the extent that that income contributed to his livelihood, not have been deriving it from agricultural work on the holding. Alternatively, an applicant who purchases livestock, fattens the animals on the holding and then sells them out finished or as stores, would appear to be engaged in agricultural work to the extent to which the profit is derived from the fattening activity. It is not easy to draw a distinction between those two activities where there is a rapid turnover in livestock which have visited the holding perhaps on little more than a 'bed and breakfast' basis.

As to whether income derived from quota leasing, where a dairy farming enterprise had been discontinued and both the milk quota and sheep quota was leased out, was qualifying income, it has been decided that 'the source of the quota rents was immaterial. The proper consideration was how the applicant had access to them. Once they had gone into the partnership account the only reason he was able to draw on them was because what he drew was in recognition of his agricultural work on the unit of which the holding formed part. He was economically dependent on that unit. His agricultural work on that unit was the source of almost the whole of his livelihood, certainly well over 50%'[2].

1   For a case in which the ALT has decided that work undertaken by an applicant as a contractor on land away from the holding, nevertheless fell to be treated as qualifying agricultural work on the holding, see *Sandercock v Sandercock* (2000) ALT, Midlands Area.
2   *Sandercock v Sandercock* (2000) ALT, Midlands Area. Also see, *Dyson Industries Ltd v Potter* (2007) ALT/Y/S/54.

LIVELIHOOD

35.39 There is a general consensus amongst ALTs that 'livelihood' is a term wider in its implication than mere income and that it covers not merely benefits which are measurable directly in cash terms, such as wages, but also benefits in kind[1]. Therefore, if the applicant has enjoyed rent and rate free living accommodation, with electricity, oil and other services paid for through the farm account and free, or subsidised, motoring, meals and the like, provided those benefits have been granted to the applicant by reason of his agricultural work upon the subject holding, or the larger agricultural unit of which it forms part, then they fall to be evaluated and added to the income received by the applicant in determining the applicant's principal source of livelihood. The first instance ALT decision was upheld by the Divisional Court[2].

In *Helm v ALIH (Properties) Ltd*[3], the ALT had to consider the treatment of board and lodgings. The ALT rejected the landlord's submission that the receipt of board and lodging was not attributable to the applicant's work on the farm but to his being his parents' son and still living at home aged 29. The ALT described this as 'inconceivable'.

The ALT approved the following passage at para 14.50 of Muir Watt and Moss on Agricultural Holdings:

'The valuation of [board and lodgings] shall not be what was the cost to the provider of the accommodation but what was the value of it to the applicant. In other words what would the applicant from time to time have had to pay in order to enjoy the benefit of the accommodation?'

The ALT also approved the valuation approach of the applicant's expert which:

'was to look at the cost of alternative accommodation in the close locality. He used 3 comparables where a room was available to let in a shared house varying in price from £80 to £122 per week to include utilities and bills. He took an average figure of £120 per week and then, to take account of the fact that the applicant had the use of 2 rooms, multiplied it by 1.5 to 2 to arrive at a range of £180 to £240 per week. Having arrived at an annual figure for 2009, he then discounted that figure to allow for the increase in house prices since 2001'.

1   *Judge v Umpleby Trustees* (1978) ALT, Yorks/Lancs Area.
2   *Littlewood v Rolfe* [1981] 2 All ER 51, 43 P & CR 262.
3   (2010) ALT, E1/1130.

SOURCES OF LIVELIHOOD

35.40 If the applicant has other sources of livelihood, apart from his agricultural work or other work upon or from[1] the subject holding or the larger agricultural unit of which it forms part, then they have to be evaluated and set against the sources of livelihood derived from the applicant's agricultural work etc, in determining the applicant's principal source of livelihood. Principal in this context means more than 50%[2].

Sources of livelihood derived from agriculture, but not from agricultural work or other work on or from[3] the holding or larger agricultural unit of which the holding forms part, constitute outside sources of livelihood for this purpose.

In *Casswell v Welby*[4], the Court of Appeal held that the proper test is not where the sums spent by the applicant come from, but why he had access to them. The court applied a test of 'economic dependence': was the applicant economically dependent for his livelihood on his work on the holding? If net profits from the business were insufficient to pay the son's drawings, it was irrelevant that they were funded by increased family loans and overdraft facilities, provided that they were in payment for his work on the farm. Section 36(3)(a) requires the applicant to establish his economic dependence on the holding. In *Casswell v Welby*[5], the applicant's work on the holding was the sole source of his livelihood. Where net profits were insufficient, it was irrelevant how his living expenses were funded.

The application of the Court of Appeal's decision is illustrated in *Collins v Spofforth*[6]. The applicant lived and, for the most part, ate at the farmhouse. He lived frugally and saved well. He had investment income of about £2,500 per year and received regular payments of about £6,700 per year from the farm accounts. In *Casswell*, where the applicant had regularly drawn more than his profit share, it was determined that capital had to be invested in the business before drawings could be regarded as qualifying income. In *Spofforth*, the ALT interpreted *Casswell* to require the applicant to demonstrate his financial dependence upon his work on the holding. The ALT decided that the application would not have received the £6,700 had he not been working on the farm. Accordingly, he derived his principal source of livelihood from work on the holding.

Another issue which arises in practice is how the ALT should assess the joint resources of, for example, a husband and wife, when considering whether the application has derived his principal source of livelihood for the relevant period from his agricultural work on the holding or on an agricultural unit of which the holding forms part.

The point arose in *Monkman v Mitchelson*[7]. Mr Monkman applied for succession following his father's death. He and his wife had bought another property, School House, in nearby Cropton. They lived in that building while another on the same site, The Old School, was being converted. Mr Monkman was now solely responsible for the farming business. His wife kept the books as well as having a part-time job of her own, doing the same thing for a local engineering company. The sole argument concerned the principal source of livelihood test and the basis of calculation on which satisfaction should be decided. Mrs Monkman's figures differentiated farming income, other income, benefits in kind, investments into and drawings from the farm business and an analysis of their joint account and expenditure on improvement of their home. On those calculations, Mr Monkman comfortably satisfied the test in all seven of the years prior to his father's death. The landlords disputed only the basis of calculation of his livelihood. They argued that joint resources should be pooled and allocated between husband and wife, on the basis of which the best result for Mr Monkman would have been 49.17% satisfaction and the worst 31.99%. The ALT preferred the approach adopted by the Monkmans, namely to determine first whether the expense was properly to be considered 'livelihood' and then to assess from whence it came: from the agricultural work on the holding (or the larger unit) or not.

1   *Littlewood v Rolfe* [1981] 2 All ER 51, 43 P & CR 262.
2   *Littlewood v Rolfe* [1981] 2 All ER 51, 43 P & CR 262.
3   See para 35.41.
4   (1995) 71 P & CR 137, [1995] 17 LS Gaz R 48, CA.
5   (1995) 71 P & CR 137, [1995] 17 LS Gaz R 48, CA.
6   (2009) ALT, SW1/1057 and 1058.
7   (2010) ALT/Y/S/59.

THE AGRICULTURAL UNIT

35.47 It was held by the Divisional Court in *Trinity College, Cambridge v Caines*[1] that the agricultural unit of which the holding had to form part must be established at the date of death. If the unit had changed in its constitution, and land which formerly, during the seven-year period, formed part of the unit, had been disposed of, or other land had been acquired, the ALT has to determine the extent of the unit at the date of death. If and in so far as the applicant's livelihood was derived from agricultural work upon land which was part of the unit at the date in question, but has ceased to be so by the date of death, that source of livelihood was deemed to be a source of livelihood derived not from the applicant's agricultural work upon the unit in question. Therefore, it fell to be aggregated with the applicant's other sources of livelihood in determining what was his principal source of livelihood.

Considerable difficulties have been experienced, despite the statutory definition in s 109(2) of the Agriculture Act 1947, in determining what constitutes an agricultural unit at any one time. It is unclear, for example, as to whether land the subject of a seasonal grazing agreement can thereby constitute part of the agricultural unit. It is probable that such land would be excluded[2].

A practical example of the difficulties arose in *Helm v ALIH (Properties) Ltd*[3], where the ALT was asked to consider whether an additional 20 hectares tenanted by the applicant personally but farmed in conjunction with the deceased's holding should be treated as part of a 'larger unit'. The ALT noted that the two areas were worked by the same machinery and adopted the same cultivation system. Income and expenditure for the two areas was dealt with together. The ALT decided in favour of the application that the 20 hectares and the subject holding were farmed as a single agricultural unit. 'Occupation' should be given a 'common sense meaning'.

1   (1983) 272 Estates Gazette 1287.
2   *Keene v Trustees for Guy's and St Thomas' Charity* (2005) ALT, South Western.
3   (2010) ALT, E1/1130.

Applicant treated as eligible

35.51 An applicant, who is not fully eligible so far as the principal source of livelihood test is concerned, may apply to be treated as eligible pursuant to the provisions of s 41 of the AHA 1986. He may do so if:

(a)   he is in all other respects an eligible person;
(b)   the principal source of livelihood test, 'though not fully satisfied', is satisfied 'to a material extent';
(c)   it would be fair and reasonable for him to be treated as fully eligible[1].

An application to be treated as eligible must, like the primary application itself, be made within three months beginning with the day after the date of death[2]. If the application is not made within that three-month period, the ALT may not subsequently entertain such an application[3]. An applicant who believes that he is fully eligible and proceeds upon that basis, only to discover later that for one reason or another he does not satisfy the primary test fully, cannot at the hearing invite the ALT nevertheless to treat him as fully eligible. If there is any doubt as to eligibility, it is wise to draft the applicant to the ALT in the alternative[4].

The primary test must have been satisfied 'to a material extent'[4A]. The problem of how one can satisfy the principal source of livelihood test to a material extent has been considered in *Littlewood v Rolfe*[5], *Wilson v Earl Spencer's Settlement Trustees*[6] and *Thomson v Church Comrs for England*[7]. The combined effect of these three cases is that for the full test to be satisfied to a material extent, the contribution to the applicant's livelihood derived from his agricultural work must be 'substantial in terms of time and important in terms of value'. A shortfall of as much as 50% from compliance with the full test can, in a proper case, amount to compliance with the full test to a 'material extent'. Conversely, it is not sufficient for the applicant merely to show that his agricultural work upon the unit or holding in question made an important contribution towards his livelihood. That is to view the matter the wrong way round. The ALT must determine the amount of the shortfall and then see whether the extent of compliance is sufficient[8].

1   AHA 1986, s 41(1)(b).
2   AHA 1986, s 41(2).
3   *Kellett v Cady* (1980) 257 Estates Gazette 494.
4   See para 35.86ff.
4A   See para 35.81.
5   [1981] 2 All ER 51, 43 P & CR 262.
6   [1985] 1 EGLR 3, 274 Estates Gazette 1254.
7   [2006] EWHC 1773 (Admin), [2006] 43 EG 180.
8   *Littlewood v Rolfe* [1981] 2 All ER 51, (1981) 258 EG 168; *Thomson v Church Comrs for England* [2006] EWHC 1773 (Admin), [2006] 43 EG 180. Also see the discussion at para 35.37.

THE FAIR AND REASONABLE TEST

35.54 It is not sufficient for the applicant to show that he has satisfied the full eligibility test to a material extent and assert that he should be treated as eligible. The applicant must go on and satisfy the ALT that in all circumstances it would be fair and reasonable for the applicant to be able to apply under s 39 of the AHA 1986 for a direction entitling him to a tenancy of the holding. This requires a wide-ranging inquiry and the ALT might, for example, determine that it would not be fair and reasonable for the applicant to be treated as fully eligible if there were substantial land holdings available to him, which did not disqualify him under the commercial unit occupation test because he had so arranged his affairs that he was not a disqualifying occupier, though he had available to him the use of that land. The provision is essentially directed to whether the applicant can satisfy the test, not to initiating a general investigation of the merits of the application. Therefore, consideration of the effect on the beneficiaries of the trustee landlords is not relevant[1].

[1]   *James Raine's Trustee v Raine* (1985) 275 Estates Gazette 374. Also see, *Fowler v Cockerill* (2007) ALT/1/S/55.

PROCEDURE

35.79 As with all features of the agricultural holdings legislation, it is vital for applicants and landlords alike to follow very strictly the procedures laid down both in the AHA 1986 itself and in the regulations passed under it. These are currently the Agricultural Land Tribunals (Rules) Order 2007, SI 2007/3105 ('the 2007 Rules Order').

Those time limits and procedures which are statutorily prescribed are mandatory and inflexible. Failure to comply with them is fatal to the defaulting party. Those time limits and procedures which are prescribed in the regulations passed under the statute are subject to variation by the Chairman of the ALT under rule 51 of the 2007 Rules Order as to time.

Application by potential new tenant

35.81 Any eligible person wishing to apply for a new tenancy must make his application within three months of the date following the date of death of the deceased tenant. Until the 2007 Rules Order came into force on 15 January 2008, the application had to be in accordance with Form 1 (Succession on Death) which appears in the Appendix to the Agricultural Land Tribunals (Succession to Agricultural Tenancies) Order 1984[1], or in a form 'substantially to the like effect'. The forms are no longer prescribed. They are now issued by the ALT in a standardised format[1A].

Before making an application for succession on death, the applicant must deliver a notice in writing of his intention to do so to all interested parties[1B]. Interested parties is defined in the 2007 Rules Order as 'every person who appears to the applicant to be an interested party'[1C].

The application must relate to the whole holding. There is no provision for applying for succession in respect of part only[2].

The three-month time limit is expressed to be 'the period of three months beginning with the day after the date of death'[3]. The corresponding day rule applies[4].

In *Townson v Executors of Waddington deceased*[5], the applicant applied for succession following his mother's death. The ALT observed that there were 'surprising gaps and shortcomings in the evidence put forward by and on behalf of the applicant'. At the substantive hearing the applicant applied to amend his application to include the alternative ground under s 41 of the AHA 1986 to be treated as eligible in that he satisfied the principal source of livelihood test to a 'material content'[6]. The ALT rejected the application to amend finding that the application under s 41 had to be made within three months after the date of death of the tenant and that the ALT had no power to extend the time limit.

If the applicant is not fully eligible, but wishes to apply under s 41 of the AHA 1986 to be treated as eligible, that application must be made within the same three-month period. The prescribed form for an application under s 41 contains a part (Part B) dealing with a person who is not fully eligible but who wishes to be treated as if he was. If there is doubt as to whether the applicant is fully eligible or not, that part of the form can be completed without prejudice to the applicant's primary contention that he is fully eligible. If he does not complete that part of the form in the belief that he is fully eligible, and he is found not to be fully eligible, he is not then able to apply at that stage to be treated as eligible: his failure to complete the form in the first place being then fatal.

1   SI 1984/1301.
1A   See para 46.7.
1B   Agricultural Land Tribunals (Rules) Order 2007, SI 2007/3105, r 40(2).
1C   Agricultural Land Tribunals (Rules) Order 2007, SI 2007/3105, rr 1 and 2(2)(f).
2   For the provisions relating to the making of a direction in respect of part only, see para 35.93.
3   AHA 1986, s 39(1).
4   *Dodds v Walker* [1981] 2 All ER 609, [1981] 1 WLR 1027, HL. See para 42.27.
5   (2009) ALT/W/S/652.
6   See para 35.51.

35.82 The time limit of three months for applying to be treated as eligible is statutorily prescribed and is, therefore, mandatory and inflexible. Neither the chairman nor the ALT has any power to extend the time.

At the same time as making an application to the ALT, the applicant must give notice of his application to the landlord. Under the rules applying before the 2007 Rules Order, failure to serve notice of the application upon the landlord is not fatal to the applicant, provided the landlord is not prejudiced[1].

As to the contents of an application to the ALT, see chapter 46[2].

Under the Agricultural Land Tribunals (Rules) Order 1978[3] the application had to be accompanied by various documents, as listed in art 16(4). These included all documents on which the party making the application intends to rely in support of his case. This rule was more honoured in the breach than in the observance. In practice, documents were often produced by the parties after the application had been made.

The 2007 Rules Order no longer prescribes the documents[4].

Normally an applicant will need to produce the following documents to establish his eligibility and suitability to be granted a new tenancy in succession to the deceased former tenant:

(a)   the deceased tenant's death certificate, so as to establish the fact and date of death;

(b)   the applicant's birth certificate – full, not shortened form – so as to establish the close relationship;

(c)   the applicant's marriage certificate – in the case of a widow or married daughter applicant;

(d)   farm partnership agreement or contract of employment (if applicable);

(e)   the farm accounts for the relevant five years, ending with the date of death. It is a wise precaution to produce seven years' accounts so that selection of the five years can be made by discarding any two where losses or problems of eligibility arise;

(f)   a statement of the applicant's wages (if applicable);

(g)   a statement setting out any outside sources of livelihood, whether agriculturally related (for example, contracting, cattle dealing, cattle haulage, share farming, etc) or non-agricultural (for example, dividend income from stock exchange investments);

(h)   a copy of any tenancy agreement or other agreement relating to any other land occupied by the applicant;

(i)   copies of certificates relating to any relevant academic qualifications of the applicant (for example, HND, City & Guilds certificates, etc);

(j)   a medical certificate stating the applicant's state of health;

(k)   a full statement of the applicant's own capital and any other capital available to be used to finance the farming in the event of the applicant being successful (for example, capital belonging to members of the applicant's family, with an appropriate statement as to the arrangements made or to be made with the financier concerned);

(l)   if an overdraft or other form of borrowing is to be relied upon, a letter from the bank or lending house specifying the facility available and the term or terms of the loan;

(m)   if any changes are to be made in the farming system, a statement of those changes and a forward farm budget and cash flow projection showing how the farm is to be farmed henceforth;

(n)   the deceased tenant's will, probate and Inland Revenue account – if the applicant is relying upon any inherited monies;

(o)   a map of the subject holding to the scale of 6' to one mile or 1/10.000, or larger;

(p)   a similar map or plan of any other land comprised in the agricultural unit of which the holding forms part and any other land occupied by the applicant;

(q)   the notice to quit given (if any);

(r)   the tenancy agreement of the subject holding.

35.82 *Succession on death*

This list is not exhaustive, but is indicative of the type of documents that a successful applicant is likely to have to adduce and which should accompany his application. If any document is unavailable at the time the application is made, it can be provided subsequently. An applicant should not delay the lodging of his application on account of unavailability of documents.

1   *Kellett v Alexander* (1980) 257 EG 494.
2   See para 46.6.
3   Agricultural Land Tribunals (Rules) Order 1978, SI 1978/259, art 16(4).
4   See para 46.7.

The landlord's reply

35.83 If the landlord wishes to oppose the whole or any part of the applicant's application, he must complete the form required by the ALT[1] and return this within one month from the date on which the copy of the application by the applicant was served by the ALT on the landlord.

1   See the Schedule to SI 2007/3105, r 9.

35.84 Frequently, the landlord will find that the applicant has not provided sufficient information to enable the landlord to determine whether the applicant is prima facie eligible and/or suitable. The landlord will require further information and the supply of further documents to make such an assessment. In those circumstances it is normal for the landlord to put the applicant to proof, while at the same time seeking through the ALT the supply of further information and the delivery of documents in support.

If the landlord fails to reply within the prescribed period of one month, or such further period as the Chairman shall allow by the exercise of his discretion provided by r 51[1], then the landlord is not entitled to dispute any matter alleged by the applicant in his application[2].

1   Agricultural Land Tribunals (Rules) Order 2007, SI 2007/3105.
2   Agricultural Land Tribunals (Rules) Order 2007, SI 2007/3105, r 4(6).

Landlord's application for consent to operation of the notice to quit

35.85 A landlord who has given notice to quit pursuant to Case G of Pt I of Sch 3 to the AHA 1986 may apply for consent to the operation of the notice to quit[1]. The time limit for the making of an application by the landlord for consent to the operation of the notice to quit is as follows:

(a)   Where only one application for the grant of a new tenancy is made, at any time after the landlord receives notice of the application until the expiration of four months after a copy of the application itself has been served upon him. The Secretary of the ALT is required to inform the landlord at the start of the period of four months[2].

(b)   If two or more applications for succession are made then the four-month period is extended until one month after the date on which the number of applications which are pending is reduced to one, or within one month of such earlier date as the ALT may direct[3].

Many landlords make applications for consent to the operation of the notice to quit almost as a matter of course, though very rarely are they well advised to do so[4]. Any application by the landlord must also be accompanied by all documents on which the landlord relies (as for the applicant's application)[5]. The landlord should also give all necessary particulars of hardship and the like, if a greater hardship ground is relied upon. Even if it is not, he should do so to satisfy the fair and reasonable landlord proviso.

[1]   For the commentary on this provision, see para 31.90 and note that even if no application for consent is made the notice to quit will still take effect regardless of the success of the application. The effect of consent is not to render a notice which would otherwise be inoperative effective but to preclude an applicant who is eligible and suitable from obtaining a direction for succession. AHA 1986, s 44.
[2]   Agricultural Land Tribunals (Rules) Order 2007, SI 2007/3105, r 41(1).
[3]   Agricultural Land Tribunals (Rules) Order 2007, SI 2007/3105, r 41(2).
[4]   See para 35.78.
[5]   See para 35.82.

Multiple applications

35.86   If more than one application is received by the ALT within the relevant period of three months from the date of death of the tenant, then the procedures to be followed by the ALT are set out in the AHA 1986.

If one of the applicants is a person 'validly designated by the deceased in his will as the person he wishes to succeed him as tenant of the holding', the ALT must first determine whether that person is both eligible and suitable. The ALT may only consider any other applicant if the ALT determines that the person designated in the will is not an eligible and/or suitable person to become the tenant of the holding[1]. It is a wise precaution for a tenant to nominate his successor in his will or codicil[2].

If more than one person claims to be a designated applicant then the ALT must consider the validity of each claim[3].

[1]   AHA 1986, s 39(4).
[2]   See para 35.89.
[3]   Agricultural Land Tribunals (Rules) Order 2007, SI 2007/3105, r 42.

35.87   If no person is designated by the will, or if the person so designated is found by the ALT to be ineligible and/or unsuitable, then the ALT must consider each of the other applicants and determine whether each is both eligible and suitable[1].

The ALT must, subject to any direction by the Chairman, consider any question of eligibility and suitability by applying the 1986 Act in a specified order[2].

[1]   AHA 1986, s 39(6).
[2]   Agricultural Land Tribunals (Rules) Order 2007, SI 2007/3105, r 43.

35.88 If the landlord consents, the ALT may give a direction specifying any two, three or four applicants as being entitled to a joint tenancy of the holding[1]. If the landlord objects to a joint tenancy, or indeed to any one of the applicants being the subject of a direction entitling him to a tenancy of the holding, then the ALT must, subject to affording the landlord and any other suitable applicant an opportunity of stating his views on the suitability of that applicant[2], determine which, in the ALT's opinion, is the most suitable person to be the subject of a direction entitling him to the tenancy of the holding[3].

The landlord will be deemed not to consent if he does not respond to the ALT within the period specified by the Chairman[4].

[1] AHA 1986, s 39(9).
[2] AHA 1986, s 39(7).
[3] AHA 1986, s 39(8).
[4] Agricultural Land Tribunals (Rules) Order 2007, SI 2007/3105, r 43(3).

35.89 It very frequently happens that multiple applications are made not because the applicants are in competition for the holding, but so as to safeguard the tenancy being lost by some technical disqualification of a sole applicant. For example, a widow and son might apply in circumstances where both wish the son to be successful but the widow's application was made in case the son might be found too inexperienced or not to have satisfied the principal source of livelihood test fully. In those circumstances, a wise precaution for the tenant to take during his lifetime is to nominate his son in his will so that the widow's application can be left in abeyance pending determination of the son's. If there is no such nomination, the ALT must hear both applications together and determine which applicant is the more suitable. If the widow is then successful, despite the views of both applicants that the son should be treated as the favoured candidate, one of the two potential rights of succession will have been 'used up'.

Where two or more applications are made, each applicant may, if he wishes to oppose any of the other applicants, file a reply to the other applications and, if he wishes to do so, must file the reply with the ALT within one month of the expiry of the relevant period[1].

If the applicants are not in competition, but wish to apply for a joint tenancy, the form, suitably adapted, must be completed within the same period of one month so as to constitute the application for a joint tenancy[2].

[1] Agricultural Land Tribunals (Rules) Order 2007, SI 2007/3105, r 41.
[2] Agricultural Land Tribunals (Rules) Order 2007, SI 2007/3105, r 41.

Interlocutory matters

35.90 Once the exchange of applications and replies has been concluded, the Secretary of the ALT is required 'as soon as practicable' to fix a date, time and place for the hearing of the application and to give at least 14 days' notice of the hearing[1].

Frequently, documents will not have been supplied by either the applicant in support of his application for a direction, or the landlord in support of his application for consent to the operation of the notice to quit, in which event the aggrieved party may apply under r 5[2], in writing, for any directions on any matter which the Chairman has power to determine, including a request for the provision of documents or other information[3].

Before making a determination in the case of any applicant, the ALT must give the landlord an opportunity to state his views as to the suitability of the applicant[4].

[1]   Agricultural Land Tribunals (Rules) Order 2007, SI 2007/3105, r 16.
[2]   Agricultural Land Tribunals (Rules) Order 2007, SI 2007/3105.
[3]   For the provisions regarding interlocutory matters generally, see Ch 46.
[4]   AHA 1986, s 39(7).

The hearing

A single applicant

35.91 If there is only one application for succession, then the applicant must open his case. If the landlord has sought consent to the operation of his notice to quit, that is treated as a counter-claim. The procedure is the same as for civil proceedings in the High Court[1].

[1]   Agricultural Land Tribunals (Rules) Order 2007, SI 2007/3105, r 23.

Multiple applications

35.92 As to the procedure as to multiple applications[1], if the ALT determines that one or more of several applicants is both eligible and suitable, but no application has been made by the landlord for consent to the operation of his notice to quit, before making any direction in favour of the applicant in question, the proceedings must first be adjourned to enable the landlord within one month thereafter to make an application if he wishes for consent to the operation of his notice to quit[2].

[1]   See para 35.86.
[2]   Agricultural Land Tribunals (Rules) Order 2007, SI 2007/3105.

Chapter 36

SUCCESSION ON RETIREMENT

THE APPLICANT'S QUALIFICATION FOR SUCCESSION

Eligibility

Principal source of livelihood test

TIME FOR SATISFYING THE TEST

36.24 Section 50(2)(a) of the AHA 1986 refers to the principal source of livelihood test in 'the last seven years'. It does not specify whether the seven-year period expires on the date of the retirement notice, on the date of the application or the date on which the retirement notice is to take effect (ie more than a year after the date of the retirement notice). In the previous edition of this book and the draft of this edition, it was submitted that, as the retirement notice must nominate a 'single eligible person'[1], the applicant must be possessed of the qualifications of eligibility at the date on which the retirement notice is given. That would support the conclusion that the seven-year period expires on the date of the retirement notice and not at any later date[2]. Section 53(5) of the AHA 1986 reinforces this view by requiring the ALT to be satisfied in due course that the applicant was 'an eligible person at the date of the giving of the retirement notice'. The contrary argument was that the principal livelihood test had to be satisfied at all times during a period from the date of service of the retirement notice until the consideration of the issue by the ALT[3]. The view expressed in this book was adopted by the ALT in *Shirley v Crabtree*[4]. The ALT stated a case for the High Court which upheld the decision of the ALT[5].

[1]   See AHA 1986, s 49(1)(b).
[2]   This would also be consistent with the decision of the House of Lords in *Jackson v Hall* [1980] AC 854, [1980] 1 All ER 177, HL, where it was held that the commercial unit occupation test had to be satisfied at the date of death and continuing thereafter.
[3]   This view is expressed by the editor of *Woodfall: Landlord and Tenant* (Looseleaf edn, 1994) Sweet & Maxwell, at para 21.195.
[4]   (2006) ALT, Midlands.
[5]   [2007] EWHC 1532 (Admin), [2008] 1 WLR 18, [2007] NLJR 975.

PROCEDURE

36.29 As with nearly all features of the agricultural holdings legislation, the procedural requirements relating to an application for succession on retirement must be most strictly complied with. Failure to satisfy the statutory time limits and procedures is fatal to the applicant's and/or landlord's case. The time limits are short.

166

Although there is limited power for the chairman or the ALT itself to relieve an applicant or landlord from non-compliance with the regulations[1], there is no such power if the failure is to comply with a statutory time limit. The procedural requirements, therefore, must be most closely studied and followed. They are as follows.

[1]   Agricultural Land Tribunals (Rules) Order 2007, SI 2007/3105, r 51.

Retirement notice

36.30   The procedural trigger for succession on retirement is the retirement notice[1] to be given by the tenant of the holding (or in the case of a joint tenancy, all the tenants)[2]. There is no prescribed form for a retirement notice. All that is required is that the tenant (or if there is a joint tenancy, all the tenants) must give notice to the landlord, in whatever terms, that he or they 'wish a single eligible person named in the notice to succeed him or them as tenant of the holding as from a date specified in the notice'[3]. That date has to be a date on which the tenancy could have been terminated by notice to quit falling not less than one nor more than two years from the date of the notice, ie the annual term date between one and two years after the date of the notice[4].

The tenant who can give a retirement notice does not include any person who is holding the tenancy in a fiduciary capacity, ie as executor, administrator, committee of the estate, trustee in bankruptcy or other person deriving title from a tenant by operation of law. This is because the definition of tenant for the purposes of the giving of a retirement notice is the same as the definition of a tenant whose death can give rise to a Case G notice to quit[5].

The retiring tenant (or each of them, if there is more than one) must have attained the age of 65 or be permanently incapacitated[6].

The AHA 1986 does not specify that the notice must be in writing. It is implied. The retirement notice has to accompany the application to be made by the nominated successor[7]. Unless the notice is in writing, that requirement cannot be satisfied.

Where the ALT considers the nominated successor's application and refuses to make a direction, the unsuccessful nominated successor is barred from applying for succession on the tenant's later death[8]. This will be the case even where a significant period has elapsed between the ALT's refusal of succession pursuant to a retirement notice and the tenant's later death, during which the unsuccessful nominated successor may have overcome the earlier obstacles to him establishing both eligibility and suitability.

If the ALT rejects the nominated successor's application, the tenancy remains vested in the retiring tenant. The retirement notice is of no effect[9]. This is described in the AHA 1986 as being without prejudice to the operation of s 51(2), as a result of which this retirement notice, even though it has become abortive by the dismissal of the application by the ALT, will have excluded any further application pursuant to a retirement notice given by the tenant[10].

It is clear that a second retirement notice cannot be given, nominating as a successor somebody who has already applied and failed to obtain a direction from the ALT because he was found to be unsuitable or because the landlord succeeded on greater hardship grounds. In the last edition of this book it was suggested that an applicant who is found to be ineligible might, upon acquiring the eligibility requirements, be able to reapply pursuant to a second retirement notice. This is because the definition of a retirement notice is a notice specifying an eligible person[11]. There remains no authority in relation to this point.

If an application for retirement succession is withdrawn or abandoned, it is treated as if it had never been made. A further retirement notice can be given[12]. This is an important safeguard for an applicant who discovers a flaw in his application at some stage up to the time when the ALT hearing takes place. Such an applicant can always withdraw, but the application must be withdrawn prior to the hearing[13]. The procedures can be gone through afresh with a new retirement notice and a fresh application then being made. Time will be lost in the process, but the applicant will not then stand to lose the opportunity to become tenant of the farm for all time.

1   AHA 1986, s 49(3).
2   AHA 1986.
3   AHA 1986, s 49(1)(b).
4   AHA 1986.
5   AHA 1986, ss 49(2) and 34(2). See para 31.95.
6   AHA 1986, s 51(3). See para 36.15ff.
7   AHA 1986, s 53(3)(a).
8   AHA 1986, s 57(4).
9   AHA 1986, s 53(9).
10   AHA 1986.
11   AHA 1986, ss 49(1)(b), 49(3), 51(2) and 53.
12   AHA 1986, s 53(10).
13   Agricultural Land Tribunals (Rules) Order 2007, SI 2007/3105, r 6.

Application for succession

36.32 Before making an application for succession on death, the applicant must deliver a notice in writing of his intention to do so to all interested parties[A1]. Interested parties is defined in the Agricultural Land Tribunals (Rules) Order 2007 as 'every person who appears to the applicant to be an interested party'[B1].

Once a retirement notice has been given, then the nominated successor must within one month apply to the ALT in the form available from the ALT[1] for the grant of a new tenancy. The time limit of one month runs from the day after the date of the giving of the retirement notice. It is a statutorily prescribed time limit which is mandatory and inflexible[2]. The application must be signed by both the retiring tenant and the nominated successor[3]. It must be accompanied by the retirement notice. These requirements are also statutory requirements[4].

The Agricultural Land Tribunals (Rules) Order 2007 requires that the application should also be accompanied by any plan[5] or other document[6] which the party making the application intends to adduce in support of his case. This provision is non-statutory. The chairman may dispense with these requirements[7]. For a commentary on the documents which should accompany the application, see para 35.82.

At the same time as the applicant applies to the ALT for the grant of a new tenancy in succession to the retiring tenant, the applicant must give notice of the application to the landlord in Form 6[8]. This requirement is not a statutory requirement and, if not satisfied, does not invalidate the application[9].

[A1]   Agricultural Land Tribunals (Rules) Order 2007, SI 2007/3105, r 40(2).
[B1]   Agricultural Land Tribunals (Rules) Order 2007, SI 2007/3105, rr 1 and 2(f).
[1]   See para 46.6.
[2]   AHA 1986, s 53(2). See *Kellett v Alexander* (1980) 257 Estates Gazette 494. For the corresponding day rule and the calculation of the one-month period, see *Dodds v Walker* [1981] 2 All ER 609, [1981] 1 WLR 1027, HL.
[3]   Signature by an agent has been found to be insufficient: see *White v de Pelet* (1993) ALT, South Western Area.
[4]   AHA 1986, s 53(3).
[5]   Agricultural Land Tribunals (Rules) Order 2007, SI 2007/3105, r 7(1)(a).
[6]   Agricultural Land Tribunals (Rules) Order 2007, SI 2007/3105, r 7(1)(b).
[7]   Agricultural Land Tribunals (Rules) Order 2007, SI 2007/3105, r 7(2).
[8]   Agricultural Land Tribunals (Rules) Order 2007, SI 2007/3105, r 40.
[9]   See *Kellett v Alexander* (1980) 257 Estates Gazette 494.

Landlord's reply

36.33 A landlord who intends to oppose the whole or any part of the application made by the nominated successor must, within one month of the service of the application upon him, serve a reply in the form available from the ALT[1]. The requirement of the landlord to file a reply within one month is not a statutory requirement. The landlord may apply to the chairman for an extension of time, which the chairman may grant on such terms and conditions, if any, as appear to him just[2].

If the landlord wishes to allege that greater hardship would be caused to him by the ALT giving the direction than would be caused to the applicant by refusing his application, he must specify such allegation in the reply and set out the reasons for the claim[3].

[1]   Agricultural Land Tribunals (Rules) Order 2007, SI 2007/3105, r 4. See para 46.2.
[2]   Agricultural Land Tribunals (Rules) Order 2007, SI 2007/3105, rr 4(5) and 51.
[3]   SI 1984/1301, Schedule r 4(2).

Chapter 42

MISCELLANEOUS PROVISIONS

SERVICE OF NOTICES

Service by post: registered post and recorded delivery

42.15 Section 93(1) of the AHA 1986 expressly authorises service by registered post or by recorded delivery[1]. If a notice, request, demand or other instrument under the AHA 1986 is 'sent' by registered post or recorded delivery, again due service (ie service in the ordinary course of post) is presumed, unless the contrary is proved. The practical advantage of sending notices and other formal communications in this way is that the sender does not need to rely upon the rebuttable presumption of due service in the ordinary course of post. If the recorded service is used, the sender should be able to prove due service positively[2]. If a notice is served by recorded delivery post, but the addressee refuses to accept the document and it is then returned through the 'dead letter post' system, it is submitted that due service has not been effected[3].

[1] AHA 1986, s 93(1) is derived from the AHA 1984, Sch 2 para 1(7), Sch 3 para 21, and AHA 1948, s 92. Although the Recorded Delivery Service Act 1962, ss 1 and 2, clearly applied to the service of notices under s 92 of the AHA 1948, the matter has now been put beyond doubt by s 93 of the AHA 1986 which extends the former s 92 by specifically referring to the recorded delivery service.
[2] For cases in which notices were held not to have been served although the registered or recorded delivery postal service were used, see *Beer v Davies* [1958] 2 QB 187, [1958] 2 All ER 255, DC; *Layton v Shires* [1960] 2 QB 294, [1959] 3 All ER 587, DC; *Hosier v Goodall* [1962] 2 QB 401, [1962] 1 All ER 30, DC; and *R v County of London Quarter Sessions Appeal Committee, ex p Rossi* [1956] 1 QB 682, [1956] 1 All ER 670, CA. NB: this was because the contrary of due service was proved.
[3] *Hallinan (Lady) v Jones* [1984] 2 EGLR 20, 272 Estates Gazette 1081. For a decision to contrary effect, see *Van Grutten v Trevenen* [1902] 2 KB 82, CA, but note that this was a decision under the 1883 Act, ie an Act passed before the Interpretation Act 1889. Note the wording of s 26 of the Interpretation Act 1889 which negatives the presumption in s 93(1) where the contrary to due service is proved. See also, *French v Elliott* [1959] 3 All ER 866, [1960] 1 WLR 40.

42.16 In *CA Webber (Transport) Ltd v Railtrack Ltd*[1], the tenancies were lettings of business premises. The landlord sent notices on a Friday to the tenant terminating the tenancies and stating that it would oppose any application to the court for new tenancies. The tenant had an arrangement with the Post Office not to receive post on a Saturday. It received the notices on the Monday or Tuesday. The tenant commenced proceedings contending that the notices were invalid because they were served less than six months before the termination of the tenancies. This argument would not have been available had the notices been received on the Saturday. The county court judge held that the service of the notices was governed by s 23 of the Landlord and Tenant Act 1927 and not s 7 of the Interpretation Act 1972. She also found that had s 7 applied, then service would have been effected on the Saturday. The tenant appealed contending:

(a)   The date of receipt was governed by s 7 of the Interpretation Act 1972.
(b)   Alternatively, on its proper construction, s 23 of the Landlord and Tenant Act 1927, meant that the notices had been served at the time of the attempt to deliver or on actual delivery.
(c)   Alternatively, s 3 of the Human Rights Act 1998 required the court to give effect to s 23 in a manner which was compatible with rights under the European Convention of Human Rights: Article 6(1) and Article 1 of the First Protocol.

The Court of Appeal dismissed the appeal[2]. It held that where a notice is served by a primary method authorised by s 23 of the Landlord and Tenant Act 1927, for example, by recorded delivery, it is immaterial whether the notice is received. Section 7 of the Interpretation Act 1978 has no application and the risk of non-receipt lies with the intended recipient. The date of service is the date on which the server puts the notice in the post[3].

In *WX Investments Ltd v Begg*[4], a tenancy of business premises incorporated the provisions as to service of notices contained in s 196(4) of the Law of Property Act 1925[5], by virtue of which notices under the lease were sufficiently served if sent by the recorded delivery service. The tenant had the right to serve a counter-notice within 14 days of the receipt of a rent notice specifying the rent that she was willing to pay. If no counter-notice was served, the rent was fixed at that in the rent notice. On 22 September the landlord sent a rent notice. The tenant's agent posted a counter-notice by first-class recorded delivery. Unsuccessful attempts were made to deliver it on 25 September and 30 September. On the second occasion, a card was left informing the landlord's agent that the Post Office was holding an item of mail. By the time that the counter-notice was collected, the 14-day period had expired. The Court of Appeal, in dismissing the landlord's appeal, held that s 196(4) of the Law of Property Act 1925 did not merely provide for service by recorded delivery at the time at which delivery was actually effected but by using the words 'and that service shall be deemed' introduced a presumed date of delivery regardless of when, or if, delivery actually took place. Service of the counter-notice was deemed to have occurred on the first occasion on which the Post Office attempted to deliver it notwithstanding the fact that it was not received until much later.

In a county court case it was found that the deemed service provisions of s 23 of the Landlord and Tenant Act 1927 do not apply to a letting of an agricultural holding under the AHA 1986 because s 93 of the AHA 1986 is subject to the provisions of the Interpretation Act 1978. Accordingly, there is deemed service in the ordinary course of post and not when the notice is committed to the postal system[6].

1   [2003] EWCA Civ 1167, [2004] 3 All ER 202, [2004] 1 EGLR 49.

2   It also decided that *Lex Services plc v Johns* (1989) 59 P & CR 427, [1990] 1 EGLR 92
     was decided per incuriam. Also see, *R v County of London Quarter Sessions Appeal
     Committee, ex p Rossi* [1956] 1 QB 682, [1956] 1 All ER 670, CA.
3   Cf *WX Investments Ltd v Begg* [2002] EWHC 925 (Ch), [2002] 1 WLR 2849, [2002]
     3 EGLR 47.
4   [2002] EWHC 925 (Ch), [2002] 1 WLR 2849, [2002] 3 EGLR 47. Also see, *Holwell
     Securities Ltd v Hughes* [1974] 1 All ER 161, [1974] 1 WLR 155, CA; *Godwin v Swindon
     Borough Council* [2001] EWCA Civ 1478, [2001] 4 All ER 641, [2002] 1 WLR 997;
     Wilderbrook Ltd v Oluwu [2005] EWCA Civ 1361, [2006] 2 P & CR 54, 149 Sol Jo LB
     1451.
5   As adapted by the Recorded Delivery Service Act 1962, s 1(1).
6   *Thompson v Bradley* (2006), Birmingham County Court. Lawtel 15 January 2007.

Service by facsimile and e-mail

42.18 Service by email or other comparable modern electronic transmission
presents a greater problem for the party seeking to rely upon such transmission as constituting due service. An e-mail communication which is available,
but not taken up, or even one which is read from a screen with no hard copy
taken, can hardly be said to have been delivered to the recipient or 'left at his
proper address'.

In some areas of law, provision has been made for service by electronic means
of communication[1]. No provisions have been introduced applying such means
to the AHA 1986.

The Agricultural Tenancies Act 1995 (ATA 1995) specifically provides that in
the case of farm business tenancies, text transmitted by 'facsimile or other
electronic means' is not to constitute due service unless service in that way is
authorised 'by written agreement made at any time before the giving of the
Notice'[2].

In a case relating to a notice given pursuant to a tenant's break clause in
relation to a commercial lease, the Court of Appeal held that a notice sent by
facsimile was not valid. The lease provided that the notice was to be valid only
when given by hand or posted to an appropriate address unless receipt by
other means was acknowledged by the landlord. The tenant posted the notice
to the incorrect address and although further copies were faxed to the
landlord's offices receipt was not acknowledged.

It was held by the Court of Appeal that the formal requirements in the lease
relating to service went to the essential validity of the notice and were not
merely evidential. The absence of any obligation on the landlord to acknowledge an informal notice did not prejudice the tenant since it could serve a
formal notice by hand or by post[3].

1   See, for example, Companies Act 1985 (Electronic Communications) Order 2000,
     SI 2000/3373. Also see, *PNC Telecom plc v Thomas* [2002] EWHC 2848 (Ch), [2004]
     1 BCLC 88, [2003] BCC 202. Also see, *Katana v Catalyst Communities Housing Ltd*
     [2010] EWCA Civ 370, (2010) 26 EG 92.
2   ATA 1995, s 36(2) and (3). See para 17.2. Note that the application of *Hastie and
     Jenkinson v McMahon* [1991] 1 All ER 255, [1990] 1 WLR 1575, CA, should not be relied
     upon as being necessarily applicable to the service of notices under the AHA 1986.

3   *Orchard (Developments) Holdings plc v Reuters Ltd* [2009] EWCA Civ 6, [2009] 1 P & CR D51, [2009] 16 EG 140.

Joint tenants

42.21 In the case of joint tenants, the common law rule is that a notice or other document addressed to all of the joint tenants served on any one of them, on behalf of them all, constitutes good service[1]. It has also been held that service of a notice addressed to a firm is good service on the partners[2].

It should be noted that, in the case of two companies being part of the same group, one trading and one dormant, it is essential to establish which of the companies must be served to establish effective service[3].

1   *Doe d Macartney (Lord) v Crick* (1805) 5 Esp 196. It is nevertheless safer to serve notices on all the joint tenants. See *Jones v Lewis* (1973) 25 P & CR 375, 117 Sol Jo 373, CA for a case in which the notice was bad because it was only addressed to one of two joint tenants and the statutorily prescribed form had strictly to be complied with. See also *Blewett v Blewett* [1936] 2 All ER 188, CA in the context of forfeiture. For a fuller discussion of the issues relating to joint tenancies, see para 29.10.
2   *Carpenter v Phelps Bros* (1979) unreported. *Sed quaere* especially in the case of a 'penal notice' such as a notice to remedy or a notice to pay. But for a case in which service on a partnership of High Court proceedings was considered, see *Marsden v Kingswell Watts* [1992] 2 All ER 239, CA.
3   In *Prudential Assurance Co Ltd v Exel UK Ltd* [2009] EWHC 1350 (Ch), [2010] 1 P & CR 90, [2009] PLSCS 200, both companies needed to be served.

Service on agent or servant

42.22 The effect of s 93(3) of the AHA 1986 is that service on an agent is due service, provided the agent was authorised to receive such notice on behalf of his principal[1]. The person responsible for the control of the management or farming, as the case may be, of the agricultural holding, is deemed to be agent for the tenant[2]. In contrast to the common law position, there is no need for the agent or servant to be authorised to receive the notices being served.

Generally a landlord's statutory notice can be served on the duly authorised agent of the tenant[3]. The agency does not survive the death of the principal[4].

1   *Hemington v Walter* (1950) 155 Estates Gazette 134, 100 L Jo 51; *Tanham v Nicholson* (1872) LR 5 HL 561; and *Wilbraham v Coclough* [1952] 1 All ER 979.
2   *Egerton v Rutter* [1951] 1 KB 472, [1951] 1 TLR 58, where son of deceased intestate tenant in possession of and running the holding, was held to be deemed to be agent for the President of the Family Division (now the Public Trustee). Also see, *Harrowby (Earl) v Snelson* [1951] 1 All ER 140, 95 Sol Jo 108 and *Sweeny v Sweeny* (1876) IR 10 CL 375.
3   *Galinski v McHugh* (1988) 57 P & CR 359, [1989] 1 EGLR 109, CA; *Yenula Properties Ltd v Naidu* [2002] EWCA Civ 719, [2003] HLR 229, [2002] 3 EGLR 28.
4   *Lodgepower Ltd v Taylor* [2004] EWCA Civ 1367, [2005] 1 EGLR 1, [2005] 08 EG 192.

Service of notice to quit on death

42.23 The combined effect of s 93 and the decisions under the former s 92 of the AHA 1948 is as follows:

(a)   If the deceased died leaving a will, service on his executors is good service, even though they have not taken out a grant of probate[1]. Alternatively, service on the person having the control of the management of farming will be good service, he being deemed to be agent for the executors[2].

(b)   If the tenant leaves no will and therefore dies intestate, or leaves a will appointing no executors, or none who survives the tenant, service must be effected on The Public Trustee, PO Box 3010, London WC2A 1AX (Tel: 020 7911 7027). A prescribed form must be used, accompanied by a fee payable to 'The Public Trustee[3]. Service on the person in control of the management of farming of the holding will be good service, he being deemed to be agent for the Probate Judge[4].

(c)   Frequently, the landlord may not know whether the tenant died testate or intestate, or who the executors were if testate, or whether they intend to renounce probate. There is also a problem that a later will may be found. In those circumstances, the safest course is to serve notices addressed to the personal representatives on the Public Trustee, the farmhouse, the person in control of the management or farming of the holding and any solicitors or agents thought to be acting. Duplication of the notice will not invalidate the notice, particularly if it is explained that the duplicated service is being effected out of an abundance of caution. In this way, with the minimum of additional effort at an early stage, the right to serve a notice to quit on death under Sch 3 Pt I to the AHA 1986 will be assured[5].

Many of the problems are now alleviated by the provision that the three-month time limit for serving notice to quit on death does not run until after notice in writing of the death from the personal representatives has been received or an application for succession has been made. In that event, service on the person giving notice to the landlord will normally suffice.

1   The grant, when obtained, operates from death; *sed quaere* if probate is renounced. Also see, *Power v Stanton* [2010] 42 EG 110.
2   See para 42.22.
3   See *Practice Direction* [1995] 1 WLR 1120. Cf, previous *Practice Direction* [1985] 1 WLR 360 which required service to be on the President of the Family Division of the High Court, c/o The Treasury Solicitor, Queen Anne's Chambers, 28 Broadway, London SW1H 9JS. That latter address is no longer applicable. Also see, *Thorlby v Olivant* (1959) 104 Sol Jo 400, 175 Estates Gazette 211, CA. The fee is currently £40.
4   See para 42.22.
5   In other words, when in doubt serve all possible recipients rather than confine service to the most probable candidate for having the tenancy vested in him by operation of law following death.

TERM DATES

42.26A One issue which arises is identifying the term date. Where, for example, the tenancy is an annual periodic tenancy, following the expiry of the fixed term, the anniversary date will be fixed on the expiry of the fixed term[1]. Where the protection arose following a failed attempt to create a *Gladstone v Bower* agreement[2], the anniversary date is the date of the signing and dating of the tenancy agreement[3].

1   See para 20.7.
2   See para 20.13.
3   *Calcott v JS Bloor (Measham) Ltd* [1998] 1 WLR 1490, [1998] 3 EGLR 1, CA.

Chapter 43

LETTINGS BY A MORTGAGOR OF AGRICULTURAL LAND

IMPEACHING A LEASE OR TENANCY GRANTED BY
A MORTGAGOR

Section 423 of the Insolvency Act 1986

43.16 Since the purpose of grants falling within case (c) (at 43.15 above) will almost invariably be to improve the position of the mortgagor or his family or associates against the mortgagee, lenders instinctively raise the question whether the transaction is a fraud on creditors under s 423 of the Insolvency Act 1986 (IA 1986)[A1].

This section confers upon the court wide powers to set aside 'transactions entered into at an undervalue', or otherwise to protect the interests of creditors or potential creditors, if the court is satisfied that the transaction was entered into for the purpose of putting assets beyond their reach, or of otherwise prejudicing their interests[B1].

Section 423(2) sets out the scope of these provisions:

'This section relates to transactions entered into at an undervalue; and a person enters into such a transaction with another person if:
(a)   he makes a gift to the other person or he otherwise enters into a transaction on terms that provide for him to receive no consideration;
(b)   he enters into a transaction with the other in consideration of marriage; or
(c)   he enters into a transaction with the other for a consideration[C1] the value of which, in money or money's worth, is significantly less than the value, in money or money's worth, of the consideration provided by himself'.

In relation to the like provision applying in the case of bankruptcy[D1], the court has a discretion to make no order setting aside a transaction where it has been established that it was at an undervalue but justice required no order to be made[E1].

Section 99 and section 423 appear to be mutually exclusive. In order to comply with the requirements of LPA 1925, s 99, the lease or tenancy must be granted 'at the best rent that can reasonably be obtained'. That would seem to preclude the possibility that the grant could at the same time be regarded as a transaction 'entered into at an undervalue' for the purposes of s 423(1). For these purposes, it is not necessary to come to a conclusion as to whether paras (a) (b) and (c) in s 423(1) are intended to stand as an exhaustive definition of the expression 'transactions entered into at an undervalue' or whether they are merely examples. It is, however, to be observed that the test of validity under s 99 is more stringent than the test of 'undervalue' under s 423(1)(c)[1]. Section 99 requires a reservation of the best rent that can reasonably be obtained. If the rent falls below that amount then, subject only to a de minimis rule, the lease will not be authorised. But the grant will not have been made at an undervalue under s 423(1)(c), unless the rent was 'significantly less' than the letting value.

This issue was considered in the *Agricultural Mortgage Corpn plc v Woodward*[2]. The facts were that the mortgagor farmed as a freehold landowner. On 18 April 1989, the mortgagor granted a legal mortgage over his farm to the Agricultural Mortgage Corporation (AMC). The mortgagor fell into arrears and shortly before a deadline set by the AMC to clear those arrears, on 16 April 1992 the mortgagor granted a tenancy of the farm to his wife. It was an annual tenancy terminable upon 12 months notice. The tenancy was protected by the AHA 1986. The annual rent reserved was agreed to represent the full market rent. The AMC sought to set aside the tenancy pursuant to s 423 of the IA 1986.

[A1]   Also, in the case of bankruptcy or liquidation, the court has additional powers under the Insolvency Act 1986, ss 339 and 238 respectively. See, for example, *Re Marsh (in bankruptcy), Casey v Whitworth* [2009] BPIR 834.

[B1]   *Godfrey v Torpy* [2007] EWHC 919 (Ch), [2007] Bus LR 1203, (2007) Times, 16 May.

[C1]   Consideration can include services: see *Re: HHO Licensing Ltd (in liquidation)* [2007] BPIR 1363. Also see, *Kali Ltd v Chawla* [2007] EWHC 1989 (Ch), [2007] EWHC 2357 (Ch), [2008] BPIR 415.

[D1]   Insolvency Act 1986, s 339.

[E1]   *Singla v Brown* [2007] EWHC 405 (Ch), [2008] Ch 357, [2008] 2 FLR 125.

[1]   See *Bacon (MC) Ltd, Re* [1990] BCLC 324, [1990] BCC 78. Cf *Hill v Spread Trustee Co Ltd* [2006] EWCA Civ 542, [2007] 1 All ER 1106, [2007] 1 WLR 2404.

[2]   (1994) 70 P & CR 53, [1995] 1 EGLR 1, CA.

43.18   The exhaustive judgment of Neuberger J (as he then was) in the High Court in *National Westminster Bank plc v Jones*[1] was followed by the Court of Appeal. The judgment recognised that, provided that the rent reserved by the s 99 tenancy was sufficient to reflect the full marriage or ransom value of the tenancy, the tenancy would be binding on the mortgagee.

It was as a consequence of the decision in *National Westminster Bank plc v Jones* that another bank sought to establish that the statutory rent review provisions of the Agricultural Tenancies Act 1995 (ATA 1995) made it impossible for the mortgagor to grant a tenancy for a term beyond three years which could sufficiently reflect the full marriage or ransom value. That is the point which was taken in *Barclays Bank plc v Bean*[2].

In *Barclays Bank plc v Bean*, there were the two separate payments reserved by the farm business tenancy. One was the open market rent (subject to a rent review provision) and the other was a premium paid over the course of the terms of the tenancy. The Deputy Judge in the High Court held that both satisfied the statutory definition of rent in s 205(1)(xxiii) of the Law of Property Act 1925. Accordingly, both the market rent and the premium payments fell within the statutory rent review formula of s 13 of the ATA

1995. As a consequence, an arbitrator would reduce the totality of the payments agreed to be made to a single market rent. This caused the transaction as a whole to be one at an undervalue, set aside under s 423[3].

The legal basis for the bank's challenge was removed upon the amendment being made to s 9 of the ATA 1995 pursuant to the RRO 2006[4]. The parties are now free to contract out of the statutory rent review provision[5]. Accordingly, the position will revert to that which applied prior to *Barclays Bank plc v Bean*, namely that it will be necessary to consider in each case (by reference to expert evidence) whether the rent reserved by the s 99 tenancy is sufficient to reflect the marriage or ransom value. If it does, then (based upon the decision in *National Westminster Bank plc v Jones*[6]) the tenancy will be binding upon the mortgagee.

There appears to be a predilection on the part of the courts to favour the mortgagee against the mortgagor in these type of cases[7]. This is reflected by another decision of the Court of Appeal in *Department for Environment, Food and Rural Affairs v Feakins*[8], where the Court of Appeal was prepared to uphold the decision of the High Court setting aside the disposal of the freehold of a farm by a bank pursuant to s 423 of the IA 1986, where the effect of the transaction was to prejudice DEFRA as a creditor with the benefit of a charging order granted by the court[8A].

There remains open the possibility of a challenge to the Court of Appeal decision in *Agricultural Mortgage Corpn v Woodward*[9], in order to establish that it is unnecessary for the rent to reflect sufficiently the marriage or surrender value. It is enough for the rent to be 'the best rent that can reasonably be obtained, regard being had to the circumstances of the case', in accordance with the statutory definition contained in s 99(6) of the LPA 1925.

1   [2001] 1 BCLC 98, [2000] NPC 73; affd [2001] EWCA Civ 1541, [2002] 1 P & CR D20, [2002] 1 BCLC 55. Also see, *Delaney v Chen* [2010] EWHC 6 (Ch), [2010] 12 EG 101, [2010] 2 P & CR D1 where, in a case relating to residential property, the court held that an arrangement involving the grant of a tenancy did not amount to a transaction at undervalue.
2   [2004] 3 EGLR 71, [2004] 41 EG 152.
3   The case was settled before hearing in the Court of Appeal.
4   Regulatory Reform (Agricultural Tenancies) (England and Wales) Order 2006, SI 2006/2805, effective from 19 October 2006.
5   See para 9.3ff.
6   [2001] 1 BCLC 98, [2000] NPC 73; affd [2001] EWCA Civ 1541, [2002] 1 P & CR D20, [2002] 1 BCLC 55.
7   See, for example, *Barclays Bank plc v Eustice* [1995] 4 All ER 511, [1995] 1 WLR 1238, CA. The correctness of this decision was doubted by Lord Neuberger in the House of Lords in *In re McE, In re M* [2009] UKHL 15 at para 109, [2009] AC 908, [2009] NI 258.
8   [2005] EWCA Civ 1513, [2007] BCC 54, (2005) Times, 22 December.
8A As to the effect of setting aside a transaction and generally, see *4 Eng Ltd v Harper* [2009] EWHC 2633 (Ch), [2010] 1 BCLC 176, (2009) Times, 6 November.
9   (1994) 70 P & CR 53, [1995] 1 EGLR 1, CA.

Sham or device

43.19 Any apparently valid legal transaction can be set aside by the courts on the ground that it is a sham. A transaction is a sham if it is designed to give the appearance to the outside world that the parties to it have entered into legal rights and obligations which are different to the legal rights and obligations which they have really undertaken: see the classic definition by Diplock LJ in *Snook v London and West Riding Investments Ltd*[1]. One of the most frequently encountered types of sham in the field of property transactions is the creation of a document which appears to suggest that parties have entered into a licence to occupy a house or flat, whereas in substance what the parties really intended to create was a tenancy[2].

The court may also be prepared to refuse to give effect to the apparent exercise of a legal power if it appears that the power is being exploited for an ulterior purpose[3]. In *Quennell v Maltby*[4], the plaintiff's husband was the mortgagor of a house let to a statutory tenant whose tenancy had been granted in breach of the terms of the mortgage deed. The husband wanted the tenant evicted, and invited the mortgagee bank to exercise its power of sale. The bank refused, and the husband and the bank transferred the mortgage to the plaintiff who then took possession proceedings against the tenant on the ground that the tenancy was not binding upon her. It was held that the court was entitled to, and would, look behind the formal legal relationship of the parties, because a mortgagee would not be granted possession unless it was sought bona fide and reasonably, for the purpose of enforcing the security. Here the mortgagee was acting with the ulterior motive of assisting her husband in obtaining vacant possession and defeating the protection afforded to the tenant by the Rent Acts. In those circumstances she was to be treated as her husband's agent, and the action failed.

[1]   [1967] 2 QB 786, [1967] 1 All ER 518, CA. Also see, *Godfrey v Torpy* [2007] EWHC 919 (Ch), [2007] Bus LR 1203, (2007) Times, 16 May, in the context of the operation of s 423 of the Insolvency Act 1986; *Kali Ltd v Chawla* [2007] EWHC 2357 (Ch), [2008] BPIR 415.
[2]   See *Street v Mountford* [1985] AC 809, [1985] 1 EGLR 128, HL.
[3]   See *Quennell v Maltby* [1979] 1 All ER 568, [1979] 1 WLR 318, CA.
[4]   [1979] 1 All ER 568, [1979] 1 WLR 318, CA.

Conspiracy to defraud or injure

43.26 Much less is there a criminal conspiracy. At the root of the crime of conspiracy to defraud is an intention 'by dishonesty to deprive a person of something which is his or to which he would be or might be entitled ...'[1] .

First, it is submitted that the conduct in question could not be described as dishonest. The test of 'dishonesty' for the purposes of the criminal law was laid down by the Court of Appeal (Criminal Division) in *R v Ghosh*[2]. A jury can convict a defendant of dishonesty but only if it is satisfied that:

(1)   the conduct in question would be regarded by reasonable persons as dishonest; and
(2)   the defendant was aware of that fact.

43.26 *Lettings by a mortgagor of agricultural land*

It is submitted that the valid exercise of a statutory power cannot be characterised as dishonest simply because it was being exploited to further the interests of one party to a commercial arrangement against the interest of the other.

Second, and in any event, when a mortgagor is validly exercising his statutory power of leasing he is not depriving the mortgagee 'of something which is his or to which he is or would be or might be entitled ...' The subject of the mortgage, being agricultural land, is land which, by virtue of LPA 1925, s 99, is capable of being burdened by a lease or tenancy binding on the mortgagee from the moment it is mortgaged. The mortgagee cannot therefore argue that he has an entrenched right to vacant possession which is being unlawfully infringed.

1   *Scott v Metropolitan Police Comr* [1975] AC 819, per Viscount Dilhorne at 1039, [1974] 3 All ER 1032, HL.
2   [1982] QB 1053, [1982] 2 All ER 689, CA. Also see *Meretz Investments NV v ACP Ltd* [2007] EWCA Civ 1303, [2008] Ch 244, [2008] 2 WLR 904.

Appointment of a receiver

43.30 Section 99(19) of the LPA 1925 provides that the statutory power of leasing given to the mortgagor shall become exercisable 'after a receiver of the income of the mortgaged property or any part thereof has been appointed by a mortgagee under his statutory power', by the mortgagee in place of the mortgagor. The statutory power to appoint a receiver arises under s 101(1) of the LPA 1925[1]:

'A mortgagee, where the mortgage is made by deed, shall, by virtue of this Act, have the following powers ...:

...

(iii)   a power, when the mortgage money has become due, to appoint a receiver of the income of the mortgaged property, or any part thereof'.

Accordingly, if the mortgagee appoints a receiver[2], the mortgagor loses the power to grant a tenancy which would be binding on the mortgagee[3].

1   See also s 109(1) of the LPA 1925 which postpones the statutory right to appoint a receiver until the time when the power of sale has arisen.
2   Note that the receiver must be appointed under a legal charge and the provisions of the LPA 1925. An appointment of a receiver under an agricultural charge governed by the Agricultural Credits Act 1928 (ACA 1928) does not have the requisite effect. Also note that the definition of charged assets under the ACA 1928, comprising 'farming stock and other agricultural assets', does not extend to Single Payment Scheme entitlements, although such entitlements may be separately charged by a farmer to a lender: see *Capell Ltd v Waterfall* [2009] EWHC (Ch), unreported (a decision of Judge McCahill QC).
3   A receiver does not have a right to possession against the mortgagor: *Patmore v Bean* [2002] EWHC (Ch), unreported (a decision of Judge Behrens QC). Note how a sale by a receiver or mortgagee may avoid the necessity for a mortgagee to bring an action for possession: *Horsham Properties Group Ltd v Clark* [2008] EWHC 2327 (Ch), [2009] 1 All ER (Comm) 745, [2008] 3 EGLR 75. This decision has been widely criticised and proposals to close the 'Horsham loophole' are contained in the Mortgage Repossessions Bill. A mortgagee may also exercise its right to recover possession without a court order by peaceable re-entry: *Aurora Leasing Ltd v S Morgan & Sons Ltd* [2009] EWHC 3066 (Ch).

Chapter 45

REMEDIES

NON-PAYMENT OF RENT

Generally

45.2 The remedies which a landlord may consider include:

(a) suing the tenant for payment;
(b) suing people other than the present tenant;
(c) demanding rent from any sub-tenant;
(d) threatening bankruptcy if the tenant is an individual;
(e) threatening winding-up if the tenant is a company;
(f) forfeiture; and
(g) levying distress.

Additionally, in the case of the AHA 1986, the landlord may serve a notice to pay, as a preliminary step to a Case D(a) notice to quit, if the tenant does not pay rent within two months of the service of a notice to pay[1].

There are a number of points which the landlord may wish to consider in choosing the appropriate remedy. These include the following:

(i) Does the landlord want possession?
(ii) Could the holding easily be re-let?
(iii) If the holding could easily be re-let, would it be to a better covenant, would it be on better rent or would the other terms be as favourable to the landlord?
(iv) The physical state of the premises, as well as the current market, may be a relevant factor.
(v) Does the landlord want to retain the current tenant?
(vi) Are there any previous tenants to be sued?
(vii) Are there are any sureties to be sued?
(viii) Is the holding or any part of it sub-let? If so, has the tenant been receiving rent from the sub-tenant and not paying it to the landlord?
(ix) Is the right to forfeit available? For example, is there a valid forfeiture clause and has the landlord waived the breach?
(x) Are there goods on the holding enabling the landlord to levy distress?
(xi) Is there a danger that there will be insufficient goods to levy distress, thereby losing the landlord the right to forfeit?
(xii) In relation to the AHA 1986, is the notice to pay route the obvious answer?
(xiii) Is there is a set-off issue?

45.2 *Remedies*

(xiv) Is any remedy affected by, or likely to be affected by, the impact of an insolvency procedure?

(xv) The recovery of interest[2].

¹ See para 31.28.
² *Yuanda (UK) Co Ltd v WW Gear Construction Ltd* [2010] EWHC 720 (TCC), 130 ConLR 133, [2010] BLR 435.

The present tenant or other people?

The original tenant

45.5 The original tenant will usually benefit from a statutory release if the tenancy was one granted after 1 January 1996, when the Landlord and Tenant (Covenants) Act 1995 (LT(C)A 1995) came into force. The exceptions are:

(a) where the tenancy is granted pursuant to an agreement or an option (including a right of pre-emption) entered into before 1 January 1996; or

(b) where it is granted pursuant to a court order made before 1 January 1996; or

(c) where it is an overriding lease granted pursuant to s 19 of the Landlord LT(C)A 1995 in relation to a tenancy which is not a tenancy protected under the LT(C)A 1995[1].

It should be noted that the LT(C)A 1995 may apply in relation to a tenancy where a variation of an existing tenancy is such so as to cause an implied surrender and re-grant[2].

The original tenant's liability will include an obligation to pay interest on late payments, but only if the tenancy agreement reserves the right to charge interest. The landlord may claim interest on late payment under s 35A of the Senior Courts Act 1981, but the court is only likely to award interest against the original tenant from the date on which it is claimed from the original tenant by the landlord and not from when the rent became due[3].

As to the effect of the death of the original tenant, generally, if a contracting party dies, he is not discharged from contractual obligations which continue to affect his estate[4]. Accordingly, if the original tenant has died, his estate is probably liable by privity of contract for the duration of the term of the tenancy agreement[5]. The general rule may be excluded by an express provision in the tenancy agreement[6].

¹ LT(C)A 1995, ss 5, 11.
² LT(C)A 1995, s 1(5). As to surrender and re-grant, see para 33.5ff.
³ *Estates Gazette Ltd v Benjamin Restaurants Ltd* [1995] 1 All ER 129, [1994] 2 EGLR 43, CA.
⁴ Law Reform (Miscellaneous Provisions) Act 1934.
⁵ *Youngmin v Heath* [1974] 1 All ER 461, [1974] 1 WLR 135, CA.
⁶ *Kennewell v Dye* [1949] Ch 517, [1949] 1 All ER 881. See para 45.10.

Sureties

45.8 A surety has been characterised as a 'quasi-tenant'[1]. The liability of a surety will depend upon the terms of the contract[1A]. There is a distinction between a contract of 'guarantee' and one of 'indemnity'. The latter is described as a 'primary' liability, whereas the former is a 'secondary' liability. In practice, surety covenants are often drafted as a hybrid, the obligation initially being that of a guarantee, but taking effect as an indemnity in the event that the tenant is discharged of liability[2]. The distinction is probably of no practical significance while the tenancy continues[3].

Usually the following rules apply in respect of sureties:

(a)   A surety is liable for rent as reviewed.
(b)   The liability of the surety continues for the period of any statutory continuation of a tenancy after the expiry of the original term[4].
(c)   The liability ceases upon forfeiture[5].
(d)   The surety's contract is with the landlord only and therefore he is not liable to the original tenant[6].
(e)   The liability of the surety continues if the landlord sells the freehold reversion[7].
(f)   Whether the surety's obligations continue beyond the death of the surety depends upon the contractual terms[8].
(g)   If the surety becomes bankrupt, the landlord can prove in his bankruptcy[9].
(h)   If the tenancy is disclaimed by a liquidator or trustee in bankruptcy[10], the tenancy does not end entirely. It does so only to relieve the insolvent tenant from liability. The position of a guarantor (and a former tenant) is unaffected[11]. The surety may be required to take a new lease[12].
(i)   Where an assignment has been consented to by the landlord upon the tenant entering into the appropriate authorised guarantee agreement (AGA) with its existing surety as guarantor, it has been held that the guarantor of the assignee's obligations under the AGA was not liable by reason of the Landlord and Tenant (Covenants) Act 1995[13].

1   *P & A Swift Investments (a firm) v Combined English Stores Group plc* [1989] AC 632, [1988] 2 EGLR 67, HL.
1A   For a general review of the law in this area, see 'Catching the Surety', Timothy Fancourt QC, Falcon Chambers Symposium: Property Law in the Recession – 4 March 2009.
2   *General Produce Co v United Bank Ltd* [1979] 2 Lloyd's Rep 255.
3   *NRG Vision Ltd v Churchfield Leasing Ltd* [1988] BCLC 624, 4 BCC 56.
4   *Junction Estates v Cope* (1974) 27 P & CR 482.
5   *Associated Dairies Ltd v Pierce* (1982) 43 P & CR 208, 259 Estates Gazette 562; *Capital and City Holdings Ltd v Dean Warburg Ltd* (1988) 58 P & CR 346, [1989] 1 EGLR 90, CA.
6   This point is not without difficulty: see *Becton Dickinson UK Ltd v Zwebner* [1989] QB 208, [1989] 1 EGLR 71.
7   *P & A Swift Investments (a firm) v Combined English Stores Group plc* [1989] AC 632, [1988] 2 EGLR 67, HL.
8   *Holme v Brunskill* (1878) 3 QBD 495, CA.
9   *Re Houlder* [1929] 1 Ch 205.
10   See para 45.60ff.

45.8　Remedies

11 *Hindcastle Ltd v Barbara Attenborough Associates Ltd* [1995] QB 95, [1994] 2 EGLR 63, CA; *Basch v Stekel* (2001) 81 P & CR DG 1; *Scottish Widows plc v Tripipatkul* [2003] EWHC 1874 (Ch), [2004] 1 P & CR 461, [2004] BCC 200; *Shaw v Doleman* [2009] EWCA Civ 279, [2009] Bus LR 1175, [2009] 2 P & CR 205.
12 *Active Estates Ltd v Parness* [2002] EWHC 893 (Ch), [2002] 3 EGLR 13, [2002] 36 EG 147. As to the impact of a CVA (see para 45.35) in relation to a guarantor's liability to a landlord, there is no automatic release: see *Prudential Assurance Co Ltd v PRG Powerhouse Ltd* [2007] EWHC 1002 (Ch), [2007] Bus LR 1771, [2007] 3 EGLR 131; *Mourant & Co Trustees Ltd v Sixty UK Ltd (in administration)* [2010] EWHC 1890 (Ch), (2010) Times, 2 November. Also generally see, *Prudential Assurance Co Ltd v Ayres* [2008] EWCA Civ 52, [2008] 1 All ER 1266n, [2008] 1 EGLR 5.
13 *Good Harvest Partnership LLP v Centaur Services Ltd* [2010] EWHC 330 (Ch), [2010] Ch 426, [2010] 2 WLR 1312. Note that the case was to be heard on appeal but settled. Also see para 45.5; *K/S Victoria Street v House of Fraser Ltd* [2010] EWHC 3006 (Ch), [2010] All ER (D) 189 (Dec) and *K/S Victoria Street v House of Fraser (Stores Management)* [2010] EWHC 3344 (Ch)[2010] All ER (D) 312 (Dec).

The present tenant

45.9 It should first be noted that rent is not 'due' until the tenant has been given written notice of the landlord's address for service of documents and notices, as required by s 48 of the Landlord and Tenant Act 1987[1].

The next question is to ensure that the rent is due. Most tenancy agreements provide for rent to be paid in advance, but if the tenancy agreement is silent, the rent is due in arrears.

The landlord also has to consider whether the tenant is entitled to make deductions from the rent and whether this explains non-payment[2]. Deductions may be made:

(a)　as authorised by the tenancy agreement;
(b)　as authorised by statute;
(c)　where the tenant has a claim to set off[3].

There are limited circumstances where a tenant can argue that, for example where the tenant has abandoned the premises, there is an obligation on the landlord to mitigate his losses[4].

1 *Dallhold Estates (UK) Property Ltd v Lindsey Trading Properties Inc* (1993) 70 P & CR 332, [1994] 1 EGLR 93, CA. See para 31.29.
2 *Televantos v McCulloch* (1990) 23 HLR 412, [1991] 1 EGLR 123, CA.
3 See para 45.10.
4 *Reichman v Beveridge* [2006] EWCA Civ 1659, [2007] Bus LR 412, [2007] 1 P & CR 20.

Set off

45.10 Originally, any deduction from rent by way of set off could only be in respect of a liquidated sum. The law has developed so that an unliquidated claim for damages for breach of covenant by the landlord can also be set off. For example, if the landlord has failed to fulfil his repairing obligations and the tenant has expended money undertaking the necessary work. The landlord's obligation to repair normally arises only on notice and therefore he should have been given notice of the disrepair. Importantly, unless the tenant relies on the equitable doctrine of set off[1], the tenant must have paid the sums that he seeks to set off[2].

As noted above, pursuant to the provisions of the LT(C)A 1995, a landlord is not able to recover any fixed charge (including rent) from a former tenant or his surety unless, within six months of the liability becoming due, he has served on that person a notice informing him that the liability is now due and that the landlord intends to recover that amount and any interest payable[3].

There is no right of set off if the tenant has not carried out and paid for the repairs but, in some circumstances, the tenant may be entitled to rely upon the doctrine of equitable set off, if he has a cross-claim for damages against the landlord. In *British Anzani (Felixstowe) Ltd v International Marine Management (UK) Ltd*[4], the tenant was able to set off £1m, following the landlord's failure to repair two warehouses, against £540,000 rent arrears, even though the landlord's obligation was not contained in the tenancy agreement, but in a prior agreement to construct the warehouses and lease them to the tenant. To rely upon this doctrine, the tenant must show the close connection between his counterclaim and the landlord's claim for rent.

Unless the tenant can show that the tenancy agreement has been frustrated[5], the tenant is not entitled to deduct rent simply because the premises have been damaged or are partially unusable. If the landlord's failure to comply with the covenants in the tenancy agreement are so serious so as to constitute a repudiation of the tenancy agreement, then the tenant may rely upon the equitable doctrine of set off[6].

[1]   See para 31.32.
[2]   *Lee-Parker v Izzet* [1971] 3 All ER 1099, [1971] 1 WLR 1688.
[3]   LT(C)A 1995, s 17. See *Scottish & Newcastle plc v Raguz* [2008] UKHL 65, [2009] 1 All ER 763, [2009] 2 All ER (Comm) 447.
[4]   [1980] QB 137, [1979] 2 All ER 1063.
[5]   *National Carriers Ltd v Panalpina (Northern) Ltd* [1981] AC 675, [1981] 1 All ER 161, HL.
[6]   *Hussein v Mehlman* [1992] 2 EGLR 87, [1992] 32 EG 59. In that case, a failure by the landlord to comply with a repairing obligation was held to allow the tenant to vacate the property and return the keys to the landlord, bringing the tenancy to an end by the tenant's acceptance of the landlord's breach repudiating the tenancy. It is submitted that such cases would be rare, even more rare in relation to agricultural holdings.

Court proceedings

45.13 It is beyond the scope of this book to provide details of the court procedure arising in relation to a claim by a landlord for the recovery of rent against either the present tenant or any other party liable to the landlord. It should be noted that, since 1 July 1991, the county court has unlimited jurisdiction and accordingly the landlord may elect between the county court or the High Court. If the landlord decides to issue proceedings in the county court, the claim may be commenced in any court, no matter where the tenant resides or where the cause of action arose. The tenant may, however, apply to transfer the action to another court and the court will subsequently give consideration as to the appropriate trial venue.

An action for the recovery of rent through the court may be appropriate where:

(a) distress[1] is unavailable;

(b) there is a prospect of a dispute, causing the statutory demand route to be inappropriate[2];

(c) there is no sub-tenancy and therefore no opportunity to recover rent from a sub-tenant[3];

(d) forfeiture is unavailable or undesirable because the landlord does not wish to recover possession of the holding[4];

(e) in the case of an AHA 1986 tenancy, the landlord does not wish to recover possession of the holding and accordingly the notice to pay route is inappropriate[5];

(f) the landlord merely wishes to recover the rent through the range of enforcement methods available in the event that the landlord obtains a judgment in the High Court or the county court;

(g) the landlord wishes to avail himself of the opportunity to apply to the court for the appointment of a receiver by the court[6].

It should be noted that, in the context of the Housing Act 1988, the Supreme Court held that a secure tenancy only ends, following an order for possession being made by the court, when the order is actually executed[7].

[1] See Ch 26 and para 45.15.
[2] See para 45.16ff.
[3] See para 45.15.
[4] See para 45.21.
[5] See para 31.28ff.
[6] See Civil Procedure Rules. Also see, *Sinclair v Glatt* [2009] EWCA Civ 176, [2009] 4 All ER 724, [2009] 1 WLR 1845 as to the remuneration of a receiver.
[7] *Austin v Southwark London Borough Council* [2010] UKSC 28, [2010] 4 All ER 16, [2010] 3 WLR 144.

Trespass

45.21A Where the occupation of property is by a person other than a tenant or other person in lawful possession or occupation, the landlord/landowner may seek possession by trespass proceedings in the court[1] or peaceable re-entry[2]. Self help in relation to trespass 'is a summary remedy, which is justified only in clear and simple cases or in an emergency'[3].

[1] Note that a possession order may be obtained to cover land which is not in unlawful occupation: *University of Essex v Djemal* [1980] 2 All ER 742, [1980] 1 WLR 1301, CA; *University of Sussex v Protestors* [2010] 16 EG 106 (CS). A possession order will not extend to cover land belonging to the landowner that was wholly distinct, even miles away from, the land occupied: *Secretary of State for the Environment, Food and Rural Affairs v Meier* [2009] UKSC 11, [2010] 1 All ER 855, [2009] 1 WLR 2780. Cf *Drury v Secretary of State for the Environment, Food and Rural Affairs* [2004] EWCA Civ 200, [2004] 2 All ER 1056, [2004] 3 EGLR 85. Also see, *School of Oriental and African Studies v Persons Unknown* [2010] 49 EG 78 (CS).
[2] *Aurora Leasing Ltd v S Morgan & Sons Ltd* [2009] EWHC 3066 (Ch).

³   Per Lloyd LJ in *Macnab v Richardson* [2008] EWCA Civ 1631, [2009] 35 EG 108, applying *Burton v Winters* [1993] 3 All ER 847, [1993] 1 WLR 1077, CA.

TENANT'S BREACH OF COVENANT OTHER THAN NON-PAYMENT OF RENT

Specific performance

45.23   Specific performance is a discretionary remedy, born of the Court of Chancery, to provide a remedy where the remedy at law is inadequate. It follows that where damages provide the injured party with full compensation, the court will not, as a general principle, order specific performance.

Conversely, the court will not automatically grant specific performance even where damages are insufficient. Specific performance is a discretionary remedy. It may be refused on grounds of laches[1], mistake or hardship which would arise to the defendant[1A].

Until 1858 the court did not have power to award damages in lieu of specific performance. It was necessary for the aggrieved party to commence separate proceedings in a common law court. The Chancery Amendment Act 1858[2] provided that where the court had jurisdiction to grant an injunction or an order for specific performance, it could (if it thought fit) award damages 'either in addition to or in substitution for' the injunction or order for specific performance.

The current jurisdiction of the court to award damages is contained in s 50 of the Senior Courts Act 1981 which provides:

> 'Where the Court of Appeal or the High Court has jurisdiction to entertain an application for an injunction or specific performance, it may award damages in addition to, or in substitution for, an injunction of specific performance'.

Damages in substitution are not available if the court has no jurisdiction to specifically enforce the contract. Damages will not be awarded if there is a defence to specific performance. Damages may be awarded if specific performance is refused pursuant to the court's discretion, for example, due to laches.

One question which does arise in practice in relation to agricultural holdings is whether a landlord can obtain specific performance of a tenant's repairing obligation. Often the landlord will first consider relying upon the law of forfeiture[3] or (in the case of an AHA 1986 tenancy) a notice to remedy to do works[4]. Alternatively, if the tenancy agreement contains a provision allowing the landlord to enter and carry out works, the landlord may choose that route for enforcement. Nevertheless, in an exceptional case, the court will order specific performance of the tenant's repairing obligation[5]. In *Rainbow Estates Ltd v Tokenhold Ltd*, it was relevant to the court's exercise of its jurisdiction that the tenancy agreement did not contain a power for the landlord to enter to carry out works or a valid forfeiture clause[6].

¹   Negligence or unreasonable delay in asserting or enforcing a right.

1A   Generally see, *Coles v Samuel Smith Old Brewery* [2007] EWCA Civ 1461, [2008] 2 EGLR 159; *Frasers Islington Ltd v Hanover Trustee Co Ltd* [2010] EWHC 1514 (Ch), [2010] 27 EG 85 (CS), [2010] 2 P & CR D49.
2   Better known as Lord Cairns' Act.
3   See para 45.21.
4   See para 31.44ff.
5   *Rainbow Estates Ltd v Tokenhold Ltd* [1999] Ch 64, [1998] 2 EGLR 34. Cf *Hill v Barclays* (1810) 16 Ves 402.
6   See para 10.12ff.

Injunction

45.24 An injunction is the usual remedy to enforce a breach of a negative prohibition in a tenancy agreement. It directs a party to do the specified act or, more usually, to refrain from doing it. There are prohibitory, mandatory, *quia timet* and interim injunctions:

(a)   a prohibitory injunction is an order not to do something[1];

(b)   a mandatory injunction is an order to do something[2];

(c)   a *quia timet* injunction can be ordered before any breach occurs on the basis that the claimant has a well founded fear of an imminent breach. This will usually be a prohibitory injunction, although it may be mandatory[3];

(d)   an interim injunction is granted in the early stages of proceedings before a final determination of the substantive issues by the court. The court will consider the balance of convenience[4].

1   *Lumley v Wagner* (1852) 1 De GM & G 604; *Medina Housing Association Ltd v Case* [2002] EWCA Civ 2001, [2003] 1 All ER 1084, [2003] HLR 536.
2   *Esso Petroleum Co Ltd v Kingswood Motors (Addlestone) Ltd* [1974] QB 142, [1973] 3 All ER 1057; *Hemingway Securities Ltd v Dunraven Ltd* (1994) 71 P & CR 30, [1995] 1 EGLR 61. Cf *Law Debenture Trust Corpn plc v Ural Caspian Oil Corpn Ltd* [1995] Ch 152, [1995] 1 All ER 157, CA.
3   *Redland Bricks Ltd v Morris* [1970] AC 652, [1969] 2 All ER 576, HL. Damages in lieu is available: *Leeds Industrial Co-operative Society v Slack* [1924] AC 851, HL; *Hooper v Rogers* [1975] Ch 43, [1974] 3 All ER 417, CA. As to injunctions and self-help, see *Ashdale Land and Property Co v Maioriello* [2010] EWHC 3296 (Ch), [2010] All ER (D) 274 (Dec).
4   *American Cyanamid Co v Ethicon Ltd* [1975] AC 396, [1975] 1 All ER 504, HL.

Damages in lieu

45.26 The court's exercise of its discretionary power to award damages in lieu of an injunction is guided by the decision of A L Smith LJ in *Shelfer v City of London Electric Lighting Co*[1]:

'... it may be stated as a good working rule that—

(1)   if the injury to the plaintiff's rights is small

(2)   and is one which is capable of being estimated in money

(3)   and is one which can be adequately compensated by a small money payment

(4)   and the case is one in which it would be oppressive to the defendant to grant an injunction

then damages in substitution for an injunction may be given'.

A key feature of the 'good working rule' is the oppressiveness test, which is applied at the date that the injunction is sought.

> 'The outcome of any particular case usually turns on the question: would it in all the circumstances be oppressive to the defendant to grant the injunction to which the plaintiff is prima facie entitled?'[2]

In relation to breaches of leasehold covenants, the starting point for the measure of damages is the cost to the landlord of performing the covenant breached.

The court also has jurisdiction to award damages in lieu based upon 'lost opportunity'. This jurisdiction emerged in relation to restrictive covenant cases in respect of freehold land[3]. It may also be relevant in the case of landlord and tenant disputes.

In the context of damages in lieu, it may also be possible to recover quasi-restitutionary damages, ie a share in profits, based upon the House of Lords decision in *A-G v Blake (Jonathan Cape Ltd, third party)*[4]. In that case, Lord Nicholls stated:

> 'The *Wrotham Park* case, therefore, still shines, rather as a solitary beacon, showing that in contract as well as tort damages are not always narrowly confined to recoupment of financial loss. In a suitable case damages for breach of contract may be measured by the benefit gained by the wrongdoer from the breach. The defendant must make a reasonable payment in respect of the benefit he has gained ...

> Circumstances do arise when the just response to a breach of contract is that the wrongdoer should not be permitted to retain any profit from the breach ...

> When, exceptionally, a just response to a breach of contract so requires, the court should be able to grant the discretionary remedy of requiring a defendant to account to the plaintiff for the benefits he has received from his breach of contract ...

> When the circumstances require, damages are measured by reference to the benefit obtained by the wrongdoer. This applies to interference with property rights. Recently, the like approach has been adopted to breach of contract.

> The court will have regard to all the circumstances, including the subject matter of the contract, the purpose of the contractual provision which has been breached, the circumstances in which the breach occurred, the consequences of the breach circumstances in which relief is being sought. A useful general guide, although not exhaustive, is whether the plaintiff had a legitimate interest in preventing the defendant's profit-making activity and, hence, in depriving him of his profit'.

It is submitted that this approach to the measure of damages fits more naturally with damages in lieu of an injunction or specific performance, rather than damages or breach of contract.

It should also be noted that mitigation of loss does apply where a landlord is seeking damages for breach of contract[5].

1   [1895] 1 Ch 287 at 322. Also see *Lunn Poly Ltd v Liverpool & Lancashire Properties Ltd* [2006] EWCA Civ 430, [2006] 25 EG 210, [2006] 12 EG 222 (CS); *Regan v Paul Properties Ltd* [2006] EWCA Civ 1391, [2007] Ch 135, [2007] 4 All ER 48; *Watson v Croft Promosport Ltd* [2009] EWCA Civ 15, [2009] 3 All ER 249, [2009] 18 EG 86.
2   Per Millett LJ in *Jaggard v Sawyer* [1995] 2 All ER 189, [1995] 1 EGLR 146, CA. Followed in *Midtown Ltd v City of London Real Property Co Ltd* [2005] EWHC 33 (Ch), [2005] 1 EGLR 65, [2005] 14 EG 130.
3   *Wrotham Park Estate Co v Parkside Homes Ltd* [1974] 2 All ER 321, [1974] 1 WLR 798; *Jaggard v Sawyer* [1995] 2 All ER 189, [1995] 1 EGLR 146, CA; *Bracewell v Appleby* [1975] Ch 408, [1975] 1 All ER 993; *Gafford v Graham* (1998) 77 P & CR 73, [1999] 40 LS Gaz R 44, CA.
4   [2001] 1 AC 268, [2000] 4 All ER 385, HL. Also see *Amec Developments Ltd v Jury's Hotel Management (UK) Ltd* (2000) 82 P & CR 286, [2001] EGLR 81; *Experience Hendrix LLC v PPX Enterprises Inc* [2003] EWCA Civ 323, [2003] 1 All ER (Comm) 830, [2003] FSR 853; *WWF–World Wide Fund for Nature (formerly World Wildlife Fund) v World Wrestling Federation Entertainment Inc* [2007] EWCA Civ 286, [2008] 1 All ER 74, [2008] 1 All ER (Comm) 129; *Crestfort Ltd v Tesco Stores Ltd* [2005] EWHC 805 (Ch), [2005] 3 EGLR 25, [2005] 37 EG 148; *Pell Frischmann Engineering Ltd v Bow Valley Iran Ltd* [2009] UKPC 45, [2010] BLR 73, [2010] 4 LRC 200.
5   *Reichman v Beveridge* [2006] EWCA Civ 1659, [2007] Bus LR 412, [2007] 08 EG 138.

Damages generally

45.27   The points made above in relation to damages in lieu of an injunction or specific performance apply generally in relation to a claim for damages for breach of contract arising from a breach of a term or condition of a tenancy agreement[1].

The Court of Appeal has held that there are three ways in which damages can be assessed for the breach of covenant[1A]:

(a)   Compensatory damages to compensate the claimant for losses resulting from the breach, without taking account of the loss of the benefit of the covenant.

(b)   Buy-out damages assessed on what reasonable people in the position of the parties would have hypothetically negotiated for releasing the right, ie for the loss of the covenant[1B].

(c)   An account for profit damages, ie a sum based on an account for the tenant's profit arising from the breach[1C].

In relation to claims for disrepair, a landlord is circumscribed by the Landlord and Tenant Act 1927[2]. Section 18 restricts the landlord to damages not exceeding the amount by which the value of the freehold reversion is diminished by reason of the breach[3].

1   *Niazi Services Ltd v Van Der Loo* [2004] EWCA Civ 53, [2004] 1 WLR 1254, [2004] 1 EGLR 62.
1A   *Lunn Poly Ltd v Liverpool & Lancashire Properties Ltd* [2006] EWCA Civ 430, [2006] 25 EG 210, [2006] 12 EG 222 (CS). Also see, *Pell Frischmann Engineering Ltd v Bow Valley Iran Ltd* [2009] UKPC 45, [2010] BLR 73, [2010] 4 LRC 200.
1B   *Wrotham Park Estate Co v Parkside Homes Ltd* [1974] 2 All ER 321, [1974] 1 WLR 798; *Bracewell v Appleby* [1975] Ch 408, [1975] 1 All ER 993; *Carr-Saunders v Dick McNeil Associates Ltd* [1986] 2 All ER 888, [1986] 2 EGLR 181.
1C   Such damages were awarded in *A-G v Blake (Jonathan Cape Ltd, third party)* [2001] 1 AC 268, [2000] 4 All ER 385, HL; but not in *Forsyth-Grant v Allen* [2008] EWCA Civ 505, [2008] 2 EGLR 161.

2   Note that the provisions of the Leasehold Property (Repairs) Act 1938, requiring a
    landlord to obtain leave of the court before commencing proceedings does not apply to a
    farm business tenancy under the ATA 1995 (ATA 1995, Schedule para 8) or an agricultural
    holding under the AHA 1986 (AHA 1986, Sch 14 para 17).
3   See para 10.12ff. Also see *Eyre v Rea* [1947] KB 567, [1947] 1 All ER 415.

Damages for trespass

45.28   An issue which arises in practice is the measure of damages recoverable
by the landlord in relation to unlawful occupation, whether because the tenant
unlawfully holds over or otherwise.

Trespass is actionable per se. A landowner may recover nominal damages for
trespass even if no loss has been suffered. This will be the case where a
landowner is wrongfully deprived of his land but suffers no direct loss[1].
Alternatively, damages may be substantial[2].

Mesne profits and damages for use and occupation are terms which are often
used interchangeably[3]. There is a difference, as explained by Lloyd LJ in
Ministry of Defence v Ashman:

> 'As to mesne profits they are, as I understand it, simply damages for trespass
> recoverable against a tenant who holds over after the lawful termination of the
> tenancy. A claim for mesne profits is thus to be distinguished from an action for
> use and occupation where the tenant holds over with the consent of his
> landlord. The former action is grounded in tort, the latter in quasi-contract'[4].

In *Ministry of Defence v Ashman*[5], the tenant had paid a subsidised rent. The
landlord claimed market rent as the appropriate measure of damages,
although there was no evidence that it would have let the property on the
open market. The Court of Appeal found that the Ministry had elected for
restitutionary damages, but determined that the market rent was not payable
because it was not the value of the land to the trespasser. The value was
limited to that sum which the defendant would have had to pay for suitable
local authority housing.

The term 'mesne profits' is not confined to the profits which have accrued to
the occupier, but extends to all loss that the landowner has suffered[5A]. This
has been the position since 1770 when Chief Justice Wilmot said, in relation
to a claim for mesne profits: 'Damages are not confined to the mere rent of the
premises; but the jury may give more, if they please ...'[5B].

In *A-G v Blake (Jonathan Cape Ltd, third party)*[6], Lord Nicholls identified
that, as a general rule:

> 'Damages are measured by the plaintiff's loss, not the defendant's gain. But the
> common law, pragmatic as ever, has long recognised that there are many
> commonplace situations where a strict application of this principle would not
> do justice between the parties. The compensation for the wrong done to the
> plaintiff is measured by a different yardstick. A trespasser who enters another's

45.28 *Remedies*

land may cause the land owner no financial loss. In such a case damages are measured by the benefit received by the trespasser, namely, by his use of the land'.

The assessment of the quantum of damages for trespass depends upon whether the landowner elects to claim damages for actual loss suffered or restitutionary damages. The election does not need to be made before bringing a claim, but before judgment[7].

The danger for a trespasser is that the court will assess the measure of damages to include a loss of opportunity (for example, to develop the holding) or, in an exceptional case, on account of profits[8].

A tenant who wrongfully remains in possession after the end of the tenancy ceases to be liable for mesne profits when he gives up possession, irrespective of notice[9].

1. *Swordheath Properties Ltd v Tabet* [1979] 1 All ER 240, [1979] 1 WLR 285, CA.
2. As to the award of aggravated damages where the trespass is accompanied by high-handed, insulting or oppressive behaviour, see *Horsford v Bird* [2006] UKPC 3, [2006] 1 EGLR 75, [2006] 15 EG 136.
3. *Dean and Chapter of the Cathedral and Metropolitan Church of Christ Canterbury v Whitbread plc* (1995) 72 P & CR 9, [1995] 1 EGLR 82.
4. (1993) 66 P & CR 195, [1993] 2 EGLR 102 at 102, CA. Also see *Phillips v Homfrey* (1871) 6 Ch App 770; *A-G v De Keyser's Royal Hotel Ltd* [1920] AC 508, HL; *Morris v Tarrant* [1971] 2 QB 143, [1971] 2 All ER 920.
5. (1993) 66 P & CR 195, [1993] 2 EGLR 102, CA. Followed in *Ministry of Defence v Thompson* (1993) 25 HLR 552, [1993] 2 EGLR 107, CA. Also see, *Inverugie Investments Ltd v Hackett* [1995] 3 All ER 841, [1995] 1 WLR 713, PC; *A-G v Blake (Jonathan Cape Ltd, third party)* [2001] 1 AC 268, [2000] 4 All ER 385, HL.
5A. *Clerk and Lindsell* (20th edn, 2010), para 19–73 and *McGregor on Damages* (18th edn), paras 34–042 to 34–066.
5B. *Goodtitle v Tombs* (1770) 3 Wils 188, 95 ER 965. Also see, *Bramley v Chesterton* (1857) 2 CBNS 592, 140 ER 548.
6. [2001] 1 AC 268 at 279, [2000] 4 All ER 385, HL. Also see, *WWF–World Wide Fund for Nature (formerly World Wildlife Fund) v World Wrestling Federation Entertainment Inc* [2007] EWCA Civ 286, [2008] 1 All ER 74, [2008] 1 All ER (Comm) 129.
7. *Ministry of Defence v Ashman* (1993) 66 P & CR 195, [1993] 2 EGLR 102, CA.
8. *Experience Hendrix LLC v PPX Enterprises Inc* [2003] EWCA Civ 323, [2003] 1 All ER (Comm) 830, [2003] FSR 853; *Severn Trent Water Ltd v Barnes* [2004] EWCA Civ 570, [2004] 2 EGLR 95, [2005] RVR 181; *Forsyth-Grant v Allen* [2008] EWCA Civ 505, [2008] 2 EGLR 161. Also, in the context of a breach of repairing obligations, where the court was prepared to order the landlord to be liable for the tenant's loss of profits, see *Hawkins v Woodhall* [2008] EWCA Civ 932, [2008] All ER (D) 375 (Jun). Also, as to economic loss generally, see *Shell UK Ltd v Total UK Ltd* [2010] EWCA Civ 180, [2010] 3 All ER 793, [2010] 3 WLR 1192.
9. *Jones v Merton London Borough Council* [2008] EWCA Civ 660, [2008] 4 All ER 287, [2009] 1 WLR 1269.

RECTIFICATION

45.32 It is beyond the scope of this book to consider in detail the remedy of rectification. It is sometimes relevant in respect of tenancy agreements and landlord and tenant relationships[A1].

Rectification is an equitable remedy causing the correction of a written document if, by mistake, it does not correctly record the true agreement between the parties[1]. Critically, what is rectified is not a mistake in the transaction itself, but a mistake in the way in which that transaction has been expressed in writing[2].

Rectification is a remedy of last resort. A court will first try to establish the true construction of a document in order to seek to give it contractual effect. Alternatively, the court will consider assistance provided by a collateral contract. The latter does not apply in relation to a contract for the sale or disposition of land governed by the Law of Property (Miscellaneous Provisions) Act 1989[3].

In *Weeds v Blaney*[4] the court identified two kinds of rectification:

> 'There are two kinds of rectification. One is where both parties are under a common mistake – that is, both of them believe that the concluded instrument expresses their common intention in regard to a particular provision or aspect of the agreement – but both of them are mistaken in that the instrument on its proper construction does not carry out that common intention. Both contribute to the mistake. The one party who sends forward a draft containing the mistake. The other party who returns it without correcting it ... The other kind of rectification is where there is a unilateral mistake by one party which is known to the other party. Such as where a party puts forward a contract or instrument for signature, but himself makes a mistake in the drafting of it – maybe a negligent mistake: and the other party spots the mistake – and turns a blind eye to it. He sees that it will or may operate to his advantage and so says nothing about it, and signs the contract as it stands. Such conduct on his part savours of sharp practice: and the court will rectify the instrument so as to correct the mistake.
>
> In both those kinds of rectification there is a negligent mistake by the plaintiff or his solicitors, but that is no bar to rectification. It is indeed the very reason why rectification is granted'.

In general the court will not order rectification unless there has been a mistake in the written document which was common to all of the parties[5].

[A1] For a general review of the law in this area, see 'Swings and Roundabouts in the Law of Rectification', Martin Rodger QC, Falcon Chambers Symposium: Property Law in the Recession – 4 March 2009.

[1] *Frederick E Rose (London) Ltd v William H Pim Jnr & Co Ltd* [1953] 2 QB 450, [1953] 2 All ER 739, CA.

[2] *Racal Group Services Ltd v Ashmore* [1995] STC 1151, 68 TC 86, CA.

[3] *Wright v Robert Leonard (Development) Ltd* [1994] NPC 49, [1994] EGCS 69, CA.

[4] [1978] 2 EGLR 84 at 85.

[5] *Hicklane Properties Ltd v Bradbury Investments Ltd* [2008] EWCA Civ 691, [2009] 1 P & CR 53; *KPMG LLP v Network Rail Infrastructure Ltd* [2007] EWCA Civ 363, [2007] Bus LR 1336, [2008] 1 P & CR 187; *Ashcroft v Barnsdale* [2010] EWHC 1948 (Ch), [2010] STC 2544, [2010] 32 EG 61 (CS).

THE EFFECT OF INSOLVENCY

Types of insolvency

Administration

45.37 Administration is a procedure whereby the court will make an order for administration, following the presentation of a petition by the company, its directors, a creditor or creditors, directing that the business and the property of the company[1] should be managed by an administrator for a specified period[2].

An administration order will only be granted if:

(a)   a company is, or is likely to become, unable to pay its debts as they fall due or the value of its assets is, or is likely to become, less than the amount of its liabilities, taking into account contingent and prospective liabilities; and

(b)   the court is satisfied that one or more of the statutorily prescribed purposes apply.

The statutorily prescribed purposes are:

 (i)   the survival of the company as a going concern; or

 (ii)   the approval of a voluntary arrangement; or

(iii)   the sanctioning under s 425 of the Companies Act 1985[3] of a compromise or arrangement between the company and any such persons mentioned in that section; or

(iv)   a more advantageous realisation of the company's assets than will be effected on a winding up.

---

[1]   The procedure is also available in the case of a partnership: see The Insolvent Partnerships Order 1994, SI 1994/2421. Note that generally an administrator will not owe a duty of care to creditors: see *Charalambous v B & C Associates* [2009] EWHC 2601 (Ch), (2009) 43 EG 105 (CS).

[2]   IA 1986, ss 8–27.

[3]   To be re-enacted as Companies Act 2006, s 895 at a date to be appointed.

Liquidation

45.38 Compulsory liquidation of a company follows non-compliance with a statutory notice demanding payment within 21 days resulting in the presentation of a winding-up petition to the court and a subsequent order for liquidation[1].

Voluntary liquidation of a company may arise for a reason mentioned in s 84 of the IA 1986, for example, pursuant to an extraordinary resolution of the company to the effect that it cannot by reason of its liabilities continue its business[2].

In both compulsory and voluntary liquidations, a liquidator is appointed, although often, pending the appointment of an insolvency practitioner, the Official Receiver will first act[3].

1   IA 1986, Pt IV, Ch VI. Also see para 45.17. As to set-off, see *Chan Sui Ko v Appasamy* [2005] EWHC 3519 (Ch), [2008] 1 BCLC 314, [2008] BPIR 18.
2   IA 1986, Pt IV, Chas II–V.
3   IA 1986, Pt IV, Chs VII–X.

Bankruptcy

45.39 Bankruptcy of an individual follows non compliance with a statutory notice demanding payment of an unsecured debt within 21 days resulting in the presentation of a petition of a creditor and the subsequent bankruptcy order made by the court[1].

1   IA 1986, ss 264–387. As to set-off, see *Chan Sui Ko v Appasamy* [2005] EWHC 3519 (Ch), [2008] 1 BCLC 314, [2008] BPIR 18.

The effect of insolvency on enforcement (other than distress)

Voluntary arrangements

45.41 A distinction needs to be drawn between an individual voluntary arrangement and a company voluntary arrangement. In the case of the former, a statutory moratorium can be imposed under an interim order so that no action can be commenced against the individual (or a partnership) without the leave of the court. In the latter case, a moratorium arises in cases of 'small companies'[1] or where an administration order has been made[2].

If a tenant is contemplating an individual voluntary arrangement, then the effect of obtaining an interim order[3] is:

(a)   forfeiture is no longer available to the landlord without the permission of the court;
(b)   no other proceedings can be instituted without the leave of the court;
(c)   there can be no distraint for rent[4]; and
(d)   disclaimer is not available[5].

Where the tenant is a company entering into a company voluntary arrangement, unless the company is a 'small company' or an administration order has been made:

(i)   forfeiture (including peaceable re-entry) are available to the landlord;
(ii)   proceedings may be issued by the landlord; and
(iii)   the landlord may distrain for rent.

The interim order ceases to have effect after 28 days[6]. Once the proposals for the voluntary arrangement are approved by the court, following a vote by the creditors, it binds all interested parties[7]. A creditor whose interests have been unfairly prejudiced by the voluntary arrangement may challenge the order in the court[8].

1   Companies Act 1985, s 247. To be replaced by Companies Act 2006, ss 382 and 465 at a date to be appointed.
2   IA 1986, ss 5(2), 6.

3   An interim order requires an application to the court. It is not an automatic consequence of a voluntary arrangement.
4   See para 45.15.
5   See para 45.60.
6   IA 1986, s 260(4).
7   IA 1986, s 260(2).
8   IA 1986, s 262. *Re Naeem (a Bankrupt) (No 18 of 1988)* [1990] 1 WLR 48. As to the effect of a CVA on guarantees and generally, see *Prudential Assurance Co Ltd v PRG Powerhouse Ltd* [2007] EWHC 1002 (Ch), [2007] Bus LR 1771, [2008] 1 BCLC 289.

Administration

45.43 No proceedings nor execution nor other legal process may be commenced or continued against a company (or a partnership) or its property without the leave of the court, and subject to such conditions as the court may impose, after an administration order has been made[1]. Previously leave was not required for peaceable re-entry[2]. That position was reversed when the Insolvency Act 2000 (IA 2000) came into force[3]. It is now necessary for a landlord to obtain permission of the court or the administrator before being able to proceed with forfeiture either by way of proceedings or peaceable re-entry.

The administrator has a power of sale[4]. If a landlord or a mortgagee considers himself to be unfairly prejudiced by the acts of the administrator, there is a procedure to enable him to apply to the court, which can then grant such relief as it thinks fit[5].

The courts have decided that administrators have the power to pay administration expenses as they fall due[6]. There was little guidance as to whether ongoing rent is to be paid as an expense. The Insolvency (Amendment) Rules 2003 and 2005[7] introduced new provisions that deal with administration expenses. It is arguable that these rules (reflecting those applying to liquidations) validate the payment of ongoing rent as an expense[8]. Since the ninth edition of this book, the issue has been considered by the High Court in *Goldacre (Offices) Ltd v Nortel Networks (UK) Ltd (in administration)*[8A]. Although the case does not specify that the continuing rents must be paid as they fall due, it provides that any rent or other liability falling due while the administrators use the property for the purposes of the administration should be payable in full as an expense of the administration.

It should be noted that where a company is in administration it has been held that business rates are an expense of the administration[9].

1   IA 1986, ss 10, 11. *Atlantic Computer Systems plc, Re* [1992] Ch 505, [1992] 1 All ER 476, CA; *Metro Nominees (Wandsworth) (No 1) Ltd v Rayment* [2008] BCC 40. Note that this does not stop a tenant continuing with an application for a new lease under the provisions of the Landlord and Tenant Act 1954, Part II: see *Somerfield Stores Ltd v Spring (Sutton Coldfield) Ltd* [2009] EWHC 2384 (Ch), [2010] 2 BCLC 452, [2009] 48 EG 104.
2   *Lomax Leisure Ltd, Re* [2000] Ch 502, [1999] 2 EGLR 37; *Metro Nominees (Wandsworth) (No 1) Ltd v Rayment* [2008] BCC 40.
3   IA 2000, s 9, with effect from 2 April 2001.

4   IA 2000, s 14 and Sch 1. As to the duty to obtain the best price, see *Bell v Long* [2008] EWHC 1273 (Ch), [2008] 2 BCLC 706, [2008] BPIR 1211. As to the administrator's personal liability, see *Coyne v DRC Distribution Ltd* [2008] EWCA Civ 488, [2008] BCC 612, [2008] BPIR 1247.
5   IA 2000, s 27.
6   *Salmet International Ltd (in administration), Re* [2001] BCC 796, [2001] BPIR 709.
7   SI 2003/1730 and SI 2005/527.
8   See Levaggi and Marsden, 'Expensive Quandry', EG 10 March 2007.
8A [2009] EWHC 3389 (Ch), [2010] Ch 455, [2010] 3 WLR 171.
9   *Toshoku Finance UK plc, Re, Khan v IRC* [2002] UKHL 6, [2002] 3 All ER 961, [2002] 1 WLR 671; *Exeter City Council v Bairstow* [2007] EWHC 400 (Ch), [2007] 4 All ER 437, [2007] Bus LR 813.

Bankruptcy

45.45 Proceedings cannot be commenced after a bankruptcy order has been made without the leave of the court. Further, the court has power to stay existing proceedings[1]. Leave is not required to commence forfeiture proceedings[2].

In the context of the recovery of possession of agricultural holdings, especially by a mortgagee, the rights of wives gives rise to particular issues[3].

1   IA 1986, s 285.
2   *Ezekiel v Orakpo* [1977] QB 260, [1976] 3 All ER 659, CA.
3   It is beyond the scope of this book to cover this. See, for example, *Avis v Turner* [2007] EWCA Civ 748, [2008] Ch 218, [2007] 4 All ER 1103; *French v Barcham* [2008] EWHC 1505 (Ch), [2009] 1 All ER 145, [2009] 1 WLR 1124; *Ball v Jones* [2008] 2 FLR 1969, [2008] Fam Law 1184; *Haines v Hill* [2007] EWCA Civ 1284, [2008] Ch 412, [2008] 2 All ER 901. As to the impact of constructive trusts, see *Holman v Howes* [2007] EWCA Civ 877, 10 ITELR 492, [2008] 1 FLR 1217.

The effect of insolvency on distress

Liquidation

45.51 Upon the compulsory liquidation of a company, following the making of a winding-up order, no action or proceedings can be proceeded with or commenced against a company or property of a company, except with the leave of the court[1]. For this purpose, the winding up is deemed to commence on the presentation of the petition[2].

Distress (or execution) after the compulsory winding-up order has been made is void[3]. The benefit of any execution against goods or land is lost by a creditor unless it is completed before the presentation of the petition, subject to the court's general discretion to override this[4].

The court will not usually restrain distress commenced before the winding up, but will restrain distress for rent due after liquidation (or after the presentation of the winding-up petition)[5].

45.51 *Remedies*

Where a liquidator retains premises to sell them, or for some other purpose, he must pay the rent in full, which will be an expense of the liquidation. If he fails to do so, then he will be liable for distress[6].

Where a liquidator abstains from doing anything with a property, it will not give the landlord the right to distrain for rent subsequent to the winding up. The rent is merely a debt for which the landlord must prove in the liquidation[7]. The landlord shall be paid in full, or be allowed to distrain, if the liquidator is continuing to use the property[8].

Where a tenant is in liquidation, but has sub-tenants, under the Law of Distress Amendment Act 1908, the sub-tenant's goods are protected from seizure by the landlord, if the sub-tenant makes a declaration that the goods are not the property of the tenant in liquidation and if the sub-tenant undertakes to pay rent directly to the superior landlord until the arrears are paid in respect of which the levy is threatened. The sub-tenant becomes the immediate tenant of the landlord. It is necessary for the landlord to serve a notice on the sub-tenant pursuant to s 6 of the Law of Distress Amendment Act 1908[9].

Upon the voluntary liquidation of a company, the liquidator can ask the court to determine the validity of any distress levied[10]. The court can stay proceedings against the company, after the commencement of a voluntary winding up, and thereby restrain any distress. There is no automatic stay[11].

[1] IA 1986, s 130. *Gresham International Ltd v Moonie* [2009] EWHC 1093 (Ch), [2010] Ch 285, [2010] 2 WLR 362.
[2] IA 1986, s 129.
[3] IA 1986, s 128.
[4] IA 1986, s 183.
[5] *Herbert Berry Associates Ltd v IRC* [1978] 1 All ER 161, [1977] 1 WLR 1437, HL; *Roundwood Colliery Co, Re, Lee v Roundwood Colliery Co* [1897] 1 Ch 373, CA.
[6] *Re Downer Enterprises Ltd* [1974] 2 All ER 1074, [1974] 1 WLR 1460.
[7] *ABC Coupler and Engineering Co Ltd (No 3), Re* [1970] 1 All ER 650, [1970] 209 EGLR 1197.
[8] *Atlantic Computer Systems plc, Re* [1992] Ch 505, [1992] 1 All ER 476, CA.
[9] *Rhodes v Allied Dunbar Pension Services Ltd, Re Offshore Ventilations Ltd* [1989] 1 All ER 1161, [1989] 1 EGLR 78, CA.
[10] IA 1986, s 112.
[11] IA 1986, ss 112(10) and 126(1).

Insolvency and forfeiture

Waiver

45.54 A landlord does not waive his right to forfeit by reason of having constructive notice of liquidation through notification of the winding-up order in the London Gazette and acceptance of rent afterwards[1].

[1] *Official Custodian for Charities v Parway Estates Developments Ltd* [1985] Ch 151, [1984] 3 All ER 679, CA. For a case of waiver in a company voluntary arrangement, see *Thomas v Ken Thomas Ltd* [2006] EWCA Civ 1504, [2007] Bus LR 429, 150 Sol Jo LB 1396. Per incuriam: it would not have been open to the landlord to seek to forfeit the lease for non-payment of sums covered by the CVA.

Disclaimer

Vesting order

45.64 The disclaimer does not take effect unless either:

(a) no application for the vesting of the lease in a third party is made within 14 days of service of the last copy of the disclaimer; or

(b) where such an application has been made, the court directs that the disclaimer shall take effect[1].

Any person who 'claims an interest in the disclaimed property' or any person 'who is under any liability in respect of the disclaimed property, not being a liability discharged by the disclaimer' may apply to the court for a vesting order[2].

An application for a vesting order must be made within three months of the applicant becoming aware of the disclaimer[3], whether he becomes aware by receipt of the notice from the trustee or liquidator or otherwise. Even if the time limits are missed, it appears that in both bankruptcy and liquidation, time can be extended[4].

The court will not make a vesting order, except on terms that the person is subject to the same liabilities as the company/bankrupt was subject to at the commencement of the winding up or bankruptcy or the same liabilities as the person would have been subject to had they taken an assignment at the commencement of the winding up. Where the vesting order is made in favour of a party other than a sub-tenant or mortgagee, the court has discretion as to the terms of the vesting order[4A].

The landlord is a person interested in the disclaimed property[5], but he cannot obtain a vesting order for the purpose of preserving sub-leases where the sub-tenants have declined to apply for a vesting order[6]. A person whose interest is discharged by the disclaimer cannot claim a vesting order, for example, a surety[7].

A vesting order can be made in respect of part only of the premises under the IA 1986[8], but on terms that the tenant of part will be subject to the same obligations as the original tenant was. If there is a disclaimer, and a person declines to accept a vesting order, that person shall be excluded from all interests in the property[9].

Unfortunately the sections in the IA 1986 do not make any clear provision for the apportionment of rent and other obligations upon the grant of a vesting order in respect of part of the premises. This may be of particular significance in the context of an agricultural holding.

---

1 IA 1986, s 179 (liquidation); s 317 (bankruptcy).
2 IA 1986, s 181 (liquidation); s 320 (bankruptcy).
3 Insolvency Rules 1986, rr 4.194 and 6.186. This extends to an equitable assignee: *Test Valley Borough Council v Minilec Engineering Ltd (in liquidation)* [2005] 2 EGLR 113.
4 IA 1986, s 376.

4A   *Beegas Nominees Ltd v BHP Petroleum Ltd and Sevington Properties Ltd* (1998) 77 P & CR 14, [1998] 2 EGLR 57, CA.
5   *Re Cock, ex p Shilson* (1887) 20 QBD 343.
6   *ITM Corpn Ltd, Re, Sterling Estates v Pickard UK Ltd (formerly Paxus Professional Systems Ltd)* [1997] 2 BCLC 389, [1997] 2 EGLR 33.
7   *Yarmarine (IW) Ltd, Re* [1992] BCLC 276, [1992] BCC 28.
8   IA 1986, s 182(2) (liquidation); s 321(2) (bankruptcy).
9   IA 1986, s 182(4) (liquidation); s 321(4) (bankruptcy); *Re AE Realisations (1985) Ltd* [1987] 3 All ER 83, [1988] 1 WLR 200.

Liability of the insolvency practitioner

Bankruptcy

45.68   In the case of bankruptcy, if there is no disclaimer, the effect is that the trustee in bankruptcy will remain liable upon the terms of the tenancy by virtue of privity of estate. If the bankrupt tenant was the original tenant, he will remain liable by privity of contract. Liability for all rent accruing after the date of the bankruptcy order will continue, notwithstanding the discharge of the tenant from bankruptcy[1]. If the trustee in bankruptcy wishes to be released from the liability, it is necessary for him to disclaim the lease or to assign it to a third party.

If the trustee in bankruptcy disclaims the tenancy[2], he is released from all liability. The landlord may prove for rent and other liabilities up to the date of the bankruptcy order and may also seek rent from the date of the bankruptcy order to the date of the disclaimer.

1   *Metropolis Estates Co Ltd v Wilde* [1940] 2 KB 536, [1940] 3 All ER 522, CA.
2   As to the position in relation to the termination of a licence upon bankruptcy, see *Perpetual Trustee Co Ltd v BNY Corporate Trustee Services Ltd* [2009] EWCA Civ 1160, [2010] Ch 347, [2010] 3 WLR 87.

SURRENDER: PRACTICALITIES

45.70A   Particularly in a recessionary economic climate, landlords are often under pressure to accept a surrender of a tenancy without due diligence. This is not often the case in relation to agricultural holdings, but is more prevalent in respect of commercial premises. These might be part of a diversified agricultural holding.

There are practical issues which need to be addressed including:

(a)   securing the keys;
(b)   receiving any title documents;
(c)   dealing with any rates payable;
(d)   addressing arrears of rent;
(e)   establishing the state and condition of the property;
(f)   dealing with any employees of the tenant[1];
(g)   arranging for the removal of chattels[2].

¹   Regard has to be had to the Transfer of Undertakings (Protection of Employment) Regulations (TUPE).
²   Notice may need to be given under the Torts (Interference with Goods) Act 1977.

FRAUD ACT 2006

45.71 The Fraud Act 2006 came into force on 15 January 2007. It applies to England, Wales and Northern Ireland. It repeals the deception offences previously contained in the Theft Acts 1968 and 1979. It replaces those offences with a single offence of fraud.

The Fraud Act 2006 states that fraud can be committed in one of three ways:

(a)   by false representation¹;
(b)   by failure to disclose information when there is a legal duty to do so²; and
(c)   by an abuse of position³.

The Fraud Act 2006 widens the scope of events that can be classed as fraud. It provides that a maximum sentence of ten years' imprisonment can be imposed on a person found guilty under the Fraud Act 2006.

The Fraud Act 2006 may arise in relation to landlord and tenant relationships and to property related transactions more generally. For example, the Fraud Act 2006 may have relevance in relation to cases of the type of *Rous v Mitchell*⁴, where the tenant relies upon the tort of deceit to set aside a landlord's notice to quit.

Under the Theft Acts 1968 and 1979, it was necessary for a party asserting reliance upon the deception offences to establish that a loss had been suffered. The Fraud Act 2006 provides that allegations of fraud can be investigated where no loss has been suffered and no gain made. Further, the representation or statement made, for the purposes of s 2 of the Fraud Act 2006, does not have to be untrue. It may be sufficient that it is merely misleading⁵.

¹   Fraud Act 2006, s 2.
²   Fraud Act 2006, s 3.
³   Fraud Act 2006, s 4.
⁴   [1989] 2 EGLR 5, [1989] 48 EG 59; affd [1991] 1 All ER 676, [1991] 1 EGLR 1, CA. See para 31.15.
⁵   As to the calculation of damages in relation to the tort of deceit, see *Parabola Investments Ltd v Browallia Cal Ltd* [2010] EWCA Civ 486, [2010] 3 WLR 1266, [2010] NLJR 697.

Chapter 46

AGRICULTURAL LAND TRIBUNALS

Note: This updated version of Chapter 46 replaces the 9th edn version in its entirety.

The publication of the ninth edition of this book was delayed in the hope that it would be possible to incorporate the promised new rules applying to the Agricultural Land Tribunals (ALT) procedure. Regrettably, at the end of August 2007, the timetable for finalising the new rules, laying them before Parliament and implementing them, remained uncertain and the book had to go to print.

In January 2007, DEFRA published a draft of the revised Agricultural Land Tribunals (Rules) Order for England and Wales for consultation. The new rules arose from the concern expressed by ALT chairmen that the existing rules were outdated and hampered their ability to carry out their activities effectively and in the best interests of the parties. The existing rules did not reflect either modern civil procedure rules or the new 'Model Rules of Procedure for Tribunals', published by the Council on Tribunals in 2003.

The draft of the new rules was substantially revised as a consequence of the consultation process. The resulting Agricultural Land Tribunals (Rules) Order 2007 ('the ALT Rules 2007') came into force on 15 January 2008.

Current indications are that the ALT will, in 2012, move into the First Tier of HM Courts & Tribunals Service. This is likely to result in a further change of rules, appeal procedure and re-structuring of administrative areas.

INTRODUCTION

46.1 The ALT were set up by s 73 of the Agriculture Act 1947. Their original role was as an appellate court hearing appeals from decisions of the Minister or the County Agricultural Executive Committees.

Following the Agriculture Act 1958, the ALT now has a very important role to play as a court of first instance determining disputes under agricultural legislation, principally the Agricultural Holdings Act 1986 ('AHA 1986'). Indeed, following the enactment of the Agricultural Tenancies Act 1995 ('ATA 1995'), and the withering on the vine of the AHA 1986, it will increasingly be the case that practitioners dealing with matters under the AHA 1986 will find that it is the ALT which maintains its residual significance as tenants continue to seek succession tenancies[1].

---

[1]   See Chs 34–36.

Current jurisdiction

46.2 The current jurisdiction of the ALT falls into three separate categories. First and foremost, the ALT deals with applications for succession to an existing AHA 1986 protected tenancy upon the death or retirement of the sitting tenant. This jurisdiction was introduced for succession upon death by the Agriculture (Miscellaneous Provisions) Act 1976, Pt II, which was extended for succession on retirement by the Agricultural Holdings Act 1984. It should be noted that although the 1984 Act extended succession to retirement of the sitting tenant, at the same time that Act withdrew succession on death and retirement in relation to tenancies granted on or after 12 July 1984 with limited exceptions[1].

In addition to its jurisdiction dealing with succession, the ALT has two other roles. First, it is the ALT which deals with applications under the Land Drainage Act 1991[2]. These provide a remedy for owners and occupiers of any land which has suffered injury or which has been prevented from being improved by drainage through a neighbour's neglect of ditches.

Second, the ALT has an additional jurisdiction in relation to agricultural holdings in eight cases:

(a) Applications for consent to the operation of a notice to quit[3].
(b) Applications for a certificate of bad husbandry as a precondition to a landlord being able to give a so-called incontestable notice to quit to the tenant under Case C of Sch 3 of the AHA 1986[4].
(c) The variation or revocation of conditions imposed on consents to the operation of a notice to quit by the ALT[5].
(d) An application for a direction to provide, alter or repair fixed equipment[6].
(e) Applications for approval, in default of consent from the landlord, for long-term improvements to be carried out by the tenant[7].
(f) An application dealing with a determination in relation to a landlord's failure to carry out improvements[8].
(g) An application for a direction that an agricultural holding be treated as a market garden[9].
(h) An application for a direction to avoid or relax a provision in a lease dealing with heather or grass burning[10].

[1] See Chs 34–36.
[2] Land Drainage Act 1991, ss 28 or 30.
[3] AHA 1986, s 27(3).
[4] AHA 1986, Sch 3 para 9(1).
[5] AHA 1986, s 27(5).
[6] AHA 1986, s 11(1).
[7] AHA 1986, s 67(3).
[8] AHA 1986, s 67(6)(b).
[9] AHA 1986, s 80.
[10] Hill Farming Act 1946, s 21 (as amended by the Agriculture Act 1958 ('AA 1958')).

Constitution

46.3 England and Wales are served by eight ALTs with separate geographical jurisdictions[1]. The areas and addresses of ALTs are, since the making of the Agricultural Land Tribunals (Areas) Order 1982[2], as follows:

46.3 *Agricultural Land Tribunals*

Area	Counties and London Boroughs	Address
Northern	Tees Valley Cumbria Durham Northumberland Tyne & Wear	Hornbeam House Electra Way Crewe Cheshire CW1 6GJ Secretary: Mr M Baker Tel: 01270 754156 Fax: 01270 754260 Email: michael.baker@defra.gsi.gov.uk
Yorkshire and Humberside	Humberside (the former county of) North Yorkshire South Yorkshire West Yorkshire	Crewe Office
Midlands	Derbyshire Hereford and Worcester Leicestershire Nottinghamshire Warwickshire West Midlands	Crewe Office
Western	Cheshire Greater Manchester Lancashire Merseyside Shropshire Staffordshire	Crewe Office
South Western	Avon (the former county of) Cornwall Devon Dorset Gloucestershire Somerset Wiltshire Isles of Scilly	Zone 2/18 Temple Quay House 2, The Square Temple Quay Bristol BS1 6EB Secretary: Mr R Gilbey Tel: 0117 372 3511/3510 Fax: 0117 372 3512 Email: ray.gilbey@defra.gsi.gov.uk
South Eastern	Berkshire Buckinghamshire East Sussex	Bristol Office

	Hampshire Isle of Wight Kent Oxfordshire Surrey West Sussex London Boroughs South of the River Thames including Richmond upon Thames	
Eastern	Bedfordshire Cambridgeshire Essex Hertfordshire Lincolnshire Norfolk Northamptonshire Suffolk London Boroughs North of the River Thames except Richmond upon Thames	Bristol Office
Welsh	Gwynedd Clwyd Dyfed Gwent Powys Mid/South/West Glamorgan	Government Buildings Spa Road East Llandrindod Wells Powys LD1 5HA Tel: 01597 828281 Fax: 01597 828385 Email: altwales@wales.gsi.gov.uk

[1] The constitution of individual ALTs is governed by the Agriculture Act 1947 ('AA 1947'), Sch 9 paras 13–16, as amended by the Agriculture Act 1958, Sch 1 para 5(1) and (2).
[2] SI 1982/07.

46.4 Where an agricultural holding falls partly within the area of one tribunal and partly within the area of another, then the tribunal for the area in which the greater part is situated has jurisdiction[1].

Since the Agricultural Land Tribunals (Areas) Order 1982, the description of the areas within which each tribunal has jurisdiction has not been revised following local government re-organisation to accord with the new local authorities and no new statutory instrument has been made. However, since re-organisation of local authorities, some of the counties no longer exist, eg Avon, Humberside and some of the Welsh counties[2].

205

Each ALT consists of panels of suitable persons appointed for each area, including a chairman and deputy chairmen and members appointed by the Lord Chancellor. For the hearing of each individual case, the ALT will consist of three people. One will be the chairman (or a deputy chairman) together with a representative of the interests of owners of agricultural land and a representative of the interests of farmers. The chairman and deputy chairmen must be qualified lawyers, being a barrister or solicitor of at least seven years standing, appointed by the Lord Chancellor. In addition to the three usual members of the ALT, the chairman may also nominate two assessors to assist at the hearing, should he deem it necessary. The assessors are selected from a panel of surveyors nominated by the President of the Royal Institution of Chartered Surveyors. The nomination of a surveyor is rarely made in practice.

A technical slip in the constitution of the ALT, or even the disqualification of a person sitting as a member, will not invalidate the decision[3]. Further, the decision of the ALT need not be unanimous[4].

[1] See the Agricultural Land Tribunals (Rules) Order 2007, SI 2007/3105, Part 1 and AA 1947, s 75 (as amended by AA 1958, Sch 1 para 4) whereby the Lord Chancellor was given power to direct, on application, that the whole of the land should be treated as being in the area of one or other of the tribunals in an appropriate case.
[2] For the earlier provisions, see Agricultural Land Tribunals (Areas) Order 1974, SI 1974/66, as amended by Agricultural Land Tribunals (Areas) (Amendment) Order 1976, SI 1976/208. The current order is the Agricultural Land Tribunals (Areas) Order 1982, SI 1982/97.
[3] Agriculture Act 1947, Sch 9 para 20(2).
[4] Cf *Brain v Minister of Pensions* [1947] KB 625, [1947] 1 All ER 892 and *Minister of Pensions v Horsey* [1949] 2 KB 526, [1949] 2 All ER 314; and the Agricultural Land Tribunals (Rules) Order 2007, SI 2007/3105, r 30(1).

Time limits

46.5 As with many aspects of the AHA 1986, time limits are of critical importance. Reference should be made to chapters 34–36 dealing with the provisions in the AHA 1986 relating to succession. It is worth noting that there are two critical and inflexible time limits which must be complied with in connection with succession applications, namely:

(a) Following the death of a sitting tenant, an application for succession *must* be made within three months from the date of death[1].
(b) If the application for succession is given pursuant to a retirement notice by the sitting tenant, the application to the ALT for succession *must* be made within one month of such notice[2].

Further, the ALT Rules 2007[3] lays down strict time limits in connection with applications to the ALT. These range from the service of all documents in connection with an application to, for example:

(i)   A one-month time limit for applying for consent to the operation of a landlord's notice to quit, where appropriate[4].
(ii) A one-month time limit for replying to an application for consent or for succession.

The time limits must also be complied with, but r 51[5] provides that the chairman may, on receiving a written application supported by reasons, extend the time for any step in connection with ALT proceedings where he considers that it would not be reasonable to expect compliance within the time limits. The chairman's discretion whether to allow, conditionally or unconditionally, or to refuse such an extension is absolute[6]. The chairman may also shorten any time limit where he considers it reasonable to do so. Before exercising this discretion to extend or shorten time limits the chairman must give affected parties an opportunity to make representations within five days or such other period as directed.

The parties may, unless the chairman otherwise directs, agree in writing to vary a time limit provided that the secretary is notified in writing before the original time limit expires. The agreed variation can, unless the chairman otherwise directs, be for a maximum of 28 days and the new deadline must expire no less than seven days before a hearing.

Any failure to comply with the provisions of the ALT Rules 2007[7] does not of itself render the proceedings, or any part of the proceedings, invalid[8]. Directions may be given by the chairman or the ALT to cure or waive any irregularity before a decision is reached.

1 AHA 1986, s 39(1) and Agricultural Land Tribunals (Succession to Agricultural Tenancies) Order 1984, SI 1984/1301, art 3(3).
2 AHA 1986, s 53(2) and the Agricultural Land Tribunals (Succession to Agricultural Tenancies) Order 1984, SI 1984/1301, art 23(2). See para 46.8 below as to the distinction between the time limits under the AHA 1986 referred to in sub-paras (a) and (b) above. These are mandatory whereas deadlines under the ALT Rules 2007 can be extended pursuant to r 51.
3 Agricultural Land Tribunals (Rules) Order 2007, SI 2007/3105.
4 Agricultural Land Tribunals (Rules) Order 2007, SI 2007/3105, r 39.
5 Agricultural Land Tribunals (Rules) Order 2007, SI 2007/3105, r 51.
6 *Moss v National Coal Board* (1982) 264 Estates Gazette 52. Also, see generally, *Kellett v Alexander* (1980) 257 Estates Gazette 494.
7 Agricultural Land Tribunals (Rules) Order 2007, SI 2007/3105.
8 Agricultural Land Tribunals (Rules) Order 2007, SI 2007/3105, r 47. Also see *Purser v Bailey* [1967] 2 QB 500, [1967] 2 All ER 189, CA.

ALT PROCEDURE

Application

46.6 A new provision has been introduced by the ALT Rules 2007[1]. Before making an application for succession, whether on death (under s 39 of the AHA 1986)[2] or on retirement (under s 55 of the AHA 1986)[3], the applicant must deliver a notice in writing of his intention to do so to all interested parties[4]. Interested parties is defined in the Rules as 'every person who appears to the applicant to be an interested party'[5].

Any application to the ALT must be made in writing and state:

(a)   the name and address of the applicant;
(b)   the name and address of every respondent;

(c)   the address, description and area of all land which is referred to in the application;
(d)   the reasons for the application including particulars of any hardship to the applicant;
(e)   the order and every other remedy which the applicant seeks;
(f)   the name and address of every person who appears to the applicant to be an interested party, with reasons for that person's interest;
(g)   where the applicant bases his application on the ground of hardship to any person other than himself, the name and address of each such person and particulars of the hardship on which the applicant relies; and
(h)   the name, address and profession of any representative of the applicant and whether the Tribunal should deliver notices concerning the application to the representative instead of to the applicant[6].

The applicant must include in his application, in addition to the information required by r 2(2) of the ALT Rules 2007 (see above), confirmation that he has notified the interested parties in accordance with r 40(2) of the ALT Rules 2007.

[1]   Agricultural Land Tribunals (Rules) Order 2007, SI 2007/3105.
[2]   See Ch 35.
[3]   See Ch 36.
[4]   Agricultural Land Tribunals (Rules) Order 2007, SI 2007/3105, r 40(2).
[5]   Agricultural Land Tribunals (Rules) Order 2007, SI 2007/3105, r 2(2)(f).
[6]   Agricultural Land Tribunals (Rules) Order 2007, SI 2007/3105, r 2(2).

46.7 The application forms are no longer prescribed following the repealing of the Agricultural Land Tribunals (Succession to Agricultural Tenancies) Order 1984, SI 1984/1301. They are now issued by the ALT in a standardised format. These are available to download from various sources although use of the old version, while not good practice, should not invalidate an application[1].

The revoking of the Agricultural Land Tribunals (Rules) Order 1978, SI 1978/259, has also resulted in the similar withdrawal of all of the prescribed forms which relate to the ALT's jurisdiction on issues other than succession.

Practitioners will find that the forms appear deceptively straightforward, but in practice require very careful and detailed consideration, together with the supply of a considerable amount of information.

Each application should be accompanied by:

(a)   two copies of a map of the land which is referred to in the application or reply on a scale of 1/10,000, or larger; and
(b)   two copies of any plan or other document which the party making the application or reply intends to rely upon in support of their case[2].

Further, in connection with an application for succession, normally an applicant will need to produce the following documents to establish his eligibility and suitability to be granted a new tenancy in succession to the deceased or retiring tenant:

(a)   the deceased tenant's death certificate;

(b)   the applicant's birth certificate;

(c)   the applicant's marriage certificate in the case of a widow or married daughter applicant;

(d)   any farm partnership agreement or contract of employment;

(e)   farm accounts for the relevant five years, ending with the date of death. In practice it is wise to produce seven years' accounts;

(f)   a statement of the applicant's wages (if any);

(g)   a statement identifying any outside sources of livelihood, whether derived from agriculture or otherwise;

(h)   a copy of any tenancy agreement or other agreement relating to any other land farmed by the applicant;

(i)   copies of certificates relating to any relevant academic and/or vocational qualifications of the applicant;

(j)   a medical certificate stating the applicant's state of health;

(k)   a full statement of the applicant's capital resources and any other capital available to be used to finance the farming;

(l)   documentation from the applicant's bank or other lender detailing any lending to the applicant and the terms of such lending;

(m)   if changes are proposed in relation to the farming system, details of those changes together with a farm budget and cashflow projection;

(n)   the deceased tenant's will, probate and Her Majesty's Revenue & Customs (HMRC) account if the applicant is relying upon any inherited funds;

(o)   the Case G notice to quit served by the landlord (if any);

(p)   the tenancy agreement of the subject holding;

(q)   copies of the applicant's tax returns for the relevant years.

A proper preparation of the documents which are necessary to be supplied to the ALT cannot be overemphasised. Although, for example, it is possible to seek a direction from the chairman to dispense with the provision of a map, plan or any other document required to be provided[3], good practice dictates that this should be avoided.

It should be noted that every application and any supporting written statement must state at the end that 'I believe that the facts stated in this document are true'[4]. The application must be signed by the party making it, or by a person authorised to do so on his behalf, and should be delivered or sent to the secretary of the ALT[5]. Sufficient copies should be enclosed to allow the secretary to retain one and serve all the respondents. On receiving from any party an application, reply or other document referred to in the ALT Rules 2007, the secretary shall forthwith acknowledge receipt, register the application and serve one copy on every other party to the proceedings[6].

---

[1]   Agricultural Land Tribunals (Rules) Order 2007, SI 2007/3105, r 2. Also see, *Morris v Patel* [1987] 1 EGLR 75, (1986) 281 Estates Gazette 419, CA, where an out of date form was used. It was held to be 'substantially to the like effect' to the forms then in use so the application was not invalid.

[2]   Agricultural Land Tribunals (Rules) Order 2007, SI 2007/3105, r 7(1).

[3]   Agricultural Land Tribunals (Rules) Order 2007, SI 2007/3105, r 7(2).

[4]   Agricultural Land Tribunals (Rules) Order 2007, SI 2007/3105, r 2(3).

[5]   Agricultural Land Tribunals (Rules) Order 2007, SI 2007/3105, r 2(4).

[6]   Agricultural Land Tribunals (Rules) Order 2007, SI 2007/3105, r 3.

Reply

46.8 A respondent who receives a copy of an application must deliver to the secretary a written reply acknowledging receipt of the application and setting out:

(a)   the title of the proceedings, the name of the applicant and the case number;

(b)   his name and address and the name and address of every person who appears to the respondent to be an interested party who is not already named in the application, with reasons for that person's interest;

(c)   a statement whether or not he intends to resist the application and, if so, the reasons for resisting it or the position he will adopt;

(d)   whether he intends to be present or be represented at any hearing; and

(e)   the name, address and the profession of any representative and whether the Tribunal should deliver notices concerning the application to the representative instead of to the respondent[1].

The reply, as with an application, must be supported by a statement of truth and signed by the respondent or his representative. The reply must be delivered to the secretary within one month of the date on which the application was delivered to the respondent[2].

It should be noted that the ALT Rules 2007 refers to applications and replies in a general sense as it has a much wider jurisdiction than succession applications under the AHA 1986. However, it is anticipated that the main reason practitioners will refer to this chapter is in relation to succession cases so an important distinction needs to be made at this point.

The succession application time limits (including the related issue of consent to operation of the landlord's Case G notice to quit) are set out earlier in this chapter[3]. These time limits are prescribed by statute, the AHA 1986, so are completely inflexible and must be adhered to. However, in respect of the ALT's wider jurisdiction[4], a reply delivered after the one-month time limit has expired must be treated as an application for an extension of time if it contains the reasons for the delay[5].

If the application for extension of time is refused (or allowed and still not complied with) then the respondent may not take any further part in the proceedings without the permission of the chairman except to:

(a)   apply for a (further) extension of time for filing a reply;

(b)   request that the applicant provide further detail of his application;

(c)   apply to review the ALT's decision in respect of why the respondent did not receive the application or was not able to file a reply in accordance with the time limit;

(d)   be called as a witness;

(e)   be delivered a copy of the ALT's decision[6].

---

[1]   Agricultural Land Tribunals (Rules) Order 2007, SI 2007/3105, r 4(1).

[2]   Agricultural Land Tribunals (Rules) Order 2007, SI 2007/3105, r 4(2).

[3]   See para 46.5.

[4]   See para 46.2(b)–(h).

⁵   Agricultural Land Tribunals (Rules) Order 2007, SI 2007/3105, r 4(5).
⁶   Agricultural Land Tribunals (Rules) Order 2007, SI 2007/3105, r 4(6).

Service

46.9 Any document required or authorised by the rules governing the procedure before the ALT to be delivered to any person, body or authority is duly served if it was delivered to them or sent to the proper address by special delivery, recorded delivery or otherwise with proof of posting[1].

The ALT Rules 2007 refer to the often contentious issue of service of documents by electronic means. A document is deemed served if it is sent to the proper address by fax or other means of electronic communication. However, electronic service is only possible where the recipient has consented in writing to the use of such means of communication. A legal representative is deemed to give such consent if the fax number or email address is shown as an acceptable means of delivery on his notepaper. The standard practice of including such details on letterheads would be enough to indicate such acceptance.

¹   Agricultural Land Tribunals (Rules) Order 2007, SI 2007/3105, r 49(1).

46.10 Although there is no definition provided of 'legal representative' it would appear to exclude both Chartered Surveyors and Fellows of the Central Association of Agricultural Valuers. This is an odd use of terminology when the rules state simply that the parties may appear at the hearing or be represented[1]. There is no distinction, as there was under the old rules, between counsel, solicitor or other representative appointed in writing[2]. The result would therefore appear to be that non-legally qualified advisers cannot give deemed consent in such circumstances. However, the adoption of the frequently used caveat 'this firm does not accept service of documents by electronic means' will prevent such deemed acceptance by all professions.

When a document has been sent it should, unless the contrary is proved, be taken to have been received by the party to whom it is addressed:

(a)   in the case of a document sent by post, on the day on which the document would be delivered in the ordinary course of post;

(b)   in the case of a document transmitted by fax or other means of electronic communication, on the day on which the document is transmitted; or

(c)   in the case of a notice or document delivered in person, on the day on which the document is delivered.

Any document to be served on a UK incorporated or registered company should be sent to the company secretary at the registered or principal office. In order to achieve service on a UK company an authorised person will need to be identified and served with the relevant documents. Any partner may be served on behalf of a partnership and an unincorporated association may be served via a member of its governing body. Where a diocesan board of finance has an interest in land a copy of any relevant documentation must also be delivered to the Church Commissioners.

In the case of an untraceable recipient, one that is outside the UK or where no Personal Representatives have been appointed following death then the chairman may dispense with delivery. A direction may also be given for substituted service by means of a newspaper advertisement or otherwise.

1   Agricultural Land Tribunals (Rules) Order 2007, SI 2007/3105, r 23(3).
2   Agricultural Land Tribunals (Rules) Order 1978, SI 1978/259, r 25.

Withdrawal of application or reply

46.11 A party may withdraw his application or reply by giving notice in writing signed by the party or his representative to the secretary of the ALT at any time before the hearing. Notice may be given at the hearing but only with the permission of the ALT[1]. Where a reply is withdrawn the ALT may exercise its discretion to award costs. Any application for such an award must be made promptly[2].

1   Agricultural Land Tribunals (Rules) Order 2007, SI 2007/3105, r 6(1).
2   Agricultural Land Tribunals (Rules) Order 2007, SI 2007/3105, r 6(2)–(3). See para 46.14.

Amendment of application or reply

46.12 An application or reply may be amended or a supplementary statement of reasons provided at any time before notification of the hearing date is received. Amendment after this date will require the permission of the chairman. Changes to a party's case can be made at the hearing itself but consent of the ALT must be obtained and that may be granted on such terms as the tribunal thinks fit. As with the original application or reply, copies of any amendments or supplementary statements must be provided to the secretary and all other parties[1].

1   Agricultural Land Tribunals (Rules) Order 2007, SI 2007/3105, r 8.

Interlocutory applications

46.13 The applicant or respondent may include in their application or reply, or by way of a separate application, a request for disclosure or additional information from the other side. This can be used to good effect by those acting for landlords by including in the reply a request for the detailed supporting information which often does not accompany an application. Additionally requests can be made for:

(a)   an early hearing of the application or any preliminary issue supported by reasons;

(b)   agreement to the matter being dealt with by written representations only;

(c)   permission to rely on the evidence of more than two experts;

(d)   a decision on any preliminary issue.

The chairman may order that a person having an interest in the proceedings be made a party. This may result from an application from an existing party to the proceedings but that is not necessary. The order may be made on the chairman's own initiative. A person can be joined as a respondent without further formality but their consent is required if they are to become an applicant in the process. Any consequential directions as are considered necessary may be given.

Directions

46.14 Despite these provisions, it is the chairman who has the greater ability to dictate how the case proceeds by the issuing of instructions to the parties in the form of directions. These may be given at any stage of the proceedings either on an application by either party or on the chairman's own initiative.

Directions shape the process of the case and can be given to:

(a)   require the production of information, statements or documents;
(b)   direct a party to produce a signed statement from any person whose evidence they wish to rely on;
(c)   determine the relevant issues and what evidence is to be heard by the ALT.

A person may apply to vary or set aside a direction if they had no opportunity to object to it being given. The chairman (or ALT as appropriate) must not set aside or vary a direction without notifying the parties of the application and considering any representations from them.

If a direction is not complied with by a party then the ALT may, before or at the hearing, dismiss the application/reply in whole or part. Where appropriate a respondent can be debarred from contesting the application altogether. The ALT must not take such action without giving notice to the defaulting party which gives it the chance to comply within a specified period or establish why the proposed dismissal or debarring should not occur.

The rules have incorporated the proactive nature of the Civil Procedure Rules with the chairman able to give directions for a case management meeting to be held. At the meeting the chairman must give all necessary directions for the conduct of the application. The chairman may encourage the parties or their expert witnesses to meet with a view to settling the dispute or, at least, narrowing the issues for the hearing.

Preliminary issues

46.15 The chairman may direct that any question of fact or law which arises out of an application may be decided at a preliminary hearing[1]. If deciding that issue substantially disposes of the whole application then the ALT may treat the preliminary hearing as the main hearing and give directions to conclude the matter[2]. The ALT may, in circumstances where the preliminary issue is not determinative of the proceedings as a whole, decide the issue and go on to consider the application without a further hearing in any event. This can only happen with the parties agreement and if the ALT has considered any representations made by them. Such a preliminary hearing, unlike the final one, would not be in public so this approach could only be taken where there were no important public interest considerations. The chairman will also have to consider the material before the ALT and the issues raised in determining that dispensing with a final hearing does not prejudice the administration of justice[3].

[1]   Agricultural Land Tribunals (Rules) Order 2007, SI 2007/3105, r 13(1).
[2]   Agricultural Land Tribunals (Rules) Order 2007, SI 2007/3105, r 13(2).
[3]   Agricultural Land Tribunals (Rules) Order 2007, SI 2007/3105, r 13(3).

Notice of hearing

46.16 Extensive interlocutory issues are not anticipated before the ALT. Therefore the secretary must, as soon as reasonably practicable and with due regard to the reasonable convenience of the parties, fix a date, time and place for the hearing of the application. The secretary must give notice of the hearing 14 clear days before the hearing is due to take place[1].

In practice, the parties to the dispute may be attempting to negotiate a settlement and, as the issues are often complex, such time can be taken in negotiations during which the parties might request that a hearing is deferred.

The secretary must include with the notice of hearing, information relating to the rules and procedure of the ALT. This will include the right of any party who is not represented or does not intend to appear at the hearing to deliver to the secretary additional written representations or evidence in support of their case[2].

When a party receives the notice of hearing he must inform the secretary whether he intends to be present or represented at the hearing and the names of any witnesses he intends to call[3].

The chairman may consolidate applications lodged in respect of the same subject matter or which involve the same or similar issues. He may take this action on his own initiative or on an application by a party[4]. Before making a direction, notice must be given to all parties who have the opportunity to make representations[5]. Subject to the chairman's directions, and any specific provision of the rules, all applications in respect of a particular holding must be heard and determined together[6].

The ALT may (except in a drainage case) deal with an application or preliminary issue without a hearing if no reply is delivered within the appointed (or extended) time and the application is unopposed. The ALT will also have to consider the administration of justice and review the materials and issues which would have been reviewed at a hearing. If there are no such concerns and there is no other important public interest consideration requiring a public hearing then the matter can be considered without a hearing[7].

The applicant must compile a hearing bundle containing all relevant documents and the respondent is required to assist in its preparation. The contents must be agreed, paginated and indexed. Four copies must be delivered to the secretary and one to each party not less than seven days before the hearing[8].

1 Agricultural Land Tribunals (Rules) Order 2007, SI 2007/3105, r 16(1).
2 Agricultural Land Tribunals (Rules) Order 2007, SI 2007/3105, r 16(2)(c).
3 Agricultural Land Tribunals (Rules) Order 2007, SI 2007/3105, r 16(3).
4 Agricultural Land Tribunals (Rules) Order 2007, SI 2007/3105, r 18(1).
5 Agricultural Land Tribunals (Rules) Order 2007, SI 2007/3105, r 18(2).
6 Agricultural Land Tribunals (Rules) Order 2007, SI 2007/3105, r 18(3).
7 Agricultural Land Tribunals (Rules) Order 2007, SI 2007/3105, r 19.
8 Agricultural Land Tribunals (Rules) Order 2007, SI 2007/3105, r 20.

Inspection

46.17 Practice differs from ALT to ALT as to whether inspection of the subject holding will take place immediately before the main hearing commences or whether the ALT convenes initially and then adjourns to carry out the inspection or whether the inspection takes place after the main hearing. An inspection of the holding is usually an important part of the hearing of any case, unless the issues have been narrowed to the extent that an inspection would not assist deliberations. The ALT is authorised to enter and inspect an agricultural holding owned or occupied by any party and to inspect fixed equipment, produce, livestock, etc. The members of the ALT panel may be accompanied by the parties, their representatives and expert witnesses including any expert appointed by the ALT itself, but, as in the case of arbitration, care should be taken not to treat the inspection as a quasi-hearing[1].

The ALT sits in public unless it is satisfied that by reason of disclosure of confidential information it is reasonable that the hearing or some part of it should take place in private. Any person may attend a hearing in private providing all parties have consented[2].

Any party may appear or be heard in person or alternatively represented by a barrister, solicitor, surveyor or otherwise[3].

At the hearing the party making the application shall begin and other parties shall be heard in such order as the ALT may determine. Further, the flexibility employed is reflected in the provision that the procedure of the hearing shall be such as the ALT may direct[4]. The ALT must, so far as it deems appropriate, avoid formality and inflexibility in the proceedings[5].

If a party fails to appear at the hearing at the time fixed, the ALT may (if it is satisfied that the party was duly notified of the hearing and there is no good reason for the absence) hear and decide the application, question in the party's absence or adjourn the hearing. Before deciding to dispose of the application or question in the absence of a party the ALT must consider the application together with any reply and accompanying representations[6]. Where the applicant has failed to attend and the ALT has disposed of the application then no fresh application may be made arising out of the same facts without the consent of the ALT[7].

1   Agricultural Land Tribunals (Rules) Order 2007, SI 2007/3105, r 25(1).
2   Agricultural Land Tribunals (Rules) Order 2007, SI 2007/3105, r 21.
3   Agricultural Land Tribunals (Rules) Order 2007, SI 2007/3105, r 23(3).
4   Agricultural Land Tribunals (Rules) Order 2007, SI 2007/3105, r 23(2)(a).
5   Agricultural Land Tribunals (Rules) Order 2007, SI 2007/3105, r 23(2)(b).
6   Agricultural Land Tribunals (Rules) Order 2007, SI 2007/3105, r 22(1), (2).
7   Agricultural Land Tribunals (Rules) Order 2007, SI 2007/3105, r 22(3).

Evidence

46.18 The ALT may admit evidence of any relevant fact notwithstanding that it would not be admissible in a court of law[1]. This is in contrast to the rule that a party cannot be directed to produce any document which they could not be compelled to produce on the trial of an action in a court of law[2]. Any such documents produced must only be used for the purposes of the proceedings in hand[3].

Any party who wishes to rely on the evidence of a witness must deliver a statement of that witness to the secretary. Any such statement must be supported by a statement of truth[4].

At any stage of the proceedings, the ALT may order the personal attendance of the maker of a written statement, deponent of an affidavit or any expert whose report has been filed[5].

The ALT will give every party an opportunity to give evidence, call witnesses and to cross-examine any witness called by, or on behalf of, any other party and to re-examine his own witnesses after cross-examination. Further, a party may, if he so desires, give evidence as a witness on his own behalf and address the ALT generally on the subject matter of the application[6].

In an application for succession on death, where two or more applications are made, each applicant may, if he wishes to oppose any of the other applicants, include in his application, or in a separate reply, the following information:

(a)   reasons why he opposes or intends to oppose that other application;
(b)   a statement indicating whether he disputes that applicant's claim to be a designated applicant and, if so, why;
(c)   a claim to be a more suitable applicant than any other;
(d)   a statement that he has agreed with one or more other applicants to request the landlord's consent to a direction entitling them to a joint tenancy of the holding[7].

1   Agricultural Land Tribunals (Rules) Order 2007, SI 2007/3105, r 23(6).
2   Agricultural Land Tribunals (Rules) Order 2007, SI 2007/3105, r 11(3).
3   Agricultural Land Tribunals (Rules) Order 2007, SI 2007/3105, r 11(2).

4   Agricultural Land Tribunals (Rules) Order 2007, SI 2007/3105, r 24.
5   Agricultural Land Tribunals (Rules) Order 2007, SI 2007/3105, r 23(5).
6   Agricultural Land Tribunals (Rules) Order 2007, SI 2007/3105, r 23(4).
7   Agricultural Land Tribunals (Rules) Order 2007, SI 2007/3105, r 40(4).

Expert evidence

46.19 Unless the chairman otherwise directs, an expert may only give oral evidence if he has previously submitted a written report and delivered it to all parties. The parties are limited to two experts each unless the chairman allows an application for additional expert evidence. Such an application must state why such evidence is required and, where practicable, who will be providing it[1].

As with court proceedings, the expert's overriding duty is to assist the ALT on matters within his expertise. This duty overrides any obligation to the party instructing or paying him[2].

The expert's report must be addressed to the ALT and must contain[3]:

(a)   details of the expert's qualifications;
(b)   a statement of the substance of all material instructions whether written or oral, on the basis of which the report was written;
(c)   details of any literature or any other material which the expert has relied on in making the report;
(d)   where there is a range of opinion on the matter dealt with in the report—
    (i)   a summary of the range of opinion; and
    (ii)   the reasons for the expert's own opinion;
(e)   a summary of the conclusions reached; and
(f)   a statement that the expert understands his duty to the ALT and has complied with that duty.

1   Agricultural Land Tribunals (Rules) Order 2007, SI 2007/3105, r 27.
2   Agricultural Land Tribunals (Rules) Order 2007, SI 2007/3105, r 28.
3   Agricultural Land Tribunals (Rules) Order 2007, SI 2007/3105, r 29(4).

Decision of the ALT

46.20 The decision of the ALT is given in writing together with, except in the case of a decision by consent, a statement of the ALT's reasons for its decision. In the event of a disagreement between the members of the panel, the decision may be a majority one. The chairman may, at or following the hearing give the parties an informal, non-binding indication of the ALT's likely decision.

At any time before the chairman signs the decision, the ALT may reconsider and if necessary reconvene the hearing or request further submissions. This may lead to a different decision to the one informally indicated.

The secretary of the ALT sends a copy of the decision and the reasons to each of the parties[1].

The chairman is able to correct any clerical mistake or error arising from an accidental slip or omission in the written record of the ALT's decision. Further, the ALT may set aside or vary its decision if:

(a)   a matter presented to the ALT during the hearing was not dealt with in the decision;

(b)   a party, entitled to be heard at the hearing, but who failed to be present or represented had a good reason for such failure;

(c)   new evidence has become available since the conclusion of the proceedings and its existence could not reasonably have been known or foreseen before then[2].

1   Agricultural Land Tribunals (Rules) Order 2007, SI 2007/3105, r 30.
2   Agricultural Land Tribunals (Rules) Order 2007, SI 2007/3105, r 32.

Costs

46.21 Originally, under the Agricultural Holdings Act 1948, the ALT had no power to make any costs order. Section 5 of the Agriculture (Miscellaneous Provisions) Act 1954 introduced a limited power for the ALT to award costs, but only against a party who had acted 'frivolously, vexatiously or oppressively'. A further extension was introduced by the Agriculture Act 1958. That gave the ALT power to order a 'reasonable contribution towards costs' against any party in proceedings relating to the enforcement of a condition attaching to the giving of consent to a notice to quit.

When the 1948 Act was repealed and re-enacted, the AHA 1986, s 27(7) included a power for the ALT, in proceedings under that section, to provide for the payment by any party of such sum as the ALT considers a reasonable contribution to costs. The width of this jurisdiction has been the subject of confusion and debate. In *Newall v Wright*[1], the ALT decided that this was not a general power to award costs against a landlord or a tenant in relation to any application for consent to the operation of a notice to quit. This is contrary to the view expressed in the previous edition of this book[2]. Section 27(7) of the AHA 1986 provides that the ALT 'may, in proceedings under this section, by order provide for the payment of any party of such sum as the [ALT] consider a reasonable contribution towards costs'. In *Newall v Wright*, it was determined that an application by a landlord for consent to the operation of a notice to quit does not involve 'proceedings under this section'. A definitive answer to the issue from the courts is awaited.

Otherwise, in proceedings before the ALT, the power to award costs is limited to cases where the ALT determines that a party has acted 'frivolously, vexatiously or oppressively'[3].

1   (2005) ALT, Eastern Area.
2   See Scammell and Densham's Law of Agricultural Holdings (8th edn, 1997), p 425, para (7).
3   Agriculture (Miscellaneous Provisions) Act 1954, s 5. It was not until the enactment of that section that the ALT had any power to award costs. The power was then extended in relation to certain cases involving consent to the operation of the landlord's notice to quit by the Agriculture Act 1958, Sch 1 para 13. See, *Harris v Stubbings* (2008) ALT/SW40/90.

Date of postponement of operation of notice to quit

46.22 When the ALT consents to the operation of a notice to quit it has power either of its own motion or on the application of the tenant to postpone the termination of the tenancy for a period not exceeding 12 months if the notice to quit would otherwise become effective on or within six months after the giving of consent[1]. The tenant's application must be made within 14 days of the consent being given[2]. It is unclear as to whether the 12-month period commences on the date that consent is given or when the notice to quit would otherwise expire[3].

[1] Agricultural Holdings (Arbitration Notices) Order 1987, SI 1987/710, art 13(1).
[2] Agricultural Holdings (Arbitration Notices) Order 1987, SI 1987/710, art 13(1).
[3] Agricultural Holdings (Arbitration Notices) Order 1987, SI 1987/710, art 13(1).

APPEALS AGAINST A DECISION OF THE ALT

Generally

46.23 There are two methods of challenging a decision of the ALT. First, either during the ALT proceedings or after their conclusion, a point of law may be referred to the High Court by way of case stated.

The second method of disputing a decision of the ALT is by way of an application for judicial review seeking a prerogative order from the High Court.

Reference to the High Court of a question of law

46.24 Section 6 of the Agriculture (Miscellaneous Provisions) Act 1954 gives the ALT the ability to refer questions of law to the High Court at the request of any party to the proceedings. These provisions are now supplemented by the ALT Rules 2007, rr 37 and 38[1]. The procedure is no longer exclusively 'an appeal by way of case stated' as the chairman *may* direct the party making a request to supply a draft of the case stated[2].

A reference lies only on a point of law and must be the subject of a request by either party[3]. The ALT cannot state a case of its own motion. The request must state:

(a) concisely the questions of law that the party wishes the ALT to refer to the High Court; and
(b) any findings of fact which the party disputes.

The chairman may invite the party to amend its request or draft statement of case if he considers that:

(a) any question of law referred to could be expressed in clearer terms; or
(b) it is desirable to add or substitute a similar or related question[4].

Any party wishing to appeal from a decision of the ALT must make a request either at the hearing, or in writing to the secretary of the ALT, not later than 28 days from the date when the decision is delivered to the said party[5].

If the ALT decides to refuse a request, the secretary must, within 14 days (or such extended period as the chairman considers necessary) of receipt of it, give a notice in writing to that effect to all parties which gives reasons for the refusal[6].

Where the ALT has refused a request to refer a question of law to the High Court, the appellant has a right to apply to the court for an order directing the ALT to state a case[7]. The method of application is by motion to the Administrative Court of the Queen's Bench Division. The procedure is that the appellant must, within 14 days after receiving notice of the refusal, serve on the secretary a notice in writing of his intended application and deliver copies to all other parties[8].

It is also necessary in cases of applications under s 11 of the AHA 1986 (the provision of fixed equipment, etc) that the application notice and case stated should be served on the authority having power to enforce the statutory requirement specified in the application. The authority has the right to be heard.

A case stated for the decision of the High Court must set out the question of law and any disputed findings of fact. A copy of the ALT's decision must also be attached. The chairman must then sign the case stated and deliver it to all parties within two months of the date of request or making of the order by the High Court directing the reference[9]. It is normally most convenient for the parties to seek to agree the form and contents of the case stated rather than to leave the matter to the ALT[10].

It is submitted that the test which the court should apply in deciding whether to require the ALT to state a case is whether the court is satisfied that there is a fairly arguable point of law which would justify ordering the ALT to refer it to the High Court for decision[11].

Any decision of the High Court will be given effect to by the ALT. This will be achieved either by it being reconvened for the purpose or by the chairman exercising his powers under s 6(5) of the 1954 Act[12]. If the ALT cannot be reconvened as originally constituted then the hearing must take place before a differently constituted tribunal[13].

1   SI 2007/3105.
2   Agricultural Land Tribunals (Rules) Order 2007, SI 2007/3105, r 37(3).
3   Cf the arbitrator's position, where the case stated lies only before the making of the award and where the arbitrator may state a case of his own motion.
4   Agricultural Land Tribunals (Rules) Order 2007, SI 2007/3105, r 37(4).
5   Agricultural Land Tribunals (Rules) Order 2007, SI 2007/3105, r 37(1).
6   Agricultural Land Tribunals (Rules) Order 2007, SI 2007/3105, r 37(5).
7   Agriculture (Miscellaneous Provisions) Act 1954, s 6(2).
8   Agricultural Land Tribunals (Rules) Order 2007, SI 2007/3105, r 37(6).
9   Agricultural Land Tribunals (Rules) Order 2007, SI 2007/3105, r 37(7).

[10]   See the remarks of Widgery LCJ in *Cooke v Talbot* (1977) 243 Estates Gazette 831 where the ALT refused to state a case when invited to do so by the tenant, the Lord Chief Justice said that it was desirable in such cases for the parties to seek to agree the statement of facts and the questions of law rather than leave this to the tribunal. As to the method of formulating an appeal by way of case stated, see the remarks of Megaw LJ in *Camden London Borough v Civil Aviation Authority* (1980) 257 Estates Gazette 273 at 277, CA. See also *R v Agricultural Land Tribunal for the South Eastern Area, ex p Parslow* [1979] 2 EGLR 1, (1979) 251 Estates Gazette 667.

[11]   *William Smith (Wakefield) Ltd v Parisride Ltd* [2005] EWHC 462 (Admin), [2005] 2 EGLR 22, [2005] 24 EG 180. Cf *Davies v Agricultural Land Tribunal (Wales)* [2007] EWHC 1395 (Admin); *Ross v Donaldson* 1983 SLT (Land Ct) 26; *Maggs v Worsley* (1982) ALT, South Western Area.

[12]   Agricultural Land Tribunals (Rules) Order 2007, SI 2007/3105, r 38.

[13]   It was held in *Cooke v Talbot* (1977) 243 Estates Gazette 831 that the Divisional Court had no power to compel the reconstitution of the ALT for the purposes of the further hearing, even if they felt it was desirable to do so. Also see *R v Agricultural Land Tribunal (Wales), ex p Hughes* (1980) 255 Estates Gazette 703.

Judicial review

46.25   Until the passing of s 6 of the Agriculture (Miscellaneous Provisions) Act 1954, the only right of appeal from the ALT lay by way of prerogative order of certiorari, mandamus or prohibition. These orders have now been amalgamated in one form of prerogative order known as judicial review. This is a restricted remedy which will only rarely be appropriate. In principle, this is still available in order to challenge the decision of the ALT on the same grounds as that of an arbitrator[1].

The uniform procedure for the exercise by the High Court of its jurisdiction to supervise the proceedings of inferior courts, tribunals or arbitrations is governed by s 31 of the Senior Courts Act 1981 and Parts 8 and 54 of the Civil Procedure Rules[2]. There is a two-tier system for making the application. First, it is necessary to obtain leave to apply for judicial review. Then, if permission is granted, the substantive application is heard. The relief sought may include one of the prerogative orders which have been renamed quashing orders, mandatory orders and prohibiting orders respectively.

[1]   *Re Jones and Carter's Arbitration* [1922] 2 Ch 599, 91 LJ Ch 824, CA; *Maxwell-Lefroy v Bracey* (1956) 167 Estates Gazette 147; and *Price v Romilly* [1960] 3 All ER 429, [1960] 1 WLR 1360; and see Tribunals and Inquiries Act 1958, s 11. See also, *Davies v Price* [1958] 1 All ER 671, [1958] 1 WLR 434, CA.

[2]   See CPR Pts 8 and 54. Reference should be made to the current edition of the Civil Procedure Rules as to the procedure to be adopted.

Chapter 47

ARBITRATION

ARBITRATION UNDER THE AGRICULTURAL TENANCIES ACT 1995

Stay of proceedings

47.2 In relation to the court's jurisdiction, regard must be had to s 9 of the Arbitration Act 1996 (AA 1996)[1], which gives the court power to stay proceedings before the court where the litigants are parties to a binding arbitration agreement[2].

The power given to the court by s 9 of the AA 1996 applies where:

(a)   a party to an arbitration agreement against whom legal proceedings are brought (whether by way of claim or counter-claim) in respect of a matter under which the agreement is to be referred to arbitration may (upon notice to the other parties to the proceedings) apply to the court in which the proceedings have been brought to stay the proceedings so far as they concern that matter[3]; and

(b)   the person applying to stay the proceedings has taken the appropriate procedural step (if any) to acknowledge the legal proceedings against him[4]; and

(c)   the person making the application to stay the legal proceedings has not taken any step in those proceedings to answer the substantive claim[5]; and

(d)   the court is satisfied that the arbitration agreement is not null and void, inoperative or incapable of being performed[6].

The courts upheld the validity of an arbitration agreement and stayed court proceedings in the face of a challenge that it contravened a party's right to have his case heard in court under Article 6 of the European Convention on Human Rights 1950. The arbitration agreement constituted a waiver of the individual's rights under Article 6(1)[7].

An application may be made to the court to stay proceedings notwithstanding that the matter is to be referred to arbitration only after the exhaustion of other dispute resolution procedures[8]. The arbitration procedure under the ATA 1995 is statutory. The power given to the court by s 9 of the AA 1996 to stay legal proceedings applies equally to statutory arbitrations[9].

---

[1]   It should not be forgotten that the court has an inherent jurisdiction to stay proceedings which can be used in circumstances outside those considered in s 9: see *Al-Naimi (trading as Buildmaster Construction Services) v Islamic Press Services Inc* [2000] 1 Lloyd's Rep 522, 70 ConLR 21, CA.

2   The provision to stay legal proceedings was formerly contained in s 4 of the Arbitration Act 1950, which was specifically referred to in s 28(4) of the ATA 1995. See the House of Lords decision in *Inco Europe Ltd v First Choice Distribution (a firm)* [2000] 2 All ER 109, [2000] 1 All ER (Comm) 674, HL.

3   AA 1996, s 9(1).

4   AA 1996, s 9(3). *Capital Trust Investments Ltd v Radio Design TJ AB* [2002] EWCA Civ 135, [2002] 2 All ER 159, [2002] 1 All ER (Comm) 514.

5   AA 1996, s 9(3). An application to set aside default judgment, applying (unnecessarily) for leave to defend and applying for consequential directions do not amount to steps in the proceedings to answer the substantive claim.

6   AA 1996, s 9(4). If the court refuses to stay the legal proceedings, any provision that an award is a condition precedent to the bringing of legal proceedings in respect of any matter is of no effect in relation to those proceedings: AA 1996, s 9(5). For a case where the court proceedings were not stayed, see *Capes (Hatherden) v Western Arable Services Ltd* [2009] EWHC 3065 (QB), [2010] 1 Lloyd's Rep 477.

7   *Stretford v Football Association Ltd* [2006] EWHC 479 (Ch), [2006] All ER (D) 275 (Mar).

8   AA 1996, s 9(2).

9   AA 1996, s 9(4).

Confidentiality

47.2A   The AA 1996 does not include a provision in respect of confidentiality. The position is governed by the common law. Arbitration is a private process[1]. In *Dolling-Baker v Merrett*[2], it was held that:

> 'Although the proceedings are consensual and may thus be regarded as wholly voluntary, their very nature is such that there must ... be some implied obligation on both parties not to disclose or use for any other purpose any documents ... disclosed or produced in the course of the arbitration, or transcripts or notes of the evidence in the arbitration or the award ... save with the consent of the other party, or pursuant to an order or leave of the court'.

In *Emmott v Michael Wilson & Partners Ltd*[3], the court found that the duty not to disclose 'is in reality a substantive rule of arbitration law reached through the device of an implied term' (at para 106). It was made clear however (para 107) that disclosure would be permissible in the following instances:

(1)   with the express or implied consent of the parties;

(2)   if there is an order, or leave of the court (although that does not mean that the court has a general discretion to lift the obligation of confidentiality);

(3)   if it is reasonably necessary for the protection of the legitimate interests of an arbitrating party;

(4)   where the interests of justice require disclosure.

1   *Russell v Russell* (1880) 14 Ch D 471.

2   [1991] 2 All ER 890 at 899, [1990] 1 WLR 1205, CA.

3   [2008] EWCA Civ 184, [2008] 2 All ER (Comm) 193, [2008] Bus LR 1361.

THE ARBITRAL PROCESS UNDER THE ARBITRATION ACT 1996

Introduction

47.18   The AA 1996 applies to:

(a)   all arbitrations conducted under the AHA 1986 save that they must be conducted by a single arbitrator;

(b)   all arbitrations under the ATA 1995 save that:

  (i)   the general provisions set out at 47.5 et seq above override any parts of the AA 1996 that are inconsistent;

  (ii) separate provisions set out in the ATA 1995 apply to general arbitrations, rent arbitrations, improvement arbitrations and compensation arbitrations and the AA 1996 only applies when it is not inconsistent with these provisions.

The fact that an arbitration under the AHA 1986 or the ATA 1995 is a statutory arbitration does not result in any different set of rules being applied in respect of the application of the AA 1996, for example, more lenient time limits[1].

[1]   *Peel v Coln Park LLP* [2010] EWCA Civ 1602, 154 Sol Jo (no 38) 29.

Appointment of the arbitrator

Dispute as to jurisdiction

47.24 Previously, under the Arbitration Acts 1950 to 1979, an arbitrator could not determine his own jurisdiction[1], but the AA 1996 provides a procedure to deal with an objection to the substantive jurisdiction of the tribunal[2] and the parties cannot alter this procedure by agreement.

If a party objects to the arbitrator's substantive jurisdiction at the outset of the proceedings, that party must raise the issue not later than the time when he takes the first step in the proceedings to contest the merits of any matter in relation to which he challenges the arbitrator's jurisdiction[3]. A party is not precluded from raising such an objection by the fact that he has appointed or participated in the appointment of an arbitrator[4].

Any objection during the course of the arbitration that the arbitrator is exceeding his substantive jurisdiction must be made as soon as possible after the matter alleged to be beyond his jurisdiction is raised[5].

The arbitrator may admit an objection to his substantive jurisdiction at a later stage if he considers the delay justified[6].

When an objection is made to the arbitrator's substantive jurisdiction, the arbitrator has power to rule on his own jurisdiction and may:

(a)   rule on the matter in an award as to jurisdiction[7]; or

(b)   deal with the objection in his award on merits[8].

If the parties agree which of these courses the arbitrator should take, the arbitration shall proceed accordingly[9].

The arbitrator may in any case, and is required to if the parties so agree, stay the arbitration proceedings whilst an application is made to the court for a determination of a preliminary point of jurisdiction[10]. The court may, on the application of either party to an arbitration (upon notice to the other parties), determine any question as to the substantive jurisdiction of the tribunal[11]. The court will only consider an application to determine jurisdiction if:

(a)   it is made with the agreement in writing of all of the other parties to the proceedings[12]; or

(b)   it is made with the permission of the arbitrator and the court is satisfied that:

    (i)   the determination of the question is likely to produce substantial savings in costs;

    (ii)   the application was made without delay; and

    (iii)   there is a good reason why the matter should be decided by the court[13].

Any claims falling within the arbitrator's terms of reference cannot be raised in subsequent court proceedings regardless of whether or not the arbitrator ruled on them at the arbitration[14].

1   *Heyman v Darwins Ltd* [1942] AC 356, [1942] 1 All ER 337, HL.
2   AA 1996, s 31.
3   AA 1996, s 31(1).
4   AA 1996, s 31(1).
5   AA 1996, s 31(2).
6   AA 1996, s 31(3).
7   AA 1996, s 31(4).
8   AA 1996, s 31(4)(b).
9   AA 1996, s 31(4).
10   AA 1996, ss 31(5) and 32.
11   AA 1996, s 32(1).
12   AA 1996, s 32(2)(a).
13   AA 1996, s 32(2)(b).
14   *LIDL GMBH v Just Fitness Ltd* [2010] EWHC 39 (Ch), [2010] All ER (D) 143 (Jun), following *Conquer v Boot* [1928] 2 KB 336.

General duty of the arbitrator

47.32 The AA 1996 imposes certain general duties upon the arbitrator. The arbitrator is obliged to act fairly and impartially as between the parties, giving each party a reasonable opportunity of putting his case and dealing with that of his opponent, and to adopt procedures suitable to the circumstances of the particular case, avoiding unnecessary delay or expense, so as to provide a fair means for the resolution of the matters falling to be determined[1]. In *Peel v Coln Park LLP*[1A], an Arbitrator decided that a Case B notice to quit was void and ineffective in broad terms because the intention on the part of the landlord to develop only occurred in respect of the time when the notice to quit took effect and not at the date of the notice to quit itself. Part of the award related to costs and provided that the landlord, who had lost, should bear the costs of the arbitrator, but otherwise the parties were to bear their own costs. The tenant sought to appeal out of time. Both the High Court and the Court of Appeal dismissed the application for an extension of time. The tenant submitted that he had not been given a reasonable opportunity to put his case in relation to costs and that the arbitrator had failed to adopt procedures for the fair resolution of the question of costs. It was submitted that this was in contravention of s 33 of the AA 1996. Some credence to the submissions was provided by a decision of HHJ Humphrey Lloyd QC in *Gbangbola v Smith & Sherriff Ltd*[1B]. In *Peel v Coln Park LLP*, Longmore LJ stated that: 'On an application for an extension of time, it does not seem to me that, in a case where the arbitrator has, pursuant to a direction of the court, given reasons that are not obviously silly or illegal reasons, that there has been any breach of Section 33'[1C]. The arbitrator must comply with those general duties in conducting the arbitration, in his decisions on matters of procedure and evidence and in the exercise of all other powers conferred upon him[2]. The duty is widely drafted and cannot be excluded by agreement of the parties.

Unlike the expert[3], the arbitrator is not entitled to go beyond the evidence adduced by the parties[4]. If the arbitrator re-works figures produced by the parties, but does not introduce new evidence to which he applies his own expertise, his award will not be capable of challenge for that reason[4A]. The arbitrator cannot be pursued for negligence if he acts in a quasi-judicial capacity[5]. If the arbitrator fails to comply with the duties set out in s 33 such that his actions cause substantial injustice, this will be a serious irregularity[6].

[1] AA 1996, s 33(1). See also *Norbrook Laboratories Ltd v Challenger* [2006] EWHC 1055 (Comm), [2006] 2 Lloyd's Rep 485, [2006] BLR 412.
[1A] [2010] EWCA Civ 1602, 154 Sol Jo (no 38) 29.
[1B] [1998] 3 All ER 730.
[1C] *Peel v Coln Park LLP* [2010] EWCA Civ 1602 per Longmore LJ.
[2] AA 1996, s 33(2).
[3] See para 48.6.
[4] *Fox v PG Wellfair Ltd* [1981] 2 Lloyd's Rep 514, [1981] Com LR 140, CA; *Top Shop Estates Ltd v Danino* [1985] 1 EGLR 9, 273 Estates Gazette 197. See paras 47.33–47.35.
[4A] *Leftbank Properties Ltd v Spirit Group Retail Ltd* [2008] PLSCS 6.
[5] *Sirros v Moore* [1975] QB 118, [1974] 3 All ER 776, CA.
[6] See para 47.66.

Privileged communications

47.32A It is good practice for the arbitrator to inform the parties at the commencement of the arbitration that they should copy correspondence sent to him to the other party and that they should not send to the arbitrator any without prejudice or otherwise privileged communications.

It should be noted that privilege which extends to legal advice given to a party by his lawyers does not include advice (whether legal or otherwise) given by, for example, the party's accountant or surveyor[1].

[1] *R (on the application of Prudential plc) v Special Commissioner of Income Tax* [2009] EWHC 2494 (Admin), [2010] 1 All ER 1113, [2010] STC 161.

Interlocutory matters

47.34 The AA 1996 provides that it should be for the arbitrator to decide on all procedural and evidential matters, subject to the right of the parties to agree any matter[1].

The procedural and evidential matters include, in addition to the provision relating to statements of cases[2], the following:

(a)   when and where any part of the proceedings is to be held;

(b)   the language or languages to be used in the proceedings and whether translations of any relevant documents are to be supplied[3];

(c)   whether any and if so which documents or classes of documents should be disclosed between and produced by the parties and at what stage[4];

(d)   whether any and if so what questions should be put to and answered by the respective parties and when and in what form this should be done;

(e)   whether to apply strict rules of evidence (or any other rules) as to the admissibility, relevance or weight of any material (oral, written or other) sought to be tendered on any matters of fact or opinion, and the time, manner and form in which such material should be exchanged and presented;

(f)   whether and to what extent the arbitrator should take the initiative in ascertaining the facts and the law; and

(g)   whether and to what extent there should be oral or written evidence or submissions[5].

The arbitrator may fix the time within which any directions given by him are to be complied with, and may if he thinks fit extend the time so fixed (whether or not it has expired)[6]. If the arbitrator departs from the agreed directions it may amount to serious irregularity[7].

[1]   AA 1996, s 34(1).
[2]   See para 47.33.
[3]   This provision might be relevant to arbitrations in Wales.
[4]   The rules that apply in court proceedings which prevent privileged communications being disclosed, also apply in relation to witness evidence. Note the restrictions on the use of documents disclosed for collateral purposes: see *British Sky Broadcasting Group plc v Virgin Media Communications Ltd (formerly NTL Communications Ltd)* [2008] EWCA Civ 612, [2008] 4 All ER 1026, [2008] 1 WLR 2854.
[5]   AA 1996, s 34(2).
[6]   AA 1996, s 34(3).
[7]   See para 47.66.

Hearings

47.35   There is no obligation on the arbitrator to determine the case at a hearing[1]. The arbitrator has the power to decide procedure and whether a hearing is appropriate.

If a hearing takes place, the arbitrator must consider how the evidence should be presented. He will need to decide whether there is any need for oral witness evidence or if it is sufficient to rely on witness statements[2]. If the arbitrator has allowed the parties to use expert evidence, the arbitrator will consider if oral evidence is required from the expert.

In the absence of an agreement to the contrary, the arbitrator is free to decide the procedure for the hearing. He can follow the usual court procedure, but there is no obligation to do so.

The party on whom the onus of proof lies (the equivalent of the claimant in a court action) should open his case. The opening address should merely outline the case. Being an address, it is not evidence and must not contain any factual allegations which are not subsequently supported by formal evidence.

Witnesses may then be called. If the onus of proof is to be discharged they must be called. The party defending may then cross-examine and the quasi-claimant may re-examine. Cross-examination, as long as it is not obviously irrelevant, should be unrestricted. Re-examination is only permissible on matters with which the witnesses' cross-examination has already dealt, except by the arbitrator's leave, which should be sparingly given. If new points are thereby introduced it means that the other party may well need the chance of further cross-examination, and so on. In this way proceedings can easily degenerate into an argument.

The defending party then, likewise, may call witnesses who are subjected to cross-examination, and then close. The final closing address is made by the party opening[3]. It is beyond the scope of this book to consider the rules of procedure in detail. The standard textbooks on this subject should be consulted.

[1] Cf the position that used to apply under Sch 11 of the AHA 1986. See *O'Donoghue v Enterprise Inns plc* [2008] EWHC 2273 (Ch), [2009] 1 P & CR 14, where the arbitrator's decision not to hold an oral hearing was found not to be a serious irregularity under s 68(2)(a) of the AA 1996: see para 47.66.
[2] AA 1996, s 34(2)(h).
[3] He has the double advantage of opening the case and closing, thereby having the last word.

Expert evidence

47.49 Unless otherwise agreed by the parties, the arbitrator may appoint experts or legal advisers to report to him and the parties, or appoint assessors to assist him on technical matters, and may allow any such expert, legal adviser or assessor to attend the arbitration[1]. The parties must be given a reasonable opportunity to comment on any information, opinion or advice offered by such person to the arbitrator[2]. The arbitrator may also permit the parties to rely on expert evidence.

The fees and expenses of an expert, legal adviser or assessor appointed by the arbitrator for which the arbitrator is liable are expenses of the arbitrator for the purposes of the AA 1996[3]. This is a mandatory provision and the parties cannot agree otherwise and deprive experts of their fees and expenses. Such fees and expenses are costs of the arbitrator and recoverable as part of the costs of the arbitration under s 64(1).

As a matter of good practice, experts should consider the rules set out in CPR Pt 35. While not binding on arbitrations, it sets out the duties of the expert and the form and content of the expert's report. The issues are the same for experts who deal with property in the courts or before an arbitrator.

The expert's overriding duty is to the arbitrator, even if he has been appointed by one of the parties. An expert must be independent and must not do anything to compromise his independence or objectivity[4].

An expert has immunity from suit in respect of evidence given in court and statements made for the purposes of giving evidence but the immunity of an expert witness does not extend to disciplinary proceedings by the professional body of which he is a member[5]. It is submitted that the same analysis will apply to an expert acting in an arbitration.

It should be noted that the High Court has held that an expert witness whose evidence had led to significant expense in reckless disregard for his duties to the court, was vulnerable to an order for costs being made against him[6].

1   AA 1996, s 37(1)(a).
2   AA 1996, s 37(1)(b).
3   AA 1996, s 37(2).
4   Any expert should also bear in mind any practice statements provided by his professional body, for example the RICS practice statement 'Surveyors Acting as Expert Witnesses' (3rd edn) and the Civil Justice Council's 'Protocol for the Instruction of Experts Giving Evidence in Civil Claims', and the accompanying Code of Practice for Experts, agreed jointly by the Academy of Experts and the Expert Witness Institute, Published June 2005.
5   *Meadow v General Medical Council* [2006] EWCA Civ 1390, [2007] QB 462, [2007] 1 All ER 1; *Lambeth London Borough Council v Kay* [2006] UKHL 10, [2006] 2 AC 465, [2006] 4 All ER 128; *Jones v Kaney* [2010] EWHC 61 (QB), [2010] 2 All ER 649.
6   *Phillips v Symes (a bankrupt)* [2004] EWHC 2330 (Ch), [2005] 4 All ER 519, [2005] 2 All ER (Comm) 538.

Settlement

47.54 The parties are able to agree provisions governing what happens in the event of a settlement being achieved in the arbitration before its determination by the arbitrator[1].

In the absence of specific agreement by the parties as to the provisions which would apply in the event of a settlement in advance of the arbitration hearing, the AA 1996 lays down rules governing the position. The arbitrator is required to terminate the substantive proceedings and, if requested by the parties and not objected to by the arbitrator himself, to record the settlement in the form of an agreed award[2].

It should be noted that where there is a dispute as to the construction of a settlement agreement, the court will not permit the admission of evidence of background without prejudice communications[3].

Parties should also be aware that if they conduct settlement discussions within Part 36 of the Civil Procedure Rules, they are submitting themselves to the self-contained code of CPR 36 where the normal rules of offer and acceptance do not apply[4].

If the parties include a confidentiality provision in a settlement agreement, they should recognise the limited remedies available for a breach of such an agreement[5].

47.54 *Arbitration*

AA 1996, s 51(1).
AA 1996, s 51(1) and (2).
Oceanbulk Shipping and Trading SA v TMT Asia Ltd [2010] EWCA Civ 79, [2010]
     3 All ER 282, [2010] 2 All ER (Comm) 176.
Gibbon v Manchester City Council [2010] EWCA Civ 726, [2010] 1 WLR 2081, [2010]
     36 EG 120. Also see, *C v D* [2010] EWHC 2940 (Ch), [2010] NLJR 1650, [2011] 03 EG
     84.
Vercoe v Rutland Fund Management Ltd [2010] EWHC 424 (Ch), [2010] PLSCS 108.

Premature termination

47.54A Where the parties to an arbitration agreed to terminate the hearing
without expressly or impliedly resolving the issues it was originally commenced to determine, the decision to terminate did not prevent a party from
seeking to commence a fresh arbitration in respect of the same issues to the
extent that he was not estopped by the terms of the agreement to abandon the
hearing[1].

Wakefield (Tower Hill Trinity Square) Trust v Janson Green Properties Ltd [1998] NPC
     104, [1998] EGCS 95. Also see, *Allied Marine Transport Ltd v Vale do Rio Doce
     Navegacao SA, The Leonidas D* [1985] 2 All ER 796, [1985] 1 WLR 925, CA.

The arbitrator's award

Date of award

47.56 Unless otherwise agreed by the parties, the arbitrator may decide what
is to be taken to be the date on which the award was made[1].

In the absence of any such decision by the arbitrator, the date of the award
shall be taken to be the date on which it is signed by the arbitrator[2].

Once an award has been made and given a date by the arbitrator, it cannot be
changed retrospectively[3].

AA 1996, s 54(1).
AA 1996, s 54(2).
Peel v Coln Park LLP [2010] EWCA Civ 1602, 154 Sol Jo (no 38) 29.

Effect of award

47.60 Unless otherwise agreed by the parties, an award made by the
arbitrator pursuant to an arbitration agreement is final and binding both on
the parties or any persons claiming through or under them[1]. This does not
affect the right of a person to challenge the award by any available process of
appeal or review under the AA 1996[2]. An award remains a private matter
between the parties and cannot directly affect the rights of third parties[3].

AA 1996, s 58(1). It should be noted that an arbitrator's decision on a point of law on, for
     example, a first rent review, will not create an issue estoppel which would settle the point
     of law for the remainder of the term of the tenancy. A dissatisfied party is able to apply to

the court in construction proceedings for a determination of the issue by the court: *British Railways Board v Ringbest Ltd* [1996] 2 EGLR 82, [1996] 30 EG 94.
2   AA 1996, s 58(2).
3   As to written reasons for an award, see para 47.69.

Costs of the arbitration

47.61   The costs of the arbitration are defined in the AA 1996 as comprising the arbitrator's fees and expenses, the fees and expenses of any arbitral institution concerned, and the legal or other costs of the parties[1]. The costs include those costs of or incidental to any proceedings to determine the amount of the recoverable costs of the arbitration[2].

An agreement which has the effect that a party is to pay the whole or part of the costs of the arbitration in any event is only valid if made after the dispute in question has arisen[3].

Subject to any agreement between the parties, the arbitrator may make an award allocating the costs of the arbitration as between them[4]. Unless the parties otherwise agree, the arbitrator shall award costs on the general principle that costs should follow the event except where it appears to the arbitrator that in the circumstances this is not appropriate in relation to the whole or part of the costs[5]. If the arbitrator decides to do something other than award costs which follow the event, the award should explain the reasons for that. Although not bound by them, the arbitrator should consider the principles which apply in the courts when determining the issue of costs[6].

Unless the parties otherwise agree, any obligation under the agreement between them as to how the costs of the arbitration are to be borne, or under an award allocating the costs of the arbitration, extends only to such costs as are recoverable[7]. The parties are free to agree what costs of the arbitration are recoverable[8]. If or to the extent that there is no such agreement, the arbitrator may determine by award the recoverable costs of the arbitration on such basis as he thinks fit. If he does so, he must specify the basis on which he has acted and the items of recoverable costs and the amount referable to each[9].

1   AA 1996, s 59(1).
2   AA 1996, s 59(2), see also s 63. Note that an arbitration may incorporate a conditional fee agreement: *Bevan Ashford v Geoff Yendle (Contractors) Ltd* [1999] Ch 239, [1998] 3 All ER 238; Courts and Legal Services Act 1990, s 58A, inserted by the Access to Justice Act 1999.
3   AA 1996, s 60.
4   AA 1996, s 61(1).
5   AA 1996, s 61(2). For a more detailed guidance as to the principles applying in respect of the arbitrator's discretion as to costs, see Mustill and Boyd, *Commercial Arbitration* (2nd edn, 1989), Butterworths, Ch 26E and the 2000 companion volume.
6   The CPR Pt 44.
7   AA 1996, s 62.
8   AA 1996, s 63(1).
9   AA 1996, s 63(2) and (3).

47.62 If the arbitrator does not determine the recoverable costs of the arbitration, any party to the arbitration may apply to the court (upon notice to the other parties). The court may:

(a) determine the recoverable costs of the arbitration on such basis as it thinks fit; or

(b) order that they should be determined by such means and upon such terms as it may specify[1].

In *Peel v Coln Park LLP*[1A], the arbitrator decided that a Case B notice to quit was void and ineffective in broad terms because the intention on the part of the landlord to develop only occurred in respect of the time when the notice to quit took effect, not at the date of the notice to quit itself. Part of the award related to costs and provided that the landlord, who had lost, should bear the costs of the arbitrator, but otherwise the parties were to bear their own costs. The arbitrator was requested to give his reasons and (in brief) those reasons were that the landlord had won on certain issues, that the tenant had been responsible for the fact that it had taken a substantial period of time to get to the stage of the award and that, although the ordinary rule was that costs should follow the event, the arbitrator thought it right to depart from the ordinary rule for those reasons. The award was the subject to an appeal made out of time. The High Court dismissed the application for an extension of time and an appeal was made to the Court of Appeal. The Court of Appeal also dismissed the application for an extension of time, but as regards the way in which the arbitrator had dealt with the costs, Longmore LJ commented: 'It seems to me that the decision of the arbitrator in relation to costs is well within the range of reasonable decisions about costs to which arbitrators up and down the land frequently have to come'[1B].

Unless the court determines otherwise the recoverable costs of the arbitration shall be determined on the basis that there shall be allowed a reasonable amount in respect of all costs reasonably incurred, and any doubt as to whether costs were reasonably incurred or were reasonable in amount shall be resolved in favour of the paying party[2].

The provisions relating to the costs of the arbitration are subject to the provisions contained in s 64 of the AA 1996 in respect of the recoverable fees and expenses of the arbitrator[3]. The recoverable costs of the arbitration shall include only such reasonable fees and expenses of the arbitrator as are appropriate in the circumstances.

Nothing contained in the AA 1996 dealing with the recoverability of costs of the arbitration affects any rights of the arbitrator, any expert, legal adviser or assessor appointed by the arbitrator, or any arbitral institution, to payment of their fees and expenses[4].

Unless otherwise agreed by the parties, the arbitrator may direct that the recoverable costs of the arbitration, or of any part of the arbitral proceedings, shall be limited to a specified amount[5]. Any direction in this regard may be made or varied at any stage of the arbitration, but it must be done sufficiently in advance of the incurring of costs to which it relates, or the taking of any steps in the proceedings which may be affected by it, for the limit to be taken into account[6].

Conditional fee agreements are permissible in arbitrations and can be allowed by arbitrators[7]. Costs of lay representatives acting in arbitrations have also been allowed[8]. The costs of lay representatives are not recoverable for any court application.

There is no express right of appeal against a court decision although it has been held that such right exists[9]. Permission to appeal can be given by the trial judge or the Court of Appeal.

[1]   AA 1996, s 63(4).
[1A] *Peel v Coln Park LLP* [2010] EWCA Civ 1602, 154 Sol Jo (no 38) 29.
[1B] *Peel v Coln Park LLP* [2010] EWCA Civ 1602 per Longmore LJ at para 18.
[2]   AA 1996, s 63(5). The procedure for determining the costs of the arbitration is therefore akin to a standard basis assessment before the court: see CPR Pt 47. The courts can also award costs on an indemnity basis. This means that any doubt as to whether costs were reasonably incurred or were reasonable in amount shall be resolved in favour of the receiving party. The AA 1996 does not rule out the possibility of indemnity costs but gives no guidance on when such an award would be appropriate. The arbitrator should consider the guidance set out in case law and must bear in mind that an unjustified departure from the standard basis may be considered to be a serious irregularity, see para 47.66.
[3]   AA 1996, ss 63(6) and 64. See para 47.63.
[4]   AA 1996, s 63(7).
[5]   AA 1996, s 65(1).
[6]   AA 1996, s 65(2).
[7]   *Bevan Ashford (a firm) v Geoff Yeandle (Contractors) Ltd* [1999] Ch 239, [1998] 3 All ER 238.
[8]   *Piper Double Glazing Ltd v DC Contracts (1992) Ltd* [1994] 1 All ER 177, [1994] 1 WLR 777.
[9]   *Inco Europe Ltd v First Choice Distribution* [2000] 2 All ER 109, [2000] 1 All ER (Comm) 674, HL.

Enforcement of the award

47.64 An award made by the arbitrator pursuant to an arbitration agreement may, by leave of the court, be enforced in the same manner as a judgment or order of the court to the same effect[1]. Where leave is so given, judgment may be entered in terms of the award[2]. Leave to enforce an award shall not be given where, or to the extent that, the person against whom it is sought to be enforced shows that the arbitrator lacks substantive jurisdiction to make the award[3]. The right to raise such an objection may have been lost[4].

[1]   AA 1996, s 66(1). Also see, *National Ability SA v Tinna Oils and Chemicals Ltd, The Amazon Reefer* [2009] EWCA Civ 1330, [2010] 2 All ER 899, [2010] 2 All ER (Comm) 257.
[2]   AA 1996, s 66(2).
[3]   AA 1996, s 66(3).
[4]   AA 1996, s 73 and see para 47.75.

Challenging the award

Substantive jurisdiction

47.65 A party to an arbitration may (upon notice to the other parties and to the arbitrator) apply to the court:

(a)   challenging any award of the arbitrator as to its substantive juris-diction; or

(b)   for an order declaring an award made by the arbitrator on the merits to be of no effect, in whole or in part, because the arbitrator did not have substantive jurisdiction[1].

Challenges on this ground arise where the original agreement to refer to arbitration is invalid, there is some defect in the appointment process or some disagreement over what matters should have been submitted to arbitration[2]. Section 30 allows the arbitrator to determine his own jurisdiction. A challenge under s 67 will only arise if the arbitrator has determined his own jurisdiction under s 30 and a party has not appeared in an arbitration, or has appeared and then registered a prompt objection that the arbitrator has not resolved by an interim award[3]. A party is not precluded from objecting by the fact that he has appointed or participated in the appointment of the arbitrator[4].

A party may lose the right to object[5] and the right to apply is subject to statutory restrictions contained in the AA 1996[6].

On an application to challenge the award as to its substantive jurisdiction, the court has power to confirm the award, vary it or set it aside in whole or in part[7].

If a party commences a challenge to an award but then unilaterally discontin-ues the challenge by issuing a notice of discontinuance, the court has jurisdiction to set aside the notice of discontinuance if the court considers it to be an abuse of process[7A].

The arbitrator may continue the arbitration and make a further award while an application to the court in respect of his substantive jurisdiction is pending[8].

After the court has made the decision, no appeal lies against the court's decision without leave. Leave will not be given unless the court considered that the question of law involves a point which is of general importance or is one which for some other special reason should be considered by the Court of Appeal.

[1]   AA 1996, s 67(1).
[2]   AA 1996, s 30.
[3]   *Amec Civil Engineering Ltd v Secretary of State for Transport* [2005] EWCA Civ 291, [2005] 1 WLR 2339, 101 ConLR 26.
[4]   AA 1996, s 31(1).
[5]   AA 1996, s 73 and see para 47.75.
[6]   AA 1996, s 70(2) and (3) and see para 47.71.

⁷   AA 1996, s 67(3). The leave of the court is required for any appeal from a decision of the court: s 67(4).
⁷ᴬ   *Sheltam Rail Co (Pty) Ltd v Mirambo Holdings Ltd* [2008] EWHC 829 (Comm), [2009] 1 All ER 84, [2009] Bus LR 302.
⁸   AA 1996, s 67(2).

Serious irregularity

47.66   A party to an arbitration may (upon notice to the other parties and to the arbitrator) apply to the court challenging an award in the proceedings on the ground of serious irregularity affecting the arbitrator, the proceedings or the award[1]. A party may lose the right to object[2] and again is subject to statutory restrictions contained in the AA 1996[3].

The AA 1996 defines serious irregularity as an irregularity which the court considers has caused or will cause substantial injustice to the applicant. It means one or more of the following:

(a)   failure of the arbitrator to comply with his general duties contained in s 33 of the AA 1996[4];

(b)   the arbitrator exceeding his powers (otherwise than by exceeding his substantive jurisdiction)[5];

(c)   failure by the arbitrator to conduct the proceedings in accordance with the procedure agreed by the parties[6];

(d)   failure by the arbitrator to deal with all of the issues that were put to him[7];

(e)   any arbitral or other institution or person vested by the parties with powers in relation to the proceedings or the award exceeding its powers[8];

(f)   uncertainty or ambiguity as to the effect of the award;

(g)   the award being obtained by fraud or the award or the way in which it was procured being contrary to public policy;

(h)   failure to comply with the requirements as to the form of the award[9];

(i)   any irregularity in the conduct of the proceedings or in the award which is admitted by the arbitrator or by any arbitral or other institution or person vested by the parties with powers in relation to the proceedings or the award[10].

An application or appeal must be brought within 28 days of the date of the award or, if there has been any arbitral process or appeal or review, of the date when the applicant or appellant was notified of the result of that process[11]. If an appeal to the High Court is unsuccessful, permission from the High Court is required to appeal beyond to the Court of Appeal[12].

¹   AA 1996, s 68(1).
²   AA 1996, s 73 and see para 47.75.
³   AA 1996, s 70(2) and (3) and see para 47.71.
⁴   See para 47.32. *Petroships Pte Ltd v Petec Trading and Investment Corpn, The Petro Ranger* [2001] 2 Lloyd's Rep 348.
⁵   AA 1996, s 67.
⁶   *Norbrook Laboratories Ltd v Challenger* [2006] EWHC 1055 (Comm), [2006] 2 Lloyd's Rep 485, [2006] BLR 412 where the arbitrator contacted witnesses direct and failed to inform the parties.

7   This could include a deficiency of reasons in a reasoned award if the arbitrator fails to deal
    with all issues put to him, see *Margulead Ltd v Exide Technologies* [2004] EWHC 1019
    (Comm), [2004] 2 All ER (Comm) 727, [2005] 1 Lloyd's Rep 324. See also *Torch Offshore
    LLC v Cable Shipping Inc* [2004] EWHC 787 (Comm), [2004] 2 All ER (Comm) 365,
    [2004] 2 Lloyd's Rep 446. Note that the arbitrator's decision not to hold an oral hearing is
    not of itself a serious irregularity: *O'Donoghue v Enterprise Inns plc* [2008] EWHC 2273
    (Ch), [2009] 1 P & CR 309.
8   In practice, in relation to agricultural arbitrations this is likely to be the RICS, although
    there is no reason why the arbitration agreement should not permit another institution to
    appoint the arbitrator, for example, the Central Association of Agricultural Valuers or the
    Law Society.
9   See para 47.55.
10 AA 1996, s 68(2).
11 AA 1996, s 70(3). As to appealing out of time, see *Kalmneft JSC v Glencore International
    AG* [2002] 1 All ER 76, [2001] 2 All ER (Comm) 577; *Nagusina Naviera v Allied
    Maritime Inc (The Maria K)* [2002] EWCA Civ 1147, [2002] All ER (D) 146 (Jul); *Squirrel
    Films Distribution Ltd v SPP Opportunities Fund LLP* [2010] EWHC 706 (Ch).
12 AA 1996, s 79(6). Also see, *Athletic Union of Constantinople v National Basketball
    Association* [2002] 1 All ER (Comm) 70, [2002] 1 Lloyd's Rep 305; *Henry Boot
    Construction (UK) Ltd v Malmaison Hotel (Manchester) Ltd* [2001] QB 388, [2001]
    1 All ER 257, CA; *Virdee v Virdi* [2003] EWCA Civ 41, [2003] All ER (D) 46 (Jan). Note
    that an appeal does lie to the Court of Appeal when a judge makes an order outside his
    jurisdiction: *Cetelem SA v Roust Holdings Ltd* [2005] EWCA Civ 618, [2005] 4 All ER 52,
    [2005] 2 All ER (Comm) 203. The Court of Appeal also has a residual jurisdiction where
    there is misconduct or unfairness on the part of the judge: *CGU International Insur-
    ance plc v Astrazeneca Insurance Co Ltd* [2006] EWCA Civ 1340, [2007] 1 All ER
    (Comm) 501, [2007] Bus LR 162. Further, the Court of Appeal may review a case if there
    are grounds for believing that, at an earlier hearing, the applicant's rights under Article 6 of
    the Human Rights convention were overridden: *North Range Shipping Ltd v Seatrans
    Shipping Corp, The Western Triumph* [2002] EWCA Civ 405, [2002] 4 All ER 390, [2002]
    2 All ER (Comm) 193; *Taylor v Lawrence* [2002] EWCA Civ 90, [2003] QB 528, [2002]
    2 All ER 353.

Appeal on a point of law

47.69 Unless otherwise agreed by the parties[A1], a party to an arbitration may
(upon notice to the other parties and to the arbitrator) appeal to the court on
a question of law arising out of an award made in the proceedings[1].

An agreement to dispense with reasons for the arbitrator's award shall be
considered an agreement to exclude the court's jurisdiction to hear an appeal
on a question of law arising out of the award[2].

An appeal to the court can only be made with the agreement of all of the other
parties to the proceedings or with the leave of the court[3]. The right of appeal
is also subject to the statutory restrictions contained in the AA 1996[4].

Leave to appeal will only be given by the court if it is satisfied that:

(a)   the determination of the question will substantially affect the rights of
      one or more of the parties;
(b)   the question is one which the arbitrator was asked to determine[5];
(c)   on the basis of the findings of fact in the award:
      (i)   the decision of the arbitrator on the question is obviously wrong;
            or

236

(ii)   the question is one of general public importance and the decision of the arbitrator is at least open to serious doubt; and

(d)   despite the agreement of the parties to resolve the matter by arbitration, it is just and proper in all the circumstances for the court to determine the question[6].

In *National Trust for Places of Historic Interest or Natural Beauty v Fleming*[6A], the question as to what constitutes 'obviously wrong' in s 69 of AA 1996 was considered.

A landowner entered into a deed of covenant with the National Trust to protect land that he owned from urban sprawl. The covenant stated 'nothing in the forebearing stipulation shall prevent the cultivation of the said land or any part thereof in the ordinary course of agricultural husbandry in accordance with the custom of this country'. The land then changed hands and was sublet to a salad crop production company, selling to national supermarkets. The site was developed with caravans, parking and an amenity area in order to cater for the seasonal migrant labour. A dispute arose between the National Trust and the landowner which centred on the true construction of the restrictions in the deed and it was referred to arbitration under the terms of the deed. The arbitrator found that the landowner was entitled to rely upon the proviso and consequently there was no breach of any of the restrictions.

The National Trust sought leave to appeal under s 69 against the interim award of the arbitrator. The proposed grounds of appeal concerned subparagraph (d) of s 69 namely whether it was just and proper in all the circumstances for the court to determine the question. The application for leave to appeal was refused. The court held that it only had jurisdiction to grant leave to appeal if it was satisfied, among other things, that on the basis of the findings of fact in the award, the decision on the question of law was 'obviously wrong'. That was a stringent test and implied that the error was demonstrable on the face of the award itself and did not require close scrutiny to expose it. The threshold was much higher than the usual test of 'real prospect of success' which would be applied in an application for permission to appeal. The case emphasises the reluctance of the court to interfere with an arbitrator's decision. The National Trust had been unable to establish that the basic steps in the arbitrator's reasoning displayed any error of law and that the decision was obviously wrong. A fair and not over critical reading of the award as a whole made it clear why the arbitrator decided the question as he did. The claimant had not given enough weight to the strong findings of fact of the arbitrator.

The issue of what constituted 'obviously wrong' was also considered in *Stodday Land Limited v Mashiter*[6B]. A landlord served a notice under the AHA 1986 requiring the tenant to enter into a written tenancy agreement. The parties disagreed over the applicable repairing obligations. At the arbitration in July 2008, the tenant was successful in showing that the responsibility for maintenance of all boundary fences, hedges and walls lay with the landlord (despite the incorporation of the model clauses into the tenancy). The arbitrator decided there was an oral term in the existing tenancy that the landlord should carry out such repairs. The landlord sought permission to appeal. His argument was that the model clauses are incorporated into every oral tenancy of an agricultural holding, without variation in accordance with s 7(3) of the AHA 1986.

Although the court acknowledged the force of the landlord's arguments, in order to allow the appeal he had to find that the arbitrator's award was 'obviously wrong'. The judge acknowledged it was possible that the arbitrator's decision was wrong, but it was impossible to say that it was 'obviously wrong'. This may seem to be a bizarre outcome but quoting from an earlier case the judge said 'The parties should be left to accept for better or worse the decision of the Tribunal that they had chosen to decide the matter in the first instance'. This is by no means new law, but is further confirmation that parties are usually stuck with an arbitrator's decision. Consequently, if there is a difficult point of law that must be decided, the parties may decide to ask the arbitrator to refer that to the court on a preliminary point.

If an application is made to the court for leave to appeal on a point of law, the applicant must identify the question of law to be determined and state the grounds on which it is alleged that leave to appeal should be granted[7]. The court will decide whether leave should be given without convening a hearing unless the court considers that a hearing is required[8].

On an appeal on a point of law, the court may by order confirm the award, vary it, remit it to the arbitrator, in whole or in part, for reconsideration in the light of the court's determination, or set aside the award in whole or in part[9].

[A1] An arbitration clause which uses the words: 'final, conclusive and binding' does not operate to contract out of the operation of AA 1996, s 69: *Shell Egypt West Manzala GmbH v Dana Gas Egypt Ltd* [2009] EWHC 2097 (Comm), [2010] 2 All ER (Comm) 442, [2010] 1 Lloyd's Rep 109.

[1] AA 1996, s 69(1). An arbitration clause which excludes an appeal to a court on a point of law under s 69 is not in breach of the right to a fair trial under Article 6 of the European Convention of Human Rights: see *Sumukan Ltd v Commonwealth Secretariat* [2007] EWCA Civ 243, [2007] 3 All ER 342, [2007] 2 All ER (Comm) 23.

[2] AA 1996, s 69(1).

[3] AA 1996, s 69(2).

[4] AA 1996, s 70(2) and (3) and see para 47.71.

[5] *Historic Buildings and Monuments Commission for England v Isambard Estates Ltd* [2005] All ER (D) 151 (Jun). It is not necessary to establish that the question had been raised in the arbitration in the same form as it is raised on appeal: *Safeway Stores v Legal & General Assurance Society Ltd* [2004] EWHC 415 (Ch), [2005] 1 P & CR 9.

[6] AA 1996, s 69(3).

[6A] [2009] EWHC 1789 (Ch), [2009] All ER (D) 192 (Jul).

[6B] [2009] EWHC (Ch), unreported. A decision of Judge Behrens QC.

[7] AA 1996, s 69(4).

[8] AA 1996, s 69(5). The leave of the court is required for any appeal from a decision of the court in respect of its decision to grant or refuse leave to appeal: s 69(6).

[9] AA 1996, s 69(7). The courts are loath to interfere. Where a decision was no more than an error of law, the court will not quash the decision of the arbitrator or remit it on the grounds that it represents an 'excess of power': *Lesotho Highlands Development Authority v Impregilo SpA* [2005] UKHL 43, [2006] 1 AC 221, [2005] 3 All ER 789. For the principles to be applied by the court to an arbitrator's award, see *Kershaw Mechanical Services Ltd v Kendrick Construction Ltd* [2006] EWHC 727 (TCC), [2006] 4 All ER 79, [2006] 2 All ER (Comm) 81.

Chapter 48

EXPERT DETERMINATION AND THE COURTS

ALTERNATIVE DISPUTE RESOLUTION UNDER THE AGRICULTURAL TENANCIES ACT 1995

Form of ADR

48.4 The ATA 1995 provides the parties with complete freedom of contract as to the method of ADR to be employed. It might be by way of a tailored arbitration agreement or, at the other end of the spectrum, mediation or some other form of ADR. Most usually it will be a determination by an expert[1].

[1] In 1996, the RICS and the Law Society together promoted the concept of PACT (Professional Arbitration on Court Terms). The aim was to introduce a form of alternative dispute resolution into the lease renewal process. The scheme was designed to apply to renewals that are not contested by the landlord. Once the tenant had made the originating application to the court (which was required within four months of the landlord's notice), the parties and the court would jointly agree to delegate the task of fixing the terms of the renewal lease to an appropriate individual. That individual might be a valuer or lawyer acting in the capacity of arbitrator or independent expert, whose qualifications and experience would be appropriate to the nature of the dispute. RICS members can download the guidance note, Lease renewals under PACT, at www.rics.org.

METHODS OF DISPUTE RESOLUTION

Determination by an expert

48.6 The following points should be noted.

(a) The words appointing an expert should be clear and unambiguous to avoid any dispute as to whether an expert or an arbitrator is intended to be appointed[1].

(b) The role of an expert is to decide upon an issue of mutual interest to the parties in order to avoid a dispute. This is in contra- distinction to the role of the arbitrator who determines the outcome of a dispute[2].

(c) The expert's role is not to perform a judicial function. That is the role of an arbitrator. The expert's duties are to investigate and to reach a decision by his own inquiries and expertise[3]. The expert could come to a decision without receiving any evidence or argument from the parties.

(d) The provisions in the ATA 1995 and the AA 1996 relating to the appointment of arbitrators do not apply to experts. The parties must ensure that the contractual provisions for appointment and determination are clear and cannot be frustrated[4].

(e) As to the role of the President of the RICS in relation to the appointment of an expert pursuant to the terms of a lease and the question of the expert's relevant experience, see *Epoch Properties Ltd v British Home Stores (Jersey) Ltd*[5].

(f) The expert may receive written representations from the parties, but he is not required to do so, unless provision is made in the terms of his appointment, and he need not take such representations into account in reaching a decision.

(g) Unlike an arbitrator[6], the expert may act entirely on his own evidence and opinion[7]. However, the expert does owe a duty of care to the parties[8] which he will be in breach of if he fails to take into account matters which he should not[9].

(h) The parties cannot require a hearing, unless provision is made in the terms of the expert's appointment. If a hearing does take place, the rules of evidence do not apply, evidence is not given on oath, and there is no provision for discovery, interrogatories or notices to admit.

(i) Unless bound to do so by the terms of his appointment, there is no requirement that the expert's decision should contain his reasons.

(j) The expert's powers as to costs and his remuneration derive exclusively from the terms of his appointment and cannot be determined or assessed by the court.

(jj) An independent expert has no power to make any orders as to his fees, or as to the costs of a party, unless such a power is conferred upon him by the lease or the agreement between the parties[9A].

(k) Although an expert's decision will usually be stated to be final and binding, the courts have been prepared to impugn an expert's decision. The position is summarised in the decision of Nourse J in *Burgess v Purchase & Sons (Farms) Ltd*[10].

'In my judgment the present state of the law can be summarised as follows. The question whether a valuation made by an expert on a fundamentally erroneous basis can be impugned or not depends on the terms expressed or to be implied in the contract pursuant to which it is made. A non-speaking valuation made of the right property by the right man and in good faith cannot be impugned, although it may still be possible, in the case of an uncompleted transaction, for equitable relief (as opposed to damages) to be refused to the party who wishes to sustain the valuation. On the other hand, there are at least three decisions at first instance to the effect that a speaking valuation which demonstrates that it has been made on a fundamentally erroneous basis can be impugned. In such a case the completion of the transaction does not necessarily defeat the party who wishes to impugn the valuation'[11].

The status of the decision of an expert has been considered more recently by Lightman J in *British Shipbuilders v VSEL Consortium plc*[12], who, considering earlier authorities[13] set out his view of the status of the expert's decision. In particular, he made it clear that the role of the expert and the ambit of his remit were essentially a matter of construction of the agreement between the parties and the expert. If the expert alone is entitled to determine the issue exclusively, the court may only intervene if he has failed to comply with the agreement and may then set aside his decision. However, the court may be asked, in advance of the expert's decision, to determine questions as to the limits of his remit. It will seldom do so, however, because the nature of the question is at that stage hypothetical[14].

1   *Langham House Developments Ltd v Brompton Securities Ltd* [1980] 2 EGLR 117, 256 Estates Gazette 719; *Safeway Food Stores Ltd v Banderway Ltd* [1983] 2 EGLR 116, 267 Estates Gazette 850.
2   *Sutcliffe v Thackrah* [1974] AC 727, [1974] 1 All ER 859, HL; *Arenson v Casson Beckman Rutley & Co* [1977] AC 405, [1975] 3 All ER 901, HL. Cf *Leigh v English Property Corpn Ltd* [1976] 2 Lloyd's Rep 298.
3   *Sutcliffe v Thackrah* [1974] AC 727, [1974] 1 All ER 859, HL.
4   In the event of a dispute the court may assist: see *Sudbrook Trading Estate Ltd v Eggleton* [1983] 1 AC 444, [1982] 3 All ER 1, HL.
5   [2004] JCA 156, [2004] 3 EGLR 34.
6   *Fox v PG Wellfair Ltd* [1981] 2 Lloyd's Rep 514, [1981] Com LR 140, CA.
7   *Belvedere Motors Ltd v King* [1981] 2 EGLR 131, 260 Estates Gazette 813.
8   *Zubaida v Hargreaves* [2000] Lloyd's Rep PN 771, [1995] 1 EGLR 127, CA.
9   *Belvedere Motors Ltd v King* [1981] 2 EGLR 131, 260 Estates Gazette 813.
9A See *Reynolds & Fetherstonhaugh: Handbook of Rent Review*, para G1.1.2.
10 [1983] Ch 216, [1983] 2 All ER 4. Also see, *Homespace Ltd v Sita South East Ltd* [2008] EWCA Civ 1, [2008] 1 P & CR 436 (where the landlord overturned an expert determination more than four years after it was made); *Level Properties Ltd v Balls Brothers Ltd* [2007] EWHC 744 (Ch), [2008] 1 P & CR 1, [2007] 23 EG 166.
11 *Burgess v Purchase & Sons (Farms) Ltd* [1983] 2 All ER 4, at p 11. Also see: *Baber v Kenwood Manufacturing Co Ltd* [1978] 1 Lloyd's Rep 175, 121 Sol Jo 606, CA; *Heyes v Earl of Derby* (1984) 272 Estates Gazette 935, CA; *Quietfield Ltd v Vascroft Contractors Ltd* [2006] EWHC 174 (TCC), 109 ConLR 29; affd [2006] EWCA Civ 1737, [2007] Bus LR D1, 114 ConLR 81.
12 [1997] 1 Lloyd's Rep 106.
13 Including the House of Lords in *Mercury Communications Ltd v Director General of Telecommunications* [1996] 1 All ER 575, [1996] 1 WLR 48, HL and whether that case had or had not overruled *Jones v Sherwood Computer Services plc* [1992] 2 All ER 170, [1992] 1 WLR 277, CA and *P & O Property Holdings Ltd v Norwich Union Life Insurance Society* (1994) 68 P & CR 261, HL (see *Woodfall: Landlord and Tenant*, Vol 1 (Looseleaf edn) Sweet & Maxwell at para 8.048).
14 See *National Grid Co plc v M25 Group Ltd* [1998] 32 EG 90, [1999] EGCS 2 where the extent of the expert's remit was looked at in the context of a rent review: it was held that where an expert was appointed to determine the rent, matters of construction relating to the rent review provision were not necessarily within the 'exclusive remit' of the expert and could, therefore, be challenged in the courts or the subject of a preliminary hearing in the court.

THE COURTS

The Agricultural Holdings Act 1986

48.8 Litigation remains the most common form of dispute resolution. This is despite the introduction of the Civil Procedure Rules (CPR) which have encouraged parties to consider ADR[A1]. The courts have penalised parties in costs at the end of a hearing for failing to address ADR procedures[1].

Under the AHA 1986, the jurisdiction of the courts is preserved by s 97 of that Act. The jurisdiction of the court is applied mainly to matters of dispute arising as to rights other than those expressly created by the agricultural holdings legislation itself and thereby referred to arbitration or the Agricultural Land Tribunal (ALT). The section is not as wide as might at first appear in its operation.

48.8 Expert determination and the courts

The principle enshrined in s 97 of the AHA 1986 is not made expressly subservient to:

(a)   the provisions of s 15(4) and (5) of the AHA 1986 which restrict a landlord's rights during the tenancy, in the case of an alleged abuse of a tenant's freedom of disposal of produce and cropping of his arable land, to the remedy of an injunction (no damages, except on quitting). The question as to whether the tenant has exercised his right so as to injure or deteriorate the holding has to be decided by arbitration (AHA 1986, s 15(6));

(b)   the provisions of s 83 of the AHA 1986, which sets out the compulsory reference to arbitration under that Act of all claims between landlord and tenant arising under the Act, custom or agreement, and 'on or out of the termination of the tenancy of the holding or any part thereof';

(c)   the other provisions of the AHA 1986 'which otherwise expressly' so provide.

These may be illustrated by the express provisions against contracting-out of the AHA 1986[2] and the provisions of s 15(1). Since the decision in *Kent v Conniff*[3], it can no longer be said, as was at one time thought, that there is, on the true construction of s 71 of the AHA 1986, any denial of a landlord's rights to claim damages during the tenancy for breaches of a tenant's obligations of any type under the tenancy agreement.

On the affirmative side, the effect of s 97 of the AHA 1986 is to preserve custom, in so far as it is permissible expressly by s 77 of the Act, as a basis for compensation claims, and so such customs as those for pre-entry or hold-over for certain purposes are saved by this section. So also are customs as to compensation for a tenant who entered on the holding before 1 March 1948 and who has not elected by notice under s 64(1) and Sch 12 para 6 to invoke the relevant provisions of this Act regarding items of tenant-right compensation which are itemised in Pt II of Sch 8 to the AHA 1986. It must be noted that it is only in respect of such items and in such circumstances that custom is preserved.

[A1]   Parties should note that if they conduct settlement discussions within Part 36 of the Civil Procedure Rules, they are submitting themselves to the self-contained code of CPR 36 where the normal rules of offer and acceptance do not apply: *Gibbon v Manchester City Council* [2010] EWCA Civ 726, [2010] 1 WLR 2081, [2010] 36 EG 120. Also see, *C v D* [2010] EWHC 2940 (Ch), [2010] NLJR 1650, [2011] 03 EG 84. Parties should also note that an offer purporting to be pursuant to Part 36 may not be if, for example, it is time restricted: *C v D* [2010] EWHC 2940 (Ch), [2010] NLJR 1650, [2011] 03 EG 84.

[1]   *Dunnett v Railtrack plc (in railway administration)* [2002] EWCA Civ 303, [2002] 2 All ER 850, [2002] 1 WLR 2434; *Cowl v Plymouth City Council* [2001] EWCA Civ 1935, [2002] 1 WLR 803, (2002) Times, 8 January; *Halsey v Milton Keynes General NHS Trust* [2004] EWCA Civ 576, [2004] 4 All ER 920, [2004] 1 WLR 3002.

[2]   For example, AHA 1986, s 3.

[3]   [1953] 1 QB 361, [1953] 1 All ER 155, CA. But note this case was decided before the making of the Agriculture (Maintenance, Repair and Insurance of Fixed Equipment) Regulations 1973, SI 1973/1473 (as amended) which expressly provides now for arbitration in the case of such disputes.

Chapter 49
MILK QUOTA

OVERVIEW OF THE SYSTEM OF MILK QUOTA

Introduction of milk quota

49.1 Milk production quotas were introduced on 2 April 1984 arising from quantitative controls imposed on the production of milk and other dairy products under the Common Agricultural Policy of the European Economic Community, now the European Community (EC)[1]. Initially the quota system, introduced on 2 April 1984, operated for five years. It has subsequently been amended and extended, particularly in 1992. Currently it is projected to expire on 31 March 2015[2].

In the United Kingdom milk quotas were first introduced by the Dairy Produce Quota Regulations 1984[3]. Occupiers of holdings identified as dairy holdings had registered against their holding an amount called a 'reference quantity' or 'quota'. The effect of the registration was to set a maximum quantity of milk production or other dairy products so that if the producer exceeds that level in any quota year, a levy may be imposed on the excess.

At one time quota was a valuable asset. More recently quota prices have fallen[4].

[1] It is beyond the scope of this book to consider the scope of the European milk quota scheme. For the definitive analysis, see Cardwell, *Milk Quotas: European and UK Law* (1996) OUP. Also see Usher, *Legal Aspects of Agriculture in the European Community* (1988) Clarendon Press; Snyder, *The Law of the Common Agricultural Policy* (1986) Sweet and Maxwell; and Wood, Priday, Carter and Moss, *Milk Quotas: Law and Practice* (1986) Farmgate Communications Limited.
[2] Council Regulation (EC) 1234/2007, OJ 2007 L 299/1, art 66(1).
[3] SI 1984/1047.
[4] See, eg, European Commission *Evolution of the Market Situation and the Consequent Conditions for Smoothly Phasing Out the Milk Quota System* COM(2010)727.

Reference quantity

49.2 Under Council Regulation (EEC) 804/68, as amended, each Member State was entitled to produce milk and dairy products to a specified ceiling described as 'a reference quantity'[A1]. If the reference quantity is exceeded, then levy becomes payable to the EC in relation to the over-production of the Member State. The system is convoluted because the levy is generally

243

recovered[1] from the individual producers by reference to their own individually allocated milk quota, but the levy is collected by purchasers of milk (ie the dairies) in the case of wholesale deliveries or from the producer in the case of direct sales[2].

[A1] Council Regulation (EEC) 804/68, JO 1968 L 148/13, art 5c (as amended by Council Regulation (EEC) 856/84, OJ 1984 L 90/10).

[1] The collection of levy was the responsibility of the Intervention Board for England and Wales until 2002. It has since been collected by the Rural Payments Agency (RPA), as agent for the Department of Environment, Food and Rural Affairs (DEFRA) in England and the National Assembly for Wales.

[2] Until the Dairy Produce Quotas Regulations 2005, SI 2005/465 (DPQR 2005) came into force on 31 March 2005, the RPA could not (other than in exceptional circumstances) collect levy direct from a producer: see Case C-230/01 *Intervention Board for Agricultural Procedure v Penycoed Farming Partnership* [2004] ECR I-937, [2004] 3 CMLR 681. This lacuna was dealt with by the DPQR 2005 to enable the RPA to collect direct from producers: SI 2005/465, reg 31. This amendment to the regulations followed an unreported county court decision, in *Duckworth v Department for Environment and Rural Affairs* (2005) Barrow-in-Furness County Court.

Direct sales and wholesale quota

49.3 The two main categories of quota are direct sales and wholesale[1]. Direct sales quota is the quantity of dairy produce which may be sold by direct sale from a holding in a quota year without the seller being liable to pay levy. Wholesale quota is the quantity of dairy produce which may be delivered by wholesale delivery to a purchaser from a holding in a quota year without the producer in occupation of that holding being liable to pay levy. Wholesale quota represents the major part of quota allocated in the UK.

The RPA is required to keep a direct sales and a wholesale register, in which are entered details of each individual producers quota, identification of the holding for which it is registered and, in the case of the wholesale register, details of the relevant wholesale purchaser. The RPA must also keep a register of purchasers, in which there must be set out, in particular, the name of each purchaser and his purchaser quota[2].

Both the original allocation of individual quotas and any later alteration must be notified to the producers concerned by the competent authority (in England, the RPA); and the principle of legal certainty requires that the communication should provide all relevant information[3].

[1] For other categories of quota, see para 49.4.
[2] See para 49.5.
[3] Joined Cases C-480/00 to C-482/00, C-484/00, C-489/00 to C-491/00 and C-497/00 to C-499/00 *Azienda Agricola Ettore Ribaldi* [2004] ECR I-2943.

Other forms of quota

49.4 There have been three other categories of quota since the introduction of milk quota in 1984:

(a)   purchaser quota;

(b)   purchaser special quota; and
(c)   'special' quota, normally known as 'SLOM' quota.

Purchaser quota is the quantity of dairy produce which can be delivered by wholesale delivery to a purchaser during a quota year without that purchaser being liable to pay levy[1].

Purchaser special quota was the quantity of dairy produce which could be delivered by wholesale delivery against a producer's special quota to a purchaser during a quota year without the purchaser being liable to pay levy[2]. The DPQR 2005 no longer makes specific reference to this type of quota. Accordingly, it is subsumed into quotas generally.

The Dairy Produce Quotas (Amendment) Regulations 1990[3] made special provision for the implementation of EC legislation to enable qualifying producers who participated in the non-marketing of milk or dairy herd conversion schemes to apply for the allocation of 'special' quota. This is usually referred to as 'SLOM' quota.

Special allocations of quota were required for producers who participated in the EC non-marketing and conversion schemes and who had reduced or ceased their dairy output in their country's reference year: 1983 in the UK. As a result of litigation before the Court of Justice of the European Union (CJEU) in the cases of *Mulder I*[4] and *Von Deetzen I*[5], it was determined that such producers had been treated inequitably and accordingly special quota should be allocated to them.

There were three rounds of SLOM quota allocations following the decisions in *Mulder I* and *Von Deetzen I*. The first SLOM quota was provided for in Council Regulation (EEC) 764/89[6]. It was allocated subject to various conditions, one of which restricted a producer's right to receive special quota limited to 60% of the amount of milk delivered during the 12 months preceding the month in which the application to participate in the non-marketing or conversion scheme was made. This limitation was ruled to be unlawful by the European Court[7]. This resulted in a second round of SLOM allocations under Council Regulation (EEC) 1639/91[8]. That in turn was challenged[9]. As a consequence, a third round of SLOM quota was allocated pursuant to Council Regulation (EEC) 2055/93[10]. As in the case of purchaser special quota, the DPQR 2005 no longer makes specific reference to this type of quota. Accordingly, it is subsumed into quotas generally.

1   DPQR 2005, SI 2005/465, reg 2(1) (as amended by SI 2008/439).
2   DPQR 2002, SI 2002/457, reg 3(1).
3   SI 1990/132.
4   Case 120/86 [1988] ECR 2321.
5   Case 170/86 [1988] ECR 2355.
6   OJ 1989 L 84/2 (amending Council Regulation (EEC) 857/84, OJ 1984 L 90/13).
7   Case C-189/89 *Spagl v Hauptzollamt Rosenheim* [1990] ECR I-4539, ECJ; Case C-217/89 *Pastätter v Hauptzollamt Bad Reichenhall* [1990] ECR I-4585, ECJ.
8   OJ 1991 L 150/35.
9   In Case C-264/90 *Wehrs v Hauptzollamt Luneberg* [1992] ECR I-6285, ECJ, a producer took over a holding subject to a non-marketing or conversion undertaking, but was barred from the SLOM allocation by reason of having obtained a reference quantity under other

provisions of the milk quota scheme. Also see Case C-81/91 *Twijnstra v Minister van Landbouw, Natuurbeheer en Visserij* [1993] ECR I-2455, ECJ.

10   OJ 1993 L 187/8.

Purchasers/producers

49.5 In the UK any levy on wholesale quota which arises as a result of the Member States production exceeding the reference quantity for the 12 months concerned (where the quota year runs from 1 April to 31 March in each year) is payable by the 'purchaser' on milk delivered to it by 'producers'[1]. The purchaser is then under a duty to recover the levy from producers proportionately to their contributions to the reference quantity being exceeded. The system is administered by the RPA[2]. In the case of direct sales, the producer processor pays the RPA direct any levy payable.

The purchasers are purchasing dairies which have operated since the deregulation of the milk market by the Agriculture Act 1993. Each purchaser has a quota, which is the quantity of dairy produce which may be delivered by wholesale deliveries to that purchaser from holdings in a region during a quota year without the purchaser being liable to pay levy. It is the ability of producers to trade their quota and transfer it which has not only given milk quota an economic value, but also has resulted in disputes in relation to transfers and matters relating to transfers.

1   As to the definition of producers, see para 49.7.
2   Formerly the Intervention Board for Agricultural Produce.

Holding

49.6 Quota is registered in relation to a producer's 'holding', often known as the Euro holding. The holding is defined as 'all of the production units managed by a farmer situated within the territory of the same Member State'[1]. The holding, therefore, may include both freehold and leasehold land. Importantly, it is not an 'agricultural holding' within the definition contained in the Agricultural Holdings Act 1986 (AHA 1986).

1   Council Regulation (EC) 1234/2007, OJ 2007 L 299/1, art 65(d), which cross refers to Council Regulation (EC) 1782/2003, OJ 2003 L 270/1 (and see now, following repeal of Council Regulation (EC) 1782/2003, Council Regulation (EC) 73/2009, OJ 2009 L 30/16, art 146(2) and Annex XVIII). See also DPQR 2005, SI 2005/465, reg 2(1) (as amended by SI 2008/439). Note that 'a farm is perfectly capable of being a holding even if the cows have all gone': per McCowan LJ in *WE & RA Holdcroft v Staffordshire County Council* [1994] 2 EGLR 1, [1994] 28 EG 131 at 134. See also para 49.17.

Farmer/producer

49.7 A 'farmer' means 'a natural or legal person, or group of natural or legal persons, whatever legal status is granted to the group and its members by national law, whose holding is situated within Community territory ... and who exercises an agricultural activity'[1].

246

A 'producer' means 'a farmer with a holding located within the geographical territory of a Member State, who produces and markets milk or who is preparing to do so in the very near future'[2].

The definition of producer is not limited to individuals, but extends to farming companies and partnerships. In the case of *R v Dairy Produce Quota Tribunal for England and Wales, ex p Atkinson*[3], two brothers, one on his own and one jointly with his wife, lodged claims before the prescribed date for a share in their region's reserved quota under the exceptional hardship provisions in the Dairy Produce Quotas Regulations 1984. In each case the applicants had purchased the farms in 1984, but were not producing milk on those farms during the year ending 31 March 1985. However, at all material times the two brothers had been in partnership with their father in relation to another farm which was an active dairy farm to which a primary quota attached. The Quota Tribunal rejected the applicants' claim on the ground that no actual dairy farming was being carried out in the year ending 31 March 1985 on either of the newly purchased farms. As such neither of the applicants were 'producers'. It was argued that the applicants were producers as they were part of a partnership on their father's farm where the main occupation was dairy farming. Accordingly, the decision of the Quota Tribunal was quashed and the case remitted for fresh consideration by a differently constituted Tribunal.

[1]   Council Regulation (EC) 1234/2007, OJ 2007 L 299/1, art 2(2)(a), which cross refers to Council Regulation (EC) 1782/2003, OJ 2003 L 270/1 (and see now, following repeal of Council Regulation (EC) 1782/2003, Council Regulation (EC) 73/2009, OJ 2009 L 30/16, art 146(2) and Annex XVIII). See also DPQR 2005, SI 2005/465, reg 2(1) (as amended by SI 2008/439).
[2]   Council Regulation (EC) 1234/2007, OJ 2007 L 299/1, art 65(c). See also DPQR 2005, SI 2005/465, reg 2(1) (as amended by SI 2008/439).
[3]   (1985) 276 Estates Gazette 1158.

Leasing

49.8 It is permissible for one producer to agree with another to make a temporary transfer to that other producer, for the period of one quota year, of part of his quota which he does not intend to use, such transactions being commonly known as 'leasing'[1]. This is not a permanent transfer of quota to which the arbitration provisions contained in the DPQR 2005 apply[2].

[1]   Council Regulation (EC) 1234/2007, OJ 2007 L 299/1, art 73(1).
[2]   For the current provisions authorising temporary transfers in England, see DPQR 2005, SI 2005/465, reg 15 (as amended by SI 2008/439).

Transfers

49.9 Individual quotas shall be transferred with the holding whenever it is sold, leased, transferred by actual or anticipated inheritance or any other means involving comparable legal effects for the producers, in accordance with detailed rules to be determined by the Member States[1]. This relates to the general rule where quota is transferred with land. As seen below[2], transfers without land are authorised for the purposes of improving the structure of milk production[3]. It is not possible to transfer quota by the grant or termination of a tenancy under which a holding, or part of a holding, is occupied for a period of less than ten months[4].

In the UK, changes to the occupation of an entire holding which has registered quota carry a transfer of the entire quota with them. Changes in occupation of part of holdings require an apportionment[5]. In default of agreement between the parties, such apportionment is made by arbitration[6].

1   Council Regulation (EC) 1234/2007, OJ 2007 L 299/1, art 74(1).
2   See para 49.29.
3   Council Regulation (EC) 1234/2007, OJ 2007 L 299/1, art 75(1)(e); DPQR 2005, SI 2005/465, reg 13 (as amended by SI 2008/439). See further para 49.29.
4   DPQR 2005, SI 2005/465, reg 16. See para 49.14.
5   SI 2005/465, reg 10.
6   SI 2005/465, reg 10(2) and Sch 1.

49.10 The arbitration rules for the apportionment of milk quota are contained in regs 9 to 12 and 39 of and Sch 1 to the DPQR 2005[1]. The Arbitration Act 1996 does not apply to arbitrations under the DPQR 2005 which has its own unique arbitration code based upon the now defunct provisions of Sch 11 to the AHA 1986.

1   SI 2005/465 (as amended by SI 2007/106 and SI 2008/439). For arbitrations in Wales, see the Dairy Produce Quotas (Wales) Regulations 2005, SI 2005/537 (W.47), regs 9–12 and 39 and Sch 1 (as amended by SI 2007/844 (W.76) and SI 2008/685 (W.72)).

End of tenancy claims

49.11 Where the tenant is a registered producer in respect of a Euro holding which consists entirely of land comprised in a tenancy, then all the quota, in principle, reverts to the landlord at the end of the tenancy. There is no question of apportionment. Subject to detailed rules, a tenant has a right under para 13 of Sch 1 to the Agriculture Act 1986 to receive compensation for such part of the quota as, in broad terms is attributable to efficient farming practices or fixed equipment introduced by the tenant or has been purchased by the tenant[1].

Claims for compensation under the Agriculture Act 1986 are settled either at the end of the tenancy, or before, by arbitration. The procedures laid down in the AHA 1986 apply, now adopting the terms of the Arbitration Act 1996[2].

In some cases the position will be complicated. The tenant may occupy land let by one landlord and other land let by another landlord or owned by the tenant himself. Upon quitting part of the milk quota holding there would be an apportionment of milk quota which must first be settled by arbitration under the DPQR 2005 and claims for compensation then have to be settled under the Agriculture Act 1986.

As regards tenancies under the AHA 1986 ending after 31 March 2005, where:

(a)   a tenant of any land in a holding[3] has quota registered as available to him;

(b)   the quota is so registered by virtue of a transfer referred to in reg 13 of the DPQR 2005[4], the cost of which was not borne by the tenant's landlord;

(c)   the tenancy of the land in question expires without any possibility of renewal on similar terms;

(d)   the tenant and his landlord have not agreed that, after the expiry of the tenancy, the quota should no longer be available to the tenant; and

(e)   the tenant continues to be a producer after the expiry of the tenancy in relation to:

    (i)   another holding; or

    (ii)   another part of the holding of which the land formed part,

the tenant may submit a notice to the Secretary of State[5] that the quota is to be available to him by virtue of his occupation of that other holding or that other part of the holding of which the land formed part[6].

The notice referred to above must:

(i)   be in such form as the Secretary of State may reasonably require;

(ii)   reach the Secretary of State no later than 31 March in the quota year in which the tenancy expires; and

(iii) include a statement by the tenant that:

    (a)   he and his landlord have not agreed that, after the expiry of the tenancy, the quota should be registered in relation to the holding which then comprises or, as the case may be, includes, the land, stating the amounts of used and unused quota[7] involved; and

    (b)   he continues to be a producer[8].

---

[1]   The complex provisions relating to the calculation of compensation are dealt with in detail in Ch 50.

[2]   Agriculture Act 1986, Sch 1 paras 10 and 11.

[3]   DPQR 2005, SI 2005/465, reg 2(1) (as amended by SI 2008/439). Note that this is the definition of 'holding' for milk quota purposes (the Euro holding) and not for the purposes of the AHA 1986. See para 49.6.

[4]   See para 49.29.

[5]   Secretary of State for Environment, Food and Rural Affairs: DPQR 2005, SI 2005/465, reg 2(1) (as amended by SI 2008/439).

[6]   SI 2005/465, reg 14(2).

[7]   'Unused quota' is 'quota remaining unused after direct sales or deliveries have been taken into account' (following any adjustment for fat content) and 'used quota' is to be construed accordingly: SI 2005/465, reg 2(1) (as amended by SI 2008/439).

[8]   SI 2005/465, reg 14(3).

LEGISLATION GOVERNING THE QUOTA SYSTEM

49.12 In the UK the milk quota system was initially governed by the Dairy Produce Quotas Regulations 1984[1], but following a series of amending and consolidating regulations, the quota system is now regulated by the DPQR 2005, as amended[2]. Formerly the milk quota regime for England and Wales was the same, contained in the Dairy Produce Quotas Regulations 1997[3]. Now the DPQR 2005 apply to England and the Dairy Produce Quotas

49.12 *Milk quota*

(Wales) Regulations 2005[4] apply to Wales. Despite the separation, the rules applying in Wales are basically the same as in England.

1. SI 1984/1047. See also the Dairy Produce Quotas (General Provisions) Regulations 2002, SI 2002/458 (as amended by SI 2005/466, SI 2007/477 and SI 2008/438).
2. SI 2005/465 (as amended by SI 2006/120, SI 2007/106 and SI 2008/439).
3. SI 1997/733.
4. SI 2005/537 (W.47) (as amended by SI 2006/762 (W.72), SI 2007/844 (W.76) and SI 2008/685 (W.72)).

THE BACKGROUND TO THE ARBITRAL PROCESS

The mechanics of transfer

49.13 Save in limited circumstances[1], in the case of a transfer of the whole or part of a 'holding', the transferee[2] must submit to the RPA a notice of transfer in such form as may reasonably be required by Secretary of State, in the case of transfers with land on or before 31 March in the quota year[3] in which the transfer takes place, regardless of whether or not by lease[4].

Such notice shall, include a statement from the transferor[5] and transferee specifying the amounts of used and unused quota transferred[6].

1. Retention of quotas at the end of a tenancy: see DPQR 2005, SI 2005/465, reg 14.
2. Transferee means '(a) where quota is transferred with a holding or part of a holding, a person who replaces another as occupier of that holding or part of a holding; and (b) in any other case, the person to whom quota is transferred': SI 2005/465, reg 2(1) (as amended by SI 2008/439).
3. The quota year means any of the periods of 12 months referred to in art 66(1) of Council Regulation (EC) 1234/2007, OJ 2007 L 299/1, these periods commencing on 1 April in any year.
4. DPQR 2005, SI 2005/465, reg 9(3) (as amended by SI 2007/106). Note that under the DPQR 2005 as originally enacted, where the transfer was by lease, the notice was to be submitted no later than 1 March in any quota year.
5. Transferor means '(a) where quota is transferred with a holding or part of a holding, a person who is replaced by another occupier of that holding or part of a holding; and (b) in any other case, the person from whom quota is transferred': SI 2005/465, reg 2(1) (as amended by SI 2008/439).
6. It may be observed that the Advocate General in Joined Cases C-230/09 and C-231/09 *Hauptzollamt Koblenz v Etling* (Opinion delivered on 14 September 2010) was of the view that, while Member States could provide otherwise in their detailed rules, the European Community legislation, in principle, permitted permanent transfer of all the quota allocated to the transferor at the beginning of the quota year, even where a part of that quota had already been delivered.

49.14 In the case of a transfer of the whole holding, the notice must include a consent or sole interest notice provided by the transferor in respect of the holding[1]. Where the transferor is a tenant, the landlord must sign the consent notice before the tenant can transfer.

Where there is a transfer of part of a holding, the DPQR 2005 require that:

(a)   an apportionment of the quota relating to the holding must either be agreed between the transferee and the transferor and contained in the notice required to be lodged with the RPA or, in the absence of such agreement, determined by arbitration in accordance with Sch 1 to the DPQR 2005 in England; *and*

(b)   any dairy produce which has been sold by direct sale or delivered by wholesale delivery from the holding during the quota year in which the change of occupation takes place and prior to that transfer shall, in principle, be deemed, for the purposes of any levy calculation, to have been sold, transferred free of charge or delivered from each part of the holding in proportion to that apportionment, unless the parties agree otherwise and notify the RPA of the agreement in such form as the RPA may reasonably require, at the time of the submission of the notice of transfer pursuant to reg 9 of the DPQR 2005[2].

There are limited circumstances in which there is no transfer of quota upon the transfer of the whole or part of a holding[3]. These include the grant or termination of a licence to occupy land or the grant or termination of a tenancy under which a holding, or part of a holding, is occupied for a period of less than ten months[4].

[1]   DPQR, SI 2005/465, reg 9(5)(c).
[2]   SI 2005/465, reg 10.
[3]   SI 2005/465, reg 16 (as amended by SI 2006/120). There are like provisions in Wales: see the Dairy Produce Quotas (Wales) Regulations 2005, SI 2005/537 (W.47) (as amended by SI 2006/762 (W.72)).
[4]   SI 2005/465, reg 16(1)(b).

The arbitral code

49.15 Milk quota arbitrations are conducted in accordance with their own self contained rules which are set out in Sch 1 to the DPQR 2005[1].

Paragraph 3 of Sch 1 requires an arbitrator to base his award on findings made by him as to the areas used for milk production[2] in the five years during which milk production took place preceding the change of occupation or, in the case of a prospective apportionment, preceding his appointment as arbitrator.

Arbitrators appointed under the DPQR 2005 are appointed either by agreement or by the President of the RICS. Prior to the TRIG[3] reforms resulting in the RRO 2006[4], the President had to appoint a member of the panel drawn up by the Lord Chancellor for the purpose of conducting arbitrations under the AHA 1986. The panel has now been abolished and so this is no longer the case.

[1]   See Ch 51.
[2]   As to areas used for milk production, see *Puncknowle Farms Ltd v Kane* [1985] 3 All ER 790, [1985] 2 EGLR 8. See para 49.28.
[3]   Tenancy Reform Industry Group.
[4]   The Regulatory Reform (Agricultural Tenancies) (England and Wales) Order 2006, SI 2006/2805.

49.16 *Milk quota*

KEY LEGAL ISSUES

The nature of a milk quota transfer

49.16 Since the introduction of milk quotas in 1984, the trading in milk quota that has arisen has been underpinned by agreements by transferors and transferees to transfer the entirety or part of the milk quota attaching to a holding.

The typical transaction, where the parties intend to effect a permanent transfer of milk quota without a permanent transfer of land, is the grant of a tenancy of a minimum of ten months by the transferor in respect of the whole or part of his holding. Upon the change of occupation occasioned by the grant of the tenancy, an agreed amount of milk quota is transferred to the transferee and becomes immediately registerable in the transferee's name. As part of the transaction, the transferee agrees that for the period of the tenancy he will not use any part of the land comprised in the tenancy for milk production, so that it is no longer an 'area used for milk production'. Accordingly, on the termination of the tenancy, the agreed amount of milk quota is apportioned to land of the transferee which has been used for dairy farming and remains registered in his name.

The extent of the holding

49.17 A holding under the European Community legislation extends to 'all of the production units managed by a farmer situated within the territory of the same Member State'[1].

It has been determined by the European Court that the definition of a holding is a broad one and, in particular, the definition is wide enough to include tenanted land, even where the production units at the date of the grant have neither dairy cows nor the necessary facilities for milk production, and the agreement imposes no obligation to engage in milk production[2].

In the UK, it has been held that land which the occupier was obliged by contract not to use for milk production could not be regarded as part of a holding[3].

---

[1] Council Regulation (EC) 1234/2007, OJ 2007 L 299/1, art 65(d), which cross refers to Council Regulation (EC) 1782/2003, OJ 2003 L 270/1 (and see now, following repeal of Council Regulation (EC) 1782/2003, Council Regulation (EC) 73/2009, OJ 2009 L 30/16, art 146(2) and Annex XVIII). See also DPQR 2005, SI 2005/465, reg 2(1) (as amended by SI 2008/439). Originally a holding extended to all such production units within the Community. The definition was changed in Council Regulation (EEC) 1560/93, OJ 1993 L 154/30.
[2] See Case 5/88 *Wachauf v Bundesamt für Ernährung und Forstwirtschaft* [1989] ECR 2609, [1991] 1 CMLR 328, ECJ (and, in particular, the Opinion of the Advocate General).
[3] *Carson v Cornwall County Council* [1993] 1 EGLR 21, [1993] 03 EG 119. Cf *WE & RA Holdcroft v Staffordshire County Council* [1994] 2 EGLR 1, [1994] 28 EG 131.

Definition of the producer

49.18 As seen above[1], a 'producer' means 'a farmer with a holding located within the geographical territory of a Member State, who produces and markets milk or who is preparing to do so in the very near future'[2]. Production units have not been defined in the European legislation.

'Producer' covers both farmers making direct sales and those more usually involved in wholesale deliveries to purchasers. It embraces tenants and freehold owners[3]. It extends to business structures, including partnerships and companies. This gives rise to two issues. First, the legal status of the producer; and second, the extent to which a producer must be actively engaged in milk production.

As to the legal status of the producer, in the case of partnerships the general practice has been to register the milk quota in the name of the partnership rather than in the name of the individual partners[4]. In the UK it was held arguably to be sufficient that it was sufficient to qualify as a producer if an individual was a member of a partnership engaged in dairy farming[5]. It is now established that this means actively engaged in milk production[6].

[1] See para 49.7.
[2] Council Regulation (EC) 1234/2007, OJ 2007 L 299/1, art 65(c). See also DPQR 2005, SI 2005/465, reg 2(1) (as amended by SI 2008/439). As to the definition of 'farmer', see para 49.7.
[3] Case C-341/89 *Ballmann v Hauptzollamt Osnabrück* [1991] ECR I-25.
[4] See Case C-98/91 *Herbrink v Minister van Landbouw, Natuurbeheer en Visserij* [1994] ECR I-223, [1994] 3 CMLR 645, ECJ; Case C-84/90 *R v Ministry of Agriculture, Fisheries and Food, ex p Dent* [1992] ECR I-2009, [1992] 2 CMLR 597.
[5] *R v Dairy Produce Quota Tribunal for England and Wales, ex p Atkinson* (1985) 276 Estates Gazette 1158.
[6] See para 49.30.

Transfer/change of occupation

49.19 Unless falling within the limited exceptions set out in the DPQR 2005[1], any transaction which involves both a 'transfer' and a 'change of occupation' of a holding, or part of it, will require a re-registration of quota. There must therefore be a transfer of a holding or part of it. As a consequence, there must also be a change of occupation. Rather, they have not sought to break down the transaction into the component parts. The courts have considered the transaction as a whole[2]. In *WE & RA Holdcroft v Staffordshire County Council*, McCowan LJ observed: 'It is plain ..., in my judgment, that when the regulations talk about 'transfer' they are talking in terms of occupation and not legal title'[3].

As has been seen above[4], the concept of transfer is defined by reference to 'transferor' and 'transferee' in the DPQR 2005. The definitions are however imprecise. The 'occupier' of a holding is defined as including the person entitled to grant occupation of that land to another[5]. The concept of change of occupation has given rise to a number of difficulties including whether physical occupation is required. It appears that the absence of physical occupation consequential upon the grant of a tenancy with the attendant right to occupy will be insufficient to give rise to a change of occupation causing the transfer of milk quota. It has also been suggested that de minimis physical occupation will be insufficient. In *R v Ministry of Agriculture, Fisheries and Food, ex p Cox*[6], the vendor sold milk quota using a grazing agreement. Subsequently, when it became apparent that the purchaser had failed to graze stock on the land during the term of the agreement, the vendor applied for the re-registration of the quota in his name. It was held that the effect of Commission Regulation (EEC) 1371/84[7] was to require actual occupation of the land, and not the acquisition of a mere right to occupy.

1   See para 49.14.
2   See, eg, *WE & RA Holdcroft v Staffordshire County Council* [1994] 2 EGLR 1.
3   [1994] 2 EGLR 1 at 134.
4   See para 49.9.
5   DPQR 2005, SI 2005/465, reg 2(1) (as amended by SI 2008/439).
6   [1993] 2 CMLR 917, [1993] 1 EGLR 17.
7   OJ 1984 L 132/11.

The nature of milk quota

Interest in land: the statutory provisions

49.20 Disputes between partners as to their entitlement in respect of milk quota, together with litigation between lenders and borrowers[1], have given rise to consideration of the juridical nature of milk quota. The starting point is that milk quota is said to attach to the land and passes with the land to which it relates[2]. It raises the question as to whether it is an interest in land, in which case the following statutory provisions would need to be considered.

Section 2 of the Law of Property (Miscellaneous Provisions) Act 1989 provides that a contract for the sale or other disposition of an interest in land can only be made in writing and only by incorporating all the terms which the parties have expressly agreed in one document or, where contracts are being exchanged, in each document. 'Interest in land' is defined as 'any estate, interest or charge in or over land'[3]. The Law of Property (Miscellaneous Provisions) Act 1989 further provides that 'nothing in this section [s 2] affects the creation or operation of resulting, implied or constructive trusts'[4].

Section 53 of the Law of Property Act 1925 provides that no interest in land can be created or disposed of except by signed writing, and that a declaration of trust in respect of any land or any interest in land must be proved by signed writing. As with the Law of Property (Miscellaneous Provisions) Act 1989, the Law of Property Act 1925 does not affect the creation or operation of resulting, implied or constructive trusts.

Section 205(1)(ix) of the Law of Property Act 1925 defines 'land' widely, as including a rent, other incorporeal hereditaments, and an easement, right, privilege, or benefit in, over, or derived from the land. An interest in land has been described as a right which has 'the quality of being capable of enduring through different ownership of the land, according to normal conceptions of title to real property'[5]. An interest in the proceeds of sale of land has been held to be an interest in land[6]. In this analysis, it should be noted that the Trusts of Land and Appointment of Trustees Act 1996 introduced trusts of land and abolished the doctrine of conversion.

Further, it may be observed that s 4(1) of the Law of Property Act 1925 provides:

> 'Interests in land validly created or arising after the commencement of this Act, which are not capable of subsisting as legal estates, shall take effect as equitable interests, and, save as otherwise expressly provided by statute, interests in land which under the Statute of Uses or otherwise could before the commencement of this Act have been created as legal interests, shall be capable of being created as equitable interests: Provided that, after the commencement of this Act (and save as hereinafter expressly enacted), an equitable interest in land shall only be capable of being validly created in any case in which an equivalent equitable interest in property real or personal could have been validly created before such commencement'.

The section has not been judicially considered in any reported case, but may well prevent parties from creating novel forms of interest in land and making them capable of binding or benefiting the land. This does not, however, prevent Parliament, or the EC, by virtue of the European Communities Act 1972, from creating a novel right which runs with land and may be an interest in land.

1   See para 49.21.
2   See, eg, Council Regulation (EC) 1234/2007, OJ 2007 L 299/1, Preamble (37); and, for statement of this principle by the CJEU, see, eg, Case 5/88 *Wachauf v Bundesamt für Ernährung und Forstwirtschaft* [1989] ECR 2609, [1991] 1 CMLR 328; Case C-98/91 *Herbrink v Minister van Landbouw, Natuurbeheer en Visserij* [1994] ECR I-223, [1994] 3 CMLR 645, ECJ; Case C-15/95 *EARL de Kerlast v Unicopa* [1997] ECR I-1961. See further para 49.21.
3   Law of Property (Miscellaneous Provisions) Act 1989, s 2(6).
4   Law of Property (Miscellaneous Provisions) Act 1989, s 2(5).
5   *Nurdin & Peacock plc v DB Ramsden & Co Ltd* [1999] 1 EGLR 119 at 124K–124L, [1998] EGCS 123.
6   *Cooper v Critchley* [1955] Ch 431, [1955] 1 All ER 520, CA.

Is milk quota an interest in land?

49.21 Milk quota was allocated to a 'producer', being a farmer supplying milk in respect of a 'holding'. The quota then attaches to the holding and passes with it. On a sale of part, it is apportioned. In *Faulks v Faulks*[1], Chadwick J held that quota was not an asset capable of being enjoyed, or transferred, independently of the land in respect of which it is registered:

> 'The fact that the transfer of a potential liability is likely to be matched by a payment to the person assuming that liability may enable it to be said that the quota transferred has an intrinsic economic value, but that does not of itself lead to the conclusion that quota is an asset separate and distinct from the holding in relation to which it was, or becomes, registered'.

That decision was followed by Blackburne J in *Davies v H & R Ecroyd Ltd*[2]:

'... while it is well recognised that in certain circumstances, milk quota may become severed from the land with which it would otherwise run, the fundamental principle is that milk quota attaches to and passes with the land to which it relates'[3].

Likewise, in *Harries v Barclays Bank plc*[4], the Court of Appeal held that a bank which held a charge over a farm, but not over the farmer's quota, was entitled to retain the proceeds of sale of the farm which were attributable to the value of the quota, and also the proceeds of leasing the quota. The proceeds of sale attributable to the value of the quota were not capable of separate treatment from that attributable to the value of the land. The proceeds from the quota leasing were an incident of possession of the farm to which the bank had become entitled under the charge. The proceeds formed part of the rents and profits of the land to which the bank was entitled as one of the products of its possession of the mortgaged property.

Further, the CJEU has affirmed a number of times the fundamental principle that milk quota attaches to and follows the land in respect of which it is registered. In *EARL de Kerlast*, the Court said:

'The Court has consistently held that the entire system of reference quantities is based on the general principle laid down by Article 7 of Regulation No 857/84 and Article 7 of Regulation No 1546/88, that a reference quantity is allocated in relation to land and must therefore be transferred with that land ...'[5].

It should also be noted that Preamble (37) of Council Regulation (EC) 1234/2007[6] refers to 'the principle that quotas are tied to farms'. Nonetheless, the EC legislation does grant certain options for the tie to be broken[7]. These include what appears to be a total break of the link with land, Member States being authorised to 'centralise and supervise transfers of quotas without land'[8]. The UK has not chosen to follow this route: in January 2004, DEFRA issued an 'Explanatory Statement' in relation to the then DPQR including the following:

'In the light of the responses to the consultation [in relation to the DPQR 2002] and the provisions of the new European Council regulation on milk quota ... we have decided not to introduce new regulations breaking the link between quota and land entirely'.

Accordingly, it would seem clear that milk quota is allocated in relation to land and that, in principle, it is transferred with land. Moreover, the CJEU has distinguished between milk quotas and payment entitlements under the Single Payment Scheme, on the basis that in the latter case any link with the land is more tenuous[9]. On the other hand, as indicated, specified policy reasons may justify departure from the general principle[10]; and it may be reiterated that one option (albeit not exercised in the UK) has been to centralise and supervise quota transfers without any reference to a land transaction. Accordingly, there would seem to be much force in the statement of Morritt LJ in *Harries v Barclays Bank plc*[11] that:

'Milk quota is the creation of the legislation both European and domestic to which I have referred. In determining where the benefit of it lies and how it got there it is necessary to apply that legislation to the facts of the case. I do not find it helpful in that context to seek to label or categorise milk quota as an asset or as an asset of a particular description, not least when the description is one of English law which may not be recognised by the domestic laws of the other member states'.

1 [1992] 1 EGLR 9, [1992] 15 EG 82.
2 [1996] 2 EGLR 5, [1996] 30 EG 97.
3 [1996] 2 EGLR 5.
4 [1997] 2 EGLR 15, [1997] 45 EG 145, CA.
5 Case C-15/95 [1997] ECR I-1961, para 17.
6 OJ 2007 L 299/1.
7 Council Regulation (EC) 1234/2007, OJ 2007 L 299/1, Preamble (37) and art 75.
8 Council Regulation (EC) 1234/2007, OJ 2007 L 299/1, art 75(1)(c). Also note the Opinion of Advocate General Ruiz-Jarabo Colomer in Case C-186/96 *Demand v Hauptzollamt Trier* [1998] ECR I-8529. See further para 52.21.
9 Case C-470/08 *Van Dijk v Gemeente Kampen* [2010] All ER (D) 141 (Feb) (Judgment delivered on 21 January 2010), para 25; and see also Case C-434/08 *Harms v Heidinga* (Opinion delivered on 4 February 2010), para 31. See further para 52.14.
10 For permanent transfers without land, see para 49.29.
11 [1997] 2 EGLR 15, [1997] 45 EG 145, CA.

49.22 Further, it may be observed that, for tax purposes at least, there is authority to the effect that milk quota is not an interest in land. Thus, in *Cottle v Coldicott*[1] the Special Commissioners held that, when assessing Capital Gains Tax on the sale of quota by means of a short-term tenancy, there was no part disposal of land; and, accordingly, no part of the acquisition cost of the land could be taken into account when calculating the tax liability. Rather, in these circumstances, milk quota was to be regarded as a separate asset. The decision was subsequently followed in *Foxton v Revenue and Customs Comrs*[2], where the Special Commissioners rejected argument that quota was land, stating that: 'While milk quota is related to holdings of land that does not mean that it is the same asset as the holding because it can be dealt with separately by the method adopted in this case of granting a short sub-tenancy, which is not itself a disposal of the land'[3].

These decisions cannot easily be reconciled with the reasoning of the courts in *Faulks v Faulks*[4], *Davies and H & R Ecroyd Ltd*[5], and *Harries v Barclays Bank plc*[6]. If they were correct, it is submitted that they were only so in the tax context. And, indeed, the Special Commissioners in *Cottle v Coldicott* were at pains to confine their determination to such context.

1 [1995] STC (SCD) 239.
2 [2005] STC (SCD) 661.
3 On the facts, there was a certain logic to this interpretation, in that the main purpose of the transfer was to sell the milk quota (as opposed to granting a permanent interest in the land).
4 [1992] 1 EGLR 9, [1992] 15 EG 82.
5 [1996] 2 EGLR 5.
6 [1997] 2 EGLR 15, [1997] 45 EG 145, CA.

49.23 Likewise, for the purposes of a milk quota security scheme, milk quota has been treated as an independent asset. In *Swift v Dairywise Farms Ltd*[1], the facts were complicated involving two sister companies trading in milk quota and the extent to which such quota could be treated as security for a loan. In short, loans were made by Dairywise Limited to farmers whose milk quota was transferred to Dairywise Farms Limited as security for the loan. After Dairywise Limited went into liquidation, its liquidators brought proceedings against Dairywise Farms Limited contending that Dairywise Farms Limited held the milk quota for the benefit of Dairywise Limited. The decision at first instance of Jacob J considered the juridical nature of milk quota. The judge held that milk quota constituted property within the definition of s 436 of the Insolvency Act 1986 and was capable of forming the subject matter of a trust between Dairywise Limited and Dairywise Farms Limited.

The decision at first instance was the subject of an appeal to the Court of Appeal. The Court of Appeal[2] did not adopt the analysis or reasoning of Jacob J, in short determining the issues as an interlocutory matter based upon the contractual arrangements between Dairywise Limited and Dairywise Farms Limited. The court held that borrowers had an equitable right to require the re-transfer of quota.

1   [2000] 1 All ER 320, [2000] 1 WLR 1177.
2   [2001] EWCA Civ 145, [2003] 2 All ER 304n, [2001] 3 EGLR 101. The Court of Appeal included Chadwick LJ, the judge in *Faulks v Faulks* [1992] 1 EGLR 9, [1992] 15 EG 82.

Milk quota and partnerships

49.24 The creation or termination of a partnership gives rise to particular problems, not least because an excluded category of transfer is a licence and many partnerships proceed on the basis of the partnership being granted a licence to occupy the holding farmed by the partnership. As indicated, the High Court in *Faulks v Faulks* held that, on the facts of the case, the milk quota was not a partnership asset[1].

In *Faulks*, two brothers farmed an agricultural holding pursuant to a tenancy granted to one brother alone. The partnership deed provided that the brother who was tenant stood possessed of the tenancy in trust for the partnership for the duration of the partnership. The issue which arose was whether the milk quota passed with the tenancy on dissolution or should be valued as a separate asset of the partnership. The court held that it passed with the tenancy. Although quota has an intrinsic economic value, that does not lead to the conclusion that quota is an asset separate and distinct from the holding in relation to which it is registered. Accordingly, the milk quota formerly registered in the name of the partnership, prior to its dissolution, could not properly be regarded as an asset of the partnership.

In *Davies v H & R Ecroyd Ltd*[2], the parties entered into a farming partnership agreement on 1 February 1983 in relation to a dairy holding. It was agreed that the holding itself, which was owned by one of the parties, was not a partnership asset. Milk quota was subsequently allocated to the holding in April 1984. The partnership was dissolved in February 1998. The non-land owning party claimed that the milk quota was an asset of the partnership. The milk quota was introduced after the parties entered into the partnership. It was impossible to attribute to the partners any intention other than the milk quota should be treated in the same way as the holding. The milk quota allocated to the holding in 1984 was not an asset of the partnership.

¹ [1992] 1 EGLR 9, [1992] 15 EG 82. It may be observed, however, that the partnership deed did not expressly address milk quotas, having been drawn up before their introduction.
² [1996] 2 EGLR 5, [1996] 30 EG 97. See also Case C-127/94 *R v Ministry of Agriculture, Fisheries and Food, ex p H & R Ecroyd Holdings Ltd* [1996] ECR I-2731, [1996] 3 CMLR 214, ECJ.

Surrender of a lease

49.25 Both the CJEU¹ and the Court of Appeal in the UK² have held that the surrender of a lease is a transaction of comparable legal effect for the purposes of occasioning a transfer of milk quota.

In *WE & RA Holdcroft v Staffordshire County Council*³, the tenant of a dairy farm with wholesale milk quota gave a notice to quit to the landlord effective on 25 March 1990. The farm was farmed in partnership with the tenant's son and wife. The tenant's son formed a new partnership with his own wife and bought another farm. The dairy herd was removed to that new farm on 1 March 1990. The original farming partnership was dissolved and possession of the tenanted farm was given up to the landlord on 25 March 1990. This gave rise to two issues. First, was the surrender a transfer entitling the landlord to a claim in relation to the quota? Second, was the re-arrangement of occupation under the partnership which took place on 1 March 1990 a transfer of comparable legal effect justifying an arbitration and the apportionment of the milk quota? It was held that the surrender of a tenancy amounts to a transaction having 'comparable legal effect' to a transfer by sale, lease or inheritance. It therefore entitled the landlord to a share of the quota. Further, the transfer of occupation which took place on the earlier dissolution of the first partnership on 1 March 1990 was also a transfer and could trigger arbitration proceedings and a possible apportionment of the milk quota pursuant to the DPQR.

¹ Case 5/88 *Wachauf v Bundesamt für Ernährung und Forstwirtschaft* [1989] ECR 2609, [1991] 1 CMLR 328.
² *WE and RA Holdcroft v Staffordshire County Council* [1994] 2 EGLR 1, [1994] 28 EG 131.
³ [1994] 2 EGLR 1, (1994) 28 EG 131.

Areas used for milk production

49.28 Milk quota attaches to such land as falls within the definition of 'areas used for milk production in the last five-year period during which production took place before the change of occupation, or, in the case of a prospective apportionment, in the last five-year period during which production took place before the appointment of the arbitrator'¹. The phrase 'areas used for milk production' was expressly considered in the case of *Puncknowle Farms Ltd v Kane*². In his award, the arbitrator took the view that they comprised:

'the forage areas used by the dairy herd and to support the dairy herd by the growing of grass and any fodder crops for the milking dairy herd, dry cows and all dairy following female young stock (and homebred dairy or dual purpose bulls for use on the premises, if applicable), if bred to enter the production herd and not for sale. In this case, maize, silage, hay and grass were the fodder crops, but consideration would have been given to corn crops, or part of corn crops, grown for consumption by the dairy herd or young stock, including the use of straw, had agreed evidence been produced'.

Likewise, the High Court adopted a broad interpretation, so as to include 'the areas which are used to support the dairy herd by the maintenance of animals between one lactation and another, and to support the animals which are destined for inclusion in the dairy herd on any holding'. In addition, it accepted that land used for milk production may be used concomitantly for other purposes in the rural context; and that the buildings and yards would also qualify (if of sufficient size to be material), together with land used for dairy and dual purpose bulls (provided that they were bred to enter the production herd).

An unresolved issue is whether an area used for milk production which is occupied pursuant to an agreement which itself would not constitute a transfer for the purposes of the DPQR 2005³ is an area which will be taken into account by the arbitrator in determining the apportionment of milk quota over the five-year period upon which he has to base his award.

In *Posthumus v Oosterwoud*⁴, the CJEU determined a case concerning the objective criteria to be applied by Member States when introducing legislation as to quota apportionment. The Advocate General's Opinion⁵ was that only a mathematical apportionment fell to be carried out unless a Member State had laid down its own objective criteria for some different approach to the apportionment. It is not an objective criterion to leave the parties free to negotiate and agree their own apportionment. Member States should not 'leave the matter to the discretion of the parties. That would be contrary both to the terms of the legislation, and especially to the notion of 'objective criteria', and contrary also to what must be assumed to be the purpose of the legislation, namely to avoid manipulation of the quota system and to prevent trading in quotas'. The Advocate General's Opinion continued to the effect that, where parties do reach agreement, Member States must take measures to see that the community legislation has been satisfied and that those measures 'might also include the scrutiny of the terms of compensation agreed in order to ensure that such agreements do not amount to a disguised form of trading quotas'.

The CJEU itself emphasised the fact that Member States had the option to lay down objective criteria in relation to the assessment of areas used for milk production. Where a Member State had not laid down such objective criteria, apportionment was to be strictly in accordance with areas used for milk production. No account could be taken of the extent to which the different areas contributed to total milk production⁶.

¹ DPQR 2005, SI 2005/465, Sch 1 para 3(1).
² [1985] 3 All ER 790, [1985] 2 EGLR 8.

³ For example, occupied pursuant to a licence.
⁴ Case C-121/90 [1991] ECR I-5833, [1992] 2 CMLR 336, ECJ. See also Case C-79/91 *Knüfer v Buchmann* [1992] ECR I-6895, [1993] 1 CMLR 692, ECJ.
⁵ Advocate General Jacobs.
⁶ The 'artistic' approach preferred by the Irish High Court was not embraced: *Lawlor v Minister for Agriculture* [1990] 1 IR 356, [1988] 3 CMLR 22.

Transfer of quota without transfer of land

49.29 Notwithstanding the basic principle that quota attaches to, and follows, the areas used for milk production, a limited concession was introduced in 1992 which allowed in specified circumstances transfers of quota separate from and without a transfer of the corresponding land[1]. This concession was extended and previously required undertakings were removed in 2002[2].

A transferee must submit a notice of transfer without land by no later than 31 March in the quota year of the transfer and must include confirmation from the transferor and transferee of the amounts of used and unused quota transferred, a consent or sole interest notice given by the transferor in respect of the holding from which the quota is to be transferred and a statement from the transferee that he is a producer[3].

1 Council Regulation (EEC) 3950/92, OJ 1992 L 405/1, art 8.
2 See now Council Regulation (EC) 1234/2007, OJ 2007 L 299/1, art 75(1)(e); and DPQR 2005, SI 2005/465, reg 13 (as amended by SI 2008/439).
3 DPQR 2005, SI 2005/465, reg 13 (as amended by SI 2008/439).

Non-producer producers

49.30 A question regularly raised between the introduction of milk quota in 1984 and 2002 was whether milk quota could be safely retained (and leased out) by a farmer who was registered as a producer but who was not engaged in milk production. From the outset, the DPQR contained confiscation provisions for non-use[1]. However, so-called 'non-producer producers' avoided confiscation by leasing out their quota on an annual basis.

In 2002 the CJEU held that those holding milk quota should be genuine producers[2].

Importantly, with specific reference to the landlord and tenant context, the CJEU in *Alois Kibler jun v Land Baden-Wurttemburg* held that, on return of a leased part of a holding, the corresponding quota for that part cannot pass to the landlord if he is not a milk producer, does not intend to carry out such an activity and does not intend to grant a lease for the undertaking concerned to a milk producer[3].

1 See now DPQR 2005, SI 2005/465, art 38 (as amended by SI 2007/106 and SI 2008/439) (and, for the current European Community provisions, see Council Regulation (EC) 1234/2007, OJ 2007 L 299/1, art 72).

2 Case C-401/99 *Thomsen v Amt für Ländliche Räume Husum* [2002] ECR I-5775. Note
that in *Harries v Barclays Bank plc* [1997] 2 EGLR 15, [1997] 45 EG 145, the Court of
Appeal did not deal with how the mortgagee in possession (as opposed to a receiver
appointed by the mortgagee) could be a producer. Also cf the enduring nature of a
'holding': see para 49.6.

3 Case C-275/05 *Alois Kibler jun v Land Baden-Wurttemburg* [2006] ECR I-10569, [2006]
All ER (D) 323 (Oct), ECJ.

The legality of the UK milk quota transfer system

49.31 The range of key legal issues identified above indicates why, in the last
edition of this book, the legality of the UK milk quota transfer system was
scrutinised. Moreover, such concerns were formally articulated in *Carson v
Cornwall County Council*[1], where it was accepted that there were sufficient
doubts about the legality of the system to render it unsafe to determine the
value of milk quota, for the purposes of compensation under the Agriculture
Act 1986, by reference to quota transfers which were taking place on the open
market. That said, in *Harries v Barclays Bank plc*, the Court of Appeal has
recognised the existence of the UK milk quota transfer system as practised by
way of a short-term grazing tenancy[2].

Although these matters exercised the courts in the 1990s, the combined effect
of the fall in value in milk quota and the introduction of the ability to transfer
milk quota without a concurrent transaction in land[3] has resulted in there
being less litigation concerning milk quota generally.

1 [1993] 1 EGLR 21, [1993] 03 EG 119. See also, in particular, Case C-121/90 *Posthumus v
Oosterwoud* [1991] ECR I-5833, [1992] 2 CMLR 336, ECJ.

2 [1997] 2 EGLR 15, [1997] 45 EG 145, CA. See also para 49.21.

3 A practice first authorised in England by the Dairy Produce Quotas Regulations 1994,
SI 1994/672, reg 13.

Milk quota 'theft'

49.32 An issue which has arisen in practice is whether a tenant can avoid the
impact of the compensation provisions contained in the Agriculture Act 1986[1]
and acquire for himself the full value of the milk quota (whether transferred
quota[2] or otherwise) before the termination of the tenancy. In the absence of
an effective quota protection clause[3], it is submitted that it may be possible for
the tenant to engage in what is inelegantly and inappropriately sometimes
described as quota 'theft' and/or quota 'massage'.

Quota 'massage' arises where the tenant engages in a course of use of an
agricultural holding protected by the AHA 1986[4] whereby he ceases using for
milk production that part of his Euro holding[5] which comprises tenanted land.
As the tenanted land will then cease to be 'areas of milk production'[6], over a
period of five years[7] the quota will cease to attach to the tenanted land upon
an apportionment of quota arising at the end of the tenancy. In the absence of
express provision in the tenancy agreement, it would appear that there is
nothing to stop a tenant engaging in this quota 'massage'.

1 See Ch 50.

2   See para 50.7.
3   See para 24.25.
4   Technically the same may apply to a farm business tenancy under the Agricultural Tenancies Act 1995 (ATA 1995), although in practice it is less likely to arise.
5   See para 49.6.
6   See para 49.28.
7   See para 49.28.

49.33 In the absence of a milk quota protection clause[1], a tenant under a tenancy within either the AHA 1986 or the ATA 1995 would also appear able, in principle, to dispose of quota registered in his name by way of permanent transfer[2]. However, until the relaxation in transfers without land, the landlord had an indirect means of ensuring that quota remained 'attached' to the holding. As has been seen, the usual practice for transfers of quota with land has been to grant a tenancy; and, as almost all tenancies contain anti-alienation provisions, the landlord would refuse consent for the grant of a sub-tenancy. If the tenant acted in breach of the prohibition against sub-letting, he would face forfeiture[3] or, in the case of the AHA 1986, alternatively a Case E notice to quit[4].

In addition to reliance upon anti-alienation provisions, under AHA 1986 tenancies landlords have considered that because of the provisions relating to compensation[5], which pre-suppose that on termination the milk quota remains with the holding for the benefit of the landlord, the tenant is not entitled to remove the quota. But this would seem to be incorrect. Unless the tenancy agreement contains an effective prohibition upon the tenant disposing of the quota, he remains, in principle, free to do so.

That said, in the case of both transfers with and without land, it is necessary for the transferor to lodge a consent or sole interest notice[6]. 'A consent or sole interest notice' is not defined, but 'interest' is defined. The DPQR 2005 provides that interest 'includes a licence to occupy land and the interest of a mortgagee and a trustee, but does not include the interest of a beneficiary under a trust or settlement'[7]. Assuming, as would seem to be the case, that a landlord has an interest in the land, and assuming that he is not a signatory to such a consent notice, it may be argued on his behalf that, without the completed notice, there should be no valid transfer. But it remains to be seen how a court would deal with this situation[8].

1   See para 24.25. Note that a general quota protection has been found not to apply to milk quota: *Lee v Heaton* [1987] 2 EGLR 12, 283 Estates Gazette 1076.
2   See para 49.9.
3   Under the ATA 1995, see Ch 13. Under the AHA 1986, see Ch 33.
4   See para 31.76ff.
5   See Ch 51.
6   DPQR 2005, SI 2005/465, regs 9 and 13 (as amended by SI 2007/106 and SI 2008/439).
7   SI 2005/465, reg 2(1) (as amended by SI 2008/439).
8   A landlord may also perhaps look to the right to property as enshrined in Article 1 of the First Protocol to the European Convention on Human Rights.

Chapter 50

THE TENANT'S CLAIMS ON QUITTING: MILK QUOTA

INTRODUCTION

50.1 Because of the restriction on production caused by the introduction of the quota system, milk quota acquired a substantial capital value. Current values are very low as the UK has only exceeded its milk quota once in the last ten years. The resulting low capital and leasing values have been exacerbated by the gradual increase in the amount of UK quota as 2015 approaches bringing with it the proposed abolition of milk quota. The idea of increasing the amount of quota is to provide a 'soft landing' when it is removed but market forces appear to be achieving that through the mechanism of supply and demand in any event[1].

The Agriculture Act 1986 (AgA 1986) was enacted to ensure that on the termination of a tenancy, the tenant should share in such part of the value as is attributable to the quota attached to the agricultural holding being vacated. The amount of that share is intended to reflect the extent to which the tenant had, by efficient farming or the provision of fixed equipment, increased the amount of quota registered in respect of the agricultural holding.

Apart from providing for compensation for efficient farming, the AgA 1986 also provides that a tenant should receive compensation for quota, the cost of which he had financed wholly or in part by buying in quota from another milk producer. The statutory provisions enabling compensation to be awarded to a tenant in these circumstances are contained in the AgA 1986, s 13[2] and Sch 1 and the Milk Quota (Calculation of Standard Quota) (Amendment) Order 1992[3], which supplements the AgA 1986[4].

Regrettably, but perhaps inevitably, the calculations necessary to arrive at the compensation payable are exceedingly complex and have given rise to many disputes[5]. In order to make these calculations, it is necessary to understand the terminology employed in the AgA 1986 and its subordinate legislation, in particular the meaning of 'holding'[6], 'relevant quota'[7], 'allocated quota'[8], 'transferred quota'[9], 'standard quota'[10], 'the relevant number of hectares'[11], 'the prescribed quota per hectare'[12] and 'the tenant's fraction'[13] and many other terms of art[14].

The AgA 1986 came into effect on 25 September 1986 and only applied to tenancies which terminated on or after 25 July 1986. Accordingly, there was

264

no provision for compensation payable to tenants who quit their holdings at any time after 2 April 1984 (the date on which milk quotas were introduced) and before 25 July 1986.

Bostock was such a farmer who, together with others, applied for judicial review of the decision of the Minister to introduce legislation providing for compensation, but excluding tenants who quit during the period prior to the coming into effect of the AHA 1986[15]. The case went to the European Court where the court followed its earlier decision in *Wachauf v Bundesamt für Ernährung und Forstwirtschaft*[16]. It held that Member States were not obliged to introduce compensation schemes for tenants on quitting.

The AgA 1986 introduced limited compensation for tenants holding under 1986 Act tenancies who satisfied the statutory criteria. Farm business tenants holding under the Agricultural Tenancies Act 1995 (ATA 1995) will only be entitled to compensation, if at all, for 'intangible benefits' or otherwise by agreement[17]. Accordingly, what follows in this chapter only relates to AHA 1986 tenancies.

[1]   European Commission *Evolution of the Market Situation and the Consequent Conditions for Smoothly Phasing Out the Milk Quota System* COM(2010)727.
[2]   Section 13 of the AgA 1986 was brought into force on 25 September 1986 by the Agriculture Act (Commencement) (No 1) Order 1986, SI 1986/1484.
[3]   SI 1992/1225.
[4]   Section 15 of the AgA 1986 also contains provisions as to the effect of milk quota on rent – for a full commentary on those provisions, see para 25.22ff.
[5]   For a surveyor's guide to milk quota compensation calculations, see Edwards, *Milk Quotas Explained* (1995) RICS.
[6]   A 'holding' in this context is not the same as an 'agricultural holding'. It is often known as a 'Euro holding', see para 49.6.
[7]   See para 50.5.
[8]   See para 50.3.
[9]   See para 50.7.
[10]   See para 50.8.
[11]   See para 50.8.
[12]   See para 50.9.
[13]   See para 50.12.
[14]   For example, 'dairy cows', 'feeding of dairy cows', 'the reasonable amount', 'prescribed average yield','dairy improvement', 'dairy fixed equipment', etc.
[15]   *R v Minister of Agriculture, Fisheries and Food, ex p Bostock* [1991] 1 CMLR 687, [1991] 2 EGLR 1, CA. The case proceeded to the CJEU by way of a reference for a preliminary ruling in the course of an application to the English High Court for judicial review: C-2/92 [1994] ECR I-955, [1994] 3 CMLR 547, ECJ.
[16]   Case C-5/88 *Wachauf v Bundesamt für Ernährung und Forstwirtschaft* [1989] ECR 2609, [1991] 1 CMLR 328, ECJ.
[17]   See para 16.6ff.

ENTITLEMENT TO COMPENSATION

Relevant quota

50.5 The first stage in the determination of the compensation to which an outgoing tenant is entitled is to identify that part of the 'registered quota' (being allocated and/or transferred quota) which is 'relevant quota'. Relevant quota is either the quota registered exclusively in relation to the land in respect of which the tenancy has terminated (ie the subject agricultural holding) or the proportion of the quota that falls to be apportioned to that land, if the registered quota extends to other land[1]. The statutory objective is to ensure that the tenant only receives compensation for quota which 'attaches to' land covered by the tenancy in question[2].

If the holding to which the registered quota attaches consists only of the tenanted land, the whole of that quota will be relevant quota[3]. If not, the quota will have to be apportioned between the tenanted land and the other land in order that the quantum of quota for compensation purposes can be determined[4]. It would seem that in cases in which arbitration is necessary in order to determine the tenant's compensation for quota, the first duty of the arbitrator, where the quota is registered in respect of land in addition to the tenanted land, will be to make a determination as to how the quota is to be apportioned between the different areas of land. The AgA 1986 does not contain any direction as to how such an apportionment should be undertaken, but it is submitted that the apportionment should be in accordance with the Dairy Produce Quotas Regulations 2005 (DPQR 2005)[5].

[1]   AgA 1986, Sch 1 Pt I para 1(2). The quota register maintained originally by the Milk Marketing Board, later the Intervention Board for England and Wales and now by the Rural Payments Agency (RPA) will only show a single quota figure for each producer, relating to the entirety of the land that he occupies, ie the holding as defined for milk quota purposes. The holding is often referred to colloquially as the 'Euro holding'.

[2]   As to whether quota attaches to land at all, cf *Faulks v Faulks* [1992] 1 EGLR 9, [1992] 15 EG 82 and *Cottle v Coldicott* [1995] STC (SCD) 239.

[3]   AgA 1986, Sch 1 Pt I para 1(2)(a).

[4]   AgA 1986, Sch 1 Pt I para 1(2)(b) and see *Puncknowle Farms Ltd v Kane* [1985] 3 All ER 790, [1985] 2 EGLR 8.

[5]   SI 2005/465. By Sch 1, para 3(1) of the DPQR 2005 the apportionment, if undertaken by the arbitration process, is 'based on findings made by the arbitrator as to areas used for milk production' in the five years preceding the change of occupation. It is to be noted that this provision is different from those contained in the Dairy Produce Quotas Regulations 1984, SI 1984/1047, reg 5(6) and Sch 2 para 6(3)(e). The meaning of 'areas used for milk production' was considered by the High Court in *Puncknowle Farms Ltd v Kane* [1985] 3 All ER 790, [1985] 2 EGLR 8. After a period of some doubt, it now is clear that in the absence of prescribed objective criteria for making the apportionment, a strictly mathematical apportionment by reference to the areas used for milk production must be employed regardless of the relative value and productive capacity of the land in question: see the European Court decisions in C-121/90 *Posthumus v Oosterwoud* [1991] ECR I-5833, [1992] 2 CMLR 336, ECJ and C-79/91 *Knüfer v Buchmann* [1992] ECR I-6895, [1993] 1 CMLR 692, ECJ. See para 49.28.

ASSESSMENT OF COMPENSATION

The statutory scheme

50.6 The provisions in the AgA 1986 covering calculation of compensation are intended to provide the outgoing tenant with compensation for the direct and indirect contributions that he made to the build up of the allocated quota through his managerial skills as a producer and the cash investments he has made in the form of dairy improvements and fixed equipment to the holding. Additionally, the provisions enable the tenant to recover the proportion of the cost of any transferred quota that he financed.

The tenant is thus eligible to receive compensation under three heads:

(a) if the tenant has acquired transferred quota, he is entitled to compensation to the extent to which he has financed the transaction[1] – 'transferred quota';

(b) if the allocated quota in respect of the tenanted land[2] exceeds the standard quota[3] the tenant is entitled to compensation in respect of the excess – 'excess over standard quota'[4];

(c) the tenant is entitled to receive compensation which is computed by reference to investments made by the tenant in dairy improvements and dairy fixed equipment[5] – 'the tenant's fraction'[6].

[1] Note that the compensation to which the tenant will be entitled is the value of that part of the transferred quota in respect of which he bore the cost of the transaction.

[2] See para 50.5 as to the meaning of relevant quota and the need for apportionment in all cases except those in which the milk quota was allocated exclusively to the land comprised in the tenancy.

[3] Details of the standard quota are contained in the Milk Quota (Calculation of Standard Quota) (Amendment) Order 1992, SI 1992/1225.

[4] See para 50.8ff.

[5] See para 50.8ff.

[6] See para 50.12.

Transferred quota

50.7 'Transferred quota' is defined as meaning milk quota transferred to the tenant by virtue of the transfer to him of the whole or part of a holding[1]. Transferred quota in most cases will consist of quota which the tenant has purchased on the open market by means of his being granted some interest such as a short-term grazing tenancy[2] by the vendor of the quota on terms that give effect to the transfer of the quota to the purchaser's holding[3]. The amount of the payment to which the tenant is entitled in respect of transferred quota depends upon whether he bore the whole or only part of the cost[4].

In a case where the tenant bore the whole cost of the transaction by virtue of which the quota was transferred to him, he is entitled to compensation amounting to the value of the transferred quota[5]. If the tenant bore only part of the cost, he is entitled to compensation in respect of the value of the corresponding part of the transferred quota[6]. It should be noted that transferred quota does not enter into the calculation for the purpose of assessing the amounts due under the next two heads of claim – 'excess over standard quota' and the 'tenant's fraction'.

[1] AgA 1986, Sch 1 Pt I para 1(2).

[2] A licence was not sufficient to effect a transfer of quota and the tenancy had to be for not less than ten months. This is no longer the case since the relaxation in the transfer of quota without land: see the Dairy Quotas Produce Regulations 2005, SI 2005/465, reg 10.

[3] Transactions of this type are now common. Despite the very large number of such transactions, and the amount of milk quota transferred in this way, there is as yet no final and definitive authority as to the legal efficacy of such quota transfer transactions. It is possible that the whole quota transfer system, prior to the relaxation in transfers of quota without land, was fundamentally flawed. See para 49.31 for further detail of the concerns formally articulated in *Carson v Cornwall County Council* [1993] 1 EGLR 21, [1993] 03 EG 119 where it was accepted that it was unsafe to use open market comparables to

determine the value of milk quota, for the purposes of compensation under the Agriculture Act 1986. See also, in particular, C-121/90 *Posthumus v Oosterwoud* [1991] ECR I-5833, [1992] 2 CMLR 336, ECJ.

However, it is submitted that this is not the case see *Faulks v Faulks* [1992] 1 EGLR 9, [1992] 15 EG 82 and *Cottle v Coldicott* [1995] STC (SCD) 239. See also the European cases of C-5/88 *Wachauf v Bundesamt für Ernährung und Forstwirtschaft* [1989] ECR 2609, [1991] 1 CMLR 328 and C-2/92 *R v Minister of Agriculture, Fisheries and Food, ex p Bostock* [1994] ECR I-955, [1994] 3 CMLR 547, at first instance, [1991] 2 EGLR 1. In *Harries v Barclays Bank plc* [1997] 2 EGLR 15 the Court of Appeal has recognised the existence of the UK milk quota transfer system as practised by way of a short-term grazing tenancy.

4   It would appear that the tenant is not entitled to compensation at all if he did not bear any part of the cost, directly or possibly indirectly (for example, if the cost was borne by a farming company). Care should be taken when structuring a transaction for the purchase of transferred quota to avoid difficulties of this kind.

5   AgA 1986, Sch 1 Pt II para 5(3)(a).

6   AgA 1986, Sch 1 Pt II para 5(3)(b).

Excess over standard quota

The 'normal case'

50.8 In order to ascertain whether compensation is due to the tenant in respect of excess of allocated quota over standard quota, it is necessary to calculate the standard quota by reference to the statutory instrument[1] and the provisions of the AgA 1986. In the case of composite holdings[2], an apportionment of the quota (being either allocated and/or transferred quota) will by this stage have already been made in order to determine the proportion of the total quota allocated to the tenant which is referable to the subject agricultural holding.

It is then necessary to apportion the relevant hectares from the remaining hectares which together constitute the subject agricultural holding in order to determine 'the relevant number of hectares'. For this purpose, 'the relevant number of hectares' is defined as 'the average number of hectares of the agricultural holding used during the relevant period[3] for the feeding of dairy cows kept on the land[4] or, if different[5], the average number of hectares of the land which could reasonably be expected to have been so used (having regard to the number of grazing animals other than dairy cows kept on the land during that period)'[6]. This definition is supplemented by it being provided that references to land used for the feeding of dairy cows kept on the land do not include land used for growing cereal crops for feeding to dairy cows in the form[7] of loose grain[8]. Also, references to dairy cows are to cows kept for dairy production. These include cows, calved heifers and in-calf cows temporarily dry but part of a milking herd, but does not include in-calf heifers or followers[9]. It should be noted that the basis of assessment of the number of hectares relevant for computing standard quota is narrower than the phrase 'areas used for milk production' contained in the DPQR and widely interpreted (in the context of the Dairy Produce Quotas Regulations 1984) in *Puncknowle Farms Ltd v Kane*[10].

It is the 'average' and not the total number of hectares used for the feeding of dairy cows kept on the land, etc, which is relevant. Even though a time apportionment between the animals kept on the land, eg cows in summer and sheep in winter, might reduce the 'average number of hectares' substantially, it is submitted that would not be a correct method of giving effect to the statutory averaging exercise. It would be more appropriate to apportion the relevant hectares between feeding dairy cows and other animals on the basis of their relative consumption from the land. This could be achieved by a livestock unit calculation[11].

1   Milk Quota (Calculation of Standard Quota) (Amendment) Order 1992, SI 1992/1225.
2   See para 50.5. Composite holding means in this case a holding which includes land additional to the subject agricultural holding itself.
3   'The relevant period' means the period in relation to which the allocated quota was determined or, where it was determined in relation to more than one period, the period in relation to which the majority was determined or, if equal amounts were determined in relation to different periods, the latter of those periods: AgA 1986, Sch 1 Pt II para 8. For wholesale producers the relevant period will normally be from 1 January 1983 to 31 December 1983. Special provision is made for the situation in which the relevant period (ie the period or periods during which the allocated quota was determined) is less than or greater than 12 months, or if rent was only payable by the tenant in respect of part of the relevant period. In these circumstances, the rent payable is annualised: AgA 1986, Sch 1 Pt II para 7(3).
4   It seems probable that the reference to 'hectares ... used ... for the feeding of dairy cows kept on the land' is both the land on which the dairy cows were physically placed and land from which they were supported during the relevant period (eg land used for hay or silage making) subject only to the exclusion of land used for growing cereal crops for 'feeding in the form of loose grain'. This phrase (contained in para 6(5) of Sch 1 of the AgA 1986) has given rise to problems in practice since grain fed to dairy cows is usually processed through a mill and mix machine and is rarely, if ever, fed 'in the form of loose grain' (see *Grounds v A-G of the Duchy of Lancaster* [1989] 1 EGLR 6, [1989] 21 EG 73, CA). Land used for growing barley when the straw is fed to the dairy cows or the whole crop is ensiled would appear not to be excluded.
5   A problem arises as to whether the alternative or 'if different' calculation requires a subjective or objective test to be applied. The reference to the other 'grazing animals ... kept on the land' makes it clear that in part at least the alternative calculation must have regard to the actual grazing system employed by the tenant during the relevant period. On the other hand, if the fixed equipment could have supported a larger number of dairy cows than were in fact kept because the tenant grew corn on the land which might reasonably have been expected to have been used to feed dairy cows, the 'if different' calculation should be applied. If the land was used for grazing sheep or beef animals or dairy followers, etc, the 'if different' calculation should not be applied. This partially subjective and partially objective test appears arbitrary.
6   AgA 1986, Sch 1 Pt II para 6(1)(a). This provision suggests that in some cases a determination should be made as to areas that might reasonably be expected to have been used for the feeding of dairy cows kept on the land, as compared with the areas actually used – as to which see post 'if different'.
7   Note the expression 'loose grain'. If the grain was crushed and compounded through a mill and mix system it is doubtful whether it was thus fed as loose grain.
8   AgA 1986, Sch 1 Pt II para 6(5)(a).
9   AgA 1986, Sch 1 Pt II para 6(5)(b).
10   [1985] 3 All ER 790, [1985] 2 EGLR 8.
11   Milk Quota (Calculation of Standard Quota) (Amendment) Order 1992, SI 1992/1225.

Special situations: the 'reasonable amount'

50.10 Schedule 1 para 6(2) of the AgA 1986 applies a different calculation in substitution for the normal calculation of standard quota[1]. This applies when by virtue of the quality of the land in question, or climatic conditions in the area[2], the amount of milk that could reasonably be expected to have been produced from[3] one hectare of land[4] during the relevant period[5] (termed 'the reasonable amount') was either greater or less than the prescribed average yield per hectare. The prescribed average yield per hectare[6] is also laid down in the statutory instrument[7] which in columns 2(b), 3(b) and 4(b) prescribes varying average yields per hectare, dependent on the quality of the land and the type of stock carried on the land[8].

It follows that in many cases the calculation of standard quota will be by reference to this formula rather than 'prescribed quota'. If these circumstances apply, the standard quota is calculated by multiplying the relevant number of hectares[9] by such proportion of the prescribed quota per hectare[10] as the reasonable amount bears to the prescribed average yield per hectare. The first amending statutory instrument, SI 1987/626 (and no doubt all subsequent amending statutory instruments), has been made to give effect to EC cut-backs in registered quota from time to time.

These provisions have been considered by the Court of Appeal in *Grounds v A-G of the Duchy of Lancaster*[11]. It was held in *Grounds v A-G of the Duchy of Lancaster* that the arbitrator, when determining the standard quota, must take into account the practice of reasonably skilled and successful farmers. This would normally include feeding bought-in concentrate. Furthermore, the expression 'land used for growing cereals for feeding to dairy cows in the form of loose grain' encompasses grain which has been processed, eg through a mill and mix machine. Cows cannot digest unprocessed loose grain.

In *Surrey County Council v Main*[12], a county court judge considered the circumstances in which the 'reasonable' calculation fell to be made.

Paragraph 6(2) of Sch 1 to the AgA 1986 provides that for the purposes of assessing standard quota the relevant number of hectares fall to be multiplied by the prescribed quota per hectare. However, an alternative calculation (the 'reasonable amount') falls to be undertaken:

> '... where, by virtue of the quality of the land in question, or climatic conditions in the area, the amount of milk which could reasonably be expected to have been produced from one hectare of the land during the relevant period, is greater or less than the prescribed average yield per acre'.

1   See para 50.8ff.
2   Note 'the reasonable' amount calculation only applies when the difference between the land in question and its productive capacity and the average is attributable to either 'the quality of the land' or 'climatic conditions'. Other considerations, such as the quality of the buildings, cannot give rise to this calculation.
3   'Milk ... produced from ... land' – another arcane expression. Land does not produce milk – cows do. It was held by the Court of Appeal that the production of milk does not have to be confined to home-grown grass and forage crops and exclude bought-in feedstuffs. See, *Grounds v A-G of the Duchy of Lancaster* [1989] 1 EGLR 6, [1989] 21 EG 73, CA.
4   It is wholly unclear as to what 'one hectare of land' means. If it requires each of the relevant hectares to be considered separately and individually that creates anomalies and difficulties (eg the absence of buildings which are not usually on the land used simply for the feeding of dairy cows). On the other hand, it may mean each of the hectares being quitted by the tenant. In that case, that would include the buildings being used for milking

as well as the land used for feeding but would also include other land used for other systems of farming. That too will distort the resultant figures. The precise meaning of the 'one hectare' provision is unclear.

⁵ See para 50.8.
⁶ Note the difference in terminology between 'the prescribed quota per hectare' and 'the prescribed average yield per hectare'.
⁷ Milk Quota (Calculation of Standard Quota) (Amendment) Order 1992, SI 1992/1225.
⁸ Note that in each case the figures are higher than those used for the normal calculation of standard quota set out in Columns 2(a), 3(a) and 4(a) of the Schedule.
⁹ See para 50.8.
¹⁰ Ie as set out in columns 2(a), (b) and (c) of the Schedule to SI 1992/1225.
¹¹ [1989] 1 EGLR 6, [1989] 21 EG 73, CA.
¹² [1992] 1 EGLR 26, [1992] 06 EG 159.

50.11 The argument mounted on behalf of the landlord in *Surrey County Council v Main*[1] was that this required, in every case, the arbitrator to carry out the 'reasonable amount' calculation, to which a fraction then had to be applied, with the resultant figure being compared to the standard quota calculated by reference to the para 6(1) calculation. It was held by the county court judge that this was not correct and that the arbitrator was entitled to approach the matter in the way that he had done in that case, ie to consider, first, the quality of the land in question and, second, the climatic conditions so as to determine whether there was anything exceptional in either, and if they were neither better nor worse than average during the relevant period (in that case, 1983), then the para 6(1) calculation had to be used so that the 'reasonable amount' calculation only fell to be undertaken in exceptional cases.

Paragraph 6(3) of Sch 1 to the AgA 1986[2] requires an adjustment to the calculation of the standard quota to be made in cases in which the quota actually allocated to the tenant in pursuance of an award of quota made by the Dairy Produce Quota Tribunal was less than the Tribunal's award. In such circumstances the standard quota is reduced by the amount by which the quota actually allocated in pursuance of the Tribunal's award falls short of the amount awarded[3].

Paragraph 6(3) is to be read together with para 6(4), the latter sub-paragraph requiring similar adjustments to be made to the computation of allocated quota where there have been subsequent allocations of milk quota. These are to be taken into account in making the adjustment described in para 6(3).

¹ [1992] 1 EGLR 26, (1992) 06 EG 159.
² The situation to which para 6(3) relates applies particularly in the case of wholesale development quota.
³ These figures have now been amended by Milk Quota (Calculation of Standard Quota) (Amendment) Order 1987, SI 1987/626 and will no doubt be amended again from time to time as further EU cut-backs are made to registered quota.

VALUATION OF THE CLAIM

50.16 The payment which the tenant is entitled to obtain from his landlord on quitting the tenanted land[1] is by reference to the value of the milk quota for which compensation is payable[2]. For this purpose, the value of the quota to be applied is the value at the time of the termination of the tenancy in question. In determining that value on termination, all available evidence is to be taken into account including evidence as to the differential in market price paid for land where milk quota is registered and where it is not registered[3]. This may well produce a substantially lower figure than the price paid for milk quota when sold independently, rather than attached to the freehold itself.

The value to be attributed to the litreage of compensatable milk quota has given rise to many of the most difficult problems of milk quota compensation.

Since 1984, a market in milk quota developed with the quota originally being transferred by means of a short-term change of occupation of the land to which the quota is 'attached' (as it is called) and subsequently without land, as the restrictions imposed by the DPQR were relaxed. Two problems arise over the application of the sums realised in that way to the milk quota compensation valuation exercise, namely:

(a)   the legality of the transactions whereby the milk quota is detached from the holding in respect of which it was originally allocated; and

(b)   the accuracy of valuing the milk quota allocated to a holding by reference to comparatively small quantities of quota acquired by milk producers so as to secure marginal increases in their production of milk.

The legality of transactions whereby milk quota has been transferred from the land to which it was originally allocated has been considered in Chapter 49[4].

Assuming that the UK quota sale system is and has been lawful, it is arguable whether, as a matter of valuation rather than law, the prices realised have reflected the overall value of milk quota for the purposes of para 9 of Sch 1 to the AgA 1986. It could be argued that the price paid by a dairy farmer, fearing payment of the levy, so as to 'top up' his available quota, does not truly reflect the value of the underlying quota attached to the holding. Valuing 'at the margin' and applying that value 'across the board' involves a distortion. However, that argument would apply to any commodity, even eg rent, when supply and demand are out of balance.

1   AgA 1986, Sch 1 Pt I para 1.
2   AgA 1986, Sch 1 Pt II para 5.
3   AgA 1986, Sch 1 Pt II para 9. It would seem that in most cases evidence will be adduced as to the market price of quota sold 'independently' of land at the date of termination. In practice, that is substantially greater than the enhanced value of the land sold with the quota still attached to it. However, the legal efficacy of quota transfer by tenants of short-term grazing tenancies has still to be tested. An arbitrator must take into account all relevant evidence, including both forms of valuation, and make his award accordingly. He may not ignore one set of values and rely exclusively on the other.
4   See para 49.31 regarding the doubts about the legality of the system and the concerns formally articulated in *Carson v Cornwall County Council* [1993] 1 EGLR 21, [1993] 03 EG 119 where it was accepted that it was unsafe to determine the value of milk quota, for the purposes of compensation under the Agriculture Act 1986 by reference to quota transfers which were taking place on the open market.

Chapter 51

DISPUTE RESOLUTION: MILK QUOTA

THE ARBITRAL PROCESS

Notices relating to the appointment of an arbitrator

51.6 Every appointment or application relating to the appointment of an arbitrator or any notice in respect of his appointment, including the revocation of his appointment, must be in writing[1].

1 DPQR 2005, SI 2005/465, Sch 1 para 10.

Dispute as to the jurisdiction of an arbitrator

51.7 If an arbitrator is appointed, whether by the President or by agreement, and there is a dispute as to his jurisdiction, either party may make an application for judicial review for an Order prohibiting him from acting[1]. Alternatively, the arbitrator may seek the opinion of the county court by way of case stated as to whether he has jurisdiction[2].

1 *R v London County Justices and LCC* [1894] 1 QB 453, CA; *Westwood v Barnett* 1925 SC 624, Ct of Sess; *R v Powell, ex p Marquis Camden* [1925] 1 KB 641, 23 LGR 391; *R v Liverpool Justices, ex p Roberts* [1960] 2 All ER 384n, [1960] 1 WLR 585.
2 DPQR 2005, SI 2005/465, Sch 1 para 28. This is the same procedure which applied to the AHA 1986 before the RRO 2006, SI 2006/2805.

The parties to an arbitration

51.11 Where an arbitration takes place to deal with the apportionment of quota upon its restoration following confiscation[1], any person with an interest in the holding who has refused to sign a statement of the agreed apportionment of quota taking account of the areas used for milk production[2] is required to be a party to the arbitration[3].

Further, in any arbitration to which Sch 1 to the DPQR 2005 applies, the arbitrator may, in his absolute discretion join as a party to the arbitration any person having an interest in the holding, whether or not such person has applied to become a party to the arbitration, provided that such person consents to be joined[4].

1 See para 51.4.
2 Pursuant to DPQR 2005, SI 2005/465, reg 39(4)(b).
3 SI 2005/465, Sch 1 para 12(2).
4 SI 2005/465, Sch 1 para 12(1).

CHALLENGING THE ARBITRATOR'S AWARD

Special case/case stated

51.23 The arbitrator may at any stage of the arbitration, and must if so directed by the judge of the county court upon an application made by any party, state in the form of a special case for the opinion of the county court any question of law arising in the course of the arbitration and any question as to the jurisdiction of the arbitrator[1]. This is commonly known as the 'case stated' procedure. The jurisdiction of the High Court is excluded in cases to which this procedure applies[2].

More than one case may be stated in the course of the arbitration[3]. The arbitrator cannot state a case after he has made his award[4].

An appeal against any direction to state a case or against the opinion of the county court on a case stated lies to the Court of Appeal. The opinion of the court is binding on the arbitrator and must be applied by him[5].

If the arbitrator is satisfied and confident that he is able to adjudicate upon an issue raised by the parties without recourse to stating a case, he may do so. Alternatively, before making his award, the arbitrator may advise the parties as to his opinion in relation to a legal issue and give the parties a limited period in which to invite him to state a case.

[1]   DPQR 2005, SI 2005/465, Sch 1 para 28.
[2]   *Jones v Pembrokeshire County Council* [1967] 1 QB 181, [1966] 1 All ER 1027.
[3]   *Public Trustee v Randag* [1966] Ch 649, [1965] 3 All ER 88.
[4]   *Tabernacle Permanent Building Society v Knight* [1892] AC 298, HL.
[5]   *Mitchell-Gill v Buchan* (1921) 58 SLR 371, 1921 SC 390, Ct of Sess.

Chapter 52

PAYMENTS TO FARMERS UNDER THE COMMON AGRICULTURAL POLICY

Note: This updated version of Chapter 52 replaces the 9th edn version in its entirety.

INTRODUCTION

52.1 Farmers have been in receipt of subsidies since the inception of the Common Agricultural Policy, but over the past two decades the regulatory framework for delivery of these subsidies has been subject to major reform[1]. Most notably, there has been a shift from support of the product to support of the producer, with the greatest stride along this road being the introduction of the Single Farm Payment under the Mid-term Review of the Common Agricultural Policy[2]. A key characteristic of the Single Farm Payment is that, as income support which is not dependent upon the production of any specific agricultural product or, indeed, upon production at all, it is apprehended to allow farmers to respond better to market signals[3].

Ab initio the Single Payment Scheme has encompassed the vast majority of direct payments under earlier regimes (such as arable area payments and livestock premiums); and, since the Mid-term Review, its coverage has been expanded to include, for example, subsidies under the sugar regime[4]. However, although it does now constitute the most significant source of Common Agricultural Policy support for farmers, there do remain a number of payments to farmers which are beyond its scope, both in respect of such limited crop-specific support as has survived and in respect of rural development measures[5].

It may be highlighted that the reform process is very much ongoing. Thus, the Mid-term Review was soon followed by the 'Health Check' of the Common Agricultural Policy, which commenced in November 2007[6]; and the current legislation governing the Single Payment Scheme, Council Regulation (EC) 73/2009, forms part of a package of measures which emerged from this initiative[7]. Further, in November 2010, the European Commission issued its Communication, *The CAP Towards 2010: Meeting the Food, Natural Resources and Territorial Challenges of the Future*, to address the direction of agricultural policy for the period 2013–2020[8]. This expressly stated that '[t]he CAP has evolved, but further changes are necessary'[9]; and among the new imperatives identified were the need to address both European Union and global food security and the need to mitigate the effects of climate change.

Broad considerations have driven such reform, at both European Union and international levels. For example, there has been a clear determination to secure greater acceptance by society of support to farmers, on the basis that they received payments in return for the provision of 'public goods', such as high standards of environmental protection and animal welfare[10]. Likewise, the new regime was intended to be more compatible with world trade obligations[11]. In particular, it was intended that, since the Single Farm Payment breaks the link with production, it should obtain exemption from domestic support reduction commitments under the Uruguay Round Agreement on Agriculture, by virtue of its qualifying as 'de-coupled income support'[12].

While such broad considerations may seem far from the day-to-day operation of agricultural tenancies, they have nonetheless shaped the way in which land is to be farmed. Not least, the receipt of both the Single Farm Payment and remaining crop-specific support is dependent upon compliance with obligations designed to ensure good farming practice (cross-compliance). And, in purely economic terms, it has become demonstrably clear that access to European Community direct payments is essential to the profitability of most farming businesses. As stated by the Scottish Land Court in *Morrison-Low v Paterson*, '[w]here SFP is included in a budget it is typically found to be at a level which makes it the dominant element in the "profit" of the whole enterprise'[13].

The result is that it may now be regarded as essential to address European Community direct payment schemes in any treatment of the law of agricultural tenancies. This may be effected in three stages:

(a)   first, examination of the European Community framework;
(b)   second, examination of the implementation of this European Community framework in England and Wales; and
(c)   third, a more detailed analysis of the landlord and tenant implications.

1   See, generally, eg, M Cardwell *The European Model of Agriculture* (2004) Oxford University Press, Oxford; and JA McMahon *EU Agricultural Law* (2007) Oxford University Press, Oxford.

2   For the Communication which launched the Mid-term Review, see European Commission *Mid-term Review of the Common Agricultural Policy* COM(2002)394. See also, generally, eg, J Moody and W Neville *Mid Term Review: a Practical Guide* (2004) Burges Salmon, Bristol; Central Association of Agricultural Valuers *Mid Term Review: a Valuer's Interim Guide* (2004) Central Association of Agricultural Valuers, Coleford; M Cardwell *The European Model of Agriculture* (2004) Oxford University Press, Oxford, pp 159–174; Central Association of Agricultural Valuers *Mid Term Review: a Valuer's Second Interim Guide* (2005) Central Association of Agricultural Valuers, Coleford; JA McMahon *EU Agricultural Law* (2007) Oxford University Press, Oxford, pp 250–259; and C Rodgers *Agricultural Law* (2008) 3rd Edition, Tottel Publishing, Haywards Heath, in particular, pp 81–91 and 600–625.

3   See, eg, European Commission *Mid-term Review of the Common Agricultural Policy* COM(2002)394, 19.

4   For the legislation which incorporated the sugar regime, see Council Regulation (EC) 1782/2003, OJ 2003 L 270/1, Annex VI (as amended by Council Regulation (EC) 319/2006, OJ 2006 L 58/32).

5   The relative scale of the Single Farm Payment as against other forms of direct payment can be judged from provisional United Kingdom figures for 2009: total expenditure on all direct payments (less levies) amounted to £3,644 million and, of this total, the Single Farm Payment accounted for some £2,950 million (Department for Environment, Food and Rural Affairs (DEFRA) *et al, Agriculture in the United Kingdom 2009* (2010) DEFRA, London, Table 11.1).

6 For the Communication which launched the Mid-term Review, see European Commission *Preparing for the 'Health Check' of the CAP Reform* COM(2007)722.

7 OJ 2009 L 30/16.

8 COM(2010)672.

9 COM(2010)672, 5.

10 See, eg, European Commission *Mid-term Review of the Common Agricultural Policy* COM(2002)394, 2 and 8–9; and European Commission *Report from the Commission to the Council on the Application of the System of Cross-compliance* COM(2007)147, 2.

11 European Commission *Mid-term Review of the Common Agricultural Policy* COM(2002)394, 20.

12 The criteria governing 'de-coupled income support' are set out in the Uruguay Round Agreement on Agriculture, Annex 2, para 6. Importantly, as indicated, no production is required in order to receive such support (on which aspect see the decision of the Appellate Body in *United States – Subsidies on Upland Cotton* (2005) WT/DS267/AB/R). On the Uruguay Round Agreement on Agriculture generally, see, eg, JA McMahon *The WTO Agreement on Agriculture: a Commentary* (2006) Oxford University Press, Oxford; and, on the compatibility of European Community direct payments with world trade commitments, see, eg, A Swinbank and R Tranter 'Decoupling EU Farm Support: Does the New Single Payment Scheme Fit within the Green Box?' (2005) 6 *Estey Centre Journal of International Law and Trade Policy* 47–61.

13 (2010) SLC/233/08, para 86.

EUROPEAN COMMUNITY LEGISLATION

Introduction

52.2 As indicated, most direct payments have been channelled into the Single Payment Scheme, which under the European Community legislation is stated to provide 'income support'[1]; and the Scheme has been implemented in the United Kingdom as from 1 January 2005[2]. It is, however, important to reiterate that, while the Single Payment Scheme formed the centre piece of the Mid-term Review reforms, a limited amount of crop-specific support was retained; and, under the European Community legislative framework both the Single Farm Payment and this crop-specific support fall subject to the same general rules (such as those on cross-compliance)[3]. In addition, as again indicated, farmers may receive payments in respect of rural development measures, the most significant of these in the United Kingdom being agri-environmental programmes[4].

The European Community legislation considered will be that applicable in the 15 'old' Member States.

1 See now Council Regulation (EC) 73/2009, OJ 2009 L 30/16, art 1. This regulation replaced Council Regulation (EC) 1782/2003, OJ 2003 L 270/1, which originally introduced the Single Payment Scheme.

2 Council Regulation (EC) 1782/2003, OJ 2003 L 270/1, art 156(2)(d). Member States were granted the option to delay implementation until either 1 January 2006 or 1 January 2007, but the United Kingdom did not avail itself of this option: art 71.

3 For crop-specific support outside the Single Payment Scheme, see para 52.13.

4 For payments in respect of rural development measures, see para 52.15. It may be noted that, in England during 2008, expenditure under the key agri-environmental measure, the Environmental Stewardship Scheme, was £222 million, whereas expenditure under the key measure at that date for support of less-favoured areas, the Hill Farm Allowance Scheme, was only £27.2 million (DEFRA *et al, Agriculture in the United Kingdom 2009* (2010) DEFRA, London, Table 11.6).

General rules: outline

52.3 Turning first to the general rules, four aspects may be examined, namely:

(a)   statutory definitions;
(b)   cross-compliance;
(c)   modulation; and
(d)   artificiality[1].

All have the capacity to impact materially upon the landlord and tenant relationship.

---

[1]   The European Community legislative framework also provides general rules to govern the integrated administration and control system: Council Regulation (EC) 73/2009, OJ 2009 L 30/16, arts 14–27. For current national implementation in the United Kingdom, see the Common Agricultural Policy Single Payment and Support Schemes (Integrated Administration and Control System) Regulations 2009, SI 2009/3263. These detailed rules are largely outside the scope of this work; but it may be noted that their application to cross-compliance has proved controversial: see, eg, European Commission *Report from the Commission to the Council on the Application of the System of Cross-compliance* COM(2007)147. See, generally, eg, J Moody and W Neville *Mid Term Review: a Practical Guide* (2004) Burges Salmon, Bristol, pp 106–112.

General rules: statutory definitions

52.4 For the purposes of the European Community legislation implementing the Single Payment Scheme and crop-specific support, Council Regulation (EC) 73/2009 provides specific definitions of 'farmer', 'holding', 'agricultural activity' and 'agricultural area'; and their interaction with national definitions in the Agricultural Holdings Act 1986 and the Agricultural Tenancies Act 1995 may, on occasion, prove difficult.

A 'farmer' is defined as 'a natural or legal person, or a group of natural or legal persons, whatever legal status is granted to the group and its members by national law, whose holding is situated within Community territory ... and who exercises an agricultural activity'[1]. Further, in order to guarantee that Common Agricultural Policy support is entirely used to ensure a fair standard of living for the agricultural community[2], as from 2010, a Member State may establish appropriate objective and non-discriminatory criteria to provide that direct payments (whether under the Single Payment Scheme or otherwise) are not granted to a natural or legal person '(a) whose agricultural activities form only an insignificant part of its overall economic activities; or (b) whose principal business or company objects do not consist of exercising an agricultural activity'[3].

In turn, a 'holding' is defined as 'all the production units managed by a farmer situated within the territory of the same Member State'[4]; and 'agricultural activity' is defined as 'the production, rearing or growing of agricultural products including harvesting, milking, breeding animals and keeping animals for farming purposes, or maintaining the land in good agricultural and environmental condition'[5]. Consistent with evolving European Community policy, extensive grazing for nature conservation and landscape management purposes may qualify as an 'agricultural activity'; and an activity remains agricultural notwithstanding that the farmer is subject to the instructions of a nature conservation authority[6].

As has been seen, there is a definition not only of 'agricultural activity', but also of 'agricultural area', this meaning 'any area taken up by arable land, permanent pasture and permanent crops'[7]. For the purposes of the Single Payment Scheme, 'arable land', 'permanent pasture' and 'permanent crops' are further defined. 'Arable land' is 'land cultivated for crop production or maintained in good agricultural and environmental condition ..., irrespective of whether or not that land is under greenhouses or under fixed or mobile cover'[8]. 'Permanent pasture' is 'land used to grow grasses or other herbaceous forage naturally (self-seeded) or through cultivation (sown) and that has not been included in the crop rotation of the holding for five years or longer' (but excluding areas set aside under a European Community agri-environmental scheme)[9]. 'Permanent crops' are 'non-rotational crops other than permanent pasture that occupy the land for five years or longer and yield repeated harvests, including nurseries, and short rotation coppice'[10].

These definitions in the European Community legislation would seem to differ from agricultural holdings legislation in two material respects. First, as noted, Article 2(b) of Council Regulation (EC) 73/2009 makes reference to 'all the production units managed by a farmer situated within the territory of the same Member State'. Accordingly, it would seem clear that, where a farmer manages production units in one or more of England, Northern Ireland, Scotland and Wales, those production units comprise the same holding for the purposes of the European Community legislation (as has long been the case with milk quotas). But it would be rare indeed if they were to comprise the same holding for the purposes of landlord and tenant legislation[11].

Second, it is very evident that the definition of 'agricultural activity' extends beyond the definition of 'agriculture' as found in s 96(1) of the AHA 1986 and s 38(1) of the ATA 1995[12]. Not least, it covers also the maintenance of land in good agricultural and environmental condition, without any obligation to engage in production[13].

---

[1] Council Regulation (EC) 73/2009, OJ 2009 L 30/16, art 2(a). The definition would seem apt, therefore, to include companies and partnerships. On the other hand, in the case of share farming agreements, it would seem less clear whether, in particular, the landowning party qualifies as a 'farmer': see, eg, *National Trust for Places of Historic Interest v Birden* [2009] EWHC 2023 (Ch), [2009] All ER (D) 154 (Sep) (where the judge did not feel that it was necessary for him to decide the issue, since it was not an issue between the parties to the case, but expressed some doubt whether the landowning party met the criteria: paras 78, 110 and 153).

[2] Council Regulation (EC) 73/2009, OJ 2009 L 30/16, Preamble (23) (ie, to meet the second objective of the Common Agricultural Policy: Treaty on the Functioning of the European Union, art 39(1)(b)).

[3] Council Regulation (EC) 73/2009, OJ 2009 L 30/16, art 28(2). This option has not been taken up in England and Wales.

[4] Council Regulation (EC) 73/2009, OJ 2009 L 30/16, art 2(b). This wording is not unlike that found earlier in the milk quota legislation: see, eg, prior to its repeal, Council Regulation (EEC) 3950/92, OJ 1992 L 405/1, art 9(d) (as amended by Council Regulation (EEC) 1560/93, OJ 1993 L 154/30); and, for interpretation of the term 'holding' by the Court of Justice of the European Union (CJEU) in the context of milk quotas, see, eg, Case

5/88 *Wachauf v Bundesamt für Ernährung und Forstwirtschaft* [1989] ECR 2609, [1991] 1 CMLR 328, ECJ. It is of interest that the term 'production unit' is retained notwithstanding that production is not required in order to receive the Single Farm Payment.

5   Council Regulation (EC) 73/2009, OJ 2009 L 30/16, art 2(c).
6   Case C-61/09 *Landkreis Bad Dürkheim v Aufsichts- und Dienstleistungsdirektion* [2010] All ER (D) 257 (Nov) (Judgment delivered on 14 October 2010), para 49.
7   Council Regulation (EC) 73/2009, OJ 2009 L 30/16, art 2(h).
8   Commission Regulation (EC) 1120/2009, OJ 2009 L 316/1, art 2(a).
9   Commission Regulation (EC) 1120/2009, OJ 2009 L 316/1, art 2(c). For the agri-environmental schemes concerned, see Council Regulation (EC) 2078/92, OJ 1992 L 215/85; Council Regulation (EC) 1257/1999, OJ 1999 L 160/80, arts 22–24; and Council Regulation (EC) 1698/2005, OJ 2005 L 277/1, art 39. It may be highlighted that, even though compulsory set-aside has now been abolished, a farmer may still elect to put land into set-aside under European Community rural development agri-environmental schemes.
10   Commission Regulation (EC) 1120/2009, OJ 2009 L 316/1, art 2(b). For the definition of short rotation coppice, see Commission Regulation (EC) 1120/2009, OJ 2009 L 316/1, art 2(n).
11   For the position where a farming enterprise operates in more than one Member State, see Case C-463/93 *Katholische Kirchengemeinde St Martinus Elten v Landwirtschaftskammer Rheinland* [1997] ECR I-255 (relating to milk quotas).
12   See paras 19.6 and 3.23.
13   On this aspect see, generally, eg, L Bodiguel and M Cardwell 'Evolving Definitions of 'Agriculture' for an Evolving Agriculture?' [2005] *Conveyancer* 419–446; and see further para 52.26.

General rules: cross-compliance

52.5 In the case of the Single Farm Payment and crop-specific support, receipt is dependent upon observance of cross-compliance obligations as stipulated in the European Community legislation. In consequence, there is great incentive for farmers to tailor their farming practices so as to meet these criteria. The cross-compliance obligations comprise:

(a)   statutory management requirements;
(b)   a requirement to maintain all agricultural land in good agricultural and environmental condition; and
(c)   an obligation to maintain land under permanent pasture[1].

The statutory management requirements relate to: public, animal and plant health; the environment; and animal welfare. They were phased in over three years, the final tranche becoming applicable as from 1 January 2007; and the detailed requirements are now listed in Annex II to Council Regulation (EC) 73/2009[2].

By contrast, the minimum requirements for good agricultural and environmental condition are defined by the Member States, at national or regional level, taking into account the specific characteristics of the areas concerned (including soil and climatic condition, existing farming systems, land use, crop rotation, farming practices and farm structures). Member States must, however, define these minimum requirements on the basis of a European Community framework, set out in Annex III to Council Regulation (EC) 73/2009. The current framework covers five issues:

(i) soil erosion, with compulsory standards imposed in relation to minimum soil cover and minimum land management reflecting site-specific conditions, together with optional standards in relation to the retention of terraces;

(ii) soil organic matter, with compulsory standards imposed in relation to arable stubble management, together with optional standards in relation to crop rotations;

(iii) soil structure, with optional standards only, relating to appropriate machinery use;

(iv) a minimum level of maintenance, with compulsory standards imposed in relation to the retention of landscape features (including, where appropriate, hedges, ponds, ditches, trees in line, in group or isolated and field margins), the avoidance of encroachment of unwanted vegetation on agricultural land and the protection of permanent pasture; and with optional standards in relation to minimum livestock stocking rates and/or appropriate regimes, the establishment and/or retention of habitats, the prohibition of the grubbing up of olive trees and the maintenance of olive groves in good vegetative condition; and

(v) the protection and management of water, with compulsory standards imposed in relation to the establishment of buffer strips along water courses and, where use of water for irrigation is subject to authorisation, compliance with authorisation procedures.

Any optional standard is nonetheless compulsory if a Member State had already defined for such standard a minimum requirement for good agricultural and environmental condition prior to 1 January 2009 and/or if national rules addressing the standard are applied in the Member State[3].

Under the European Community framework as enacted prior to Council Regulation (EC) 73/2009, it has been held to be possible for a Member State to lay down, among its standards for good agricultural and environmental condition, requirements relating to the maintenance of visible public rights of way, so long as such requirements contributed to the retention of the rights of way as landscape features or to the avoidance of the deterioration of habitats[4].

Since agriculture is, in principle, administered on a devolved basis in the United Kingdom, separate cross-compliance rules have been implemented for England, Northern Ireland, Scotland and Wales[5]. Those currently applicable in England are contained in the Agriculture (Cross compliance) (No 2) Regulations 2009[6] and those currently applicable in Wales are contained in the Common Agricultural Policy Single Payment and Support Schemes (Cross Compliance) (Wales) Regulations 2004[7]. A matter of some importance is that, although more onerous obligations were imposed in England than in Northern Ireland, Scotland and Wales, the CJEU held in *R (on the application of Horvath) v Secretary of State for Environment, Food and Rural Affairs* that, where it is the devolved administrations of a Member State which have the power to define the minimum requirements for good agricultural and environmental condition, divergences between the measures laid down by the various administrations cannot, alone, constitute discrimination[8].

Additionally, in the case of old Member States, such as the United Kingdom, land which was under permanent pasture as at 15 May 2003 must be maintained under permanent pasture[9]. In this context, the legislation adopts the general definition of 'permanent pasture', as already noted[10]. By way of exception, Member States can choose in duly justified circumstances to dispense with this obligation, provided that they take action to prevent any significant decrease in their total permanent pasture area[11]. Under the detailed rules, this would mean a decrease to the detriment of land under permanent pasture of more than 10% as compared with the ratio of land under permanent pasture in 2003[12]. By way of further exception, the obligation to maintain land under permanent pasture does not apply where the land is to be afforested, so long as the afforestation is compatible with the environment (and, in this context, the afforestation must not be plantations of Christmas trees or fast-growing species cultivated in the short term)[13].

[1]   Council Regulation (EC) 73/2009, OJ 2009 L 30/16, arts 5–6.
[2]   These detailed requirements are as follows:
    (1)   Council Directive 79/409/EEC (Wild Birds Directive), OJ 1979 L 103/1, arts 3(1), 3(2)(b), 4(1), (2) and (4) and 5(a), (b) and (d);
    (2)   Council Directive 80/68/EEC (protection against groundwater pollution), OJ 1980 L 20/43, arts 4 and 5;
    (3)   Council Directive 86/278/EEC (use of sewage sludge in agriculture), OJ 1986 L 181/6, art 3;
    (4)   Council Directive 91/676/EEC (Nitrates Directive), OJ 1991 L 375/1, arts 4 and 5;
    (5)   Council Directive 92/43/EEC (Habitats Directive), OJ 1992 L 206/7, arts 6 and 13(1)(a);
    (6)   Council Directive 2008/71/EC (identification and registration of pigs), OJ 2008 L 213/31, arts 3, 4 and 5;
    (7)   Regulation (EC) 1760/2000 of the European Parliament and of the Council (identification and registration of bovine animals and the labelling of beef and beef products), OJ 2000 L 204/1, arts 4 and 7;
    (8)   Council Regulation (EC) 21/2004 (identification and registration of ovine and caprine animals), OJ 2004 L 5/8, arts 3, 4 and 5;
    (9)   Council Directive 91/414/EEC (the placing of plant protection products on the market), OJ 1991 L 230/1, art 3;
    (10)   Council Directive 96/22/EC (prohibition of the use in stockfarming of certain substances having a hormonal or thyrostatic action and of beta-agonists), OJ 1996 L 125/3, arts 3(a), (b), (d) and (e), 4, 5 and 7;
    (11)   Regulation (EC) 178/2002 of the European Parliament and of the Council (Food Law Regulation), OJ 2002 L 31/1, arts 14, 15, 17(1), 18, 19 and 20;
    (12)   Regulation (EC) 999/2001 of the European Parliament and of the Council (prevention, control and eradication of certain transmissible spongiform encephalopathies), OJ 2001 L 147/1, arts 7, 11, 12, 13 and 15;
    (13)   Council Directive 85/511/EEC (control of foot-and-mouth disease), OJ 1985 L 315/11, art 3;
    (14)   Council Directive 92/119/EEC (control of certain animal diseases, together with specific measures relating to swine vesicular disease), OJ 1992 L 62/69, art 3;
    (15)   Council Directive 2000/75/EC (control and eradication of bluetongue), OJ 2000 L 327/74, art 3;
    (16)   Council Directive 91/629/EEC (minimum standards for the protection of calves), OJ 1991 L 340/28, arts 3 and 4;
    (17)   Council Directive 91/630/EEC (minimum standards for the protection of pigs), OJ 1991 L 340/33, arts 3 and 4(1); and
    (18)   Council Directive 98/58/EC (protection of animals kept for farming purposes), OJ 1998 L 221/23, art 4.

[3]   Council Regulation (EC) 73/2009, OJ 2009 L 30/16, art 6(1).

4   Case C-428/07 R *(on the application of Horvath) v Secretary of State for Environment, Food and Rural Affairs* [2009] ECR I-6355. For the earlier European Community framework, which was the subject matter of this case, see Council Regulation (EC) 1782/2003, OJ 2003 L 270/1, Annex IV.
5   External relations, however, remain within the competence of the United Kingdom Parliament and Government, with the result that DEFRA has primary responsibility for agriculture negotiations at European Union level; and, in addition, United Kingdom ministers enjoy reserve powers to intervene, where necessary, to ensure correct implementation of obligations under European Community law where they concern devolved matters.
6   SI 2009/3365 (as amended by SI 2010/2941). See further para 52.19.
7   SI 2004/3280 (W.284) (as amended by SI 2005/3367 (W.264), SI 2006/2831 (W.252), SI 2007/970 (W.87) and SI 2010/38 (W.11)). See further para 52.19.
8   Case C-428/07 R *(on the application of Horvath) v Secretary of State for Environment, Food and Rural Affairs* [2009] ECR I-6355, [2009] NLJR 1106, ECJ. For the English legislation concerned, see the Common Agricultural Policy Single Payment and Support Schemes (Cross Compliance) (England) Regulations 2004, SI 2004/3196. See further para 52.19.
9   Council Regulation (EC) 73/2009, OJ 2009 L 30/16, art 6(2).
10 Commission Regulation (EC) 1122/2009, OJ 2009 L 316/65, art 2(2) (cross-referring to Commission Regulation (EC) 1120/2009, OJ 2009 L 316/1, art 2(c)); and see para 52.4.
11 Council Regulation (EC) 73/2009, OJ 2009 L 30/16, art 6(2).
12 Commission Regulation (EC) 1122/2009, OJ 2009 L 316/65, art 3(2).
13 Council Regulation (EC) 73/2009, OJ 2009 L 30/16, art 6(2).

General rules: modulation

52.6 Under the European Community legislation a proportion of all direct payments to farmers is to be compulsorily deducted each year, so as to increase the level of financing for rural development measures[1]. Such transfer of resources, known as 'modulation', is intended to redress, at least partially, the disproportionately low percentage of overall Common Agricultural Policy expenditure devoted to rural development[2].

As a general rule, this compulsory deduction throughout the Member States commenced following the Mid-term Review at 3% in 2005, rose to 4% in 2006 and was then to remain at 5% for the period 2007 to 2012[3]. These rates did not, however, survive the 'Health Check', when modulation was identified as the key mechanism for realising the policy imperative of strengthening support for rural development[4]. The compulsory rates were, accordingly, applied to amounts in excess of 5,000 Euros per year and raised to 7% in 2009, 8% in 2010, 9% in 2011 and 10% in 2012, with a further 4% being deducted for amounts in excess of 300,000 Euros[5].

Against this background, the position in the United Kingdom has been somewhat complicated by the appetite of the Government for voluntary modulation[6]. Indeed, even prior to the introduction of compulsory modulation under the Mid-term Review, the option of implementing voluntary modulation as granted by European Community legislation had already been taken up in England, Northern Ireland, Scotland and Wales[7]. The voluntary rate must now be added to the compulsory rate; and the European Community legislation which currently governs voluntary modulation is Council Regulation (EC) 378/2007[8]. It grants the option of imposing voluntary modulation to those Member States which, upon its coming into force, were already applying additional modulation (as was the case in the United Kingdom)[9]. The maximum rate is 20%[10]; and rates can be regionally differentiated according to objective criteria if the Member State was operating the Single Payment Scheme on a regional basis, which has been the policy choice for the United Kingdom[11].

The detailed rules in England and Wales will be considered later[12]. For the time being, it may be noted that regionally differentiated rates were indeed applied, with farmers in England being placed subject to the heaviest reductions: thus, in their case, voluntary modulation commenced at 12% in 2007, rose to 13% in 2008 and was then to continue at 14% from 2009 to 2012[13]. When the compulsory rates were increased as from 2009 by the 'Health Check', the overall burden was then apprehended to be too great and, in consequence, the European Community legislation reduced the levels of voluntary modulation[14]. Nonetheless, farmers in England will remain subject to a 19% deduction for the period 2009–2012[15], whereas, for example, a farmer in France will be subject to a maximum 10% deduction in 2012 (provided that the 300,000 Euros threshold is not exceeded). This imbalance has the potential to create distortions in competition, as is evident on the face of the European Community legislation. For example, Member States applying voluntary modulation and the European Commission are to monitor closely the impact of the measures, 'in particular as regards the economic situation of the farms, taking into account the need to avoid unjustified unequal treatment between farmers'[16]. That said, for United Kingdom producers to show discrimination may be no easy task; and this will be especially so in circumstances where all producers within a Member State, or a region of a Member State, are subject to the same constraints on the basis of objective criteria[17]. Nonetheless, the extent of such reductions in direct payments cannot fail to impact heavily upon freehold owners and tenants alike.

---

[1]   Council Regulation (EC) 73/2009, OJ 2009 L 30/16, art 7. For the legislation now governing rural development, see Council Regulation (EC) 1698/2005, OJ 2005 L 277/1; and see also para 52.15.

[2]   At the time of the Agenda 2000 reforms, when modulation was first introduced on a voluntary basis, it was projected that only 4,370 million Euros would be spent on rural development and ancillary measures by 2006, as opposed to 37,290 million Euros on other Common Agricultural Policy costs: European Commission, *Bulletin of the European Union, 3–1999*, at I.12.

[3]   Council Regulation (EC) 1782/2003, OJ 2003 L 270/1, art 10(1). An additional amount of aid had the effect of reimbursing farmers for any modulation on up to 5,000 Euros of direct payments: Council Regulation (EC) 1782/2003, OJ 2003 L 270/1, art 12.

[4]   See, eg, European Commission *Preparing for the 'Health Check' of the CAP Reform* COM(2007)722, 10.

[5]   Council Regulation (EC) 73/2009, OJ 2009 L 30/16, art 7(1) and (2).

[6]   Policy documentation has even favoured an increase in the rate of modulation to 20%: see, eg, Policy Commission on the Future of Farming and Food, *Farming and Food: a Sustainable Future (Curry Report)* (2002) Cabinet Office, London, p 77.

[7]   For the European Community legislation, see Council Regulation (EC) 1259/1999, OJ 1999 L 160/113, arts 4–5. For the English legislation, see the Common Agricultural Policy Support Schemes (Modulation) Regulations 2000, SI 2000/3127 (as amended by SI 2001/3686 and SI 2004/2330); and, for the Welsh legislation, see the Common Agricultural Policy Support Schemes (Modulation) (Wales) Regulations 2000, SI 2000/3294 (W.216) (as amended by SI 2001/3680 (W.301) and SI 2004/2662 (W.233)).

8   Council Regulation (EC) 378/2007, OJ 2007 L 95/1. See Preamble (1): '[r]eductions of direct payments applied in respect of voluntary modulation should be additional to those resulting from the application of compulsory modulation provided for in Article 10 of Regulation (EC) No 1782/2003 [now Article 7 of Council Regulation (EC) 73/2009]'.
9   Council Regulation (EC) 378/2007, OJ 2007 L 95/1, art 1(1)(a). This option was also available where a Member State was granted a derogation (under art 70(4a) of Council Regulation (EC) 1698/2005, OJ 2005 L 277/1) from the requirement to co-finance European Community support: art 1(1)(b).
10   Council Regulation (EC) 378/2007, OJ 2007 L 95/1, art 1(4).
11   Council Regulation (EC) 378/2007, OJ 2007 L 95/1, art 3(1). For operation of the Single Payment Scheme on a regional basis, see para 52.9.
12   See para 52.22.
13   Common Agricultural Policy Single Payment and Support Schemes Regulations 2005, SI 2005/219, reg 11 (as amended by SI 2007/3182).
14   Council Regulation (EC) 378/2007, OJ 2007 L 95/1, art 1 (as amended by Council Regulation (EC) 73/2009, OJ 2009 L 30/16); and see also Council Regulation (EC) 73/2009, OJ 2009 L 30/16, art 8.
15   For a useful breakdown of the interaction between compulsory and voluntary modulation rates in England, see, eg, DEFRA, *Further Information: Modulation Question & Answers* (available at http://archive.defra.gov.uk/foodfarm/farmmanage/singlepay/furtherinfo/modulation.htm, accessed on 2 May 2011).
16   Council Regulation (EC) 378/2007, OJ 2007 L 95/1, art 5.
17   See, eg, Case C-292/97 *Karlsson, Re* [2000] ECR I-2737, ECJ; and Case C-428/07 *R (on the application of Horvath) v Secretary of State for Environment, Food and Rural Affairs* [2009] ECR I-6355, [2009] NLJR 1106, ECJ. It may be highlighted that, in the latter case, as with voluntary modulation, regional implementation was expressly authorised. Further, at the time when the differentiated rates of voluntary modulation were introduced under Council Regulation (EC) 378/2007, the United Kingdom Government produced extensive justification for this action: see the Communication to the European Commission from the United Kingdom Government attached to the Common Agricultural Policy Single Payment and Support Schemes (Amendment) Regulations 2007, SI 2007/3182.

General rules: artificiality

52.7 The European Community legislation provides that 'no payment shall be made to beneficiaries for whom it is established that they artificially created the conditions required for obtaining such payments with a view to obtaining an advantage contrary to the objectives of that support scheme'[1]. This provision reflects concern on the part of the European Community institutions that assets created under the umbrella of the Common Agricultural Policy should not become the subject of speculation. Thus, in the context of milk quotas, the CJEU has emphasised that producers could not 'expect that a common organisation of the market would confer on them a commercial advantage which did not derive from their occupational activity'[2]; and that it was necessary 'to prevent a reference quantity from being claimed for the sole purpose of deriving a purely financial advantage therefrom'[3]. Similar sentiments have now been expressed in the context of the Single Payment Scheme, the Advocate General in *Harms v Heidinga* observing that '[i]t appears that the Community legislature was concerned about manoeuvres to circumvent the provisions of [Council Regulation (EC) 1782/2003] and that there was a real desire to prevent and repress fraud, not least because the risk of speculation is omnipresent in a regime which is decoupled from production'[4].

Indeed, the CJEU has generated judicial momentum in addressing abusive practices by economic operators[5]. These abusive practices may be characterised as 'transactions carried out not in the context of normal commercial

285

operations, but solely for the purpose of wrongfully obtaining advantages provided for by Community law'[6]; and, to constitute an abusive practice, two elements must be satisfied[7]. First, notwithstanding formal observance of the legislative conditions, the transaction concerned must objectively result in the accrual of an advantage whose grant would be contrary to the purposes of European Community law: in other words, the commercial operation was not carried out for an economic purpose. Second, subjectively, there must be an intention to obtain such an advantage. With regard to this second element, it is the responsibility of the national court to determine the real substance and significance of the transactions concerned. In this regard, it may take account of their purely artificial nature and the links of a legal, economic and/or personal nature between the operators involved[8].

Accordingly, both landlords and tenants should ensure that their dealings are not tainted by any artificiality; and, as indicated, this imperative is only reinforced by the fact that the CJEU has shown a willingness to extend its jurisprudence on abusive practices from taxation to the receipt of European Community support by farmers.

1   Council Regulation (EC) 73/2009, OJ 2009 L 30/16, art 30.
2   Case C-44/89 *von Deetzen v Hauptzollamt Oldenburg* [1991] ECR I-5119, para 21.
3   Case C-236/90 *Maier v Freistaat Bayern* [1992] ECR I-4483, para 26.
4   Case C-434/08 *Harms v Heidinga* (Opinion delivered on 4 February 2010), para 36.
5   See, generally, eg, HL McCarthy 'Abuse of Rights: the Effect of the Doctrine on VAT Planning' [2007] *British Tax Review* 160–174. See also, in the national court, eg, *WHA Ltd v Revenue and Customs Comrs* [2007] EWCA Civ 728, [2008] 1 CMLR 522, [2007] STC 1695.
6   Case C-255/02 *Halifax plc v Revenue and Customs Comrs* [2006] ECR I-1609, [2006] Ch 387, para 69 (a VAT case).
7   See, eg, Case C-110/99 *Emsland-Stärke GmbH v Hauptzollamt Hamburg-Jonas* [2000] ECR I-11569, paras 52–53; Case C-255/02 *Halifax plc v Revenue and Customs Comrs* [2006] ECR I-1609, [2006] Ch 387, paras 74–75: Case C-196/04 *Cadbury Schweppes plc v Revenue and Customs Comrs* [2006] ECR I-7995, [2007] Ch 30, para 64 (a corporate tax case); and Case C-277/09 *Revenue and Customs Comrs v RBS Deutschland Holdings GmbH* [2011] SWTI 262 (Judgment delivered on 22 December 2010) para 49 (a VAT case).
8   Case C-255/02 *Halifax plc v Revenue and Customs Comrs* [2006] ECR I-1609, [2006] Ch 387, para 81.

Single Farm Payment: introduction

52.8 While these general rules apply to all direct payments, their greatest impact is in relation to the Single Payment Scheme, unquestionably the greatest innovation of the Mid-term Review. As has been seen, this measure is characterised as income support. It is also apprehended to be decoupled from production, with consequent benefits in terms of permitting farmers to produce for the market and in terms of exemption from domestic support reduction commitments under the Uruguay Round Agreement on Agriculture. In addition, it forms part of an overall drive to achieve simplification of European Community legislation[1].

Against this policy background, the Single Payment Scheme already replaces the vast majority of earlier direct payment schemes; and, since its commencement under the Mid-term Review, the intention has been that it should become ever more all-embracing[2]. In the case of the United Kingdom, the most significant earlier direct payment schemes to have become comprised under its umbrella were those in respect of: arable crops; beef and veal; milk and milk products (dairy premium and additional payments); sheep and goats; and sugar[3].

[1] See, eg, European Commission *Mid-term Review of the Common Agricultural Policy* COM(2002)394, 2 and 10; and European Commission *Simplification and Better Regulation for the Common Agricultural Policy* COM(2005)509.

[2] See, eg, European Commission *Mid-term Review of the Common Agricultural Policy* COM(2002)394, 19–20.

[3] The list of direct payment schemes comprised within the Single Payment Scheme were originally set out in Annex VI to Council Regulation (EC) 1782/2003, OJ 2003 L 270/1, which was much amended as new schemes were added: for example, as indicated, the sugar regime became incorporated as a result of Council Regulation (EC) 319/2006, OJ 2006 L 58/32. With particular reference to England and Wales, three aspects may be highlighted. First, under the general rule, dairy premium and additional payments, as introduced by the Mid-term Review, only became comprised in the Single Payment Scheme as from 2007: Council Regulation (EC) 1782/2003, OJ 2003 L 270/1, art 50. (For the provisions implementing the dairy premium and additional payments see arts 95–97). However, where the Single Payment Scheme was implemented on a regional basis, then the decision could be taken to comprise them within the Single Payment Scheme ab initio: art 62; and this course of action was adopted in England and in Wales: the Common Agricultural Policy Single Payment and Support Schemes Regulations 2005, SI 2005/219, reg 7; and the Common Agricultural Policy Single Payment and Support Schemes (Wales) Regulations 2005, SI 2005/360 (W.29), reg 7 (and see further para 52.18). Second, even though certain of the earlier direct payment schemes, in principle, became comprised within the Single Payment Scheme, the European Community legislation permitted Member States to retain varying levels of payment coupled to production. In particular, Member States could opt to retain coupled to production, inter alia, up to 25% of arable area payments, up to 50% of sheep and goat payments and up to 100% of suckler cow premiums: Council Regulation (EC) 1782/2003, OJ 2003 L 270/1, arts 64–68. A matter of some importance is that this option of retaining support coupled to production was not exercised in the United Kingdom. Third, Member States were granted the option to retain up to 10% of national ceilings in any of the sectors comprised within the Single Payment Scheme so as to make additional payments for specific types of farming which are important for the protection or enhancement of the environment or for improving the quality and marketing of agricultural products: art 69. Again this option was not exercised in England and Wales, but in Scotland it was exercised so as to introduce the Beef Calf Scheme: the Common Agricultural Policy Single Farm Payment and Support Schemes (Scotland) Regulations 2005, SI 2005/143, regs 19–25.

Single Farm Payment: allocation

52.9 Under the European Community legislation, allocation of the Single Farm Payment could be made either nationally on an historic basis or on a regional basis.

In the former case, the allocation was based upon the total amount of direct payments which the farmer had received under the support schemes listed in Annex VI to Council Regulation (EC) 1782/2003, these being averaged over a three-year reference period[1]. The reference period covered the calendar years 2000, 2001 and 2002[2]. Specific provisions conferred access to the payment entitlements where the farmer received the holding or part of the holding by way of actual or anticipated inheritance[3]; or where the farmer received a payment entitlement from the national reserve or by transfer[4]. Specific provisions also addressed the position where a farmer had changed his legal status or denomination prior to the date by which application forms were to be lodged in the first year of the application of the Single Payment Scheme[5]; or where there had been a 'merger' or 'scission' prior to that date[6]. Further, where the production of a farmer was adversely affected by force majeure or exceptional circumstances before or during the reference period, the farmer was entitled to request that allocation be calculated on the basis of the calendar year or years in the reference period which were not so affected[7]. Force majeure and exceptional circumstances were defined, non-exhaustively, to include: the death of the farmer; long-term professional incapacity of the farmer; a severe natural disaster gravely affecting the agricultural land of the holding; the accidental destruction of livestock buildings on the holding; and an epizootic affecting part or all of the livestock of the farmer[8]. Similar accommodation was afforded to farmers who during the reference period were subject to agri-environmental commitments[9]. To meet the requirement that production be 'adversely affected', it has been held sufficient to show that production was lower than it would otherwise have been in the reference period, with there being no difference in principle between the case of a farmer whose production was halved through force majeure or agri-environmental commitments and the case of a farmer who for the same reasons was prevented from doubling production[10].

While, as a general rule, allocation would be made nationally on an historic basis, Member States could opt in the alternative to allocate the Single Farm Payment on a regional basis[11]. If this option was implemented, Member States enjoyed further discretion. They could permit the historic basis to apply; or, in duly justified cases and according to objective criteria, they could divide all, or some, of the Single Farm Payments falling within a particular regional ceiling between all the farmers whose holdings were located in that region[12]. Any such allocation was to be made by dividing the regional ceiling by the number of eligible hectares, established at regional level[13]; and, for this purpose, 'eligible hectare' was defined as 'any agricultural area of the holding taken up by arable land and permanent pasture except areas under permanent crops, forests or used for non agricultural activities'[14]. Accordingly, farmers would receive a flat-rate payment per eligible hectare.

In the United Kingdom allocation has been made on a regional basis. This aspect will be considered in greater detail later[15]. For the time being, it may be noted that, in the case of Wales, historic entitlements have been retained, whereas, in the case of England, the decision was at once taken to opt for the phasing in a flat-rate payment over the period 2005–2012[16].

In addition, two separate forms of direct payment were allocated within the Single Payment Scheme: payment entitlements subject to special conditions[17]; and set-aside entitlements[18].

The former (now termed 'special entitlements'[19]) have remained of relatively slight importance in the United Kingdom, in that they address the situation of farmers who were granted specified payments in the livestock sector, but who had no historic area in the reference period, or whose entitlement per hectare would be higher than 5,000 Euros[20]. In other words, they are primarily concerned with intensive livestock operations, such as the feed lots more commonly found in the United States.

Set-aside entitlements, by contrast, were of much wider importance. However, unlike special entitlements, they lost their distinctiveness when the compulsory set-aside obligation was abolished in response to the global food crisis in 2007–2008[21]. In consequence, the current legislation expressly provides that set-aside entitlements 'shall not be subject to previous set aside obligations'[22]. That said, notwithstanding the abolition of these obligations, the importance of set-aside entitlements prior to their abolition merits identification of the salient features of the separate (yet similar) rules which they enjoyed under the Single Payment Scheme.

First, these rules varied depending upon whether the Single Payment Scheme was being operated on an historic or on a flat-rate basis[23]. If it was being operated on an historic basis, the total number of set-aside entitlements to be allocated to the farmer equalled the average number of hectares that he compulsorily set aside over the 2000–2002 reference period[24]. If the Single Payment Scheme was being operated on a flat-rate basis, the number of set-aside entitlements was established by multiplying the amount of eligible land declared by a farmer in the first year of the Single Payment Scheme by a set-aside rate. The set-aside rate was calculated by multiplying the basic 10% compulsory set-aside rate by the proportion of eligible land in the region which received arable area payments in the reference period[25]. Second, for the purposes of the rules governing set aside, eligible land enjoyed a separate definition, to be distinguished from that for 'eligible hectares' under the general rules governing the Single Payment Scheme[26]. By way of derogation from that general definition, a 'hectare eligible for set-aside entitlement' meant 'any agricultural area of the holding taken up by arable land, except areas which at the date provided for the area aid applications for 2003 were under permanent crops, forests or used for non-agricultural activities or under permanent pasture'[27]. On the other hand, exceptions were made for land set aside under specified agri-environmental schemes or afforested as a result of an application made after 28 June 1995[28]. Accordingly, 'hectares eligible for set-aside entitlements' extended beyond areas that had been eligible for arable area payments, so as to include, for example, temporary grass and fodder crops. As shall be seen, the fact that more land was therefore brought within the set-aside scheme resulted in a lower set-aside rate in England[29]. Third, where the Single Payment Scheme was being operated on a flat-rate basis, as in England, no allocation was made to farmers declaring less hectares eligible for set-aside entitlements than would have been required to produce 92 tonnes of cereals on the basis of regional yields in the year before the year of application of the Single Payment Scheme (as adjusted to take account of the lower set-aside rate)[30]. Fourth, land set aside was also to be maintained in good agricultural and environmental condition[31]. However, although it might be subject to rotation, it was not as a general rule to be used for agricultural purposes and was not to produce any crop for commercial purposes[32].

[1]   Council Regulation (EC) 1782/2003, OJ 2003 L 270/1, art 37(1). Where a farmer commenced an agricultural activity during the reference period, the average was based on the payments that he was granted in the calendar year or years during which he exercised the agricultural activity: art 37(2).

2   Council Regulation (EC) 1782/2003, OJ 2003 L 270/1, art 38.

3   Council Regulation (EC) 1782/2003, OJ 2003 L 270/1, art 33(1)(b).

4   Council Regulation (EC) 1782/2003, OJ 2003 L 270/1, art 33(1)(c). The national reserve could not amount to more than 3% of total allocations: art 42(1).

5   Council Regulation (EC) 1782/2003, OJ 2003 L 270/1, art 33(2). The cut-off date was supplied by Commission Regulation (EC) 795/2004, OJ 2004 L 141/1, art 14(2).

6   Council Regulation (EC) 1782/2003, OJ 2003 L 270/1, art 33(3) (and see, for the cut-off date, Commission Regulation (EC) 795/2004, OJ 2004 L 141/1, art 15(3)). A 'merger' was the merger of two or more separate farmers; and a 'scission' was the scission of one farmer into at least two new separate farmers or the scission of one farmer into at least one new separate farmer (for the detailed rules see Commission Regulation (EC) 795/2004, OJ 2004 L 141/1, art 15(1) and (2)).

7   Council Regulation (EC) 1782/2003, OJ 2003 L 270/1, art 40(1).

8   Council Regulation (EC) 1782/2003, OJ 2003 L 270/1, art 40(4).

9   Council Regulation (EC) 1782/2003, OJ 2003 L 270/1, art 40(5).

10 *R (on the application of Gwilim and Sons) v Welsh Ministers* [2010] EWCA Civ 1048, (2010) Times, 2 November (relating to agri-environmental commitments). See also Case C-152/09 *Grootes v Amt für Landwirtschaft Parchim* [2010] All ER (D) 206 (Nov) (Judgment delivered on 11 November 2010).

11 Council Regulation (EC) 1782/2003, OJ 2003 L 270/1, art 58. Following the 'Health Check', Member States which had implemented the Single Payment Scheme nationally on an historic basis have been granted a further opportunity to move to the regional basis: Council Regulation (EC) 73/2009, OJ 2009 L 30/16, art 46; but, as shall be seen, this provision did not affect the United Kingdom (which had already opted for the regional basis).

12 Council Regulation (EC) 1782/2003, OJ 2003 L 270/1, art 59(1).

13 Council Regulation (EC) 1782/2003, OJ 2003 L 270/1, art 59(2).

14 Council Regulation (EC) 1782/2003, OJ 2003 L 270/1, art 44(2).

15 See para 52.17.

16 Importantly, the Welsh Assembly Government decided to continue to operate the Single Payment Scheme on the basis of historic entitlements, notwithstanding that the reforms effected by the 'Health Check' offered the opportunity to modify such entitlements: see, eg, *Answers to the Written Assembly Questions for Answer on 12 February 2010* (available at http://www.assemblywales.org/bus-home/bus-chamber/bus-chamber-third-assembly-written.htm?act=dis&id=168114&ds=2/2010, accessed on 26 February 2011); and, for the European Community legislation, see Council Regulation (EC) 73/2009, OJ 2009 L 30/16, art 45.

17 Council Regulation (EC) 1782/2003, OJ 2003 L 270/1, arts 47–49.

18 Council Regulation (EC) 1782/2003, OJ 2003 L 270/1, arts 53–57.

19 Council Regulation (EC) 73/2009, OJ 2009 L 30/16, art 44.

20 Council Regulation (EC) 1782/2003, OJ 2003 L 270/1, art 48. The specified livestock payments were set out at art 47. They included, in particular: slaughter premium; beef special premium and suckler cow premium, where the farmer was exempted from the stocking rate requirement on the basis that he had not more than 15 livestock units (unless he had applied for extensification premium); and dairy premium and additional payments. For fuller consideration of payment entitlements subject to special conditions, and the difficulties that arose on their implementation in England, see, eg, J Moody and W Neville *Mid Term Review: a Practical Guide* (2004) Burges Salmon, Bristol, pp 129–132.

21 This obligation was first removed in respect of 2008 by Council Regulation (EC) 1107/2007, OJ 2007 L 253/1. And it was then permanently removed under the 'Health Check': see European Commission *Preparing for the 'Health Check' of the CAP Reform* COM(2007)722, 6–7; and Council Regulation (EC) 73/2009, OJ 2009 L 30/16, Preamble (30).

22 Council Regulation (EC) 73/2009, OJ 2009 L 30/16, art 33(3).

23 The historic basis is applicable either under the general rule or, alternatively, where the Single Payment Scheme is operated regionally, but no decision has been taken to implement the flat-rate basis of allocation (as is the case in Wales). The flat-rate basis is applicable only where the Member State opts to implement the Single Payment Scheme regionally and to implement the flat-rate basis (as is being phased in throughout England).

24 Council Regulation (EC) 1782/2003, OJ 2003 L 270/1, art 53.

25 Council Regulation (EC) 1782/2003, OJ 2003 L 270/1, art 63(2).

[26] For the general definition, see Council Regulation (EC) 1782/2003, OJ 2003 L 270/1, art 44(2).

[27] Council Regulation (EC) 1782/2003, OJ 2003 L 270/1, art 54(2).

[28] For the agri-environmental and afforestation schemes in question, see respectively Council Regulation (EC) 1257/1999, OJ 1999 L 160/80, arts 22–24 and art 31.

[29] See para 52.20.

[30] Council Regulation (EC) 1782/2003, OJ 2003 L 270/1, art 63(2).

[31] Council Regulation (EC) 1782/2003, OJ 2003 L 270/1, art 56(1).

[32] Council Regulation (EC) 1782/2003, OJ 2003 L 270/1, art 56(1) and (2). That said, it may be noted that two major exemptions from the set-aside obligation applied: (a) where the entire holding was managed organically for the totality of its production; and (b) where the land set aside was used for the provision of materials for the manufacture within the European Community of products not primarily intended for human or animal consumption: art 55. Further, energy crops could be grown on land set aside and Member States were authorised to pay national aid up to 50% of the costs associated with the establishment of multi-annual crops intended for biomass production: art 56(4). On the other hand, where land was subject to an application for specific aid for energy crops (available under arts 88–92 prior to its abolition under the 'Health Check'), that land could not be counted as land set aside: art 90; and see para 52.13.

Single Farm Payment: unlocking payment entitlements

52.10 Where a farmer has been allocated a payment entitlement under the Single Payment Scheme, it can only be unlocked when matched against 'eligible hectares'[1]. Accordingly, there is a 'link' to land, with landlord and tenant implications[2].

For this purpose, 'eligible hectares' is defined as 'any agricultural area of the holding, and any area planted with short rotation coppice ... that is used for an agricultural activity or, where the area is used for non-agricultural activities, predominantly used for agricultural activities', together with any area which gave a right to payments under the Single Payment Scheme in 2008 and which satisfies one of three criteria[3]. The first is that the area is no longer eligible through implementation of the Wild Birds Directive[4], the Habitats Directive[5] or the Water Framework Directive[6]; the second is that the area was subject to first afforestation under a European Community or national rural development scheme[7]; and the third is that the area was set aside under a European Community agri-environmental scheme[8]. As has been seen, 'agricultural area' is defined as 'any area taken up by arable land, permanent pasture and permanent crops'[9]; and 'agricultural activity' is defined as 'the production, rearing or growing of agricultural products including harvesting, milking, breeding animals and keeping animals for farming purposes, or maintaining the land in good agricultural and environmental condition'[10].

Accordingly, the definition of 'eligible hectares' is very broad. It covers land used not just to grow standard combinable crops, such as cereals, but also to grow, inter alia, sugar beet, potatoes, fruit and vegetables, vines, multiannual crops (including artichokes, asparagus, raspberries and blackberries), nursery crops and short rotation coppice, together with permanent pasture. In this context, two aspects may be highlighted. First, it is possible to match payment entitlements against land used to grow certain energy crops, such as short rotation coppice, but, as indicated, the 'Health Check' saw abolition of the specific aid for energy crops as previously granted outside the Single Payment

Scheme[11]. Second, what constitutes an 'eligible hectare' has been considerably extended in the context of the fruit and vegetables sector. When this sector was first incorporated into the Single Payment Scheme, it had been possible to match payment entitlements against land used to grow certain fruit, vegetables and potatoes (other than starch potatoes), but only where the Single Payment Scheme was implemented regionally on a flat-rate basis (as in England)[12]. The current legislation removes this constraint, with the result that it is now also possible to match payment entitlements against land growing such crops in Wales. Further, as indicated, the definition of 'agricultural area' in Council Regulation (EC) 73/2009 includes any area taken up by permanent crops, whereas formerly they were excluded (with the exception of multiannual crops and the nurseries of multiannual crops)[13]. In consequence, by way of illustration, under the original legislation apples and pears were excluded, but the multiannual exemption permitted raspberries and blackberries to qualify. By contrast, the new definition of 'agricultural area' is apt to provide blanket coverage of land taken up by permanent fruit and vegetables (including apples and pears and, indeed, commercial orchards generally), as well as by nursery crops and vines.

Importantly, the definition of 'eligible hectares' does not require that the land be in production, since 'agricultural activity' includes maintaining the land in good agricultural and environmental condition. Further, in *Landkreis Bad Dürkheim v Aufsichts- und Dienstleistungsdirektion* it was held that, so long as the agricultural area is used for an agricultural activity, it is irrelevant for the purposes of its meeting the criteria for 'eligible hectares' whether the activity has an essentially agricultural or nature conservation objective[14]. It may also be reiterated that use for non-agricultural activities is permitted, provided that the predominant use remains for agricultural activities. For such purposes, the test is whether the 'agricultural activity can be exercised without being significantly hampered by the intensity, nature, duration and timing of the non-agricultural activity'[15]; and the detailed criteria are to be established at the level of the Member States[16].

In addition, for an eligible hectare to unlock payment, it must be 'at the farmer's disposal', except in case of force majeure or exceptional circumstances, on a date fixed by the Member State, which must be no later than the date fixed in that Member State for amending the aid application[17]. In *Landkreis Bad Dürkheim v Aufsichts- und Dienstleistungsdirektion* the CJEU was required to consider the criterion that the land should be 'at the farmer's disposal'[18]. First, it made clear that there was no requirement for the land to be held pursuant to a lease or other similar transaction, since the legislation did specify the nature of the legal relationship involved[19]. Second, land could remain 'at the farmer's disposal' notwithstanding that the farmer was subject to certain restrictions (such as restrictions imposed for conservation purposes on the nature and duration of his activities); but the farmer must still enjoy a degree of autonomy sufficient for the carrying-out of his agricultural activity (including maintenance of the land in good agricultural and environmental condition), this being a matter for the national court to decide[20]. Third, while the agricultural activity must be carried out in the name of the farmer and on his behalf, this being again a matter for the national court to decide, it was

292

irrelevant that the farmer be required to carry out tasks for a third party (such as a nature conservation authority) in return for payment[21].

Finally, it may be noted that, prior to the abolition of set-aside, set-aside entitlements could only be matched against hectares eligible for set-aside entitlements[22]; and they were to be claimed before any other entitlement[23].

1   Council Regulation (EC) 73/2009, OJ 2009 L 30/16, art 34(1).
2   On first implementation of the Single Payment Scheme, Council Regulation (EC) 1782/2003, OJ 2003 L 270/1, Preamble (30) recited that: '[t]he overall amount to which a farm is entitled should be split into parts (payment entitlements) and linked to a certain number of eligible hectares to be defined, in order to facilitate transfer of the premium rights. To avoid speculative transfers leading to the accumulation of payment entitlements without a corresponding agricultural basis, in granting aid, it is appropriate to provide for a link between entitlements and a certain number of eligible hectares, as well as the possibility of limiting the transfer of entitlements within a region'. See also now Council Regulation (EC) 73/2009, OJ 2009 L 30/16, Preamble (28). For the landlord and tenant implications, see para 52.25.
3   Council Regulation (EC) 73/2009, OJ 2009 L 30/16, art 34(2). For what amount to 'non-agricultural activities', see para 52.21.
4   Council Directive 79/409/EEC, OJ 1979 L 103/1.
5   Council Directive 92/43/EEC, OJ 1992 L 206/7.
6   Directive 2000/60/EC of the European Parliament and of the Council, OJ 2000 L 327/1.
7   For the legislation concerned, see Council Regulation (EC) 1257/1999, OJ 1999 L 160/80, art 31; and Council Regulation (EC) 1698/2005, OJ 2005 L 277/1, art 43.
8   For the legislation concerned, see Council Regulation (EC) 1257/1999, OJ 1999 L 160/80, arts 22–24; and Council Regulation (EC) 1698/2005, OJ 2005 L 277/1, art 39. It may be reiterated that, even though compulsory set-aside has now been abolished, a farmer may still elect to put land into set-aside under European Community rural development agri-environmental schemes.
9   Council Regulation (EC) 73/2009, OJ 2009 L 30/16, art 2(h), with definitions of 'arable land', 'permanent pasture' and 'permanent crops' being provided by Commission Regulation (EC) 1120/2009, OJ 2009 L 316/1, art 2(a), (b) and (c); and see further para 52.4.
10 Council Regulation (EC) 73/2009, OJ 2009 L 30/16, art 2(c); and see further para 52.4.
11 See further para 52.13. This specific aid for energy crops was granted under Council Regulation (EC) 1782/2003, OJ 2003 L 270/1, arts 88–92. It may be noted that support for energy crops is, however, still available under the rural development regime: see para 52.15.
12 Council Regulation (EC) 1782/2003, OJ 2003 L 270/1, art 60 (as amended by Council Regulation (EC) 2012/2006, OJ 2006 L 384/8).
13 Under Council Regulation (EC) 1782/2003, OJ 2003 L 270/1, art 44(2), 'eligible hectares' were defined as 'any agricultural area of the holding taken up by arable land and permanent pasture except areas under permanent crops, forests or used for non-agricultural activities': and, for the multi-annual exemption, see Commission Regulation (EC) 795/2004, OJ 2004 L 141/1, art 2(c).
14 Case C-61/09 [2010] All ER (D) 257 (Nov) (Judgment delivered on 14 October 2010), para 47.
15 Commission Regulation (EC) 1120/2009, OJ 2009 L 316/1, art 9.
16 For the detailed criteria in England and Wales, see para 52.21.
17 Council Regulation (EC) 73/2009, OJ 2009 L 30/16, art 35(1). For the relevant date in England and Wales, see para 52.25. It may be highlighted that, prior to the 'Health Check', it was a requirement that the land be 'at the farmer's disposal' for a period of at least ten months: Council Regulation (EC) 1782/2003, OJ 2003 L 270/1, art 44(3).
18 Case C-61/09 [2010] All ER (D) 257 (Nov) (Judgment delivered on 14 October 2010). The legislation concerned was Council Regulation (EC) 1782/2003, OJ 2003 L 270/1, art 44(2) and (3), which likewise employed the wording 'at the farmer's disposal'.
19 Case C-61/09 [2010] All ER (D) 257 (Nov) (Judgment delivered on 14 October 2010), para 54.
20 Case C-61/09 [2010] All ER (D) 257 (Nov) (Judgment delivered on 14 October 2010), paras 62–65. As indicated, the earlier legislation required that the land be 'at the farmer's disposal' for a period of at least ten months and the CJEU held that during this period no third party should carry out any agricultural activity on the land in question: para 66.

21 Case C-61/09 [2010] All ER (D) 257 (Nov) (Judgment delivered on 14 October 2010), paras 69–70.
22 Council Regulation (EC) 1782/2003, OJ 2003 L 270/1, art 54(1).
23 Council Regulation (EC) 1782/2003, OJ 2003 L 270/1, art 54(6). See Case C-153/09 *Agrargut Bäbelin GmbH v Amt für Landwirtschaft Bützow* [2011] All ER (D) 221 (Jan) (Judgment delivered on 2 December 2010) (which considers also the position where a farmer has insufficient hectares eligible for set-aside to meet his obligation).

Single Farm Payment: non-use

52.11 Payment entitlements that have not been used for a period of two years are to revert to the national reserve, except in cases of force majeure and exceptional circumstances[1]. As under the original legislation, force majeure or exceptional circumstances are defined, non-exhaustively, to include: the death of the farmer; long-term professional incapacity of the farmer; a severe natural disaster gravely affecting the agricultural land of the holding; the accidental destruction of livestock buildings on the holding; and an epizootic affecting part or all of the livestock of the farmer[2].

The fact that payment entitlements are not lost for two years may provide some comfort for tenants who lack security, since, in the event that their tenancy comes to end, they are granted a period of grace either to find new eligible hectares against which they may match their entitlements or to dispose of them[3].

1 Council Regulation (EC) 73/2009, OJ 2009 L 30/16, art 42. Under the original legislation, the period was three years: Council Regulation (EC) 1782/2003, OJ 2003 L 270/1, art 45; and, when the shorter period was introduced for 2009, transitional provisions covered the position both for that year and for 2010. Thus, for 2009, if payment entitlements were not activated over the two-year period 2007–2008, they were not to revert to the national reserve if activated in 2006; and, for 2010, if payment entitlements were not activated over the two-year period 2008–2009, they were not to revert to the national reserve if activated in 2007: Council Regulation (EC) 73/2009, OJ 2009 L 30/16, art 42.
2 Council Regulation (EC) 73/2009, OJ 2009 L 30/16, art 31. For the original definition, see Council Regulation (EC) 1782/2003, OJ 2003 L 270/1, art 40(4).
3 See, eg, J Moody and W Neville *Mid Term Review: a Practical Guide* (2004) Burges Salmon, Bristol, p 118.

Single Farm Payment: transfers

52.12 Under the European Community legislation provision is made for the transfer of payment entitlements[1]. Such transfers may occur at any time in the year; and it is for the transferor to inform the competent authority of the Member State within a period established by that Member State[2]. However, transfer may only occur in favour of another farmer established within the same Member State, except in the case of transfer by actual or anticipated inheritance (and, even in these cases, the payment entitlements may only be used within the same Member State)[3]. Further, Member States may decide that payment entitlements may only be transferred within the same region[4]. As indicated, throughout the operation of the Single Payment Scheme a theme expressly underpinning such provisions has been the need to avoid 'speculative transfers'[5]; and, in this context, a matter of some importance is that transfers may only be made in favour of farmers exercising an agricultural activity. Although, as has been seen, the criteria for what constitutes an 'agricultural activity' are not onerous, it being sufficient to maintain the land in good agricultural and environmental condition, there may be danger in treating these provisions too lightly. In the past, the CJEU has shown a robust attitude towards the requirement that those holding milk quota should be genuine producers[6]; and there is every sign that this pattern will be replicated in the case of the Single Payment Scheme[7].

Payment entitlements may be transferred by sale or by any other definitive transfer, with or without land[8]. On the other hand, where the transfer is effected by lease or similar types of transactions, then the payment entitlements transferred must be accompanied by the transfer of an equivalent number of eligible hectares[9]. These transfer provisions were considered by the CJEU in *Harms v Heidinga*[10]. In particular, the CJEU was required to address whether the requirements for a 'sale or other definitive transfer' could be satisfied by a contractual arrangement whose object was to effect a definitive transfer of payment entitlements, but in circumstances where the transferee, in his capacity as the person formally entitled to the payment entitlements, was required to activate them and pass on to the transferor all or part of the payments received. It was stated that, although as a rule parties may arrange their own affairs in accordance with the principle of freedom of contract, they could not enter into commitments which contradicted the objective of the Single Payment Scheme; and the objective of the Single Payment Scheme was to provide income support for farmers[11]. In this context, emphasis was laid upon the requirement that farmers observe cross-compliance obligations in order to secure payment, with it also being necessary for them to hold a sufficient number of eligible hectares, against which the payment entitlements were to be matched[12]. Thus, if there were a contractual arrangement under which the transferor was to retain, on an ongoing basis, a part of the entitlements which he had formally transferred, this would offend the transfer rules in that the transferor would continue to benefit from the Single Payment Scheme without being subject to its cross-compliance obligations (or, indeed, holding eligible hectares)[13]. However, the position would be different if, instead, the contractual arrangement was to determine, by reference to the value of that part of the payment entitlements, an agreed price for the transfer of all the payment entitlements; and it was for the national court to assess, on the facts, which of these two alternatives was the true intention of the parties[14].

In the case of a sale (but not a lease) of payment entitlements, whether or not with land, Member States can, acting in compliance with the general principles of European Community law, decide that part of the payment entitlements sold should revert to the national reserve or that their unit value should be reduced in favour of the national reserve[15]. In the United Kingdom this discretion has not been exercised. If it were exercised, then care would be required to ensure that there was indeed compliance with the general principles of European Community law: for example, the measure must be proportionate[16].

52.12 *Payments to Farmers under the Common Agricultural Policy*

In addition, there continue to be specific restrictions on the transfer of special entitlements. For 2009, 2010 and 2011, their special status will be preserved only where they are all transferred to the same transferee; and thereafter their special status will be preserved only in cases of actual or anticipated inheritance[17]. By contrast, there are no longer specific restrictions on transfer of payment entitlements received from the national reserve[18].

---

1   Council Regulation (EC) 73/2009, OJ 2009 L 30/16, art 43.
2   Commission Regulation (EC) 1120/2009, OJ 2009 L 316/1, art 12(1) and (2).
3   Council Regulation (EC) 73/2009, OJ 2009 L 30/16, art 43(1). It is possible that guidance as to what constitutes 'inheritance' may be sought by analogy from milk quota cases: see, eg, Case C-44/89 *von Deetzen v Hauptzollamt Oldenburg* [1991] ECR I-5119, [1994] 2 CMLR 487, ECJ. What would seem tolerably clear, in any event, is that the CJEU would be reluctant to give more than general guidance, leaving detailed consideration of particular instances to national courts: [1991] ECR I-5119, para 40. See also Commission Regulation (EC) 1120/2009, OJ 2009 L 316/1, art 3.
4   Council Regulation (EC) 73/2009, OJ 2009 L 30/16, art 43(1). Similarly, under the earlier sheep annual premium and suckler cow premium regimes, Member States could restrict the transfer of sheep and suckler cow quotas from sensitive zones or regions where sheep or beef and veal production were particularly important for the local economy. For implementation of such provisions in the United Kingdom, see the Sheep Annual Premium and Suckler Cow Premium Quotas Regulations 2003, SI 2003/2261, regs 7 and 8.
5   See now Council Regulation (EC) 73/2009, OJ 2009 L 30/16, art 43(2).
6   See, eg, Case C-401/99 *Thomsen v Amt für Ländliche Räume Husum* [2002] ECR I-5775; and Case C-275/05 *Alois Kibler jun v Land Baden-Wurttemburg* [2006] ECR I-10569, [2006] All ER (D) 323 (Oct), ECJ.
7   See, eg, Case C-434/08 *Harms v Heidinga* (Judgment delivered on 20 May 2010).
8   Council Regulation (EC) 73/2009, OJ 2009 L 30/16, art 43(2).
9   Council Regulation (EC) 73/2009, OJ 2009 L 30/16, art 43(2). Prior to the 'Health Check', transfers were subject to a further general restriction. Except in the case of force majeure or exceptional circumstances, a farmer could only transfer his payment entitlements without land after he had used at least 80% of them during at least one calendar year or after he had voluntarily surrendered to the national reserve all the payment entitlements that he had not used in the first year of application of the Single Payment Scheme (in the United Kingdom, this being 2005): Council Regulation (EC) 1782/2003, OJ 2003 L 270/1, art 46(2). This further restriction was abolished as from 1 January 2009.
10   Case C-434/08 *Harms v Heidinga* (Judgment delivered on 20 May 2010). The case related to the transfer provisions as set out in the original legislation (Council Regulation (EC) 1782/2003, OJ 2003 L 270/1, art 46(2)), but the material wording was identical to that in Council Regulation (EC) 73/2009, OJ 2009 L 30/16, art 43(2).
11   Case C-434/08 (Judgment delivered on 20 May 2010), paras 36–38.
12   Case C-434/08 (Judgment delivered on 20 May 2010), para 38.
13   Case C-434/08 (Judgment delivered on 20 May 2010), paras 43–45.
14   Case C-434/08 (Judgment delivered on 20 May 2010), paras 46–49. It may be noted that the Advocate General was clearly of the view that such a contractual arrangement would offend the transfer rules, in that the right to receive payment was inseparable from legal ownership of the payment entitlements.
15   Council Regulation (EC) 73/2009, OJ 2009 L 30/16, art 43(3). Under the earlier sheep annual premium and suckler cow premium regimes, a similar 'siphon' was authorised in the case of a transfer of rights without transfer of the holding. For its implementation at the full rate of 15% in the United Kingdom, see the Sheep Annual Premium and Suckler Cow Premium Quotas Regulations 2003, SI 2003/2261, reg 5. A 'siphon' is also currently authorised under the milk quota regime (but not implemented in the United Kingdom): Council Regulation (EC) 1234/2007, OJ 2007 L 299/1, art 76.
16   See, eg, in the context of milk quotas, Case C-313/99 *Mulligan v Minister for Agriculture and Food (Ireland)* [2002] ECR I-5719, ECJ.
17   Council Regulation (EC) 73/2009, OJ 2009 L 30/16, art 44(3).
18   These restrictions were introduced under Council Regulation (EC) 1782/2003, OJ 2003 L 270/1, art 42(8) (as amended by Council Regulation (EC) 2012/2006, OJ 2006 L 384/8).

Crop-specific direct payments not within the Single Payment Scheme

52.13 As indicated, the Single Payment Scheme does not cover all direct payments to farmers. When it was first implemented under the Mid-term Review, a variety of crop-specific support was preserved, in large part to maintain production in areas traditionally associated with such crops[1]. That said, there has been a continuing drive to extend decoupling of support from production, with ever more direct payments being brought within the umbrella of the Single Payment Scheme. Perceived advantages for this policy include greater market orientation, simplification of the legislative framework and increased world trade compatibility[2].

The 'Health Check' has marked a further significant step forward in this direction and, in England and Wales, the extent of crop-specific support is now relatively small. In particular, as has been seen, on the introduction of payment entitlements the option was not exercised to retain support coupled to production in, for example, the arable and the sheepmeat and goatmeat sectors[3]; and at the same time the decision was taken to integrate dairy premiums and additional payments into the Single Payment Scheme ab initio[4]. Moreover, as indicated, the 'Health Check' saw support for energy crops confined to the rural development regime (with no specific aid being available under Council Regulation (EC) 73/2009)[5]. In consequence, under Council Regulation (EC) 73/2009 the only crop-specific support of significance remains the protein crop premium[6]; and even this is to be phased out by 2012 at the latest[7]. In England the last year of the protein crop premium is 2011, while in Wales it was 2010.

Thus, for the present, in England the protein crop premium remains available in the case of specified types of peas, field beans and sweet lupins[8]. The amount of the premium is 55.57 Euros per hectare of protein crops harvested after the stage of lactic ripeness[9]. As at 1 January 2009 a maximum guaranteed area of 1,648,000 hectares was established at European Community level, but this has been reduced as and when Member States integrated the protein crop premium into the Single Payment Scheme[10]. Scaleback provisions apply if this maximum guaranteed area is exceeded[11].

---

[1] European Commission *Mid-term Review of the Common Agricultural Policy* COM(2002)394, 20.

[2] See, eg, Council Regulation (EC) 73/2009, OJ 2009 L 30/16, Preamble (40).

[3] See para 52.8.

[4] See para 52.8. For the European Community legislation, see Council Regulation (EC) 1782/2003, OJ 2003 L 270/1, art 62; and, for implementation in England and Wales, see the Common Agricultural Policy Single Payment and Support Schemes Regulations 2005, SI 2005/219, reg 7; and the Common Agricultural Policy Single Payment and Support Schemes (Wales) Regulations 2005, SI 2005/360 (W.29), reg 7.

[5] See para 52.10. As recited in Council Regulation (EC) 73/2009, the need for specific aid had been rendered otiose by recent developments in the bioenergy sector and, in particular, strong demand for energy crops on international markets and the introduction of binding targets for the share of bioenergy in total fuel by 2020: OJ 2009 L 30/16, Preamble (42). Aid had been paid at the rate of 45 Euros per hectare: Council Regulation (EC) 1782/2003, OJ 2003 L 270/1, art 88. As a rule, it could only be granted in respect of areas whose production was covered by a contract between the farmer and the processing industry, although exemption was conferred where the farmer himself undertook the processing: Council Regulation (EC) 1782/2003, OJ 2003 L 270/1, art 90. For the detailed provisions,

see Commission Regulation (EC) 1973/2004, OJ 2004 L 345/1, arts 23–44 (as amended by Commission Regulation (EC) 270/2007, OJ 2007 L 75/8). Originally, a maximum guaranteed area of 1,500,000 hectares was established at European Community level, with scaleback provisions in the event of it being exceeded: Council Regulation (EC) 1782/2003, OJ 2003 L 270/1, art 89. However, with the increased emphasis on biofuel production, this maximum guaranteed area had been raised to 2 million hectares: Council Regulation (EC) 1782/2003, OJ 2003 L 270/1, art 89 (as amended by Council Regulation (EC) 2012/2006, OJ 2006 L 384/8).

6 OJ 2009 L 30/16, arts 79–81. In England there is also an area payment for nuts under Council Regulation (EC) 73/2009, OJ 2009 L 30/16, arts 82–86. Again 2011 will be the final year of the Scheme.

7 Council Regulation (EC) 73/2009, OJ 2009 L 30/16, Annex XI. Earlier incorporation into the Single Payment Scheme is expressly authorised by Council Regulation (EC) 73/2009, OJ 2009 L 30/16, art 67.

8 Council Regulation (EC) 73/2009, OJ 2009 L 30/16, art 79.

9 Council Regulation (EC) 73/2009, OJ 2009 L 30/16, art 80. A derogation is available where the crops are grown on areas which are fully sown and which are cultivated in accordance with local standards, but which do not reach lactic ripeness as a result of exceptional weather conditions recognised by the Member State (provided that the areas in question are not used for any other purpose up to the growing stage): Council Regulation (EC) 73/2009, OJ 2009 L 30/16, art 80. A further derogation is available where protein crops are traditionally sown in a mixture with cereals, provided that the protein crops are predominant: Commission Regulation (EC) 1121/2009, OJ 2009 L 316/27, art 14.

10 Council Regulation (EC) 73/2009, OJ 2009 L 30/16, art 81(1) and (3).

11 Council Regulation (EC) 73/2009, OJ 2009 L 30/16, art 81(2).

The nature of the asset

52.14 Under Council Regulation (EC) 73/2009, the Single Payment Scheme is stated to be an 'income support scheme for farmers'[1]. Its introduction under the Mid-term Review was expressly understood 'to complete the shift from production support to producer support'[2]; and, prioritising one of the objectives of the Common Agricultural Policy, the particular target remains to ensure a fair standard of living for the agricultural community[3]. Moreover, such categorisation as 'income support' has repeatedly been emphasised by the CJEU[4]; and, similarly, in the Scottish Land Court case of *Morrison-Low v Paterson* there was no dispute that the effect of the Single Farm Payment was to decouple subsidy from production, with it being properly described as ' "income support" for farmers'[5]. This is also consistent with the European Community imperative that the payment entitlements should qualify as 'de-coupled income support' for the purposes of the Uruguay Round Agreement on Agriculture, so securing exemption from domestic support reduction commitments[6].

On the other hand, the Single Farm Payment would not appear to be straightforward income support. In particular, there is no conventional assessment of the financial resources of the beneficiary[7]. Detailed eligibility criteria focus rather on agricultural activity and agricultural area; and four examples of such provisions may be given. First, as has been seen, the definition of 'farmer' in this context also includes a requirement that there be the exercise of an agricultural activity (although to meet this criterion it is sufficient to maintain the land in good agricultural and environmental condition)[8]. Second, the key objective of the Single Payment Scheme, namely to ensure a fair standard of living for the agricultural community, is closely related to the maintenance of rural areas[9]; and, as highlighted by the CJEU, this brings in train the requirement that receipt of the Single Farm Payment is conditional upon observation of cross-compliance obligations in relation to the agricultural area of the holding[10]. Third, a 'link' with agricultural areas is also established by the requirement that payment entitlements be matched against eligible hectares[11]. Thus, encapsulating these second and third examples, the Advocate General in *Harms v Heidinga* declared that 'the mere fact that a farmer has obtained payment entitlements does not automatically result in him receiving actual support connected with those entitlements. To benefit from single payments, the farmer is required not only to hold the payment entitlements but also to activate them by having at his disposal a corresponding amount of hectares of agricultural land and by complying with other management requirements – such as conditions imposed under environmental and animal protection and food safety laws (so-called cross-compliance)'[12]. Fourth, as has again been seen, the transfer rules require that, in the case of leases or similar types of transactions, payment entitlements may only be transferred when accompanied by the transfer of an equivalent number of eligible hectares[13]. As recited in the Preamble to Council Regulation (EC) 73/2009, this addresses the need to 'prevent speculative transfer and the accumulation of payment entitlements without a corresponding agricultural basis'[14].

Nevertheless, it would seem prudent to recognise the limitations of any such link. Not least, definitive transfers may be made without land[15]; and payment entitlements are not attached to individual parcels of land: a farmer (including a tenant) can in principle match them against any eligible hectares at his disposal[16]. Indeed, as stated by the Advocate General in *Harms v Heidinga*, 'payment entitlements may in principle be freely transferred and are not linked to specific agricultural land'[17]; and in *Van Dijk v Gemeente Kampen* the CJEU had earlier held that the requirement for payment entitlements to be matched against eligible hectares did not lead to the conclusion that they were 'linked to specific parcels'[18].

Further, the CJEU has explicitly distinguished income support under the Single Payment Scheme from milk quotas[19]. Perhaps most significantly, in the case of milk quotas the general rule remains rather that they are transferred with the holding[20]; and, consistent with this approach, the current legislation refers to 'the principle that quotas are tied to farms'[21]. As with the Single Payment Scheme, the purpose has been to avoid 'speculative operations'[22]. The Advocate General in *Harms v Heidinga* also distinguished payment entitlements from earlier premiums available in the livestock sector, on the basis that payment entitlements were 'solely "an income support for farmers" '[23]; and, likewise, for the purposes of rent review, in *Morrison-Low v Paterson* the Scottish Land Court did not accept that 'sheep quota cases are directly comparable': rather, '[t]he effect of the quota was to determine the potential limits of entitlement. The payment itself was, however, based on the stock actually held. There would be no payment of subsidy if the land was not available for use for keeping the stock. We have no doubt that the value from keeping sheep is properly to be taken to be a fruit of the use of the land'[24]. That said, the similarities between the Single Farm Payment and livestock premiums would seem considerably greater than its similarities with milk quotas. For example, in *R v Minister of Agriculture, Fisheries and Food, ex p Country Landowners Association* the CJEU unequivocally affirmed that livestock premiums were linked to producers (as opposed to being tied to farms)[25]; and, in similar fashion to the Single Farm Payment, such premiums were introduced in order to offset loss of income (albeit by reference to a specific common organisation of the market)[26].

In this context it is also possible to note the interpretation adopted by HM Revenue and Customs[27]. They do not countenance that receipt of the Single Farm Payment may be regarded as income from land. Instead, in the usual case, it will be treated as income from farming (under Schedule D, Case 1 of the Income and Corporation Taxes Act 1988 or s 9 of the Income Tax (Trading and Other Income) Act 2005)[28]. Likewise, the payment entitlements themselves are considered separate chargeable assets for Capital Gains Tax purposes (although not wasting assets, since there is no clarity as to the future of the Single Payment Scheme after 2012)[29].

Accordingly, while the overriding purpose of the Single Farm Payment is undoubtedly to provide income support for farmers, free from any requirement of production, it would be hard to deny that the more detailed eligibility criteria, which associate it with both agricultural activity and agricultural areas, generate genuine landlord and tenant issues; and these will be explored later[30].

[1]   OJ 2009 L 30/16, art 1(b). Likewise, the original legislation referred to the Single Payment Scheme as 'income support': Council Regulation (EC) 1782/2003, OJ 2003 L 270/1, art 1. On this aspect generally, see, eg, D Rennie 'The Legal Nature of Single Farm Payment Entitlement' (2011) 171 *Farm Law* 16–20.

[2]   Council Regulation (EC) 1782/2003, OJ 2003 L 270/1, Preamble (24). See also, eg, European Commission *A Long-term Policy Perspective for Sustainable Agriculture* COM(2003)23, 3.

[3]   Council Regulation (EC) 73/2009, OJ 2009 L 30/16, Preamble (25) (the second objective of the Common Agricultural Policy being '(b) thus to ensure a fair standard of living for the agricultural community, in particular by increasing the individual earnings of persons engaged in agriculture': Treaty on the Functioning of the European Union, art 39(1)(b)). It may also be noted that it has long been established that the European Community institutions may temporarily accord greater weight to one of these objectives, in order to meet the demands of economic factors or conditions: see, eg, Case 5/73 *Balkan-Import-Export GmbH v Hauptzollamt Berlin-Packhof* [1973] ECR 1091; and Case C-280/93 *Germany v Council* [1994] ECR I-4973.

[4]   See, eg, Case C-470/08 *Van Dijk v Gemeente Kampen* [2010] All ER (D) 141 (Feb) (Judgment delivered on 21 January 2010), para 27; and Case C-434/08 *Harms v Heidinga* (Judgment delivered on 20 May 2010), para 38.

[5]   (2010) SLC/233/08, para 92.

[6]   See para 52.1.

[7]   That said, it may be noted that a higher rate of modulation is applied when a farmer receives in excess of 300,000 Euros under the Single Payment Scheme in one year, a further 4% being compulsorily deducted from all amounts above that threshold: see para 52.6. This is justified on the basis that 'larger beneficiaries do not require the same level of unitary support for the objective of income support to be efficiently attained' and that 'the potential to adapt makes it easier for larger beneficiaries to operate with lower levels of unitary support': Council Regulation (EC) 73/2009, OJ 2009 L 30/16, Preamble (11).

[8]   Council Regulation (EC) 73/2009, OJ 2009 L 30/16, art 2(a) and (c); and see para 52.4.

[9]   Council Regulation (EC) 73/2009, OJ 2009 L 30/16, Preamble (25).

[10] See, eg, Case C-434/08 *Harms v Heidinga* (Judgment delivered on 20 May 2010), para 38; and, for cross-compliance obligations generally, see para 52.5.

11 See, eg, Case C-470/08 *Van Dijk v Gemeente Kampen* [2010] All ER (D) 141 (Feb) (Judgment delivered on 21 January 2010), para 29: 'Article 44(1) of that regulation [Council Regulation (EC) 1782/2003, OJ 2003, L 270/1 (now, with amendment, Council Regulation (EC) 73/2009, OJ 2009 L 30/16, art 34(1)] recognises that there is a link between payment entitlements and agricultural areas in that each payment entitlement which corresponds to an eligible hectare gives a right to payment of the amount fixed by the payment entitlement'; and see generally para 52.10.

12 Case C-434/08 *Harms v Heidinga* (Opinion delivered on 4 February 2010), para 24.

13 Council Regulation (EC) 73/2009, OJ 2009 L 30/16, art 43(2); and see further para 52.12.

14 Council Regulation (EC) 73/2009, OJ 2009 L 30/16, Preamble (28). It may be noted that the equivalent provision in the earlier legislation (Council Regulation (EC) 1782/2003, OJ 2003, L 270/1, Preamble (30)) made express reference to the 'link between entitlements and a certain number of eligible hectares'.

15 Council Regulation (EC) 73/2009, OJ 2009 L 30/16, art 43(2).

16 Council Regulation (EC) 73/2009, OJ 2009 L 30/16, art 34(1).

17 Case C-434/08 *Harms v Heidinga* (Opinion delivered on 4 February 2010), para 32.

18 Case C-470/08 *Van Dijk v Gemeente Kampen* [2010] All ER (D) 141 (Feb) (Judgment delivered on 21 January 2010), para 32.

19 Case C-470/08 *Van Dijk v Gemeente Kampen* [2010] All ER (D) 141 (Feb) (Judgment delivered on 21 January 2010), para 25; and see also Case C-434/08 *Harms v Heidinga* (Opinion delivered on 4 February 2010), para 31.

20 See now Council Regulation (EC) 1234/2007, OJ 2007 L 299/1, art 74. For earlier provision to like effect, see, eg, Council Regulation (EEC) 3950/92, OJ 1992 L 405/1, Preamble, which referred to 'the principle linking reference quantities to holdings'.

21 Council Regulation (EC) 1234/2007, OJ 2007 L 299/1, Preamble (37). The general rule that milk quota is attached to land has also been consistently defended by the CJEU: see, eg, Case C-98/91 *Herbrink v Minister van Landbouw, Natuurbeheer en Visserij* [1994] ECR I-223, [1994] 3 CMLR 645, ECJ; and Case C-15/95 *EARL de Kerlast v Unicopa* [1997] ECR I-1961; and see further para 49.21. On the other hand, as also recognised in the current legislation, the general rule that milk quotas are transferred with the holding has been subject to numerous exceptions (for example, temporary transfers and transfers with a view to improving the structure of milk production: see now Council Regulation (EC) 1234/2007, OJ 2007 L 299/1, art 73 and art 74(1)(e)); and this has prompted advocacy that milk quota may be regarded as an asset distinct from the land: see, eg, Case C-186/96 *Demand v Hauptzollamt Trier* [1998] ECR I-8529, Opinion, para 39, where Advocate General Ruiz-Jarabo Colomer stated that 'the relaxation of the conditions governing the transfer of quotas reinforces the concept which traders legitimately have of the quota as an autonomous valuable asset. In those circumstances, and in spite of the great differences in regard to this matter between the individual national legal orders, I believe that milk quotas must currently be regarded as authentic intangible assets'.

22 See, eg, the written observations of the European Commission in Case 5/88 *Wachauf v Bundesamt für Ernährung und Forstwirtschaft* [1989] ECR 2609, [1991] 1 CMLR 328, ECJ.

23 Case C-434/08 *Harms v Heidinga* (Opinion delivered on 4 February 2010), para 31.

24 (2010) SLC/233/08, para 103.

25 Case C-38/94 [1995] ECR I-3875, [1996] 2 CMLR 193, ECJ.

26 See, eg, Council Regulation (EEC) 1837/80, OJ 1980 L 183/1, Preamble and art 5(1).

27 HM Revenue and Customs, *Tax Bulletin: Special Edition – Single Payment Scheme* (June 2005).

28 HM Revenue and Customs, *Tax Bulletin: Special Edition – Single Payment Scheme* (June 2005), 4. The position may, however, be more complex. For example, as shall be seen, the level of activity may be considered insufficient to constitute the carrying on of a trade (as when the land is simply being maintained in good agricultural and environmental condition): see para 52.26. In such circumstances, status as trading income may be denied. See also D Rennie 'The Legal Nature of Single Farm Payment Entitlement' (2011) 171 *Farm Law* 16–20, 20.

29 HM Revenue and Customs, *Tax Bulletin: Special Edition – Single Payment Scheme* (June 2005), 5. Comparison may be drawn with the treatment of milk quota as a separate asset for Capital Gains Tax purposes in *Cottle v Coldicott* [1995] STC (SCD) 239; and *Foxton v Revenue and Customs Comrs* [2005] STC (SCD) 661. See para 49.22.

30 See paras 52.24–52.33.

Rural development

52.15 The Agenda 2000 reforms saw formal constitution of rural development as the 'Second Pillar' of the Common Agricultural Policy, taking its place alongside the 'First Pillar', which comprises market management measures and direct payments (and which includes now the Single Farm Payment)[1]. That said, notwithstanding the transfer of funds from the 'First Pillar' to the 'Second Pillar' through modulation, expenditure on rural development remains significantly less than that on market management measures and direct payments. As has been seen, provisional United Kingdom figures for 2009 indicated that the Single Farm Payment accounted for some £2,950 million, as compared with just £630 million in total for the two main rural development schemes (namely, agri-environmental schemes and less-favoured areas support schemes)[2].

The current regulatory framework for rural development was originally laid down by Council Regulation (EC) 1698/2005[3], as supplemented by Strategic Guidelines for Rural Development, adopted on 20 February 2006[4]. This regime has in essence preserved the pre-existing range of rural development measures, but they are now ordered under four heads or 'Axes':

(a)   Axis 1 addresses improving the competitiveness of the agricultural and forestry sector;
(b)   Axis 2 addresses improving the environment and the countryside;
(c)   Axis 3 addresses the quality of life in rural areas and diversification of the rural economy; and
(d)   Axis 4 addresses the Leader initiative[5].

As between these Axes it is expressly provided that, in principle, at least 10% of European Community funding must be spent on Axis 1 and Axis 3, at least 25% on Axis 2 and at least 5% on Axis 4[6].

At the time of the 'Health Check', 'new challenges' faced by the Common Agricultural Policy were identified as climate change, bio-energy and water management[7]. Accordingly, Council Regulation (EC) 1698/2005 was amended to place Member States under an obligation, as from 1 January 2010, to provide in their rural development programmes, in accordance with their specific needs, for types of operations having as their priorities, inter alia, climate change, renewable energies and water management[8]. Similarly, the Strategic Guidelines for Rural Development were amended, so as to highlight, for example, the important contribution that agriculture and forestry could make in the provision of feedstock for bio-energy, carbon sequestration and, more generally, the further reduction of greenhouse gas emissions[9].

The English and Welsh rural development measures which have proved of greatest relevance to tenants are as follows:

(i)   under Axis 1, measures to modernise agricultural holdings, measures to help farmers to adapt to demanding standards based on European Community legislation and measures to support farmers who participate in food quality schemes;

(ii) under Axis 2, payments to farmers in areas with handicaps (other than mountain areas)[10], Natura 2000 payments[11], payments linked to the Water Framework Directive[12], agri-environmental payments and animal welfare payments; and

(iii) under Axis 3, measures to support diversification into non-agricultural activities.

It may also be reiterated that such rural development support should be clearly distinguished from direct payments (including the Single Farm Payment) under Council Regulation (EC) 73/2009. As highlighted, they fall under separate 'Pillars' of the Common Agricultural Policy; and of particular note is the fact that receipt of agri-environmental payments or animal welfare payments is dependent upon undertaking voluntary obligations which extend beyond the compulsory cross-compliance requirements as attached to both the Single Farm Payment and other direct payments[13].

[1] For the policy document which initiated the Agenda 2000 reforms, see European Commission *Agenda 2000: For a Stronger and Wider Union* COM(1997)2000 (and, in particular, Part One, III). For the legislation first implementing the 'Second Pillar', see Council Regulation (EC) 1257/1999, OJ 1999 L 160/80; and Commission Regulation (EC) 445/2002, OJ 2002 L 74/1. See also, generally, eg, J Moody and W Neville *Mid Term Review: a Practical Guide* (2004) Burges Salmon, Bristol, pp 176–179; and M Cardwell (2004) *The European Model of Agriculture* (2004) Oxford University Press, Oxford, pp 57–129.

[2] See para 52.1; and DEFRA *et al, Agriculture in the United Kingdom 2009* (2010) DEFRA, London, Table 11.1.

[3] OJ 2005 L 277/1. For the detailed rules, see, in particular, Commission Regulation (EC) 1974/2006, OJ 2006 L 368/15.

[4] Council Decision 2006/144/EC of 20 February 2006, OJ 2006 L 55/20.

[5] 'Leader' is the acronym for '*Liaison entre actions de développement de l'économie rurale*'; and its focus has been the promotion of local rural development action groups. The regime as enacted under Council Regulation (EC) 1698/2005 had been preceded by: Leader I (EC Commission notice at OJ 1991 C 73/33); Leader II (EC Commission notice at OJ 1994 C 180/48); and Leader+ (EC Commission notice (as amended) at OJ 2000 C 139/5).

[6] Council Regulation (EC) 1698/2005, OJ 2005 L 277/1, art 17 (as amended by Council Regulation (EC) 74/2009, OJ 2009 L 30/100).

[7] See, eg, European Commission *Preparing for the 'Health Check' of the CAP Reform* COM(2007)722, 8–10. See also now European Commission *The CAP Towards 2010: Meeting the Food, Natural Resources and Territorial Challenges of the Future* COM(2010)672, which envisages that these new challenges will feature large in rural development programmes for the period 2013–2020.

[8] OJ 2005 L 277/1, art 16a (as amended by Council Regulation (EC) 74/2009, OJ 2009 L 30/100). See also the new Annex II, which contains an indicative list with types of operations and potential effects related to these priorities.

[9] Council Decision 2006/144/EC of 20 February 2006, OJ 2006 L 55/20 (as amended by Council Decision 2009/61/EC of 19 January 2009, OJ 2009 L 30/112); and, in particular, Annex, para 2.5(i).

[10] These payments replace payments in respect of less-favoured areas and areas with natural restrictions which were implemented under Council Regulation (EC) 1257/1999, OJ 1999 L 160/80, arts 13–21 (as amended by Council Regulation (EC) 1783/2003, OJ 2003 L 270/70). Introduction of the new regime under Council Regulation (EC) 1698/2005 has, however, proved problematic. In particular, the European Community institutions have been critical of the generous interpretation accorded to 'less-favoured areas' by some Member States: see, eg, Court of Auditors *Special Report No 4/2003 Concerning Rural Development Support for Less-favoured Areas* (2003). In order to resolve these difficulties of designation, it was initially provided that the earlier less-favoured areas regime was to continue until 1 January 2010: Council Regulation (EC) 1698/2005, OJ 2005 L 277/1, art 93; but it would now seem that the new designation system will not be implemented until 2014: see, eg, European Commission, *Rural Development Policy 2007–2013 –*

Commission Communication: 'Towards a Better Targeting of the Aid to Farmers in Areas with Natural Handicaps' (available at http://ec.europa.eu/agriculture/rurdev/lfa/comm/index_en.htm, accessed on 23 March 2011).

11   Natura 2000 payments are those made in order to advance the objectives of the Wild Birds Directive (Council Directive 79/409/EEC, OJ 1979 L 103/1) and the Habitats Directive (Council Directive 92/43/EEC, OJ 1992 L 206/7).

12   Directive 2000/60/EC of the European Parliament and of the Council, OJ 2000 L 327/1.

13   Council Regulation (EC) 1698/2005, OJ 2005 L 277/1, arts 39(2) and (3) and 40(1) and (2).

IMPLEMENTATION IN ENGLAND AND WALES

Introduction

52.16 In European Community law there has been increased focus on the principle of subsidiarity when implementing policy, this finding clear expression in the Treaty on European Union, where Article 5(3) now provides that 'in areas which do not fall within its exclusive competence, the Union shall act only if and in so far as the objectives of the proposed action cannot be achieved by the Member States, either at central level or at regional and local level'[1]. Thus, in the agricultural context, the Mid-term Review was understood to promote subsidiarity[2]; and the legislation governing the rural development regime, Council Regulation (EC) 1698/2005, expressly requires that 'Member States shall be responsible for implementing the rural development programmes at the appropriate territorial level, according to their own institutional arrangements, in accordance with this Regulation'[3]. On the other hand, the European Community institutions have consistently resisted the notion that this trend amounts to renationalisation of the Common Agricultural Policy[4]. Not least, even as the Single Payment Scheme was first introduced, specific measures addressed the potential for differing national implementation to lead to distortions of competition; and a clear illustration of such measures would be the requirement that Member States respect a framework at European Community level when implementing their cross-compliance obligations[5].

Against this background, seven areas may be identified where the European Community legislation has afforded particular discretion for the purposes of implementing the Single Payment Scheme in England and Wales:

(a)   regional implementation;
(b)   dairy premium and additional payments;
(c)   cross-compliance;
(d)   set-aside;
(e)   the detailed rules with which a farmer must comply in order to unlock payment entitlements;
(f)   additional modulation; and
(g)   determination of the minimum size of holding that may qualify for payment entitlement.

In this regard, it may be noted that, while the rules governing dairy premium and additional payments and set-aside are now largely of historic importance, they have had a material impact upon the number of payment entitlements which may currently be held by individual farmers and, for that reason, would seem worthy of consideration.

1   On subsidiarity, generally, see, eg, A Estrella, *The EU Principle of Subsidiarity and its Critique* (2002) Oxford University Press, Oxford.
2   See, eg, European Commission *Mid-term Review of the Common Agricultural Policy* COM(2002)394, 3.
3   OJ 2005 L 277/1, art 7.
4   See, eg, European Commission *Mid-term Review of the Common Agricultural Policy* COM(2002)394, 2; and Commissioner Fischler, Speech/03/356, *CAP Reform*, Brussels, 9 July 2003 (available at http://europa.eu/rapid).
5   For the original legislation, see Council Regulation (EC) 1782/2003, OJ 2003 L 270/1, art 5 and Annex IV; and see further para 52.5.

Regional implementation

52.17 As has been seen, the major choice for Member States was whether or not to implement the Single Payment Scheme on a regional basis[1]. In the case of the United Kingdom, the decision was taken to do so[2]. Northern Ireland, Scotland and Wales each became a separate region[3]; and England has been divided into three further regions: moorland; the severely disadvantaged area, excluding moorland; and all other land[4].

In turn, as has also been seen, regional implementation permitted the Member State, in duly justified cases and according to objective criteria, to opt for allocation of the Single Farm Payment on a flat-rate basis per eligible hectare within a particular region[5]. This option was exercised in respect of the three English regions. However, rather than imposing the flat-rate basis immediately as from 2005, it was also decided that there should be a phased transition from the historic basis over an eight-year period[6]. This graduated approach was designed to prevent too swift redistribution of support away from farmers with high historic entitlements and to allow the industry better to adapt to the market[7]. Accordingly, in 2005 the flat-rate element of support was only 10%, as opposed to an historic element of 90%; but annual increases in the flat-rate element will remove any historic element by 2012[8].

Year	Flat-rate element	Historic element
2005	10%	90%
2006	15%	85%
2007	30%	70%
2008	45%	55%
2009	60%	40%
2010	75%	25%
2011	90%	10%
2012	100%	0%

In Wales the historic basis was retained, as also in Scotland; but in Northern Ireland a 'hybrid static' model was adopted, with a fixed proportion of flat-rate and historic entitlements[9]. In consequence, there is a significant level of variation throughout the United Kingdom, which has the capacity to impact adversely on individual farmers, most particularly in border areas[10]. In this context, it may be recalled that the Welsh Assembly Government has decided to continue to operate the Single Payment Scheme on the historic basis even after the 'Health Check'[11].

As indicated, where the flat-rate basis was adopted, the amount of entitlement enjoyed by a farmer is determined by multiplying the total flat-rate amount for the region by the number of 'eligible hectares'[12]. As a general rule, the number of eligible hectares was to be established using the number of hectares declared for the first year of application of the Single Payment Scheme[13]. Accordingly, for English (and Northern Irish) farmers their 2005 declarations were critical. Further, during the English 2005–2012 transition period, any historic element will be loaded onto those same eligible hectares. This land should be entered on the Rural Land Register, whose creation pre-dated the Mid-term Review.

[1] Council Regulation (EC) 1782/2003, OJ 2003 L 270/1, art 58; and see further para 52.9.
[2] By July 2003 it was already clear that regional implementation would be the policy choice: see, eg, Department for Environment, Food and Rural Affairs Press Release 301/03, *Government Presses Ahead With Consultation on Farm Reforms*, 22 July 2003.
[3] For Northern Ireland, see the Common Agricultural Policy Single Payment and Support Schemes Regulations (Northern Ireland) 2005, SR 2005/256, reg 3 (and see now the Common Agricultural Policy Single Payment and Support Schemes Regulations (Northern Ireland) 2010, SR 2010/161, reg 3); for Scotland, see the Common Agricultural Policy Single Farm Payment and Support Schemes (Scotland) Regulations 2005, SSI 2005/143, reg 3 (as now amended by the Common Agricultural Policy Single Farm Payment and Support Schemes and Cross-Compliance) (Scotland) Amendment Regulations 2009, SSI 2009/391); and, for Wales, see the Common Agricultural Policy Single Payment and Support Schemes (Wales) Regulations 2005, SI 2005/360 (W.29), reg 3 (and see now the Common Agricultural Policy Single Payment and Support Schemes (Wales) Regulations 2010, SI 2010/1892 (W.185), reg 3).
[4] Hansard (HC) 22 April 2004, Vol 420, Cols 26–28WS (Written Statement: Secretary of State for Environment, Food and Rural Affairs); and the Common Agricultural Policy Single Payment and Support Schemes Regulations 2005, SI 2005/219, reg 3 (and see now the Common Agricultural Policy Single Payment and Support Schemes Regulations 2010, SI 2010/540, reg 2). Originally it had been proposed that there be two regions (severely disadvantaged areas and all other land): Announcement by the Secretary of State for Environment, Food and Rural Affairs, Hansard (HC) 12 February 2004, Vol 417, Col 1586.
[5] Council Regulation (EC) 1782/2003, OJ 2003 L 270/1, art 59; and see further para 52.9.
[6] This was permitted by Council Regulation (EC) 1782/2003, OJ 2003 L 270/1, art 63(3); and, for current authority to like effect, see Council Regulation (EC) 73/2009, OJ 2009 L 30/16, art 48(2).
[7] Announcement by the Secretary of State for Environment, Food and Rural Affairs, Hansard (HC) 12 February 2004, Vol 417, Col 1586.
[8] The Common Agricultural Policy Single Payment and Support Schemes Regulations 2005, SI 2005/219, reg 8 and Sch 1 (and see now the Common Agricultural Policy Single Payment and Support Schemes Regulations 2010, SI 2010/540, reg 6 (which addresses also the further integration of coupled support into the Single Payment Scheme)).
[9] For the Northern Irish provisions, see the Common Agricultural Policy Single Payment and Support Schemes Regulations (Northern Ireland) 2005, SR 2005/256, reg 8 and Sch 1.
[10] Concern at potential distortion of competition was articulated from the moment that these decisions were announced: Hansard (HC) 12 February 2004, Vol 417, Col 1588 (Theresa May).
[11] See, eg, *Answers to the Written Assembly Questions for Answer on 12 February 2010* (available at http://www.assemblywales.org/bus-home/bus-chamber/bus-chamber-third-assembly-written.htm?act=dis&id=168114&ds=2/2010, accessed on 26 February 2011); and see further para 52.9.

¹² For the definition of 'eligible hectares', see Council Regulation (EC) 1782/2003, OJ 2003 L 270/1, art 44(2) (and see now Council Regulation (EC) 73/2009, OJ 2009 L 30/16, art 34(2)); and see further paras 52.9 and 52.10.
¹³ Commission Regulation (EC) 795/2004, OJ 2004 L 141/1, art 38(1).

Dairy premium

52.18 Another choice for Member States which opted for the regional basis of allocation was whether or not to incorporate the dairy premium and additional payments into the Single Payment Scheme ab initio (rather than, under the general rule, as from 2007)¹. In both England and Wales, this derogation was exercised². For English dairy producers such decisions have not worked to their advantage. The dairy premium and additional payments were directed to compensate them specifically for reductions in the intervention price in the dairy sector; and yet those payments have been subsumed within regional flat-rate payments which will benefit equally all farmers.

¹ Council Regulation (EC) 1782/2003, OJ 2003 L 270/1, art 62; and see further para 52.13. It may be noted that, where a Member State opted for the regional basis of allocation, these payments could be incorporated into the Single Payment Scheme ab initio, whether or not payment entitlements were allocated within a particular region on an historic or on a flat-rate basis.
² For England, see the Common Agricultural Policy Single Payment and Support Schemes Regulations 2005, SI 2005/219, reg 7; and, for Wales, see the Common Agricultural Policy Single Payment and Support Schemes (Wales) Regulations 2005, SI 2005/360 (W.29), reg 7. Indeed, the same approach was adopted in both Northern Ireland and Scotland: see respectively the Common Agricultural Policy Single Payment and Support Schemes Regulations (Northern Ireland) 2005, SR 2005/256, reg 7; and the Common Agricultural Policy Single Farm Payment and Support Schemes (Scotland) Regulations 2005, SSI 2005/143, reg 7.

Cross-compliance

52.19 As again indicated, under the Mid-term Review a wide range of cross-compliance obligations became applicable; and these affect all direct payments, not just the Single Farm Payment¹. Importantly, the cross-compliance obligations extend not just to the statutory management requirements, but also to the maintenance of all agricultural land in good agricultural and environmental condition: and, in this latter context, Member States have been accorded considerable discretion, provided always that they respect the framework established at European Community level, which expressly stipulates that they must take into account the specific characteristics of the areas concerned, including soil and climatic condition, existing farm systems, land use, crop rotation, farming practices and farm structures².

In the United Kingdom such discretion has been reflected in the imposition of different cross-compliance obligations in England, Northern Ireland, Scotland and Wales³. However, as recognised by the European Commission, '[s]triking the appropriate balance between a common EU framework, on the one hand, and local specific situations, on the other, is one of the most important challenges faced by the system'⁴. Indeed, in the case of *R (on the application of Horvath) v Secretary of State for Environment, Food and Rural Affairs* the variation between the English and other cross-compliance obligations gave rise to challenge, on the basis of discrimination[5]. In particular, the English regulations required farmers to maintain visible public rights of way, a requirement not found elsewhere in the United Kingdom[6]. The CJEU first considered whether a Member State could in any event include the maintenance of visible public rights of way among its standards for good agricultural and environmental condition[7]. This question was answered in the affirmative: *visible* public rights of way were found to constitute 'landscape features', with the result that, in accordance with the European Community legislation, the maintenance requirements would be valid inasmuch as they contributed to their retention as landscape features or, as the case may be, to the avoidance of the deterioration of habitats. The CJEU then went on to consider the broader issue, namely whether devolved administrations (as in Northern Ireland, Scotland and Wales) could impose different obligations. In this regard, it was held to be 'settled case-law that each Member State is free to allocate powers internally and to implement Community acts which are not directly applicable by means of measures adopted by regional or local authorities'[8]. Accordingly, 'where the constitutional system of a Member State provides that devolved administrations in a Member State are to have legislative competence, the mere adoption by those administrations of different [good agricultural and environmental condition] standards ... does not constitute discrimination contrary to Community law'[9]. And since, in principle, agricultural matters fall within the competence of the devolved administrations of the United Kingdom, the contested provisions did not give rise to discrimination. That said, it may also be noted that there was no discussion whether divergences between measures laid down by devolved administrations should be justified in accordance with objective criteria[10].

On the other hand, more generally the United Kingdom Government has been swift to affirm that the burden imposed by cross-compliance obligations is 'relatively light ... representing a mixture of common-sense farming practice and support for existing legislation'[11]. In this may be detected an awareness of criticism that the United Kingdom has 'gold-plated' legislation emanating from Brussels. And, as has been seen, the detailed cross-compliance rules applicable in England are currently set out in the Agriculture (Cross compliance) (No 2) Regulations 2009[12], while those currently applicable in Wales are set out in the Common Agricultural Policy Single Payment and Support Schemes (Cross Compliance) (Wales) Regulations 2004[13].

Many of the detailed rules for maintenance of the land in good agricultural and environmental condition are no more than might be expected as an integral part of good farming practice: for example, the control of field thistles or Japanese knotweed[14]. Likewise, other provisions do no more than reinforce existing legislation: for example, obligations relating to crop burning under the Crop (Residues) Burning Regulations 1993[15] and obligations relating to the removal of hedges under the Hedgerows Regulations 1997[16]. This has led to more general criticism that cross-compliance obligations realise little public benefit[17]; and such criticism would appear particularly strong in the case of the statutory management requirements, which are limited to pre-existing measures: indeed, the European Commission has expressly acknowledged that they do not create new obligations[18].

That said, in the case of the requirement that farmers maintain all agricultural land in good agricultural and environmental condition, there is more than an element of novelty. Perhaps most notably, land must be so maintained even if it is not in agricultural production; and in this regard both the English and Welsh implementing legislation impose specific obligations[19]. By way of example, a farmer must generally cut down any scrub or cut down or graze any rank vegetation on all agricultural land not in agricultural production at least once every five years; and, with only limited exception, there must be no application of inorganic fertiliser. Moreover, even where the land is in agricultural production, more extensive environmental protection may be accorded. Thus, as a general rule, in England a farmer must not cultivate or apply fertilisers or pesticides to land within two metres of the centre of a hedgerow, watercourse or field ditch[20].

A significant factor is that the penalties for breach of cross-compliance obligations are additional to those exacted under any of the European Community legislation which together comprise the statutory management requirements[21]. Accordingly, they constitute a further and robust incentive to reach the standard of good agricultural practice, not least because the penalties for their breach may, in an extreme case, lead to total exclusion from one or several aid schemes for one or more calendar years[22].

[1]   See para 52.5; and, for first implementation in England and Wales, see C Rodgers *Agricultural Law* (2008) 3rd Edition, Tottel Publishing, Haywards Heath, pp 607–620.

[2]   Council Regulation (EC) 73/2009, OJ 2009 L 30/16, art 6(1) (replacing Council Regulation (EC) 1782/2003, OJ 2003 L 270/1, art 5(1)).

[3]   See respectively the Agriculture (Cross compliance) (No 2) Regulations 2009, SI 2009/3365 (as amended by SI 2010/2941) (replacing the Agriculture (Cross compliance) Regulations 2009, SI 2009/3264, which in turn replaced the Common Agricultural Policy Single Payment and Support Schemes (Cross-compliance) (England) Regulations 2005, SI 2005/3459 (as amended by SI 2006/3254, SI 2007/2003, SI 2007/2500 and SI 2008/80), which in turn replaced the Common Agricultural Policy Single Payment and Support Schemes (Cross Compliance) (England) Regulations 2004, SI 2004/3196 (as amended by SI 2005/918)); the Common Agricultural Policy Single Payment and Support Schemes (Cross Compliance) Regulations (Northern Ireland) 2005, SR 2005/6 (as amended by SR 2006/459, SR 2009/316 and SR 2010/174); the Common Agricultural Policy Schemes (Cross-Compliance) (Scotland) Regulations 2004, SSI 2004/518 (as amended by SSI 2005/143, SSI 2005/225, SSI 2007/99, SSI 2008/100, SSI 2008/184 and SSI 2009/391); and the Common Agricultural Policy Single Payment and Support Schemes (Cross Compliance) (Wales) Regulations 2004, SI 2004/3280 (W.284) (as amended by SI 2005/3367 (W.264), SI 2006/2831 (W.252), SI 2007/970 (W.87) and SI 2010/38 (W.11)).

[4]   European Commission *Report from the Commission to the Council on the Application of the System of Cross-compliance* COM(2007)147, 3.

[5]   Case C-428/07 R *(on the application of Horvath) v Secretary of State for Environment, Food and Rural Affairs* [2009] ECR I-6355, [2009] NLJR 1106, ECJ; and see also M Cardwell and J Hunt 'Public Rights of Way and Level Playing Fields' (2010) 12 *Environmental Law Review* 291–300.

[6]   For the regulations concerned, see the Common Agricultural Policy Single Payment and Support Schemes (Cross Compliance) (England) Regulations 2004, SI 2004/3196 (the requirement to maintain visible public rights of way being set out in the Schedule, paras 26–29).

[7]   For the European Community legislation concerned, see Council Regulation (EC) 1782/2003, OJ 2003 L 270/1, Annex IV (and see now Council Regulation (EC) 73/2009, OJ 2009 L 30/16, Annex III).

[8]   Case C-428/07 R *(on the application of Horvath) v Secretary of State for Environment, Food and Rural Affairs* [2009] ECR I-6355, para 50.

9   Case C-428/07 R *(on the application of Horvath) v Secretary of State for Environment, Food and Rural Affairs* [2009] ECR I-6355, para 58.
10   It may be observed that, if a Member State imposes regionally differentiated rates of voluntary modulation, such differentiation must be in accordance with objective criteria: Council Regulation (EC) 378/2007, OJ 2007 L 95/1, art 3(1); and see further para 52.22.
11   Hansard (HC) 22 July 2004, Vol 424, Col 69WS (Written Statement: Secretary of State for Environment, Food and Rural Affairs).
12   The Agriculture (Cross compliance) (No 2) Regulations 2009, SI 2009/3365 (as amended by SI 2010/2941).
13   The Common Agricultural Policy Single Payment and Support Schemes (Cross Compliance) (Wales) Regulations 2004, SI 2004/3280 (W.284) (as amended by SI 2005/3367 (W.264), SI 2006/2831 (W.252), SI 2007/970 (W.87) and SI 2010/38 (W.11)).
14   See, eg, in the case of England, the Agriculture (Cross compliance) (No 2) Regulations 2009, SI 2009/3365, Sch 1 para 6 (as amended by SI 2010/2941).
15   SI 1993/1366 (and, for the relevant cross-compliance provision in England, see the Agriculture (Cross compliance) (No 2) Regulations 2009, SI 2009/3365, Sch 1 para 1).
16   SI 1997/1160 (as amended by SI 2003/2155) (and, for the relevant cross-compliance provision in England, see the Agriculture (Cross compliance) (No 2) Regulations 2009, SI 2009/3365, Sch 1 para 1).
17   See, eg, GFA-RACE Partners Limited in Association with IEEP, *Impacts of CAP Reform Agreement on Diverse Water Pollution from Agriculture* (Department for Environment, Food and Rural Affairs, London, 2004) (which concluded that the pressure to impose light cross-compliance obligations would preclude any major effect on nitrate pollution).
18   European Commission *Report from the Commission to the Council on the Application of the System of Cross-compliance* COM(2007)147, 3.
19   See respectively the Agriculture (Cross compliance) (No 2) Regulations 2009, SI 2009/3365, Sch 1 para 5 (as amended by SI 2010/2941); and the Common Agricultural Policy Single Payment and Support Schemes (Cross Compliance) (Wales) Regulations 2004, SI 2004/3280 (W.284), Sch para 7 (as amended by SI 2010/38 (W.11)).
20   The Agriculture (Cross compliance) (No 2) Regulations 2009, SI 2009/3365, Sch 1 para 8(1)(a). It was recognised by the United Kingdom Government ab initio that such measures would be controversial, but it was pointed out that there would be the benefit of 'double counting', in that their observance would also meet the requirements of the hedgerow management options for the purposes of Entry Level Stewardship, as was to be introduced under the Environmental Stewardship (England) Regulations 2005, SI 2005/621: Hansard (HC) 22 July 2004, Vol 424, Col 69WS (Written Statement: Secretary of State for Environment, Food and Rural Affairs).
21   For clear statement to this effect in the legislation which first implemented the statutory management requirements, see, eg, Council Regulation (EC) 1782/2003, OJ 2003 L 270/1, Preamble, Recital (2): '[i]f those basic standards are not met, Member States should withdraw direct aid in whole or in part on the basis of criteria that are proportionate, objective and graduated. Such withdrawal should be without prejudice to sanctions laid down now or in the future under other provisions of Community or national law'.
22   See now Council Regulation (EC) 73/2009, OJ 2009 L 30/16, art 24.

Set-aside

52.20   Since the decision was taken in the case of England to implement the Single Payment Scheme on a flat-rate basis (albeit over a 2005–2012 transitional period), it became necessary to determine the set-aside rate under the detailed rules contained in Article 63(2) of Council Regulation (EC) 1782/2003, as opposed simply to applying under the general rule a three-year average over the 2000–2002 reference period[1].

The operation of these detailed rules resulted in there being no set-aside obligation for the moorland region, a 1.3% rate for the region comprising severely disadvantaged areas (excluding moorland) and an 8% rate for the region comprising all other land[2]. Thus, even the highest rate was lower than the general 10% rate. The reason for this was that a greater proportion of land has become subject to set-aside obligations, since, as has been seen, they now extend to, for example, temporary grass and fodder crops[3]. In consequence, the lower rates have secured the same overall volume of land set aside.

In addition, national legislation provided detailed rules governing the management of land set aside. In England these rules were contained in the Common Agricultural Policy Single Payment Scheme (Set-aside) (England) Regulations 2004[4]; and in Wales they were contained in the Common Agricultural Policy Single Payment Scheme (Set-aside) (Wales) Regulations 2005[5]. In large part they continued the obligations applicable under the earlier Arable Area Payments Scheme[6].

It may be reiterated that the compulsory set-aside obligation was first temporarily lifted for 2008 and then permanently abolished at the time of the 'Health Check', with the result that set-aside entitlements have now lost their distinctiveness[7].

[1] Council Regulation (EC) 1782/2003, OJ 2003 L 270/1, art 63(2); and see para 52.9.
[2] Hansard (HC) 22 July 2004, Vol 424, Col 71WS (Written Statement: Secretary of State for Environment, Food and Rural Affairs).
[3] See para 52.9.
[4] SI 2004/3385 (as amended by SI 2005/3460 and SI 2007/633).
[5] SI 2005/45 (W.4) (as amended by SI 2006/3101 (W.285)).
[6] The Arable Area Payments Regulations 1996, SI 1996/3142 (as amended by SI 1997/2969, SI 1998/3169 and SI 1999/8).
[7] See Council Regulation (EC) 1107/2007, OJ 2007 L 253/1; and Council Regulation (EC) 73/2009, OJ 2009 L 30/16, Preamble (30). See further para 52.9.

Detailed rules for unlocking payment entitlements

52.21 The European Community rules which govern the unlocking of payment entitlements are relatively generous. As already seen, farmers can receive payment by matching their payment entitlements against 'eligible hectares'; and 'eligible hectares' are broadly defined[1]. Production is not a pre-requisite; and, if a farmer does undertake production, payment entitlements may be matched against land used to grow a wide range of crops, including certain energy crops, with this range having recently been expanded following general incorporation of the fruit and vegetables sector into the Single Payment Scheme.

Detailed rules, however, afford some discretion to Member States. First, as noted, non-agricultural activities on 'eligible hectares' are permitted, so long as the predominant use remains for agricultural activities, with the relevant test being whether the 'agricultural activity can be exercised without being significantly hampered by the intensity, nature, duration and timing of the non-agricultural activity'[2]. Importantly, in this context, the detailed criteria are to be established at the level of the Member States[3]. As a consequence, in both England and Wales extensive guidance has been provided[4].

311

In essence, non-agricultural activities are divided into three categories. The first category comprises activities which are permitted without restriction, such as walking, bird watching and school or university nature or farm visits. The second category comprises activities which are allowed up to a 28-day limit, such as clay shooting, car boot sales, country fairs and shows, festivals and events, car parking and motor sports. The third category comprises activities which preclude payment entitlements being matched against the land, such as golf courses, other permanent sports facilities, gallops or airstrips. The restrictions in respect of the second and third categories apply throughout the calendar year.

Secondly, Member States also enjoy some latitude when determining the date at which the 'eligible hectares' must be at the disposal of the farmer. In this context, it may be reiterated that, under the current regime, it is no longer necessary for the land to be at the disposal of the farmer for a period of at least ten months[5]. In any event, the date fixed by the Member State must be no later than the date fixed in that Member State for amending the aid application[6]. In England the date currently fixed is the last day when the single application for direct payments can be submitted to the competent authority[7]; and in Wales the date currently fixed is 15 May[8].

[1]   See now Council Regulation (EC) 73/2009, OJ 2009 L 30/16, art 34(2); and see para 52.10.
[2]   Commission Regulation (EC) 1120/2009, OJ 2009 L 316/1, art 9.
[3]   Commission Regulation (EC) 1120/2009, OJ 2009 L 316/1, art 9.
[4]   See, respectively, Rural Payments Agency *Single Payment Scheme Handbook for England 2011 and 2012*, Rural Payments Agency and DEFRA, 2011, pp 20–22; and Welsh Assembly Government *2010 Single Application Rules Booklet*, Welsh Assembly Government, 2010, pp 16–17 (these rules, subject to amendment, also being applicable for 2011).
[5]   For the earlier legislation, see Council Regulation (EC) 1782/2003, OJ 2003 L 270/1, art 44(3); and see para 52.10.
[6]   Council Regulation (EC) 73/2009, OJ 2009 L 30/16, art 35(1).
[7]   The Common Agricultural Policy Single Payment and Support Schemes Regulations 2010, SI 2010/540, reg 5. This is determined by Council Regulation (EC) 1122/2009, OJ 2009 L 316/65, art 11 (and would generally be 15 May).
[8]   The Common Agricultural Policy Single Payment and Support Schemes (Wales) Regulations 2010, SI 2010/1892 (W.185), reg 6.

Voluntary modulation

52.22   It has been seen that under European Community rules a proportion of all direct payments are to be compulsorily deducted each year, so as to increase the level of financing for rural development measures[1]; and that, following the 'Health Check', the compulsory rates were applied to amounts in excess of 5,000 Euros per year and raised to 7% in 2009, 8% in 2010, 9% in 2011 and 10% in 2012, with a further 4% being deducted for amounts in excess of 300,000 Euros[2].

However, it may also be re-emphasised that Member States have for some time been granted the option to impose voluntary modulation, over and above compulsory levels. Initially, such option was granted where Member States had already introduced voluntary modulation prior to the Mid-term Review[3]. The United Kingdom met this criterion and in England an additional 2% was transferred to finance rural development measures in 2005, the proportion being increased to 6% in 2006[4]. When combined with the compulsory rate, this led to an overall reduction of 5% in 2005 and 10% in 2006. In Wales voluntary modulation was likewise imposed, but the additional percentages were lower: 1.5% in 2005 and 0.5% in 2006[5].

It may further be recalled that European Community legislation enacted in 2007 authorised far more extensive voluntary modulation, at rates of up to 20%, where the Member State was already applying additional reductions[6]. The European Community legislation also authorised Member States to differentiate rates between regions according to objective criteria if the Single Payment Scheme was being operated on a regional basis[7]. Since in the United Kingdom additional reductions were already being applied and the Single Payment Scheme was being operated on a regional basis, there was the opportunity both to impose such voluntary modulation and to differentiate rates between regions. In England an additional rate of 12% was introduced in 2007, rising to 13% in 2008 and then to remain at 14% from 2009 to 2012[8]. As justification for this decision, much weight was placed upon the need to secure funding for the Rural Development Programme for England 2007–2013 and, in particular, agri-environmental schemes[9]. In Wales the additional rates were again to be lower: 0% in 2007; 2.5% in 2008; 4.2% in 2009; 5.8% in 2010; and 6.5% in 2011 and 2012[10].

More recently, it has been necessary to address the consequences of the increase in compulsory rates as imposed by the 'Health Check'. As has been seen, these new compulsory rates, when combined with voluntary modulation, were considered capable of creating an excessive burden for farmers, so leading to a reduction in the levels of voluntary modulation under European Community legislation[11]. Accordingly, the amounts of modulation as currently authorised in England and Wales are as follows[12]:

England
Amounts up to and including €5,000

Year	EU modulation	Voluntary modulation	Total modulation
2009	0%	14%	14%
2010	0%	14%	14%
2011	0%	14%	14%
2012	0%	14%	14%

Amounts over €5,000 and up to and including €300,000

Year	EU modulation	Voluntary modulation	Total modulation
2009	7%	12%	19%
2010	8%	11%	19%
2011	9%	10%	19%
2012	10%	9%	19%

52.22 *Payments to Farmers under the Common Agricultural Policy*

Amounts over €300,000

Year	EU modulation	Voluntary modulation	Total modulation
2009	11%	8%	19%
2010	12%	7%	19%
2011	13%	6%	19%
2012	14%	5%	19%

Wales

For amounts up to and including €5,000

Year	EU modulation	Voluntary modulation	Total modulation
2009	0%	4.2%	4.2%
2010	0%	5.8%	5.8%
2011	0%	6.5%	6.5%
2012	0%	6.5%	6.5%

For amounts over €5,000 and up to and including €300,000

Year	EU modulation	Voluntary modulation	Total modulation
2009	7%	2.2%	9.2%
2010	8%	2.8%	10.8%
2011	9%	2.5%	11.5%
2012	10%	1.5%	11.5%

For amounts over €300,000

Year	EU modulation	Voluntary modulation	Total modulation
2009	11%	0%	11%
2010	12%	0%	12%
2011	13%	0%	13%
2012	14%	0%	14%

1   See para 52.6.
2   Council Regulation (EC) 73/2009, OJ 2009 L 30/16, art 7 (replacing Council Regulation (EC) 1782/2003, OJ 2003 L 270/1, art 10).
3   For the European Community legislation concerned, see Commission Regulation (EC) 1655/2004, OJ 2004 L 298/3.
4   The Common Agricultural Policy Single Payment and Support Schemes Regulations 2005, SI 2005/219, reg 11.
5   The Common Agricultural Policy Single Payment and Support Schemes (Wales) Regulations 2005, SI 2005/360 (W.29), reg 10.
6   Council Regulation (EC) 378/2007, OJ 2007 L 95/1; and see para 52.6.
7   Council Regulation (EC) 378/2007, OJ 2007 L 95/1, art 3(1). For operation of the Single Payment Scheme on a regional basis, see para 52.9.
8   Common Agricultural Policy Single Payment and Support Schemes Regulations 2005, SI 2005/219, reg 11 (as amended by SI 2007/3182).
9   Hansard (HC) 29 March 2007, Vol 458, Col 131WS (Written Statement: Secretary of State for Environment, Food and Rural Affairs).

¹⁰ For the voluntary modulation rates as then implemented in Northern Ireland, Scotland and Wales (as well as England), see Commission Decision 2007/679/EC of 22 October 2007, OJ 2007 L 280/25.

¹¹ Council Regulation (EC) 378/2007, OJ 2007 L 95/1, art 1 (as amended by Council Regulation (EC) 73/2009, OJ 2009 L 30/16); and see also Council Regulation (EC) 73/2009, OJ 2009 L 30/16, art 8. For the reduced amounts realised, see Commission Decision 2009/519/EC of 2 July 2009, OJ 2009 L 173/13.

¹² See, respectively, the Common Agricultural Policy Single Payment and Support Schemes Regulations 2010, SI 2010/540, Schedule; and the Common Agricultural Policy Single Payment and Support Schemes (Wales) Regulations 2010, SI 2010/1892 (W.185), Schedule.

Minimum size of holding

52.23 When the new direct payments regime was introduced under the Mid-term Review, Commission Regulation (EC) 795/2004 provided that Member States could decide to fix a minimum size per holding for which the establishment of payment entitlements might be requested, subject to the proviso that the minimum size was not to be higher than 0.3 of a hectare[1]. In both England and Wales the decision was taken to implement a minimum size of 0.3 of a hectare[2]. By the time of the 'Health Check', there was concern that a large number of farmers received small amounts of payments, these often being less than the administrative costs involved, while not all the recipients were genuine farmers[3]. In consequence, the legislation was revised to provide that Member States are not, in principle, to grant direct payments to a farmer either: (a) where the total amount in a calendar year is less than 100 Euros (this condition being applicable to farmers holding special entitlements)[4]; or (b) where the eligible area of the holding is less than one hectare[5]. The detailed provisions permit Member States to adjust these thresholds within specified limits in order to take account of the structure of their agricultural economies, with the specified limits in the United Kingdom being respectively 200 Euros and 5 hectares[6]. The policy choice in both England and Wales has been not to depart from the general rule laying down a minimum size of one hectare: but, in the case of farmers holding special entitlements, the minimum claim is 200 Euros in England, as opposed to only 100 Euros in Wales[7]. In this context, it may also be reiterated that neither the English nor the Welsh legislation impose criteria to ensure that direct payments are not granted to a natural or legal person whose agricultural activities form only an insignificant part of its overall economic activities or whose principal business or company objects do not consist of exercising an agricultural activity[8].

¹ OJ 2004 L 141/1, art 12(6). An exception was made in the case of payment entitlements subject to special conditions: art 12(7).

² See, respectively, the Common Agricultural Policy Single Payment and Support Schemes Regulations 2005, SI 2005/219, reg 5; and the Common Agricultural Policy Single Payment and Support Schemes (Wales) Regulations 2005, SI 2005/360 (W.29), reg 5. The same limit was imposed in Northern Ireland and in Scotland.

³ European Commission *Preparing for the 'Health Check' of the CAP Reform* COM(2007)722, 5.

⁴ For special entitlements, see para 52.9.

⁵ Council Regulation (EC) 73/2009, OJ 2009 L 30/16, art 28(1).

⁶ Council Regulation (EC) 73/2009, OJ 2009 L 30/16, art 28(1) and Annex VII.

⁷ See respectively the Common Agricultural Policy Single Payment and Support Schemes Regulations 2010, SI 2010/540, reg 4; and the Common Agricultural Policy Single Payment and Support Schemes (Wales) Regulations 2010, SI 2010/1892 (W.185), reg 5.

⁸ Council Regulation (EC) 73/2009, OJ 2009 L 30/16, art 28(2); and see further para 52.4.

LANDLORD AND TENANT ISSUES

General

52.24 While the Single Payment Scheme has had a major impact on the way agricultural land is farmed and on the profitability of farming enterprises, landlord and tenant issues do not feature large in the legislative framework itself. For example, unlike in the case of the milk quota legislation, there is no specific provision dealing with the position of payment entitlements on the termination of tenancies[1]. This would seem consistent with the fact that the Single Payment Scheme is characterised as 'income support scheme for farmers'[2]. Moreover, the CJEU has affirmed that, as a rule, landlord and tenant issues remain within the competence of the Member States[3].

That said, under the European Community legislation payment entitlements are not completely divorced from the land. For example, as has been seen, they must be matched against eligible hectares for their value to be unlocked; and, by reason of the cross-compliance regime, receipt is conditional upon performance of land management obligations[4]. Consequently, in the landlord and tenant context there is arguably the potential for a symbiotic relationship: the tenant, as the farmer exercising the agricultural activity[5], will be entitled to apply for the direct payments; and the landlord, owner of the eligible hectares[6], will be able to provide the land to unlock them. It is perhaps no coincidence, therefore, that a spirit of co-operation has been advocated. For example, in 2004 the Tenancy Reform Industry Group stressed that 'the parties should treat each other fairly in these matters as the best way to unlock value to their mutual benefit'[7].

For these reasons, the current legislative framework for direct payments has the capacity materially to affect numerous aspects of the landlord and tenant relationship; and seven such aspects may be considered:

(a) occupation of the land;
(b) use of the land and user clauses;
(c) termination of tenancies;
(d) quota protection clauses;
(e) rent review;
(f) transfers; and
(g) succession[8].

1   For the current provision governing the treatment of milk quotas on the termination of a tenancy, see Council Regulation (EC) 1234/2007, OJ 2007 L 299/1, art 74(4): '[w]here there is no agreement between the parties, in the case of tenancies due to expire without any possibility of renewal on similar terms, or in situations involving comparable legal effects, the individual quotas in question shall be transferred in whole or in part to the producer taking them over, in accordance with provisions adopted by the Member States, taking account of the legitimate interests of the parties'.
2   Council Regulation (EC) 73/2009, OJ 2009 L 30/16, art 1(b); and see para 52.14.
3   See, eg, Case C-2/92 *R v Ministry of Agriculture, Fisheries and Food, ex p Bostock* [1994] ECR I-955 at I-985: 'legal relations between lessees and lessors, in particular on the expiry of a lease, are, as Community law now stands, still governed by the law of the Member States in question'.
4   See para 52.14.

⁵ For the current definitions of 'farmer' and 'agricultural activity', see Council Regulation (EC) 73/2009, OJ 2009 L 30/16, art 2(a) and (c); and see para 52.4.
⁶ For the current definition of 'eligible hectares', see Council Regulation (EC) 73/2009, OJ 2009 L 30/16, art 34(2); and see para 52.10.
⁷ *Notes to Aid Tenants and Landlords on CAP Reform* (2004), para 35.
⁸ See generally, eg, J Moody and W Neville *Mid Term Review: a Practical Guide* (2004) Burges Salmon, Bristol, pp 196–213; Central Association of Agricultural Valuers *Mid Term Review: a Valuer's Interim Guide* (2004) Central Association of Agricultural Valuers, Coleford, pp 97–99; Central Association of Agricultural Valuers *Mid Term Review: a Valuer's Second Interim Guide* (2005) Central Association of Agricultural Valuers, Coleford, pp 119–130 and 135–137; and C Rodgers *Agricultural Law* (2008) 3rd Edition, Tottel Publishing, Haywards Heath, pp 81–91 and 600–625.

Occupation of the land

52.25 Where a farmer is a tenant, whether under the AHA 1986 or the ATA 1995, in the usual course he will be seeking to match his payment entitlements against the land comprised within the tenancy so as to secure receipt of the Single Farm Payment. For this purpose, the land should be entered on the Rural Land Register¹.

Under the legislation as first enacted, payment entitlements could only be matched against eligible hectares which were at the disposal of the farmer for a period of at least ten months (except in case of force majeure or exceptional circumstances)². However, this ten-month rule led to management difficulties, as was soon recognised by the European Commission³. By way of illustration, in the case of short-term tenancies for specialist cropping, there was the potential for both the landowner and the tenant mutually to exclude each other from meeting this criterion, in that, for example, a six-month tenancy for the growing season from 1 March to 31 August would leave neither party able to unlock the value of payment entitlements. The current legislation, accordingly, requires only that the land is at the disposal of the farmer (except in case of force majeure or exceptional circumstances) on a date fixed by the Member State, which must be no later than the date fixed in that Member State for amending the aid application⁴. As has been seen, in England and Wales, this will generally be 15 May in any given year⁵; and it would be wise for both landowners and tenants to ensure that there is a 'farmer' at that date with the eligible hectares at his disposal so as to make the requisite claim under the Single Payment Scheme⁶.

The position may be more complex if there is an agreement or arrangement for less than a tenancy. As a preliminary matter, it will be necessary to determine whether, notwithstanding the label, the agreement is indeed a tenancy under the test established in *Street v Mountford*⁷. Many of the grazing 'licences' which are still being granted would seem vulnerable on this account⁸. Accordingly, where there is grazing land and the landowner wishes himself to claim the Single Farm Payment, a better course might be an agistment agreement. This should arguably preserve the land at his disposal.

While in the absence of a tenancy it must be recognised that the term 'disposal' is likely to prove an elusive concept, in that the legislation itself gives no indication as to the degree of exclusivity required, considerable guidance has now been provided by the CJEU in *Landkreis Bad Dürkheim v Aufsichts- und Dienstleistungsdirektion*, which would seem to establish three propositions[9]. First, the parcels in question need not be at the disposal of the farmer pursuant to a lease or other similar transaction, with the parties also being free to provide, in the absence of a provision to the contrary, that such parcels be made available without monetary consideration[10]. Second, there was no requirement that the farmer should have unlimited power over the area in question, which could remain at his disposal despite the presence of certain restrictions (such as, on the facts, contractual restrictions imposed by a conservation authority on the nature and duration of his activities)[11]. Yet, it may also be highlighted that the CJEU emphasised that the farmer 'must enjoy a degree of autonomy with regard to that area sufficient for the carrying-out of his agricultural activity'[12]. While this was a matter for the national court to assess, it was stated that such agricultural activities would include maintenance of the land in good agricultural and environmental condition[13]. In this light, it would be wise for any agreement to be explicit as to which party is to undertake cross-compliance obligations; and there would be danger of artificiality if the same party does not, on the basis that the eligible hectares are at their disposal, make the claim for direct payments. Third, the CJEU held that 'the agricultural activity must be carried out on the land concerned in the farmer's name and on his behalf', this again being a matter for the national court to decide[14]. For such purposes, however, it was irrelevant that the farmer was also required to carry out certain tasks for a third party in return for payment[15]. Since the third party in question was a conservation body, this determination would tend to confirm that, even if a farmer were subject to multiple conditions as a result of his land having been dedicated as, for example, a Site of Special Scientific Interest, the land would still remain at his disposal for the purposes of the Single Payment Scheme.

Even more difficult considerations would seem to arise in the case of share farming and contracting agreements[16]. The case of *Landkreis Bad Dürkheim v Aufsichts- und Dienstleistungsdirektion* is of less assistance in such circumstances, since, as observed by the Advocate General, it related rather to the effect of conditions imposed on the use of the land[17]. The inherent complexity of competing claims was, nevertheless, expressly noted by the CJEU, where it affirmed that 'it is essential that no third party carry out any agricultural activity on the disputed areas [during the ten-month period]. In order to avoid the situation where a number of farmers claim allocation of the parcels concerned to their holding, those areas may not, during that period, be considered as allocated to other farmers' holdings for the purposes of the single payment scheme'[18]. In consequence, it becomes essential to ascertain which of the persons concerned qualifies as the 'farmer' of the eligible hectares. Much will depend on the individual terms of the contract and the manner in which the contract is then performed in practice, with the emphasis on substance rather than form. Otherwise, there would be a danger of artificiality, contrary to Article 30 of Council Regulation (EC) 73/2009[19].

As a rule, share farming agreements are not intended to confer exclusive possession and, accordingly, a tenancy on the working farmer. While, under the law of England and Wales, the land may thus instinctively appear to remain at the disposal of the landowner, such an interpretation may be difficult to square with the position that the Single Farm Payment is in essence an income support scheme for farmers carrying out an agricultural activity[20]. Such tension may be illustrated by the facts of the 1989 decision of the Court of Appeal in *McCarthy v Bence*[21]. In that share farming case, no tenancy agreement was found, yet in terms of the criteria for qualifying as a farmer under the Single Payment Scheme the activities undertaken by the landowner were relatively limited, the share farmer being responsible for exercising good husbandry over the area allocated. On the other hand, the activities under-taken by the landowner did include having dead elms felled and removed, having scrub and roots grubbed out and burned, ditching and spraying for thistles; and these may be equated with English and Welsh cross-compliance obligations[22], whose performance, as has been seen, the CJEU regard as a key factor in determining which party has the eligible hectares at their disposal[23]. Like principles would seem to apply to contracting agreements. Where the contractor simply undertakes operations at a fixed rate per hour, there should be sufficient control vested in the landowner to maintain the land at his disposal: for example, where a landowner without a combine employs a contractor to harvest his cereals. By contrast, if the landowner has in effect handed over control of the farming operations to the contractor, then it would be hard to show that the land was not at the disposal of the contractor[24].

Accordingly, so far as share farming and contracting agreements are con-cerned, there would seem to be no substitute for ensuring that both the agreement and subsequent practice determine with sufficient clarity that the land is at the disposal of one party. Further, as established by the CJEU, that party should not only have sufficient autonomy to be able to carry out their agricultural activity, but also be in a position to perform the required cross-compliance obligations[25]. However, achieving such certainty for the purposes of the Single Payment Scheme may generate uncertainty under landlord and tenant legislation.

[1] Land may be added to the Rural Land Register; but in England it was that registered for 2005 which fixed the total number of eligible hectares against which payment entitlements may be matched.

[2] Council Regulation (EC) 1782/2003, OJ 2003 L 270/1, art 44(3); and see para 52.10.

[3] See, eg, European Commission *Report from the Commission to the Council on the Application of the System of Cross-compliance* COM(2007)147, 9.

[4] Council Regulation (EC) 73/2009, OJ 2009 L 30/16, art 35(1).

[5] See para 52.21.

[6] C Rodgers *Agricultural Law* (2008) 3rd Edition, Tottel Publishing, Haywards Heath, pp 90–91.

[7] [1985] AC 809, [1985] 2 All ER 289, HL. For analysis of the decision and its importance, see, eg, S Bright, '*Street v Mountford* Revisited', in S Bright (ed.) *Landlord and Tenant Law: Past, Present and Future* (2006) Hart Publishing, Oxford, pp 19–39.

[8] See para 19.34ff.

[9] Case C-61/09 [2010] All ER (D) 257 (Nov) (Judgment delivered on 14 October 2010) (the case concerning Council Regulation (EC) 1782/2003, OJ 2003 L 270/1, art 44, which, just as Council Regulation (EC) 73/2009, OJ 2009 L 30/16, art 35, employed the wording 'at the farmer's disposal').

[10] Case C-61/09 [2010] All ER (D) 257 (Nov) (Judgment delivered on 14 October 2010), paras 54–55. On the facts, the land was made available free of charge, subject only to the occupier making contributions to a trade association.

[11] Case C-61/09 [2010] All ER (D) 257 (Nov) (Judgment delivered on 14 October 2010), paras 57–66.

12   Case C-61/09 [2010] All ER (D) 257 (Nov) (Judgment delivered on 14 October 2010), para 62.

13   Case C-61/09 [2010] All ER (D) 257 (Nov) (Judgment delivered on 14 October 2010), paras 62 and 65.

14   Case C-61/09 [2010] All ER (D) 257 (Nov) (Judgment delivered on 14 October 2010), para 69.

15   Case C-61/09 [2010] All ER (D) 257 (Nov) (Judgment delivered on 14 October 2010), para 70.

16   On share farming agreements generally, see paras 19.34 and 19.35.

17   Case C-61/09 (Opinion delivered on 11 May 2010), para 44.

18   Case C-61/09 [2010] All ER (D) 257 (Nov) (Judgment delivered on 14 October 2010), para 66.

19   OJ 2009 L 30/16, art 30; and see para 52.7.

20   On this aspect, see, eg, P N di C Willan, 'Share Farming', in A A Lennon and R E O McKay *Agricultural Law, Tax and Finance* (looseleaf) Sweet & Maxwell, at D4.3.

21   [1990] 1 EGLR 1, [1990] 17 EG 78, CA. See also C Rodgers 'Share Farming, Joint Venture and Problems of Exclusive possession' [1991] *Conveyancer* 58–65.

22   See para 52.19.

23   In this context may be noted the case of *National Trust for Places of Historic Interest v Birden* [2009] EWHC 2023 (Ch), [2009] All ER (D) 154 (Sep). While the court was not required to decide which party to a share farming agreement was the 'farmer' with the land at their disposal for the purposes of the Single Payment Scheme, the case does illustrate more generally the difficulties in making claims for agricultural subsidies under such arrangements. For example, share farming agreements as a rule preclude one party holding himself out as agent for the other; and this creates a significant barrier to any argument that the share farmer is making the claim on behalf of both himself and the landowner, a barrier raised yet higher by the requirement, as has been seen, that the agricultural activity must be carried out in the name of the farmer and on his behalf: Case C-61/09 *Landkreis Bad Dürkheim v Aufsichts- und Dienstleistungsdirektion* [2010] All ER (D) 257 (Nov) (Judgment delivered on 14 October 2010), para 69.

24   For discussion of contract farming agreements in the context of Inheritance Tax, see, eg, *Arnander, Lloyd and Villiers v Revenue and Customs Comrs* [2006] STC (SCD) 800, [2007] RVR 208: a farmhouse was held not to be occupied for the purposes of agriculture where the contractors undertook the day to day farming activities; and it may also be noted that it was the contractors who made the claim for arable area payments.

25   See, in this regard, eg, Rural Payments Agency *Single Payment Scheme Handbook for England 2011 and 2012*, Rural Payments Agency and DEFRA, 2011, p 12.

Use of the land and user clauses

52.26 Most tenancy agreements will contain a clause requiring the tenant to use the land for agricultural purposes only[1]. Moreover, these clauses have been interpreted relatively strictly by the courts. For example, in *Jewell v McGowan* there was held to be breach where the tenant had diversified into open farm activities, which were estimated to contribute one third of the income of the farm[2]. However, in this context there may be tensions between national law in England and Wales and the European Community legislation which governs the various direct payment regimes.

Perhaps most importantly, for a farmer to qualify for any direct payments under the 'First Pillar' of the Common Agricultural Policy (not just the Single Farm Payment), he must undertake 'agricultural activity'. As has been seen, this term is broadly defined as 'the production, rearing or growing of agricultural products including harvesting, milking, breeding animals and keeping animals for farming purposes, or maintaining the land in good agricultural and environmental condition'[3]. Accordingly, the definition extends beyond 'production agriculture' and the definition of 'agriculture' found in both the AHA 1986 and the ATA 1995[4]. More specifically, it includes maintaining the land in good agricultural and environmental condition, with the result that a farmer undertaking agricultural activity for the purposes of the European Community direct payment regimes may not qualify as an agricultural tenant under either the AHA 1986 or the ATA 1995[5].

While this mismatch may be thought to give rise only to theoretical difficulties, it may be noted that in the Scottish landlord and tenant case of *Cambusmore Estate Trustees v Little* absence of production was found *prima facie* to amount to a breach of Rule 1 of the rules of good husbandry, which imposes on the occupier an obligation, inter alia, to maintain a reasonable standard of efficient production[6]. Against this background, perhaps surprisingly the United Kingdom Government declined to update the definition of 'agriculture' during the passage of the Agricultural Tenancies Bill through Parliament, so as to include, for example, crops for industrial and fuel uses and set-aside[7]. Further, although detailed tax considerations are beyond the scope of this work, a matter of some significance is that HM Revenue and Customs do not regard the simple maintenance of the land in good agricultural and environmental condition as a trade for income tax purposes[8].

Nonetheless, in order to meet the business condition, which is a prerequisite for any farm business tenancy, it is sufficient:

'(a)   that all or part of the land comprised in the tenancy is farmed for the purposes of a trade or business; and
(b)   that, since the beginning of the tenancy, all or part of the land so comprised has been so farmed'[9].

Importantly, 'farming' is defined more broadly than 'agriculture':

'[r]eferences in this Act to the farming of land includes references to the carrying on in relation to land of any agricultural activity'[10].

This might bring some comfort to tenants choosing simply to maintain the land in good agricultural and environmental condition, not least since the words 'agricultural activity' are found in both the national and European Community legislation. On the other hand, to qualify as a farm business tenancy, it is also necessary to satisfy either the agriculture condition or the notice condition[11]; and in each case reference is made to the character of the tenancy being primarily or wholly 'agricultural' (as opposed to any reference to 'farming')[12].

---

[1]   For a useful analysis of the contents of farm business tenancies, see, eg, I Whitehead, A Errington, N Millard and T Felton *An Economic Evaluation of the Agricultural Tenancies Act 1995* (2002) University of Plymouth, Plymouth, pp 28–38.
[2]   [2002] EWCA Civ 145, [2002] 3 EGLR 87; and see, generally, eg, W Barr 'Agricultural Law Update' (2002) 146 Sol Jo 657. Considerable weight was placed upon the fact that the clause was to use the land for agricultural purposes *only*.
[3]   Council Regulation (EC) 73/2009, OJ 2009 L 30/16, art 2(c); and see para 52.4.
[4]   Under both the AHA 1986 and the ATA 1995 'agriculture' is non-exhaustively defined so as to include 'horticulture, fruit growing, seed growing, dairy farming and livestock breeding and keeping, the use of land as grazing land, meadow land, osier land, market gardens and nursery grounds, and the use of land for woodlands where that use is ancillary

to the farming of land for other agricultural purposes': AHA 1986, s 96(1); and ATA 1995, s 38(1). See further para 19.6 and para 3.23.

5   See, eg, L Bodiguel and M Cardwell 'Evolving Definitions of "Agriculture" for an Evolving Agriculture?' [2005] *Conveyancer* 419–446.

6   1991 SLT (Land Ct) 33. The rules of good husbandry applicable in Scotland mirror those applicable in England and Wales: see respectively the Agriculture (Scotland) Act 1948, Sch 6; and the Agriculture Act 1947, s 11.

7   Such amendment was expressly advocated: Hansard (HC) 6 February 1995, Vol 254, Col 82 (Mr Clifton-Brown). Likewise, the Tenancy Reform Industry Group did not propose a change in the definition of 'agriculture', on the basis that no recognisable redefinition could include all forms of diversification: *Tenancy Reform Industry Group (TRIG): Final Report* (Department for Environment, Food and Rural Affairs, London, 2003), para 4.3.3.

8   HM Revenue and Customs *Tax Bulletin: Special Edition – Single Payment Scheme* (June 2005), 4.

9   ATA 1995, s 1(2). See further para 3.23.

10   ATA 1995, s 38(2).

11   ATA 1995, s 1(3) and (4). See further paras 3.23 and 3.28ff.

12   In the case of the notice condition it may be emphasised that it is only necessary to show that the character of the tenancy was primarily or wholly agricultural at its commencement, leaving substantial scope for change of use.

52.27   In the context of land use, this would not appear to be the only tension between national law governing agricultural tenancies and European Community law governing the Single Payment Scheme. As has been seen, in order to unlock payment entitlements, they must be matched against 'eligible hectares'; and the European Community law definition of 'eligible hectares', as interpreted in national guidance, displays some differences from land considered agricultural for the purposes of the AHA 1986 and the ATA 1995[1].

Prima facie, there is considerable coherence between the European Community law definition and what constitutes agriculture in English and Welsh law, since 'eligible hectares' are, in principle, 'any agricultural area of the holding, and any area planted with short rotation coppice … that is used for an agricultural activity or, where the area is used as well for non-agricultural activities, predominantly used for agricultural activities'[2]. Moreover, this coherence has been reinforced by the fact that, following the 'Health Check', the European Community law definition now makes express reference to predominant use, whereas previously it seemed to address each area of the holding individually[3]. In consequence, the revised definition accords more closely with the AHA 1986, under which an agricultural holding can include non-agricultural land, provided that the use is substantially agricultural[4]. Indeed, s 1(1) defines 'agricultural holding' as 'the aggregate of the land (whether agricultural land or not) comprised in a contract of tenancy …'. And, similarly, it is better aligned with the ATA 1995, under which the agriculture condition looks to whether the character of the tenancy is primarily or wholly agricultural, while the notice condition looks to whether it was so at the commencement of the tenancy[5].

However, as indicated, some differences do remain. First, the European Community law definition makes no reference to woodland or forest, whereas under both the AHA 1986 and the ATA 1995 woodlands are included if their use is ancillary to the farming of land for other agricultural purposes. That said, a degree of flexibility is conferred by national guidance, which permits payment entitlements to be matched against, for example, grazeable woodland (interpreted, in principle, as woodland with fewer than 50 trees per hectare)[6]; and arguably this is not too far from ancillary use under the AHA 1986 and the ATA 1995.

Second, the European Community law definition does not require commercial use[7]. Accordingly, provided that they are maintained in good agricultural and environmental condition, paddocks used to graze ponies or horses for recreational purposes would seem to qualify as 'eligible hectares'; but they do not qualify as an agricultural holding or as land comprised in a farm business tenancy[8].

Third, national guidance on the extent of non-agricultural activities permitted on eligible hectares may be more generous than case law under the AHA 1986. For example, school or university nature or farm visits are permitted without restriction[9]; but the tenant in *Jewell v McGowan* was in breach of the covenant to use the land for agricultural purposes only, notwithstanding that approximately half of those visiting the open farm activities were local schoolchildren[10]. On the other hand, in this context there is also considerable overlap between European Community and national legislation. Thus, racehorse gallops would fail to qualify both as 'eligible hectares' and as an agricultural holding[11].

In consequence, where the land is tenanted no general assumption can be made that all the eligible hectares, against which payment entitlements can be matched, would necessarily fall within the agricultural holdings or farm business tenancy regimes: the example of a pony paddock may be reiterated. Likewise, there may be land comprised within agricultural holdings and farm business tenancies which does not qualify as an eligible hectare, as where on a large agricultural holding there are small areas of woodland whose tree density is too high to qualify as grazeable woodland.

1   See paras 52.10 and 52.21.
2   Council Regulation (EC) 73/2009, OJ 2009 L 30/16, art 34(2). As has been seen, the definition extends also to any area which gave a right to payments under the Single Payment Scheme in 2008 and which satisfies one of three criteria relating to rural development measures: see para 52.10.
3   Council Regulation (EC) 1782/2003, OJ 2003 L 30/16, art 44(2).
4   See, generally, para 19.6.
5   Section 1(3) and (4).
6   See, eg, Rural Payments Agency *Single Payment Scheme Handbook for England 2011 and 2012*, Rural Payments Agency and DEFRA, 2011, pp 17–20; and Welsh Assembly Government *2010 Single Application Rules Booklet*, Welsh Assembly Government, 2010, pp 14–15 (these rules, subject to amendment, also being applicable for 2011).
7   It may be reiterated that in England and Wales no decision has been taken to enact criteria to ensure that direct payments (whether under the Single Payment Scheme or otherwise) are granted to a natural or legal person '(a) whose agricultural activities form only an insignificant part of its overall economic activities; or (b) whose principal business or company objects do not consist of exercising an agricultural activity': Council Regulation (EC) 73/2009, OJ 2009 L 30/16, art 28(2).
8   See paras 19.2 and 3.2ff. It may be noted, however, that under the agricultural holdings legislation it is not necessary that the trade or business be agricultural, so long as there is a trade or business: see, eg, *Rutherford v Maurer* [1962] 1 QB 16 (where land used to graze horses for a riding school was held to be agricultural). Again, HM Revenue and Customs have indicated that, although land used for grazing horses or ponies for leisure purposes

may unlock the Single Farm Payment, they do not regard such activity as a trade for income tax purposes: HM Revenue and Customs *Tax Bulletin: Special Edition – Single Payment Scheme* (June 2005), 4.

9   See, eg, Rural Payments Agency *Single Payment Scheme Handbook for England 2011 and 2012*, Rural Payments Agency and DEFRA, 2011, p 20; and Welsh Assembly Government *2010 Single Application Rules Booklet*, Welsh Assembly Government, 2010, p 16 (these rules, subject to amendment, also being applicable for 2011).

10   [2002] EWCA Civ 145, [2002] 3 EGLR 87.

11   See, in respect of national guidance, eg, Rural Payments Agency *Single Payment Scheme Handbook for England 2011 and 2012*, Rural Payments Agency and DEFRA, 2011, p 21; and Welsh Assembly Government *2010 Single Application Rules Booklet*, Welsh Assembly Government, 2010, p 17 (these rules, subject to amendment, also being applicable for 2011). See, in respect of the AHA 1986, *Bracey v Read* [1963] Ch 88, [1962] 3 All ER 472; and *University of Reading v Johnson-Houghton* [1985] 2 EGLR 113, 276 Estates Gazette 1353.

Termination of tenancies

52.28   On the termination of tenancies it is necessary to ascertain whether, in principle, the payment entitlements and other forms of direct payment will revert with the land to the landowner or whether, as separate assets, they will remain at the disposal of the tenant. In this regard, much would seem to depend more generally upon how they are to be characterised in law.

The Single Payment Scheme is stated in Council Regulation (EC) 73/2009 to be an 'income support scheme for farmers'[1]; and this characteristic materially influenced the CJEU in *Van Dijk v Gemeente Kampen*, when holding that 'Community law does not require a lessee, on the expiry of the lease, to deliver to the lessor the leased land, including the payment entitlements accumulated thereon or relating thereto, or to pay compensation'[2]. Indeed, in the view of the CJEU, it was 'apparent from both the objectives and the scheme' of the legislation 'that, in the absence of a clause to the contrary, payment entitlements remain with the lessee on the expiry of the lease'[3]. In addition to such function as income support, it was also considered significant that payment entitlements were not linked to specific parcels of land and that they could only be held by farmers, a status not universally enjoyed by lessors. Further, the CJEU highlighted that, unlike the legislative framework for milk quotas, the Single Payment Scheme contained no express provision requiring the lessee to deliver the payment entitlements to the lessor on the expiry of the lease[4]. Any claim for unjust enrichment was swiftly despatched on the ground that, to sustain such a claim, there must be no valid legal basis for the enrichment; and, in these circumstances, it was clear that a valid legal basis was supplied by the legislation establishing the Single Payment Scheme.

The decision of the CJEU in *Van Dijk v Gemeente Kampen* may also be regarded as consistent with its earlier decision in *R v Minister of Agriculture, Fisheries and Food, ex p Country Landowners Association*, which concerned premiums in the sheep and goat and beef and veal sectors[5]. These were unequivocally held to be linked to producers, as opposed to the holding; and, with specific reference to the landlord and tenant context, it was confirmed that neither the regulatory framework nor any general principle of European

Community law required Member States to provide a mechanism for compensating detriment caused to owners of agricultural land by the introduction of such a system of premium rights, even where premium rights were transferred by producers who did not own the land on which they farmed[6].

Accordingly, on the termination of a tenancy, it would appear to be established that a tenant should be free to match his payment entitlements against other eligible hectares at his disposal, since they are not associated with individual parcels of land or, in the terminology of milk quotas, 'tied to farms'[7]. This interpretation also chimes with the overriding objective of the legislation, namely to provide decoupled income support for producers. Yet it may be highlighted that the CJEU in *Van Dijk v Gemeente Kampen* did countenance scope for contractual modification of this general principle, it applying 'in the absence of a clause to the contrary'[8].

[1] OJ 2009 L 30/16, art 1(b); and see further para 52.14.
[2] Case C-470/08 [2010] All ER (D) 141 (Feb) (Judgment delivered on 21 January 2010), para 43. The case concerned Council Regulation (EC) 1782/2003, OJ 2003 L 270/1 (as opposed to Council Regulation (EC) 73/2009, OJ 2009 L 30/16), but there were no significant differences in respect of the relevant provisions.
[3] Case C-470/08 [2010] All ER (D) 141 (Feb) (Judgment delivered on 21 January 2010), para 26.
[4] In the case of milk quotas, see now Council Regulation (EC) 1234/2007, OJ 2007 L 299/1, art 74(4): '[w]here there is no agreement between the parties, in the case of tenancies due to expire without any possibility of renewal on similar terms, or in situations involving comparable legal effects, the individual quotas in question shall be transferred in whole or in part to the producer taking them over, in accordance with provisions adopted by the Member States, taking account of the legitimate interests of the parties'.
[5] Case C-38/94 [1995] ECR I-3875, [1996] 2 CMLR 193, ECJ; and see para 52.14.
[6] Case C-38/94 [1995] ECR I-3875, para 21.
[7] Council Regulation (EC) 1234/2007, OJ 2007 L 299/1, Preamble (37).
[8] Case C-470/08 [2010] All ER (D) 141 (Feb) (Judgment delivered on 21 January 2010), para 26. See further para 52.29.

Quota protection clauses

52.29 In consequence, it would appear that, if a landlord is to have any prospect of taking over the payment entitlements on the termination of the tenancy, he must rely on express contractual provision. As seen, this possibility was countenanced by the CJEU with specific reference to the Single Payment Scheme in *Van Dijk v Gemeente Kampen*[1], with it likewise being regarded as an option in the case of livestock premium quotas by the CJEU in *R v Minister of Agriculture, Fisheries and Food, ex p Country Landowners Association*[2].

The grounds for such express contractual provision would seem strongest where the landlord has made available the payment entitlements to the tenant, in which case their reversion without compensation to the landlord on termination of the tenancy would not seem objectionable[3]. On the other hand, if the payment entitlements are considered to have been generated by the efforts of the tenant, it is possible that a quota protection clause to this effect may offend European Community law. Although analogies with milk quota are imprecise, it may be observed that in the milk quota case of *Wachauf v Bundesamt für Ernährung und Forstwirtschaft* the CJEU stated that:

325

'... it must be observed that Community rules which, upon the expiry of the lease, had the effect of depriving the lessee, without compensation, of the fruits of his labours and of his investments in the tenanted holding, would be incompatible with the requirements of the protection of fundamental rights in the Community legal order'[4].

This statement would be particularly apposite where the Single Farm Payment is based upon historic production carried out by the tenant, as is the case in Wales (and, for the time being, at least partially, in the case of England).

In addition, any clause seeking to transfer the payment entitlements to the landlord on the termination of a tenancy would only appear to be valid in circumstances where this conformed to the overriding objective of the Single Payment Scheme. For example, it would seem to be a prerequisite that the payment entitlements should be transferred to a person who qualified as a farmer[5]. Further, it would be wise to consider phrasing the clause in such a way as to capture not just the Single Farm Payment, but also other forms of direct payment.

The position is likely to be even more complex where the tenancy agreement was negotiated and entered into before the announcement of the Mid-term Review on 10 July 2002, since quota protection clauses in all probability will fail to address the Single Farm Payment. Indeed, the difficulty for the draftsman in anticipating future forms of support was expressly recognised by the CJEU in *R v Minister of Agriculture, Fisheries and Food, ex p Country Landowners Association* (where it highlighted that problems would be likely to arise if contractual relationships were already in existence when new forms of support were introduced)[6].

Further, United Kingdom courts have shown themselves relatively strict in construing quota protection clauses. For example, in *Lee v Heaton* a clause drafted by reference to 'any basic quota under a marketing scheme' was held insufficient to capture wholesale milk quota[7]. The milk quota system did not establish, or seek to establish, a scheme for regulating the marketing of milk. Rather, it imposed a levy on disposals of milk products. Likewise, in the specific context of the Single Payment Scheme, in *National Trust for Places of Historic Interest v Birden* the court was required to address a quota protection clause in a share farming agreement which provided that '[a]ny production grants or subsidies paid to either party in respect of livestock or other agricultural production or cessation of production on all or part of the land or otherwise' was to be shared in fixed proportions between the landowner and the share farmer[8]. On the facts, the share farming agreement had ended prior to the Single Payments Scheme becoming effective in the United Kingdom, with the result that any payment was in respect of agricultural activity by the former share farmer as a farm business tenant on another farm; and, accordingly, any claim by the landowner under this clause did not succeed. The landowner was no more successful with an alternative claim that it was an implied term of the contract that any subsidy system introduced by the United Kingdom Government to replace the existing system would be dealt with in the same proportions as under the share farming agreement. Significantly, it was held that the Single Payment Scheme was 'wholly different' from the previous regime[9]; and, as a result, neither was such a term to be implied on the basis that it was so obvious as to go without saying, nor was it necessary to give business efficacy to the share farming agreement. In addition, even if such a term could be implied, it could only be binding during the currency of the share farming agreement (which, by the relevant date, had terminated); and, in any event, any implied terms were precluded by a clause providing that the agreement contained the whole agreement between the parties.

Accordingly, for such purposes any quota protection clause would need to be very carefully drafted. The CJEU has confirmed that it must respect the overriding purpose of the Single Payment Scheme as 'income support'; and national courts have indicated that such a provision framed by reference to a marketing scheme, production quotas or production rights attached to land would not be effective in the case of the current direct payments regime. Moreover, in the light of *National Trust for Places of Historic Interest v Birden*, there must be doubt whether a clause drafted prior to the Mid-term Review so as to include 'successor' regimes would be held to cover payment entitlements: it may be reiterated that the Single Payment Scheme was regarded as wholly different from earlier subsidies[10].

[1]   Case C-470/08 [2010] All ER (D) 141 (Feb) (Judgment delivered on 21 January 2010), para 26; and see para 52.28.
[2]   Case C-38/94 [1995] ECR I-3875, para 24.
[3]   It would be normal to record the number of payment entitlements made available in the tenancy agreement.
[4]   Case 5/88 [1989] ECR 2609, para 19. See also, eg, JHH Weiler and NJS Lockhart, ' "Taking Rights Seriously" Seriously: the European Court and its Fundamental Rights Jurisprudence' (1995) 32 *Common Market Law Review* 51–94 and 579–627.
[5]   See also *Morrison-Low v Paterson* (2010) SLC/233/08, where the Scottish Land Court, referring to the judgment of the CJEU in *Van Dijk v Gemeente Kampen*, regarded as significant 'the stress placed on the intention to benefit farmers and the recognition that a landlord while owning land is not necessarily a farmer': para 131.
[6]   Case C-38/94 [1995] ECR I-3875, para 24.
[7]   [1987] 2 EGLR 12, 283 Estates Gazette 1076.
[8]   [2009] EWHC 2023 (Ch), [2009] All ER (D) 154 (Sep).
[9]   [2009] EWHC 2023 (Ch), para 148.
[10] That said, the original allocation of payment entitlements did track levels of support under, for example, the Arable Area Payments Scheme; and, although this historic element is fast disappearing in England, the historic basis is still employed in Wales. It may also be noted that, in the context of the Uruguay Round Agreement on Agriculture, some guidance as to what constitutes a 'successor regime' may be found in the decision of the Appellate Body in *United States – Subsidies on Upland Cotton* (2005) WT/DS267/AB/R.

52.30 Over and above provision for the destination of payment entitlements on the termination of the tenancy, it would be prudent for the landlord to oblige the tenant to use those entitlements annually. As has been seen, if they have not been used for a period of two years, they are to revert to the national reserve, except in cases of force majeure or exceptional circumstances[1]. Such a provision would be of particular importance where the landlord had made the payment entitlements available to the tenant at the commencement of the tenancy agreement[2].

[1]   Council Regulation (EC) 73/2009, OJ 2009 L 30/16, art 42; and see para 52.11.
[2]   C Rodgers *Agricultural Law* (2008) 3rd Edition, Tottel Publishing, Haywards Heath, pp 89–90.

Rent review

52.31 From first implementation of the Single Payment Scheme, there has been considerable evidence that the income support which it provides has a material impact upon the profitability of farms[1]. In this regard, it may be observed that, as the flat-rate basis has been phased in throughout the 'lowland' English region, relatively unproductive land where margins were tight has acquired the same rate of support per eligible hectare as land which had enjoyed high levels of historic support. Further, farmers have enjoyed the viable option of simply maintaining their land in good agricultural and environmental condition, so long as any cross-compliance costs are less than the amount of direct payments received[2]. However, as indicated, a tenant farmer will need to ensure that adopting this course will not breach any user clause[3].

With the profitability of farms at least partially dependent upon receipt of the Single Farm Payment (and other direct payments), their treatment on rent review has inevitably proved to be an important issue.

Under the AHA 1986, the rent properly payable in respect of a holding is to be the rent at which the holding might reasonably be expected to be let by a prudent and willing landlord to a prudent and willing tenant. All relevant factors are to be taken into account, including (in every case): the terms of the tenancy (including those relating to rent); the character and situation of the holding (including the locality in which it is situated); the productive capacity of the holding and its related earning capacity; and the current level of rents for comparable lettings[4]. In the case of payment entitlements, the terms of the tenancy may be relevant: for example, if they restrict the ability of the tenant to dispose of payment entitlements; or if there is a user clause which obliges the tenant to use the land for agricultural purposes only (which, as seen, may affect the ability of the tenant to pursue the option of simply maintaining the land in good agricultural and environmental condition)[5]. On the other hand, following the decision of the Scottish Land Court in *Morrison-Low v Paterson*, it would seem to be established that the income stream from the Single Farm Payment should not be included when assessing 'productive earning capacity'[6]; and that it 'cannot properly be viewed as part of the earnings of the farm'[7].

The implications of *Morrison-Low v Paterson* have been considered earlier, both in the context of rent review more generally[8] and when considering the nature of the Single Farm Payment as an asset[9]; but, with regard to its specific treatment on rent review, it may be of advantage to highlight three further findings of the Scottish Land Court. First, since it was not appropriate to assume the willing tenant to be a newcomer to farming, such a tenant would have the requisite level of payment entitlements for the farm[10]. Second, cases in relation to livestock premium quotas were not directly comparable and the treatment of milk quota on rent review had no bearing on the issue[11]. Third, payment entitlements could not be turned to account without land against which to match them; and '[t[hat must have value in the rental process'[12]. Accordingly, a tenant would make an allowance for the convenience of being able to use the holding to unlock his payment entitlements. Such allowance would be assessed by reference to the rental costs of adopting the alternative course of leasing 'naked acres' (ie land which satisfies the criteria for 'eligible hectares', but against which, for the time being, no farmer is matching payment entitlements); and it would also include a sum for the saving of time and effort (reflecting, inter alia, the added responsibility which would be incurred if the tenant were to maintain the naked acres in good agricultural and environmental condition)[13].

In addition, in the broader context of direct payments under rural development programmes, reference may be made to the decision of the Court of Appeal in *Childers (JW) Trustees v Anker*, where one of the issues was the correct treatment on rent review of compensation payments in respect of a Site of Special Scientific Interest[14]. The Court of Appeal was clear that the ability to restrict normal agricultural operations by virtue of a management agreement and the existence of compensation payments were both 'relevant factors'[15]. Accordingly, there would seem to be authority to the effect that direct payments in respect of both Natura 2000 measures and agri-environmental measures more generally should fall to be taken into account on rent review[16]; and, as agri-environmental payments acquire greater priority, the importance of this finding is likely to increase: in particular, payments under the Environmental Stewardship (England) Regulations 2005[17] have been identified as the future focus of the rural development programme for England[18].

A matter of some interest is that in *Childers (JW) Trustees v Anker* the Court of Appeal also endorsed the approach taken by the judge that non-farming income was a relevant factor, an endorsement which arguably has the capacity to impact on the treatment of the Single Farm Payment on rent review[19]. That said, the analogy between sums received in respect of a Site of Special Scientific Interest and the Single Farm Payment is not precise. In particular, a factor determining the amount received in respect of the former is income foregone[20], whereas the latter is characterised as income support. On the other hand, in both cases production is not necessarily a pre-requisite and land management obligations are imposed (albeit at a low level in the case of cross-compliance under the Single Payment Scheme).

In the case of farm business tenancies under the ATA 1995, on any reference in pursuance of a statutory review notice, the arbitrator is to determine the rent properly payable in respect of the holding[21]; and, for these purposes, the rent properly payable in respect of the holding is the rent at which the holding might reasonably be expected to be let on the open market by a willing landlord to a willing tenant[22], with 'all relevant factors' again to be taken into account[23]. Accordingly, similar considerations would apply; but, unlike the AHA 1986 (and therefore more in line with the Scottish legislation), there is no mention of the productive capacity of the holding and its related earning capacity.

---

[1] See, eg, Deloitte Press Releases, 'Farm Incomes Set for Roller Coaster Ride, Warns Deloitte', 14 October 2005; and 'Farmers Predicted to Produce Food at Loss', 3 November 2005. See also, more recently, eg, *Morrison-Low v Paterson* (2010) SLC/233/08, para 86.

2   See, generally, eg, J Moody and W Neville *Mid Term Review: a Practical Guide* (2004) Burges Salmon, Bristol, p 199.
3   See para 52.26.
4   The AHA 1986, Sch 2 para 1(1); and see further para 25.30ff.
5   For the extent that maintaining the land in good agricultural and environmental condition constitutes 'agriculture', see para 52.26. See also C Rodgers *Agricultural Law* (2008) 3rd Edition, Tottel Publishing, Haywards Heath, p 88.
6   *Morrison-Low v Paterson* (2010) SLC/233/08, para 107. It may be noted that the relevant Scottish provision, the Agricultural Holdings (Scotland) Act 1991, s 13 (as amended by the Agricultural Holdings (Scotland) Act 2003, s 69) does not make express reference to the 'productive capacity' or 'related earning capacity', as found in the Agricultural Holdings Act 1986, Sch 2 paras (1) and (2). See also, eg, J Moody *Rent Review under the Agricultural Holdings (Scotland) Acts: Morrison-Low v Paterson – Scottish Land Court: CAAV Discussion Paper 12 June 2010*; and D Rennie 'The Legal Nature of Single Farm Payment Entitlement' (2011) 171 *Farm Law* 16–20.
7   (2010) SLC/233/08, para 138.
8   See para 25.18A.
9   See para 52.14.
10   See, in particular, (2010) SLC/233/08, paras 97–98.
11   See, in particular, (2010) SLC/233/08, paras 102–106: and, for comparison of livestock premium quotas and milk quota with the Single Farm Payment, see para 52.14.
12   (2010) SLC/233/08, para 138.
13   See, in particular, (2010) SLC/233/08, paras 138 and 141. It was agreed that the rent for naked acres would be £6.50 per acre, with the Scottish Land Court assessing the sum for the saving of time and effort at £2.50 per acre. The position in England may be considerably different, in that there is a far closer balance between the number of payment entitlements and the number of eligible hectares: for helpful discussion of this aspect, see J Moody *Rent Review under the Agricultural Holdings (Scotland) Acts: Morrison-Low v Paterson – Scottish Land Court: CAAV Discussion Paper 12th June 2010*.
14   (1995) 73 P & CR 458, [1996] 1 EGLR 1, CA.
15   For a broad interpretation of relevant factors see, eg, *Enfield London Borough Council v Pott* [1990] 2 EGLR 7, [1990] 34 EG 60 (relating to a farm shop).
16   For such measures, see para 52.15. It may also be noted that in *Morrison-Low v Paterson* (2010) SLC/233/08 it was accepted, in principle, that the income from an environmental scheme was to be taken into account on rent review: paras 175–177.
17   SI 2005/621 (as amended by SI 2005/2003, SI 2006/991 and SI 2006/2075).
18   DEFRA, *Comprehensive Spending Review*, 20 October 2010 (available at http://ww2.defra.gov.uk/news/2010/10/20/comprehensive-spending-review/, accessed on 3 April 2011).
19   A matter of some importance is that the Scottish legislation considered in *Morrison-Low v Paterson* differs materially from the legislation applicable in England and Wales. In particular, reference is instead made to 'information about rents of other agricultural holdings (including when fixed) and any factors affecting those rents (or any of them) except any distortion due to a scarcity of lets': Agricultural Holdings (Scotland) Act 1991, s 13(4)(a) (as amended by the Agricultural Holdings (Scotland) Act 2003, s 63).
20   See generally, eg, C Rodgers *Agricultural Law* (2008) 3rd Edition, Tottel Publishing, Haywards Heath, pp 543–546.
21   ATA 1995, s 13(1). The rent review procedure under the ATA 1995 does not, however, apply in two circumstances. First, it is open to the parties to agree expressly in the tenancy agreement that the rent is not to be reviewed; and, second, the agreement can provide that the rent be varied, at a specified time or times during the tenancy, either (i) by or to a specified amount or (ii) in accordance with a specified formula which does not preclude a reduction and which does not require or permit the exercise by any person of any judgment or discretion in relation to the determination of the rent of the holding: ATA 1995, s 9. See further para 9.6ff. It is possible to envisage that a specified formula could be employed to take account of, for example, a declining Single Farm Payment as a high historic element is replaced by the flat-rate element.
22   ATA 1995, s 13(2).
23   This obligation to take into account all relevant factors is subject to exceptions: ATA 1995, s 13(3) and (4). For example, the arbitrator is to disregard any effect on the rent of the fact that the tenant is in occupation of the holding. See further para 9.20.

Transfer

52.32 It has been seen that payment entitlements may be transferred by sale or by any other definitive transfer, with or without land[1]. As stated by the Advocate General in *Harms v Heidinga*, 'it is clear that the Community legislature intended payment entitlements to be transferable and traded in. The single farm payment was broken down into payment entitlements precisely so as to facilitate its transfer. Indeed, contrary to milk quotas for example, payment entitlements may in principle be freely transferred and are not linked to specific agricultural land'[2]. Accordingly, as a general rule, tenants would appear freely able to effect transfers, with no obligation to compensate landlords being imposed by European Community law. In this regard, it may be observed that, in *R v Minister of Agriculture, Fisheries and Food, ex p Country Landowners Association*, the CJEU held that, where livestock premium quotas linked to tenant-producers were transferred, land-lords could not look to either the regulations or any general principle of European Community law for compensation[3]; and such quotas share several characteristics with payment entitlements[4].

On the other hand, as has also been seen, such transfers are subject to limitations, of which three may be highlighted. First, a Member State may decide that payment entitlements may be transferred or used only within a single region[5]; and payment entitlements attributable to and established in Wales may only be used or transferred within Wales[6]. Second, as established in *Harms v Heidinga*, payment entitlements may only be transferred to a farmer, who is capable of carrying out the cross-compliance obligations, with dis-bursement of the aid being dependent upon him holding the requisite number of eligible hectares[7]. Third, any transfer of payment entitlements by lease or similar types of transactions must be accompanied by the transfer of an equivalent number of eligible hectares. The purpose of such measures has been to prevent speculative transfers and accumulation of payment entitlements without a corresponding agricultural basis[8].

In consequence, the scope for a landlord to restrict transfers is somewhat circumscribed. Where a land transaction is required, as is the case with any transfer of payment entitlements by lease or similar types of transactions, he may possess a powerful lever either to prohibit the transfer altogether or to extract value from the tenant. By contrast, no land transaction is required for a sale or any other definitive transfer; and, in this respect, comparison may be drawn with milk quotas: under that regime, a tenancy for a period of ten months or more is, as a general rule, required to effect permanent transfer, with such requirement permitting landlords a much greater degree of control[9]. It may be reiterated that the CJEU in *Harms v Heidinga* did establish that, by reason of the principle of freedom of contract, the parties remain free to arrange their own affairs; but, at the same time, crucially, the CJEU affirmed that 'limitations on freedom of contract may none the less arise from the applicable European Union rules', with the result that, '[i]n particular, the contractual freedom of a person having payment entitlements does not permit him to enter into commitments which contradict the objectives of Regulation

331

No 1782/2003 [now Council Regulation (EC) 73/2009]'[10]. Accordingly, the three limitations mentioned above would seem to be beyond modification by the parties.

A matter of considerable practical importance is that, when transferring payment entitlements, both landlords and tenants take care to ensure compliance with communication deadlines. The European Community legislation provides that payment entitlements may be transferred at any time in the year, with it being for each Member State to establish the period within which the transferor shall inform the competent authority[11]. In England, the transferor must notify the transfer to the competent authority that allocated the payment entitlement at least six weeks before the transfer is to take place and at least six weeks before the last day for lodging an application under the Single Payment Scheme[12]. In Wales, notification must take place at least six weeks before the transfer comes into effect[13].

[1] Council Regulation (EC) 73/2009, OJ 2009 L 30/16, art 43(2); and see further para 52.12.
[2] Case C-434/08 *Harms v Heidinga* (Opinion delivered on 4 February 2010), para 32 (footnotes omitted). The case related to the transfer provisions as set out in the original legislation (Council Regulation (EC) 1782/2003, OJ 2003 L 270/1, art 46(2)), but the relevant wording is identical to that in Council Regulation (EC) 73/2009, OJ 2009 L 30/16, art 43(2).
[3] Case C-38/94 [1995] ECR I-3875, [1996] 2 CMLR 193, ECJ. It may be noted that one of the regulations implementing livestock premium quotas, Commission Regulation (EEC) 3567/92, provided that 'Member States may, if necessary, take appropriate transitional measures with a view to finding equitable solutions to problems which might arise in contractual relationships existing at the time this Regulation enters into force between producers who do not own all the land they farm, in the event of a transfer of premium rights or of other actions having equivalent effect. Such measures may only be taken in order to resolve the difficulties connected with the introduction of a premium rights system linked to the producer and must in any event respect the principles governing that link': OJ 1992 L 362/41, art 13. The CJEU did not feel that the provision extended to the introduction of a mechanism to compensate detriment to landlords; and, moreover, it was for Member States to assess the need for protective measures, having regard in particular to national arrangements for implementing the rules in question and national rules governing the legal relationship between landlord and tenant. It may also be noted that no such provision was to be found in the context of the Single Payment Scheme.
[4] See para 52.14.
[5] Council Regulation (EC) 73/2009, OJ 2009 L 30/16, art 43(1).
[6] Common Agricultural Policy Single Payment and Support Schemes (Wales) Regulations 2010, SI 2010/1892 (W.185), reg 9.
[7] (Judgment delivered on 20 May 2010); and see further para 52.12.
[8] Council Regulation (EC) 73/2009, OJ 2009 L 30/16, Preamble (28); and, for the original legislation, see Council Regulation (EC) 1782/2003, OJ 2003 L 270/1, Preamble (30). See also, eg, Case C-470/08 *Van Dijk v Gemeente Kampen* [2010] All ER (D) 141 (Feb) (Judgment delivered on 21 January 2010), para 36.
[9] For the current legislation see, in the case of England, the Dairy Produce Quotas Regulations 2005, SI 2005/465, reg 16(1)(b); and, in the case of Wales, the Dairy Produce Quotas (Wales) Regulations 2005, SI 2005/537 (W.47), reg 16(1)(b).
[10] (Judgment delivered on 20 May 2010), paras 36–37.
[11] Commission Regulation (EC) 1120/2009, OJ 2009 L 316/1, art 12(1) and (2).
[12] The Common Agricultural Policy Single Payment and Support Schemes Regulations 2010, SI 2010/540, reg 7; but note that Commission Regulation (EC) 1120/2009, OJ 2009 L 316/1, art 12(3) provides that '[a] Member State may require that the transferor shall communicate the transfer to the competent authority of the Member State where the transfer will operate, within a time period to be established by that Member State but not earlier than six weeks before the transfer takes place and taking into account the last date for lodging an application under the single payment scheme'.

¹³ Welsh Assembly Government *2010 Single Application Rules Booklet*, Welsh Assembly Government, 2010, p 22 (these rules, subject to amendment, also being applicable for 2011).

Succession

52.33 The Single Farm Payment and other direct payments have inevitably had a material impact upon succession. In particular, they are crucial to any assessment of net annual income for the purposes of determining whether the applicant meets the criterion that 'he is not the occupier of a commercial unit of agricultural land'[1]. As has been seen, a 'commercial unit of agricultural land' is 'a unit of agricultural land which is capable, when farmed under competent management, of producing a net annual income of an amount not less than the aggregate of the average annual earnings of two full-time, male agricultural workers aged twenty or over'[2]. Central to this calculation have been the units of production orders, issued annually, by reference to whose provisions the net annual income is ascertained[3].

For such purposes, the economic and financial importance of the Single Farm Payment and other direct payments was soon recognised. Indeed, in a 2005 consultation paper, DEFRA stated that '[s]ubsidies as a percentage of net farm income typically range from between 25 to 125%'[4]. Moreover, it also affirmed that 'an assessment, which excluded [the Single Farm Payment], would not be meaningful'[5]. Following this consultation exercise, the Agricultural Holdings (Units of Production) (England) Order 2006 included values for eligible hectares under the Single Payment Scheme[6]; and it also included, for example, specific sums in respect of the protein crop premium for beans and dried peas[7]. This approach continues under the current legislation, the Agricultural Holdings (Units of Production) (England) Order 2010, applicable from 7 November 2010[8]. It may be observed that the express purpose of the units of production orders is to assess 'productive capacity'[9], yet the Single Farm Payment, although characterised as income support, is still regarded as a factor in that calculation, a legislative choice which may be contrasted with the line taken by the Scottish Land Court in the context of rent review[10].

The Single Farm Payment and other direct payments may also generate complications when determining whether the applicant meets the principal source of livelihood test. In particular, for these purposes there may be doubt as to the consequences of the applicant having limited his activities to maintenance of the land in good agricultural and environmental condition.

Under the principal source of livelihood test, the applicant must show that, in the seven years ending with the date of death of the former tenant (in the case of succession on death) or in the previous seven years (in the case of succession on retirement), his only or principal source of livelihood throughout a continuous period of not less than five years (or two or more discontinuous periods together amounting to not less than five years) derived from his agricultural work on the holding or on an agricultural unit of which the holding forms part[11]. Under the Regulatory Reform (Agricultural Tenancies) (England and Wales) Order 2006 there has been expansion of what amounts to agricultural work carried out by a person on the holding or on an agricultural unit of which the holding forms part[12]. This now includes: (i) agricultural work carried out by him from the holding or an agricultural unit of which the holding forms part and (ii) other work carried out by him on or from the holding or an agricultural unit of which the holding forms part. In either case there must be approval in writing by the landlord after 19 October 2006.

As noted, it is not clear that maintenance of the land in good agricultural and environmental condition qualifies as 'agriculture' for the purposes of the AHA 1986[13]. Accordingly, an applicant who restricts his operations in this way could fail the principal source of livelihood test, notwithstanding that he is conforming with European Community policy. On the other hand, it could be argued that maintaining the land in good agricultural and environmental condition amounts to 'other work carried out' by the applicant on the holding, so as to take advantage of the amendment effected by the Regulatory Reform (Agricultural Tenancies) (England and Wales) Order 2006. That said, it must be reiterated that the applicant would need to show approval in writing by the landlord after 19 October 2006. The safer option must be to remain in production if there is any possibility of succession; and, indeed, there is some logic in preserving succession rights for those who engage in farming as their profession as opposed to those who meet relatively light cross-compliance obligations in return for European Community support[14].

[1]   For the 'commercial unit test' see the AHA 1986, s 36(3)(b) (in the case of succession on death) and s 50(2)(b) (in the case of succession on retirement); and see further para 35.55ff.
[2]   AHA 1986, Sch 6 para 3(1).
[3]   AHA 1986, Sch 6 paras 3(2) and 4.
[4]   DEFRA, 'Consultation Paper on Proposed Changes to the Annual Agricultural Holdings (Units of Production) (England) Order Required Under Schedule 6 of the Agricultural Holdings Act 1986' (DEFRA, London, 2005), para 6.
[5]   DEFRA, 'Consultation Paper on Proposed Changes to the Annual Agricultural Holdings (Units of Production) (England) Order Required Under Schedule 6 of the Agricultural Holdings Act 1986' (DEFRA, London, 2005), para 6.
[6]   SI 2006/2628, Schedule para 6. Cf the Agricultural Holdings (Units of Production) (Wales) Order 2006, SI 2006/2796 (W.235).
[7]   SI 2006/2628, Schedule para 2.
[8]   SI 2010/2504, Schedule paras 2 and 5. For the equivalent provisions in Wales, see Agricultural Holdings (Units of Production) (Wales) Order 2010, SI 2010/2825 (W.232), Schedule paras 2 and 5.
[9]   See now the Agricultural Holdings (Units of Production) (England) Order 2010, SI 2010/2504, reg 2.
[10] *Morrison-Low v Paterson* (2010) SLC/233/08; and see para 52.31.
[11] AHA 1986, s 36(3)(a) (in the case of succession on death) and s 50(2)(a) (in the case of succession on retirement); and see further para 35.33ff.
[12] SI 2006/2805.
[13] See para 52.26.
[14] See also Council Regulation (EC) 73/2009, OJ 2009 L 30/16, Preamble (23) (although it may be noted that in England and Wales no decision has been taken to implement, as from 2010, criteria to ensure that direct payments are not granted to natural or legal persons whose agricultural activities form only an insignificant part of their overall economic activities or whose principal business or company objects do not consist of exercising an agricultural activity: art 28(2)).

Chapter 53

COMPENSATION FOR COMPULSORY PURCHASE OF AN AGRICULTURAL HOLDING

INTRODUCTION

53.1 The rules and procedures which apply generally to the assessment of compensation for the acquisition of land apply equally when agricultural land is the subject of a compulsory purchase order (CPO)[1]. Therefore, where agricultural land is taken by compulsion, compensation shall be based on the value of land, which shall be *'taken to be the amount if sold in the open market ... a willing seller might be expected to realise*[2]'. When ascertaining that value, any restrictions on the land or on existing tenancies must be taken into account, as should existing planning permissions and, in some cases, the 'hope value' of securing a planning consent. Equally, any increase attributable to any use which is contrary to the law must be disregarded[3] as should any value which is attributable entirely to the scheme underlying the compulsory acquisition[4].

As with any other claim for compensation pursuant to a CPO, compensation for the acquisition of agricultural land is also payable for *'disturbance or for any other matter not directly based on the value of land*[5] and where land is severed, compensation can be claimed where that severance impacts on the value of the land retained[6]. However, special rules apply to the assessment of compensation where, as a consequence of the compulsory acquisition, an acquiring authority[7] either acquires the interest of the landlord in an agricultural holding or any part of it, or it acquires the interest of the tenant in, or takes possession of, an agricultural holding or part of it[8].

This chapter looks at the special rules which apply to the entitlement to and assessment of compensation for either a landlord or tenant of an agricultural holding.

[1] For an overview of compulsory purchase generally, see Soloman and Messent, *Property Transactions: Planning and Environment* (1st edn, 2007) Sweet and Maxwell.
[2] Land Compensation Act 1961 (LCA 1961), s 5, Rule (2).
[3] LCA 1961, s 5, Rule (4).
[4] *Pointe Gourde Quarrying and Transport Co Ltd v Sub-Intendent of Crown Lands* [1947] AC 565, 63 TLR 486, PC and LCA 1961, s 6.
[5] LCA 1961, s 5, Rule (6).
[6] Compulsory Purchase Act 1965 (CPA 1965), s 7.
[7] An 'acquiring authority' is any person authorised by enactment to acquire or take possession of land compulsorily, Agriculture (Miscellaneous Provisions) Act 1968 (A(MP)A 1968), ss 12(1), 17(1).
[8] Land Compensation Act 1973 (LCA 1973), s 48(1).

COMPENSATION TO A LANDLORD

53.2 As highlighted above, in assessing the value of the landlord's interest in an agricultural holding, the tenancy agreement must be taken into account. In this respect, if the tenancy is one to which the AHA 1986 applies, any right of the landlord to serve a notice to quit must be disregarded, as should any notice to quit already served by the landlord, which would not be or would not have been effective if:

(a)   in Case B[1] (land required for a non-agricultural use for which planning permission has been granted) the reference to the land being required did not include a reference to it being required by an acquiring authority; and

(b)   the reference in the AHA 1986[2] to the landlord's proposal to terminate the tenancy for a use other than agriculture, not falling within Case B, did not include a reference to its being used by an acquiring authority.

If the tenant has quitted the holding (or any part of it) by reason of a notice to quit which should be disregarded, for the purposes of assessing the compensation it must be assumed that he has not done so[3]. If the notice to quit is not one which needs to be disregarded pursuant to the above, then this can be taken into account in assessing the value of the landlord's interest. If the land to be acquired by the acquiring authority results in a reduction in value of land retained by the landlord (ie through severance), the landlord can claim compensation for such reduction[4]. He may also be able to require acquisition of the whole of the land[5]. A landlord may also be entitled to a basic loss payment[6].

For Farm Business Tenancies governed by the ATA 1995 the usual rules for assessing compensation apply and the landlord will be entitled to the value of the reversionary interest, taking into account the terms of the tenancy agreement.

[1]   AHA 1986, s 26(2), Sch 3 Pt 1 Case B.
[2]   AHA 1986, s 27(3)(f). This is one of the matters as to which the Agricultural Land Tribunal must be satisfied before giving consent to a notice to quit.
[3]   LCA 1973, s 48(2).
[4]   CPA 1965, s 7.
[5]   See paras 53.14 to 53.18.
[6]   See para 53.9.

COMPENSATION TO A TENANT UNDER THE AHA 1986

53.3 Where a tenant holds a yearly tenancy, compensation is based either upon service of a notice to quit or service of a notice of entry.

Notice to quit compensation

53.4 Where the acquiring authority has acquired the landlord's interest, then effectively it steps into the shoes of the landlord and can serve a notice to quit under the AHA 1986. Under the AHA 1986, the period of notice must not be less than 12 months from the end of the current year of the tenancy[1] (although a shorter period will apply if the tenancy agreement contains an early resumption clause in respect of a non-agricultural use)[2].

The basis of compensation pursuant to a notice to quit is the AHA 1986 which provides for a basic disturbance payment and an additional compensation payment[3]. The basic payment shall be an amount equivalent to one year's rent of the holding at the rate at which rent was payable immediately before termination of the tenancy[4]. This payment can increase to up to two year's rent where the tenant has, not less than one month prior to termination of the tenancy, given notice in writing to the landlord of his intention to make a claim for additional compensation and, before their sale, the tenant has given the landlord a reasonable opportunity of making a valuation of any household goods, implements of husbandry, fixtures, farm produce or farm stock which the tenant unavoidably needs to remove or sell as a result of quitting the holding[5]. The additional compensation payment shall be an amount equal to four year's rent of the holding at the rate at which rent was payable immediately before the termination of the tenancy of the holding[6].

Improvements and any just allowance which ought to be made by the tenant to an incoming tenant (tenant-right) can be claimed[7]. If the land to be acquired results in a reduction in value of land retained by the tenant (ie through severance), the tenant can claim compensation for such reduction[8] or can require the acquiring authority to acquire the whole of the land[9]. A tenant may also be entitled to one or more of the statutory loss payments[10].

[1]   AHA 1986, s 25(1).
[2]   AHA 1986, s 25(2)(b).
[3]   AHA 1986, s 60(2).
[4]   AHA 1986, s 60(3)(a).
[5]   AHA 1986, s 60(3), (5) and (6).
[6]   AHA 1986, s 60(4).
[7]   AHA 1986, s 64 and s 65 and Schedules 7 and 8.
[8]   CPA 1965, s 7.
[9]   See paras 53.14 to 53.18.
[10] See paras 53.9 to 53.12.

Notice of entry compensation

53.5 If the acquiring authority serves a notice of entry, the tenant is entitled to compensation under s 20 of the Compulsory Purchase Act 1965 (CPA 1965). In this case the tenant will be compensated for the value of his unexpired term or interest in the land[1]. In the same way as assessing the value of the landlord's interest, in assessing the tenant's compensation in this respect there must, in certain circumstances, be disregarded any right of the landlord to serve a notice to quit, and any notice to quit already served by the landlord[2]. The effect is that the tenant's security of tenure is taken into account for the purposes of assessing compensation. If the notice to quit is not one which needs to be disregarded, it can be taken into account.

53.5 Compensation for compulsory purchase of an agricultural holding

Formerly, where a tenant's interest was compulsorily acquired by an acquiring authority under statutory powers, any provision in the tenancy which authorised the resumption of possession of the holding at short notice for non-agricultural purposes was to be treated as though it authorised resumption on the usual 12 months notice to quit. Where a tenant was compulsorily dispossessed by an acquiring authority, the resumption clause was to be disregarded for the purpose of calculating the payment of additional compensation under the Agriculture (Miscellaneous Provision) Act 1968 (A(MP)A 1968)[3]. However, that provision has been repealed, except, effectively, where compensation to a tenant shall be increased under s 48(6) of the Land Compensation Act 1973 (LCA 1973).

The tenant will be entitled to a payment for disturbance in respect of losses incurred between the date of entry and expiry of the term. He shall also be entitled to compensation for damage done to him by severing land or otherwise injuriously affecting it[4]. As with the notice to quit basis of compensation, a claim can be made for any just allowance which ought to be made by him as an incoming tenant (tenant-right) and for any loss or injury he may sustain[5].

By virtue of the A(MP)A 1968[6], the additional compensation provisions in the AHA 1986 also apply to compensation claimed under s 20 of the CPA 1965 (ie an amount equal to four year's rent of the holding). However, additional compensation under these provisions shall not be payable[7] where the acquiring authority requires the land comprised in the agricultural holding or part of it for the purposes of agricultural research or experiment or for demonstrating agricultural methods or for the purposes of the enactments relating to smallholdings, or where the Minister[8] acquires the land to ensure full and efficient use of it[9].

Where the tenancy is for a term of two years or more, the additional compensation payment will be limited to such amount as brings the aggregate compensation payable in such case up to what would be payable, including the additional payment, in the case of a tenancy from year to year[10]. To avoid a double payment, the tenant's compensation should be reduced by a sum equivalent to the additional payment, save that if the tenant's compensation so calculated amounts to less than it would have been had s 48 of the LCA 1973 not been enacted, then it must be increased by the amount of the deficiency[11]. In assessing the tenant's compensation, no account is to be taken of any benefit which might accrue to the tenant by virtue of the additional compensation provisions for disturbance contained in the AHA 1986[12]. A tenant may also be entitled to one or more of the statutory loss payments[13].

1   CPA 1965, s 20(1).
2   LCA 1973, s 48(3).
3   A(MP)A 1968, s 15(1).
4   CPA 1965, s 20(2).
5   CPA 1965, s 20(1).
6   A(MP)A 1968, s 12.
7   A(MP)A 1968, s 13(2).
8   A(MP)A 1968, s 50(1).

9 Ie under the Agriculture Act 1947, s 84(1)(c). But where an acquiring authority acquires or takes possession pursuant to s 226 or s 230 of the Town and Country Planning Act 1990, then it shall be deemed that they have not acquired for any of the purposes specified in s 13(2).
10 A(MP)A 1968, s 12(2).
11 LCA 1973, s 48(6).
12 LCA 1973, s 48(6A). The additional compensation provisions in this context mean s 60(2)(b) of the AHA 1986.
13 See paras 53.9 to 53.12.

Electing the basis of compensation

53.6 It should be noted that where a notice to quit is served on a tenant, in certain circumstances he may elect to have his compensation determined as if a notice of entry had been served, that is to say pursuant to s 20 of the CPA 1965[1]. The LCA 1973 specifies those circumstances, which include where the acquiring authority has served notice to treat on the landlord or has agreed to acquire his interest in the holding and where the tenant gives up possession of the holding to the acquiring authority on or before the date on which his tenancy terminates in accordance with the notice[2]. Although in most cases compensation under s 20 will yield greater compensation than the notice to quit basis, this will depend on the precise circumstances. If the tenant does elect to have his compensation assessed in this way then such election must be made in writing and be served on the acquiring authority no later than the date possession of the holding is given up[3].

1 LCA 1973, s 59.
2 LCA 1973, s 59(1) and (2).
3 LCA 1973, s 59(4).

Compensation to a tenant under the ATA 1995

53.7 Farm Business Tenancies of a fixed term with less than a year left to run, or yearly tenancies, can be dealt with by an acquiring authority as outlined above (ie by notice to quit or notice of entry). Where the acquiring authority has acquired the landlord's interest, then effectively it steps into the shoes of the landlord and can serve a notice to quit. A claim for value of the interest and disturbance can be made but given that there is no security of tenure, the assessment of compensation is likely to be small. Where a notice of entry is served, because there is no security of tenure, the right of the landlord to serve a notice to quit is not to be disregarded. The other heads of compensation (above) can be claimed by the tenant although this does not apply to the additional compensation payment[1]. With fixed term tenancies with over a year to run, the acquiring authority is required to serve a notice to treat in order to acquire the tenant's interest. In this case, the tenant's value will include the unexpired term.

1 LCA 1973, s 48(1A).

53.8 *Compensation for compulsory purchase of an agricultural holding*

LOSS PAYMENTS

53.8 Loss payments for disturbance are governed by the LCA 1973.

Basic loss payment

53.9 A person who has a qualifying interest in land acquired compulsorily is entitled (to the extent that he is not entitled to a home loss payment) to a basic loss payment[1]. This can apply to both landlords and tenants of an agricultural holding. The basic loss payment is calculated by reference to the owner's claim for compensation for the value of his interest. The payment is calculated as the lower of 7.5% of the value of the claimant's property acquired or £75,000[2].

1   LCA 1973, s 33(A).
2   LCA 1973, s 33A(2).

Occupier's loss payment

53.10 A person in occupation (usually the tenant) is additionally entitled to an occupier's loss payment for agricultural land[1]. The occupier's loss payment for agricultural land is calculated by reference to the greater of (subject to a maximum of £25,000):

(a)   2.5% of the value of the occupier's interest;
(b)   the 'land amount'; or
(c)   the 'building amount'.

The 'land' and 'building' calculations are contained in the LCA 1973[2].

If additional compensation is payable under the AHA 1986[3], then only one payment can be made (ie either the additional compensation payment or the occupier's loss payment). The claimant is entitled to whichever is the greater[4].

1   LCA 1973, s 33B.
2   LCA 1973, s 33B(8), (9) and (10).
3   AHA 1986, s 60 by virtue of A(MP)A 1968, s 12.
4   A(MP)A 1968, s 12(4).

Home loss payment

53.11 If the acquisition involves a dwelling then, in certain circumstances, a displaced occupier (usually the tenant) may be entitled to a home loss payment for the loss of that dwelling[1]. A home loss payment is calculated by reference to the value of the claimant's interest. A tenant with a leasehold interest of greater than three years is entitled to a market value equivalent to 10% of the value of the interest, subject to a minimum of £4,700 and a maximum of £47,000. An occupier with any lesser interest is entitled to £4,700[2].

1   LCA 1973, s 29.
2   LCA 1973, s 30.

Loss payments generally

53.12 All of the amounts and percentages referred to above are capable of change by statutory instrument[1]. Claims should be made in writing and supported by sufficient information to enable the claim to be calculated[2]. Provision is made for claims arising on the insolvency or death of the claimant[3].

[1] LCA 1973, s 33K.
[2] LCA 1973, s 33E.
[3] LCA 1973, ss 33F and 33G.

Farm loss payments

53.13 Prior to the amendments made by the Planning and Compulsory Purchase Act 2004 to the LCA 1973, which introduced the above loss payments, the LCA 1973 dealt with a scheme of farm loss payments. The farm loss payment scheme applied to acquisitions prior to 31 October 2004, and therefore is now principally of historic interest.

Under the old provisions[1], where a person in occupation of land constituting or included in an agricultural unit had an owner's interest then, if as a consequence of compulsory acquisition of his interest in the whole of the land ('the land acquired'), he was displaced from that land on or after 17 October 1972 and not more than three years after the date of displacement he began to farm another agricultural unit elsewhere in Great Britain then he was, subject to a number of exceptions, entitled to receive a payment known as a farm loss payment from the acquiring authority. The amount of the farm loss payment was equal to the average annual profit derived from the use for agricultural purposes of the agricultural land comprised in the land acquired (minus a reasonable rent and any loss of profit which would be compensatable pursuant to a disturbance claim). In most cases, that profit was calculated by reference to the profits to the three years ending with the date of displacement or, if the person concerned had been in occupation for a shorter period, that shorter period. A reduction was also made in certain circumstances, for example where the value of the land acquired was greater than the value of the new agricultural unit.

[1] LCA 1973, ss 34–36.

SEVERANCE OF AN AGRICULTURAL UNIT

53.14 As noted above, compensation can be claimed where severance impacts on the value of the land retained[1]. In addition to this, a landlord or tenant can in certain circumstances require the acquiring authority to purchase the remaining land.

[1] CPA 1965, s 7.

Severance following notice to treat

53.15 Where an acquiring authority serves notice to treat in respect of any agricultural land on a person, whether in occupation or not, who has a greater interest in the land than as tenant for a year or from year to year, and that person has such an interest in other agricultural land comprised in the same agricultural unit, that person (the claimant) may, within two months beginning on the date of service of the notice to treat, serve a counter-notice[1] on the acquiring authority claiming that the other (retained) land is not reasonably capable of being farmed, either by itself or in conjunction with other relevant land, as a separate agricultural unit and requiring the acquiring authority to purchase his interest in the whole of the other land[2].

Other relevant land means land comprised in the same agricultural unit as to which the notice to treat relates and land comprised in any other agricultural unit occupied by the claimant on the date of service of the notice to treat, being land in respect of which he is entitled to a greater interest than as a tenant for a year or from year to year[3]. Where an acquiring authority has served a notice to treat in respect of land in the holding, other than that to which the notice relates or in respect of other relevant land[4], then unless and until the notice to treat is withdrawn, it shall be treated as if that land did not form part of a holding or did not constitute other relevant land[5].

[1]   Where a counter-notice is served, the claimant must, within the same period of two months, serve a copy on any other person who has an interest in the land to which the requirement in the counter-notice relates: LCA 1973, s 53(2).
[2]   LCA 1973, s 53(1).
[3]   LCA 1973, s 53(3).
[4]   Or where such a notice is deemed to have been served by virtue of the Town and Country Planning Act 1990, ss 137–144 (purchase notices).
[5]   LCA 1973, s 53(4).

53.16 If within two months beginning with the date of service of a counter-notice, the acquiring authority does not agree in writing to accept the counter-notice as valid, the claimant or the acquiring authority may, in the two months after that period, refer the issue to the Upper Tribunal[1]. The Upper Tribunal must determine whether the claim in the counter-notice is justified and make a declaration as to its validity[2]. Where the counter-notice is declared valid, the acquiring authority is deemed to be authorised to acquire compulsorily the land to which the claim relates and to have served a notice to treat in respect of it on the date of the original notice to treat[3].

A counter-notice may be withdrawn by the claimant at any time before the Upper Tribunal has determined compensation or during the six weeks beginning with the date of such determination[4]. Where a counter-notice is withdrawn, any notice to treat deemed to have been served as a consequence of a counter-notice is also deemed to be withdrawn[5].

The compensation payable pursuant to a notice to treat which is deemed to have been served by the acquiring authority will be assessed by reference to certain statutory assumptions relating to planning permission[6].

Where, as a consequence of a counter-notice requiring any acquiring authority to purchase the whole of a claimant's interest in land[7], the acquiring authority becomes entitled to a lease of any land, but not to the interest of the landlord, the acquiring authority must offer to surrender the lease to the landlord on such terms as the acquiring authority considers reasonable[8]. If the landlord refuses to accept any sum offered, or refuses or fails to make out his title to the acquiring authority's satisfaction, the acquiring authority may pay the sum payable to the landlord into court[9]. Where an acquiring authority which becomes entitled to the lease of any land in these circumstances is a corporate body or does so under any enactment, the corporate powers of the acquiring authority include (if they would not otherwise do so) power to farm the land[10].

[1]   Formerly the Lands Tribunal: see Transfer of Tribunal Functions (Lands Tribunal and Miscellaneous Amendments) Order 2009, SI 2009/1307.
[2]   LCA 1973, s 54(1).
[3]   LCA 1973, s 54(2).
[4]   LCA 1973, s 54(3).
[5]   LCA 1973, s 54(3). Note, the general power to withdraw a notice to treat pursuant to s 31 of the LCA 1961 is not exercisable in the case of a notice to treat which is deemed to have been served as a consequence of a counter-notice: LCA 1973, s 54(4).
[6]   LCA 1973, s 54(5).
[7]   counter-notice under ss 53 and 54 of the LCA 1973.
[8]   LCA 1973, s 54(6)(a). The question of what terms are reasonable may be referred by the acquiring authority or the landlord to the Upper Tribunal. If the issue has not been resolved by agreement between the acquiring authority and the landlord at the end of three months after the offer of surrender, the reference to the Upper Tribunal is compulsory: LCA 1973, s 54(6)(b) and (c).
[9]   LCA 1973, s 54(7).
[10]   LCA 1973, s 54(8).

Severance following notice of entry

53.17 Where the acquiring authority serves a notice of entry[1] on the person in occupation of an agricultural holding, being a person with no greater interest than as a tenant for a year or from year to year, and the notice relates to part only of that holding, then that person (the claimant) may, within two months beginning on the date of service of the notice of entry, serve on the acquiring authority a counter-notice[2] claiming that the remainder of the holding is not reasonably capable of being farmed, either by itself or in conjunction with other relevant land, as a separate agricultural unit, and electing to treat the notice of entry as a notice relating to the entire holding[3].

Other relevant land means land comprised in the same agricultural unit as the agricultural holding and land comprised in any other agricultural unit occupied by the claimant on the date of service of the notice of entry, being land in respect of which he is then entitled to a greater interest than as a tenant for a year or from year to year[4]. Where an authority has served a notice to treat in respect of the land in the holding, other than that to which the notice of entry relates or in respect of other relevant land, then unless and until the notice to treat is withdrawn, it shall be treated as if that land did not form part of a holding or did not constitute other relevant land[5].

[1]   A notice of entry under the CPA 1965, s 11(1); LCA 1973.

2   Where a counter-notice is served, the claimant shall also serve a copy on the landlord of the holding, but failure to do so will not invalidate the counter-notice: LCA 1973, s 55(2).
3   LCA 1973, s 55(1).
4   LCA 1973, s 55(3).
5   LCA 1973, s 55(4).

53.18 If within the period of two months from service of the counter-notice, the acquiring authority does not accept the validity of the counter-notice in writing, the claimant or the acquiring authority may, within the two months after the end of that period, refer the counter-notice to the Upper Tribunal. The Upper Tribunal must determine whether the claim in the counter-notice is justified and make a declaration as to its validity[1]. Where the counter-notice is accepted or declared valid by the Upper Tribunal, if before the end of 12 months after such acceptance or declaration, the tenant has given up to the acquiring authority possession of every part of the holding, then the notice of entry is deemed to have extended to the part of the holding to which it did not relate. The acquiring authority is deemed to have taken possession of that part pursuant to the notice of an entry on the day before the expiration of the year of the tenancy which is current at the date of acceptance or declaration[2].

Where the claimant gives up possession of a holding to the acquiring authority, but the acquiring authority has not been authorised to acquire the landlord's interest in the land not subject to compulsory purchase[3], then:

(a)   neither the claimant nor the acquiring authority shall be liable to the landlord by reason of the claimant giving up possession of the land not subject to the compulsory purchase or the acquiring authority taking possession of it[4];

(b)   immediately after the date on which the acquiring authority takes possession of that land, it must give up possession of it to the landlord[5];

(c)   the tenancy is treated as terminated on the date on which the tenant gives up possession of the holding[6];

(d)   any rights and liabilities of the tenant in relation to the landlord arising under sub-paragraph (c)[7] are transferred to the acquiring authority, and any question as to payments in respect of such rights and liabilities must be determined by the Upper Tribunal in the absence of agreement[8]; and

(e)   any increase in value of the land, not subject to the compulsory purchase, which is attributable to the landlord taking possession under (b) above must be deducted from the compensation payable in respect of the acquisition of his interest in the remainder of the holding[9].

1   LCA 1973, s 56(1).
2   LCA 1973, s 56(2).
3   'The land not subject to compulsory purchase' is the part of the holding to which the notice of entry does not relate: LCA 1973, s 56(3).
4   LCA 1973, s 56(3)(a).
5   LCA 1973, s 56(3)(b).
6   LCA 1973, s 56(3)(c). If a claimant gives up different parts of the holding at different times, the tenancy is treated as terminated on the date of the claimant giving up the last part. The provisions relating to the date on which the tenancy is to be treated as terminated are without prejudice to any rights or liabilities of the landlord or the claimant accruing before that date: LCA 1973, s 56(3)(c). As to the application of s 70 of the AHA 1986

(compensation payable to the landlord for deterioration of the holding), to a tenancy terminated under this provision, see LCA 1973, s 56(4).
7   ie rights under the contract of tenancy, the AHA 1986 or otherwise.
8   LCA 1973, s 56(3)(d).
9   LCA 1973, s 56(3)(e).

Electing the basis of compensation for remainder of the holding

53.19 Where a notice to quit relates to only part of an agricultural holding and it is served on a tenant who is entitled to have compensation determined under s 20 of the CPA 1965[1], provided the tenant makes an election that his compensation will be determined in this way within two months of service of the notice to quit, then he may serve a notice on the acquiring authority requiring the authority to take the remainder of the holding as well, with compensation being assessed under s 20 of the CPA 1965 (ie on a notice of entry basis), if the remainder of the holding is not reasonably capable of being farmed as a separate agricultural unit (either on its own or with other land)[2].

1   See para 53.6.
2   LCA 1973, s 61.

OPEN CAST COAL MINING

53.20 Where the British Coal Corporation[1] compulsorily acquires temporary rights of occupation and use of agricultural land for the purposes of open cast coal mining by means of a compulsory rights order[2], the occupier is entitled to receive from the Corporation compensation based on the annual value of land, adjusted by reference to expected profit or loss, and also compensation for the cost of removal and in relation to forced sales of property[3].

On the termination of the occupation by the British Coal Corporation, the occupier is entitled to compensation by way of payment of the cost of works for restoring the land and compensation for diminution in the value of the holding. There may be additional compensation payable upon re-occupation[4]. Where the land subject to the compulsory rights order consists of, or includes, land which constitutes or forms part of an agricultural holding, the provision is made for modifying the right of the tenant to receive compensation from his landlord in respect of long-term improvements and the adoption of a special farming system, ie high farming[5]. Compensation is payable by the Corporation to a tenant in respect of short-term improvements and tenant-right matters and in relation to market garden improvements[6].

1   Formerly the National Coal Board: see the Coal Industry Act 1987, s 1.
2   Opencast Coal Act 1958 (OCA 1958), Pt 1, ss 4, 5, 7–12 and 14–16.
3   OCA 1958, ss 17–20, 27, Sch 3.
4   OCA 1958, ss 21–23 and 23A (added by the Coal Industry Act 1975, s 6(1)).
5   OCA 1958, ss 24, 25, 37 and Sch 7 Pt 1. As to long-term improvements and high farming, see paras 38.17–38.22 and 38.87–38.88 respectively.
6   OCA 1958, ss 26, 28 and Sch 4.

STATUTORY INSTRUMENTS

AGRICULTURAL LAND TRIBUNALS (RULES) ORDER 2007

SI 2007/3105

The Lord Chancellor makes the following Order, in exercise of the powers conferred on him by section 73(3) and (4) of the Agriculture Act 1947, section 6(4) and (6) of the Agriculture (Miscellaneous Provisions) Act 1954 and section 67(7) of the Agricultural Holdings Act 1986, and after consultation with the Council on Tribunals in accordance with section 8 of the Tribunals and Inquiries Act 1992.

A1.727A

1   Citation and commencement

This Order may be cited as the Agricultural Land Tribunals (Rules) Order 2007 and comes into force on 15th January 2008.

NOTES

Initial Commencement

Specified date: 15 January 2008: see above.

A1.727B

2   Agricultural Land Tribunals Rules

(1)   The Schedule (Agricultural Land Tribunals Rules) has effect.

(2)   The Rules set out in that Schedule may be cited as the Agricultural Land Tribunals Rules 2007.

NOTES

Initial Commencement

Specified date: 15 January 2008: see art 1.

A1.727C

3   Revocations and savings

(1)   The Agricultural Land Tribunals (Rules) Order 1978 and the Agricultural Land Tribunals (Succession to Agricultural Tenancies) Order 1984 are revoked.

(2)   Where an application to an Agricultural Land Tribunal—

    (a)   has been made before the commencement of this Order;

    (b)   is made after the commencement of this Order for a direction entitling the applicant to a tenancy of an agricultural holding on the death or retirement of the tenant when the date of death or the giving of the retirement notice was before the commencement of this Order; or

    (c)   is made after the commencement of this Order for the Tribunal's consent to operation of notice to quit when the date on which the tenant served a counter-notice in writing requiring section 26(1) of the Agricultural Holdings Act 1986 shall apply to the notice to quit was before the date of the commencement of this Order,

the Agricultural Land Tribunals (Rules) Order 1978 or the Agricultural Land Tribunals (Succession to Agricultural Tenancies) Order 1984, as the case may be, continue to apply to that application as if they had not been revoked.

NOTES

Initial Commencement

Specified date: 15 January 2008: see art 1.

SCHEDULE
AGRICULTURAL LAND TRIBUNALS RULES

Article 2

A1.727D

CONTENTS

PART 1
INTERPRETATION

NOTES

Initial Commencement

Specified date: 15 January 2008: see art 1.

PART 1
INTERPRETATION

A1.727E

1   Interpretation

In these Rules, unless the context otherwise requires, the following definitions apply—

'the 1947 Act' means the Agriculture Act 1947;
'the 1954 Act' means the Agriculture (Miscellaneous Provisions) Act 1954;

'the 1986 Act' means the Agricultural Holding Act 1986;

'the 1991 Act' means the Land Drainage Act 1991;

'application' means an application to the Tribunal and 'apply' and 'applicant' have corresponding meanings;

'Chairman' means—

    (a)   the Chairman of the Tribunal;

    (b)   a person nominated under paragraph 16(1) of Schedule 9 to the 1947 Act to act as Chairman at any hearing; or

    (c)   a person appointed under paragraph 16(A) of that Schedule to act as Chairman;

'confidential matter' means any matter that relates to intimate personal, medical or financial circumstances or national security, or is commercially sensitive, or consists of information communicated or obtained in confidence;

'costs' means any costs that the Tribunal has the authority to award under section 5 of the 1954 Act or section 27(7) of the 1986 Act;

'decision' means a decision of the Tribunal on the application before it or any substantive issue that arises in it, and includes a dismissal of an application or reply;

'decision document' has the meaning given by rule 30(4);

'designated applicant' means a person who is validly designated by the deceased in his will in accordance with section 39(4) of the 1986 Act;

'direction' means any order or other determination by a Tribunal or the Chairman other than a decision;

'document' includes information recorded in any form and, in relation to information recorded otherwise than in legible form, references to its production include references to producing a copy of the information—

    (a)   in legible form; or

    (b)   in a form from which it can be readily produced in a legible form;

'drainage case' means proceedings started by an application under the 1991 Act;

'holding' means land (including a ditch) in respect of which an application is made;

'interested party' includes—

    (a)   in the case of an application under section 39 of the 1986 Act—

        (i)   any other applicant under that section or any other person eligible to be such an applicant;

        (ii)   any personal representative of the deceased tenant, any person eligible to apply to be the personal representative of the deceased tenant or any person administering the estate of the deceased tenant;

    (b)   in the case of an application under section 53 of the 1986 Act, the tenant of the holding,

but does not include the applicant or the respondent;

'the landlord' means the landlord of the holding;

'other applicant' means any person who is also making an application in respect of the same or some of the same land;

'the official expert' means a person who for his agricultural, drainage or similar expertise is engaged by the Secretary of State or the Welsh Ministers, as the case may be, to report or act on behalf of the Secretary of State or Welsh Ministers in connection with the application;

'party' means the applicant or respondent;

'register' means the register of applications and decisions kept by the Secretary;

'reply' includes a reply by a respondent or interested party as provided for in rule 4 of these Rules;

'respondent' means a person against whom any application is made or any person added or substituted as a respondent;

'the Secretary' means the person for the time being acting as Secretary of the Tribunal and includes any assistant Secretary or other officer or servant appointed under paragraph 22 of Schedule 9 to the 1947 Act;

'the Tribunal' means the Agricultural Land Tribunal for the area in which the whole or the greater part of the holding is situated, or, where the proceedings are transferred, means the Agricultural Land Tribunal to which they have been transferred.

NOTES

Initial Commencement

Specified date: 15 January 2008: see art 1.

PART 2
APPLICATIONS AND REPLIES

A1.727F

2   Making an application

(1)   An application to the Tribunal must be made in writing.

(2)   The application must state—

- (a)   the name and address of the applicant;
- (b)   the name and address of every respondent;
- (c)   the address, description and area of all land which is referred to in the application;
- (d)   the reasons for the application including particulars of any hardship to the applicant;
- (e)   the order and every other remedy which the applicant seeks;
- (f)   the name and address of every person who appears to the applicant to be an interested party, with reasons for that person's interest;
- (g)   where the applicant bases his application on the ground of hardship to any person other than himself, the name and address of each such person and particulars of the hardship on which the applicant relies; and
- (h)   the name, address and profession of any representative of the applicant and whether the Tribunal should deliver notices concerning the application to the representative instead of to the applicant.

(3)   The application and any supporting written statement must state at the end 'I believe that the facts stated in this document are true' and be signed by the applicant or the applicant's representative.

(4)   The application, any supporting written statement and any accompanying material must be delivered to the Secretary, together with copies of those documents for all respondents.

A1.727G

3   Acknowledgement, registration and delivery of applications

(1)   Upon receiving an application the Secretary must—

- (a)   deliver an acknowledgement of its receipt to the applicant or the applicant's representative;
- (b)   enter brief particulars of it in the register; and
- (c)   deliver copies of the application to the named respondents.

(2) The Secretary must, at the same time, advise the applicant or the applicant's representative, the respondents and interested parties in writing of the following information—

    (a)   the title of the proceedings;

    (b)   the case number of the application entered in the register;

    (c)   the address to which notices and other communications to the Tribunal must be delivered;

    (d)   any further steps which they must take; and

    (e)   that general procedural guidance in relation to the proceedings may be obtained from the office of the Tribunal.

A1.727H

4   Action by respondent on receipt of an application

(1) A respondent who receives a copy of an application must deliver to the Secretary a written reply acknowledging receipt of the application and setting out—

    (a)   the title of the proceedings, the name of the applicant and the case number;

    (b)   his name and address and the name and address of every person who appears to the respondent to be an interested party who is not already named in the application, with reasons for that person's interest;

    (c)   a statement whether or not he intends to resist the application and, if so, the reasons for resisting it or the position he will adopt;

    (d)   whether he intends to be present or be represented at any hearing; and

    (e)   the name, address and the profession of any representative and whether the Tribunal should deliver notices concerning the application to the representative instead of to the respondent.

(2) The reply must state at the end 'I believe that the facts stated in this document are true' and be signed by the respondent or the respondent's representative and must be delivered to the Secretary within one month of the date on which the application was delivered to the respondent by the Secretary.

(3) Copies of the reply and any accompanying material must be provided to the Secretary for all applicants.

(4) The Secretary must deliver copies of the reply to the applicant.

(5) A reply which is delivered to the Secretary after the time appointed by paragraph (3) which contains the respondent's reasons for the delay must be treated as including an application for an extension of the time so appointed.

(6) Subject to rules 39 and 40(6), a respondent who has not delivered a written reply within the time appointed or extended may not, without the approval of the Chairman, take any part in the proceedings before the Tribunal on the application except—

    (a)   to apply for an extension of time for delivering a reply;

    (b)   to apply for a direction that the applicant provide further particulars of his application;

    (c)   to apply under rule 32 for a review of the Tribunal's decision for the reason that the respondent did not receive the application or statement of reasons or was not able to deliver a reply;

    (d)   to be called as a witness; or

    (e)   to be delivered a copy of a decision or corrected decision.

A1.727I

5 Additional matters

The applicant or respondent may include in the application or reply, or in a separate application to the Tribunal, as appropriate—

(a) a request for disclosure of any document or additional information about an application or reply;

(b) a request for an early hearing of the application or of any question relating to the application, with the reasons for that request;

(c) consent to the matter being dealt with on written representations only;

(d) an application under rule 27(2) for permission to rely on the evidence of more than two experts;

(e) a request for a decision on any question as a preliminary issue.

A1.727J

6 Withdrawal of application or reply

(1) A party may withdraw his application or reply—

(a) at any time before the hearing of the application by delivering to the Secretary a notice signed by the party or the party's representative stating that the application or reply is withdrawn; or

(b) at the hearing of the application, with the permission of the Tribunal.

(2) The withdrawal of an application or reply does not prevent the Tribunal from exercising its power to award costs.

(3) Any application for such an award of costs must be made promptly.

A1.727K

7 Documents and other material to accompany application or reply

(1) A party must deliver with his application or reply two copies of the following documents (with copies for all other parties)—

(a) maps of any land which is referred to in the application or reply on a scale of 1/10,000 or larger;

(b) every other map (which, where possible, should be on a scale of 1/10,000 or larger), plan, certificate, report or other document which he intends to rely upon for the purposes of his application or reply.

(2) The Chairman may excuse a party from providing any document referred to in paragraph (1) where the document could more conveniently be provided by some other party or where it would be unreasonable on the grounds of expense or otherwise to require it to be delivered at this stage.

(3) A party need not provide a document if copies have already been delivered to the Secretary.

NOTES

Initial Commencement

Specified date: 15 January 2008: see art 1.

PART 3
PRELIMINARY PROCEDURES

A1.727L

8   Amendment of application or reply

(1)   A party may, at any time before he is notified of the date of the hearing of the application, amend his application or reply, or deliver a supplementary statement of reasons for the application or reply.

(2)   A party may amend his application or reply with the permission of the Chairman at any time after he has been notified of the date of the hearing of the application or at the hearing itself with the permission of the Tribunal and such permission may be granted on terms that the Chairman or Tribunal thinks fit.

(3)   A party must deliver a copy of every amendment and supplementary statement to the Secretary and to all other parties.

A1.727M

9   Action by interested parties on receipt of copy of application or reply

(1)   An interested party may give notice to the Secretary that he wishes to take part in the proceedings as a respondent.

(2)   That person must include in the notice—

- (a)   the title of the proceedings, the name of the applicant and the case number;
- (b)   his name and address and the name and address of every person who appears to him to be an interested party who is not already named in the application, with reasons for that person's interest;
- (c)   a statement whether or not he intends to resist the application and, if so, the reasons for resisting and or the position he will adopt;
- (d)   whether he intends to be present or be represented at any hearing; and
- (e)   the name, address and the profession of any representative and whether the Tribunal should deliver notices concerning the application to the representative instead of to him.

(3)   A person who wishes to take part in the proceedings must deliver to the Secretary copies of the notice and accompanying documents to enable the Secretary to send a copy to each of the other parties.

(4)   A notice given under this rule shall, if the person giving it is made a respondent to the proceedings, be treated as that person's reply to the application.

A1.727N

10   Addition of new parties to the proceedings

If the Chairman considers, whether on the application of a party or otherwise, that it is desirable that a person having an interest in the proceedings be made a party, the Chairman may order that person to be joined as a respondent or, with the consent of that person, as an applicant and may give any consequential directions which may be just including directions as to the delivery of documents.

A1.727O

11 Directions

(1)   At any stage of the proceedings the Chairman may, either of his own initiative or on the application of a party, give the directions he considers necessary or desirable in the conduct of the application, and may in particular—

   (a)   direct any party to provide, to the Tribunal and to the other parties, any further information or supplementary statements or to produce any documents or copies of any documents which may reasonably be required;
   (b)   where a party has access to information which is not reasonably available to the other party, direct the party who has access to the information to prepare and file a summary recording the information;
   (c)   direct a party who wishes to rely on the evidence of any witness to deliver a signed statement or report of that witness to the Secretary and to the other parties;
   (d)   give a direction as to—
      (i)   the issues on which the Tribunal may require evidence;
      (ii)   the nature of that evidence; and
      (iii)   the way in which the evidence is to be placed before the Tribunal;
   (e)   by direction exclude evidence that would otherwise be admissible if the evidence is irrelevant, unnecessary or improperly obtained;
   (f)   by direction limit cross-examination;
   (g)   direct any party to lodge before the hearing an outline argument; or
   (h)   give any direction necessary in the exercise of any of powers conferred by these Rules.

(2)   It is a condition of the supply of any document that a party must only use the document supplied for the purposes of the proceedings.

(3)   A party cannot be directed to produce any document which a party could not be compelled to produce on the trial of an action in a court of law.

(4)   In giving effect to this rule, the Chairman must take into account the need to protect any matter that relates to confidential material.

A1.727P

12 Case management meeting

(1)   If the Chairman concludes that any proceedings would be facilitated by holding a case management meeting, he may, on the application of a party or on his own initiative, give directions for a case management meeting to be held.

(2)   The Secretary must give the parties not less than 14 days' notice, or a shorter time if agreed by all parties, of the time and the place of the case management meeting.

(3)   At a case management meeting the Chairman must give all directions which appear necessary or desirable for the conduct of the application and where appropriate set a time and place for the hearing of the application and a timetable for the hearing.

(4)   The Chairman may encourage parties or their expert witnesses to meet with a view to resolving the dispute without a hearing or with a view to narrowing the issues for the hearing.

A1.727Q

13   Preliminary issues

(1)   The Chairman may direct that any question of fact or law which appears to be in issue in the application be decided at a preliminary hearing.

(2)   If, in the opinion of the Tribunal, deciding that question substantially disposes of the whole application, the Tribunal may treat the preliminary hearing as the hearing of the application and may give such direction as it thinks fit to dispose of the application.

(3)   The Tribunal may decide the question and may also dispose of the application without a further hearing, but, in each case, only if—

(a)   the parties so agree and the Tribunal has considered any representations made by them;

(b)   having regard to the material before it and the nature of the issues raised, to do so would not prejudice the administration of justice; and

(c)   there is no important public interest consideration that requires a hearing in public.

(4)   Rule 30 applies to the Tribunal's decisions on a preliminary issue.

A1.727R

14   Varying or setting aside of directions

Where a person to whom a direction issued under these Rules is addressed had no opportunity of objecting to the giving of the direction, that person may apply to the Tribunal, or Chairman as appropriate, to vary it or set it aside, but the Chairman or Tribunal must not do so without first notifying the parties and considering any representations made by them.

A1.727S

15   Failure to comply with directions

(1)   If any direction given to a party under these Rules is not complied with by that party, the Tribunal may, before or at the hearing—

(a)   dismiss the whole or part of the application; or

(b)   strike out the whole or part of a reply and, where appropriate, direct that a respondent is debarred from contesting the application altogether or some part of it.

(2)   But a Tribunal must not dismiss, strike out or give such a direction unless notice has been delivered to the party who has not complied, giving that party an opportunity to comply within the period specified in the notice or to establish why the Tribunal should not dismiss, strike out or give such a direction.

A1.727T

16   Notice of date, time and place

(1)   Subject to any direction of the Chairman, the Secretary must, with due regard to the reasonable convenience of the parties, and as soon as reasonably practicable, fix the date, time and place of a hearing and, where appropriate, set a timetable for the hearing and, not less than 14 days before the first date fixed (or a shorter time if agreed

by the parties), deliver to each party a notice that the hearing is to be or commence on that date and at that time and place and the details of any timetable for the hearing.

(2)   The Secretary must include with the notice of hearing—

(a)   information and guidance as to attendance at the hearing of the parties and witnesses, the bringing of documents, and the right of representation or assistance by another person and the procedure applicable to the hearing, having regard to any applicable burden and standard of proof and rules of evidence;

(b)   a statement of the right of the parties to receive reasons in writing for a decision of the Tribunal unless the decision is made by consent of all parties;

(c)   a statement explaining the advantages of attendance, the consequences of non-attendance, and the right of an applicant and of any party who has presented a reply, who does not intend to be present or represented at the hearing, to deliver to the Secretary and the other parties, before the hearing, additional written representations or evidence in support of their case; and

(d)   a request to be informed of any special requirements, such as for wheelchair access, which a party, representative or witness may have.

(3)   When a party receives the notice of the date, time and place of the hearing, he must inform the Secretary whether or not he intends to be present or represented at the hearing, and whether he intends to call witnesses and, if so, their names.

A1.727U

17   Public notice of hearings

The Secretary must provide for public inspection at the office of the Tribunal or through other media a list of all applications for which a hearing is to be held and of the time and place fixed for the hearing.

A1.727V

18   Consolidation or hearing together of applications

(1)   Where two or more applications have been lodged in respect of the same subject matter, or in respect of several interests in the same subject matter, or which involve the same or similar issues, the Chairman may, on the application of any party to the applications or on his own initiative, direct that the applications or any particular issue or matter raised in the applications be consolidated or heard together or consecutively.

(2)   Before giving a direction under this rule, unless all parties have consented, the Secretary must give notice to the parties to the applications and the Chairman must consider any representations made in consequence of the notice.

(3)   Subject to any specific provisions of these Rules or directions by the Chairman, all applications to the Tribunal in respect of any particular holding, whether made by the landlord or tenant, must be heard and determined together.

A1.727W

19   Power to decide application without a hearing

(1)   The Tribunal may (except in a drainage case) deal with an application or preliminary issue without a hearing if—

(a) no reply is delivered to the Secretary within the time appointed by rule 4 or any extension of time granted under rule 51 or the parties agree in writing or the respondent states in writing that he does not oppose the application;

(b) there is no other opposition to the application;

(c) having regard to the material before the Tribunal and the nature of the issues raised by the application the Tribunal considers that to do so will not prejudice the administration of justice; and

(d) there is no important public interest consideration that requires a hearing in public.

(2) Before deciding an application in the absence of a party, the Tribunal must consider any representations in writing submitted by that party in response to a notice of hearing.

(3) Nothing in this rule prevents a party from making an application for a review of the Tribunal's decision under rule 32.

A1.727X

20   Hearing bundles

(1) When practicable and subject to any directions that the Chairman may make, the applicant must compile a hearing bundle containing copies of all relevant documents.

(2) The respondent must assist with the preparation of the hearing bundle.

(3) The contents must be agreed, indexed and paginated.

(4) The applicant must deliver four copies of the bundle to the Secretary and one copy to each of the parties not less than 7 days before the start of the hearing.

NOTES

Initial Commencement

Specified date: 15 January 2008: see art 1.

PART 4
HEARINGS AND DECISIONS

A1.727Y

21   Hearings to be in public

(1) All hearings by the Tribunal must be in public unless the Tribunal is satisfied that, by reason of disclosure of confidential matters it is just and reasonable to hold the hearing or part of a hearing in private.

(2) Subject to any direction by the Tribunal hearing the proceedings, any Chairman of any Agricultural Land Tribunal or any member of a panel for the Tribunal, notwithstanding that he is not part of the Tribunal for the purpose of the hearing, and the Secretary is entitled to attend a hearing whether or not it is in private.

(3) The Tribunal, with the consent of the parties, may permit any other person to attend the hearing of an application which is held in private.

A1.727Z

22   Failure of parties to attend

(1)   If a party fails to attend or be represented at a hearing, the Tribunal may, if it is satisfied that the party was duly notified of the hearing and that there is no good reason for such absence—

(a)   hear and decide the application or question in the party's absence; or
(b)   adjourn the hearing,

and may give such directions as it thinks fit.

(2)   Before deciding to dispose of any application or question in the absence of a party, the Tribunal must consider the application and any reply, as appropriate, and any written representations or evidence supplied.

(3)   Where an applicant has failed to attend or be represented at a hearing of which he was duly notified, and the Tribunal has disposed of the application, no fresh application may be made by the applicant to the Tribunal for relief arising out of the same facts without the prior permission of the Tribunal.

(4)   Nothing in this rule prevents the applicant making an application for a review of the Tribunal's decision under rule 32.

A1.727ZA

23   Procedure at hearing

(1)   At the beginning of any hearing the Chairman may explain the manner and order of proceeding, having regard to any applicable burden and standard of proof and rules of evidence.

(2)   The Tribunal—

(a)   may conduct the hearing in the manner it considers most suitable to the clarification of the issues before it and generally to the just handling of the proceedings; and
(b)   must, so far as it appears to it appropriate, seek to avoid formality and inflexibility in its proceedings.

(3)   The parties may appear at the hearing and may be represented.

(4)   The parties may give evidence, call witnesses, question any witnesses and address the Tribunal both on the evidence and generally on the subject matter of the application.

(5)   The Tribunal may at any stage of the proceedings direct the personal attendance of any maker of a witness statement or deponent of an affidavit, or any expert whose report has been filed.

(6)   The Tribunal may receive evidence of any fact which seems to the Tribunal to be relevant even if the evidence would be inadmissible in law but, subject to rule 27, must not refuse to admit any evidence presented in due time which is admissible in law and is relevant and necessary and has not been improperly obtained.

A1.727ZB

24   Evidence of witnesses

(1)   Except where the Chairman otherwise directs, any party who wishes to rely on the evidence of any witness must deliver a statement of that witness to the Secretary and must deliver copies to every party at least 10 days before the date of the hearing.

(2)   The witness statement must state at the end 'I believe that the facts stated in this witness statement are true' and be signed by the witness.

A1.727ZC

25   Entry on land or premises

(1)   For the purpose of enabling the Tribunal to understand the issues in any proceedings before it, the Chairman may give a direction requiring the occupier of any land or premises which are relevant to the proceedings to permit the Tribunal (and any party, party's representative, expert witness, official expert and any of the Tribunal's officers or members of its staff as the Chairman considers necessary) to enter and inspect the land or premises.

(2)   The direction must specify a date and time for the entry and inspection at least 24 hours (or 7 days in drainage cases) after the date when a copy of the direction is delivered to the occupier or the occupier is notified of any change in the date specified.

(3)   This direction can be given in a notice of hearing.

(4)   If notice of the Tribunal's intention to enter and inspect any land or premises is given orally at a hearing, the Tribunal may waive the 24 hours' minimum notice requirement under paragraph (2).

(5)   The Secretary must deliver a copy of the direction to the parties and must notify them of any change in the date or time specified.

A1.727ZD

26   Inspection of land or premises by official expert

(1)   The Chairman may direct any person who owns or occupies any land or premises which are relevant to the proceedings to permit the official expert to enter and inspect the land or premises for the purpose for which he was appointed.

(2)   Every such direction must, unless the occupier was present when the direction was made, contain a statement informing the occupier that he may apply to the Chairman to vary or set aside the direction.

(3)   The occupier of the land or premises and the other parties must be given at least seven days notice of any inspection, unless the occupier and the other parties agree in writing to a shorter period of notice.

(4)   That inspection must take place during the hours of daylight and must take place on a business day unless there is good reason or the occupier and parties consent for the inspection to take place on another day.

(5)   The Secretary must deliver a copy of the report of the official expert and any written statement made by or on behalf of the Secretary of State or the Welsh Ministers to each of the parties and inform them that they may make written comments (with

copies for all other parties and the official expert) as to the contents of the report within one month (or such other period as the Chairman directs) of receiving the report.

(6)   Rules 27, 28 and 29 apply to the report and evidence of the official expert.

(7)   In this rule, 'business day' means any day except Saturday, Sunday, Christmas Day, Good Friday or a bank holiday under the Banking and Financial Dealings Act 1971.

A1.727ZE

27   Expert evidence

(1)   No expert may give oral evidence unless he has provided a written report which has been previously delivered to all parties or the Chairman otherwise directs.

(2)   No party may rely on the evidence of more than two experts without the Chairman's permission.

(3)   An application for permission must state—

(a)   the reasons why the party wishes to rely on further expert evidence; and
(b)   where practicable, the name and address of the experts on whose evidence the party wishes to rely.

(4)   If permission is granted it must be in relation only to the experts named and the reasons identified under paragraph (3).

A1.727ZF

28   Expert's overriding duty to the Tribunal

(1)   It is the duty of an expert to help the Tribunal on the matters within his expertise.

(2)   This duty overrides any obligation to the person from whom the expert has received instructions or by whom the expert is paid.

A1.727ZG

29   Form and content of expert's report

(1)   Expert evidence must be given in a written report unless the Chairman directs otherwise.

(2)   Every expert must attend the oral hearing for cross-examination unless the Chairman directs otherwise.

(3)   An expert's report must be addressed to the Tribunal and not to the party from whom the expert has received instructions.

(4)   The expert's report must contain—

(a)   details of the expert's qualifications;
(b)   a statement of the substance of all material instructions whether written or oral, on the basis of which the report was written;
(c)   details of any literature or any other material which the expert has relied on in making the report;
(d)   where there is a range of opinion on the matter dealt with in the report—
    (i)   a summary of the range of opinion; and

     (ii) the reasons for the expert's own opinion;

(e) a summary of the conclusions reached; and

(f) a statement that the expert understands his duty to the Tribunal and has complied with that duty.

(5) The expert report must be restricted to that which is reasonably required to resolve the proceedings.

A1.727ZH

30   Decision of Tribunal

(1) A decision of the Tribunal may be taken by a majority.

(2) The Chairman may, at or following the hearing, give the parties an informal, non-binding indication of the decision that the Tribunal is minded to make.

(3) At any time before a decision document is signed by the Chairman, the Tribunal may reconsider of its own accord and if necessary may reconvene the hearing or request further submissions and may decide to make a different decision than previously informally indicated.

(4) Whether there has been a hearing or not, every decision must be recorded in a document (the 'decision document') which, except in the case of a decision by consent, must also contain a statement of the reasons for the decision and must be signed by the Chairman and dated.

(5) The Secretary must deliver a certified copy of the decision document to each party.

(6) Where any document refers to any evidence that has been heard in private, the material relating to that evidence must be omitted from the decision document as the Tribunal may direct.

(7) Every copy of a document or entry delivered to the parties under this rule must be accompanied by a notification of the provisions in these Rules relating to review of the Tribunal's decision and reference to the High Court on a question of law.

A1.727ZI

31   Duty to adjourn part of hearing where time limits have not expired

(1) Where on the date appointed for the hearing the time allowed for a response has not expired, or has not started to run, the Tribunal must not proceed to hear the application except with the consent of the party whose response has not been received.

(2) Where consent is required but is not given, the Tribunal must adjourn the proceedings and the Chairman must give such directions as he considers appropriate for the further hearing of the proceedings.

A1.727ZJ

32   Review of Tribunal's decision

(1) If, on the application of a party or on its own initiative, a Tribunal is satisfied that—

(a) its decision contains a clerical mistake or error arising from an accidental slip or omission or contains an ambiguity that should be clarified or removed;

(b) it should make an additional order or direction which relates to a matter which was presented to the Tribunal but was not dealt with in its decision or which is consequential to its decision;

(c) a party, who was entitled to be heard at a hearing but failed to be present or represented, had a good reason for failing to be present or represented; or

(d) new evidence, to which the decision relates, has become available since the conclusion of the proceedings and its existence could not reasonably have been known or foreseen before then,

the Tribunal may set aside or vary the relevant decision.

(2) An application under paragraph (1) must—

(a) be made in writing stating the reasons in full; and

(b) unless made at the hearing, be delivered to the Secretary within 28 days of a certified copy of the decision document being delivered to the person making the application.

(3) When the Tribunal proposes to review its decision on its own initiative, the Secretary must deliver notice of that proposal to the parties.

(4) The parties must have an opportunity to be heard on any application or proposal for review under this rule and the review must be decided by the Tribunal which decided the case or, where it is not practicable for it to be heard by that Tribunal, by a differently constituted Tribunal.

(5) If having reviewed the decision, the decision is set aside, the Tribunal must substitute the decision it thinks fit or order a rehearing before either the same or a differently constituted Tribunal.

(6) On the setting aside or variation of the Tribunal's decision, the Secretary must immediately make such correction as may be necessary in the register and deliver a copy of the entry so corrected and the decision document to each of the parties.

(7) Rule 30 applies to the Tribunal's decision on the review.

NOTES

Initial Commencement

Specified date: 15 January 2008: see art 1.

PART 5
ADDITIONAL POWERS AND PROVISIONS

A1.727ZK

33   Power to regulate procedure etc

(1) Subject to the provisions of the 1947 Act, the 1954 Act, the 1986 Act, and the 1991 Act and of these Rules—

(a) the Tribunal may regulate its own procedure;

(b) the Chairman may regulate procedure at a case management meeting and any other meeting chaired by him alone.

(2) The Tribunal may exercise any power which these Rules give to the Chairman.

A1.727ZL

34 Power to strike out

(1)   On the application of any party, the Tribunal may order that all or part of the application, reply or any document supplied in the course of an application be struck out if it appears to the Tribunal that it—

  (a)   discloses no reasonable grounds for making or defending the application; or
  (b)   is an abuse of the Tribunal's process or is otherwise likely to obstruct the fair disposal of the proceedings.

(2)   The Secretary must deliver to the parties copies of an application for an order under this rule, and inform the parties of their opportunity to reply within 28 days or such period as the Chairman considers appropriate explaining why such an order should or should not be made.

A1.727ZM

35 Exclusion of persons disrupting proceedings

(1)   This rule applies to any of the following events—

  (a)   a hearing before the Tribunal;
  (b)   an inspection by the Tribunal;
  (c)   any meeting chaired by the Chairman alone;
  (d)   an inspection conducted by an official expert.

(2)   Without prejudice to any other powers it may have, the Chairman or Tribunal, as appropriate, may—

  (a)   exclude from any event, or part of it, any person (including a party or a party's representative) whose conduct has disrupted the event, threatens to disrupt the event, or whose conduct has otherwise interfered with the administration of justice; or
  (b)   limit the number of persons attending the event in the interests of disease prevention or for other good reason.

(3)   In deciding whether to exercise the power conferred by paragraph (2), the Chairman or Tribunal as appropriate, must, apart from other considerations, have regard—

  (a)   to the interests of the parties;
  (b)   in the case of the exclusion of a party, to the extent to which the proceedings involve an assessment of the party's conduct, character or manner of life; and
  (c)   in the case of the exclusion of a party or a party's representative, to whether the interests of that party will be adequately protected.

(4)   If the Chairman or Tribunal decides to exclude a party it must allow the party's representative sufficient opportunity to consult the party.

A1.727ZN

36 Enquiries of local authorities etc

The Chairman or the Tribunal either before or during a hearing may direct that enquiries are made of any local or other public authority or utility within whose area the land in question is situated, and the Tribunal may adjourn the hearing until the response to such enquiries has been received and copies supplied to the parties.

A1.727ZO

37   Reference to the High Court of a question of law

(1)   A request under section 6(1) of the 1954 Act must, unless made at the hearing, be made in writing to the Secretary within 28 days of a certified copy of the decision being delivered to the person making the request.

(2)   The request must state concisely—

   (a)   the questions of law that the party making the request wishes the Tribunal to refer to the High Court; and

   (b)   any issues of fact in respect of which that party contends the findings (in addition to those contained in any decision made by the Tribunal) should accompany the case stated.

(3)   The Chairman may direct the party making the request to supply a draft of the case stated.

(4)   If the Chairman considers that any question of law referred to in the request (or draft case stated) could be better framed or that it is desirable or expedient to add or substitute a similar or related question, he may invite the party making the request to amend the request (or draft) accordingly.

(5)   If the Tribunal decides to refuse the request, the Secretary must notify all parties within 14 days of the receipt of the request giving reasons for such refusal or within such extended period as the Chairman may consider necessary.

(6)   A person who intends to apply to the High Court under section 6(2) of the 1954 Act for an order directing the Tribunal to refer a question of law to the High Court—

   (a)   must deliver notice of his intended application to the Secretary within 14 days of receiving notification of the refusal; and

   (b)   must deliver copies of his notice to all other parties.

(7)   A case stated for the decision of the High Court must—

   (a)   set out the questions of law;

   (b)   attach a copy of any decision document issued by the Tribunal in relation to the proceedings;

   (c)   set out such findings of fact by the Tribunal additional to those contained in the decision document as the Chairman considers relevant to the question or questions of law;

   (d)   be signed by the Chairman; and

   (e)   be delivered to all parties within 2 months of the date of the request or, as the case may be, the making of an order by the High Court directing the reference.

A1.727ZP

38   Modification of Tribunal's decision following High Court proceedings

(1)   Following a decision of the High Court the Chairman may exercise the powers of the Tribunal under section 6(5) of the 1954 Act in any case if he considers that it is not necessary to convene the Tribunal for the purpose.

(2)   In every other case he must direct the Secretary to fix a date, time and place for the Tribunal to convene.

(3)   Where it is not possible or convenient to re-convene the Tribunal as originally constituted, the hearing must take place before a differently constituted Tribunal.

(4) These Rules apply to any proceedings which are consequent on the reference of any question to the High Court under section 6 of the 1954 Act or on the decision on such a reference.

NOTES

Initial Commencement

Specified date: 15 January 2008: see art 1.

PART 6
SPECIFIC APPLICATIONS

A1.727ZQ

39   Consent to operation of notice to quit

An application for the Tribunal's consent to the operation of a notice to quit under section 26(1) or 28(2) of the 1986 Act which is made by the landlord after service upon him by the tenant of a counter-notice must be made within one month of the service of the counter-notice.

A1.727ZR

40   Succession on death or retirement

(1) This rule applies to an application made under section 39 or section 53 of the 1986 Act.

(2) Before making such an application, the applicant must deliver a notice in writing of his intention to do so to all interested parties.

(3) The applicant must include in his application, in addition to the information required by rule 2(2), confirmation that he has notified the interested parties.

(4) In the case of proceedings under section 39 of the 1986 Act, an applicant who opposes or intends to oppose any other application under that section may include in his own application, or in a separate reply, the following information, in addition to the information required by rule 2(2)—

  (a) reasons why he opposes or intends to oppose that other application;
  (b) a statement indicating whether he disputes that applicant's claim to be a designated applicant and, if so, why;
  (c) a claim to be a more suitable applicant than any other;
  (d) a statement that he has agreed with one or more other applicants to request the landlord's consent to a direction entitling them to a joint tenancy of the holding.

(5) If any person entitled to make an application under section 39 of the 1986 Act supplies the information under paragraph (4), he may present evidence and make representations to the Tribunal that he is more suitable to be a tenant than any other applicant.

(6) If the landlord does not reply to an application under section 39 or 53 of the 1986 Act within the time allowed by rule 4(3), he is not entitled to dispute any matter alleged in the application form but—

  (a) in the case of an application under section 39 or 53, the landlord is entitled to give his views on the suitability of the applicant; and

366

(b)   in the case of an application under section 39, the landlord may where appropriate make an application under section 44 of the 1986 Act for consent to the operation of a notice to quit.

A1.727ZS

41   Applications under sections 44, 46 or 55 of the 1986 Act

(1)   Where, at the expiry of the period specified in section 39(1) of the 1986 Act, only one application under that section in respect of the holding has been made, any application by the landlord under section 44(1) of that Act must be made before the expiry of one month after the end of that period or, if later, one month after a copy of the application under section 39 is delivered to him.

(2)   Where at the expiry of that period more than one application under section 39 of the 1986 Act has been made, any application by the landlord under section 44(1) of that Act must be made before the expiry of one month after notice is delivered to him by the Secretary that the number of applications under section 39 of the 1986 Act is reduced to one or such earlier date as the Chairman directs.

(3)   Any application under section 44(6), section 46(2)(a) or section 55(8)(a) of the 1986 Act must be made in writing to the Secretary before the hearing, or orally at the hearing.

A1.727ZT

42   Procedure at hearing in case of multiple applicants where designation is claimed

(1)   In the case of proceedings under section 39 of the 1986 Act, the Tribunal must (in such order as the Tribunal considers appropriate) consider and determine the validity of each applicant's claim, if any, to be a designated applicant, giving all other parties and all other applicants for succession the opportunity to be heard.

(2)   If the Tribunal determines that any such claim is valid, the Tribunal must then hear that applicant's application as if that applicant were the only applicant and, if the Tribunal determines that the applicant is a suitable person to become the tenant of the holding, the Tribunal must dismiss all other applications under section 39(1) of the 1986 Act in respect of the same holding.

(3)   If the Tribunal determines that the designated applicant is not a suitable person to become a tenant of the holding, the Tribunal must dismiss his application.

A1.727ZU

43   Multiple applications under the 1986 Act where there is no designated applicant

(1)   The Tribunal must, subject to any direction by the Chairman, consider any question of eligibility or suitability by applying the 1986 Act in the following order—

(a)   any question arising under section 41(3) of the 1986 Act (treatment as eligible person);

(b)   any question of eligibility under section 39(2) of the 1986 Act, as applied by section 39(3) of that Act;

(c)   any question of suitability under section 39(2) of the 1986 Act, as applied by section 39(3) of that Act;

(d) any exercise of discretion under section 39(9) of the 1986 Act (direction for joint tenancy);

(e) any question of relative suitability under section 39(6) of the 1986 Act;

(f) any question arising under section 39(10) of the 1986 Act (tenancy of part of holding);

(g) any question arising under section 44 of the 1986 Act (consent to operation of notice to quit).

(2) Before giving a direction under section 39(9) of the 1986 Act, the Tribunal must—

(a) ask the landlord if he consents to the giving of a direction; and

(b) consider any representations made by other suitable applicants.

(3) The landlord will be deemed not to consent under section 39(9) of the 1986 Act if he does not respond to the Secretary within the period specified by the Chairman.

(4) Before giving a direction under section 39(10) of the 1986 Act, the Tribunal must ask each applicant whether he agrees.

A1.727ZV

44   Applications under section 67 of the 1986 Act

The period prescribed by these Rules within which a landlord may serve a notice under section 67(5) of the 1986 Act that he proposes himself to carry out an improvement is one month from the date on which notice in writing of the Tribunal's approval of the carrying out of the improvement is delivered to him.

A1.727ZW

45   Applications under the Land Drainage Act 1991

(1) On receipt of an application in a drainage case, the Secretary must request the Secretary of State or the Welsh Ministers, as the case may be, to provide the Tribunal with a report on the matters to which the application relates.

(2) A report made under this rule may make recommendations to the Tribunal regarding the application.

(3) The reply delivered under rule 4 may state the respondent's position pending receipt of the report from the official expert and the applicant's comments on the recommendations in that report.

(4) On receipt of the report, the Secretary must deliver a copy to every party.

(5) The applicant must, within one month of delivery of a copy of the report to him, deliver to the Secretary written comments on the report (with copies for all other parties and the official expert), including in particular whether, and if so, why they dispute any of the facts or recommendations.

(6) The Secretary must deliver to the respondent a copy of the applicant's comments and request written comments from the respondent within one month including whether, and if so, why they dispute any of the facts or recommendations.

(7) At the expiry of the one month period referred to in the preceding paragraph, the Secretary must deliver to each party a copy of comments received from every other party.

(8)   Each party has a further month from the date of receipt of copies of the comments to write to the Secretary supplementing their original comments and paragraph (7) applies as to delivery of any supplementary comments received by the Secretary.

(9)   A report under this rule is prima facie evidence of the facts to which it refers.

(10)   Where a report under this rule recommends that an order be made, the Tribunal may make such an order without a hearing if the following conditions are met—

- (a)   the report recommends that a specified party to the proceedings should be required or authorised to carry out any work or authorised to enter any land;
- (b)   that person has notified the Secretary of his acceptance of the recommendation; and
- (c)   every other party has—
    - (i)   notified the Secretary of his acceptance of the recommendation;
    - (ii)   failed to reply to the application within the time allowed; or
    - (iii)   withdrawn their reply.

(11)   The Tribunal may, after giving all parties an opportunity to be heard, vary an order made following a decision in a land drainage case, whether as to the time within which any work is to be carried out or otherwise.

(12)   An application for such a variation must set out the variation sought and the reasons for the application.

(13)   For the purposes of an application under the 1991 Act, the interested parties include the owner and occupier of any land which may be entered or on which any work may be done in pursuance of the proposed order or which could be adversely affected in consequence of the proposed work or improvement.

(14)   Where an application is made under section 28 but not section 30 of the 1991 Act the Chairman may direct that the application is to be treated as if it had been made under section 30 for the same or substantially the same work.

NOTES

Initial Commencement

Specified date: 15 January 2008: see art 1.

PART 7
SUPPLEMENTAL PROVISIONS

A1.727ZX

46   Review of directions

The Chairman or the Tribunal may at any time reconsider any direction and may revoke, amend or replace the direction.

A1.727ZY

47   Irregularities

(1)   Any irregularity resulting from a failure to comply with any provisions of these Rules or any direction of the Tribunal or of the Chairman before the Tribunal has reached its decision does not of itself render the proceedings invalid.

(2)   Where any such irregularity comes to the attention of the Tribunal, the Tribunal or the Chairman as appropriate may give any directions it thinks just, before reaching its decision, to cure or waive the irregularity.

(3)   Clerical mistakes in any document recording a direction or decision of the Tribunal or the Chairman, or errors arising in such a document from an accidental slip or omission, may be corrected by the Chairman by certificate in writing.

A1.727ZZ

48   Proof of documents and decisions

(1)   Any document purporting to be a document signed or issued by the Secretary on behalf of the Tribunal is, unless the contrary is proved, deemed to be a document so executed or issued as the case may be.

(2)   A document purporting to be certified by the Secretary to be a true copy of a decision of the Tribunal or of any entry of a decision in the register is, unless the contrary is proved, sufficient evidence of the decision of the Tribunal or the entry and of matters contained in it.

A1.727ZZA

49   Method of delivering and receipt of documents

(1)   Any document required or authorised by these Rules to be delivered to any person, body or authority is duly delivered to that person, body or authority—

  (a)   if it is sent to the proper address of that person, body or authority by post, by special delivery, by recorded delivery or otherwise with proof of posting;
  (b)   if it is sent to that person, body or authority at that address by fax or other means of electronic communication which produces a text which is received in legible form; or
  (c)   if it is delivered to or left at the proper address of that person, body or authority,

provided that it will only duly be delivered by fax or other means of electronic communication if the recipient consents in writing to the use of that means.

(2)   For the purposes of the proviso in paragraph (1), a legal representative is deemed to consent in writing if the reference or address for the means of electronic communication is shown as an acceptable means of delivery on the legal representative's notepaper.

(3)   Where a document has been sent in accordance with paragraph (1) it shall, unless the contrary is proved, be taken to have been received by the party to whom it is addressed—

  (a)   in the case of a document sent by post, on the day on which the document would be delivered in the ordinary course of post;
  (b)   in the case of a document transmitted by fax or other means of electronic communication, on the day on which the document is transmitted; or
  (c)   in the case of a notice or document delivered in person, on the day on which the document is delivered.

(4)   Any document required or authorised to be delivered may—

  (a)   in the case of a company or other body incorporated or registered in the United Kingdom, be delivered to the secretary or clerk of the company or body;
  (b)   in the case of a company or other body incorporated outside the United Kingdom, be delivered to the person authorised to accept it;
  (c)   in the case of a partnership, be delivered to any partner; or

(d)   in the case of an unincorporated association other than a partnership, be delivered to any member of the governing body of the association.

(5)   The proper address of any person, body or authority to whom any document is required or authorised to be delivered is—

(a)   in the case of a secretary or clerk of an incorporated company or other body registered in the United Kingdom, that of the registered or principal office of the company or body;

(b)   in the case of the person authorised to accept it on behalf of a company or other body incorporated outside the United Kingdom, the address of the principal office or place of business of that company or other body in the United Kingdom;

(c)   in the case of the Tribunal or the Secretary, the address of the office of the Tribunal;

(d)   in the case of any other person, the usual or last known address of that person.

(6)   Where any document is to be delivered to a diocesan board of finance as having an interest in land, a copy must also be delivered to the Church Commissioners.

A1.727ZZB

50   Substituted delivery of documents

If any person to whom any document is required to be delivered for the purposes of these Rules—

(a)   cannot be found or has died and has no known personal representative; or

(b)   is out of the United Kingdom,

or if for any other reason delivery to that person cannot be readily effected, the Chairman may dispense with the delivery to that person or may give a direction for substituted delivery to another person or in any other form (whether by advertisement in a newspaper or otherwise) which the Chairman may think fit and may make such consequential directions as he considers appropriate.

A1.727ZZC

51   Variation of time limits

(1)   The Chairman may extend any time limit under these Rules or in any direction whether or not it has already expired, where he considers that it would not be reasonable to expect or have expected compliance with the time limit and he may shorten any time limit where he considers that it would be reasonable to expect compliance within a shorter time limit.

(2)   Before deciding whether to extend or shorten the time limit the Chairman must give persons whose interests might be affected an opportunity to be heard or to make objections in writing and responses must be made within five days or such period as the Chairman considers appropriate.

(3)   Unless the Chairman otherwise directs, a time limit may be varied once by the written agreement of all parties provided that the Secretary is notified in writing of the agreement before the original time limit expires.

(4)   Unless the Chairman otherwise directs, a variation of a time limit under paragraph (3) must end not more than 28 days after the original time limit and end no less than seven days before a hearing.

(5) Any application for an extension or shortening of time must be in writing, stating reasons for the delay and enclosing copies for all other parties.

NOTES

Initial Commencement

Specified date: 15 January 2008: see art 1.